MESSAGE TO JUDAH

making sense

of the Black American experience

from a Biblical perspective

Trenét Worlds

MESSAGE TO JUDAH

Table of Contents

Chapter I   Identity Questions

Chapter II   Identity Crisis

Chapter III   Identity Theft

Chapter IV   The Black Man in Covenant with God

Chapter V   Captivity, Deliverance, Testing, Consecration and Covenant

ACKNOWLEDGEMENTS

I dedicate this book to my Father in Heaven who gave me a heart desiring wisdom, understanding, truth, and a hunger to search out things prophetic.

"It is the glory of God to conceal a thing: but the honour of kings is to search out a matter..." Proverbs Chapter 25 verse 2

I Corinthians Chapter 2 verses 9-10 state, "But as it is written, eye hath not seen, nor ear heard, neither have entered into the heart of man, the things which God hath prepared for them that love him. But God hath revealed them unto us by his Spirit: for the Spirit searcheth all things, yea, the deep things of God." Through His Spirit, God grants us a preview of the restored dignity, honor, and prosperity for the Black man in His Enduring Kingdom. Through Biblical scripture, He provides a gentle but firm understanding of the meaning of our suffering and present low estate.

This book could not have been written without the insight gleaned from the labor of those who studied long-ignored history. I am also indebted to the anthropological work of Joseph J. Williams, and many other researchers who have chronicled the events surrounding the Middle Passage, Antebellum period, and Jim Crow era. But a special gratitude extends to my brothers and sisters who searched the Holy Scriptures; and upon understanding their forgotten identity, boldly shared this truth with others despite opposition, ridicule, and great personal loss.

It is true that some people author books with the sole intent of igniting discord or being controversial for the sake of controversy. That is not the case with this publication. I write from the position of prophetic covering; a mantle that demands I speak the truth to the generations who will likely witness the bodily return of the Lord Jesus Christ.

Judgment begins at the house of God, and God has shown me there are specific steps which must be taken if we are to stand in the judgment, and in the congregation of the righteous. This book is not for the public at large, but to the household of faith, especially to the Black Church in America. The only scripturally correct prayer to pray at this point is, "Thy Kingdom come; thy will be done on earth, as it is in Heaven." But are we really ready for the Lord to return and execute judgment on the earth? If we have blinded our eyes and stopped our ears to historical truth, how will we face the one who is the embodiment of Truth?

This book has not been written to induce guilt, present a convincing argument for reparations, or exalt any race above another. Neither should it be dismissed as a platform for 'Black Liberation Theology'. It was written with the intent of correctly interpreting the Biblical scriptures and prophecies. It was written to a people who are 'like sheep without a shepherd'; puzzled as to why their plight has changed little since they first stepped onto the shores of the West some 450 years ago. To a people still shackled—in many cases both mentally and physically, this book was written to lift the veil that prevents them from understanding their true identity and purpose. It was written to reveal the checklist for preparation for the Lord's return: repentance for the sins of the forefathers, renunciation of new idolatries adopted while in Captivity, and embracement of a lifestyle of personal holiness and sanctification.

And lastly, it was written to serve notice to the reigning kingdoms of the earth that the apple of God's eye has been right in their midst for several hundred years. Divine judgment will be meted out based on their treatment of Israel and Judah during Captivity; as God cannot lie, and He is no respecter of persons.

The household of faith as a whole must begin to understand the unique role of the Black Church in the closing days of this age. And this understanding and acknowledgment is offered in a spirit of humility as I relay this message to the Black church in the West, and the Black Christian brethren scattered throughout the world.

To the elders among my people who have known decades of history characterized by oppression and humiliation. To the mothers and grandmothers who have shed so many tears, and whose short and sporadic seasons of rejoicing are always muted by the sober reality that the lives of their children and grandchildren daily hang in jeopardy. To the embittered young men who are losing hope in a society that grudgingly tolerates their presence, bristles alarmingly at the prospect of their collective success, and rejoices to see them hidden away in prisons. To the young women who dream of an elusive reality and seek to capture it in the false offerings of the culture; only to find emptiness and reproach. To the children who still dream and imagine, and hope for a hero and a leader; to these I write.

I count myself but a small and humble voice in the wake of impressive intellectuals and spiritual leaders who have already penned notable works addressing the incurable wound of the Black man in the Western world. These writers have inspired me in my quest to understand the dilemma of our people—authors such as Dr. Claud Anderson, founder of the Harvest Institute and author of "PowerNomics: The National Plan to Empower Black America." He speaks eloquently to the economic disparities facing us; offering a structured solution to reverse the pattern of dependency and stagnation. Dr. Joy DeGruy sheds compassionate and remarkable insight into the psychological and psychosocial elements influencing the Black mentality as a result of the horrors of slavery, in her groundbreaking book "Post Traumatic Slave Syndrome."

We know as a people something is wrong with the inability to collectively progress in American society. We know historically we have been used, defrauded, despised and hated in the country built on our unpaid labor. We know we have adopted ways of thinking and behaving to help us cope with the hatred and disenfranchisement...patterns and methods of dealing with our existence which sabotage our declared objectives but nevertheless enable us to bear up under the second rate status. In short, we recognize there is a problem.

But have we ever considered why the factors that negatively influence our life in America never seem to go away? Black Americans themselves will lament, "We never got our forty acres and a mule. Nothing from nothing leaves nothing. We were disenfranchised from the beginning." Others would say, racial hatred; but what would continuously fuel decade after decade of animosity in such an "enlightened" and "progressive" nation? Many white Americans and recent generation immigrants take the position Black Americans do not put forth enough effort; anyone—they say—with enough determination can succeed in America, the land of equal opportunity. However, despite the numbers of Black Americans who have jumped through all the required hoops and followed all the correct strategies, success appears to be on a limited basis, and somehow it is never enough to bring the entire culture up as a whole on par with the rest of the society.

Could it be not so much a matter of our cultural and societal specifics as opposed to who we are? Do we even know who we are? Is there a spiritual significance over the life of the so-called "Negro" that is causing upheaval in the unseen realm, spilling over into the natural realm manifesting as hatred and oppression? Is it possible it was never meant for us to "succeed" as success is defined in the Western mindset? If so, what in the world did Black people in the Americas do to trigger such a bizarre set of circumstances, and what can be done to reverse them? This book holds the key to those answers.

Since the introduction of Christianity to slaves brought from Africa, Black people in the Americas have always spiritually identified with the sufferings and persecutions of the Biblical Israelites. But in the late 19th century, certain men became convinced—not out of the need for identity, but by careful analysis of the Old Testament prophecies fulfilled to date—that a deep and definite ancestral link existed between the descendants of the African slave trade and the ancient twelve tribes of Israel. Careful connecting of the scriptural and historical puzzle pieces revealed the fate of at least one of the tribes—Judah, and identified their posterity as the subjects of the West African slave trade into the American colonies. The zeal of these men to return to the patriarchal foundation of Abraham, Isaac, and Jacob led them to embrace a new identity as the true descendants of the Hebrews.

Meanwhile, the Black Church in America, founded on New Testament teachings and principles, continues to flourish as a fundamental part of Black communities. For the most part, the Black church, in the quest for equality and acceptance—has simply modeled the Western white church in mode of service, government affiliation, and interpretation of end time prophecy. Black Christians seem to give little thought to their ancestry, and few know what the Bible teaches about them or the critical role they play in the countdown of this age and the coronation of the Kingdom of God on earth.

The Black Church openly professes love for the Lord Jesus Christ—the Lion of the Tribe of Judah, and trusts Him as their risen Savior. They look to Him as the Author and Finisher of their faith, and soon returning King. Yet, salvation is on an individual basis, and the Church demonstrates limited influence in stemming the destructive forces assaulting the Black community as a whole.

Members of the Hebrew Israelite community have grasped the spiritual and historical truths revealing the circumstances which brought the Black man to America, and possess remarkable scriptural discernment regarding the evils plaguing us as a people. But in strictly embracing Old Testament theology and stopping short of the New Covenant, many reject their Kinsman Redeemer, the Lion of the Tribe of Judah. Jesus said, "No man cometh to the Father, except by me."

Psalm Chapter 85 verse 10 reads, "Mercy and truth are met together," and Jesus told the people of Judah during his day that they would know the truth, and the truth would make them free. New life in Christ via His saving mercies is priceless, but knowing the entire truth of our history brings closure, renewed confidence, and enables us to address the problems that threaten our existence at the spiritual root, rather than just pruning branches.

History is often brutal and unpleasant, because the heart of man is deceitful and desperately wicked. Nevertheless, the complete story must be told, so that those who possess the truth of history might taste and see that the Lord is good; and those who have tasted of His tender mercies might not perish for lack of knowledge.

Mizraim (Egypt) was one of Ham's sons...the Greek historian Herodotus repeatedly referred to the Egyptians as being dark-skinned with woolly hair and skin tone similar to that of Ethiopians ...and Joseph, Moses, young Jesus and his parents, and the Apostle Paul (all descendants of Shemitic Abraham) were physically indistinguishable from the Egyptians.

Chapter I...Identity Questions

Who Do You Perceive Yourself to Be?

Black. African American/Afro-American. Person of Color. These are terms we use to describe ourselves as descendants of slaves brought over unwillingly from the African continent. Have you ever wondered why that is the extent of what you know about your ancestry?

Who Do Others Perceive You to Be?

Black. African American. Negro. Colored. I must stop here, because going further it would be necessary to list over forty derogatory names used to address the Black man, woman, and child in the West and around the world. These names are what the Bible refers to as "bywords," and will be discussed further on in the book.

Who Does the God of the Bible Say You Are?

God recognizes the descendants of the slave trade and the African Diaspora as his people, his own special portion. God says you are Israel; his firstborn, his sons, and his daughters. He sees you as the last end of the generations of people who fulfilled his prophetic word that they would be driven out of the land (of Israel), scattered among the nations, and brought into Egypt—the house of bondage, by ships—with a yoke of iron around their necks. Take a moment from reading this book to look up Deuteronomy the 28th Chapter, verses 48 and 68. The fact that we are in the Western half of the world is a testimony to the reality of the God of the Bible and the truth of his word. This existence in a land where we are despised, hated, and disenfranchised is the result of a Captivity that was foretold thousands of years ago by the Old Testament prophets. The idolatry of our ancient forebears, and their ultimate rejection and murder of their prophesied Messiah—Jesus Christ, of the tribe of Judah—set a curse in motion which was plainly archived in the law given to them by Moses. Whether they didn't believe the divine spoken Word, or just didn't care whether it came to pass as long as it didn't take place in their generation is of little consequence now. The important thing is that you:

*realize your true identity

*understand how you came to be in this situation

*conform to God's standards in preparation for transitioning from Captivity to restored dominion, and

*begin to exercise the ministry of reconciliation and sound doctrine with signs following by the power of the Holy Ghost, following the example of the original Hebrew Apostles in the first century church.

I realize this is somewhat of a tall order, especially after having just received the shock of being told you are the descendants of the original Hebrews—the stock of Abraham. And while the Captivity/slavery link isn't difficult to comprehend, the whole idea of Black Americans today as descendants of the people you read about in the Bible may be hard for you to wrap your head around. I understand, because not only is this not taught in traditional churches, it is actively denied in media, education, and culture. I myself had to come to grips with it.

So as much as I would like for us to jump right into the true 'flavor' of the book, we will have to first entertain a brief historical synopsis; for if you are not firmly assured of your identity, you won't know what your purpose is. And you won't understand that in spite of centuries of persecution and low estate, God is very much for you, and has always loved you with an everlasting love. And you won't place yourself in the pivotal position to prepare the way of the Lord and make straight the paths for His return—that Ultimate Event—which will bring our Captivity to a grinding halt and restore us to a glory and joyous life vastly exceeding the legendary reign of King Solomon.

You might be thinking, greater than the days the Solomon?? You're really dreaming now. Actually, yes, greater days than Solomon's; when Judah and Israel were many, as the sand which is by the sea in multitude, eating and drinking, and making merry. Because when Christ—our Kinsman Redeemer returns, we will be in the company of One greater than Solomon, with a Kingdom which is everlasting, and a dominion that has no end. And did you catch that? I said Kinsman—as in next of kin—as in related to us. And as far as dreaming, you're not too far off on that, either. In fact, the Psalmist foresaw our day of deliverance when he wrote Psalm Chapter 126, verses 1-4:

"When the Lord turned again the Captivity of Zion, we were like them that dream.

Then was our mouth filled with laughter, and our tongue with singing: then said they among the heathen, The Lord hath done great things for them.

The Lord hath done great things for us; whereof we are glad. Turn again our Captivity, O Lord, as the streams in the south."

There will be laughter, and singing, and tears of joy streaming down people's faces. People will say to each other, "Am I dreaming? Is this just a dream? Is this real?" Someone will likely say, "I don't want to wake up...leave me alone," and someone else will answer them saying, "You don't have to wake up—it's not going away... it's REAL." Imagine living in a world where everyone loves you, and you are welcome and respected wherever you go. Life outside of this Captivity and the current wicked, oppressive world system is difficult to imagine, but God's Kingdom will come, and His divine will ultimately will be done on earth. It's just that you—descendants of slaves, have not known this Kingdom was always intended for you; and to you first, as to the first dominion—and secondly to the Gentiles, as many as are grafted in via the Blood and Love Covenant of Jesus Christ.

2

In establishing the truth of our heritage, our foundation is the 'Table of Nations' found in the tenth Chapter of Genesis, and our standard of measure is to "let God be true, and every man a liar." Using these metrics, we can determine our identity as a people; and not only ours, but those of other nationalities as well. This 'Table of Nations' is a comprehensive breakdown of the descendants of Noah's three sons: Shem, Ham, and Japheth. By the offspring of these three the entire earth was populated after their generations in their nations, and by them the nations were divided in the earth after the flood. Japheth was the oldest, Shem the middle son, and Ham, the youngest.

<u>Japheth</u>

Sons: Gomer, Magog, Madai, Javan, Tubal, Tiras, Meschec, Ashkenaz

Grandsons: Elishah, Riphath, Tarshish, Togarmah, Kittim, Dodanim

By these were the isles of the Gentiles divided in their lands, every one after his language, after their families, in their nations. The "isles" are historically identified as lands to the north and west of the Mediterranean Sea; and areas we would recognize today as Europe, the northern isles, and northern to central Asiatic land mass. The important thing to remember, is that centuries before Abram—a descendant of Shem—was called into covenant with God, the 'Table of Nations' had already clearly established who the families of the Gentiles were, and their Euro-Asian geographic location.

Next, the genealogy of <u>Ham</u>, the youngest.

Sons: Cush, Mizraim, Phut, Canaan

Grandsons: Luddim, Havilah, Sabtah, Raamah, Sheba, Dedan, Sabtechah, Nimrod, Ludim, Anamin, Lehabim, Naphtuhim, Pathrusim, Casluhim (Philistim), Caphtorim, Sidon, Heth, (progenitors of the Jebusites, Amorites, Girgasites, Hivites, Arkites, Sinites, Arvadites, Zemarites, Hamathites)

Great-grandsons: Sheba, Dedan

The Bible tells us the beginning of Nimrod's kingdom was Babel (Babylon), Erech, Accad, and Calneh, and these were located in the land of Shinar (Mesopotamia, and the territory of modern day Iraq.) From that land he went further and built Nineveh, Rehoboth, Resen, and Calah. Many readers will also recognize Nineveh as part of ancient Mesopotamia.

The (now extinct) Canaanites inhabited the land area extending as far north as the Mediterranean shore to south of the Dead Sea. This included the areas of Tyre, Sidon, Palestine, Sodom, Gomorrah, and the cities of the plain. Later in the book, we will examine the unusual circumstances of how this came about, and the ultimate outcome.

As difficult as it may be to conceive based on the current arrangement of nations and ethnicities, the black and brown Hamitic peoples of antiquity inhabited and controlled a vast land area covering the geographical expanse we know today as the entire top portion of the

African continent in addition to Egypt, Sudan, Ethiopia, Somalia, Lebanon, Palestine, Iraq, and the southern Mediterranean coast. They were certainly no strangers to technology, evidenced by the architectural undertaking of the construction of the tower of Babel in Shinar—a venture requiring detailed schematics and advanced engineering skills.

But as great as the mighty Hamitic civilizations were, they are not the root of the Black man in the West today. The Black man's ancestral heritage hearkens from Noah's middle son, Shem.

<u>Shem</u>   The Father of All the Children of Eber (Heber-Hebrews).

Sons: Elam (Persia), Asshur, Arphaxad, Lud, Aram

The Hebrew lineage descends through Arphaxad, and is traced from the Lord Jesus Christ in retrocession to Shem. The Shemites traversed the land of the Arabian Peninsula from Mesha to Sephar; their territory also extended clear to India. The patriarchs Abraham, Isaac, and Jacob sojourned and conducted commerce with the Hamitic territories, but did not attempt to build permanent cities. This is clearly illustrated by Abram (Abraham) being called by God to depart from his father's house in Ur of the Chaldees (Land of Nimrod-Chaldean-Babylonia-Iraq). The first place he sojourned was Canaanite (Hamitic) territory. Later, due to famine, he removed and went to another Hamitic territory—Egypt. He then returned to Canaan, and was there at least ten years. When Abraham's wife Sarah died, he negotiated with a prominent Hittite (Hamitic) living among the descendants of Heth (Hamitic) for a specific plot of burial land. Two final examples are found in Genesis Chapter 24 verse 10, where Abraham's servant makes a journey to Mesopotamia, to the city of Nahor, Abraham's brother, and in Genesis Chapter 31 verse 20, where Abraham's nephew Laban is referred to as "Laban the Syrian."

To recap, Biblical Shemitics lived and moved freely among the Hamitic peoples; repeatedly appearing in such geographical disparities as Egypt, Canaanite territories, and Mesopotamia (Iraq). They were indistinguishable by skin color, and defined rather by specific cultural distinctions and religious practices. It is noteworthy to mention that the original dark Arabs—descendants of Ishmael from the union between Abraham and the Egyptian Hagar, were a mixture of Hamitic and Shemitic.

The Table of Nations clearly indicates that Ethiopians, Egyptians, Libyans, and the Canaanite peoples who inhabited the Afri-Mediterranean coastal areas are the direct descendants of Ham, and to a great degree the first three groups retained their ancient land boundaries and remained confined to their original geographical area. Yet, neither the Bible nor secular history teaches that the above mentioned groups were brought by ships to slavery. Deductive reasoning then, infers that even though the African continent today is populated with diverse people of black and brown skin, not everyone on the continent descended from the line of Ham. There must have been a different group of dark skinned people dwelling in the African interior that were kidnapped and brought into bondage to the Americas and other regions of the world: a people neither Hamitic nor Japhethic. The identity of these dark-skinned people who were led out in chains from the African interior and the West African coast is a critical piece of the puzzle in the quest for understanding what God has done in the past, and the place of the Black man and woman as latter day prophecy unfolds.

We constantly hear Western 'prophecy' teachers and speakers advise us to "watch Israel. Israel is the timepiece." But when they strive to interpret prophecy by events currently taking place in the Middle East, they are focusing on a fraudulent clock. Before Bible prophecy can ever be correctly interpreted, one must have discernment of who Israel and Judah really are.

All Figures in the Bible Are Black/Brown

Popular culture would have you believe the only black/dark brown skinned people in the Bible were various Ethiopians, one of the kings of the East who came to pay homage to the prophesied Redeemer born in Bethlehem, and a man from Cyrene who happened to be nearby when the Lord Jesus Christ stumbled under the weight of the cross. But is this an accurate depiction of the people to whom the scriptures were written to and about?

Virtually all significant names and events recorded in Scripture reference black/brown Shemitics, with a sprinkling of Hamitics. So when you read the pages of your Bible, you are reading about people whom you would recognize today as Black, so-called 'negro', or African American. And while much of the Biblical evidence for the dark skin color of Shem's descendants is anecdotal, the unique circumstances surrounding each piece of evidence build a solid case in support of black/brown Shem.

Ham means "burnt" or "warm." Yet, in instance after instance Biblical observers were unable to distinguish between Hebrews (descendants of Jacob through Isaac and Abraham) and Hamites. Following are some examples:

*In the story of Joseph in the book of Genesis, Joseph's jealous brothers sell him into slavery in Egypt (Mizraim; also called The Land of Ham.) Some years later a severe famine arises, and the brothers go to Egypt to purchase food. As Joseph had prophesied in his youth, his brothers bow down before him, for Joseph had become second in command in Egypt. Joseph recognized his brethren, but they were unable to distinguish him from the surrounding Egyptians.

*Years pass and a new ruler ascends the Egyptian throne; a ruler who did not honor the memory of Joseph as the divine vessel sent by God to preserve Egypt during the period of famine. A tide of ill will surges against the descendants of Jacob's sons whose population by now has exploded, and their status as guests in the land of Goshen degenerates to forced slavery.

*The new ruler employs male infanticide as a tactic to weaken the Hebrew population and dilute the race. It is during this pogrom on Hebrew baby boys that Moses is drawn out of the river by Pharaoh's daughter. Had Moses been extremely fair skinned or white, he would have been suspected of having leprosy or a genetic malformation, as a subsequent example will demonstrate, and probably left for the crocodiles. Yet, Pharaoh's daughter adopted Moses and raised him in the house of royalty as her own son, implying that he could pass for her natural offspring.

*Moses becomes a wanted man after involvement in an incident directly stemming from identifying with his true Hebrew heritage. He flees to the land of Midian, and while resting beside a well, overhears a commotion. Shepherds are harassing the daughters of the priest of Midian who have come to the well to water their flocks. Moses intervenes and assists them in completing their task. When asked by their father why they were able to return home so early, they reply "An Egyptian delivered us out of the hand of the shepherds..."

*Moses is commissioned to go before the powerful Pharaoh and his royal court to deliver the decree from God to release the Hebrews. Knowing Pharaoh will be difficult to persuade, Moses asks God for miracles which will prove that the power of God is with him. God instructs Moses to put his right hand inside his garment at the chest, and then remove it. When he takes

it out, it is described as "leprous, and white as snow." When he repeats the process, the skin color becomes once again as his other hand. There would have had to be a very drastic pigment change, for had Moses already been white or very light-skinned, the miracle would have had little impact on Pharaoh.

*Samson tells Delilah he has "seven locks" on his head. The word used for "locks" in the Hebrew translates to "ringlets." Since Samson was a Nazarite and his hair had never been cut since birth, it is not hard to envision an immense thicket of ringlets in extremely long masses separated into seven sections on his head. If one looks closely at the hair of people of African American heritage, it is easy to see individual strands are like a tightly coiled spring— essentially miniature ringlets. This is a defining characteristic of our hair although the degree of the tightness of the coil varies from person to person.

*In the Song of Solomon, when the Shulamite describes herself as "black yet comely" (beautiful), Solomon responds by calling her fairest among women. The canticle goes on to describe King Solomon's hair as "black and bushy." Lest any reading stumble at the verse preceding where he is described as white and ruddy," the definition of the original Hebrew word used there for "white" translates to "dazzling", and ruddy speaks to the blood showing through the skin as would be possible under intense emotion. The best Biblical comparisons to this "dazzling" speak to radiating brilliancy; such as the appearance of Moses' face when he came down from the mount after communing with God, and the Lord Jesus Christ on the Mount of Transfiguration. People with white skin do not glow with luminosity or rays of light as the Hebrew translation for this particular usage of white implies.

*The Apostle Paul is mistaken for the Egyptian leader of a terrorist movement during his last visit to Jerusalem. When a Roman squadron intervenes to rescue Paul from a raging mob, the commander attempts to ascertain Paul's identity, and asks him, "Aren't you that Egyptian that some time back started an insurrection and led four thousand men who were murderers out into the wilderness?" (paraphrase mine)

Evidence Points to a Black Jesus Christ

Many readers will be familiar with the account in the second Chapter of Matthew where Joseph, Mary, and young Jesus fled to Egypt to escape the murderous wrath of Herod. They had just received valuable gifts from the Wise Men of the East, and combined with Joseph's carpentry vocation they were likely able to live comfortably until they could return to Israel.

But what good are skills and resources if you stick out like a sore thumb? The survival of Joseph, his wife, and child depended on their ability to seamlessly blend into Egyptian society. God would not have warned them to flee to a place where they could be easily distinguished as outsiders. The Greek historian Herodotus repeatedly referred to the Egyptians as being dark-skinned with woolly hair and skin tone similar to that of Ethiopians. Joseph, Mary, and Jesus moved freely in Egypt without arousing suspicion. If 'color doesn't matter', why aren't they correctly portrayed in modern print and media?

At the end of the Bible, in the Book of the Revelation, the Lord Jesus Christ appears in a glorified, resurrected body. The Apostle John speaks of the blinding radiance emanating from the Lord, but he is still able to discern other distinctive features; among them, feet the color of fine brass as if burning in a furnace, and hair white like wool. Since all wool is not white, we should search the scriptures for additional clarity—and we find it in the seventh Chapter of Daniel. In a vision, the prophet Daniel sees God, whom he identifies as "the Ancient of Days" seated on the throne of judgment. The hair of the Ancient of Days is described as "like the pure wool." The Hebrew word used in this passage for wool is closely associated with another Hebrew word which means shaggy. Daniel also sees "one like the Son of Man" coming on the clouds of heaven. This "one like the Son of Man" was brought near to the Ancient of Days, and received glory, an indestructible kingdom and an everlasting dominion. This entity the prophet Daniel saw is none other than the Lord Jesus Christ—the Lion of the Tribe of Judah!

Several "ancient letters" allegedly from the first and second centuries have surfaced containing descriptions of Jesus with Nordic European features. It appears these letters were written to refute the original translation of the historian Josephus' testimony describing Jesus. But, first, to explain about Josephus. He was born Joseph ben Mattiyahu (son of Matthias), a Black Hebrew of noble birth who first fought alongside the Judæan Zealots in the rebellion against Rome; but defected upon realizing the struggle against a world empire was a lost cause. He saved his skin by approaching the Roman ruler Vespasian and advising him that he (Vespasian) was the fulfillment of the ancient Hebrew prophecy (found in Numbers Chapter 24 verse 17) foretelling the conquering Star of Jacob. Josephus knew just enough of what to say to preserve his life. Like many today, he quoted the word, but took it out of context to support his immediate agenda. Properly interpreted, the prophecy refers to the Lord Jesus Christ—the Lion of the Tribe of Judah, and reads like this:

"I shall see him, but not now: I shall behold him, but not nigh: there shall come a Star out of Jacob, and a Sceptre shall rise out of Israel, and shall smite the corners of Moab, and destroy all the children of Sheth." Apparently Josephus stopped there, for had he continued, it would have been obvious it was Israel—not Rome—that was prophesied to be the victor... "And Edom shall be a possession, Seir also shall be a possession for his enemies; and Israel shall do valiantly."

Rome never came forth out of Israel; it could only hold a ruling scepter over Israel. But the Romans were firm believers in oracles, and in the wake of the impending clash with a foe that would rather die than surrender, this prophetic green light was exactly what Vespasian needed to boost the morale of his forces. In God's timing and providence, the Roman victory was already a foregone conclusion, because the prophetic clock had already progressed into the times of the Gentiles. Nevertheless, for Josephus' apparent accuracy, he was granted Roman citizenship and given the Roman name Flavius.

Josephus went on to become translator and advisor to Vespasian's son Titus, the general responsible for the siege of Jerusalem A.D. 66-70 which resulted in the destruction of Jerusalem and the Temple. He is invaluable to our history as descendants of the original Hebrews because he himself was Hebrew and thoroughly schooled in the history, culture, and political intrigue of the era. Do not be fooled by the white European sculptures and paintings of Josephus which the oppressor has circulated in his reinvention of history. Josephus was a Black Hebrew.

Having said that, I now present evidence of a Black Jesus based on Josephus' own testimony. An interesting discovery was made by the Austrian historian Robert Eisler, which findings he published in 1931. Eisler located a Slavonic (Old Russian) translation, "Slavische Uebersetzung der Halōsis tēs Ierousalēm des Flavius Josephus"[1] ...the Capture of Jerusalem. The Slavonic manuscript was transcribed from the original Greek text, and had not been modified by Western European Christian translators. After carefully reconstructing and translating the manuscript, Josephus' description of our Elder Brother and Kinsman Redeemer contained the following observations. He was:

*A man of simple appearance

*Black-skinned

*short of stature

*prognathic—meaning a protrusion of either the upper or lower jaw

*had a long nose

*eyebrows that met in the middle

*scanty hair (an archaic description for short tight curls) parted in the middle in the Nazarene custom

*an undeveloped beard

This is much more in line with the description found in Isaiah Chapter 53 verse 2 which says: "he hath no form nor comeliness; and when we shall see him, there is no beauty that we should desire him...," as opposed to the tall, pale, silken-haired substitute produced by European culture. As participation in the New Covenant devolved from a living organism rooted in the heavenly dimension and animated by the Holy Ghost, to the religious window dressing of worldly empire, it was necessary to make Christianity attractive and appealing to the masses. In the midst of the Renaissance and European self-actualization, a short, dark, unattractive man would have defeated the purpose of religious iconography. The Slavonic manuscript is,

---

[1] Die slavische Uebersetzung der Halōsis tēs Hierousalēm des Flavius Josephus, Eisler, Robert, Prague, 1930.

however, significantly more in line with the later Russian painting 'Maundy Thursday—Christ Washes the Disciple's Feet' which is archived at the Pskov School in Pskov, Russia.[2]

February is Black History Month...but the Bible is the Black History Archive

Gentile society in the West devotes just one month out of the year (February) in recognition of Black History. They would have you believe your history began only in the late 1600's with the arrival of the slave ships. Actually, Black history goes much further back; back to the Biblical patriarchs, back through Shem to Noah, back through the godly line of Seth, even to the very beginning.

Some archaeologists intimate that no groups inhabiting the Biblical land during the Old Testament era were negroid. Perhaps these same researchers can explain then why only the negroid peoples today collectively suffer the Biblical curses of Deuteronomy 28, a position which would make them the descendants of a group who prophetically fulfilled verses 48 and 68 of that chapter.

Which Perception Will You Choose to Believe?

So far, I have

*demonstrated a mysterious void exists in the knowledge of ancestry among Black people inhabiting the Americas today

*pointed out that verifiable history demonstrates the descendants of the ancient Hamitic kingdoms have historically remained in their designated territories, and were not the subjects of the Trans-Atlantic slave trade taking place between the 17th and mid-19th centuries

*sourced the Table of Nations to prove that the people inhabiting the area of present day Palestine known as the State of Israel are descended from Japheth—who the Bible identifies as "Gentiles", a term for people the Lord Jesus Christ himself said would be inhabiting Jerusalem when He returned to judge the earth, and

*shown that the Biblical scriptures—written to and by Hebrew people—present compelling evidence that Hebrews are a dark race; ranging in complexion from brown light enough for the blood to show through the skin, to a deepness that rendered them indistinguishable from their dark brown and black Hamitic neighbors. I have also pointed out

---

[2] The ethnicity of the original Hebrews in Jerusalem is captured in a Russian iconography dated to the fourteenth century, and painted in tempura on wood panel. The painting, titled Maundy Thursday (Jesus washes the feet of the Disciples) is kept at the Pskov School of iconography in Pskov, Russia. The work is well preserved and the colors still vibrant. Clearly shown is the dark brown skin and black, curled hair of the Lord Jesus Christ and his disciples.

that the visions of the prophet Daniel and the Apostle John speak of the wool-like hair of the Ancient of Days and the Lord Jesus, and bronze/burned brass skin of the risen Lord Jesus.

WHAT'S IMPORTANT

We need to be aware of how God has chosen to reveal Himself and his Son based on the visions in the books of Daniel and Revelation. If God himself was revealed to the prophet Daniel having hair with the texture and appearance of wool, and God calls ancient Israel his son (Hosea Chapter 11 verse 1) and admonishes them to "look to the Rock from whence they are hewn, and the pit (quarry) from which they are dug", this clearly speaks of a special familial bond—a relation—even to the extent that the physical features bear resemblance; in this case, such as the hair. Similar to when the remark is made, he looks just like his father, or he has his father's features. This confession of identity with the black/brown descendants of Abraham was revealed by the Lord to the prophets Daniel and Hosea, and archived in the scriptures thousands of years before Japhethic Europeans or Euro-Asians who proselytized to Judaism began to rise as a significant culture. Further, Afro-centric adversaries to the faith who enjoy tossing around the phrase, "Jesus is the white man's God" need to understand the Lord Jesus Christ was/is the Black man's God long before any white people came into the picture. He is our near kin; our Kinsman.

The Gentiles have literally devoted centuries to depicting God, Jesus, and the heavenly angels in their own image. Even the latest biblically themed cinematic offerings at the time of the writing of this book have been carefully designed to ignore all traces of true Shemitic and Hamitic blackness. They are demeaning in a subtle manner, when Blacks who are present in the film are depicted as servants or criminals; whereas Moses, the Israelites, and the Hamitic Egyptians are white! Even as God awakens the sons of Zion against the sons of Greece, the Gentiles are intensifying their efforts to maintain the historic deception. But your Bible gives the true and accurate depiction of Hebrews, and you O Judah—the modern day descendants of the slave trade—can be encouraged and rejoice in the knowledge that our Lord is not ashamed to identify with us in physical features and characteristics!

Hebrews Chapter 2 verse 11 states, "both he that sanctifieth and they who are sanctified are all of one: for which cause he is not ashamed to call them brethren," and goes on in verses 16 and 17 to say, "For verily he took not on him the nature of angels; but he took on him the seed of Abraham. Wherefore in all things it behoved him to be made like unto his brethren, that he might be a merciful and faithful high priest in things pertaining to God, to make reconciliation for the sins of the people." It doesn't get any clearer than that. The Lord Jesus Christ—The Lion of the Tribe of Judah, was made after our lineage as Hebrews and is not ashamed to identify physically with us as Black and Brown people. Read it once again. It does not say he chose to identify with the human race as a whole: it specifically states, the seed of Abraham (the Shemite), and that in all things he was made like unto his brethren.

Knowledge is pleasant to the soul...but you must call out for insight and lift your voice to understanding, and look for it as for silver and search for it as for hidden treasure. In the spirit of a truth seeker, let's go further in tracing the path of circumstances and prophetic directives that brought us to our present state.

Chapter II...Identity Crisis

God shall enlarge Japheth, and he shall dwell in the tents of Shem.

Divine Decree: A Temporary Removal from Heritage

Before we can understand the bond between God and our forefathers, and the circumstances which affected it, it is helpful to have a brief review of their historical relationship. A specific set of sequences characterized the unique union between the Lord God and the Black man descended through the patriarchs and the twelve tribes of Israel. This pattern involved calling, relationship, covenant, choice of the called to honor covenant, blessing or punishment based upon the choice, provisional resource in the case of violation of covenant, punishment for deliberate rejection of covenant, deliverance from persecution resulting from punishment for rejection of covenant, renewal of covenant, and further opportunities of testing with option to obey or disobey covenant. This is the manner in which God chose to deal with our ancient forebears; with the intended end that they would be a people peculiar to Him, a chosen priesthood, and a light to the rest of the nations. This constant balance of testing, corrective discipline, divine provision and protection, and atonement through sacrificial offerings was designed to incrementally bring God's people to a stature of virtual godhood in the earth.

If this statement seems like a stretch of the imagination, consider Psalm Chapter 82 verses 6-7... "I have said, You are gods; and all of you are children of the most High, But you shall die like men, and fall like one of the princes." Compare this to the words of the Lord Jesus Christ found in John Chapter 10 verses 34-36... "Is it not written in your law, I said, Ye are gods? If he called them gods, unto whom the word of God came, and the scripture cannot be broken; Say ye of him, whom the Father hath sanctified, and sent into the world, Thou blasphemest; because I said, I am the Son of God?"

Jesus was talking to the religious elite of his brethren—the tribe of Judah, and he specifically stated it was in their law that God had called them gods. The Hebrew translation of this particular instance of 'gods' implies a deity, great, judges, magistrates, and angelic; incidentally the same word translated for the attributes Satan promised Eve she would attain if she ate of the fruit of the Tree of the Knowledge of Good and Evil. These attributes were already intended for God's created image and likeness in the earth, and it was never necessary to disobey God to achieve them.

God has never dealt with any people on earth the way he dealt with our forefathers. The calling and privileges of a god-like status on earth were manifested time and time again through the godly line of Shem that would bring the promised Messiah. Some examples are:

*Enoch bodily translated to the heavenly dimension

*Abraham's conversational relationship with God and ability to intercede for others

*Wives of such beauty that God had to personally intervene to prevent them from being violated

*Tremendous material wealth and success in sowing/reaping/animal husbandry

*Supernatural ability to defeat five kings and their armies with only three hundred eighteen men

*Encounter with the theophany Melchizedek (a manifestation of God visible to the human senses; the pre-Incarnate Christ)

*Procreative abilities past the normal age

*Jacob's direct encounter with the angels of God

*Wrestling with an Angel of God and prevailing

*The terror of God surrounding Jacob and keeping his enemies at bay

*Supernatural preservation in the wilderness—shoes and clothing indestructible; eating (manna) angel's food

*Ability to command the celestial powers during battle

*Many, many other miracles wrought by the judges and prophets of Israel

The patriarchs walked closely with God and learned to trust Him through situations of testing and uncertainty. Over the passage of time, the progeny of Jacob found themselves once again in the Land of Ham when they reunited with their brother Joseph and were welcomed by a benevolent Pharaoh. They were given the land of Goshen as a separate dwelling place, for Jacob's people were pastoral, and every shepherd is an abomination to the Egyptians. Still, life was good in Egypt; good enough that the Hebrew population exploded exponentially. A subsequent Pharaoh ascending the throne saw the Hebrews as a disposable human resource to be exploited, and idyllic pastoral life transitioned to rigorous forced labor. The Hebrews were resigned to building the great treasure cities of Egypt, all while population control measures were enforced; in much the same way as the wealth of the Americas was built on the unpaid labor of ancient Israel's future descendants. They groaned under the oppression, and the stage was set for divine intervention and deliverance.

If you are reading this book, you are probably familiar with the story of the plagues of Egypt, the Passover, and the Deliverance through the Red Sea. The Lord manifested His power on behalf of His people in a manner never before seen. But while God brought the people out of Egypt, much of Egypt was still in the people. Egypt was a polytheistic society, meaning many gods were worshipped for different purposes. Not only that, but images were crafted of these gods to provide a focal point of worship. This new concept of an invisible God who demanded sole worship and a specific hierarchy to communicate to the masses was difficult for many to accept. Within hours of the great deliverance, the people demanded a tangible idol to worship; a worship which would begin with feasting and end with sexual immorality. It is no wonder then, that the very first commandment forbids idolatry, and is expanded by the Lord Jesus Christ to encompass love for one's neighbor as ones' self. If you will make a conscious effort to refrain from sinning against God, you will make a conscious effort not to sin against your neighbor. A people who modeled these commandments would have indeed been a light to the nations of the world.

Idolatry was always the sin that plagued our forebears and the tipping point that angered God and caused Him to forcefully remove them from the land and scatter them to the four winds. Because God has already declared the end from the beginning, He knew exactly how this loss of heritage would take place, who it would involve, how long it would last, and the time of eventual restoration. Now, let's go further to see just how this unfolded.

Rise of the Gentiles...Noah's Prophecy over Japheth Manifests

That Jacob's descendants would abdicate the land of their inheritance to another people was decreed in the Bible as far back as the ninth Chapter of Genesis. Verses 18 through 27 set the stage for this concession, but demand careful inspection and interpretation lest the reader follow the same error as the oppressor of God's people.

18 And the sons of Noah, that went forth of the ark, were Shem, and Ham, and Japheth: and Ham is the father of Canaan.

19 These are the three sons of Noah: and of them was the whole earth overspread.

20 And Noah began to be an husbandman, and he planted a vineyard:

And he drank of the wine, and was drunken; and he was uncovered within his tent.

And Ham, the father of Canaan, saw the nakedness of his father, and told his two brethren without.

And Shem and Japheth took a garment, and laid it upon both their shoulders, and went backward, and covered the nakedness of their father; and their faces were backward, and they saw not their father's nakedness.

And Noah awoke from his wine, and knew what his younger son had done unto him. 25 And he said, Cursed be Canaan; a servant of servants shall he be unto his brethren. 26 And he said, Blessed be the Lord God of Shem; and Canaan shall be his servant.27 God shall enlarge Japheth, and he shall dwell in the tents of Shem; and Canaan shall be his servant. Noah was drunk, and uncovered in his tent. The Hebrew word used for uncovered in this instance is defined as 'to denude in a disgraceful sense'. The following verse starts in an interesting manner: "And Ham, the father of Canaan..." Ham was also the father of Cush, Mizraim, and Phut; but twice in this discourse a specific emphasis is placed on Ham as the father of Canaan. The word 'saw' used in this verse can be defined in the Hebrew as to gaze, spy or stare. The word 'told' in this verse is defined in the Hebrew "to announce out loud". This trespass resulted in a curse not upon Ham, but his son Canaan, and only Canaan. God had already blessed Noah and his sons upon disembarking from the ark, as demonstrated in the first verse of Genesis Chapter nine; so it was not possible for Ham to be cursed.

The terms of Canaan's curse demanded servitude to his Hamitic relatives, and his uncles Shem and Japheth. To Black people as descendants of Shemites, this means Canaan served our forebears, rather than the misconception that the Black people in the West today are descendants of Ham who must serve all other people, for Ham never served anybody.

We also know that the Canaanites as a distinct people were driven out of the land promised to Abraham, and either wiped out in warfare, or eventually absorbed into neighboring cultures, and no one can locate a Canaanite today. As important as it is to set the Ham/Canaan curse record straight, the first part of the final verse is the one demanding our closest scrutiny:

God shall enlarge Japheth, and he shall dwell in the tents of Shem...

Lest any Japhethic descendant read this verse and exclaim, "Aha! You see, I have every right to be where I am and exploit the Shemitic peoples and their resources," we employ the same meticulous exposition of the Hebrew translation used to bring clarity to the verses about Canaan. Remember also that in Noah's entire response after the incident, Shem was the only son with a reference to a blessing...and that blessing being the God Shem would worship; the statement about Japheth is a proclamation—but as we shall see, not something one would call a blessing, and nothing at all is said about Ham.

In every other instance where the word 'enlarge' appears in the Old Testament, the word rachab is used, with a meaning of to broaden, make room, or open wide. But in this passage where Noah spoke over his son Japheth, enlarge "pathah" in the Hebrew translation—means to open, be roomy in a mental or moral sense; to be or make simple or in a sinister way delude, to allure, deceive, enlarge, entice, flatter, persuade, silly (one).

This Hebrew word "pathah" with its inference of a large mental and moral sense, delusion, deception, enticement, and persuasion aptly describe the unregenerate Gentile mindset; the deluded sense of mental and moral superiority, the deception used in dealing with other ethnicities, and the persuasive manipulation that characterizes their control of the Western culture and society during this their time. In the mildest sense, the implication is an overinflated sense of self-esteem; in the most extreme sense, replacement of God as one's creator and savior, an obsessive preoccupation with dominating unlike nations, and a sense of entitlement whereby the exploitation of other's resources is justified. This is why Paul—a Black Hebrew, was able to speak authoritatively in I Thessalonians Chapter 4 verse 5 when he characterized the Gentiles as a people who know not God. That was true then, and it is still true today. While the Black Hebrews are the original sons to whom first dominion is granted, and have traditionally been in a covenant relationship with God, and still are—albeit placed on a temporary earthly "time out" on disciplinary grounds, the only way any Gentile can know God is through a saving relationship resulting from genuine repentance from sin and submission to the blood covenant of the Lord Jesus Christ, and obedience to His teachings.

One can easily see then, why the Gentiles as a whole are in a precarious position in these end times. The same pride and self-delusion which convinces them to ignore and obscure obvious history influences them to re-create the Lord Jesus Christ in their own image, replace the people of the original covenant with people who mirror their own physical image, and use the word of God to justify oppression and atrocity against their Hamitic and Shemitic brethren throughout the world. This narcissistic deception has persuaded them such actions are justifiable and will invoke no wrath or judgment from God. Indeed, God foresaw Japheth's attitude in the last days when He spoke through the Psalmist in Psalm Chapter 50 verses 15-22 saying,

"But unto the wicked God saith, What hast thou to do to declare my statutes, or that thou shouldest take my covenant in thy mouth?

Seeing thou hatest instruction, and castest my words behind thee.

When thou sawst a thief, then thou consentedst with him, and hast been partaker with adulterers.

Thou givest thy mouth to evil, and thy tongue frameth deceit.

Thou sittest and speakest against thy brother; thou slanderest thine own mother's son.

These things you have done, and I have been silent; you thought that I was one like yourself.

But now I rebuke you and lay the charge before you.

Now consider this, ye that forget God, lest I tear you in pieces, and there be none to deliver."

Pride goes before a fall, and a haughty spirit before destruction. Noah said, "God shall enlarge Japheth". God has done this in part that He might be glorified in the ends of the earth in the Day of the Lord. Remember that God spoke of Pharaoh, "And in very deed for this cause have I raised thee up, for to shew in thee my power; and that my name may be declared throughout all the earth." The Hamitic peoples were the first to experience the avenging power of God on behalf of the people God refers to as "His Portion", and the Japhethic peoples will experience it last. The old saying comes into play, 'We can do this the easy way, or we can do this the hard way.' The sons of Japheth can take the easy yoke of compassion and brotherly love which the Lord Jesus Christ offers or they can choose the hard way of the transgressor—which will ultimately lead to destruction beyond remedy.

Biological Genetics: Japhethic Black, Brown, and yes...White

Although the nations of the world as a whole are set against the posterity of the descendants of the Hebrews, the harshest treatment in the West emanates from the "white man." Yet, history and recovered artifacts from the most distant millennia are virtually silent about people of white or pale skin. And while all white people can be traced to Japheth, most Japhethic peoples are not white. All three brothers—Shem, Ham, and Japheth—had the same parents; in fact, Japheth was the firstborn. And while Ham's name does imply that he was the darkest of the brothers, there is nothing recorded to indicate a radical skin color difference among them. Another factor to consider is that at some point, the brothers and their collective families delayed occupying their apportioned territories in favor of attempting a single world power base. This mega-city—site of a technological endeavor designed to connect earth to space, was situated in Shinar (modern day Iraq); a climate that would be difficult for people with sparse melanin to tolerate.

The divine intervention at the Tower of Babel split up the family confederacy, but something else occurred over subsequent generations which further divided the posterity of the brothers and their families. That something was albinism.

Albinism is defined in medical dictionaries as the "congenital absence of normal pigmentation or coloration in the eyes only or in the skin, hair, and eyes." Congenital means "of or pertaining to a condition present at birth". It is the result of a recessive gene. Albinism lightens hair from black and dark brown to light brown, blond, and red. Differing expressions of the gene influence blue and green eyes. In some cases, hair that is kinky or tightly curled will straighten. There are differing degrees of albinism, and in the most extreme form—tyrosinase deficiency—no melanin is produced.

A striking example of the contrast between albinism and normal melanin among modern Japhethic peoples can be found in the comparison of people from two modern day Pakistani groups: the Koli tribe, and albinos from the Bhatti tribe. The facial structures and features are all basically the same, but the skin of the Koli people is a rich dark brown and the hair deep black, while the albinos of the Bhatti tribe have fair (white) skin, and blond or red hair.

The people aligned most closely today with the original dark Japhethic stock are the current inhabitants of Central Asia, such as the inhabitants of the 'stan' regions—Kurdistan, Pakistan, Afghanistan, Uzbekistan, and groups in the Indus Valley. (The far eastern and southeast Asian peoples are yet another subgroup established from very ancient times, stemming from mixture between Sinite Hamitics and albino Japhethics.)

The stigma associated with loss of pigment in the ancient world may have stemmed from fear of disease (association with leprosy) or fear of a curse. As a matter of fact, horrific treatment of albinos still goes on today—particularly in some regions of Africa. At any rate, individuals with albinism were driven out from the general populace and forced to band together for support and survival. Rather than the fallacy taught by some that white people gradually lost melanin as they migrated to cooler climates, simple logic dictates the recessive albinism gene was the catalyst that forced them north. If the degree of sunlight was the controlling factor, they would gradually darken to deep brown again when residing in tropic and sub-tropic climates. But that does not occur. Migration out of Africa and into the highlands of the Asian steppes would have provided some respite from the tropical and sub-tropical climates. Inter-breeding due to isolation only served to perpetuate the hypopigmentation. During the era of the Phoenicians, white people were not known to occupy the Levant, but were recognized to dwell in the lands to the north, northeast, and northwest of the Mediterranean Sea. The name 'Europe' is said to stem from the Phoenician word 'Ur-Appa,'[3] by which they sought to explain the division of the world from where the 'people with fair faces' dwelt in contrast to the darker skin of the Africans.

---

[3] PINNOCK'S GUIDE TO KNOWLEDGE, August 17 1883.

Japheth Increases...Melanin Decreases

Most Black Americans find it difficult to believe when told they are the descendants of the original Hebrews, and that their ancestors once blended seamlessly with the Hamitic peoples surrounding them in Egypt and Mesopotamia. The images they see in the news of people in the Mediterranean and North African regions are mostly light brown to almost white, and many of the facial features have a distinctly European look. The images they see of people in the modern day state of Israel are practically all white. Digital and print religious media also seem to support this as fact. Thumb through the pages of illustrated Bible story publications in any Christian bookstore and you will not find the Old or New Testament subjects correctly depicted with dark to medium dark brown skin and kinky, bushy, or tight wavy hair and negroid features. In the Apocrypha, Book of I Maccabees Chapter 3 verse 48, the writer tells us the heathen sought to paint their images in the book of the Law. The same strategy is still going on today. It is easy to understand how this color and ethnicity dissonance triggers a huge disconnect when speaking to Black brothers and sisters about their true heritage.

You Can Change the Population, but Not the Prophecy

The lightening of the skin color of the Mediterranean and North African regions observed today can be traced directly to events such as the Crusades, Moorish conquests, and European immigration into Africa. The whiteness of the inhabitants of the modern day state of Israel is verifiably traced to their immigration from Europe. However, no matter how concerted the effort to replace the Black Hebrew heritage with a white substitute, it is impossible to change the prophecies of Deuteronomy Chapter 28 verses 48 and 68, and the fact that the Black man in the Americas is the only ethnic group who—in the latter times, came by ships to Egypt (the house of bondage) with a yoke of iron around his neck.

The Bible consistently references incidences of Shemitic and Hamitic people mingling, trading, and warring; and on rare occasions Japheth is mentioned. However, there is never any specific mention of "people of white skin"; even throughout the gospels of the New Covenant. The Apostle Paul mentions the 'Scythians', and gold relics from the period representing the height of their culture depict them with straight hair. In 2005, a blond-haired, elaborately tattooed Scythian mummy dated to the eighth century B.C. was unearthed from the permafrost in the area near where Russia, Mongolia, and China converge. The writings of the ancient Greek historian Herodotus tell us that a nomadic tribe called the Budini made a confederacy with the Scythians to repel an invasion of the Medes. Herodotus described the Budini as a large and powerful nation with deep blue eyes and bright red hair. This group and tribes similar to them—cultures with practices we would recognize as pagan—overspread Russia to the north, and Europe to the northwest and west; eventually displacing the black Hamitics who were already living as far north as Germania and the British Isles.

The emergence of people of white skin as a collective and significant force in the shaping of society as we have come to know it is actually a relatively recent occurrence on the vast time-line of world history. The fact that their origin is due to a genetic deviation is supported by the fact that in terms of world population they have always been a minority, with declining numbers moving forward into the future. While the Japhethic peoples as a whole have burgeoning populations, this particular sub group is losing ground. That the smallest group would wield the greatest power in the end of days is a construct of God alone. At the same time, that the wrath of God is prophetically destined to fall heaviest on the power controlling the world at the end of the age should sound an alarm to the one wielding that power.

WHAT'S IMPORTANT

None of us get to choose how we come into the world. The families of Japheth who received and propagated the recessive albinism gene are no less loved of God, despite the humiliation and persecution they originally endured in being driven out from their darker brethren and likewise made unwelcome among the Hamitic and Shemitic peoples. The condemnation upon many of them in these latter days (basically from the 17th century forward) stems from the sin of pride: taking something that is a physical defect, essentially evidence of the effect of sin and fall from perfection—and exploiting it as a badge of superiority and entitlement whereby all others are deemed inferior and worthy of subjugation. This sin of pride holds a strong spiritual grip on the end time powers of the Anglo, European, Australian, and European migrants to Palestine. But it is rooted in the legacy and mindset of a very real person who lived many thousands of years ago.

Spiritual Genetics: Identified by Fruits over Flesh

Before revealing the identity of this person whose spiritual outlook characterizes the subgroup of Japhethic people controlling the world at the end of this age, it is necessary to briefly take a look at the interaction of human personalities, earthly kingdoms, and ruling spiritual principalities. This is a theme that plays out over and over again in scripture, and is most pronounced during the period the Bible calls the latter days. Here is how it works:

God sometimes refers to a kingdom by its founder, the family it proceeded from, or its defining characteristic. Thus, 'Israel' compasses both Jacob as an individual, and the Hebrew nation collectively under all twelve tribes, and Judah. Esau, brother of Jacob and progenitor of the Edomite nation (also called Idumea and Mount Seir) corresponds to Edom. Egypt is variously referred to in scripture as Mizraim (Ham's second son), the land of Ham, and "the house of bondage".

Whenever a kingdom no longer exists, or is still geographically intact—but stripped of the immense power it wielded in ancient times, God will still reference that kingdom as viable and a force to be judged, because of the malevolent spiritual principality associated with it. This means an area far removed from the ancient geographical location can literally take on the spiritual attributes of that original power, and a people generationally or racially different from the original can be influenced spiritually to emulate the original offending person/nation. The ruling powers of the West as a whole are collectively called "Grecia"; the lands where oppressive bondage and disenfranchisement hold the descendants of the Hebrews can correctly be called "Egypt"; the culture of media mind control (witchcraft) drug proliferation (sorcery) and obsession with materialism that characterizes the West can aptly be referred to as "Babylon"; its obsession with military exploits and empirical expansion is synonymous with "Chaldea" and "Assyria"; the pleasure loving lifestyle and aggressive perversion in the West can rightly be called "Sodom"; and the people/system involved with perpetuating the persecution and disenfranchisement of the Hebrew posterity of Jacob can accurately be called "Esau, Edom, mount Seir, or Idumea."

In other words, where all antagonists of Israel are concerned, matching the spiritual character of the named people or nation to the ancient power is more accurate than attempting to trace ancestral lineage or geographical location. Knowing this principle is the key to understanding how Gentiles of a different bloodline became the modern personification of Esau and Edom; the nemesis who opposed and obstructed the Israel of God from time immemorial, and kept his hatred forever.

That the rulers of this earth actively communicate and collaborate with the high wicked spiritual powers that controlled the original geographic territories of Israel's enemies is demonstrated in Isaiah Chapter 24 verses 21-22. We know the context of these verses refers to the Great Day of God's Wrath because verses 19-20 describe the cataclysmic rending of the earth, and verse 23 describes the darkening of the sun and moon.

"And it shall come to pass in that day, that the Lord shall punish the host of the high ones that are on high, and the kings of the earth upon the earth. And they shall be gathered together in the pit, and shall be shut up in the prison, and after many days shall they be visited."

The Hebrew word for high in this text means elevated and haughty, but is also linked to another word that means 'to breed worms.' The word prison denotes a smith, or fastener to a person. Imagine as a human being manacled and leg-shackled to a filthy, wicked, demonic being that hated you even as he promised you the power to rule the world, and still hates you. Imagine being confined in a hot, dark place with this and a multitude of other entities like him for 'many days.' These consequences are the fruit of the deadly deal the rulers of this present world have made with the kingdom of darkness; even as they persecute the people of God, and shed the blood of innocents by the millions.

The rulers of the earth are confederate with the wicked spiritual principalities and powers. But our battle as a people is not with the kings of the earth, nor do we attempt to incite rebellion against them. Our battle bypasses the kings of the earth and goes straight to the spiritual wickedness in high places that influences these men who are willing to sell their soul to gain the world. We put on the whole armor of God, and stand firm with our sword, the Word of God—on the defensive and offensive, praying for His kingdom to come, and His will to be done on earth. This is the only way to deal with the lethal, perpetual hatred that drives our primary spiritual antagonist—Esau.

Esau Then, and Esau Now

To understand the force that opposes and exalts itself against the knowledge of God and the Israel of God serving the final years of Captivity in the West and scattered throughout the nations, we need to look at the story of Esau and Jacob as told in Genesis Chapter 25 verse 19. God called Abraham out of his father's house and made a covenant (agreement) with him. One of the conditions of the covenant was circumcision of every male child on the eighth day of life. Another was explicit obedience in all things commanded (I am the Almighty God; walk before me, and be thou perfect; my covenant will I establish with Isaac.) Abraham understood clearly that even though Ishmael was the firstborn, the covenant was to be established through Isaac.

Benefits of this covenant involved a dedicated geographical territory, a legacy as progenitor over many nations, spiritual blessings which would impact the entire earth, and victory over enemies. So it was of no small concern when Isaac discovered his wife Rebekah was barren. Being the godly man he was, and taught of his father in the ways of the Lord, Isaac prayed for his wife, and she became pregnant.

Any woman who has ever carried a baby to quickening (ability to feel the baby's movements) and beyond knows an active fetus can cause quite a ruckus internally. But in Rebekah's case, she was carrying twins—Jacob and Esau, and this pregnancy was characterized by a violent struggling in her womb. The Hebrew word for struggled is râtsats, pronounced raw-tsats—and means 'to crack in pieces, literally or figuratively; to break, bruise, crush, discourage, oppress, struggle together. The striving was intense, and this was taking place before the twins even saw the light of day. Being the godly woman she was, Rebekah prayed to God for insight into what was going on. This was God's answer:

Two nations are in thy womb, and two manner of people shall be separated from thy bowels; and the one people shall be stronger than the other people; and the elder shall serve the younger.

At Rebekah's delivery, Esau was the first to be born; he came out red all over like a hairy garment. He retained this excessive body hair throughout his life; and in fact when Isaac was aged and his vision began to fail, it was his way of distinguishing between his sons, because Jacob was smooth-skinned. We can see from God's reply to Rebekah that Jacob was predestined to have the upper hand even though he was the youngest. But the first words of His answer set the tone for events that are impacting us as a people today.

Esau and Jacob signified two nations, and two manner of people. Moving forward momentarily to after the Exodus out of Egypt, God gave Moses an important message to tell the elders of the people:

Thus shalt thou say to the house of Jacob, and tell the children of Israel; Ye have seen what I did unto the Egyptians, and how I bare you on eagle's wings, and brought you unto myself.

Now therefore, if you will obey my voice indeed, and keep my covenant, then ye shall be a peculiar treasure unto me above all people: for all the earth is mine:

And ye shall be unto me a kingdom of priests, and an holy nation. These are the words which thou shalt speak unto the children of Israel.

This illustrates that of the two children/nations in Rebekah's womb, Jacob was predestined to inherit the covenant, and the nation associated with him was to be a holy nation. In contrast, his brother Esau was also destined to be progenitor over a nation, but it would be a nation associated with the heathen, or Gentiles. Esau would not be a kingdom of priests unto God, for he was of a different manner. The Hebrew definition for manner is 'a road trodden, a course of life, or mode of action'. In other words, there would be a distinct difference in Esau's system of values, his outlook on life, and his estimation of spiritual matters.

Esau was a cunning hunter; in fact, the Hebrew root word for manner also means archer, or to string a bow by treading on it or bending it. Esau loved the thrill of the hunt and would spend whatever length of time it took in the field to bag his prey. Jacob was a plain man with a gentle spirit who opted to remain close to his elderly parents.

You may already be familiar with the account of how Esau came in from the field faint, and was so desperate to eat that that he sold his birthright as the eldest for a bowl of red lentil soup. While it is true Rebekah and Jacob schemed together to usurp the blessing which followed the Abrahamic covenant, Esau had already despised the birthright: he considered it a thing of insignificance compared to the immediate demands of his belly. Neither should we feel sorry for Esau. The human body can survive for thirty to forty days before acute starvation sets in, and since at least some type of wild fruits and herbs and water source are typically available wherever herbivores are hunted, his willingness to give up the birthright for a bowl of bean soup was unconscionable. The covenant was only three generations old, and the sons had been well educated in it. In the New Testament Book of Hebrews, the Apostle Paul describes Esau as a profane person. This usage of the word profane is defined in the Greek as to walk; to cross a threshold, as a heathenish, wicked person. This means that Esau was a godless person; and not only that—despite the fact he had previously trashed his claim to the birthright, he had no problem with approaching his father to request a blessing...a blessing that, as we saw—was ultimately reserved for the establishment of a kingdom of priests, and a holy nation.

Jacob had to flee to his maternal uncle Laban to avoid Esau's wrath; Esau's anger was at the point of a murderous rage. Apparently scheming was a family trait on the mother's side, because Laban managed to extract twenty years of labor from Jacob for what was originally a seven-year oral contract. When Jacob decided he'd had enough, he stealthily took his family and possessions and left. But he knew he would have to pass through his brother Esau's territory to get back to Canaan. Jacob prayed for God's protection, but as a precaution prepared a huge conciliatory gift to placate Esau. Despite the fact Esau met him escorted by a four-hundred-man private army, the reunion was ultimately a peaceful event. The brothers reunited again some years later, to bury their father; then went their separate ways. It was at some point between this last reunion and the Exodus from Egypt, that the simmering flames of Esau's hatred were stoked and fanned. Israel did not want this enmity, and God did not want this enmity, for He commanded Israel under the law, "Thou shalt not abhor (loathe, detest) an Edomite; for he is thy brother."

Jacob went down into Egypt after the reunion of Joseph and his other sons. He died there, but was interred in Canaan. In passage of time Joseph also died in Egypt; by this time the population of the Hebrews had grown from just seventy persons to hundreds of thousands. It was not until after the miraculous deliverance from Egypt that we see the first indications of renewed enmity surface between Israel and Edom. The prophet Moses must have sensed this as he sang out after the deliverance at the Red Sea; because one of his exultations was, "Then the Dukes of Edom shall be amazed." The Hebrew translation for amazed is to tremble inwardly or be suddenly alarmed. Indeed, when the Israelites appealed to Edom on the basis of kinship and asked permission to pass through a city located on the extreme edge of their territory, the Edomites steadfastly refused. Even though Israel promised to keep to the road, and offered to pay for anything that might inadvertently be used, Edom firmly denied access. Not only that, they came out with a huge contingent of heavily armed personnel to intimidate Israel, so the people—already weary, were forced to take a detour.

Later, during the era of the Hebrew kings, Saul and David subdued the Edomites. But Solomon's idolatry eventually opened the door for an Edomite adversary, Hadad—who had a personal vendetta against the house of David for the earlier slaughter of his male countrymen.

An incident which took place under the waning rule of King Saul shows the depth of the godlessness of the Edomites. Saul was determined to kill David, and David and his band of men were on the run. David came to Nob, a city of priests—and asked Ahimelech, the head priest, for bread. The only bread that was available was the shewbread the priests ate, but Ahimelech gave it to him anyway. Unfortunately, there was also an observer present who was a chief servant to King Saul and loyal to him, one Doeg—an Edomite. Doeg wasted no time telling the king how he had observed David come to Ahimelech for food. When King Saul heard this, he summoned Ahimelech and interrogated him.

Ahimelech did not lie about the encounter, but he did remind Saul that David had been faithful to the king, and assured him he (Ahimelech) was not in a conspiracy against him. Yet for all this, Saul pronounced a death sentence on Ahimelech, and commanded his guards to kill him.

The guards knew better than to kill the priests of the Lord and refused, so Saul turned to Doeg and told him to do it. Doeg obligingly killed Ahimelech, along with eighty-four other priests. But that was not enough to satisfy his blood lust. He went to the priest's city, and there went on a killing spree of men, women, children, infants, and animals.

In later years, the Philistines joined in persecution of Judah by taking them captive and delivering them to Edom, and Edom is described by the prophet Joel as having done violence to the children of Judah, and shedding innocent blood in their land.

Not even the passage of generations could mute the hatred; it even surfaced through Esau's distant relatives. Many years later during the reign of King Ahaseurus and Queen Esther, Haman, a descendant of Agag through Amalek, Esau's grandson, attempted to craft a genocidal scheme designed to eradicate the Hebrews in whatever nation they were found.

During the time of Jerusalem's invasion, the Edomites came and stood by and casually observed as the foreigners came into the city and attacked the people. They even joined the attackers in placing bets on who would get what out of the city. Not only this, but they were elated about the humiliation of Judah, and rejoiced greatly. They made proud and boastful statements. Further, in the spirit of true looters, they helped themselves to Judah's possessions. As if that wasn't enough, they blocked the way of those trying to escape, and searched out and turned in those who were attempting to hide.

For this God prophesies through Obadiah, "For thy violence against thy brother Jacob shame shall cover thee, and thou shalt be cut off for ever." The prophet Isaiah further defines Edom's end: There is Edom, her kings, and all her princes, which with their might are laid by them that were slain by the sword: they shall lie with the uncircumcised, and with them that go down to the pit (Hell).

As the times of the Gentiles unfolded, Greece was subdued and Rome came to the fore as the ruling world power. The territories of Judah and Israel were effectively conquered, but pockets of resistance survived among some of the priests who remained faithful, and courageous men such as the Maccabee clan who fought to resist the pressure to Hellenize (adopt Greek customs) and strove to maintain the purity of worship. The Roman method of establishing empire was to maintain Pax Romana (the peace of Rome) and experience had taught them this was accomplished more effectively by setting up proxy rule (a personage native to the area) rather than bringing in a foreigner from Rome. Edom—also known as Idumea, accepted the position with no questions asked, for to have the backing of Rome meant coveted prestige and a guaranteed seat on the throne as long as the Roman tax was paid and peace kept in the province.

The Edomite kings of those days—the Herodian dynasty—were quite wicked, and became adept at navigating the tricky course that called for simultaneously placating a population that despised them, forcibly quelling the more violent civil uprisings, and maintaining good relations with Rome. And like Doeg, they had no problem murdering the people or the prophets of God.

Thus, Judah's idolatry eventually caused the tables to turn on them, and Edom gained the upper hand. In the end, Isaac's left over blessing to Esau became reality: "… and it shall come to pass when thou shalt have the dominion, that thou shalt break his yoke from off thy neck."

That was Edom then. An analysis of ancient Edom reveals:

*A predatory spirt. Esau was a cunning hunter.

*A callous disregard for matters of deep spiritual significance with long term ramifications.

*A propensity to be ruled by the demands of the flesh.

*A sense of entitlement to the blessing (regardless of legal right of possession.)

*Desire of gain over nurturing of family.

*A mentality of aggression (by thy sword shalt thou live.)

*A violent and murderous spirit (evidenced by the murder of priests, prophets, and children.)

*Intimidation and obstruction of Israel in their time of distress.

*Pride which deludes him into believing he is invincible.

*Willingness to execute the wishes of a wicked or pagan power for gain or prestige.

So where is Edom now? The answer, present and quite active in these last times. Remember, kingdoms rise and fall; nations appear and are later absorbed into other nations. If permitted under divine oversight, the spiritual principality influencing them will establish another base of operations and continue its diabolical efforts... especially where the persecution of Judah and interference with the establishment of the Kingdom of God on earth are concerned. Our ancient forebears repeatedly struggled in violent physical clashes with Edom, but the Apostle Paul reminds us that as saints and members of the body of Christ, we no longer wrestle with flesh and blood.

During the wilderness temptation, Satan showed the Lord Jesus Christ all the kingdoms of the world in a moment of time and told him, "All this power will I give thee, and the glory of them: for that is delivered unto me and to whomsoever I will I give it." We know, of course, that the Lord Jesus did not fall for that ruse, for He already knew at the end of the age all the kingdoms of the world would be in his and his Father's possession. The point is there are always men who will fall for the ruse. They will accept what seems like a huge, unreal gift even if it means losing their soul for eternity, or if receiving the gift is conditional on vicious requirements like human sacrifice (bloodshed through wars.)

Satanic hatred for the entire human race exists because man was created in the image and likeness of God. But a special enmity comes into play for the descendants of the twelve tribes who were called out to be a light to the nations. When they failed, One from the tribe of Judah appeared on the scene who fulfilled every point of the Law of Moses perfectly. He took a day for every year his brethren trekked in the wilderness and devoted it to fasting and prayer. Israel murmured against God and Moses about their limited diet, but the Lord Jesus Christ exalted the word of God over food as sustenance. Whereas Israel desired an idolatrous image even after deliverance from the oppression of Egypt, the Lord Jesus Christ reminded Satan that the first commandment was to worship the Lord God and serve only Him. Israel repeatedly tempted God in the wilderness, but Jesus spoke, "Thou shalt not tempt the Lord thy God." And He didn't stop there. He taught His disciples the principles of the Kingdom, and ministered to the people continually. He was sent first to the lost sheep of the house of Israel, but His compassion moved Him to minister to the Gentiles who reached out to Him, too. The days of His earthly ministry were an example of what it would be like to have God right here with us, *because He was God in the flesh*. The Apostle John said He did so many works that the world would not be sufficient to hold the books if all His deeds were recorded.

After all this, He submitted to an illegal trial, mockery, humiliation by man and death by crucifixion as a substitutionary sacrifice, not for His—for He did no sin—but for our sin. He was three days in the grave; but while His body lay mangled wrapped in burial cloths, His spirit preached to those spirits who perished in the Flood because of their disobedience in the days of Noah. He victoriously took the keys of Hell and Death, set them free, and led them out into paradise. After three days, His spirit reunited with His body; a body now glorified and not subject to decay or death. He was the first fruit of the resurrection, showing the type of body we will receive at His return. He was seen by over five hundred people over the next forty days before ascending to heaven at His Father's right hand: as our High Priest and Intercessor.

All this by the God-Man from the tribe of Judah! Is there any wonder then why such intense rage is directed toward the seed of His brethren? He dealt a fatal blow to the kingdom of darkness and sealed its fate with three words: "It is finished!" Every time Satan, the adversary—looks at the descendants of Judah, he is reminded of the ancestry of his conqueror. And every time he looks at one of these kinsmen or kinswomen who have entered into the New

Covenant with his Conqueror, he sees the image of Christ in various stages of formation in them.

The adversary knows his time is short. But he has persuaded those to whom he promises rulership of the world that they have plenty of time, and even if the clock should stop on them, they can perfect technology which will allow them to continue on... even to the point of storing their consciousness in cloud technology when their bodies fail. Their pride has deluded them, and they are more than willing to execute the wishes of a wicked power for gain and prestige.

In return for the rulership of this present world, the adversary has convinced its leadership that they are entitled to the highest positions of religious esteem in the eyes of the people; positions whereby they represent the voice of God on earth, or represent the chosen people of God on earth.

In return for the rulership of this present world, they are expected to aggressively live by the sword, and understand that they are entitled to control and manage all that the earth and heavens have to offer. If this means using predatory practices so that the backs of the people are always bowed down under oppression, this is acceptable. The point is to destroy the people's faith in a righteous God; that the rulers of this world alone might be heralded as saviors and providers, and push the people to give in and become as degenerate as they themselves are.

In return for the rulership of this present world, they are required to use technology to propel themselves into a position where they see everything, amass all knowledge, and exercise formidable military might on earth and in space; that they might attempt equality to the Omniscient, Omnipresent, and Omnipotent God. And most importantly, they are obligated to replace the Anointed Christ of the Bible and create another in their image. They are required to replace the people of the Bible with another in their own image, and distort the original words of God. They must oppress the people of God they have sought to replace, and continue to inflict persecutions on them, all to satisfy the millennia old personal vendetta of the Wicked Power who granted their position. Should they fail in executing this, or show compassion, they will be replaced.

Thus, they must be willing, on this earth—to stand in the place, or room, of God and Christ. The Greek word which matches this definition is antichristos—an opponent of the Messiah. The prefix 'anti' means "instead of, because of, or in the room of." It is used to denote contrast and substitution. The suffix 'Christo' signifies the Anointed Christ. Esau/Edom—the ancient archenemy with a perpetual hatred of Israel, is synonymous with the spirit of antichrist in the world today.

Match the current rulership of this world with the representations above, and you will easily see who spiritual Esau/Edom is in this last age. At this point, it is not a singular individual, but a collective in terms of religious and temporal might. Observe who controls the systems and institutions that oppress you in your Captivity; observe who claims to be the human representative of God on earth, observe who shapes the culture via social engineering designed to destroy the Black people, observe who makes claim to the ancestral lineage of Hebrew Abraham when in fact their lineage is clearly Gentile Japhethic, and you will see the correlation. That the current world leadership is controlled by a confluence of the sorcerous

Babylon/Egyptian Mystery Cult/Church of Rome/Euro-Judaic Palestinian occupancy/Anglo-American empire is no coincidence. The first entity seeks to corrupt us in our Captivity, and entice our minds away from the self-examination and repentance which will bend God's ears to our cries for deliverance. The second two act to discourage any hope of recognition of our heritage—the one by substituting a false mental image of our Elder Brother and Kinsman-Redeemer, and the other by attempting to replace us in our ancestral land; intimating that we are a people with no hope, no savior, and no deliverance. The third manifests in the iron-fisted treatment which disproportionately affects us in the courts and in society. The historical success of this aggregate is due to the fact that a threefold cord is not quickly broken.

The combined forces of these institutions act to break the people spiritually, mentally, and physically. In these last times, this united assault on the Captivity is the vent for Esau's perpetual hatred, and can be summed up as the mystery of iniquity[4] spoken of in II Thessalonians Chapter 2 verse 7. Of critical importance is the need to understand his last day base of operation—the Anglo-American powers ruling the revived Roman empire—is spiritual Great Babylon: a habitation of devils, a hold of every foul spirit, and a cage of every unclean and hateful bird. This means devils are at home here in the West, along with foul and persecuting spirits. Hence the ubiquitous architectural, marketing, and entertainment symbolism displaying the eye within the circle or triangle, mark of Cain, winged sun, owl, phoenix, and eagle. This is the manifestation of Esau today.

Knowing who these key players are however, does not mean we should plot sedition or attempt to overthrow their institutions. They are the rulers of this present world, and we are a people still under Captivity status until our King and Kinsman Redeemer appears to intervene on our behalf. Recalling the Apostle Paul's words in Ephesians Chapter 6 verse 12: "we wrestle not against flesh and blood, but against principalities, against powers, against the rulers of the darkness of this world, against spiritual wickedness in high places." These four levels of spiritual entities direct the mystery of iniquity, but our job, especially as covenant believers—is to suit up in the complete armor of God and pray without ceasing that He would turn our Captivity, and hasten His kingdom on earth. Despite the constant chaos and fear gripping the West and the world in general, God wants us to rest in Him in quietness and confidence. In stark contrast to the lukewarm Laodicean church, the captives of Judah must gird up the loins of their mind and be sober, for we are destined to be part of the purest and final witness before the end.

A final thought on this subject. There have been numerous film productions and much prophecy chatter about the fabled 'Antichrist.' At this time, there is not yet a solitary individual manifested to represent the unity of wickedness known as the mystery of iniquity. God holds the times and the seasons, and it is not yet the day for the man of sin—the son of perdition—to be revealed. In time however, it will come to pass.

---

[4] RULERS OF EVIL: Useful Knowledge About Governing Bodies, F. Tupper Saussy, Ospray Bookmakers, 1999.

Japheth's position in the last days is by no means a blanket condemnation of all Gentiles, all white people, or all people descended from European Judaics. Remember, the purpose of this book is to interpret Bible prophecy correctly in terms of how it relates to the descendants of the Trans-Atlantic and African slave trades. In order to do that, all relevant entities must be presented and properly identified. The Apostle Peter declared, "Of a truth I perceive that God is no respecter of persons; But in every nation he that feareth him and worketh righteousness, is accepted with him." Additionally, Revelation Chapter 7 verse 9 shows us people from all nations, kindreds, and languages among the redeemed of the Lord. God loves to judge righteously, and will judge everyone on an individual basis.

But all sons of Japheth must understand they can take no glory in their exalted status during these last days, for he that glorieth must glory in the Lord who alone is worthy to be exalted. God will not give His glory to another, but He will permit it to rest upon an individual who has entered into covenant with the Lord Jesus Christ through genuine repentance of sin. The terms of the covenant are clearly defined and demand entering a strait gate and walking a narrow path. That path is strewn with obstacles of suffering, persecution, and humbling circumstances. Further, those who travel it must depart from iniquity and genuinely love their neighbor and their brother. These stringent requirements are in diametric contrast to the Laodicean mentality typical of much of the Western church today.

Whatever the injuries of the past and persecutions of the present, we of the Captivity must never judge any one solely on skin color. In every place where Judah sojourns, God always has His Roman centurions (Luke 7:1-5) and Cornelius's (Acts 10:1-4.) And He strategically positions individuals of influence and authority such as the prince of the eunuchs (Daniel 1:9) and Ebedmelech (Jeremiah 38:15) to minister to us in our Captivity. Even as the lukewarm Laodicean church merges with the state, seeks to fellowship light and darkness via ecumenism, and accommodates sin in the church as politically correct and acceptable, a remnant of white brothers and sisters remain who are earnestly contending for the faith once delivered to the saints, practice a lifestyle of holiness and sanctification, and do not buy into the 'cursed seed of Ham' and 'state of Israel as fulfillment of bible prophecy' myths. Pray for these brethren because they will likewise walk alone and be persecuted in this world. But these are the same people who, during the darkest hours before the return of the Lord Jesus Christ, will hazard their lives for the faith; and if need be, lay down their lives for their brothers and sisters of color. As it is written, all who live godly in Christ Jesus shall suffer persecution.

The Lord Jesus Christ never said 'ye shall know them by their race', or 'ye shall know them by their lack of skin pigmentation'. He did say, "Ye shall know them by their fruits". Jesus is the propitiation (or reconciliation) for not only the sins of the Hebrews, but for the sins of the entire world. Since God is commanding men everywhere to repent, the choice to embrace the Edomite spirit is exactly that—a choice... and one with horrific eternal consequences.

Some may feel God is making a difference between the Hebrew descendants and the saved Gentiles. Isn't every one considered the same where salvation is concerned during the Church age? Yes, Paul writing in both Galatians Chapter 3 verse 28 and Colossians Chapter 3 verse 11 assures us there is no Jew (Hebrew) or Greek (Gentile), male or female, bond or free, circumcision or uncircumcision; all are one in Christ Jesus. But a careful reading of both the

Old and New Testament—especially Paul's letter to the Romans—clearly shows God has always had a special covenant relationship with the seed of Abraham through the line of Promise. The Gentiles (compared by the Apostle Paul to a wild olive tree) were grafted in to the native tree (Israel) by virtue of the New Covenant established by the sacrificial atonement of Jesus Christ. And while many of Judah in parts of Africa and the Americas have partaken of the New Covenant, Paul makes it very plain in the book of Romans, and the Apostle John in the Book of Revelation—that a work is yet to be done where Israel as a whole is concerned.

All things spoken prophetically over Israel in the Old Testament must be fulfilled, including punishment for idolatry and rejection of the Messiah—(which is the Captivity that has been going on in the West since the 17th century), re-gathering from the four winds, and re-establishment in the land. A good way to grasp this concept is to consider that while the first three chapters of the Book of Revelation are devoted to the Church—the Body of Christ in the earth—chapter seven verses one through eight speak of the sealing of twelve thousand men from each of the twelve tribes of Israel before cataclysmic judgment is released upon the earth. This indicates there is a distinct status that the descendants of the original Hebrew tribes still hold with God, and this status is so high ranking it influences the very timing of the apocalyptic events scheduled to take place at the end of the age.

Merger of State and Religion, Dark Ages, Renaissance to the Present

The Apostle Paul blazed the trail in taking the Gospel to the Gentiles. Everywhere he traveled and preached, he planted churches, and visited or wrote letters to guide and encourage them. The fellowships he founded were his joy and crown, yet our brother Paul had a troubling premonition that once he had gone home to be with the Lord, wolves would come in, not sparing the flock. This threat eventually manifested under the rulership of Constantine the Great, and the consensus of the Council of Nicea.

The unholy alliance of church and state so familiar today can be traced to Constantine the Great who ruled the Western Roman Empire from A.D. 306 to 337. Together with the emperor Licinius who ruled the Eastern (Byzantine) portion of the Roman territories, he crafted the Edict of Milan. This directive went into effect in A.D. 313; legitimizing the previously banned sect of Christianity and alleviating the persecution associated with it. The Edict provided for restoration of confiscated property and reparations for those who suffered loss under the persecutions of emperors Galerius and Diocletian.

The Edict of Milan was not necessarily a pro-Christian proclamation. While it emphasized guaranteeing "the reverence paid to the Divinity", it also strictly stipulated "no diminution must be made from the honor of any religion." Since most of Rome's populace was pagan, this newfound tolerance was an ideal vehicle to unify the masses, and a brilliant socio-political maneuver on Constantine's part.

The emperor himself, while 'officially converting' to Christianity, actually remained a pagan and sun-worshipper. In fact, just eight years after the signing of the Edict of Milan, and three years before declaring Christianity the official religion of Rome, Constantine issued the decree, "On the venerable Day of the Sun let the magistrates and people residing in cities rest, and let all workshops be closed."[5]

No chorus of dissent was heard among the church leaders, for the possibility of the almost unlimited power awaiting them as overseers of a state religion was irresistible. Soon after this, iconography began to appear with the halo or solar disk behind the heads of Biblical figures. In the centuries that followed, the state sanctioned church went even further and gave a "Christianized" covering to the pagan holy days, although these events were marked by fertility rites and sacrilegious acts. This idolatrous endorsement is why you see churches today celebrate Easter and Christmas with the same pageantry as secular institutions.

The Roman church leaders also introduced the unbiblical doctrine of apostolic succession from the Apostle Peter by popes; and the prohibition against priests marrying—a heresy foreseen by the Apostle Paul and documented in his first epistle to Timothy.

The Nicaean Council, an event which emperor Constantine himself attended, convened A.D. 325 in an area we would today recognize as part of Turkey. This group, composed of bishops and church leaders from throughout the Roman Empire, met to gain consensus on doctrinal matters. From this meeting would issue the key pillars which would define the Christian faith. The main issue of contention concerned the deity of the Lord Jesus Christ in relation to God the Father. Unanimity (with the exception of two dissenting) was reached affirming the Lord Jesus Christ as equal with the Father. But there is another very important matter which the council did not address. To understand how serious it was, we have to revisit the formation of the first century church.

Before Jesus gave Himself as the sacrifice for the sins of the world, He told his disciples that although He was going back to the Father, He would not leave them comfortless, but would come to them. This Presence with them would be none other than God's Spirit, the Holy Ghost, which would lead them into truth, guide them, speak what He heard from the Father, and take from that which was the Father's and give to them. How important was this relationship with the Holy Ghost to be? So critical that after His resurrection, Jesus admonished his disciples to remain at Jerusalem until they were endued with this power from on High. These were men who had lived with Jesus, and had been personally instructed by Him. They had observed His miracles first hand, and understood the principles of the Kingdom of Heaven. Yet, they were told to stay put and do nothing—until they received divine empowerment. It was imperative to have this promise revealed in them, because through it alone they would have power to be His witnesses.

This Power did indeed manifest via a rushing mighty wind, cloven tongues of fire, and the ability to speak in other languages which were understood by Hebrews who had come to Jerusalem from all parts of the known world to observe the Feast of Pentecost. Peter preached

---

[5] The issue here is not whether Christians should worship God on Sunday, for New Covenant believers are free to worship God any day and at any time they choose, as long as they worship in spirit and truth. The point is that Constantine's desire was to honor the sun—a created thing—as opposed to the One who created it—and invoke the power of the state to enforce the idolatry upon the populace.

a dynamic sermon that day that garnered three thousand souls for the Kingdom of God. We find in subsequent early church events that people would get baptized in the Holy Ghost, and the observers would recognize immediately what was taking place because they heard them speak with tongues. Yet, just two and a half centuries later, there is no mention of the fire baptism that energized the first century church; producing miracles, healings, discernment, and deliverance.

It is one thing to understand the deity of the Lord Jesus Christ; even demons acknowledge it, and tremble. But it is another thing to actually have God's power from on high fill you and enable you to become His witness. Since the Holy Ghost is the Spirit of Truth, leading and guiding the follower of the Lord Jesus Christ into all truth, it is indispensable in protecting the believer from deception. And lest any be convinced this 'baptism of fire' was only for the first century church, remember that Peter in his Pentecost sermon told his Hebrew brethren the promise was

*to them

*their children

*those who were afar off

*and as many as God would call.

Following is an interesting quote from the eighteenth century preacher John Wesley: "It does not appear that these extraordinary gifts of the Holy Ghost were common in the Church for more than two or three centuries. We seldom hear of them after that fatal period when the Emperor Constantine called himself a Christian...From this time they almost totally ceased...The Christians had no more of the Spirit of Christ than the other heathens...This was the real cause why the extraordinary gifts of the Holy Ghost were no longer to be found in the Christian Church; because the Christians were turned Heathens again, and had only a dead form left."

The baptism of the Holy Ghost was initially given to our black Hebrew ancestors of the first century church in Jerusalem and endorsed as a perpetual gift to the House of Israel first and their children; next to Israel and Judah who were removed among the nations, and lastly to as many as God would call (the Gentiles). The initial evidence of tongues, and signs and miracles following for the building up of the Church in a hostile world were never intended to cease. The cessation occurred because the Gentile sons of Japheth turned to idolatrous ways; they did no better than Shemitic Israel in that sense. But whereas Israel went after the inferior gods of the nations around them, Japheth's idolatry was of the sort where he began to worship himself. The narcissism and flattery associated with his rise and enlargement led him to pay lip service to God in the form of elaborate worship edifices and powerful spiritual potentates, but in actuality his trust was in his own ability, philosophy, military prowess and scientific and geographical discoveries... things which by the way, were new to him; but had long been common knowledge to the civilizations preceding him.

Thus we see that the union of church and state effectively neutralized the vibrant apostolic witness that energized the church under the fires of persecution. A form of godliness began to emerge, but it was a religiosity aligned with the power of the state rather than the anointing of the Holy Ghost. Without the influence of the Spirit of God, covenant and intimate fellowship with the Father and Son could not be known. Mandatory yet powerless religious observance and the need to recreate a tangible God in man's image and likeness rushed to fill the void created by the quenching of the Spirit.

Distortion of the Gospel for Temporal Power

As the times of the Gentiles continued to unfold, the hybrid church/state increasingly accumulated wealth and power, and with these was able to wield a powerful influence over rulers and their subjects. The common people did not have access to copies of the gospels and letters to the first century churches to discern the error. Those manuscripts were confiscated by religious rulers and the precious guidance contained therein supplanted by the authority of the popes. The simplicity of the apostolic gospel was replaced with the Roman church's definition of service to God. Jesus had told his followers, "My kingdom is not of this world", but this directive conflicted with the empirical goals of the Roman church. Under the aegis of popery, vast armies could be raised, bolstered by the belief that all sin would be forgiven and eternal glory the reward of their loyal service. It is not difficult to see how three major and five lesser crusades were fought under the misguided notion of claiming Jerusalem, Damascus, and parts of the Mediterranean and North Africa for the Roman Church.

Our Elder Brother and Kinsman Redeemer the Lord Jesus Christ wept over Jerusalem, and prophesied that Jerusalem would be trodden down of the Gentiles until the times of the Gentiles were fulfilled. This trampling down of His beloved city began with the sacking of Jerusalem by the armies of Titus in 66-70 AD, carried on with the Crusades, and—if the word of God is pure and true, continues even to this day with the construct of the modern day state of Israel. The times of the Gentiles—which will not expire until the second return of the Lord Jesus Christ, are yet to be completed.

WHAT'S IMPORTANT

It is critical to understand this historical background, because Christianity is often maligned as a bloodthirsty and hateful religion. These accusations are directly traceable to events such as the Crusades. Detractors need to understand that those actions did not represent the teachings of the Lord Jesus Christ, or the original Black Hebrew-founded New Testament church of the Book of Acts which is His body and called to be His visible presence on earth until His return. The witness of the true Church has always been to unreservedly love God and their brothers and sisters in the faith, and love their neighbor as themselves. There is no provision in that mandate to kill and maim for the purpose of forced conversion, maintaining the power base of the rulers of this world, gaining coveted land or resources, or to avenge one's self for real or perceived injustices. The logic behind conducting war and bloodshed under the pretext of claiming lands for Christ is seriously flawed because God already owns everything anyway: the earth is His and the fullness thereof; also He proclaims that all souls are His.

The New Covenant went into effect the moment Jesus cried out, "It is finished!" on the cross and the veil in the temple was ripped from top to bottom. This nullified the Old Covenant and the door was opened for the Gentiles to come under blood covenant with the Risen Christ. Under the Old Covenant, Israel had been redeemed from Egypt and brought into the Promised

Land, dispersed to Babylon as punishment for idolatry, and brought back into the land during the reigns of Darius the Mede and Cyrus of Persia. Despite the pleadings of successive prophets, the idolatry resumed, joined by a general disregard for love of one's neighbor.

Meanwhile, in the heavenlies, the high spiritual principality of Persia was subdued, but the next offensive involved the spiritual Prince of Grecia. On earth, the times of the Gentiles began to unfold. By the time the Lord Jesus Christ manifested in the flesh, Judæa and the territories of Israel were under Roman jurisdiction, ruled by proxy Edomite kings. Because the scripture cannot be broken, all prophesies regarding the scattering of Judah for idolatry and rejection of their Messiah were in queue for fulfillment; but were not triggered until the Roman siege around 70 A.D.

An honest reading and interpretation of Old and New Testament prophecy makes it very clear redemption and restoration of Israel is concurrent only with the return of the Lord Jesus Christ. The Lord Jesus Christ has not returned yet, for when He does, every eye will behold Him. Further, He states He is returning to be admired in those who love His appearing, as the Apostle John said in the closing of the Revelation, "Even so come, Lord Jesus."

There are many in the West and around the world that love the risen Lord Jesus Christ and earnestly long for his return. However, neither the early Judaic European Gentiles who began the movement to Palestine nor their current descendants acknowledge the risen Lord Jesus Christ and would actually resent the interference of His return. The ancient Edomite king Herod the Great executed a horrific infanticide to eliminate the threat of Judah's prophesied King, and the modern day Gentiles who manifest spiritually as Edomites likewise have no intention of abdicating rule to Judah's prophesied King. Will their declared objectives and long range strategies enable them to remain firmly entrenched? Not if the word of God in Revelation Chapter 11 verse 15 and Daniel Chapter 7 verse 27 is true:

"And the seventh angel sounded; and there were great voices in heaven, saying, The kingdoms of this world are become the kingdoms of our Lord, and of his Christ; and he shall reign for ever and ever...And the kingdom and dominion, and the greatness of the kingdom under the whole heaven, shall be given to the people of the saints of the most High, whose kingdom is an everlasting kingdom, and all dominions shall serve and obey Him."

Lastly, we must realize if our forefathers were evicted from the land due to idolatry and refusal to believe on the Lord Jesus Christ as the only means of access to God, and their descendants brought into Egypt (slavery) again by ships, it is a gross misinterpretation of scripture to teach that Gentiles who likewise refuse to believe on the Lord Jesus would be substituted to inherit the land. The present day occupation of Palestine and Jerusalem can only be understood in the context of Jesus' words when he referred to Jerusalem as being "trodden (trampled) down of the Gentiles" in the days just prior to His Return.

The Making of God in the Image of Japheth

Everyone is familiar with the blonde, blue-eyed image of Jesus found on the walls of many Western churches. Some twenty-first century Black Churches even display these pictures. But as we learned in the section *"Evidence Points to a Black Jesus Christ"*, biblical scripture does not support such a physical appearance. Even secular history supports the Bible in the case for a Black Jesus. Numerous fresco paintings exist in the ancient Roman catacombs (underground burial galleries) dated between the first and third centuries. These works clearly depict Jesus and other Biblical figures as Black men with easily recognizable Negroid features. From paintings by the early Coptic Christians in Egypt, to as late as fourteenth century Russian iconography[6], the ethnicity of the Hebrew Christians and Old Testament personages is historically verified. This proof can also be found by conducting a simple Internet search. Additionally, if there is no veracity to the account of dark Hebrews with Negroid features, one is left to ponder why a medieval white Russian artist would choose to illustrate them in this manner. The altering of the ethnicity of the Lord Jesus Christ was a Satanic attempt to so align the image of the oppressor with latter day Israel's perception of Christ, that they would revile and hate Him, and continue to reject Him just as their forefathers did.

If the Light that is in Thee Be Darkness

History books describe the Renaissance—the period between the fourteenth and seventeenth centuries—in glowing terms due to the surge in learning; and the famed art, literary, and architectural masterpieces produced during that time. The works of this era are permanently enshrined in the conscience of modern Western culture, for the achievements of the men who are household names today represent the accomplishment of white Japhethians operating in a much higher culture than the nomadic pagan existence that characterized their early entry into Europe. The advent of the printing press accelerated the exchange of thought, and also paved the way for the Biblical scriptures to reach the hands of the common people. Moorish influence from Northern Africa and cross cultural exchange from the Eastern Roman empire expanded the knowledge base and opened the way for new perception of self and the rest of the world.

But beneath the veneer of culture, artistic expression, and learning, a dangerous current was lurking; for man can increase learning exponentially, but wisdom only comes from God. The fear of the Lord is the beginning of wisdom; thus learning that contradicts the established wisdom of God is flawed. Flawed wisdom results in an intelligence which is earthly, sensual, and gives rise to thoughts that exalt themselves against the knowledge of God. Thus, men who profess themselves as wise effectively become fools, and deceive many people who are seeking guidance and understanding.

The stifling control over the word of God exercised by the Roman church in the centuries leading up to the Renaissance contributed to the Dark Ages, because the Word of God is a light to the path and a lamp to the feet. Without the wisdom that comes from the Word and a knowing relationship with the Creator, man—with his limited insight—is left to his own devices to navigate life and stand against Satan, the hater of the human race. But even as many gave their lives in martyrdom in their stand against the Roman church during persecutions such as the various Inquisitions, an entirely different threat was emerging under the guise of academics

---

[6] The ethnicity of the original Hebrews in Jerusalem is captured in a Russian iconography dated to the fourteenth century, and painted in tempura on wood panel. The painting, titled Maundy Thursday (Jesus washes the feet of the Disciples) is kept at the Pskov School of iconography in Pskov, Russia. The work is well preserved and the colors still vibrant. Clearly shown is the dark brown skin and black, curled hair of the Lord Jesus Christ and his disciples.

and groundbreaking discoveries. The sinister motive behind this was to dismantle the foundational principles of Scripture, and circumvent the declared precepts of God for obtaining eternal life. This two-pronged attack involved Heliocentrism and Alchemy.

Heliocentrism is the teaching that the earth revolves around the sun. It became widely accepted to this day via the strategy that if a lie is told often enough and loudly enough, it will become accepted as truth. However, Heliocentrism is nothing more than an attack on God's divine order established during the creation week. The book of Genesis clearly shows that the earth was created in the beginning, but the sun (and moon and stars) were not created until the fourth day. One is left to wonder what the earth was revolving around for the first three days; neither is there any place in the scriptures indicating that after God made the sun He gave the earth a push to get it started, and somehow it has circled undeviatingly ever since!

The word 'planet' is translated from the archaic 'wanderer', or 'wandering star', alluding to stars that appear to wander across the heavens. Earth however, does not belong to this category, because according to the Biblical scriptures it is fixed, immoveable, and hung upon nothing. Esau seeks to change the ordinances of God to reflect his version of the firmament's order. The power of his lie comes not in his ability to scientifically prove his position, but rather in repeatedly stating his theory until it becomes firmly entrenched in academia and culture as fact. Once he has accomplished that, anyone who suggests anything to the contrary is mocked, ridiculed, and laughed to scorn. It is a strategy that has been used repeatedly throughout history, and often resorted to because of its effectiveness.

Regarding the sun, God designed it with three specific purposes:

*To give light upon the earth

*To divide the day and night (light and darkness)

*To function as a master timekeeper registering signs, seasons, days, and years.

*The Hebrew word for signs 'oth' indicates a signal, beacon, or an omen.

At this point, some will wonder why Genesis does not speak of God creating the sun to foster and maintain plant growth. We all learned in school about photosynthesis, and how chlorophyll and sunlight act synergistically to synthesize carbohydrates from carbon dioxide and water. All this is true. But God in His wisdom did not want man to look to the sun as the giver and sustainer of life, and end up falling into idolatry worshiping the created thing rather than the Creator. To demonstrate His power and that He himself is the Source of all life, He created every grass, herb, and fruit tree the day before he created the sun. Further, when He created this plant life, it already had the seed in it. In other words, God created greenery—full grown—and the fruit trees—with ripe fruit containing the seeds for future propagation. There was no need to wait for a growth cycle from sapling to maturity, or a harvest season.

It is interesting to observe how geocentrists (or people who hold to the Creation account of a fixed, immoveable earth) are ridiculed by mockers as ignorant, and backward. Yet these same gainsayers will marvel at the precision by which the ancient Egyptian pyramids were constructed. Do they not realize these architectural marvels were created using calculations based on a fixed earth? And while some may scoff at the Biblical account, countless photographic images have been produced using rapid timed exposures over a protracted period that show the sun traversing the heavens from east to west, while all else remains stationary in the foreground and background. The same photography technique can be used to capture the rotation of the stars around the heavens. The star at the center of the star trail arc is the North Star. God tells us that heaven is His throne, and the earth is His footstool, that He sits in the 'sides of the north' and that He fills heaven and earth. As much as modern astronomers would like you to believe the universe is a chaotic ever expanding morass with no defined limits, the spheres of the two lower heavens do have set boundaries. The third heaven, which is a spiritual dimension—would more properly answer to the description of immeasurable; but even there, chaos does not exist. Everything is in its proper order at all times.

It is better to believe God than mortal man. And it is better to believe what your own eyes show you than to let someone speaking lofty words with an air of authority convince you that you didn't really see what you know you saw. True science will always verify God's account. Conflict arises when man has a dark agenda, and needs a supporting theory to back it up and cast doubt on God's version. In this case, the agenda involved worship of the sun, the idolatry Constantine indulged in even as he played the friend and advocate of the Christians. In striking down God's account of the divine order whereby He established all things, it is a short leap to attacking the authority of the rest of God's word: such as the reality of man's fallen nature; death as the penalty for sin; identity of the people He called out as His own to be a light to the nations; the miracle of manifesting Himself in the flesh genealogically through those same people to give Himself as a living sacrifice and redeem them back to Himself; in addition to God's testimony of divine judgment of the Old World by water, and His declared intention of judging this present world by fire. It is man's attempt to change the ordinance of God.

Secular science has precious little to say about the men who tried to scientifically show us God's pattern and order in the universe, but much praise is heaped on those who brought a contrary theory. This oppositional-defiant approach is typical of the unregenerate heart of those influencing and implementing much of the scientific and technological research today.

The attack on God's foundational creative laws and principles was just one side of the assault. The Renaissance also saw a heightened, almost frenzied interest in alchemy. Alchemy has been called the rudimentary beginnings of modern chemistry, but it was also characterized by a philosophical seeking of how man's nature related to the universe, a search for the 'Philosopher's Stone'... a substance that was purported to generate a universal healing remedy —an elixir of life, and a method by which metals of little value could be transmuted (or turned) into gold. A brief examination of this strange science will reveal it to be nothing more than a Middle Ages rehash of the lie Satan told Eve in the garden of Eden.

The Bible clearly explains man's nature and purpose. Man was created in the image and likeness of God to bring praise and glory to God and reflect the image of His eternity. God created the heaven and earth, and everything in them, but the creation of Man in His own image and likeness was the crowning achievement. God reserved the heavens for Himself, but gave man dominion over the earth. Man's duty is to be a good steward over the earth. This does not mean becoming a radical environmentalist. It does mean, that between the bounty God set up at creation and the wisdom He imparted to man, no one on the earth should be going cold, or hungry, or have no access to clean water. Man's hatred of his fellowman, wicked inventions, greed, and dereliction of duty has brought the earth to its present state. So the question of man's relation to other created matter is found in scripture and has already been answered.

The Philosopher's Stone, from which it was hoped the elixir of life or universal panacea could be extracted, was a study in self-delusion. The word philosopher in the Greek language means lover of wisdom, but as we saw earlier, only the fear of the Lord is the beginning of wisdom. Without that, man will be ever learning, but never coming to a knowledge of the truth. In the Old English, philosopher actually meant an alchemist or devotee of occult science. So, out of dark science, Renaissance man imagined he could find one cure that would address all ills—a panacea, and a potion that would renew him to eternal life. 'Panacea' was actually a mythological figure; a minor Greek goddess of healing who gave birth to a daughter gendered by an incestuous liaison with her father. Behind every idol stands a demon receiving worship. You can see how far off course man was straying in chasing such vain dreams. God reveals Himself to His people as Jehovah Rapha: the Lord Who Heals. Healing often comes as a result of repentance. But man imagines he is wiser and seeks to bypass God by resorting to his own devices. Transmutation of tin and lead to gold was a feat the Renaissance alchemists hoped to achieve. Success in this endeavor would have paved an easy road to riches, perhaps, until gold became as common as dirt and lost its intrinsic value. We should view these vain alchemic attempts for what they actually were: the lie "ye shall be as gods" repackaged in the Middle Ages.

How much has really changed since the Renaissance? The practice of alchemy continues, under the cloak of modern technology. We see the seeking for the connection of man to the cosmos via the logos of the space programs; the attempt to bring something valuable from something of no value (example: alleged life-saving vaccines made from viruses cultured on the cells of aborted fetal tissue) and the race to find the elixir of life (a means to enable man to continue existing forever) in the endeavor to mainstream trans-humanism, and preserve the intellect forever via cloud technology.

WHAT'S IMPORTANT

The Renaissance set the moral and spiritual tone for the end of days. When man does not acknowledge God, by default he has two options: worship idols, or worship himself. The European whites, for the most part—had a distorted view of scripture because of the people who suppressed the dissemination of the word of God, and misrepresented what they did reveal for power and gain. This was also the era when the Black Hebrew Christ miraculously changed his ethnicity, to become the representative icon which by virtue of His similitude to the Europeans, provided a sort of moral covering and authoritative endorsement for their actions and ventures. Simultaneously, the culture was being drawn into adulation of the Greek mythological pantheon, and men of higher learning were seeking for understanding from every angle except praying to their Creator. Pursuing knowledge, enlightenment, and the ability to control human destiny and achieve eternal life apart from repentance of sins and new life in Christ Jesus is ultimately an exercise in futility.

Yes, there were certainly men who swam against the tide and held true to what gospel truth was revealed to them... one has only to read Foxe's Book of Martyrs to learn of their testimonies, but these were the rare few. Just as in our time, the majority followed the prevailing culture. Whenever God is pushed to the side as irrelevant or treated as something only to be taken down from the shelf on special occasions, fleshly pride rushes in to fill the vacuum. Such a mindset of pride permeated the society, and held full sway on the hearts of the men who would soon sail the earth in search of riches for their monarchs, and eventually—traffic in human cargo.

The Attempt at Religious Justification: The Cursed Seed of Ham

When a man's conscience convicts him of wrongdoing, he has two choices. He can repent of the transgression and change his ways, or he can rationalize a justification for his actions. This is essentially what took place when our ancestors began to be enslaved on the American continent. The Founding Fathers and statesmen of the fledgling republic had much to say on how different the new colonial enterprise would be from the oppressive rule in England. Preachers established churches purported to be founded on Scripture alone; indeed, the purpose of 'New England' was to escape the corruption they disdained in the state church of "Old England." That a document could be drafted declaring all men to be created equal, and signed by people who owned other human beings, is a feat of unrivaled hypocrisy.

The oldest churches in the Southern states were represented across a spectrum which included Catholic, Baptist, Episcopalian, and Lutheran congregations. Presumably the first duty of a church where a congregation meets in the name of the Lord Jesus Christ is to preach and exhort adherence to the principles He taught. Fundamental New Testament doctrine is to love the Lord with all your heart, and your neighbor as yourself. That members of these churches could own and treat other human beings contemptibly and still attend their services and 'worship' God with no conviction points to a warped conscience.

The only way the new states could justify their hypocrisy was to change the concept of the word 'human' where the slaves were concerned, and only where the slaves were concerned. In an attempt to absolve their conscience regarding the abuse of humanity, they enacted laws that relegated the captives to mere chattel property. Chattel refers to property that is movable as opposed to real estate (land.) The entire logic in dealing with slavery was intellectually flawed: on one hand, slaves were equivalent to animals and possessed no human rights; on the other hand, it was recognized they could scheme, take revenge, or learn the forbidden art of reading—things animals are incapable of doing. This shows the schizophrenic mindset of the southern culture and also those in the north who saw slavery as an embarrassing, yet necessary evil.

What could have convinced people who considered themselves upright and moral Christians to be so double minded? Simply put, by elevating to the height of doctrine a distortion of scripture that supported white superiority. In this case, it was the false interpretation of scripture that the slaves were the descendants of the cursed seed of Ham. In the mind of the slaveholders, since Ham had done something reprehensible enough to invoke a curse on his son, kidnapping, enslaving, forced labor, torture, and even death were justifiable and deserved. Even if that meant ignoring other Old Testament teaching such as a curse extending only to a limited number of generations. In other words, Jesus' New Testament command to "Love thy neighbor as thyself" went out the window in favor of one Old Testament historical event that referenced one lineage (Canaanite) and that from a genealogy entirely different from that of the slaves!

Of course, in dehumanizing the slaves, the owners would also have to divest themselves of the natural human empathy which activates in response to suffering. Once the built-in moral safeguards of compassion and respect are dismantled and removed, malevolent and sinister forces rush to occupy the void. So effectively, the slave-owners also dehumanized and demonized themselves in the process. The result was a distorted, sadistic personality that could degrade and humiliate other human beings, while at the same time priding themselves on their Christian morality and genteel culture. I realize this sounds harsh, but demonization is the only way to characterize behavior associated with lynchings such as conducting outdoor luncheons with a body hanging from a tree in the midst, or cutting off pieces of the body to sell as souvenirs. This was nothing short of pagan worship and human sacrifice: going on right in the heart of southern 'Christian America', and not that many years ago. You probably never thought of it that way, but that's exactly what it was. As the apostle Paul said, the Gentiles know not God...and sacrifice unto devils. Of course, this should not be surprising in a place that is spiritually a habitation of devils, a hold of every foul spirit, and a cage of every unclean and hateful bird. Their true heart allegiance was revealed in the manner in which they treated those of the Captivity.

Inevitably, the question will be raised: didn't Blacks also own slaves? Compared to white ownership, a fraction of a percentage of free Blacks in the very earliest days of slavery were land holders and did purchase slaves to work their holdings. However, this appears to be basically a matter of self-preservation in a hostile environment. Any freedman who could not prove his status could be kidnapped and sold into slavery. The ability to purchase slaves meant a Black man already owned land capable of generating income, and a taxpaying landholder had a vastly reduced risk of mistakenly winding up a slave.

Secondly, a Black slave owner often used his earnings to bring other slaves to the safety of his estate, or purchase the redemption of relatives. Ultimately, it was a matter of weighing options based on the circumstances at hand. We can compare it to Josephus—the zealot who formerly fought alongside his fellow Hebrew comrades; defecting to the Romans when he saw Judah was fighting a losing battle. In terms of survival, it simply made more sense to be on the winning side if one could. It is obvious Black slave-holding was not in the same spirit as that of the oppressor, because upon the emancipation of slaves, you do not see the descendants of former Black slaveholders on a campaign of domestic terror; pillaging, burning, and doing everything within their power to disenfranchise and subvert their brethren.

Wrong People, Wrong Curse

Unfortunately, foolish and uniformed people spanning the spectrum from clergy to secular business were clinging to this misinterpretation of Hamitic identity. Because the fallacy was so convenient, and the nation was becoming accustomed to the wealth and life of ease associated with a free labor force, there was no incentive to search the scriptures, or examine history written to date to determine the slaves true background. One may ask, if our ancestors were not of Ham, when they learned this was how they were perceived, why did they not attempt to speak up and refute this misidentification? Simply put, the first generation of captives did not themselves know who they were past the name of the particular village they were kidnapped from, because in the sixteen or more centuries they had dwelt in the wilderness of Africa after exile from the land of Israel, they themselves had forgotten their heritage. Obviously, captives born on American soil had no historical reference whatsoever; although as they became exposed to the Old Testament passages, they found themselves identifying strongly with the Israelites in their bondage to ancient Egypt. Little did they know they were the same people replaying the same history...in a land that in the future would even imprint the image of an Egyptian pyramid on its currency!

This amnesia was also from God and part of the judgment He pronounced on our forefathers for walking away from Him. In Jeremiah Chapter 17 verse 1, God tells the prophet, "The sin of Judah is written with a pen of iron, and with the point of a diamond: it is graven upon the table of their heart, and upon the horns of your altars..." He goes on to say in verse four, "And thou, even thyself, shalt discontinue from thine heritage that I gave thee; and I will cause thee to serve thine enemies in the land which thou knowest not..." Here are important points you don't want to miss. Since iron and diamonds are two of the hardest substances known to man, the hearts of our forefathers had turned extremely rigid toward God, in order for Him to use that kind of terminology to describe sin written on the heart. Also, he tells Judah they are going to serve their enemies in a land which they don't know.

Judah was familiar with Egypt, and Judah knew well of the existence of Babylon. But now a Captivity was prophesied to be fulfilled in a land they knew absolutely nothing about. And, they were told they would be discontinued from their heritage. The Hebrew word for discontinue, sha(w)mat—means to fling down, jostle, to let alone, desist, let rest, release, shake, or stumble; as opposed to a complete and final disinheritance. It is best understood in the context of a parent who, after continually disciplining and admonishing a rebellious teen, finally just backs off and lets them experience the consequences of their choices and learn the hard way. It is what we as parents in this age refer to as 'tough love.' We never stop loving our child, and he still retains his position as our heir, but he cannot be trusted with the inheritance we have laid up for him until he honors us as the parent, provider, and benefactor, and demonstrates complete and willing obedience.

Consider the post-traumatic stress our ancestors must have experienced after leaving ancestral homelands and/or fleeing a war zone, loved ones lost and dying, facing starvation, eking out survival in a strange land, and trying to reestablish some semblance of culture. During the final movement out of Israel, they had to move as far west as possible into the interior of Africa, because Egypt—now under Roman control—was not an option. As time progressed, they buried the pain of the past, in order to survive and develop purpose in their present. In the wilderness jungle, there was no hostile Gentile aggressor, but there was also no temple, no priests, no sacrifices, and no high holy days. The common thread that had knit them together as a people was Jerusalem, and that thread had been severed. As prophesied in Deuteronomy Chapter 28 verse 64, they found themselves serving other gods, which neither they nor their fathers had known: gods of wood and stone.

The Correct Curses...Deuteronomy 28 and Leviticus 26

During the mid-1990's, the author attended several non-denominational churches. The prevailing message themes during those years seemed to revolve around the blessings of Abraham, and the blessings upon Israel as found in Deuteronomy Chapter 28 verses 1 through 13. The teaching sought to instill the principle that being as all the promises of God are yea and amen, and being as those in Christ the Seed of Abraham are grafted in by faith to Israel, this abnormally high level of material prosperity should be the rule rather than the exception for Christians. This type of teaching patently ignored the fact that although Moses laid out these blessings and curses before Israel entered the Promised Land, they failed to achieve this level of wealth until the reigns of David and Solomon, and once the kingdom split, never attained the equivalent of that success again.

The fixation on the blessings of Deuteronomy Chapter 28 also overlooked the fact that they were conditional on refraining from idolatry. Since the same text also outlined curses associated with idolatry, and since most Christian churches have long incorporated pagan practices, this was potentially dangerous territory to tread on.

Fortunately, the Mosaic admonition of blessings and curses was Hebrew Israel specific and not transferable to the New Covenant Christians; as attractive as the blessings might have been. In contrast, the New Testament church—while also called to be a royal priesthood and holy nation, is blessed with all spiritual blessings, and is admonished that godliness with contentment is great gain.

In retrospect, I realized that no matter who preached from this Chapter, they always stopped at verse thirteen where the last blessing was spoken... and never carried forward to the curse portion. Almost two decades would pass before I would understand why the chapter was never read in its entirety: it would have manifested clearly to both white and Black Christians who the children of Israel were—and the fact that they were right in their midst!

The ignorance of lay people—though inexcusable because everyone should be a Berean and search the scriptures, is somewhat understandable as few professing Christians actually read their Bibles today; preferring to trust their pastor or preacher to expound the word. But what would make leaders in the churches—both white and Black—tiptoe around this section of the chapter, particularly verses forty-eight and sixty-eight? Is it because so much has been vested in the 'cursed seed of Ham' and 'state of Israel as fulfillment of bible prophecy' myths that there is too much at stake to admit that both of these premises are false? And if we know something is false, should we not set the record straight? Has a 'chilling effect' gone out to intimidate churches into remaining silent on the subject? If so, where is this coercion coming from? Is fear of losing 501(c)3 status the gag that prevents men of God from proclaiming a truth which would cause the descendants of the Captivity to turn to God with their whole heart, and prompt those saved among the Gentiles to seek God earnestly with self-examination and repentance? Neither denial nor self-imposed silence will make a reality go away, and there is a Judge to whom every one of us must give account: whether of sins of commission, or sins of omission.

The long list of curses is indeed depressing and difficult to read with us as a people in mind. Nevertheless, we need to take God seriously and not repeat the same mistakes as our forebears. We should also understand that although they fell upon Israel as a whole, it has been God's discretion as to the specific timing and location of each curse. Remember, Israel was scattered to the four winds (four cardinal directions.) So certain things that happened, for instance, in South Africa under apartheid did not necessarily happen the same way in the Americas.

Some of the curses can be traced to the various sieges Israel endured under the reigns of their apostate kings (cannibalism due to starvation), some are manifest today in the areas of central and west Africa where Israel is scattered (plagues) many correspond to slavery in the West (brought by ships to Egypt... the house of bondage, hunger/thirst/nakedness during the Middle Passage, yoke of iron around the neck, giving birth to children who are then sold) others involve being only oppressed and spoiled evermore (non-consensual experimentation such as the Tuskegee Experiment) several are universal wherever Israel is found in the world (bywords/cursing, vexation, rebuke in endeavors) some speak to the Jim Crow era (carcass as meat to the fowls and beasts of the earth from lynching) and still others are specific to day to day life in America now (no ease in any place, no assurance of life, life constantly hanging in doubt via police brutality, corrupt sentencing system, and vigilantism.)

The reader can reference the entire list of curses themselves by reading Deuteronomy Chapter 28 verses 14 through 68, Authorized KJV. Later, we will revisit the actual manifestation of these curses in Chapters Ten, Eleven, and Thirteen of the book.

Chapter III   Identity Theft

Hebrew-Judah-Jacob-Israel-Israelite-Zion and Jew-Jewish-Judaism-Israeli-Zionism
are as different as day and night, black and white, right and left, and life and death.

A Conspiracy of Denominational (and Institutional) Proportions

God is not the author of confusion: a troubling state linked to envy, strife, and evil works. So it is imperative for the Black man and woman in America to understand they are the descendants of the tribe of Judah; from the seed of Abraham, and related by blood (kin) to the Lord Jesus Christ—who, had He manifested during the Jim Crow era, would likely have been called 'boy' and 'nigger' by the genteel southern Christians, and if it were possible, been subject to being hung on a tree again. Black people must reach the point where they have no doubt in their mind regarding their Shemitic Hebrew heritage; for this is key to formalizing your purpose in being a true and faithful witness, and making the way straight for the return of our Redeemer-King.

But, like walking into a blizzard, it will initially be a struggle to maintain your footing and not become lost in the storm of word play and transposed identities the world bandies about. However, once you are firmly grounded in the understanding of who the Lord Jesus Christ really is, who you are, who your ancestors were, and why they ended up here, no amount of sophistry or incorrect historical depiction will ever reverse your consciousness.

Do not expect to receive clarity from traditional historical sources or modern day mainstream media. The duplicity and deception will continue until the Lord Jesus Christ is revealed from heaven and causes those who appropriated themselves of our identity to acknowledge the truth, and know that the Lion of the Tribe of Judah has loved us with a special love. Actually, the language the Lord Jesus Christ uses to communicate this sentiment in Revelation Chapter 3 verse 9 is much stronger than this, but will be addressed at a later point.

Understand then, there is a clear and distinct difference between 'Judah'—a dark-skinned people who (along with the tribe of Benjamin and the Levites) comprised the Southern Kingdom of Israel and inhabited Jerusalem; and 'Jew' or 'Jewish' as you hear about in European history and modern Middle East reference. Judah is a people who were easily recognized as dark with negroid features. God explicitly stated on more than one occasion that He would uproot Judah and Israel from the land because of their sin, and scatter them throughout the nations, where they would serve their enemies, never being able to accumulate a secure future and prosper, and succumb to serving the gods of those nations—wood and stone. He also said they would remain in that state until the latter times; and at that point, after they considered their doings and the sins of their forefathers, He himself would turn their Captivity and send His angels to gather them from the four winds (cardinal directions) and the outermost reaches of heaven. These directives are directly correlated to God dealing with us as sons, and specific to us as recipients of an everlasting covenant. So unless God is lying (which it is impossible for God to do—Titus Chapter 1 verse 2 /Hebrews Chapter 6 verse 18) no true Judæan remained in the land after the fall of Jerusalem in 70 A.D., neither was anyone of Judah or any of the other tribes able to sneak back into the land and reestablish business as usual.

Therefore, when you read of Jews being killed in Jerusalem during the Crusades, or Jews as merchants and traders or money lenders during the early centuries of Europe, understand these were either pagan Japhethic (such as Turkish) people who adopted what they understood to be the religion of Judah—the Old Covenant given by Moses—and made it their state religion, or if in Palestine and the neighboring regions, Hamitic such as (Ethiopian/Yemenite) and mixed Hamitic/Japhethic peoples who were proselytes to the Old Covenant before the fall of Jerusalem.

That it was common for people of other ethnic groups to proselytize to the Mosaic covenant is verified in the Book of Acts by the accounts concerning the Ethiopian eunuch who came to Jerusalem to worship (Hamitic) and Cornelius the centurion (Gentile.) What made these two proselytes different was that once the gospel of the kingdom was preached to them, they called upon the name of the Lord Jesus, and were baptized. In the case of the centurion, the baptism of the Holy Ghost came upon him while Peter was still preaching and before he was water baptized. In the case of the Ethiopian, Philip baptized him, and as soon as they came up out of water, the Holy Ghost caught Philip away. But as the Ethiopian went on his way rejoicing, it is quite logical to assume he was also filled with the Spirit, because great joy and praise are hallmarks of the language spoken by the Spirit.

Regarding the European pagan Gentile proselytization to the Mosaic Covenant around the 7th century, this was more about a brilliant strategic political move than adulation for God, because the ancient kingdom of Khazaria was facing pressure from the west to convert to Christianity, and from the east to convert (by the sword) to Islam. Adopting a religion which was acknowledged and respected by both antagonists provided a safe haven. With this new identity, they could travel, trade, and act as ambassadors between countries and warring factions, and were able to prosper even as the peoples around them annihilated each other. The descendants of these same people, after coming to the Americas, bought, sold, and traded the true Judah—our ancestors, and operated plantation enterprises which prospered from the labor of our forebears. All this is documented history, much of it in the writings of the proselytes themselves.

Concerning the identity of the physical genetic seed of Jacob, it cannot be both ways. Either God forced Black Judah out of the land for idolatry and rejecting their Kinsman-King and brought them by ships into Egypt the house of bondage with a yoke of iron around their neck as punishment like He said He would do through Moses and the prophets, or He turned their skin white, permitted them to remain in the land so that they never had to wear the yoke of iron and be sold on a slave block, and later orchestrated yet another migration to the land under the bond of a covenant already fulfilled and abolished by the blood sacrifice of his Son. Either, or. But it cannot be both ways. Let God be true and every man a liar. The curses prophesied in Deuteronomy 28 and Leviticus 26 just don't fit the Japhethic people who adopted the Old Covenant; no matter how one struggles to interpret their claim. And if it doesn't fit, it's not legit.

The rarely mentioned truth is that a significant number of Euro-Judaic descendants really do know the truth about the Abrahamic lineage of the Black man in the West, but choose to keep it under wraps for obvious reasons. The practice of cloaking truth in art, cinema, or entertainment so that it is hidden in plain sight is a popular tactic of spiritual Esau during this end time domination. A prime example of this was a stand-up comedy routine where the provocative suggestion was made that Blacks were responsible for the crucifixion of Jesus. While on the surface this may appear to be just another shock value statement, the speaker is actually divulging a historical truth revealing the reality of our Hebrew lineage from Abraham and blood lineage to the Lord Jesus Christ![7]

Centuries of depicting the ancient Israelites in art as little more than suntanned white people place a distorted image in the minds of the Hebrew Captivity. Some of the oppressor's people knew differently, but chose to remain close-lipped about it. Others just went along with the revised history which was being rewritten based on the strategy that if a lie is told often enough it will eventually become accepted as truth. The inaccurate image became firmly entrenched in 1948 when white Europeans descended from the ancient pagan tribe that mass converted to Judaism centuries earlier suddenly moved into the Biblical land. Their occupancy—which was established and confirmed by military might, has resulted in bloodshed and apartheid-like conditions for over half a century now. Referring to themselves with true colonial flair as 'settlers', they said they had a divine 'right to return' and in turn extended that right to anyone in the world under the banner of Judaism, to encourage population of the land. Apparently it only occurred to the surrounding Arab nations to question how these Europeans could be 'returning' somewhere they had never left in the first place; or how they could leave Black, but return white.

The very fact that the State of Israel must perpetually resort to military aggression and repressive social policies to maintain their claim on the land proves they cannot be Jacob's true descendants, for when the Lord Jesus Christ returns and sends His angels to gather His elect out of the four winds to return to the land, there will be no need for artillery and munitions. In fact, the Lord says He alone treads the winepress of wrath; no one from the nations is with Him when He executes this judgment, and He appears before His people wearing garments bloodstained from the carnage in Edom (Isaiah Chapter 63 verse 3.)

However, true manifestations of prophecy can take centuries to fulfill, and who has time to wait that long? If carnal, unregenerate man can bring it to pass, or at least make it appear to be a literal fulfillment, all the better. The takeover of Palestine was legitimized in the world's eyes by a United Nations resolution, and marketed to the Christian church as the Bible coming to life in the end times. At this point, the Protestant churches should have sought God for discernment as to what was taking place. But two things blinded the eyes of clergy and parishioners alike in the white Western congregations: pride, and zeal to see prophecy fulfilled.

Pride influenced the endorsement of the 'modern day State of Israel is the fulfillment of prophecy' line of thinking because it gave a huge boost to a people who had little significant history until about the 9th century A.D.; a very short span when measured against the backdrop of Creation and the ancient African and Asian dynasties. Western Europe had succeeded in molding the image of the New Testament Christ into their image and likeness with white skin, blue eyes and blond or light brown hair. Now, they were also able to point to the inhabitants of the new state religion creation and postulate the legitimacy of the image; there was no reason to believe Christ did not look like his ancestors, if the descendants looked like Christ. Having

---

[7] Sarah Silverman, Jesus is Magic (2005).

made themselves the face and exemplification of a strange hybrid: 'Judeo-Christianity'—their conscience could be somewhat absolved from the true nature of the West; empirical and materialistic for the purpose of domination and wealth. Never mind that this sacralization only benefitted the conscience of the Anglo/Western Christians, for the particular set of Gentiles who moved to the land had no use for the Christian's Jesus. The sentiment of many of the Zionists was that they were their own Messiah.

Ultimately, the Protestant church did not seek God's face regarding what was taking place in the 'holy land'. Instead, it convinced itself the occupation was the fulfillment of Israel restored, and the more they would endorse and finance the new venture, the more quickly the Lord would return. And thus the Great Deception has taken root, which disables the white Western churches from accurately interpreting prophecy. Yes, they can wax eloquent about the wickedness of these last days, and the cataclysmic upheavals taking place in nature, and the conflict between nations, but they are effectively blind when it comes to understanding anything about the Israel of God, since they have already recreated Him in the only image they are comfortable with, and cherry-picked scriptures to support this fallacy instead of examining the whole counsel of God. The crux of the matter is that when Western churches acknowledge the Old Testament prophecies about Israel's restoration, they only interpret them within the context of events that have occurred from 1948 and forward. This is like biting off part of a puzzle piece section to force it to fit with a non-matching piece.

Perhaps I should not state so strictly that the occupation of Palestine is not a fulfillment of prophecy, for actually it is. It's just not the 'Israel restored' prophecy the white Western churches cling to. Here are just two of the prophecies illustrating the overrunning of that region:

God shall enlarge Japheth, and he shall dwell in the tents of Shem. Genesis Chapter 9 verse 27 ...and Jerusalem shall be trodden down of the Gentiles, until the times of the Gentiles be fulfilled...Luke Chapter 21 verse 24.

You will never observe such intricate footwork as watching the Western churches dance around Luke Chapter 21 verse 24. They would love to pin the trampling of Jerusalem on the Palestinian Arabs, but the Gentile Judaics controlling the land perpetually maintain the upper hand politically and militarily, so that explanation falls flat. Rather than admit the Judaics are the Gentiles Jesus is referring to, they just ignore that verse as though it doesn't exist. Has so much been invested in the fallacy that men now fear other men and durst not lift their voice?

*The fear of man bringeth a snare...Proverbs Chapter 29 verse 25

*For do I now persuade men, or God? or do I seek to please men? for if I yet pleased men, I should not be the servant of Christ...Galatians Chapter 1 verse 10

Perhaps they fear being censured, sanctioned, or ostracized; and in the extreme, permanently silenced for correctly interpreting Luke Chapter 21 verse 24. While these are certainly possibilities, Matthew Chapter 10 verse 28 and Romans Chapter 3 verse 4 speak to those concerns:

*And do not fear those who kill the body but cannot kill the soul. Rather fear him who can destroy both soul and body in hell...

*...let God be true, but every man a liar...

It doesn't require an advanced degree to read the word of God and see that Israel is not restored as a nation <u>until the bodily return of the Lord Jesus Christ</u>—which corresponds with the resurrection—which doesn't occur until the Last Day. <u>All of these things have yet to take place</u>.

Since these specific and linked events are yet future, we can draw three conclusions:

*The Kingdom has not yet been restored and is still yet to come

*The present carnal creation is a pseudo-kingdom representing one of two interpretations of the parable of the wheat and the tares[8]

*Someone or something has a tremendous stake in maintaining the present interpretation even if it means ignoring Bible scripture and world history, and persecuting or killing those who would dare to challenge and refute it

We can refer back to the Table of Nations, to confirm the identity of the settlers migrating from Europe to Palestine as descendants of Japheth. Remember, the "isles" are identified in Biblical context as lands to the north and west of the Mediterranean Sea, and Japheth's lineage is defined as the Gentiles. The lineage of Ashkenaz (root of Ashkenazi) ties his progeny to Japheth and clearly identifies the people as Gentile.

Another important issue to point out is the unnecessary persecution the Euro and Central Asian proselytes brought on themselves by assuming the identity of the Hebrew people. Apparently it was not a huge issue when the subjects of the ancient and powerful kingdom of Khazaria first adopted the remnants of Mosaic Law observance. But as the centuries advanced and they migrated further into Western Europe, they began to be referred to as 'Christ-killers' and often became targets of virulent persecution. It did not seem fair to some Christians that the descendants of the people who occasioned the violent and tortuous death of their Savior should reside among them, have a say in the civil affairs of Christian nations, or be prosperous. This persecution was a burden never intended to be borne on the shoulders of any Gentile; an unanticipated consequence of linking themselves to the lineage of Abraham and the patriarchs.

---

[8] Traditionally, modern Christians have interpreted the parable of the wheat and tares as an allegory of those in church who are just 'looking the part'—spiritual pretenders—intermingled with believers who are totally sold out for Christ. But Jesus says the field is the world—rather than a local fellowship. This implies that the difficulty in discerning the true from the false is a global phenomenon. This then reduces the question to the identity of the true spiritual body of Christ worldwide i.e., the Roman state church and nominal Christianity vs the ecclesia, and the true genealogical descendants of the Abrahamic Covenant promised end time restoration; Black descendants of slavery answering to the Old Testament prophecies of Captivity and by ships vs the Euro-Judaics under the politically constructed Zionist settlement campaign.

The people known to the world today as Jews rightfully take umbrage when accused of being "Christ killers", because their forebears were nowhere near the vicinity of Jerusalem during the Roman domination of Israel.

However, the reality of the Black man residing among the Gentiles—his voice in civil affairs equivalent to an ignored whisper—and failing to prosper as a collective, is much more in line with the punishment levied on a people who rejected their Messiah and by default must serve the sentence of the dispersion and Captivity.

An analogy that can be used is a scenario where an alert goes out that a triple homicide has been committed in the area. A description is provided to the citizens in the vicinity where the suspect is thought to be. For whatever reason, someone who hears the alert studies the suspect in great detail, and then disguises themselves to fit the description and ventures out into the public venue. A case of mistaken identity is likely to occur and the impersonator can expect to suffer harsh treatment at the hands of the authorities until he can prove he is not the murderer. Worse, there is the risk a vigilante may get to him first and take matters into his own hands.

Regarding the Palestinian/Arab peoples in the land, they too, albeit suffering at the hands of the Gentile Euro-Judaics—are in the position of trespasser and must return to their original territories at the homecoming of Israel. These people are a mixed multitude of Hamitic/Shemitic/Japhethic in various combinations of the groups, but not the Israel of God. The reason we can know of a surety they are not of the Israel of God as expressed through Hebrew stock is that God specifically said He would scatter Israel and Judah out of the land and into the nations. In other words, God did some housecleaning, and He didn't miss one speck of dust. Every one 'hewn from His rock' had to vacate until He himself issues the order to reoccupy.

But here is something else nobody talks about in discussions about the 'holy land'. A careful reading of Leviticus Chapter 26 verses 33 through 35 indicates God didn't want anybody in the land after He banished Israel and Judah from it. He wanted the land to rest and enjoy her sabbaths, but He states the land's enjoyment of her sabbaths is contingent on two things: Israel being out of it and in their enemies' land, and the land itself lying desolate. The Hebrew word for enjoy in these verses means to be pleased with, to approve; specifically, to satisfy a debt, and sabbaths speaks of an intermission or rest. The Hebrew word for desolate in this verse alludes to being stunned, stupefied, growing numb, or lying waste. A good modern analogy would be such as when a person cannot move or respond because he is in a state of shock. Thus, God wanted the land to lie undisturbed... in a state of suspended animation, so to speak, because she was owed that respite—until such time as He remembered the land and had His angels gather His elect from the four winds to return to it.

Presently Israel is out of the land, in Captivity in the land of their enemies; and reigned over by those who hate them. That part of God's directive has been satisfied. But the land itself is not at rest nor enjoying her sabbaths, because it is not desolate. From the neighboring peoples who early on appointed themselves inheritances in it, to the Crusades, to the present day State of Israel, the land has not experienced the relief God desired for it. Instead, it is bowed down under a Gentile power; and characterized by bloodshed, oppression, and hatred of His Son. In light of this, it is easy to understand why the Lord Jesus Christ spoke of the Gentile occupation of Jerusalem in the last days as a "trampling down".

We have seen how the Western Protestant church promoted the European Jesus image, and the 'modern day State of Israel as fulfilled prophecy' postulation as undisputed fact. But are there any other clues that might indicate a conspiratorial effort was underway to erase Black Israel from association with the covenants of God and restoration to their ancestral land?

We find a damning link in the work of Cyrus I. Scofield,[9] 1843-1921. Scofield was the author of the Scofield Reference Bible. He is highly praised by many Western Protestant luminaries, but the truth of the fact is that people are known by their fruits. Scofield's fruit shows he should never have been entrusted with the word of God at all, based on his violation of I Timothy Chapter 4 verse 8, and the admonition of II Corinthians Chapter 6 verse 15.

Why it was necessary for Scofield to make a trip to the British Isles to conduct research for his bible version seems odd, until one realizes he was recruited to give legitimacy to some of the interpretations Westcott and Hort had engineered into their revision of the New Testament. Not as well-known is that these men he was collaborating with, Fenton Hort and Brooke Westcott—were also involved in secretive groups—one at least—which required the taking of an oath. They looked to Scofield to bring their edition up to an equal footing with the popular King James Version. Scofield met this challenge by adding 'margin notes' and commentary which purported to abridge the text. The problem was that over time, Scofield's notes began to take precedence over scripture itself. Thus, the slippery slope of teaching the commandments of men as doctrine became characteristic of ministries who relied on his annotations.

The development of Scofield's reference bible was synchronous with the Zionist movement to occupy Palestine; which Britain had wrested from the Ottoman Turks. The first version was published in 1909. After that, versions were strategically released to coincide with events shaping (or taking place inside) the newly occupied Palestinian region. For instance, the Balfour Declaration, proposing British assistance with the European Jewish settlement of Palestine was announced in 1917. That same year, the next edition of the Scofield Reference Bible was released. In 1967, the year of the Israeli-Arab Six Day War, another edition was released. And in 1998—the year of the State of Israel's fiftieth anniversary, yet another edition was released. The timing of these editions—which present the modern day State of Israel and its Euro-Judaic occupants as representative of 'all of Israel', could not have been by mere chance.

Another of Scofield's insightful commentaries was that "A prophetic declaration is made that from Ham will descend an inferior and servile posterity." Because of the popularity of the Scofield Reference Bible, this perspective has been communicated to millions of readers who found it easier to accept Scofield's musings as fact rather than conduct due diligence and go

---

[9] A Little History: Cyrus I Scofield and the Tribulation. Don Nicoloff, May 2009 Idaho Observer.

back and read what Noah actually said, and seek diligently to determine whether everyone in Africa is truly descended from Ham.

Moving on from there, we turn to Catholicism.

One of the easiest clues to spot in the Catholic contribution to obscuring Israel's identity as a Black people is the fact that Rome is fully aware of both the true ethnicity of the ancient Hebrews, and the fact that the descendants of the Trans-Atlantic slave trade are their posterity. The Catholic Church had a better handle on the true Hebrew identity than the Protestants, due to the lengthy historical association between the Western and Eastern Roman empires, and the Crusades. They were aware of the artifacts, frescoes, and historical descriptions of Jesus, the disciples, the early church fathers, and the people of Jerusalem. None of this was lost on them. Even at this present day, there is a black Madonna and child enshrined at the Vatican, and images similar to it are also scattered across Europe.

What would motivate Rome then, to participate in the cover-up? Simply put, coveting the Land promised by covenant to Abraham's seed, desire for the worship of this present world, and lust for material wealth. The years 1099 A.D. and 1101-1102 A.D. saw much bloodshed in Jerusalem by the Crusaders, and Rome has longed desired to establish headquarters in Jerusalem. Current events show that this may eventually become a reality without armies and bloodshed; for recently, the Pope negotiated for and was granted a special seat in the room where the Last Supper is thought to have taken place. However, God tells us in Psalm Chapter 132 verses 13-14 that Zion is special to Him; the place He has chosen to dwell, and the place of His Name. God will not share His glory with another, and there is only one mediator between God and man—Christ Jesus. God does not have one chosen representative on earth; His representatives are every one of His children who have entered into covenant with Him via the sacrifice of His Son, those filled with His Spirit, and walking out a life of obedience, love, and sanctification. One Mediator: many ambassadors and representatives. The saints of the most High God should watch this development in Jerusalem carefully, as it may be the precursor of Matthew Chapter 24 verse 15.

Regarding worship, Catholicism is a longtime proponent of the European Jesus. One of the most widely recognized representations of this is the Image of Divine Mercy; from an apparent vision received by a Polish convent nun in 1931, whereby she reported she was instructed by a white, long-haired Jesus to paint an image of Him with the signature "Jesus, I trust in You." Allegedly she was told by this Jesus that he desired the image be venerated, first in her chapel, and later throughout the world, and that through that image, worshippers would receive mercy. Regardless of the fact that this is a blatant trespass of the Second Commandment, and something the Lord Jesus Christ would have never done or endorsed, as He fulfilled all the Law and Commandments without fail on any point—the emphasis here is on the ethnicity of the image. Jesus was a Hebrew who identified in physical characteristics with His tribe, and was dark enough to blend in with the neighboring Egyptians. Today his descendants are in Captivity; the most despised and disrespected people on the earth. At the time of this writing, there are estimated to be over one billion Catholics worldwide. If an image is to be promoted for these adherents to relate to God, it certainly can't be an image representing the dregs of society. Thus, Catholicism agrees in the obfuscation of Judah's ethnicity and the ethnicity of his Kinsman (his blood relative.)

The lust for material wealth becomes apparent when one considers the Papal decrees which were made to religiously sanction the marketing of human beings and the vast wealth generated from such a practice. In the 1400's, three Papal bulls (formal papal documents) were issued sanctioning the slave trade and hereditary slavery. As late as 1866 (less than one hundred fifty years ago) Catholicism issued a statement expressing that slavery did not conflict with natural and divine law, and that there could be several just titles of slavery. One hundred fifty years is really not that distant in the past. In the interest of fairness, it should be mentioned that from time to time different popes spoke out against slavery, but in general they could only enforce their edicts in lands they controlled.

Mormons further helped cloud our identity by the promotion of two bizarre doctrines. One was that during the war in heaven, spirit beings that were indifferent to the conflict and didn't fight whole-heartedly were given bodies with black skin as a punishment. The other was that black skin was the curse of Cain. Although there were also Protestant churches who taught the twisted 'curse of Cain' deceit as fact, it was the Latter Day Saints who attempted to authenticate it with a story from scriptures written—not by Moses, the prophets, or the Apostles, but by Joseph Smith himself, in his discourse on Abraham in the "Pearl of Great Price". To support his case for a curse, he haphazardly combines the genealogies of Ham's son Mizraim, and that of his younger brother Canaan.

According to Smith's account Ham married 'Egypt's'[10] one of the daughters of Cain. However, dissecting the logic used to craft the story exposes the fraud. First off, 'Egyptus' speaks to the feminine form of Egypt; the territory established by Ham's son Mizraim. This territory was traditionally referred to as 'the Land of Mizraim' or the Land of Ham, and not settled until quite some time after the flood, because Noah's sons and their progeny did not even spread abroad across the earth until after the divine intervention at Babel. So the name 'Egypt' or any variation thereof came into usage subsequent to the flood. Secondly, in Genesis Chapter 9 verse 1, God blessed Noah's sons in procreation, how then was Joseph Smith to curse any of them? Thirdly, the book of Jasher—which is referenced in both Joshua and II Samuel, reveals that the wives Noah selected for his sons were none other than his own first cousins.

"And thou shalt choose for thy sons three maidens, from the daughters of men, and they shall be wives to thy sons.

And Noah rose up, and he made the ark, in the place where God had commanded him, and Noah did as God had ordered him.

In his five hundred and ninety-fifth year Noah commenced to make the ark, and he made the ark in five years, as the Lord had commanded.

Then Noah took the three daughters of Eliakim, son of Methuselah, for wives for his sons, as the Lord had commanded Noah." Jasher Chapter 5:32-34

---

[10] Pearl of Great Price: Abraham: Chapter 1 vs 21-25 Joseph Smith, Founder of Mormonism.

Methuselah was Noah's grandfather. Noah's father, Lamech—predeceased his father, Methuselah. Methuselah lived to see his granddaughters married to Noah's sons, then died the year of the flood, not in it, but just prior to it. Since Eliakim was the father of the son's wives, and Methuselah's son, that would make him Lamech's brother, and Noah's uncle. Thus, the bloodline was kept pure through the godly line of Seth for transition to the New World. Finally, if God says eight souls were saved, it means exactly that—eight souls were saved i.e., found righteous enough in God's eyes to escape the judgment upon the wicked. To attack Ham's wife, would be tantamount to attacking Japheth and Shem's wives, too, since they were all sisters. Just as none of the native inhabitants of Sodom and Gomorrah escaped in Abraham's day, none of Cain's people escaped the flood. His entire lineage perished in the deluge.

Not that this is even foundational to our roots as Hebrew people who issued forth from Shem. But when foolish, hateful, and unlearned men attempt to build with blocks of lies, their tower deserves to be demolished. This just goes to show the length white people were willing to go in twisting the scripture to present people of color as sinful and worthy of degradation.

British Israelism endeavored to depict the Anglo/Americans as the Lost Ten Tribes of Israel. It also identified Great Britain as Ephraim and the United States as Manasseh and sought to eliminate Judah from the equation altogether. Proponents of this line of thinking wrestled with scripture and cobbled together events representative of Britain's rise in power during the nineteenth century, in an effort to prove that all nations would serve Great Britain. In the midst of the error, sound doctrine went out of the window and the proponents forgot that Israel, Hebrews, and Judah are terms which are used interchangeably to refer to the same people, and most importantly, that God refused the tabernacle of Joseph and did not choose the tribe of Ephraim; preferring instead to choose the tribe of Judah. It was just one more of man's prideful attempts to exalt himself using racism and nationalism.

We have already put forth some discussion of the replacement of Hebrew Israel with the Euro-Judaics. The presence of a people in the historic Holy Land who are Gentile but announce themselves to the world as Abraham's posterity and God's Chosen causes confusion for those in the Captivity attempting to understand their roots and purpose. This misrepresentation was furthered by the 1960's movie Exodus and its signature theme song performed by Pat Boone, 'This Land Is Mine.' Stirring though the rendition may have been, the premise it was based on is false. The land belongs to the people who were scattered out of it for disobedience and idolatry and taken by ships into slavery in the latter days...not to be redeemed until the bodily return of the Lord Jesus Christ at the end of the age.

The misconception is furthered when 'Messianic Jews' (Judaics who acknowledge Jesus as the risen Son of God) are added to the dynamic. In spite of confession of faith in the finished work of Christ, this group also carefully avoids the prophecies of slavery with a yoke of iron and coming over on ships as punishment for idolatry. Instead, zeal for Christ is eclipsed by an obsession with the prosperity of the modern day State of Israel and desire to see the incorporation of the additional land promised to Abraham—Erezt Israel. The imperviousness to the treatment of the Arab Muslims and Arab Christians in the land seems eerily reminiscent to the attitude the American north had about slavery in the antebellum South: that it is embarrassing, but necessary.

This dichotomy continues although there are those among their own scholars and rabbis who have advised them they are not the original Hebrews of the Bible. Also, many who live in the West today are fully aware their early American ancestors bought, sold, and worked our ancestors.[11] The strategy employed to keep the deception firmly entrenched appears to be that of labeling any who challenge it 'anti-Semitic' and a 'disseminator of hate speech.'

This is why I stated earlier the assumption of identity is one of two interpretations of the parable of the wheat and the tares. Treading down the land God has reserved as His own as an inheritance for His son Israel until the chastening is fulfilled, and assuming and attempting to obscure the identity of His son whom He will call out of Egypt once again is a dangerous position to occupy. It is one more example of man changing the ordinance of God. Far from hate, I am speaking the truth in love and sounding a warning; for the present day occupants of the land are in a position of unlawful detainer, and it is a fearful thing to fall into the hands of the Living God.

It is never prudent to assume that just because God permits something to take place, it is okay and will incur no negative consequences. God has a permissive will, and a good, perfect, and acceptable will. And for all the talk of peace, unity, and world solidarity, the kingdoms of this world will never submit to the fear of God apart from divine intervention. Fear, distrust, anger, threats of military strikes, and bloodshed will continue to plague the region until the day God comes out his place to punish the inhabitants of the earth for their iniquity, and gathers all nations together to battle. Common sense dictates that a nation in the throes of this type of turmoil does not represent fulfilled prophecy of a restored Israel, for with the true restoration comes profound peace and tranquility: a true Sabbath rest.

Many churches and prophecy teachers will stubbornly cling to the current occupation as prophecy fulfilled; bolstered by the sheer volume of tradition and media conditioning supporting it. Is there any way to challenge and refute this line of thinking using history, scripture, and solid logic? To this endeavor, I will present seven arguments which the critical Bible scholar can contrast, compare, and evaluate, based on:

*A Return to Egypt (the House of Bondage) by Ships Under a Yoke of Iron

*The Right of Return

*Willingness to Regather

*Awareness of Identity

*Wilderness Layover

*Establishment of the Nation

---

[11] February 18, 2012 "Why Do So Many Jews Hate Black People?" by Alcibiades Bilzerian. thebilzerianreport.com.

*Law of the Bloodline

*<u>A Return to Egypt (the House of Bondage) by Ships Under a Yoke of Iron</u>

This was only experienced by Black Israel: generational, institutionalized slavery for which the descendants have never been compensated; fulfilling the prophecy that they would be only oppressed and crushed always until restored

Judaics were not placed on the slave blocks shackled with iron under an institutionalized slavery; any slavery experienced was not generational, and they were even able to negotiate reparations for forced labor in Germany

*<u>The Right of Return</u>

Moses told Black Israel that they would be evicted from the land and dispersed to their enemies; and that God's intention was for the land to remain desolate (empty) until He sent His angels to re-gather them at the end of the world. In other words, no right of return. This desolation could not have referred to the earlier Babylonian Captivity, since Nebuchadnezzar left some of the poorest of the people in the land to cultivate it

The Euro-Judaics granted themselves—and by extension all other Judaics—permission to occupy the land

*<u>Willingness to Regather</u>

Psalm Chapter 110 shows that on the day the Lord intervenes—in the day of His power (day of His wrath) the people shall be willing... denoting spontaneity, as to volunteer as a soldier, freely offer ones' self as a gift

In contrast, many Euro-Judaics were reluctant to leave their homes to migrate to Palestine; but the suspicious timing of British and American moratoriums on immigration left Palestine as the only option to leave Germany

*<u>Awareness of Identity</u>

God told Black Israel that they would discontinue from their heritage, and serve their enemies in a land they couldn't recognize; however, at the end of the age He would awaken them (restore conscious identity) against the sons of Greece

However, Western prophecy teachers love to point out how that throughout the centuries 'the Jews have always maintained their unique identity no matter where they have gone'

*<u>Wilderness Layover</u>

Prophecies in Psalms, Hosea, Ezekiel, and the Revelation all point to a stopover in the wilderness for those gathered from the four winds before repatriation in the land; also God commands a covenant with the wild animals, birds, and insects so that none of the people are harmed

Regardless of the continent the Judaic immigrants hailed from, they never convened as a single massive assembly in the wilderness with animals, birds, and insects reverting to an Eden-like trust

*Establishment of the Nation

Isaiah Chapter 66 verses 7-24 reference the end of this present age when the nations of the world are conquered and there is only peace in Jerusalem. At that time, God tells Israel their nation will be born instantly: in one day—and that all their brethren will be brought out of all nations; to appear before the Lord as a clean offering—this is after he has judged the earth with fire in his fury

In contrast, immigration to the modern State of Israel has been an ongoing process—spanning well over a century; during a time which has seen no Divine cataclysmic encounter resulting in world-wide rebuke and carnage

*Law of the Bloodline

In the Scriptural Hebraic genealogy, descent is reckoned through the father

The Euro-Judaic teaching is that due to the child's link to the mother during gestation, the mother's Jewishness actually defines the child's soul

But the collusion in hiding the truth about the Black man as the original Hebrew goes further than spurious theology or re-written history. While some 'truth' and 'discernment' ministries correctly point out the Euro-Judaics are not the original descendants of Abraham, they conveniently neglect to explain who the true Hebrews are; thus further clouding the issue. Neither do they attempt to search the scriptures and compare them with history to solve the puzzle. Or, the claim is made that the Palestinian Arabs are the true descendants of Judah.

Moveable geography is another interesting twist in the effort to prevent disclosure. Traditional 'Holy Land' tours have long shown pilgrims and sightseers a mountain in Egypt which they identify as Sinai where God spoke to Moses and gave him the commandments. But in 1985 researcher and archaeologist Ron Wyatt[12] correctly identified Sinai (Horeb) right where the Bible said it was: in Arabia. When he was legally able to obtain permission to explore the area, he observed that the mountain's peak was soot black—in sharp contrast to the surrounding summits. This answers to Exodus Chapter 19 verse 18: "And mount Sinai was

---

[12] Wyatt Archaeological Research Mt. Sinai www.wyattmuseum.com/mt-sinai.htm.

altogether on a smoke, because the Lord descended upon it in fire: and the smoke thereof ascended as the smoke of a furnace, and the whole mount quaked greatly."

Wyatt also observed firsthand the Rock in Horeb where God stood before Moses as he struck the rock that gushed water for the children of Israel. The rock features a huge vertical split, with multiple gullies which clearly show evidence of downstream water erosion. And he found the huge altar that was constructed for the idolatrous worship of the golden calf, complete with the etching of an Egyptian calf hieroglyphic. This area however, known as Jebel el Lawz in the Arabic, is off limits to tourists and Saudi Arabia prohibits access to the site. These geographical and historical landmarks stand as open witnesses to the truth of the Bible and God's interaction with our forefathers. This is our history, and man labors diligently to suppress it. But...there is nothing covered, that shall not be revealed; neither hid, that shall not be known.

Thus far, we have seen proof of the conspiracy to deny or obscure the true ethnic identity of Hebrew people ranging from individual ministries to governments, to religious groups. What may be even more difficult to grasp however, is the dynamic by which the faith-oriented groups are amalgamating, and fusing themselves together with yet a third, more sinister component.

In 1994, a document was drafted: Evangelicals and Catholics Together—which was endorsed by numerous heads of ministries, seminaries, and Christian universities. The language of this declaration essentially realigned the position of evangelical churches as one of cooperation and unity rather than emphasizing doctrinal differences and seeking to convert Catholics. A few years later, an updated declaration was released signed by additional evangelical leaders. Around the same time, another ecumenical movement, Promise Keepers, was organized. Attendees to these conferences included men from both mainstream and evangelical churches, Mormon, and Catholic groups. On the heels of this, an accord was signed between the Roman Catholic Church and the Lutheran World Federation which brought resolution to the doctrinal dispute between these two systems stemming from the Reformation.

Popular and influential speakers continue to attempt to sway the charismatic churches to lay aside all differences and rejoin the Catholic Church. But there is no way to accomplish this without handling the word of God deceitfully. For instance, when a speaker compares himself to John the Baptist as a prophet in the spirit of Elijah to turn the hearts of the sons to the fathers that the way might be prepared for the coming of the Lord; but the 'sons' represent fellowships which have not yet come back to the 'fathers' of Rome, the scriptural reference is taken out of context. When individuals in powerful positions argue that Luther's protest is archaic and obsolete, thereby nullifying the raison d'etre for the Protestant Church, dissenters risk being kicked to the curb and ostracized. When Christians are told that the charismatic churches and the Roman Church preach the same gospel, and they fail to examine New Testament doctrine as revealed in the Gospels, the Acts of the Apostles, and the Epistles to see if this is indeed true, the appeal of unity and strength in numbers begins to eclipse the true model of a persecuted yet faithful body of believers called out from the world to shine as lights and represent holiness, without which no man shall see the Lord.

Most people buying a used car recognize the wisdom of obtaining a vehicle history report, regardless of how nice the body looks and how clean the interior is. When will professing

Christians exercise the same due diligence in discerning truth from error, doctrine from tradition, and holiness from idolatry?

The neutralization and re-absorbing of the Protestant Church into the Roman fold is escalating at a feverish pace, at the same time the Pope has been granted permission to establish an official presence on Mount Zion in Jerusalem, and plans have been drafted for construction of an interfaith temple where the present Dome of the Rock sits. The impetus for a new temple continues, endorsed by Western Christians, despite the fact that New Testament doctrine teaches that each son born into the kingdom by the blood covenant of Christ is a living stone, built up as a spiritual house whose foundation and chief corner stone is the Lord Jesus Christ; also the Apostle Paul tells us our bodies are the temple of the Holy Ghost. The theme of an other-dimensional temple endures even into the age to come of the New Heaven and New Earth:

And I saw no temple therein: for the Lord God Almighty and the Lamb are the temple of it... Revelation Chapter 21 verse 22.

The commission to turn the hearts of the sons to the fathers is found in the Book of Malachi, and refers to the original Black Hebrew people turning back to the unwavering faith of their ancestors Abraham, Isaac, and Jacob. This is another example of a Hebrew specific prophecy. Also note that the directive is not to turn the hearts of the sons back to the Mosaic Law, but to the fathers—who predated the Law. The emphasis is on the faith, obedience, and fellowship the patriarchal fathers had with God in their time. God is calling the sons to emulate these qualities in this day and walk them out in the midst of a crooked and perverse generation. Who will answer the call?

The fact that the Western churches—void of the Spirit—are heeding the siren call of Rome is a prophetic signal that the end of Esau's age is approaching, and the everlasting age of Jacob dawning. In light of the events transpiring in the realm we see, and realizing they are influenced and driven by powers in a realm we cannot see, now is the time for the true Israel of God: the descendants of the Trans-Atlantic slave trade—to purify our hearts and minds, and consecrate ourselves as salt and light. This can be done—even in Captivity—through a lifestyle of repentance and holy living. Earnestly contending for the faith as our first century Hebrew brethren did is the only way to counteract the unrelenting spiritual darkness. And we have these precious words from our brother Daniel for encouragement:

"the people that do know their God shall be strong, and do exploits" and "they that understand among the people shall instruct many" and...

"they that be wise shall shine as the brightness of the firmament; and they that turn many to righteousness as the stars for ever and ever."

We will have to know God, we will have to be willing to show others the good and the right way, and we will have to be wise and win souls.

What these ecumenical developments mean is that before we behold our Kinsman-Redeemer face to face, we will be living in a world where all faiths are integrated. The way this is shaping up, Rome will rule from Jerusalem. Even if diverse groups maintain their individual worship rituals, all will still be expected to acknowledge themselves as under the authority of the 'universal church'. Those who refuse will be singled out and persecuted. We must remember that the servant is not greater than his master, and if they persecuted our Lord, and our brethren in the first century church, they will surely persecute us, too. The darkest hour is just before the dawn, but at that time Michael—the prince of our people—will stand up for us, and we will be delivered: every one who is found written in the book.

Earlier, I alluded to a sinister force tying these religious institutions together. This dark energy predates any of the organizations themselves and has always been in defiance of and in opposition to God and the establishment of His people and His kingdom on earth. This force is the Egyptian and Babylonian mystery religions: the antithesis of the holy and pure wisdom which is from above. The mystery religion relies heavily upon symbolism, ritualism, and secret communication. There is a vast amount of research available on this subject; for the purposes of this book I want to point out that many of the symbols associated with Freemasonry and the Egyptian mystery occult schools can also be found in or on brick and mortar churches: symbols such as sun/sun rays, pyramid/triangle, all seeing eye, the hex/interlocked triangles, and obelisk (male phallic symbol—best recognized as steeples.)

Proverbs Chapter 6 verses 12-13 tells us a naughty (wicked, ungodly) person teacheth with his fingers. Adherents to the mystery religion signal to each other by means of hand signs. The Hebrew word for teacheth means to point out, direct, or inform. They are pointing out, or informing each other and the world that their allegiance is really to the kingdom of darkness; regardless of their outward import. The exact same hand signs are used by prominent figures in government, corporate, and big-name religious circles, as those in satanic groups and the wicked entertainment industry.

An entrance to a Mormon Temple in Salt Lake City, Utah features a large all seeing eye above it, another entrance on the same building shows the eye shape containing what strikingly resembles a Masonic handshake. Whether Eastern Orthodox, Roman Catholic, Methodist, or Lutheran, representations of the eye in a triangle with the sun rays can be found in toto or in various combinations. Steeples on top of church buildings are a type of the Egyptian obelisks, and the six-sided star has nothing to do with David and is an occult symbol—the hex—or Seal of Solomon.

Many of you already know about these symbols, but when one considers how they represent idolatry and rebellion against God and the subverting of His Kingdom, and take into account how they are so prevalent in institutional, religious, government, and secret society architecture and décor—even the currency itself, it follows that wherever the symbolism is, oppression, injustice, and persecution are also present and actively targeted on the seed of the Captivity and all who live godly in Christ Jesus. We are surrounded by an ever present reminder of Satanic hatred; and a world system that uses symbolism to constantly advertise the desire to throw off all restraints imposed by God's mercy, justice, and compassion. But we are loved with an everlasting love; the Eternal God is our refuge, and underneath are the everlasting arms.

In linking Edom to the conspiracy—for Esau's power and influence continue until the physical return of the Lord Jesus Christ, we find a cryptic connection to the financial might which enabled development of infrastructure and economic base in the newly created State of

Israel. The Balfour Declaration, dated November 2nd, 1917, was submitted to Lord Lionel Rothschild, who was at that time president of the British Zionist Federation. Lionel Rothschild was the oldest son of Mayer Amschel Rothschild, the international banking magnate. The name Rothschild means 'rich person', and the surname is literally 'red shield'—a house name. *The Hebrew word for Edom means red*. In addition to funding the fledgling state, money from the House of Rothschild financed the construction of the Masonic themed Israeli Supreme Court building (a structure which features an Illuminati pyramid with sun symbol/all-seeing eye at the top of it) and a major thoroughfare in Tel Aviv is named in honor of Baron Rothschild.

An additional conspiratorial action to obscure our heritage is the removal of the Apocrypha from the Bible. The books of the Apocrypha, originally situated between the Old and New Testaments of the King James Bible, were removed in 1885. The justification for the deletion was that the books were 'not inspired', yet our early Hebrew brethren alluded to them in their epistles extensively. A more plausible explanation for the shunning of the Apocrypha is that the holy inspiration exposed the mystery of iniquity at work in the last days. Case in point:

Many are familiar with the story of Jacob and Esau's birth. Esau came out first, and as Jacob emerged, his hand was grasping his brother's heel. In other words, at the very end of Esau (his heel) Jacob appeared (the hand.) II Esdras Chapter 6 verses 7-10 explain this event as the parting of ages: "For Esau is the end of the world, and Jacob is the beginning of it that followeth." In the subsection *Esau Then and Esau Now*, we learned the twins represented two diametrically opposing archetypes. But there is a deeper meaning beyond even that. They also symbolize two distinct ages. Esau's time is representative of the current era, a day which thankfully is drawing to a close. Symbolically, in the compressed airspace of Jacob's grip on Esau's heel lies all the time from the beginning of the struggle between them to the return of the Lord Jesus.

Esdras Chapters 11 and 12 provide a very insightful look at how the reigning power at the end of days is subdued and annihilated, never to trouble the earth and the people again. The focus of the Chapters is an eagle who reigns over the earth with formidable power. This eagle is destroyed by a mighty lion. Consider who has chosen the eagle as its symbol, and consider that our Lord is the Lion of the Tribe of Judah, and you have a clear understanding of the ultimate victory which will be won on behalf of the saints of the most High, and the inspiration for the cover art of this book.

Could that have been the reason for removing the Apocrypha... the powers in control at the time did not want a prophecy of their ultimate defeat in the hands of the common folk, lest people be reluctant to die in wars of greed and aggression? While this may be true, an equally valid explanation was the need to keep the hope of redemption out of the hearts of the true Israel. In the late 1800s, the Zionist movement was just beginning to gain momentum. Having no way of knowing at what point in the future God was going to awaken the true sons of Zion against the sons of Greece, wicked men may have decided it was better to suppress the truth in unrighteousness, than risk dealing with an awakening at a time others were staking a claim to the land of Israel.

The melding of the mystery religion (false god/false spirit), apostate church, (false bride of Christ) and spiritual Edom (Talmudic-based deception of a counterfeit Hebrew people) is the three-fold cord binding the hearts and minds of people in these last days...it is the spiritual manifestation of the Mystery of Iniquity.

The Conspiracy Foretold in Ancient Prophecy

It is easy to mock and call a person a conspiracy theorist, but I would hope most people would exercise restraint before applying that term to God. What God does do, is expose the schemes of sinful man long before those designs are implemented. God can do this with accuracy because He has already declared the end from the beginning and knows who all the players are and have been down through history. Absolutely nothing gets past Him. God is the one who said in the second Psalm, 'The kings of the earth set themselves, and the rulers take counsel together against the Lord, and against his Anointed.' The Hebrew word 'set' in this instance means, anything so as to stay. This means they will do anything to remain in power, even if it means plotting against God himself. The irony is that all of the players who are willing operatives for the mystery of iniquity have access to the same Bible you and I have. Do not fool yourself into thinking they do not know the prophecies and the predicted outcomes. Rather, they are operating on the premise of Ecclesiastes Chapter 8 verse 11: 'Because sentence against an evil work is not executed speedily, therefore the heart of the sons of men is fully set in them to do evil.'

We have already covered Noah's prophecy that God would enlarge Japheth in the subsection *Rise of the Gentiles—Noah's Prophecy over Japheth Manifests*. The apostate church and man-created State of Israel are almost exclusively represented by white Japhethians. The next prophecy found alluding to theft of identity is found in Ezekiel Chapter 35 and Chapter 36 verses 1-7. Chapter 35 is devoted solely to the rebuke and destruction of Edom. In these chapters, Edom is referred to respectively as mount Seir and Idumea; remember we learned in the subsection *Spiritual Genetics—Identified by Fruits Over Flesh* that these terms are also used interchangeably for Esau and Edom.

A synopsis of Chapter 35 details God's wrath against Edom, because of Edom's perpetual hatred against the children of Israel, the shedding of their blood, and the envy against them. Because they have enjoyed bloodshed, now bloodshed will pursue them. The execution will be complete and efficient: the inhabitants will be trapped before the slaughter begins so that no one can escape and no one can enter. Their cities will never be established again. But verse 10 is key:

Because thou hast said, these two nations and these two countries shall be mine, and we will possess it; whereas the Lord was there...here I will parse this out, for there is a lot more here than initially meets the eye. Because Edom has said, these two nations (Judah and Israel) and these two countries (the areas of the former northern kingdom and the southern kingdom) shall be mine, and we will possess it—possess—yârêsh—to occupy—by driving out previous tenants and possessing in their place, to seize, to rob, to inherit, to expel, to impoverish, to ruin, cast out, destroy, consume, disinherit, dispossess, driving out, enjoy, expel x without fail, give to/leave for inheritance + magistrate (implying enforced by law) make poor, come to poverty, take possession, seize upon, succeed x utterly whereas the Lord wast here (instead of the Lord being there)...God is going to make Himself known to them and judge them. In verse 12 God says, "...I have heard all thy blasphemies (scorn) which thou hast spoken against the mountains of Israel, saying, They are laid desolate, they are given us to consume."

This word desolate is the same Hebrew word used to communicate how God wanted the land to lie in a state of rest and numbness while He was disciplining his Hebrew sons with chastisement in Captivity. But this was the mantra the Zionists repeated, 'a land without a people for a people without a land.' On the contrary, this is one land they should have given a wide berth to; nobody should have set foot in it—not the Euro-Judaics; nor the neighboring Arabs. The land was holy to God, even if Israel and Judah had defiled their inheritance with bloodshed and repeated idolatries, He wanted it left alone until their corrective discipline was up and He supernaturally brought them back.

He goes on to say the mountains of Israel are taken up in the mouths of talkers and an infamy among the people. In Chapter 36 verse 5, God speaks:

"Therefore thus saith the Lord God; Surely in the fire (flaming anger) of my jealousy (zealous in a bad sense) have I spoken against the residue (remaining) of the heathen (Gentiles), and against all Idumea (Edom), which have appointed (assigned, bestowed) my land into their possession with the joy (blithesomeness or glee—religious or festival-mirth, pleasure, rejoice) of all their heart, with despiteful (to push aside, contempt) minds, to cast (in the sense of a suburb) it out for a prey (to plunder.)

Prophesy therefore concerning the land of Israel, and say unto the mountains, and to the hills, to the rivers, and to the valleys, Thus saith the Lord God; Behold, I have spoken in my jealousy and in my fury, because ye have borne the shame (confusion, confounded) of the heathen:

But ye, O mountains of Israel, ye shall shoot forth your branches, and yield your fruit to my people of Israel; for they are at hand (bring near, cause to approach) to come." This prophecy of the return of "my people of Israel" has yet to be fulfilled.

Ezekiel Chapter 7 verse 24: Wherefore I will bring (cause, pull in) the worst of the heathen (Gentile, a foreign nation), and they shall possess their houses: I will also make the pomp of the strong to cease; and their holy places shall be defiled.

Psalms Chapter 83 verses 1-7 very clearly explains a conspiracy among the nations to cut Israel off from being a nation, with the specific intent that the name of Israel may be no more in remembrance. Not surprisingly, we find the usual suspect—Edom—heading the list of those involved in the treachery. Based on the breakdown of this psalm:

Who: the enemies of God

What: took crafty counsel against God's people; consulted against his covered ones; formed a confederacy against God himself; consulted together with one consent;

Why: because they literally hate God, and want to blot out Israel, even to the extent of obliterating Israel's name. If you didn't catch it, the true Israel is inseparable from God. Hatred of God is manifested by the conspiracy and treachery against the descendants of the first Hebrews up to and including the generations coming after the Trans-Atlantic slave trade.

Lastly, the prophecies of the Lord Jesus Christ...

"Jerusalem shall be trodden (trampled) down of the Gentiles, until the times of the Gentiles be fulfilled..." Luke Chapter 21 verse 24. And Jesus speaking to the angels (messengers) of the churches:

"I know thy works, and tribulation, and poverty, (but thou art rich) and I know the blasphemy (speech which is impious or vilification against God) of them which say they are Jews (resembling a Judæan), and are not, but are the synagogue of Satan." Revelation Chapter 2 verse 9.

"Behold, I will make them of the synagogue of Satan, which say they are Jews (resembling a Judæan), and are not, but do lie; behold, I will make them to come and worship (to kiss, like a dog licking his master's hand; to fawn or crouch, to prostrate oneself in homage, do reverence to) before thy feet, and to know that I have loved (great fondness, personal attachment, as to kiss tenderly) thee." Revelation Chapter 3 verse 9.

These statements from the Lord Jesus Christ are very insightful, because there is a distinct difference in the word used to refer to the members of the body of Christ in the seven churches and the word used for the gathering place of those who say they are Judæan (of Judah) and are not. The Greek word used for synagogue basically means a religious gathering or meeting place. In contrast, the word used for church—ecclesia—means called out ones; a Christian community of members on earth, or saints in heaven or both.

The Revelation was given to the Apostle John for the benefit of those living at the end of the age:

"The Revelation of Jesus Christ, which God gave unto him, to shew unto his servants things which must shortly come to pass; and he sent and signified it by his angel unto his servant John...Blessed is he that readeth, and they that hear the words of this prophecy, and keep those things which are written therein: for the time is at hand." Revelation Chapter 1 verses 1 and 3.

These words of Jesus show then that there will be a definite period at the end of days when a people will exist that will claim to be Jews (of Judah) but are not. He also classifies their worship as a worship of Satan. Finally, He concludes with saying they will ultimately have to worship those whom they have lied to. It is reasonable to believe that statements such as these are the precise reason the authors of the Jewish Talmud make such abusive and reviling remarks about the Lord Jesus Christ. However, regardless of the great hatred, every knee will bow, and every tongue will confess that Jesus is Lord to the glory of God the Father.

For many years after slavery, it was common to find all types of advertisements and novelty items that depicted Blacks in insulting and humiliating ways. What was going on in white America's conscience that they could produce and mass market such hideous portrayals of Blacks without the slightest hint of remorse? The answer is, subconsciously, *many felt religiously justified*. This is because their actions were religiously influenced. America considers its religious foundations to be Judeo-Christian. And it is the Euro-Judaic holy book—the Talmud—where the account of Ham and Canaan became nauseatingly twisted and embellished with actions and commentary designed to debase the Black man in Captivity in the West; who as we have pointed out—is not even Hamitic, but Shemitic. The Talmud draws a direct link between the Black man's dark skin, full lips, and kinky hair and Ham's dishonorable attitude toward his father. One commentary even has Ham sexually abusing Noah. This warped foundational perspective of the Black man goes a long way in explaining the knee-jerk like contempt expressed by whites.

Because these damaging fables were held up as truth by people who claimed to be chosen of God, this root of bitterness has defiled entire nations. It was based on a degradation of imagination that boggles the mind, and was directed at an ethnicity that wasn't even Hamitic. But the true irony of the matter is that even as white Christian America denigrated the Black man with demeaning caricatures and stereotypes, they knew not that the Talmud likewise depicted them as animals, dirt, and dung; and described the Lord Jesus Christ in an even filthier and scornful manner.

Satan has constructed a complex maze where one lone segment of Gentiles calls themselves Shemites and calls the true Shemites Hamites, while degrading all the people of Ham in the process including the progeny of Cush, Phut, and Mizraim. While most white Gentiles are rightfully proud of their heritage, a select group feels they have replaced the black Shemites. This is a spirit of envy because the Bible declares the kingdom is decreed to Judah; though he be temporarily set aside by chastisement. But speaking of the Day of the Lord, the prophet Isaiah warns:

"Lord, when thy hand is lifted up, they will not see: but they shall see, and be ashamed for their envy at the people; yea, the fire of thine enemies shall devour them." Isaiah Chapter 26 verse 11.

Remembering too, that a nation in prophecy is judged not necessarily by where they are or who they call themselves, but by how they treat Judah and Israel in the latter days, we can see Moab and Ammon also answer to the present day Euro-Judaic state of Israel, because (through the Talmud) they have reproached and reviled the genuine Hebrews. The word reproached is defined as 'charaph,' meaning to expose; as if to pull off by stripping, to defame, to carp at. Magnify themselves against means to twist or make large in body, mind, estate, or honor. This is borne out in Zephaniah Chapter 2 verses 1-11:

"Gather yourselves together, yea, gather together, O nation not desired;

Before the decree bring forth, before the day pass as the chaff, before the fierce anger of the Lord come upon you, before the day of the Lord's anger come upon you.

Seek ye the Lord, all ye meek of the earth, which have wrought his judgment; seek righteousness, seek meekness: it may be ye shall be hid in the day of the Lord's anger.

For Gaza shall be forsaken, and Ashkelon a desolation: they shall drive out Ashdod at the noon day, and Ekron shall be rooted up.

Woe unto the inhabitants of the sea coast, the nation of the Cherethites! The word of the Lord is against you; O Canaan, the land of the Philistines, I will even destroy thee, that there shall be no inhabitant.

And the sea coast shall be dwellings and cottages for shepherds, and folds for flocks.

And the coast shall be for the remnant of the house of Judah; they shall feed thereupon: in the houses of Ashkelon shall they lie down in the evening: for the Lord their God shall visit them, and turn away their Captivity.

I have heard the reproach of Moab, and the revilings of the children of Ammon, whereby they have reproached my people, and magnified themselves against their border.

Therefore as I live, saith the Lord of hosts, the God of Israel, Surely Moab shall be as Sodom, and the children of Ammon as Gomorrah, even the breeding of nettles, and saltpits, and a perpetual desolation: the residue of my people shall spoil them, and the remnant of my people shall possess them. This shall they have for their pride, because they have reproached and magnified themselves against the people of the Lord of hosts.

The Lord will be terrible unto them: for he will famish all the gods of the earth; and men shall worship him, every one from his place, even all the isles of the heathen."

It is clear this is speaking of the time of the end because the day of the Lord will be the first time that all men on the earth worship God wherever they are. Also the prophet alludes to Judah's Captivity being turned away and the coast given to the remnant of the tribe. Realizing that everyone in the land does not reproach and revile his people, and that there are those there who have striven to be just, God exhorts them to seek righteousness and meekness, that they might be hidden when his wrath arrives.

While Moab and Ammon are a spiritual representation of a people, Ashkelon and Ashdod are actual populated cities that currently exist in Israel. Ekron is even there; it has been identified as the site of Tel Miqne—23 miles southwest of Jerusalem. When one observes who controls that region today, and what their holy book states about the true Black Hebrews, the Lord Jesus Christ, and authentic Christians, it is not difficult to understand why God has decreed this horrific prophecy.

Egypt, Assyria, and Israel in the Middle: The True Africa vs 'The Middle East'

The last factor contributing to the disconnection of Black Hebrew identity is the artificial construct referred to as the 'Mid East or Middle East'. Although you constantly hear the term bandied about on the news media and in the context of political affairs, the truth is that the Middle East is a newly created entity, in much the same way as the modern day state of Israel; and for much the same reason—a white Gentile military presence strategically positioned in a region populated by Hamitic and mixed Hamitic-Shemitic or Hamitic-Japhethic peoples. An equally important reason is to disassociate descendants of the Trans-Atlantic slave trade from any historical link to the region. But as the sovereign Lord God originally established the nations, there is no such valid order, and God declares in Isaiah Chapter 19 verses 23-25 that He is going to reverse this derangement of nations and realign them in the original and proper sequence.

Viewing a map of Africa today, you will see the continent dissected into roughly fifty-four countries; most of which did not exist until the advent of European exploration, colonialism, and exploitation of resources. The borders on some of these countries have abnormally straight lines—partitions that cannot be found in the ancient maps of Africa, where cartographers were merely concerned with accurately mapping the land mass and correctly identifying the regions, rivers, and people.

So it is understandable that most people have no idea sixteenth century mapmakers charted Libya (Phut) far into north central and northwestern Africa...this region was called Libya Interior and literally encompassed almost half of the entire African land mass. Ancient Egypt had its own territory; to its northeast lay the land of Canaan, and further due east and south east was Assyria in Mesopotamia (Nimrod's land.) If you recall from the subsection *Who Does the God of the Bible Say You Are?* all these names I have referenced are connected to Noah's son Ham.

Thus, ancient geography was much more complex than the orderly arrangement the Europeans attempted to construct in the interest of conquering and convenience. In other words, 'The Land of Ham' encompassed the entire top half of the continent of Africa, plus the land above the Arabian and Red Seas and extended clear into the entire region of modern day Iraq. Tribes and ethnicities were not arranged in a tidy, systemic fashion; rather, they took possessions around each other and established confirmed borders which were well understood by the people of the time. Hence, Shem was found in Syria with Ham to his east and west, Hamitic-Shemitic Ishmael to his south, and Japhethian Torgormah (Turkey) to his north. In Mesopotamia, Ham was bordered by Hamitic-Shemitic peoples to the west, Shem (Elam-Persia) on the east, and Hamitic-Shemitic Ishmael on the south. The indigenous peoples of these regions looked entirely different (much darker) than they appear today. They have lightened due to the mixing of white Japhethians during the European expansion.

Black Americans in the Captivity may have trouble understanding where they fit into the equation, until recalling that God drove seven nations out of Canaan (for their wickedness and idolatrous practices) and placed the Hebrews there in their stead. This was essentially one people of dark skin replacing another people of dark skin. Israel has always been part of Africa.

An intriguing prophecy is found in Isaiah Chapter 19 verses 23-25; the construction of a tri-national thoroughfare. A northeast-southwest highway will be built spanning from Egypt to Iraq, crossing directly through the land of Israel:

"In that day shall there be a highway out of Egypt to Assyria, and the Assyrian shall come into Egypt, and the Egyptian into Assyria, and the Egyptians shall serve with the Assyrians.

In that day shall Israel be the third with Egypt and with Assyria, even a blessing in the midst of the land:

Whom the Lord of hosts shall bless, saying, Blessed be Egypt my people, and Assyria the work of my hands, and Israel mine inheritance."

Notice verse 23 states "the Egyptian shall serve with the Assyrian" (Iraqis). No mention is made of Israel serving although Israel is smack in the middle between them. Why are the Egyptians and Iraqis serving? It is because of the way Israel was treated when they were in

Captivity in those nations. Wherever Israel was scattered, they were treated as the dregs of society. At our redemption, all other nations will serve Israel. Nevertheless, we will be a blessing and refreshing to the Hamitic peoples to the east and west of us, and unlike it was for our ancestors during slavery in the Western nations, those bearing the yoke of servitude will experience the Father's care and compassion for He says of them "Blessed be Egypt my people, and Assyria the work of my hands." This prophecy of an atmosphere of brotherly love, peace, security, and closeness of the Father is in stark contrast to the sentiments of the current occupiers of the land where Egypt and Iraq are concerned.

All who entered into the body of Christ by grace through faith, both of Israel and Gentile, will be delegated positions of authority 'in that day' based upon how they built on the Foundation of Christ. Therefore, let us build with works of gold, silver, and precious stones, for He is coming quickly, and his reward is with him.

WHAT'S IMPORTANT

The dynamics involved in steering the mind of the Black man in American away from the truth of his identity are myriad and complex. The conspiracy involves a false Christ; alien from His genealogy, and depicted in the image and likeness of the oppressor of the Captivity. It includes a foreign presence in the land apportioned to Israel and Judah; a presence consistently supported by media, culture, most of the Western Protestant church, and endorsed by Rome in the form of an official Vatican presence in Jerusalem and joint support for an interfaith temple.

We learned a popular reference bible exists that released editions in tandem with the progress of the alien presence in the land. We also saw this version supports the erroneous "curse of Ham/slaves are of Hamitic descent" teaching. We found that someone or some group removed books from the canon which provide critical insight into the last days—the time we currently live in. It became clear there is a complicity to control the land promised to Israel, and exploitation of the rightful heirs for the riches of this world. Permeating all of this is the mystery religion with its signs, symbols, and secret societies. And lastly, assumption of our Hebrew identity by Gentiles was foreseen and articulated to both Old and New Testament prophets.

Both Black and white churches in the West must take to heart Jesus' declaration about a group of people impersonating His brethren and receive it as words which have eternal consequences, or He would not have spoken them to John. The Lord Jesus Christ was not dictating under a word count quota and didn't need to make idle statements just to fill up empty space on a scroll. He said these things because He knew as history played out how much of a negative effect the deception would have on His brethren. He wanted them to know that even if the entire world was speaking to the contrary, He knew who was who, and the final outcome was going to have a surprise ending. He also said outside the kingdom was whosoever loveth and maketh a lie. The Greek word used in this instance for lie is the same word used in II Thessalonians Chapter 2 verse 11 to describe the lie people will end up believing as a result of the strong delusion God will send them. The Greek word for delusion in this verse alludes to fraudulence, or an impostor or misleader. If one follows the speaker's trail in Chapter 2, it is clear both the delusion and the lie are a culmination of the mystery of iniquity.

You cannot love the Kinsman-Redeemer without loving His kinfolk. You cannot hate the kinfolk without also hating their Kinsman-Redeemer. The Kinsman-Redeemer stated He came forth and proceeded from the Father, and that He and His Father are one. God told the Hebrews in the Old Testament that they are hewn from Him (the Rock) and that He is the quarry they are dug from, and called Israel His son. Net, this is a family affair. Gentiles can join the family, but only through true repentance and blood covenant with the Lord Jesus Christ. However, they cannot join the family, and then confederate with those who hate the natural family while continuing to enjoy the table and amenities of the family house—lest they find themselves banned from the premises. There will be weeping and gnashing of teeth as they present their original invitations, only to find they are now void and expired. On the contrary, when they enter the house, they owe a debt of love, for it was through the seed of the Hebrew nation that the payment for their sin manifested. Neither can any Gentile join the family gathering by forging an invitation or entering the house at some entrance other than The Door. Jesus said whoever does this is a thief and a robber.

He will ever be mindful of His covenant... He hath commanded his covenant forever.

Chapter IV...The Black Man in Covenant with God

God is a God of covenant.

Often when people speak of God, they acknowledge him in terms of being a God of love, or power, or mercy. All of this is true of him. But as the people he called and has a special love for, we need to both know and understand Him as a God of covenant. The very essence of our relationship to God and with God revolves around covenant. If we are to understand God's heart, and his sense of honor, it is imperative to understand the principle of covenant.

In the most basic sense, a covenant is a formal agreement between two parties. Where God's covenants were concerned, God sets the terms and conditions, and clearly defines the benefits for obedience and penalties for violation. God's covenants with our forefathers were non-negotiable; but God could always be trusted to honor his obligation to the agreement, whether it involved releasing blessing, or actuating a curse. Because of the gravity of such an instrument, covenants were always initiated by God.

The Hebrew words associated with covenant translate in English as to choose, select, create, cut down (as with wood) in the sense of cutting; a compact made by passing between pieces of flesh, a confederacy, a league. These terms will become more relevant as we go on.

The first recorded covenant is the promise God made to Noah that all flesh would never be destroyed by a flood again. The covenant was between God and Noah and every living creature with him for perpetual generations. Right at this juncture, we have to stop and marvel at how great a God we serve, that he could create a covenant of blessing and assurance that was binding on his entire creation forever.

While many covenants today are formalized with ink signatures or apostilles, the Lord God certified his covenant with Noah by placing his own bow (which we recognize as the rainbow) in the cloud. Also, God told Noah that when he saw the bow, he would remember his covenant with all flesh. Try to wrap your mind around how faithful God is, when you consider how many rainbows have appeared at any point and time on the earth since that first display. God never ceases thinking of us, and the earth he created.

Today we see the seal of this covenant co-opted to represent one of the attitudes that summoned the wrath of God in the antediluvian era. For, if the rainbow appeared as a token to confirm a covenant following judgment for sin, it is a misrepresentation to now associate it with a lifestyle of sin. Also of concern is the confusion the modern day Edomites have caused in trying to instate a legally binding code known as the Noahide Commandments, which sound biblical to the novice, but actually have nothing at all to do with the Noahic covenant we are discussing here. Rather, the Noahide Laws are strict obligations interpreted by the Judaic Talmud, which the proponents hope to eventually enforce upon the entire world. One of these "Noahide Laws" is a prohibition against blasphemy. The penalty for breaking these laws is decapitation. Now please remember that the Talmud maligns the Lord Jesus Christ in unspeakable terms; and that the Apostle John saw a vision at the end of the age of the souls that were beheaded for the witness of Jesus, and for the word of God, who had refused to worship the beast or his image or receive his mark.

Black Shemitic Abraham Called Out of Hamitic Mesopotamia

We saw that 'choose' and 'select' were two of the definitions related to the Hebrew word for covenant. Sometime after the failed construction of the Tower of Babel and the dispersion of the nations, God chose our forefather Abram and called him out of his father's house to go into the land of Canaan. The family had originally lived in Mesopotamia (modern day Iraq—a Hamitic territory) and Abram's father Terah actually left Mesopotamia with Abram, Sarah, and Lot with the intention of going to Canaan, but for whatever reason they stopped in Haran, before reaching Canaan. Terah died in Haran; and it was at that time God called Abram to leave his kindred and people in Haran and journey into Canaan, with the promise he was going to give that land to his descendants. Abram was seventy-five years old when he accepted this commission from God. This is an important example. We don't serve God in our youth and the prime of our life, then rest on our laurels when we are old. And we don't fritter away our life during our youth, then try to make up for it in our waning years. We order our lives so our ear is open to hear God's call and we are ready to serve him at any point in our lives.

Abram did something at that point that we need to take note of. Up until then, God had spoken, and Abram obeyed. Now, God appeared (made his presence known/felt) to Abram and reaffirmed the promise. And Abram did not just acknowledge the reaffirmation verbally. He built an altar to the Lord, in memorandum of the Lord appearing to him. An altar is built for the purpose of sacrifice, and a sacrifice is offered either to pay homage or for conciliation. Abram had not sinned; this altar was to honor God. He then began to act in faith on God's promise and moved out even further into the territory, and built another altar there, and called on the name of the Lord.

Abram's journey took a detour into Egypt because of a famine in Canaan. When he was able to return, he went back to the place of his original altar. After separating from his nephew Lot, God spoke to Abram again and reaffirmed the promise a second time; this time telling him to get up and walk the length and breadth of the land. Abram obeyed, packed up and moved as far as Hebron, and built an altar to the Lord there. I think it is important to notice, at every encounter, Abram is demonstrating faith by treading upon the territory God is promising, and each time, acknowledging the Lord with an altar of memorial.

The next encounter we read of is the meeting with Melchizedek, King of Righteousness, King of Peace and priest of the most High God. This Melchizedek was a theophany—a manifestation of the pre-incarnate Christ, because Hebrews Chapter 7 verses 1-3 tells us he had no father, no mother, no descent, neither beginning of days or end of life; but made like unto the Son of God; abideth a priest continually. This is how Jesus could tell the Pharisees, "Your father Abraham rejoiced to see my day; and he saw it, and was glad...Before Abraham was, I am."

I could have launched right into listing the various covenants, but I thought it was important to illustrate the background dynamics operating between God and Abram long before their first covenant was established. We can see a pattern of exposure and communication to

Abram by God, and a consistent response of faith, obedience, and honor by Abram. These were preparatory steps leading up to the formal action, but Abram demonstrated an understanding of the commitment involved, and his belief in God was counted as righteousness. This foundational trust and right standing was critical, because significant time would elapse between God's first covenant with Abram, and his second.

Covenant Established and the End Time Captivity Foretold

ABRAHAM

God has his signature ways.

When God gets ready to establish a covenant, he uses a unique preface. He announces who he is, and clarifies what he has already done for the party to be bound by the agreement. This is what happened with the first covenant, "I am the Lord that brought thee out of Ur of the Chaldees, to give thee this land to inherit it."

Abram prepared a sacrifice according to God's instructions—dividing the larger animals but leaving the birds whole, and waited before the Lord. He did not burn the sacrifice, but waited for God. At sunset, Abram fell into a deep sleep, and a horror of thick darkness fell upon him. I Timothy Chapter 6 verse 16 tells us God dwells in the light no man can approach unto, therefore it was of his mercy that he cloaked himself in thick darkness.

First God gives the prophecy: "Know of a surety that thy seed shall be a stranger in a land that is not theirs, and shall serve them; and they shall afflict them four hundred years, And also that nation, whom they shall serve, will I judge: and afterward shall they come out with great substance." This is a dual prophecy; with two fulfillments over two different time periods. The first fulfillment occurred during the enslavement in Egypt under Pharaoh, and was referenced in Acts Chapter 7 verses 6-7 during Stephen's testimony before he was martyred. Egypt was judged, and the Hebrews left there with great substance, to enter the wilderness, before possessing the Promised Land.

The last fulfillment is yet to come. This prophecy also correlates to another: "Out of Egypt have I called my son", which has a triple fulfillment: first in the Exodus, secondly after Joseph, Mary, and the young Jesus had to flee from Herod, and the final fulfillment is yet to take place. Because our ancestors came into Egypt again (by ships) and Israel is called God's son, the prophecy to Abram will come to fruition once again. God will call his sons out of the house of bondage—saving the tents of Judah first—and the angels gathering the rest of the tribes from the four winds.

Remember now how one of the definitions of covenant was, a compact made by passing between pieces of flesh? When it was fully dark, a smoking furnace and burning lamp passed between the pieces of flesh. God now confirms the covenant with Abram; that the land is confirmed for his descendants, and defines the boundaries by river borders, and names of each nation which will have to leave.

When Abram was ninety-nine years old, the covenant of circumcision was given. Again, God announces his exalted position: "I am the Almighty God..." This covenant confirmed the former promises concerning the future geographical territory to be possessed by the descendants, but incorporated additional benefits; new names for Abram and Sarai (now to be Abraham and Sarah) and a new requirement: circumcision of the foreskin of every male on the eighth day of life. Here we see the concept of cutting; a compact made by passing between pieces of flesh. This cutting of the flesh was to be a sign and monument to the covenant; God's covenant was to be in their flesh for an everlasting covenant. Failure to honor this requirement would result in death for the male; for example, as exceptional a man as Moses was in God's sight, the failure to obey this requirement where his son was concerned almost cost him his life. So at this command Abraham, his son Ishmael, and every male in Abraham's household were circumcised. Look at the urgency with which Abraham acted when he received this directive. There was no lingering or delay to perform the command that would seal the covenant between God and the seed of Abraham forever.

Covenant Directed Through Isaac, Jacob; Christ, the Seed of Abraham

During this same encounter, God said, "But my covenant will I establish with Isaac, which Sarah shall bear unto thee at this set time in the next year." Later, even with a sure covenant in place, Abraham is tested in the matter of offering Isaac as a sacrifice. In response to his willingness to obey, the agreement is made irrevocable by God swearing by himself—for there is none greater—"that in blessing I will bless thee, and in multiplying I will multiply thy seed as the stars of the heaven, and as the sand which is upon the sea shore; and thy seed shall possess the gate of his enemies; And in thy seed shall the nations of the earth be blessed; because thou hast obeyed my voice."

ISAAC

The covenant was further confirmed with Isaac:

"And the Lord appeared unto him, and said, Go not down into Egypt; dwell in the land which I shall tell thee of: Sojourn in this land, and I will be with thee, and will bless thee; for unto thee, and unto thy seed, I will give all these countries, and I will perform the oath which I sware unto Abraham thy father; And I will make thy seed to multiply as the stars of heaven, and will give unto thy seed all these countries; and in thy seed shall all the nations of the earth be blessed; Because that Abraham obeyed my voice, and kept my charge, my commandments, my statutes, and my laws.

And the Lord appeared unto him the same night, and said, I am the God of Abraham thy father: fear not, for I am with thee, and will bless thee, and multiply thy seed for my servant Abraham's sake.

And he builded an altar there, and called upon the name of the Lord, and pitched his tent there: and there Isaac's servants digged a well."

Here, we see God looking back to Abraham's obedience and dedication. We see God's signature salutation, and this is really beautiful as we see of the many names and attributes God is worthy to claim, he chooses to announce himself as the God of Abraham thy father. And, we see the appropriate response, in that Isaac erects an altar at the place God spoke to him.

What I am attempting to illustrate is the closeness with which our forefathers walked with God. For many today, relationship with God has degenerated to the point where showing up for church service or performing assigned tasks within the local fellowship are the sum of duty, and the remainder of ones' life belongs to self to live as one suits. The patriarchs were men who also handled business and family life, but the covenant and promises always remained front and center. When God spoke, he had their full attention and they took careful note of what he said. Afterward, they would erect an altar to commemorate that interaction. If you could have followed the route of their trek in those days, every place you saw an altar they had built would represent when God spoke to them. Can we ask ourselves what kind of memorials we are leaving in our own life journey as a testimony to others of our covenant with God, and that God has met with us, and communed with us?

JACOB

Jacob was well-versed regarding the covenant, but it was testing in adversity that brought home the glory and presence of God to him.

"And Jacob went out from Beer-sheba, and went toward Haran. And he lighted upon a certain place, and tarried there all night, because the sun was set; and he took of the stones of that place, and put them for his pillows, and lay down in that place to sleep.

And he dreamed, and behold a ladder set up on the earth, and the top of it reached to heaven: and behold the angels of God ascending and descending on it.

And, behold, the Lord stood above it, and said, I am the Lord God of Abraham thy father, and the God of Isaac: the land whereon thou liest, to thee will I give it, and to thy seed; And thy seed shall be as the dust of the earth, and thou shalt spread abroad to the west, and to the east, and to the north, and to the south: and in thee and in thy seed shall all the families of the earth be blessed. And, behold, I am with thee, and will keep thee in all places whither thou goest, and will bring thee again into this land; for I will not leave thee, until I have done that which I have spoken to thee of.

And Jacob awaked out of his sleep, and he said, Surely the Lord is in this place; and I knew it not. And he was afraid, and said, How dreadful is this place! this is none other but the house of God, and this is the gate of heaven. And Jacob rose up early in the morning, and took the stone that he had put for his pillows, and set it up for a pillar, and poured oil upon the top of it. And he called the name of that place Beth-el (which means literally House of God): but the name of that city was called Luz at the first."

The lives of the patriarchs were characterized by circuitous journeys throughout the land; here we can see this playing out again as Jacob journeys toward Haran, the area his grandfather Abraham originally left. Again, God's signature salutation, but notice he is acknowledging the patriarchal procession: I am the Lord God of Abraham thy father, and the God of Isaac...Jacob acknowledges the encounter by constructing a pillar with the stones he had used for pillows, and pouring oil on them. He also vows that place will be God's house if he returns in peace. Are these just interesting anecdotes to Bible history, or did God take that memorial seriously? We find the answer in Hosea Chapter 12 verses 4-5 where it was written many generations in the future:

"...he found him in Beth-el, and there he spake with us; Even the Lord God of hosts; the Lord is his memorial."

God holds all of our days in his hand. He has never forgotten his covenant with our forefathers, and he remembers every memorial we place before him in our prayers and actions.

And why is God rehearsing the genealogy associated with the covenant each time he references it? God is looking at sonship...both backward in time and forward in time. In referencing Abraham, God acknowledges the descent from Shem, which predates the Flood and connects to the godly line of Seth through Adam, who we see in Luke's detailed lineage (Chapter 3 verse 38) was the son of God. As we will see shortly, Israel is also the son of God, for Israel translates prince with God; and a prince is the son of a King. From Israel's descent a child will be born, and a son given, and the government will be upon his shoulder: whose name is called Wonderful, Counseller, The mighty God, The everlasting Father, The Prince of Peace. Of the increase of his government and peace there will be no end, upon the throne of David, and upon his kingdom, to order it, and to establish it with judgment and with justice from henceforth even for ever...this is none other than the Lord Jesus Christ: the Son of the Living God.

Fear motivated Jacob to pray to God for protection against his brother Esau, but faith in God's promise of the covenant enabled him to counterbalance his distress. Let's listen as he cries out to God:

"O God of my father Abraham, and God of my father Isaac, the Lord which saidst unto me, Return unto thy country, and to thy kindred, and I will deal well with thee: I am not worthy of the least of all the mercies, and of all the truth, which thou hast shewed unto thy servant; for with my staff I passed over this Jordan; and now I am become two bands. Deliver me, I pray thee, from the hand of my brother, from the hand of Esau: for I fear him, lest he will come and smite me, and the mother with the children. And thou saidst, I will surely do thee good, and make thy seed as the sand of the sea, which cannot be numbered for multitude."

*In analyzing Jacob's prayer, we see that first, just as God does, he acknowledges the paternal genealogy.

*He reminds God that he is going back to his homeland in obedience to God

*In humility, he acknowledges God's mercies and truth to him thus far, and graciousness in blessing him, for he left just one man, but is returning with a clan

*He admits he is afraid Esau might respond with a revengeful attitude, and he fears for the safety of his family

*He concludes by reminding God of the covenant affirmation at Beth-el

Now God answers Jacob's prayer, but in a very unusual manner. The struggle moves from the natural realm to the spiritual realm:

"And Jacob was left alone; and there wrestled a man with him until the breaking of the day. And when he saw that he prevailed not against him, he touched the hollow of his thigh; and the hollow of Jacob's thigh was out of joint, as he wrestled with him. And he said, Let me go, for the day breaketh. And he said, I will not let thee go, except thou bless me. And he said unto him, What is thy name? And he said, Jacob. And he said, Thy name shall be called no more Jacob, but Israel: for as a prince hast thou power with God and with men, and hast prevailed."

Jacob is facing the confrontation with Esau by himself. His family is defenseless. His parents couldn't come to his rescue. Laban had returned home, and he wasn't part of the conflict anyway.

Abraham's faith was tested with Isaac; now Jacob's steadfastness is being tested. He couldn't pin his opponent, but he refused to let his challenger overcome him. He has no choice but to obey God and return to his home, and there is no way to do that without confronting possible death. He is powerless to change either God's directive or his route home. At the same time, he can't allow fear to paralyze him. He will have no choice but to resist the fear and keep moving forward.

With a mere touch, Jacob's opponent inflicts a disabling injury on him. Struggling now in what must have been excruciating pain, Jacob is at a distinct disadvantage. This mirrors Jacob's position in the natural realm. As one man with only a small cadre of servants he will be no match for Esau and his four hundred-man private security force.

The first rays of dawn shoot over the horizon and Jacob's assailant asks to terminate the match. In spite of exhaustion from what has to have been the longest recorded wrestling bout in history combined with a sports injury that would put a normal man out of commission for a couple of months, Jacob refuses to let go. This speaks to faith in the covenant. The promise of the covenant and the knowledge that God cannot lie was all he had to hold on to—and he could not afford to let it go. The covenant promised blessing. Jacob knows this is no ordinary man wrestling with him; he realizes this is someone greater who can bestow a blessing: as Hebrews Chapter 7 verse 7 says: 'beyond all contradiction, the less is blessed of the better.'

He is asked what his name is. He responds as he has always been identified. He is informed that he has a new name, for he has power with God and men as a prince, and he has prevailed: meaning 'to be able, to attain, to overcome.' Jacob was powerless to change the circumstances he was going to have to face later that day. God had the power to change the circumstances, but he didn't choose to work that way. **Instead, he changed Jacob**.

Not only was the covenant reaffirmed, but Jacob could go now forward without fear. He still approached his brother in a spirit of humility, but this encounter with God was a major turning point in his life. It also sets an example for us as his descendants. We need to remember and honor this covenant, also.

We need to remember and honor this covenant because the covenant made to Abraham, Isaac, and Jacob has never been annulled, and has yet to be fulfilled. Some hearing this will think, the New Testament (or New Covenant) through Jesus Christ disannulled this covenant. A covenant was done away with, but not this covenant. The covenant that was done away with was the covenant associated with the Exodus. Deuteronomy Chapter 5 verses 2-3 explain:

"The Lord our God made a covenant with us in Horeb.

The Lord made not this covenant with our fathers, but with us, even us, who are all of us here alive this day."

Compare this to Deuteronomy Chapter 4 verses 27-31:

"...the Lord shall scatter you among the nations, and ye shall be left few in number among the heathen, whither the Lord shall lead you. (We are always a minority.)

And there ye shall serve gods, the work of men's hands, wood and stone, which neither see, nor hear, nor eat, nor smell.

But if from thence thou shalt seek the Lord thy God, thou shalt find him, if thou seek him with all thy heart and with all thy soul.

When thou art in tribulation, and all these things are come upon thee, even in the latter days, if thou turn to the Lord thy God, and shalt be obedient unto his voice;

(For the Lord thy God is a merciful God;) he will not forsake thee, neither destroy thee, nor forget the covenant of thy fathers which he sware unto them."

Here it is again in Psalms Chapter 105 verses 8-12:

"He hath remembered his covenant forever, the word which he commanded to a thousand generations.

Which covenant he made with Abraham, and his oath unto Isaac;

And confirmed the same unto Jacob for a law, and to Israel for an everlasting covenant:

Saying, Unto thee will I give the land of Canaan, the lot of your inheritance: When they were but a few men in number; yea, very few, and strangers in it."

In total, four major covenants are on record: the first is the one made to the patriarchs—which the Lord God refuses to relinquish. The second is the one made at Sinai which our forefathers failed to keep. That one was abolished in favor of the third—the New Blood and Love Covenant which many of us have already entered into through Jesus Christ. The fourth is reserved for the Captivity gathered from the four corners of the earth as the final witness is underway just prior to the end of the age, and this covenant is sealed by the blood of the Lord Jesus Christ. It is discussed in detail in Chapter 15; subsection, *I Will Gather You Out of the Nations—the Israel They Don't Tell You About.* It is a covenant promising supernatural spiritual regeneration to the seed of the house of Israel and the house of Judah.

All things must be fulfilled which are written in the Law and the prophets, because the Scripture cannot be broken. Heaven and earth will pass away, but God's word will not pass away. It does not go out of his mouth and return void, but accomplishes that which he sent it to do. God will save our people; the descendants of the Trans-Atlantic slave trade, and those driven east out of Africa into slavery, and gather us out of the nations.

"Behold, the days come, saith the Lord, when I will make a new covenant with the house of Israel and with the house of Judah:

Not according to the covenant that I made with their fathers in the day when I took them by the hand to lead them out of the land of Egypt; because they continued not in my covenant, and I regarded them not, saith the Lord.

For this is the covenant that I will make with the house of Israel after those days, saith the Lord; I will put my laws into their mind, and write them in their hearts: and I will be to them a God, and they shall be to me a people:

And they shall not teach every man his neighbour, and every man his brother, saying, Know the Lord: for all shall know me, from the least to the greatest..." Hebrews Chapter 8 verses 8-11.

While all can only be purged by the blood of the Lord Jesus Christ—as there remains no other sacrifice for sins, this last covenant speaks to a work commencing at the close of the age; and is linked to the promise originally made to the patriarchs. It will manifest with a divine recall from the scattering among the nations. Reading Luke Chapter 8 verse 10, Philippians Chapter 1 verse 29, and II Timothy Chapter 2 verse 12 in sequence defines how those under the covenant of the blood of Christ (represented by his body—the church) differ from those who are gathered out of winds to reoccupy the land...

"And he said, Unto you it is given to know the mysteries of the kingdom of God... For unto you it is given in the behalf of Christ, not only to believe on him, but also to suffer for his sake... If we suffer, we shall also reign with him."

The millions gathered out of the four winds have endured humiliation and hardship by virtue of Hebrew descent under divine exile, whereas the tiny minority called out to rule and reign with Christ may also be of Hebrew descent, but a significant portion of their suffering and persecution is directly linked to their intimate relationship with God for the name of Jesus.

Right now we are still teaching and preaching the gospel—and rightly so—this is what we are supposed to do until the end of the age. This preaching of the gospel is for the purpose of calling out a people from both Israel and Judah and the Gentiles (the ecclesia) to rule and reign with Christ. It can be compared to Jesus' testimony that he was sent to the lost sheep of the house of Israel as a whole; yet from the masses that thronged him he singled out a select group to be in close fellowship, learn the hidden truths of the kingdom of God, and relate these principles back to the entire house of Israel. Many are called, but few chosen, and strait is the gate, and narrow is the way, which leadeth unto life, and few there be that find it. The great gathering of Israel is a blessed and momentous event indeed; but as the Apostle Paul recognized—the ultimate goal is the high calling of God in Christ Jesus. That achievement is to be desired above all!

Chapter V...Captivity, Deliverance, Testing, Consecration and Covenant

I have set before you life and death...Choose you this day whom ye will serve.

Black Shemites in Bondage to Black Hamites

What an exciting and intriguing time of fellowship it will be at the Great Family Reunion as the saints of the ages share their unique stories of what it was like during their time, and the faithfulness God showed them. The Lord will be glorified over and over as his great works are rehearsed among his people! I'm sure it will be moving to listen to Amram, Jochebed, Shiprah, and Puah as they recount the Hebrew's reaction to Pharaoh's genocidal decree. Proverbs Chapter 28 verse 15 says: As a roaring lion, and a ranging bear; so is a wicked ruler over the poor people.

It certainly didn't start out that way. The Pharaoh over Joseph had welcomed Jacob and Joseph's extended family:

"And the fame thereof was heard in Pharaoh's house, saying, Joseph's brethren are come: and it pleased Pharaoh well, and his servants.

And Pharaoh said unto Joseph, Say unto thy brethren, This do ye; lade your beasts, and go, get you unto the land of Canaan;

And take your father and your households, and come unto me: and I will give you the good of the land of Egypt, and ye shall eat the fat of the land.

Now thou art commanded, this do ye; take you wagons out of the land of Egypt for your little ones, and for your wives, and bring your father, and come.

Also regard not your stuff; for the good of all the land of Egypt is yours."

Jacob's clan had a long history of animal husbandry, and shepherds were an abomination to the Egyptians, so Joseph advised his brothers to request grazing grounds in the land of Goshen.

"Then Joseph came and told Pharaoh, and said, My father and my brethren, and their flocks, and their herds, and all that they have, are come out of the land of Canaan; and, behold, they are in the land of Goshen.

And he took some of his brethren, even five men, and presented them unto Pharaoh. And Pharaoh said unto his brethren, What is your occupation? And they said unto Pharaoh, Thy servants are shepherds, both we, and also our fathers.

They said moreover unto Pharaoh, For to sojourn in the land are we come; for thy servants have no pasture for their flocks; for the famine is sore in the land of Canaan: now therefore, we pray thee, let thy servants dwell in the land of Goshen.

And Pharaoh spake unto Joseph, saying, Thy father and thy brethren are come unto thee:

The land of Egypt is before thee; in the best of the land make thy father and brethren to dwell; in the land of Goshen let them dwell: and if thou knowest any men of activity among them, then make them rulers over my cattle.

And Joseph placed his father and his brethren, and gave them a possession in the land of Egypt, in the best of the land, in the land of Rameses, as Pharaoh had commanded."

But with the advent of a new monarch, forced labor, beatings, and population control by infanticide made the days of Joseph a distant memory. Initially, Egypt had been a blessing to the family of promise that would have otherwise starved. But God is a moving on God. God's timetable for bringing the seed of Abraham into the land was right on track. Further, God was due the glory in miraculously delivering them, because the surrounding nations knew God, but refused to glorify him as such; choosing rather to worship objects of creation or hybrids of man and animal and their images. God was calling out a people to be representative of him, his goodness, and his mercy among the nations.

If you are reading this book, you are probably already familiar with the story of Moses' birth, and his rescue from the water by Pharaoh's daughter. Something I like to point out however, is how God honored Jochebed's faith and obedience by basically giving her baby boy back to her until he was weaned. The wisdom he gave little Miriam in prompting her to ask Pharaoh's daughter if she needed one of the Hebrew women to nurse the crying child is priceless. Additionally, Jochebed was paid to nurse her own child. Who can dispute that all things work together for good to them that love God, to them who are the called according to his purpose!

Despite the prestige and privilege associated with an upbringing of royalty, Moses identified with his own people. The scripture says he looked on their burdens. The mistreatment of his brethren grieved him. He took out one Egyptian for abusing a brother. But the people were not ready for him as a deliverer; probably due to resenting his cushy upbringing in the royal house. Moses' manner of avenging wrongdoing was not God's way, either. God needed to groom Moses to communicate Divine directives to a stubborn and arrogant ruler, act as the conduit of God's supernatural power, and assume the mantle of authority that would enable him to lead over a million people out of a lifestyle of bondage into a place where God could prepare them to be a light to the nations. When you are being taught by God, you don't set the time, place, or the lesson curriculum. Moses sat in God's class for forty years until God considered him ready to lead Israel's exodus. It seemed like an incredibly long time, but from God's perspective, everything was moving right along according to plan:

"...and the children of Israel sighed by reason of the bondage, and they cried, and their cry came up unto God by reason of the bondage.

And God heard their groaning, and God remembered his covenant with Abraham, with Isaac, and with Jacob.

And God looked upon the children of Israel, and God had respect unto them..." Exodus Chapter 2 verses 23-25. Respect in this usage indicates God saw them in the sense of recognition and care, as from the perspective of a kinsman or relative.

In the sixth Chapter of Exodus, we read where God told Moses he had "heard the groaning of the children of Israel, whom the Egyptians keep in bondage; and I have remembered my covenant." The word 'keep' used in this instance means to hedge in, as with thorns. This means the Egyptians had no intention of ever letting the Hebrews go; their desire was that they would be slaves forever. They had basically designed a system which had no provision for disengagement. Most likely, the borders were also monitored to prevent escape. And if they did manage to get out, escape to where? To begin anew as a slave somewhere else? All the surrounding peoples had already established nationhood and had set territorial boundaries. Outright refusal to work would bring harsh repercussions. To bring children into the world meant consigning them to a life-time of bondage. And the life of the boys hung in jeopardy from the moment they drew their first breath.

In seeing all this, God gave Moses a message to give to the people. In the message, He begins by identifying himself as the Lord, and he concludes by identifying himself as the Lord. This speaks to him being the Alpha and the Omega, the beginning and the end. Of all that has ever happened to his people, is happening to them now, or will happen to them in the future, he is on both ends of it, to watch over his word to perform it where his covenant is concerned that he made with our forefathers. Here are the ten things Moses was to communicate:

*I am the Lord

*I will bring you out from under the burdens of the Egyptians

*I will rid you out of their bondage

*I will redeem you with a stretched out arm and great judgments

*I will take you to me for a people

*I will be to you a God

*You shall know that I am the Lord your God, which bringeth you out from under the burdens of the Egyptians

*I will bring you into the land concerning the which I did swear to give it to Abraham, to Isaac, and to Jacob;

*I will give it (to) you for a heritage

*I am the Lord.

The next verse says Moses spoke all these things to the children of Israel, but they wouldn't listen to him for anguish of spirit, and for cruel bondage. The Hebrew word for anguish in this instance means to be grieved, much discouraged, and impatient in spirit. And this is pretty much an exact duplication of scenario when talking to people today about their true heritage as Hebrews and descendants of the patriarchs. "That's great to know" they say, "but how's that going to help me now? What good can that do for me today?"

And that is where you have to understand our presence in the West is a case of history repeating itself, and truth being stranger than fiction. If you want the spoiler, you have only to read the Book of Revelation to see that many of the same plagues and others quite worse are scheduled to befall spiritual Egypt at the time of the end. The people have a short space in the wilderness again until the land is ready to enter. Once you grasp that this is basically a replay of history, you have no option except to take all the focus off of yourself, and re-direct it to God and his promise concerning the covenant he made with Abraham, Isaac, and Jacob.

In this short message given to Moses, God says "I am" twice, "I will" seven times, and "You shall know that I am" once. Well, he still is, he still will, and we are still going to know that he is. Do not be faithless and quickly lose hope like our forefathers did. Rather, remember patience, and have faith in God. Our forefathers were in Egypt four hundred and thirty years. We are currently on the last laps of reaping for the faithlessness of their descendants. Let's not repeat their mistakes, for the things that happened to them are meant to be an example for us in the latter days. This is the time of Jacob's trouble... but he will be delivered out of it!

Deliverance, but Problems in the Wilderness

Before devastating Egypt with dreadful signs and wonders, God instructed Moses to tell Pharaoh that it was the Lord God of the Hebrews who was demanding the people be set free to sacrifice. This is very important, because we are their descendants, we are the true Hebrews. And just as Egypt is geographically positioned west of the Land of Covenant on the earth, we are currently in the Egyptian house of bondage in the western half of the world. He was the Lord God of the Hebrews then, and he is still the Lord God of the Hebrews now. Notice that when God speaks to the world about us, he presents himself as the 'Lord God of the Hebrews': he identifies with his people. But when he speaks to the people, he references the patriarchal genealogy of Abraham, Isaac, and Jacob and the covenant he made with them. It may seem like I'm beating a dead horse here, but if there was not such an intense effort to obscure our true identity, I wouldn't have to keep emphasizing it. It takes time to undo the lifetime of conditioning that has convinced us we have nothing to do with Biblical history and are just the Black version spin off of the white Western church. We have to learn to see ourselves as God knows us.

After punishing the Egyptians severely with plagues and dealing a death blow to the firstborn among their population and livestock, the people were more than willing to let the Hebrews depart. In the matter of the rod transforming into a serpent, water turning to blood, and frogs appearing, Pharaoh had taken the attitude these were mere parlor tricks, because his magicians could also imitate the feats. But when God upped the ante with lice, flies, cattle murrain (which was likely anthrax or something similar) skin boils, hail mixed with fire, consuming locusts, and darkness that could be physically felt, the devastating power of the God of Abraham, Isaac, and Jacob could not be duplicated or denied. The last nail in the coffin was the death of the firstborn of both man and beast in Egypt. At that point, God made it clear this was not just about Israel's deliverance, but that he was also judging the idol gods of Egypt. This is important to acknowledge because the land of our present Captivity is filled with symbols and references to the ancient idols invoked in the Egyptian mystery religion.

God's display of raw, unmatched power convinced some Egyptian citizens and those of mixed Hamitic and Shemitic heritage that it was in their best interest to align themselves with the winning side, and they joined the families of Jacob's descent on the march out. The journey south out of Egypt to the crossing point of the Red Sea was no stroll in the park. Remember, this was easily over a million people with what goods they could carry on their back in addition to herds of animals. Nevertheless, God guided his flock safely with a pillar of cloud by day, and a pillar of fire by night. This pillar was like a standing column, and must have extended across the horizon as far as the eye could see on either side.

Pharaoh knew the route Moses would take, and plotted to overtake the Hebrews at a point where they would be trapped between the sea and the wilderness, with nowhere to turn. But as the people neared the crossing point of the Red Sea, the Angel of the Lord removed from going before them and strategically positioned Himself at the rear of the exodus, erecting an impenetrable barrier between them and the Egyptians. The side of the pillar facing the Egyptians was cloud and darkness, but the side facing the Hebrews gave light.

As soon as the people became aware the Egyptian army was in pursuit, they began to turn on Moses and question his leadership capabilities. We need to look at their knee-jerk reaction for a minute. They had all seen the recent plagues God sent on Egypt; they were all aware each time they had been miraculously protected. Why should now be different? It is important to remember their response to danger or deprivation, because this type of reaction would become typical of them throughout the wilderness journey. Moses was dealing with a double-minded people. They basically operated on a premise of unbelief (I'll believe it when I see it; or, he couldn't have really meant no manna was going to fall on the seventh day; I'm going to see if I can find some) presumptuousness (who made you a ruler and a judge over us) and instant gratification (Who shall give us flesh to eat? i.e., who's going to bring some meat up in here—some real food?)

When the Psalmist speaks of the deliverance from Egypt in Psalm Chapter 106 he says: They soon forgat his works. But, we cannot afford to have memory loss or amnesia in a covenant relationship with God. God wants us to archive and periodically recall his miraculous works and interventions in our lives, because that builds faith. Each instance of answered prayer and supernatural involvement is like a grappling hook thrown on the rocky ledges of the mountain of life. It enables us to ascend to the next level. Our forefathers sabotaged themselves by operating in unbelief during the wilderness journey. It does not take forty years to get from the Red Sea to Canaan. But the patriarchs received the promise of the land by faith, and that was the way God wanted their progeny to enter in, too—by faith. James lets us know in Chapter 1 verse 8 that when you are asking anything of God it has to be done in faith, or don't count on receiving anything. A double minded man is unstable in all his ways. The instability of the people's outlook, in that they couldn't be depended upon to follow through, even with small faith like a grain of mustard seed—and their constant negative reaction to adverse circumstances—was a source of untold misery and constant divine rebuke in the wilderness; and eventually provoked Moses to the point where he spoke unadvisedly with his lips; and forfeited his right to enter the Promised Land with the people.

Getting back to the panic at the brink of the Red Sea, Moses told the people not to be afraid; that God would fight for them and they would never see the Egyptians again. But at this point, God basically flipped the script back to Moses and said, "What are you crying to me for? Tell the children of Israel to move on out, but you lift up the rod and stretch out your hand over the sea, and divide it: and the children of Israel shall go on dry ground through the midst of the sea." God had already sent the east wind which had blown all through the night, driving the waters back. When Moses lifted the rod and stretched out his hand over the sea, the waters parted to either side. Our forefathers stood facing a massive dry footpath as wide as the sea itself. Surrounded by the roar of standing waters on each side, and back-lit by the immense bright cloud, the scenario had to have been both awesome and eerie at the same time.

Every one of the Hebrews escaped safely to the other shore. Every one of the Egyptian army perished in the waters which remembered their natural state when Moses stretched his hand back over them once the people were safely on the other side. As for me, I will say that the bottom of the sea is a long way to go for a slave, but pride goes before a fall, and a haughty spirit before destruction. Pharaoh learned this the hard way.

Out of immediate danger from the Egyptian forces, it did not take long before the people began to complain about their diet selection. The scripture actually says the whole congregation murmured against Moses and Aaron. The Hebrew word used for murmured in this instance means 'to stop', and 'permanently' and implies obstinateness. In other words, they were just going to dig in their heels and refuse to cooperate unless something changed. At this juncture, God sent quails, and they had an opportunity to taste flesh, but later they were sorry they asked. They were to be content with the manna sent from heaven; as the scripture says— the food of angels—for this food came from a different dimension and had different properties than food harvested from the earth. That the manna was not from this dimension is shown by the commandment to fill up an omer and preserve it as a testimony to the generations to come of God's provision. Sure, God could have spoken and brought forth an abundance of fruit bearing trees and bushes, and streams teeming with fish. However, he chose to feed the people in this manner. With the manna also came specific instructions for the gathering and storage of it; that the people might learn that man does not live by bread alone, but by every word that proceeds forth from the mouth of God.

Moving forward, they challenged Moses because there was no water found in the area to drink. Notice how instead of praying individually to God, or praying for God to guide Moses, it was so much easier to turn on the human agent they could see; the person who was flesh and blood just like they were. The pattern of challenging of authority, resentment, and outright blatant refusal to honor the commandments God was relaying through Moses would play out again and again until the entire generation twenty years old and up that had been part of the Red Sea exodus perished in the wilderness.

It didn't have to go down that way. They didn't have to die like that. Their shoes didn't wear out, and their clothing didn't wear out in forty years of trekking in the wilderness. Like stepping into and out of a time machine, the wardrobe of those who entered into the promise land looked pretty much the same as when they crossed the border out of Egypt. If their clothes didn't wear out, their bodies didn't have to either. This is proven by the fact that when Moses died, his natural physical force was not abated. The stubbornness and hardheartedness of many of our forebears brought them to their untimely death.

Perhaps the most notorious offense associated with our forebears was the worship of the golden calf. God had summoned Moses to the summit of Mount Sinai to give him the two tables of testimony, tables of stone, written with the very finger of God. Here is the actual text from Exodus Chapter 32 verses 1-6:

"And when the people saw that Moses delayed to come down out of the mount, the people gathered themselves together unto Aaron, and said unto him, Up, make us gods, which shall go before us; for as for this Moses, the man that brought us up out of the land of Egypt, we wot not what is become of him.

And Aaron said unto them, Break off the golden earrings, which are in the ears of your wives, of your sons, and of your daughters, and bring them unto me.

And all the people brake off the golden earrings which were in their ears, and brought them unto Aaron.

And he received them at their hand, and fashioned it with a graving tool, after he had made it a molten calf: and they said, These be thy gods, O Israel, which brought thee up out of the land of Egypt.

And when Aaron saw it, he built an altar before it; and Aaron made proclamation, and said, Tomorrow is a feast to the Lord.

And they rose up early on the morrow, and offered burnt offerings, and brought peace offerings; and the people sat down to eat and to drink, and rose up to play."

In looking at this verse by verse, we see the impatience and the need for immediate gratification (Up, make us gods, which shall go before us; for as for this Moses, the man that brought us up out of the land of Egypt, we don't know what's happened to him.) The implication is in telling Aaron, 'Come on! Do something! We need some action here; we need to keep moving if we're ever going to get out of this wilderness, and we need some kind of deity we can procure favor with to lead us on our journey.'

What can we say on this side of the event? No one can ever say what they would or would not have done unless they were in the same situation as the person. One thing we do know is that Aaron was of a different make-up than his brother Moses. Aaron was the more eloquent speaker of the two, but he was intimidated by the people. Then again, when you consider literally thousands of people converging on him and demanding immediate action, perhaps he feared for his life. Perhaps his line of thinking was he didn't personally have plans to worship an idol, but he would try to pacify the mob in order to preserve his life and keep the people in check until Moses got back. The account only gets stranger as we read on. Although the Bible never mentions Aaron's vocation while he was in the land of Egypt, apparently he was a metalworker, and the people must have been aware of his smithing abilities. It stands to reason if you are a slave, you learn and execute whatever duties are demanded of you. This seems obvious by the way they approached him with the conviction he could produce the image, the fact that he quickly had a plan... 'Break off the golden earrings, which are in the ears of your wives, of your sons, and of your daughters, and bring them unto me', and the outcome of his efforts; he made it a molten calf, and fashioned it with a graving tool. To make the molten image he would have had to make a cast form, and dig a pit with enough space to hold a fire hot enough to melt all that gold. Fashioned with a graving tool indicates he used a chisel to form the physical structure and bovine features which would make the image realistic. He then made an altar for sacrifice in front of it, and proclaimed the following day as a feast unto the

Lord. Deuteronomy Chapter 9 verse 20 tells us God was so angry with Aaron he would have destroyed him if Moses hadn't interceded on his behalf.

Now, this is interesting. Notice that in spite of the previous attitude of just stubbornly shutting down and digging in their heels when things didn't go their way, the people seem to have a fresh zeal and motivation for the anticipated celebration... 'they rose up early on the morrow, and offered burnt offerings, and brought peace offerings.' The people sat down to eat and to drink...this implies planning the night before because remember we are talking about a huge number of people participating in this event...and rose up to play. The word play in this instance means laughter and sport of merriment or scorn; in other words, it was a raucous party. We know this because Moses' servant Joshua heard the noise clear up in the mountain where he and Moses were, and he thought the camp was being attacked by outsiders. But here the narrative takes yet another twist.

Verse 19 says the people were singing, verse 20 says they were dancing, and verse 25 says they were doing all this in the nude. The word dancing in this particular instance is related to another Hebrew word 'Khool/kheel' which means twisting or whirling in a circular or spiral manner; to dance, to writhe in pain—especially of parturition (childbirth), to wait, to pervert, to bear, make to bring forth, calve. To get an idea of what they were doing, think pole dancer and drop it low moves, and the raunchiest of R&B and hip hop choreography...you get the idea. Add to this the tambourines and whatever other instruments they had brought with them from Egypt and they had the makings for the biggest party ever.

Why so much emphasis on sexually themed dancing? Well, they were emulating pagan fertility rites they had become familiar with in Hamitic Egypt. Remember, they were idolizing a calf, and this particular heifer was Hathor, the cow deity. One of her goddess attributes was the ability to bless fertility. In fact, this was one reason so many pagan nations established fertility idols—because the "worship" of them permitted them to indulge their fleshly lusts at the same time.

Moses confronts his brother about this, and Aaron is in an awkward position to justify his actions.

Listen carefully to how the exchange is worded in Exodus Chapter 32 verses 21-24:

"And Moses said unto Aaron, What did this people unto thee, that thou hast brought so great a sin upon them?

And Aaron said, Let not the anger of my lord wax hot: thou knowest the people, that they are set on mischief.

For they said unto me, Make us gods, which shall go before us: for as for this Moses, the man that brought us up out of the land of Egypt, we wot not what is become of him.

And I said unto them, Whosoever hath any gold, let them break it off. So they gave it me: then I cast it into the fire, and there came out this calf."

Moses tells Aaron that he (Aaron) has brought a great sin upon the people. Aaron replies, 'Let not the anger of my lord wax hot: thou knowest the people, that they are set on mischief.' In explaining the formation of the calf, and attempting to distance his involvement as the craftsman, his response is almost childlike '...I cast it into the fire, and there came out this calf.' The golden calf debacle cost the camp of Israel the lives of three thousand men that day alone, and caused the people to receive a plague from the Lord. This angered God so much he told Moses he would send his angel to lead them into the land, rather than he himself go...he did not want to be in the midst of them, lest he consume them. But Moses interceded for the people, for he did not want to attempt possession of the Promised Land without God's presence. Thank God for faithful intercessors; God relented and agreed to accompany them, for he told Moses, "thou hast found grace in my sight, and I know thee by name."

I have spent so much time on this initial period following the deliverance from Egypt because there are some serious points to highlight when drawing the parallels between ourselves and our ancient forbears. Why such a spirit of unbelief? Why the constant need to challenge spiritual authority? Why the readiness to participate in a form of worship that only indulges the flesh? Why did Aaron say, "You know these people; that they are set on mischief?" (paraphrase mine) Mischief as used in this verse means bad, evil, wretchedness; and comes from another Hebrew word râ-a which means to spoil by breaking to pieces, to make or to be good for nothing, i.e. bad, physically, morally, or socially.

There can be no doubt we see some of these same inclinations in our people today. The nations of the Gentiles and the oppressor in this present Captivity definitely opine we are a people who are good for nothing and bad—physically, morally, and socially. But to those holding this view, I submit that severe and difficult to eradicate character traits are a result of spiritual confusion and compromise acquired under the abnormal conditions of prolonged Captivity. I support my contention based on the fact that the people in question were/are the direct descendants of Abraham, Isaac, and Jacob.

The patriarchs were men of great faith who honored God in their lives and actions. Also, they were careful to remember God's work in their lives, and kept the testimony of the Abrahamic Covenant alive, referencing it in communications with their progeny. Abraham did not soon forget about the encounter with Melchizedek, the miraculous birth of Isaac, and the ram provided for a sacrifice on Mount Moriah. Isaac did not soon forget his father's unfailing trust in God, or the seconds he hung between heaven and earth, and life and death as he lay bound on the altar. Jacob did not soon forget the angelic encounters, and the wrestling match that earned him the title 'Prince with God.' Even Joseph, who was separated many years from his family, referenced the Abrahamic Covenant by faith (Hebrews Chapter 11 verse 22.)

Neither can the case be made for this negative transformation in Captivity based upon retribution for their own misdeeds or those of other generations, as can be said about the present Captivity in the West, because the descendants of the patriarchs were divinely guided into Egypt by God's hand to be preserved, and to increase as a force to be reckoned with. Therefore, if the people are of the same stock as the patriarchs who both honored God and were men of honor themselves, we must conclude that change came not from being inherently bad, but from both the destructive spiritual influence that permeated Egypt, and the oppression of slavery.

When you consider ancient Egypt or Khemet as they called themselves, you are looking at a civilization that on the face of it appeared an ideal place to live. The Nile Valley was well watered; the growing seasons allowed for an abundance of crops and the people had long ago learned how to deal with the hot climate. The common folk had their day to day duties in cultivation and craftsmanship; but the civilization was well enough developed that there were physician specialists, beer breweries, and massive public works projects. Also much technology existed that has been obscured by the current keepers of history to downplay the achievements of a Black race. But the real power lay with royalty and the priest class. That the rulers could indulge in building treasure cities and colossal monuments, and that the magicians and sorcerers had such great time to devote to the study and practice of dark arts speaks to societal stability and a relatively high standard of living. Far from being a people struggling to eke out an existence in a harsh environment, life for the Egyptians was relatively uneventful barring any unforeseen catastrophes such as war or famine.

It was this bucolic and laid-back environment that our forebears found themselves in after the reunion with their brother Joseph. It is probably fair to say the family legacy of a promised covenant remained intact at least throughout the life of Jacob and his twelve sons. Additionally, through the progression of years, tribal identity survived, and it is obvious from the account of Moses' parents and the Hebrew midwives that the fear of God was among a significant portion of the people.

But at some point as the old guard passed on and the progeny multiplied, it appears some important concepts faded from memory as the deleterious effects of living in a polytheistic nation took its toll on the people's hearts and minds. The oral traditions passed down about the God of Abraham, Isaac, and Jacob were eclipsed by many strange gods, some of whom were hybrids of animal and human form. And have we considered where the Hebrews learned to worship Hathor in the manner which they did? Obviously they had observed it in their surroundings, and Joshua Chapter 24 verse 14 indicates some of them had indeed been partakers of these idol fests in Egypt. My point being, generally people just don't wholeheartedly jump into something they have absolutely no familiarity with... especially where worship is concerned. Not only that, but the fact that they desired a tangible idol to go before them is a dead giveaway that they were accustomed to seeing these images in processionals.

Egypt was not an environment that fostered the need to develop faith. The gods of Egypt did not love the Egyptian people to the point that they would make a spectacle out of a challenger's deities, and personally lead their people out of oppression by flexing the forces of nature; nor did they even possess that kind of power. It was not about a love relationship; it was only about obeisance to the deity.

Egypt had lots of perks and goodies though; and probably for some time it was just a matter of counterbalancing the oppression with whatever the captives might want to eat or drink. You will recall how shortly after leaving Egypt the people murmured and cried for fish and fowl, and leeks, and onions, and garlic and melons. How troubling it is when we attempt to communicate with our people regarding spiritual matters and they only seem to want to look at the glitz and glamour the culture parades before them.

The concept of serving an invisible God they had heard bits and pieces about, and the acceptance of ecclesiastical hierarchy and a firm code of conduct stuck in the craw of many of the people. Remember the pre-Exodus incident where Moses tried to break up the fight between two of his brethren and the response was, 'who made you a ruler and a judge over us?' Now imagine this same attitude toward him, except multiplied by many thousands of individuals. However, Moses was the meekest man who ever lived after God got finished training him in the desert for forty years. He had great strength but he kept it under control. Acts Chapter 7 verse 35 says, "This Moses whom they refused, saying, Who made thee a ruler and a judge? the same did God send to be a ruler and a deliverer by the hand of the angel which appeared to him in the bush." Still, this resistance to Moses' authority would crop up again and again, at one point even from his own family.

When Moses came down from the mountain and saw the debauchery taking place, he threw down the two tablets in anger and destroyed the gold calf—grinding it to dust; he then mixed the dust with the water supply and forced the people to drink it. To some this may seem like a gross overreaction, until you consider Moses' perspective. Hebrews Chapter 11 verse 25 tells us that when Moses came of age, he refused to be known any longer as the son of Pharaoh's daughter, and chose rather to suffer affliction with the people of God, rather than enjoy the pleasures of sin for a season. The definition of the word pleasures used in this verse is sensual lust. This means, he—the leader—had turned his back on this exact type of lifestyle and behavior, because he was looking forward into time for the reward of the fulfillment of the Abrahamic Covenant. If the leader forsakes wickedness and draws close to God to the extent God can say, "thou hast found grace in my sight, and I know thee by name", it logically follows that those being led must strive to attain the same measure. And incidentally, this is the goal we should all be shooting for: that God would say of us on that day, "thou hast found grace in my sight, and I know thee by name."

Now this is important. Notice how Paul tells us in this verse in Hebrews that Moses chose rather to suffer affliction with the people of God. It is imperative that you don't miss this label of identification, because despite the way the people were conducting themselves, with the murmuring, complaining, stubbornness, fleshly cravings, desire to usurp authority, and tendency toward idolatry, God still recognized them as **his people**. The covenant made with the patriarchs cannot be annulled, nor the progeny beneficiaries disinherited. When we see these wilderness traits in our brothers and sisters today who have not come under the Blood and Love Covenant of the Lord Jesus Christ, and submitted themselves under his easy yoke and light burden, it is easy to slip into the same mindset the Gentiles have toward us, and begin to despise our own people. This is made all the more likely by the manner in which the Gentiles constantly present themselves as the epitome of intelligence, piety, and favorable status; whereas for the most part, only actions resulting from the negative traits of our people are highlighted to shape public opinion and policy. **But the covenant does not stand or fall based on Gentile opinion**.

In comparing the actions of our forefathers in the wilderness with the mentality and behavior of their descendants today, we need to recognize and acknowledge that the same dynamic of spiritual compromise and prolonged Captivity is at work. God understood what was going on with his people; in fact, Acts Chapter 13 verse 18 describes it by saying, "And about the time of forty years suffered he their manners in the wilderness." This means he endured, like a burden, their manner of deportment and actions. Therefore, going forward, train your mind to see your fellow brothers and sisters—descendants of the Trans-Atlantic slave trade— as the people of God who are yet to be gathered back to the Father through Jesus Christ the

Lion of the Tribe of Judah; thus fulfilling the Abrahamic Covenant: because Christ, the Seed of Abraham—is the Kinsman-Redeemer; and all things must be fulfilled which are written in the Law and the Prophets concerning him. Here are two verses that bear this out; found in the Book of Acts Chapter 3 verses 25-26.

"Ye are the children of the prophets, and of the covenant which God made with our fathers, saying unto Abraham, And in thy seed shall all the kindreds of the earth be blessed.

Unto you first God, having raised up his Son Jesus, sent him to bless you, in turning away every one of you from his iniquities."

These verses prove that even after the crucifixion and resurrection of the Lord Jesus Christ, <u>he is still sent first to the descendants of Abraham</u>: the Black man brought West by Europeans, and his brethren carried east out of Africa by Islamists.

If you are already under the Blood and Love Covenant of the Lord Jesus Christ, just keep building on the Foundation; gold, silver, precious stones...and keep interceding for your brethren who have not yet been set free in their spirit by repentance of sins and calling on the name of Lord. The Covenant must be and will be fulfilled regardless; but the clarion call of the moment is to press toward the mark for the prize of the high calling of God in Christ Jesus...the short form of the Greek synopsis of that phrase is to 'aim for the award of the invitation which is at the very top'; that is, to rule and reign with Christ as kings and priests.

A Prophet from Among Your Own Brethren: By Default,
This Future Prophet is Black

There is a prophet. He is Black. A Shemitic Hebrew; descended from Abraham the Hebrew. He is the Root and Offspring of Jesse, and the Lion of the Tribe of Judah.

Moses knew his time on earth was drawing to a close, so he reiterated the commandments of God to the people. At this point, he has fulfilled his charge and been a diligent leader and a faithful intercessor. He has struck the difficult balance between being a courageous commander and the meekest man who ever lived. He has refrained from reacting in anger toward the people in spite of their constant vexing, with the exception of the matter at the waters of Meribah-Kadesh, where he struck the rock, instead of speaking to it. That was the tipping point; they finally pushed his buttons and triggered a fleshly reaction. In failing to sanctify the Lord in the presence of the people, he forfeited his opportunity to physically enter the Promised Land. We all know people who seem like they exist solely for the purpose of tormenting and subverting us, and the only way to deal with them is to put on the mantle of meekness, lift the shield of faith, and understand that the fires of persecution are painful, but ultimately they refine us as the pure gold.

It is easy to become really disgusted with our forebears for this turn of events...after all Moses did, and his determined perseverance in the face of what often appeared to be a lost cause. Moses' faithfulness mirrored God's dedication to us as a people. Then again, to whom much is given, much is required. God spoke to Moses as a man speaks to his friend; God revealed his glory to Moses, shielding him from seeing his front to protect his life. The power of God was wrought through Moses on a level exceeding Abraham, Isaac, and Jacob. Yes, the denial into the Promised Land was probably painful and humiliating, but the next time we see Moses, he appears with the prophet Elijah talking with the Lord Jesus Christ on the Mount of Transfiguration. I'm sure at that point, Moses wasn't thinking about the land, but looking forward to the permanent establishment of the Kingdom. So we can thank God that his ultimate plans and purposes exceed our earthly failures, and the day is coming when he will wipe every tear away and the former things will be remembered no more.

Moses tells the people that God will raise up a prophet from among their own brethren—a prophet like him—which they were to hear; with very severe consequences if they failed to acknowledge him...

"The Lord thy God will raise up unto thee a Prophet from the midst of thee, of thy brethren, like unto me; unto him ye shall hearken. And God said to Moses, I will raise them up a Prophet from among their brethren, like unto thee, and will put my words in his mouth; and he shall speak unto them all that I shall command him. And it shall come to pass, that whosoever will not hearken unto my words which he shall speak in my name, I will require it of him" ...Deuteronomy Chapter 18 verses 15, 18 and 19.

This prophet was none other the Lord Jesus Christ; the Lion of the Tribe of Judah manifested in the flesh; the final Passover Lamb to take away the sins of the world. This is why Jesus could say in John Chapter 5 verse 43, "I am come in my Father's name," and in Chapter 8 verse 28, "I do nothing of myself; but as my Father hath taught me, I speak these things."

That the Black Hebrew saints and apostles of the New Covenant assembly recognized the Lord Jesus Christ as that Prophet who would be raised up from among his brethren is shown in the testimony of the Apostle Peter in Acts Chapter 3 verses 22-23:

"For Moses truly said unto the fathers, A prophet shall the Lord your God raise up unto you of your brethren, like unto me; him shall ye hear in all things whatsoever he shall say unto you.

And it shall come to pass, that every soul, which will not hear that prophet, shall be destroyed from among the people."

And the testimony of Stephen in Acts Chapter 7 verse 37:

"This is that Moses, which said unto the children of Israel, A prophet shall the Lord your God raise up unto you of your brethren, like unto me; him shall ye hear."

But there is another similarity I want to point out over and above the fact that both Moses and this future prophet to come were Black Hebrews. God says he is raising up a prophet 'like unto Moses.' What is Moses most known for? The name Moses is synonymous with the deliverance of our forefathers from bondage in Egypt. So, we should understand this Prophet Moses spoke of who will arise from among the people is on an identical mission to execute great judgments upon a nation and/or system which has his people in bondage, and bring them out to a judgment in the wilderness before leading them into a cleansed and restored land.

Yes, there is a prophet. He is Black. A Shemitic Hebrew; descended from Abraham the Hebrew. He is the Root and Offspring of Jesse, and the Lion of the Tribe of Judah.

This man in his eternal form has no beginning and no end; but when he desired a human body so he could walk among his people, love them, teach them, heal them, and ultimately become a living sacrifice to take away their sins and the sins of the world, it was gendered by the Holy Ghost, and placed inside the womb of a virgin.

He lived a perfect, sinless life, but was executed as though he were a criminal. He rose from the grave after three days with all power in heaven and earth granted to him. He lives forever more, seated at the right hand of his Father, as a faithful High Priest making intercession for the saints.

Before he ascended back to heaven, he petitioned his Father to send the Holy Ghost to lead, guide, teach, and give his followers power to be his witnesses, until the restitution of all things. Then, he will return, gather his living genealogical seed from the four winds of the earth, and resurrect and translate both those of his seed under the Old Covenant and those born into his kingdom under the New Covenant—both Hebrew and Gentile.

He will purge and purify this earth of all idolatrous things that offend and cause stumbling, and it will be possible to once again know the earth as it was at the beginning of creation.

There will also be a simultaneous resurrection of those raised to everlasting shame and contempt, who will serve this Prophet's brethren whom they so shamefully treated and misused during the heyday of sinful man on earth.

At the end of a thousand years, those bearing this rightful yoke of servitude will rebel, having been deceived by Satan, once he is released from the pit prison. He will go immediately to muster a rebellion of all those disgruntled and resentful of their slave status, their forced submission to the genealogy of Abraham, their forced submission to the kings and priests of the Bride of the Lamb, and Messiah's rod of iron that rules them.

The fire of God will consume them and terminate this final resistance against the Kingdom of God and the People of God. The New Heavens and New Earth will be created, and the New Jerusalem will appear like a brilliant multifaceted jewel. God will dwell with man, and the saved of the nations will walk therein, amidst the Tree of Life and the crystal clear Water of Life that proceeds from the throne of God.

Warnings of a Return to Captivity and Bondage for Idolatry

"I told you so." "I tried to warn you!" "Didn't I tell you this would happen? Why wouldn't you listen to me?"

How many times in our lives have we heard these words? These are statements no one wants to hear, because generally if it comes to the point these words are spoken, something bad has happened. Bringing it closer to home, it could be the person who insisted on driving under the influence of alcohol. Maybe it is the person despondent with crushed feelings and a broken heart who wouldn't believe you when you tried to tell them not to get involved with an individual of questionable character. Whatever the case, someone has been faced with a choice, and they have selected the option with the negative outcome. And since no man is an island, their choices will affect the lives of others. Depending on the gravity of the circumstance, the ramifications may be light and short-term, or very grievous and long ranging.

An example of a light and short term consequence would be the case of a juvenile who steals from a store. In addition to court costs and fines, the store has the option to ban the juvenile from their premises for say—two years. After that time, he will be extended the opportunity to visit the establishment and if he sees something he wants, fork over cash like everyone else. In contrast, an example of a grievous and long ranging consequence is the outcome of what happens when a people special to God continually dishonor him.

We must understand that although God doesn't "need" any of us, once he becomes involved by virtue of love and a covenant, his honor is at stake if the other party flagrantly violates the agreement. So in his predetermined wisdom, God established a perpetual covenant with Abraham, Isaac, Jacob, and their seed after them. After their seed had multiplied and been brought into bondage, God delivered them and established a second covenant under Moses:

"And he declared unto you his covenant, which he commanded you to perform, even ten commandments; and he wrote them upon two tables of stone" ...Deuteronomy Chapter 4 verse 13.

Penalties for breaking the second covenant had some pretty severe consequences. Once the first commandment was broken (prohibition against idolatry) like dominoes, all the rest fell into disregard, because an idolater must needs follow the inclination of his idol, and lacking that, of his own unregenerate heart which is deceitful and desperately wicked. Experience is the best teacher, but the smartest person is the one who learns from the mistakes of others. Our forefathers should have realized if God cast the Canaanites out for their wicked practices, the same thing would happen to them for idolatry. Spiritual unfaithfulness would ultimately lead Israel to reproduce the same evil works of the exiled Canaanites; then, Israel itself would be vomited out of the land.

Eventually, this is exactly what ended up happening. We need to give God great praise and thanksgiving for His foreknowledge in establishing an everlasting covenant with Abraham, Isaac, and Jacob: looking down through time and seeing you and I in our present state of Captivity. All things must be fulfilled written in the Law and prophets concerning the Hebrew people, including a Captivity in the latter days that they would be re-gathered from. When will the Abrahamic Covenant be consummated? At the time of the restitution of all things at the end of the age, specifically, when the Kingdom is restored to Israel at the return of their Kinsman-Redeemer.

Now, let's look at the myriad warnings of dispersion for disobedience that were given in the wilderness even before our   forefathers set foot in the Promised Land. Because there are so many consequences attached to violation of the covenant, I will provide a sample of references to cursing and scattering in the latter days, the promise of re-gathering, and the book and chapter where they are found.

Leviticus Chapter 26

"I am the Lord your God, which brought you forth out of the land of Egypt, that ye should not be their bondmen; and I have broken the bands of your yoke, and made you go upright.

But if ye will not hearken unto me, and will not do all these commandments;

And if ye shall despise my statutes, or if your soul abhor my judgments, so that ye will not do all my commandments, but that ye break my covenant:

I will scatter you among the heathen, and will draw out a sword after you: and your land shall be desolate, and your cities waste.

Then shall the land enjoy her sabbaths, as long as it lieth desolate, and ye be in your enemies' land; even then shall the land rest, and enjoy her sabbaths.

As long as it lieth desolate it shall rest; because it did not rest in your sabbaths, when ye dwelt upon it.

And upon them that are left alive of you I will send a faintness into their hearts in the lands of their enemies;

And ye shall perish among the heathen, and the land of your enemies shall eat you up.

And they that are left of you shall pine away in their iniquity in your enemies' lands; and also in the iniquities of their fathers shall they pine away with them…"

"If they shall confess their iniquity, and the iniquity of their fathers, with their trespass which they trespassed against me, and that also they have walked contrary unto me;

And that I also have walked contrary unto them, and have brought them into the land of their enemies; if then their uncircumcised hearts be humbled, and they then accept of the punishment of their iniquity:

Then will I remember my covenant with Jacob, and also my covenant with Isaac, and also my covenant with Abraham will I remember; and I will remember the land.

And yet for all that, when they be in the land of their enemies, I will not cast them away, neither will I abhor them, to destroy them utterly, and to break my covenant with them: for I am the Lord their God. But I will for their sakes remember the covenant of their ancestors, whom I brought forth out of the land of Egypt in the sight of the heathen, that I might be their God: I am the Lord.

These are the statutes and judgments and laws, which the Lord made between him and the children of Israel in mount Sinai by the hand of Moses."

Deuteronomy Chapter 4

"When thou shalt beget children, and children's children, and ye shall have remained long in the land, and shall corrupt yourselves, and make a graven image, or the likeness of anything, and shall do evil in the sight of the Lord thy God, to provoke him to anger:

I call heaven and earth to witness against you this day, that ye shall soon utterly perish from off the land whereunto ye go over Jordan to possess it; ye shall not prolong your days upon it, but shall utterly be destroyed. And the Lord shall scatter you among the nations, and ye shall be left few in number among the heathen, whither the Lord shall lead you.

And there ye shall serve gods, the work of men's hands, wood and stone, which neither see, nor hear, nor eat, nor smell.

But if from thence thou shalt seek the Lord thy God, thou shalt find him, if thou seek him with all thy heart and with all thy soul.

When thou art in tribulation, and all these things are come upon thee, even in the latter days, if thou turn to the Lord thy God, and shalt be obedient unto his voice; (For the Lord thy God is a merciful God;) he will not forsake thee, neither destroy thee, nor forget the covenant of thy fathers which he sware unto them."

Deuteronomy Chapter 28

"But it shall come to pass, if thou wilt not hearken unto the voice of the Lord thy God, to observe to do all his commandments and his statutes which I command thee this day; that all these curses shall come upon thee, and overtake thee:

The Lord shall send upon thee cursing, vexation, and rebuke, in all that thou settest thine hand unto for to do, until thou be destroyed, and until thou perish quickly; because of the wickedness of thy doings, whereby thou hast forsaken me.

The Lord shall bring thee, and thy king which thou shalt set over thee, unto a nation which neither thou nor thy fathers have known; and there shalt thou serve other gods, wood and stone.

And thou shalt become an astonishment, a proverb, and a byword, among all nations whither the Lord shall lead thee. Thy sons and thy daughters shall be given unto another people, and thine eyes shall look, and fail with longing for them all the day long: and there shall be no might in thine hand.

Thou shalt beget sons and daughters, but thou shalt not enjoy them; for they shall go into Captivity.

The stranger that is within thee shall get up above thee very high; and thou shalt come down very low.

He shall lend to thee, and thou shalt not lend to him: he shall be the head, and thou shalt be the tail.

Moreover all these curses shall come upon thee, and shall pursue thee, and overtake thee, till thou be destroyed; because thou hearkenedst not unto the voice of the Lord thy God, to keep his commandments and his statutes which he commanded thee:

And they shall be upon thee for a sign and for a wonder, and upon thy seed for ever.

Because thou servedst not the Lord thy God with joyfulness, and with gladness of heart, for the abundance of all things;

Therefore shalt thou serve thine enemies which the Lord shall send against thee, in hunger, and in thirst, and in nakedness, and in want of all things: and he shall put a yoke of iron upon thy neck, until he have destroyed thee.

If thou wilt not observe to do all the words of this law that are written in this book, that thou mayest fear this glorious and fearful name, THE Lord THY GOD;

Then the Lord will make thy plagues wonderful, and the plagues of thy seed even great plagues, and of long continuance, and sore sicknesses, and of long continuance.

Moreover he will bring upon thee all the diseases of Egypt, which thou wast afraid of; and they shall cleave unto thee.

Also every sickness, and every plague, which is not written in the book of this law, them will the Lord bring upon thee, until thou be destroyed. And ye shall be left few in number, whereas ye were as the stars of heaven for multitude; because thou wouldest not obey the voice of the Lord thy God.

And it shall come to pass, that as the Lord rejoiced over you to do you good, and to multiply you; so the Lord will rejoice over you to destroy you, and to bring you to nought; and ye shall be plucked from off the land whither thou goest to possess it.

And the Lord shall scatter thee among all people, from the one end of the earth even unto the other; and there thou shalt serve other gods, which neither thou nor thy fathers have known, even wood and stone.

And among these nations shalt thou find no ease, neither shall the sole of thy foot have rest: but the Lord shall give thee there a trembling heart, and failing of eyes, and sorrow of mind:

And thy life shall hang in doubt before thee; and thou shalt fear day and night, and shalt have none assurance of thy life:

In the morning thou shalt say, Would God it were even! and at even thou shalt say, Would God it were morning! for the fear of thine heart wherewith thou shalt fear, and for the sight of thine eyes which thou shalt see.

And the Lord shall bring thee into Egypt again with ships, by the way whereof I spake unto thee, Thou shalt see it no more again: and there ye shall be sold unto your enemies for bondmen and bondwomen, and no man shall buy you."

Deuteronomy Chapter 30

"And it shall come to pass, when all these things are come upon thee, the blessing and the curse, which I have set before thee, and thou shalt call them to mind among all the nations, whither the Lord thy God hath driven thee,

And shalt return unto the Lord thy God, and shalt obey his voice according to all that I command thee this day, thou and thy children, with all thine heart, and with all thy soul;

That then the Lord thy God will turn thy Captivity, and have compassion upon thee, and will return and gather thee from all the nations, whither the Lord thy God hath scattered thee.

If any of thine be driven out unto the outmost parts of heaven, from thence will the Lord thy God gather thee, and from thence will he fetch thee:

And the Lord thy God will bring thee into the land which thy fathers possessed, and thou shalt possess it; and he will do thee good, and multiply thee above thy fathers.

And the Lord thy God will circumcise thine heart, and the heart of thy seed, to love the Lord thy God with all thine heart, and with all thy soul, that thou mayest live.

And the Lord thy God will put all these curses upon thine enemies, and on them that hate thee, which persecuted thee.

And thou shalt return and obey the voice of the Lord, and do all his commandments which I command thee this day.

And the Lord thy God will make thee plenteous in every work of thine hand, in the fruit of thy body, and in the fruit of thy cattle, and in the fruit of thy land, for good: for the Lord will again rejoice over thee for good, as he rejoiced over thy fathers: If thou shalt hearken unto the voice of the Lord thy God, to keep his commandments and his statutes which are written in this book of the law, and if thou turn unto the Lord thy God with all thine heart, and with all thy soul."

Idolatrous Inhabitants Removed; Black Israel Established in the Land

After the death of Moses, the Hebrews were under the leadership of Joshua. The Lord magnified Joshua and gave him respect in the eyes of the people, and began to work miracles on his behalf so that the people would know he was with Joshua even as he had been with Moses.

Most people are familiar with the story of the siege of Jericho and the walls falling straight down, but not as many know about the water miracle that was duplicated so the people could cross over Jordan. The priests went before the people, and as they carried the ark of the covenant of God's testimony, the waters rose up like a wall, and the people crossed over on dry land. Not only did this permit the people to cross safely, but it struck great fear into the hearts of the nations that were slated to be conquered.

The people were re-consecrated to God, and the males among them circumcised. They kept the Passover, and shortly after that, the manna ceased. You can see from this how faithful God was; to care for them, feed them, protect them, and bring them safely to the land to possess it.

Seven nations stronger and mightier than the Hebrews were scheduled to be vanquished. Often you hear uninformed and unspiritual people allude to how cruel God must be for the eviction and slaughter of these nations. The truth about it was—as I have stated earlier—these nations knew God, but when they had knowledge of him, they chose rather to create idols to worship—permitting them to serve a deity who placed few restraints on their behavior, and whose worship involved fertility rites or bloody human sacrifice. Remember, all the patriarchs sojourned in Canaan and were conversant with the inhabitants; it was no secret that the God whom Abraham, Isaac, and Jacob served was the same God who brought the Flood judgment in the times of old, and obliterated Sodom and Gomorrah for their wickedness. The Hamitic people residing in Canaan occupied some of the best real estate in the region, and a comprehensive knowledge of the past, yet they were ungrateful and chose to establish idols rather than glorify the Creator of all.

Someone with limited knowledge of how things operate in the spiritual realm may still question what is so wrong with a nation choosing what god it will serve. There is only one true God, eternal and self-existent, all knowing, all present, and all powerful. God is light, and in him is no darkness at all... John Chapter 1 verse 5. Therefore, if a man or nation creates an idol by their own hand or imagination, by default it is confusion and darkness, for man was born in sin and shapen in iniquity. Subsequently, any deity he could create would also bear the taint of his corrupted imagination; hence darkness. Remember, God was calling Israel to be a light to the nations. The nations all had idol gods. If they were already in light by virtue of their idols, there would have been no reason for God to raise up a people to be a light.

Secondly, whenever an idol or associated image is created, it provides a portal—a point of contact—for a demonic entity. This means the Canaanite nations were demonic strongholds; also the people were under demonic influence. Because of Satan's great hatred for God and the people of God, it is unlikely Israel would have been left alone in peace. Satan had not forgotten God's prophecy that the Seed of the woman would crush his head. He didn't know exactly who and when, but he likely figured it was somehow connected to the Abrahamic Covenant and the people God was calling out as a personal possession.

He had tried working through Pharaoh to get the male children killed, and he had succeeded in compromising the men of war who originally came up out of Egypt. In the wilderness, he incited the nation of Amalek to attack the people without provocation. One of the nations in Canaan—the Amorites—had been occupying themselves with wickedness since the days of Abraham, for God told Abraham that even though his seed was going into bondage, they would be coming back to Canaan in the fourth generation when the 'iniquity of the Amorites was full.' This means the Amorites had over four hundred years to repent and turn from their ways, but they kept the evil going full steam generation to generation. It was only a matter of time until the resistance in the spiritual realm would spill over into the flesh and blood realm and the nations around the Hebrews would converge on them to wipe them out.

The seven Canaanite nations God promised to cast out before Israel were the

*Hittites

*Girgashites

*Amorites

*Canaanites

*Perizzites

*Hivites

*Jebusites

At one point, the Amorites had come out and surrounded Israel like bees. Because of this, the Lord sent hornets which drove the Amorites out of their land. In some cases, the Canaanites proved to be a stubborn people to dislodge. In at least one instance, they used deception to trick Israel into making a covenant of peace with them. When the deceit was discovered, Israel could not kill them, because of the oath they had made, but they relegated them to forced servitude. The irony of it was they were forced to serve in the land they called home. Thus the prophecy of Noah over his grandson Canaan was fulfilled:

Cursed be Canaan; a servant of servants shall he be unto his brethren...

Blessed be the Lord God of Shem; and Canaan shall be his servant.

Because of Joshua's faithfulness, the tribes were able to enter the land and establish their apportioned boundaries. Joshua Chapter 24 verse 31 tells us that...Israel served the Lord all the days of Joshua, and all the days of the elders that overlived Joshua, and which had known all the works of the Lord, that he had done for Israel.

WHAT'S IMPORTANT

Any time a people are thrust into a strange environment where the spiritual beliefs are antithetical to their own, and distanced from the values of their ancestral ties, there is bound to be a degrading of the original principles and a slow but steady assimilation into the surrounding culture and belief system. Add bondage into the mix, and the mind becomes absorbed with seeking relief from oppression. When permanent relief is unobtainable, temporary respite is sought and often aggressively pursued. The moral code of the surroundings is adopted, and what remains are a people who not only realize they are different and despised by those who rule over them, but find themselves trapped in a frustrating cycle of mere existence times negative value.

Fulfillment of destiny is tied to a sense of purpose. When purpose is reduced to a street blocked at one end by nominal existence and at the other by pleasurable release, we see people whose lives are stagnated, preyed upon by others, and many times, cut short. The answer is not in trying to stand in the middle of the street to avoid the extremes at either end, but rather in soaring up and above to the knowledge of who we are as a people.

The recognition that we are a people wrapping up the final years of a prophecy that had to be fulfilled, and that we are very much loved of God, and that we are the beneficiaries of a multi-millennia old covenant drawn up by the Creator of heaven and earth himself should cause us to view ourselves, our people, the world, and the holy scriptures of God from an entirely new perspective. By observing the behavior of our forefathers before, during, and after the Exodus, we can see the particular sins that tend to beset us as a people; and these will be ingrained in any of us who do not become a new creation in Christ Jesus.

But repentance, infilling of the Holy Ghost and bearing of its fruits will transform us into a people who can overcome these spiritual deficits and find grace in the sight of God. A thankful spirit will overcome murmuring and complaining. Meekness, peace, and a spirit of humility will address stubbornness and the desire to usurp authority. A complete love for the Lord and the joy of the Lord—which is our strength—will guard us against idolatry. Dying daily to our flesh, guarding our heart and mind and what we permit to enter them will protect us from succumbing to fleshly cravings.

Living this way in Christ Jesus is living by example. But that is not the be all and the end all of it. That is just being salt and light. But salt makes people thirsty; light indicates to them that there really is hope in this dark world. Descendants of the Trans-Atlantic slave trade are looking for a better answer than "Come to Jesus." Granted, there is no way to the Father except by Him, but that is not explaining the cloud of hatred, the continual economic sabotage, and the eagerness to eradicate young Black male life that permeates America. It's time now to tell the entire story of our history and heritage.

Lastly, we cannot make the mistake of forgetting God's goodness in our life. We need to remind ourselves of answered prayer and divine intervention; and that, frequently. We need to rehearse the covenant promise to gather us out of the nations and reestablish us back in the land. And by the way, did you catch the prerequisites for being gathered from the nations and reinstated in the kingdom?

If they shall confess their iniquity, and the iniquity of their fathers, with their trespass which they trespassed against me, and that also they have walked contrary unto me;

And that I also have walked contrary unto them, and have brought them into the land of their enemies; if then their uncircumcised hearts be humbled, and they then accept of the punishment of their iniquity ...Then will I remember my covenant with Jacob, and also my covenant with Isaac, and also my covenant with Abraham will I remember; and I will remember the land. God is saying we must:

*Confess our iniquity

*Confess the iniquity of our forefathers

97

*Admit/articulate their trespass (idolatry /murder/witchcraft/adulteries, etc.)

*Acknowledge that what they did was contrary to God's principles and desires

*Admit that God has been walking contrary to us (as a people)

*Acknowledge that you realize he brought you here into the land of your enemies

*Humble yourself

*Accept this punishment of your iniquity

This is important, because so many of us have the attitude, what did we do to deserve all this? It is true; we are being maligned, mistreated, and murdered. But God says he requires that which is past... read it yourself in Ecclesiastes Chapter 3 verse 15. Since God requires the past, it is in our best interest to pray according to the conditions above.

This is also about honor. During the periods our forebears constructed temples, groves, and altars, practiced infant sacrifice, pagan fertility rites, worshipped the sun, moon, and starry hosts, baked cakes to the Queen of Heaven, and desecrated the Sabbath, God did not receive the honor he was due in the heavens and earth. Therefore, let us repent on behalf of our forefathers and foremothers, and offer God the sacrifice of praise and honor. Then we can ask with a blameless heart, "Turn again our Captivity, O Lord, as the streams in the south."

Chapter VI...The Struggle with Idolatry and the Need to Fit In

Fear not: ye have done all this wickedness: yet turn not aside from following the LORD, but serve the LORD with all your heart.

"How many times have I told you not to do that?" "I'm sorry...I promise I won't do it again...I promise!"

Have you ever heard this exchange between a parent and a child?

Israel in their youth as a nation was like a child who does well in class as long as the teacher is in the room, but if the instructor steps out for any length of time, he leaves off what he is supposed to be doing. Then, at some point, he is no longer just slacking, but actively involved in something he has absolutely no business doing.

Judges Chapter 2 verse 7 tells us: the people served the Lord all the days of Joshua, and all the days of the elders that outlived Joshua, who had seen all the great works of the Lord, that he did for Israel. However, like a creeping vine, dereliction of duty was spreading through the new nation. Several of the tribes failed to drive out the inhabitants of the land, opting rather to put them to forced labor. This was not God's ideal plan, because he knew the inhabitants of the land would become a snare to his people. Even a stranger joining the congregation would have to do so because he loved the Lord and desired to serve the God of Israel. He would have to be willing to consecrate himself by circumcision and obey the Mosaic Law. The Canaanites in the land had no intention of proselytizing to the faith of the God of Abraham, Isaac, and Jacob. Thus, they would be thorns in the sides of the people, and their gods would be snares.

Once the generation that came up with Joshua was deceased, another generation arose after them which knew not the Lord, nor yet the works which he had done for Israel. It was that generation that began serving Baalim, and bowed themselves down to Baal and Ashtoreth. It was to be the start of a disturbing pattern. Like a line on a graph that alternately dips and peaks, the instability of Israel's commitment to serve God was not only an affront to the Lord, but obvious to the nations round about them. Those nations were like the crowd that invites you to come enjoy yourself with them when in actuality they are planning to destroy you. Israel's values on the faithfulness chart would rally during the reigns of David and Solomon, but take a devastating plunge following the kingdom split between the north and the south.

Of Judges, Kings and Prophets

The period following the death of the last person familiar with Joshua's generation and the mighty works God wrought through him is best described as an era of self-determination and spiritual anarchy. The writer of the book of Judges states at least four times, "In those days there was no king in Israel," and in two of those instances follows by saying, "every man did that which was right in his own eyes." This was a drastic departure from the agreement the people had made with Joshua during his last exhortation to them:

And the people said unto Joshua, Nay; but we will serve the Lord...And the people said unto Joshua, The Lord our God will we serve, and his voice will we obey ...Joshua Chapter 24 verses 21 and 24.

That the writer would point out there was no king in Israel is disturbing within itself, because the Lord their God was to be king over them. God's ideal was that Israel would not follow the example of the nations. God's model was for the people to observe the Law and commandments (which if obeyed would protect the people from social and domestic disorder) avail themselves of the priests where sacrifices and the order of the service to God was concerned, and heed his prophets whenever a more advanced directive was to be communicated to the people. Throwing a king into the mix—a man like themselves whose heart would be divided between the people's spiritual well-being, his own desire for might and wealth, and the administration of his domain—only served to put another degree of separation between God and the people.

That the prophetic office was the preferred mode of God dealing with his people is obvious just by considering Israel's history thus far. Abraham was a prophet. Both Isaac and Jacob spoke prophetically over their sons. Joseph was a prophet. Moses is probably the best known; in fact, Hosea Chapter 12 verse 13 tells us by a prophet the Lord brought Israel out of Egypt, and by a prophet was he preserved.

Additionally, when a covenant with specific stipulations and penalties for violation is in effect, there is absolutely no room for self-determination. Therefore, we should not be surprised that in the first thirteen chapters alone of Judges there are seven separate and distinct occasions where Israel "did evil" in the sight of the Lord. The snare they had been warned about for failure to drive out the residue of the nations had entrapped them, because they began serving the idols of the very nations they had vanquished. We have already mentioned the vile rites associated with the worship of these entities. So God was justified into selling them into the hands of their enemies.

Israel would end up being oppressed and tormented by their enemies eight years here, eighteen years there, twenty more years later...and each time there would be an intervention when the oppression became too great and the people cried out to God for deliverance. God would send judges to deliver them out of the hand of their enemies, and typically the land would have peace and rest for as long as the judge lived. Once the judge died, the people would revert to their old ways. We should remember though, that even during the worse periods of apostasy, God always had a remnant that remained faithful. The most famous judges were Othniel, Ehud, Deborah, Gideon, Jepthah, and Samson, although all twelve that God called were a blessing during their tenure. The valor of these leaders kept Israel from being swallowed up by the pagan nations surrounding them.

Valiant and devoted judges represented the righteous end of the spectrum. At the other end lurked the idolatry and immorality associated with spiritual anarchy and self-determination. This attitude of discarding the Law and Commandments in favor of self-rule incited some in Israel to lead lifestyles more in common with the idolatrous nations around them than the goal of being a peculiar treasure to the Lord. The deception that accompanies apostasy led them to believe they were still serving God and could invoke his help while simultaneously serving idols. How far off the path is it possible to go once you begin picking and choosing how you will serve God? Nothing illustrates that better than the case of Micah and his mother, who lived in Mount Ephraim.

Micah's mother had eleven hundred pieces of silver that came up missing. When she couldn't find her money, she went to cursing about it. Unlike the times we live in now, in those days, when someone spoke a curse, people actually believed there was life and death in the power of the tongue: as the Bible says there is. That was likely what motivated Micah to fess up and return the silver to his mother.

You would think she was upset because she needed that money in case something happened to Micah and she had to fend for herself. But instead she tells him she had dedicated the silver to the Lord... and if we could stop there, that would be wonderful. But she said, "I had wholly dedicated the silver unto the Lord from my hand for my son." Now, that is confusion already. Is the silver for the Lord, or is it for her son? It must be one or the other, but it can't be both. But that was only the first part of her sentence. The entire statement was, "I had wholly dedicated the silver unto the Lord from my hand for my son, to make a graven image and a molten image: now therefore I will restore it unto thee." In other words, she told him she dedicated the silver to the Lord, but it's really for Micah, and specifically for the purpose of making a graven and a molten image for him.

Nevertheless, Micah gave his mother back all the money. So she still takes part of it, and goes to a silver smelter, and has him make a graven and a molten image, which end up on display in Micah's house. Apparently these silver images joined a menagerie of other idols, because the verse tells us Micah had a house of gods. He also had a healing god—a teraphim—and an ephod, a garment the priests wear. In his idolatry-blinded mind, the only thing that was missing now was a priest. So he solved that problem by consecrating one of his sons, and his son became his priest.

Sometime later, he becomes acquainted with a transient Levite, and convinces him to move in with him and become their family priest in exchange for food, clothing, lodging, and wages. Micah consecrated the Levite, and he became his priest. Micah feels he is set for life, for he says, "Now know I that the Lord will do me good, seeing I have a Levite to my priest."

That arrangement worked until soldiers from the tribe of Dan happened into the area and recognized the voice of the Levite who was in Micah's service. Apparently this particular Levite was making the rounds of the territory, because when he meets Micah, he is coming from the area of Bethlehem-Judah, but yet he is no stranger to the tribe of Dan, either. When these men went back and told their brethren about Micah's house of idols, the Danites basically said to each other, "You know what we have to do, right?" and they organized a force and went back and raided Micah's house, taking the ephod, the teraphim, and the molten and graven images. When the Levite went to protest, they essentially told him to just be quiet and come with them. They convinced him with this logic: "...is it better for thee to be a priest unto the house of one man, or that thou be a priest unto a tribe and a family in Israel?" And the priest's reaction? "...the priest's heart was glad, and he took the ephod, and the teraphim, and the graven image, and went in the midst of the people."

How did this all end up playing out? "...the children of Dan set up the graven image: and Jonathan, the son of Gershom, the son of Manasseh, he and his sons were priests to the tribe of Dan until the day of the Captivity of the land.

And they set them up Micah's graven image, which he made, all the time that the house of God was in Shiloh."

Many commandments broken, and many things regarding the corruption of priestly function caused a vicious circle that ultimately developed into a downward spiral. Starting with relationships in the family, ignoring the fifth commandment (Micah dishonored his mother) led to violating the eighth commandment (thou shalt not steal), and extending to relationship between man and God breaking the first and second commandments (Micah's mother has the graven and molten images produced, and Micah adds them to his household collection.) Micah is in no position to consecrate anyone, for consecration involves the setting aside of someone or something to be holy for service to God by someone who is holy, but that doesn't stop him. The Levite appears as a priest for hire; this is a distortion of his office—not that the Levites were not to be cared for since they had no inheritance among the tribes, but rather because when he saw the idols, that was the signal to pass on Micah's house and keep moving. We see Micah viewing the Levite as a sort of good-luck charm... he actually thinks God is in the midst of this despite the fact that he is trashing the first two commandments.

The encounter with the Danites shows the level of loyalty of the priest for hire...he's going to go with whoever is the highest bidder...granted he may have feared for his life, but the fact that he joyously went right along with the stolen idols indicates his fear of God was not where it should have been.

By the way, when Micah finally catches up with the Danites and sees they have no intention of returning either the Levite or his household idols, he acts like a wealthy investor who has just learned all of his stocks have severely devalued. He laments, "Ye have taken away my gods which I made, and the priest, and ye are gone away: and what have I more?" I guess he clean forgot about the God of Israel. And regarding his little idols, did it occur to him if his gods were really gods, they could have escaped the Danites and returned to his house and got back up on their pedestals? But he admits himself that he made them; apparently not realizing if a man can make a god, it is no god. Not only that, the Danites were ready to fight and take him and his family out if he made a move to reclaim the priest and the images. Once they were established in their territory, the Danites consecrated men to be priests to their tribe, and the image remained there all the time that the house of God was in Shiloh. Like a spreading cancer, the detestable thing moved further over the territory where it could touch and taint more lives.

How do we as a people get so far away from God's precepts and desires? Based on this story, it starts with 'doing what is right in our own eyes.' Once we begin calling the shots, we have made ourselves god, and exalted ourselves over the Lord. The first commandment is foundational, all the rest build upon it. So actions like dishonor, covetousness, and theft are now not far off. When people start down the slippery slope of idolatry, they will attempt to legitimize their actions by saying God is with me, or God is blessing me. If they can just work God into it, maybe there is a way to worship and live as one pleases, yet still be blessed. And if they can hook up with a person who is a representative of God—why, that's all the better. But all such spiritual enterprises are doomed to failure, for light has no fellowship with darkness. Further, any person professing godliness that tolerates idolatry will also be for sale to the highest bidder. The corruption and compromise of those who are called to represent the Lord only further emboldens the wayward and the rebellious. **Lastly, it is a sad fact that some**

people are devastated when their lie is taken from them, and still others are willing to fight and kill to hold on to a lie.

This was just one dark story from a period when our forefathers tried to go it alone without really following hard after God with all their heart, soul, and strength. Surrounded by nations that hated and resented them, and facing an adversary in the spiritual realm with a personal vendetta, the Hebrews could not afford to have a half-hearted commitment toward God. But even as idolatry, tribal warfare, and violent crime threatened to destabilize the nation, God in his manifold wisdom was preparing a priest and prophet who would love him with all his heart, judge the people righteously, and renew their faith and dedication.

The Lord never leaves himself without a witness. The birth of Samuel, whose name means "Heard of God" was an answer to a barren wife's prayer. In exchange for God's blessing, she dedicated her son to the Lord's service. After he was weaned, he went to live with the priest Eli at the house of the Lord in Shiloh to begin his internship in the duties of a priest. So if you can imagine a young brother wearing a linen ephod that fit his tiny frame, you have a picture of Samuel in training.

God was raising Samuel up because Eli's sons, Hophni and Phineas, were abusing the priests' office. They were much like men of God today entrusted with the gospel who instead make merchandise of the flock, are spiritually abusive, and care little about maintaining a blameless testimony or nurturing the people who come to them for counsel. The scripture says they were men of Belial, knew not God, abhorred the offering of the Lord, and caused the people to transgress. That individuals this dark inside were acting as intermediaries between the people and their God both grieved and angered the Lord. Thank God that under the New Covenant we are all called to be a royal priesthood; subject only to the Great High Priest that is passed into the heavens, Jesus the Son of God—the only Mediator between God and man.

Similar to the times we are living in now, in those days the word of the Lord was precious. But God confirmed his seal of approval on Samuel, in that none of his words fell to the ground. And all Israel from Dan even to Beersheba knew that Samuel was established to be a prophet of the Lord. Further, God revealed himself to Samuel there in Shiloh. Samuel was probably the first 'circuit preacher'…he made a yearly round covering all the areas of Israel to judge them.

In those years the Philistines rose up in battle against Israel. After an initial defeat, the elders of Israel agreed that in the next engagement, the ark of the covenant should go out before them into the battle. But wicked men—Hophni and Phineas, were the ones carrying the ark, and when the battle was joined, these two apostate priests were killed, along with over seven times as many Hebrews than in the first clash, and the ark of God was taken.

The ark of God, wherein was the Glory of God's presence, caused myriad problems for the people who had no business being in possession of it. From causing the Philistine's idol Dagon to fall down and break in obeisance in front of the ark, to painful and debilitating disease breaking out in the Philistine males, to outright death, they soon realized the heavy liability associated with keeping the ark. So they consulted with their priests and diviners as to the best way to get the ark back to Israel.

Now, the response of the priests and diviners is important to note (the actual account is found in I Samuel Chapters 5 and 6) because unlearned and unspiritual people often think it is so cruel and aggressive the way Israel had to deal with the idolatrous nations surrounding them. But this response (which I have paraphrased to focus on the main points) shows the nations knew full well who the God of Israel was, and that they themselves were idolaters and willfully chose to worship gods they created themselves—carved and molten images.

"What shall we do to the ark of the Lord? And they said... ye shall give glory unto the God of Israel: peradventure he will lighten his hand from off you, and from off your gods, and from off your land. Wherefore then do ye harden your hearts, as the Egyptians and Pharaoh hardened their hearts? when he had wrought wonderfully among them, did they not let the people go, and they departed?"

So it is obvious the memory of Egypt's torment and humiliating defeat was a historical fact in the region, and still fresh in the memory of surrounding nations. A demonic force represented by an idol can never overcome God himself, but it operates for the purpose of destroying God's people. Under the New Covenant of grace and peace, we put on the armor of God, wield our shield of faith and sword of the Spirit—the word of God, take our stand in prayer and praise, and the gates of hell cannot prevail against us. In the days of our forefathers, they had to conduct actual flesh and blood warfare to hold back the evil gates. God never called Israel to war for mere blood sport or show of military prowess. It was literally a matter of preserving the bloodline through which the Seed of the woman would one day manifest to take away the sins of the world, and redeem his people Israel. The ark was eventually returned to its rightful place, and Samuel led the people in repentance and re-consecration. The people put away Baalim and Ashtoreth. God gave the people deliverance from the Philistines and they had peace for a season. The point here is that all that live godly in Christ Jesus will suffer persecution, but we must be careful we are not being buffeted for our own faults because we brought the oppression on ourselves by our own wrong actions.

Samuel was growing old, and he commissioned his sons Joel and Abiah to judge Israel. These two men however, had such a love for money that they accepted bribes which in turn perverted judgment. Many of us can relate to how devastating it is to serve the Lord and live by example, only to have your children turn out of the way. I want to speak a word of encouragement to you here. In looking at godly Samuel's life, and the life of his godly mother Hannah, it is obvious a subsequent generation can go wrong and not necessarily because their parents sinned. While there can be generational tendencies and besetting sins over families, at the end of the day it is still about choices, and God gives everyone the ability to choose, right and wrong, life and death, good and evil. So if you are facing a heartbreak of this nature, encourage yourself in the Lord, and continue to intercede for your loved ones and trust God to intervene in their lives. Ask God to place godly people in their path to intercept them, and ask God to give them an intense hunger and thirst for righteousness. We cannot control the future and what our loved ones will or will not do, but we can trust God to keep his hand over their lives. As the Lord Jesus admonished us, have faith in God. There is nothing too difficult for him, and no sinner too hard for God to break and save.

But getting back to Samuel's errant sons...when the elders of Israel saw how they were conducting the office of judge, they approached Samuel as a collective and said, "Behold, thou art old, and thy sons walk not in thy ways: now make us a king to judge us like all the nations."

This might have caught Samuel off guard, but God had already spoken to Moses about this back in the wilderness when the people were told, "When thou art come unto the land which the Lord thy God giveth thee, and shalt possess it, and shalt dwell therein, and shalt say, I will set a king over me, like as all the nations that are about me; Thou shalt in any wise set him king over thee, whom the Lord thy God shall choose: one from among thy brethren shalt thou set king over thee: thou mayest not set a stranger over thee, which is not thy brother." Deuteronomy Chapter 17 verses 14 and 15.

The story continues "...But the thing displeased Samuel, when they said, Give us a king to judge us. And Samuel prayed unto the Lord. And the Lord said unto Samuel, Hearken unto the voice of the people in all that they say unto thee: for they have not rejected thee, but they have rejected me, that I should not reign over them. According to all the works which they have done since the day that I brought them up out of Egypt even unto this day, wherewith they have forsaken me, and served other gods, so do they also unto thee."

So it was against this backdrop that Israel's first flesh and blood king was anointed: a Benjamite; Saul, the son of Kish. The people later admitted to Samuel that "we have added unto all our sins this evil, to ask us a king", but we can only wonder how long it took for them to realize he was just a flesh and blood man like themselves, subject to egotism, poor judgment, and outbursts of anger. Saul was a very striking figure to look at—taller up from the shoulders than any of the people—but he had some troubling spiritual character defects...among them presumptuousness and disobedience—that ultimately cost him the throne.

It is one thing to be of Hebrew lineage, but altogether another thing to be a man or woman of God with a heart open to his voice, and bearing the spiritual fruits of faith and trust. Saul, though a valiant warrior, did not have that kind of trust in God: the faith his forefather Abraham had when asked to relinquish Isaac; so when he had waited and waited for Samuel, and the people began panicking and scattering because the Philistines were converging on them, Saul also began to panic and forgot something his son Jonathan knew: that there is no restraint to the Lord to save by many or by few. So he offered the burnt offering that only Samuel was supposed to offer.

This act in and of itself was the determining factor that caused God to reject Saul as king. His later neglect in refusing to utterly slay Amalek according to the word of the Lord merely confirmed there was always going to be a problem with Saul executing divine directives exactly as they were given. God was very serious about this; he spoke through Moses that when they were situated in the land and had rest from their enemies, they were to "blot out the remembrance of Amalek from under heaven." Even Balaam's prophecy was that "Amalek was the first of the nations; but his latter end shall be that he perish for ever." How serious was God about the annihilation of Amalek? Serious enough that an altar was built with a name many are familiar with:

"And the Lord said unto Moses, Write this for a memorial in a book, and rehearse it in the ears of Joshua: for I will utterly put out the remembrance of Amalek from under heaven.

And Moses built an altar, and called the name of it Jehovah-nissi:

For he said, Because the Lord hath sworn that the Lord will have war with Amalek from generation to generation."

So if God himself has declared war on a nation, what man will rise up to question God's judgment, and if entrusted to execute the mission on his behalf, dare to return with only a partial victory?

God rejected Saul from being king, and David was anointed in his stead. This had to have been one of more complex arrangements in the nation's history, for although David was anointed and Saul was rejected, Saul remained a force to be reckoned with for many years; largely because he would not voluntarily step down even though he knew he had no way to go but out. During those years when David was forced to be a fugitive in his own land, God was testing him and preparing him so that when he did ascend the throne, he would rule with a balance of justice and compassion.

Like all men born of women, David sinned, albeit quickly acknowledging and repenting of it and throwing himself on the mitigating mercies of God. We all know the account involving Bathsheba, which brought a sword to David's house; resulting in attempted coup d'états on both his and Solomon's reigns, and the death of three of his sons. The matter of the numbering of the people was also a dark hour during his time in power. Nevertheless, he completed the mission his forebears had left undone...he secured the territories of Israel, subdued their enemies, and established a reign of peace and prosperity for forty years. He was a man of faith, valor, mercy, and justice: truly a man after God's own heart. When only a shepherd, he was faithful over a few things, and became lord over many. David's life represented the faith and humility that precedes conquest and dominion.

If David's life was a tribute to the faith and valor that subdues both wild beasts and wild nations, Solomon—whose name means peace—was representative of the harmony and prosperity associated with a kingdom secure from all enemies and blessed with the very presence of God. These were the halcyon days of Israel; a time of joyfulness and serenity in the fairest kingdom on earth, unrivaled in beauty and ruled by the wisest of men. Solomon literally made silver at Jerusalem as plenteous as stones, and he surpassed all the kings of the earth in riches and wisdom. Further, all the kings of the earth sought the presence of Solomon, to hear his wisdom, that God had put in his heart.

David was the ultimate worship leader and worship musician, and a prolific writer of psalms. His psalms take us into a deep intimacy with God, and set the example for our approach to God in times of trouble, distress, fear, and uncertainty. By them he also teaches us how to exalt God and conduct spiritual warfare with the weapon of high praise. Many of his songs were prophetic, pointing to the coming Messiah, God's vengeance on his enemies, and the establishment of the Kingdom of God on earth. His son Solomon spoke three thousand proverbs, and wrote one thousand and five songs. We are familiar with many of his sayings in the Book of Proverbs, but how many know four hundred thirty-six more verses of his are found in The Book of Wisdom in the Apocrypha?

David set the pace in leading us into the presence and praise of God. Solomon endeavors to show us the fear of the Lord as the beginning of wisdom, and how godly wisdom will cause us to have favor with God and man, and enable us to navigate around the pitfalls and treacherous places of life. Taken together, these priceless spiritual treasures are powerful resources in building and maintaining us as a new creation in Christ Jesus.

The pinnacle of achievement was the building and dedication of the temple in Jerusalem. Solomon's humble prayer for Israel was answered by the awesome presence of the Lord filling the temple—His massive Glory. As in the manner of Elijah's sacrifice, the fire of God came down from heaven and consumed the burnt offering and the sacrifices; and the glory of the Lord filled the house. "And the priests could not enter into the house of the Lord, because the glory of the Lord had filled the Lord's house." The scripture continues, "And when all the children of Israel saw how the fire came down, and the glory of the Lord upon the house, they bowed themselves with their faces to the ground upon the pavement, and worshipped, and praised the Lord, saying, For he is good; for his mercy endureth forever. This brief chapter in Israel's history was a tiny foretaste of the glory to come when God's kingdom is manifested here on earth. This was what the disciples were yearning for when they asked Jesus, "Lord, wilt thou at this time restore again the kingdom to Israel?" This kingdom is to be desired, because the very first petition in the prayer Jesus taught the disciples to pray is "thy kingdom come, thy will be done on earth, as it is in heaven." The kingdom could not yet manifest, because the Gentiles who were to be called out and grafted into the commonwealth of Israel were not yet in place. And he said unto them, "It is not for you to know the times or the seasons, which the Father hath put in his own power."

What Jesus said next is critical and should not be missed in the context of waiting for the physical manifestation of the kingdom "...But ye shall receive power, after that the Holy Ghost is come upon you: and ye shall be witnesses unto me both in Jerusalem, and in all Judæa, and in Samaria, and unto the uttermost part of the earth." The kingdom is coming, and the kingdom is to be desired and prayed for, but the immediate call is to receive the power that the Holy Ghost brings: and this power will do what? enable the disciples to be witnesses for Jesus... where? in all Judæa, in all Samaria, and unto the uttermost part of the earth.

Why is this directive so profound? Because in Jesus' words here, we see the hierarchy of blessing exactly as explained in Romans Chapter 1 and 2 ...that the gospel is the power of God unto salvation to everyone that believeth; to the Jew (Hebrew) first, and also to the Greek. The proper sequence of the preaching of the gospel is to Judah, then to the alienated tribes of Israel, and lastly to the uttermost parts of the earth. This promise was fulfilled among the disciples and one hundred twenty other Black Hebrew worshippers on the Day of Pentecost following the ascension of the Lord Jesus Christ. The promise is to each Hebrew, our children, as many as are far off, and as many as the Lord our God shall call. According to Jesus, the baptism of the Holy Ghost as a prerequisite for effective witnessing holds preeminence over the arrival of the kingdom. And I am convinced before our Lord's return and the commencement of the kingdom, we will need to experience another outpouring of his Spirit, in order to be effective witnesses. What made John the Baptist so effective in turning many of the children of Israel to the Lord their God, and preparing people for the ministry of the Lord Jesus Christ? Because from his mother's womb, he was filled with the Holy Ghost...Luke Chapter 1 verses 15-17.

It is wonderful to have our eyes opened and come to an understanding of our identity and heritage, but it will take this baptism of fire to reach our brothers and sisters on the massive scale needed to seal the brethren who will dedicate themselves solely to the service of the Lord.

The men and brethren in Judah on the Day of Pentecost fully knew who they were, but knowledge of their ancestry and heritage was not enough to save them. But once Peter—anointed and filled with the power of God—preached his sermon, "they were pricked in their heart, and said unto Peter and to the rest of the apostles, Men and brethren, what shall we do?"

They knew who they were, and they knew who Jesus was, and that he had been crucified. But it took the anointing of the Holy Ghost to move this head knowledge to a spiritual awareness that deeply convicted their hearts and brought them to a moving repentance. The Greek word 'pricked' in this instance implies, "to pierce thoroughly, to agitate violently, to sting to the quick." This means Peter's sermon brought a painful conviction and remorse, and caused them to realize the prophecies of the prophets were coming to pass before their eyes, and that Jesus was both Lord and Christ. He stressed this to our forefathers saying, "Therefore let all the house of Israel know assuredly" that God had made the same Jesus they crucified Lord and Christ. As a result of that message, three thousand souls were saved. These were all Black Hebrew brethren that populated the first assembly of the ecclesia—the called-out ones.

The gospel must be preached to all nations before the kingdom can be restored. According to Jesus' words and the result of Peter's first altar call, the baptism of the Holy Ghost is the only vehicle by which the gospel can be preached with a witness effective enough to reach the hearts of the men and brethren of Israel. Based on this, should we not each be repenting, and making a public confession of our faith and belief in Jesus as Lord by water immersion, and receiving this spiritual fiery baptism? This is not about Pentecostalism or the Charismatic movement, because the original assembly that was called out and sealed by the infilling of the Holy Ghost on the Day of Pentecost took place in the first century and predates any modern denomination, as does the promise that it is to Israel, their children, as many as are far off, and as many as God calls. This is about the revelation to the worshippers at Jerusalem of who the Lord Jesus Christ is, and how to enter into the new covenant as a new creation. God has already given us everything we need to make straight the paths of the Lord and prepare our hearts and the hearts of the people for the Lord's return. We have the heavenly resources. We just need to deploy them: to Judah first, then Samaria, and lastly, the uttermost parts of the earth!

The Kingdom Split

Solomon's sin in his old age was the catalyst for the permanent kingdom split, though hints of schism had already surfaced toward the close of King David's reign. When his son Absalom moved to usurp the kingdom, David had to flee for his safety. After Absalom was killed attempting to escape, the men of David's tribe Judah and half of the people of Israel went to meet the king in exile to escort him back. But when the king had crossed the Jordan, the rest of the men of Israel arrived and demanded to know of David why the tribe of Judah had stolen him away from them. The men of Judah answered:

"Because the king is near of kin to us: wherefore then be ye angry for this matter? have we eaten at all of the king's cost? or hath he given us any gift?

And the men of Israel answered the men of Judah, and said, We have ten parts in the king, and we have also more right in David than ye: why then did ye despise us, that our advice should not be first had in bringing back our king?

And the words of the men of Judah were fiercer than the words of the men of Israel."

Now at least one individual, Sheba son of Bichri—tried to capitalize on the division and create a separate nation of the ten tribes, but his seditious attempt only led to his death at the hands of David's captain. So the seeds of secession had already been planted when Solomon passed away and his son Rehoboam ascended the throne.

The legacy of the Hebrew kings is best described by the cliché, 'the good, the bad, and the ugly'. The prevailing rule was the spirituality of the monarch set the tone for the conduct of the people. During the dynasty of the kings, the throne generally passed to a son, and it was common for the heir to continue in the ways of his father. But a wicked queen or individuals not of the original line could also have great sway on the people and the affairs of state. At times the two kingdoms existed side by side quietly, on other occasions they went to war with each other, and if necessary became confederate against a common threat. Periodically, prophets and priests by divine appointment brought a word from the Lord and took a stand for righteousness. Here we will highlight the first few kings on either side to illustrate the trajectory of kingship in Israel and Judah, then summarize the general outcome. Nineteen kings held the throne in Israel—the northern kingdom, until they were taken away captive into Assyria, and twenty reigned in Judah, before it was taken captive to Babylon.

Sheba's attempt at sedition was premature in God's divine timeline, for God had already predetermined that the first of two kings named Jeroboam would assume the throne over the ten tribes of Israel. Jeroboam's reign was confirmed by the prophet Ahijah even before Solomon's death, causing Jeroboam to have to flee to Egypt. After Solomon died, and his son Rehoboam took the throne in his stead, Jeroboam came with the tribes of Israel and petitioned Rehoboam to lighten the tax and compulsory service burdens imposed on them by his father. Apparently Rehoboam did not inherit his father's wisdom, because he listened to young inexperienced men like himself instead of the elders of Israel, and replied to the people that they should prepare for even harsher measures, to put it mildly. This was the tipping point that caused the kingdom to split. At first Rehoboam planned to take the other ten tribes back by force, but God spoke to him not to do it, and he obeyed God in that matter.

Rehoboam controlled Jerusalem, and the tribes that were confederate with him were Benjamin and the Levites. The Levites left off service with the other ten tribes because they were kicked out by Jeroboam from executing their duties. That's because Jeroboam had quickly sunk into idolatry and made two golden calves and repeated the terrible error in the wilderness; saying to the ten tribes,

"It is too much for you to go up to Jerusalem: behold thy gods, O Israel, which brought thee up out of the land of Egypt.

And he set the one in Beth-el, and the other put he in Dan. And this thing became a sin: for the people went to worship before the one, even unto Dan. And he made an house of high places, and made priests of the lowest of the people, which were not of the sons of Levi." The reason Jeroboam did this was because he feared losing the allegiance of the people if they went to Jerusalem to worship as ordained. This shows us Jeroboam was not a man of faith, because through the prophet Ahijah, God had told him, "if thou wilt hearken unto all that I command thee, and wilt walk in my ways, and do that is right in my sight, to keep my statutes and my commandments, as David my servant did; that I will be with thee, and build thee a sure house, as I built for David, and will give Israel unto thee."

God had already promised to give Jeroboam Israel and guide him with his presence; all he had to do was walk uprightly before the Lord. But being a faithless individual, he did not trust God, and instead made molten images. We know from way back in the days of the judges that the tribe of Dan was already a stronghold for idolatry, because Micah's silver graven and molten images were there the entire time the house of God was in Shiloh. Now there were golden calves there. The true shame of it is that Jeroboam falsely attributed the great works of the Lord God to these metal bovine images. And the lowlife priests he set up were for three functions; priests for the high places, priests for the devils (yes—you heard that correctly), and priests for the calves. So the Levites and anyone else in Israel who didn't want to be a part of this madness came to Jerusalem and resorted to Rehoboam, and this made Rehoboam's kingdom strong.

I wanted to bring out the point about just how low Jeroboam had sunk, because many times people wonder why in Jesus' day it was said the Jews (which is Judah) had no dealings with the Samaritans (the northern kingdom.) But now you can see why, because the northern tribes were sacrificing to devils, but still calling it the worship of the Lord. That's why Jesus could tell the woman at the well that the people of Judah knew what they worshiped, but the people of Samaria didn't know what they worshiped.

The multitude of people who joined Rehoboam made his kingdom strong, and for three years the people in Judah served the Lord as in the days of David and Solomon. But when he was strong, he clean forgot about the Lord, and the people followed suit. They began building high places, images, and groves. The spiritual atmosphere relaxed to the extent sodomites felt at ease in the land, and they committed the same kind of abominations as the nations God had driven out of Canaan in the days of Joshua.

For this reason, God sent Shishak king of Egypt against Rehoboam and Judah. God sent a prophet—Shemaiah—to tell them their trespass brought this misfortune upon them. It took this for Rehoboam and the elders of Judah to humble themselves, and God lessened the punishment against Judah. This was one of the first examples of how the leader is like a domino which if toppled, causes all the others to fall. Rehoboam and Jeroboam were at war with each other as long as they reigned. The Chronicle's closing remark on Rehoboam is that he did evil, because he prepared not his heart to seek the Lord. Rehoboam's rating falls under bad.

Jeroboam continued with his idolatrous ways to the point of building an altar which was designed to imitate the altar in Jerusalem, except that he—Jeroboam—decided which day and month the sacrifice would be held, instead of the day God had appointed. The day he went to burn incense on this illegal altar, a prophet appeared to him and foretold a person would be born that would sacrifice Jeroboam's idolatrous priests on that same altar. The prophet said the sign this would come to pass would be the altar splitting apart and the ashes pouring out from it. When Jeroboam heard this, he lifted up his hand to command those with him to take the prophet into custody. But then he couldn't pull his hand back in again. While his hand was in this frozen state, the altar split just as foretold, and the ashes poured out. Jeroboam begged the prophet to intercede to God for him, that his hand would be restored. This in and of itself proves Jeroboam knew the Lord God was the supreme God.

You would think the frozen hand experience would have been enough to bring Jeroboam to repentance, but he kept his idolatry up, continuing to consecrate lowlife priests to sacrifice at the high places. This would eventually cause his lineage to be cut off from the face of the earth.

Jeroboam was still reigning in Israel when Rehoboam of Judah died, and Rehoboam's son Abijah took the throne. Apparently Jeroboam wanted to keep the conflict going from generation to generation. He marshalled eight hundred thousand chosen men of valor and initiated a conflict with Abijah. Abijah only had half as many chosen men, but he had something Jeroboam lacked—right standing with God. Abijah told Jeroboam, "we keep the charge of the Lord our God; but ye have forsaken him. And, behold, God himself is with us for our captain, and his priests with sounding trumpets to cry alarm against you. O children of Israel, fight ye not against the Lord God of your fathers; for ye shall not prosper."

Jeroboam thought he had the upper hand by bringing up an ambushment to completely surround Judah, but:

"They cried unto the Lord, and the priests sounded with the trumpets. Then the men of Judah gave a shout: and as the men of Judah shouted, it came to pass, that God smote Jeroboam and all Israel before Abijah and Judah."

The outcome of that battle was that Judah took out over half of Jeroboam's forces and subdued Israel at that time, because they relied upon the Lord God of their fathers. God struck Jeroboam's son and he died while still a youth, and God struck Jeroboam for his unrepentant idolatrous ways, and he died also. Jeroboam's rating falls under ugly. As for Abijah, he prospered after that event and grew mighty. Abijah's rating falls under good.

After Abijah's death, his son Asa reigned. God gave Asa peace in the land for the first ten years. Asa got busy and wisely redeemed that time by taking away the altars of the strange gods, removing the high places, breaking down the images, and cutting down the groves. He also proactively built up the cities in Judah and fortified them. It was a good thing he did that, because Zerah the Ethiopian came up against Judah with a million-man army and three hundred chariots. Once again, Judah was drastically outnumbered, but Asa cried unto God and testified to him that it was nothing to God to help whether by many or with those who have no power. He invoked their relationship to God and petitioned him to not let man prevail against him. In praying this way, Asa was identifying Judah as one with God. Well, God did fight for our forefathers, and that million-man army and their three hundred chariots turned tail and ran, but they couldn't outrun Judah and they were overtaken and overthrown.

After this, a prophet—Azariah, came to exhort Asa to continue to seek the Lord. And the principle is very simple, the Lord is with you, while you be with him, and if you seek him, he will be found of you, but if you forsake him, he will forsake you. Then the prophet makes a statement that gives great insight into the condition of Judah in those days: "Now for a long season Israel hath been without the true God, and without a teaching priest, and without law.

But when they in their trouble did turn unto the Lord God of Israel, and sought him, he was found of them." He ends his exhortation by telling Asa,

"Be ye strong therefore, and let not your hands be weak: for your work shall be rewarded."

Sometimes all it takes is a word spoken in due season to renew our courage and dedication. Asa put away all the abominable idols found in any of the territories he controlled, and renewed the altar of the Lord. People from other tribes started rallying to him, when they saw the Lord was with him. At that time, a huge sacrificial offering was made to the Lord, and Judah entered into a covenant with God to seek the Lord God of their fathers with all their heart and with all their soul; That whosoever would not seek the Lord God of Israel should be put to death, whether small or great, whether man or woman. Judah rejoiced in this oath, because they had sought the Lord with their whole desire; and he was found of them: and he gave them rest round about.

Some of the hardest conflicts to overcome in life are those stemming from the people closest to us. But when Asa rallied up with God, he received courage to not worry about how family felt about his zeal for the Lord. He deposed his own grandmother (the queen mother) from her position of royalty because she had made an idol in a grove. Asa demolished her idol and burned it.

Now in the meantime, the northern kingdom had made themselves another king, Nadab, son of Jeroboam. He did evil in the sight of God like his father. He was only on the throne for two years until Baasha from the tribe of Issachar conspired against him and not only killed him, but wiped out his entire house. This was to fulfill the prophecy of Ahijah the Shilonite against the house of Jeroboam for his wickedness. Then Baasha assumed the throne. Apparently Baasha didn't review the history archives about Jeroboam's defeat and he began a tactical attack on Judah. Baasha's strategy was to establish a military fort city that would block entrance to and from Judah. This was an hour of testing for Asa, and in this matter he did not choose the right response; opting to take treasures from the temple of the Lord and from his own possessions as an incentive for the king of Syria to break his league with Baasha and take Asa's side against him. King Ben-hadad of Syria accepted the bribe and attacked certain cities of the northern kingdom, causing Baasha to abandon construction on his military outpost, but it displeased the Lord in that Asa had failed to trust in him, especially in light of the great deliverance in the battle against Zerah the Ethiopian. God sent the prophet Hanani to rebuke him saying, "the eyes of the Lord run to and fro throughout the whole earth, to shew himself strong in the behalf of them whose heart is perfect toward him. Herein thou hast done foolishly: therefore from henceforth thou shalt have wars."

This reproof enraged Asa and he put Hanani in prison; also he oppressed some of the people at the same time. He must have really nursed a grudge about this, because he developed an illness that progressed to the terminal stage, but the entire length of his illness, he wouldn't seek God, only the doctors. Well, we all know if you want to hold out, who is able to hold out longest without ever having to cry uncle. Nevertheless, Asa is chronicled as a king that did that which was good and right in the eyes of the Lord his God, and whose heart was perfect all his days. If God gave him the seal of approval, let the record stand. Asa's rating falls under good.

The vivid contrast between the blessing of God on the southern kingdom of Judah and the constant turmoil and cloak and dagger that characterized the northern kingdom is illustrated by the fact that during the reign of Asa alone, Israel went through six kings: Nadab, Baasha, Elah, Zimri, Omri, and Tibni. A prophet name Jehu pronounced the destruction over the house of Baasha, who continued the wickedness of Jeroboam, although he was not related to him. After Baasha's death, his son Elah took the throne, but he likewise did evil, and was only in power for two years when one of his servants, Zimri—killed him and usurped the throne.

As soon as Zimri came into power, he executed all of Baasha's male relatives up to and including friends of the family. This fulfilled the prophecy Jehu brought against Baasha. At the time Zimri committed these assassinations, Israel was at war with the Philistines. When word filtered back of the massacre, the people made the current military leader, Omri, king. Omri was coronated right in the camp while on duty. He left the conflict with the Philistines to dethrone Zimri. But before he could get to him, Zimri apparently barricaded himself in the king's house, and torched it from within. Thus he died in infamy for his treason.

Then further division arose among the northern kingdom of who should be king—a man named Tibni favored by some of the people, or the hastily crowned Omri. Although it was described as a fifty/fifty popularity split, the people following Omri were able to prevail and Tibni lost his life as a result. Omri is the person responsible for establishing Samaria as it came to be known. In just six years Omri wrought more evil than all those that were before him. Nadab, Baasha, Elah, Zimri, and Omri all have a rating of bad.

In stark contrast to the stifling evil of the northern kingdom, the light of the glory of God blazed brightly in the reign of Jehoshapat, son of Asa. Jehoshapat is described as a king who walked in the first ways of his father David, and sought not unto Baalim; But sought to the Lord God of his father, and walked in his commandments, and not after the doings of Israel. For this reason, the Lord was with him and greatly established the kingdom in his hand. This is also the era during which the prophet Elijah began his ministry to the northern kingdom.

In the reign of Jehoshaphat, we are refreshed to see the blessing on Judah that existed under the rule of David and Solomon. Jehoshaphat was serious about reform, and commissioned the Levites and priests to go round about Judah with the scriptures, and teach the people. God responded by placing the fear of the Lord on the nations around Judah, and they would not go to war against them. The Arabians gave Jehoshaphat great gifts of flocks, and even some of the Philistines brought him presents and tributes of silver. Here we see the outworking of Proverbs Chapter 16 verse 7: When a man's ways please the Lord, he maketh even his enemies to be at peace with him. This added wealth was a great blessing, because the very first thing Jehoshaphat had to do when he ascended the throne was strengthen himself against Israel.

In the meantime, a new but dark star was rising over the northern kingdom: Ahab, the son of Omri. Ahab holds the infamous distinction of doing evil in the sight of the Lord above all that were before him, and of provoking the Lord to anger more than all the kings before him. Not only did he continue the sinful practices of Jeroboam, he married the Zidonian princess we know of as Jezebel. This was a Hamitic woman who was a devoted worshiper of Baal. Baal was venerated both as a sun god and a fertility deity. While conducting the research for this book, I found many sources wanted to identify Baal with ancient Semitic peoples. Meaning Shemitic. But we should be clear that although there may have been some people of Shemitic ancestry who elected to worship this deity, this was basically a Phoenician concept, and the Phoenicians were a Hamitic people.

How he ever convinced the righteous king Jehoshaphat to join in league with him is incredulous, considering Ahab's track record in his own domain long before they agreed to go up to battle together against Ramoth-gilead. Besides his offenses in marrying an idolatrous high priestess and rearing an altar to her idol, understanding of God's precepts was so far away from the people he reigned over that a man attempted to rebuild Jericho again, costing the lives of two of his sons. In other words, Ahab did nothing to bring the word of the Lord to the people to protect them from folly and tempting the Lord. He let Jezebel call the shots in the land, and she took full advantage of this by instituting a pogrom on the prophets of the Lord. A godly man who was under the king, Obadiah—hid one hundred of these prophets in two caves by fifty each, and brought them food and water during that dangerous time.

On top of all this, a drought had been going on for three years because of Israel's wickedness, but that didn't stop Ahab and Jezebel. Once Elijah had his showdown with the four hundred and fifty prophets of Baal (one man against four hundred fifty) and the rain returned, Jezebel voiced her determination to kill Elijah, and Ahab didn't even protest.

In spite of this, God wrought a great victory for Ahab, when Ben-hadad, the king of Syria, came against him. The Syrians took a severe beating, and Ben-hadad escaped. However, he planned another campaign against Ahab in about a year, thinking foolishly that Israel's God was only God of the hills, and not a God of the valleys. This new war cost him one hundred thousand footmen in one day, and the rest of his forces fled to a city, but a wall fell on twenty-seven thousand of them there; only Ben-hadad and a few of his servants escaped. The king and his remaining servants approached Ahab and appealed for mercy. Ahab's response was to make a covenant of peace with him. Now this is the same Syrian king that earlier with no provocation had sent messengers to taunt Ahab saying, "Thy silver and thy gold is mine; thy wives also and thy children, even the goodliest, are mine." And when Ahab agreed in hopes of staving off a confrontation, Ben-hadad sent messengers again, saying:

"Although I have sent unto thee, saying, Thou shalt deliver me thy silver, and thy gold, and thy wives, and thy children; Yet I will send my servants unto thee tomorrow about this time, and they shall search thine house, and the houses of thy servants; and it shall be, that whatsoever is pleasant in thine eyes, they shall put it in their hand, and take it away."

Did you catch that? Ben-hadad was really beside himself with arrogance. He didn't say the servants would take whatsoever was pleasant in their eyes...he wants them to take whatever is of most value in Ahab's eyes. In other words, he is trying to really get him where it hurts the most. Yet, Ahab made a covenant of peace with Ben-hadad, because Ben-hadad agreed to restore the cities his father had taken away from Israel, and agreed to let Israel makes streets in Damascus as Ben-hadad's father had made in Israel. So with this agreement he sent him away to his home. This thing displeased the Lord and he sent a prophet to let Ahab know that since he had let go out of his hand a man whom God had appointed to utter destruction, Ahab's life would go for his life, and Ahab's people for Ben-hadad's people. Remember—as in the case of Saul and the Amalekites—God was very serious about the kings in war accomplishing the mission in its entirety.

Ahab must have been depressed in realizing his days were numbered and the doom he had brought upon Israel. But to pile on more transgression by pressuring a man to part with his family inheritance is certainly not the way to make a recovery from sin. Yet this was exactly what the spirit of covetousness incited Ahab to do. Like many in power today, he was totally out of touch with the common laboring man who does not have vast wealth at his disposal and only possesses that which he works for or has been left to him by family.

Pouting and sulking, he said no more to Naboth, the man whose property he wanted, but he knew his melancholy would spur his wife into action. Ultimately, Jezebel framed Naboth using false witnesses and he was stoned to death for blasphemy. Ahab hasted to go claim his ill-gotten possession, but little did he know the prophet Elijah would be waiting there to meet him with a blood-chilling prophecy of his death, that of his posterity, and that of his wicked wife. It took this word from the Lord to bring Ahab to repentance, and because of that, God reserved the bulk of his wrath for Ahab's posterity. So, all this had taken place prior to the time Jehoshaphat and Ahab made a league, because Jehoshaphat was a godly man who desired peace; therefore he made peace with the kings of Israel. It was in this context that Jehoshaphat king of Judah and Ahab king of Israel agreed to go up against the Syrians at Ramoth-gilead. And they called for the prophets of Israel to prophesy and they all prophesied the battle would be victorious.

However, Jehoshaphat had his suspicions, so he asked if there was any other prophet other than these who were all saying the same thing. And Ahab replied there was, but he hated him, because he never said anything good about him, only evil. When a messenger was sent to summon this prophet whose name was Micaiah, the escort tried to prep him to say something good like all the other prophets had. But Micaiah was a true man of God, and he had already made up his mind he was going to speak what God said regardless of the cost. Well, Micaiah first parroted an identical answer, which Ahab could tell was insincere. So he asked for the truth and Micaiah gave it to him. Micaiah's revelation that the Lord had put a lying spirit in the mouth of all the other prophets earned him an assault from one of the lying prophets and a prison sentence of undetermined length, since his release was predicated on Ahab's victorious return from the battle, and Micaiah knew Ahab would not be coming back alive.

Despite the fact the king of Syria had commanded his chariot captains to fight neither with small nor great, save only with the king of Israel, and despite the fact Ahab attempted to disguise himself as a common soldier rather than a king, a certain man shot him, and he continued in the battle until sunset, although he was bleeding heavily the entire time. So in that slow and horrible way, he died. Ahab's rating falls under ugly.

As for Jehoshaphat, he returned to his house in peace. But he was met by a prophet who rebuked him saying, "Shouldest thou help the ungodly, and love them that hate the Lord? therefore is wrath upon thee from before the Lord. Nevertheless there are good things found in thee, in that thou hast taken away the groves out of the land, and hast prepared thine heart to seek God."

Returning safely from battle did not cause Jehoshaphat to become careless and rest on his laurels. He actually went out himself throughout the land and evangelized the people to return to the Lord God of their fathers. Also he set up judges and priests to handle the controversies of the people and exhorted them to judge righteously at all times. Thus,

Jehoshaphat was found in right standing when an adversarial trio conspired to vanquish Judah. This event was the combined assault of Moab, Ammon, and Edom.

Before touching on what has to be one of the most inspirational and oft told stories of the Old Testament, I want to take a moment to remind the people to whom this book is written—the descendants of the Trans-Atlantic slave trade—that these are *our* people we have been talking about in the trials and victories of Judah. When you see how enemies conspired to subdue and annihilate our forefathers out of pure envy and resentment and rejoiced whenever hardship or negative circumstances affected them, it is easy to draw the connection to our present day alienation, the subtle contempt, the veiled disgust and hatred suppressed on the job or during commercial transactions but given full vent in Internet blogs, news article comments, and talk show discourses. Indeed, people themselves may not understand why they feel the way they feel...they just know that's how they feel about the Black person in America. And while they may not be able to put their finger on it, the spirit influencing their outlook knows very well the who, what, and why; because it is a spirit that has kept its hatred forever.

"And Jehoshaphat feared, and set himself to seek the Lord, and proclaimed a fast throughout all Judah. And Judah gathered themselves together, to ask help of the Lord: even out of all the cities of Judah they came to seek the Lord.

And Jehoshaphat stood in the congregation of Judah and Jerusalem, in the house of the Lord, before the new court, And said, "O Lord God of our fathers, art not thou God in heaven? and rulest not thou over all the kingdoms of the heathen? and in thine hand is there not power and might, so that none is able to withstand thee?

Art not thou our God, who didst drive out the inhabitants of this land before thy people Israel, and gavest it to the seed of Abraham thy friend for ever?

And they dwelt therein, and have built thee a sanctuary therein for thy name, saying, If, when evil cometh upon us, as the sword, judgment, or pestilence, or famine, we stand before this house, and in thy presence, (for thy name is in this house,) and cry unto thee in our affliction, then thou wilt hear and help.

And now, behold, the children of Ammon and Moab and mount Seir, whom thou wouldest not let Israel invade, when they came out of the land of Egypt, but they turned from them, and destroyed them not;

Behold, I say, how they reward us, to come to cast us out of thy possession, which thou hast given us to inherit. O our God, wilt thou not judge them? for we have no might against this great company that cometh against us; neither know we what to do: but our eyes are upon thee. And all Judah stood before the Lord, with their little ones, their wives, and their children

Then upon Jahaziel the son of Zechariah, the son of Benaiah, the son of Jeiel, the son of Mattaniah, a Levite of the sons of Asaph, came the Spirit of the Lord in the midst of the congregation; And he said, Hearken ye, all Judah, and ye inhabitants of Jerusalem, and thou king Jehoshaphat, Thus saith the Lord unto you, Be not afraid nor dismayed by reason of this great multitude; for the battle is not yours, but God's.

Tomorrow go ye down against them: behold, they come up by the cliff of Ziz; and ye shall find them at the end of the brook, before the wilderness of Jeruel. Ye shall not need to fight in this battle: set yourselves, stand ye still, and see the salvation of the Lord with you, O Judah and Jerusalem: fear not, nor be dismayed; tomorrow go out against them: for the Lord will be with you.

And Jehoshaphat bowed his head with his face to the ground: and all Judah and the inhabitants of Jerusalem fell before the Lord, worshipping the Lord. And the Levites, of the children of the Kohathites, and of the children of the Korhites, stood up to praise the Lord God of Israel with a loud voice on high. And they rose early in the morning, and went forth into the wilderness of Tekoa: and as they went forth, Jehoshaphat stood and said, Hear me, O Judah, and ye inhabitants of Jerusalem; Believe in the Lord your God, so shall ye be established; believe his prophets, so shall ye prosper.

And when he had consulted with the people, he appointed singers unto the Lord, and that should praise the beauty of holiness, as they went out before the army, and to say, Praise the Lord; for his mercy endureth for ever. And when they began to sing and to praise, the Lord set ambushments against the children of Ammon, Moab, and mount Seir, which were come against Judah; and they were smitten.

For the children of Ammon and Moab stood up against the inhabitants of mount Seir, utterly to slay and destroy them: and when they had made an end of the inhabitants of Seir, every one helped to destroy another.

And when Judah came toward the watch tower in the wilderness, they looked unto the multitude, and, behold, they were dead bodies fallen to the earth, and none escaped.

And when Jehoshaphat and his people came to take away the spoil of them, they found among them in abundance both riches with the dead bodies, and precious jewels, which they stripped off for themselves, more than they could carry away: and they were three days in gathering of the spoil, it was so much.

And on the fourth day they assembled themselves in the valley of Berachah; for there they blessed the Lord: therefore the name of the same place was called, The valley of Berachah, unto this day. Then they returned, every man of Judah and Jerusalem, and Jehoshaphat in the forefront of them, to go again to Jerusalem with joy; for the Lord had made them to rejoice over their enemies.

And they came to Jerusalem with psalteries and harps and trumpets unto the house of the Lord. And the fear of God was on all the kingdoms of those countries, when they had heard that the Lord fought against the enemies of Israel. So the realm of Jehoshaphat was quiet: for his God gave him rest round about."

We should look at this event, and analyze it step by step, because there are many lessons for us as a people trusting God in this Captivity. This was the perfect conflict, countered by the perfect response, dealt with using the perfect battle strategy, resulting in the perfect outcome, and commemorated with the perfect celebration. This was the ideal conflict, because any battle we are able to win on our own does not present the opportunity for faith and trust in

God. Judah was hopelessly outnumbered, and one of the three antagonists was Judah's major hater, Edom.

Jehoshaphat responded to this threat in the perfect manner, because he was already in a position of right standing with God. He had done everything in his power to consecrate himself and the people in holiness to the Lord. He had removed the idols, and commissioned the priests and judges to teach and arbitrate on behalf of the people. Still, rather than trust in his own righteousness before God, he humbled himself in fasting and prayer. Jehoshaphat took the lead in seeking God for help. There was no indication of pride or self-justification. No prophet had to come to him as in the case of Rehoboam, and admonish him or counsel him what steps to take as he was facing this imminent threat. He did not have to preface his petition with, 'O Lord God, we have sinned greatly …'

Jehoshaphat begins with an Old Testament version of the Disciples Prayer…similar to 'Our Father, which art in heaven,' he intones, "O Lord God of our fathers, art not thou God in heaven?" Jehoshaphat knows his history and his heritage, and reminds God of the covenant with Abraham, and Abraham's relationship to God as a friend. He reminds God of the content of Solomon's prayer at the dedication of the temple; that they could stand before the house where God's presence was, and call on him for help in the time of need. Lastly, he reminds God that when his forefathers came up from Egypt, they avoided all conflict with Ammon, Moab, and Edom. These parties know the land Judah occupies was taken from the Canaanites by divine order for Israel, and they already have their own territories and their own gods, yet they still want to take away from Israel what was designated to God's people as a place of worship to God and a light to the nations.

When you peel back all the layers, the core issue is that Ammon, Moab, and Edom hate God, because Judah is synonymous with God. They cannot reach into the heavens and strike down God, so the next best option is to strike God's people. This is why the Lord God would say, "the battle is not yours, but God's." Jehoshaphat asks God to judge this confederacy. He admits he and his people are powerless against such a great multitude, and they have no idea of what to do, and they are looking to God for deliverance.

What happens next is an example of the spiritual way God likes to show forth his power on behalf of his people. The anointing of the Holy Ghost brings the very mind of God concerning this situation to the people. Not a written commandment which has to passed from a mediator to the people, but a direct word from God. To summarize:

*Do not be afraid or dismayed because they are so many

*It's not even your battle…I got this one; this is my battle

*Go down against them tomorrow…this is where you will find them

*You won't even have to fight this battle: stand still and see the salvation of the Lord with you

*Don't be afraid or dismayed; go out against them tomorrow

*For the Lord will be with you

A fitting conclusion to this visitation from God was the worship of the king and people, and the loud resounding praise of the Levites. One can almost feel the sense of excitement in the heavenly realm in the anticipation of what is slated to be a landmark battle in the annals of Judah's history. For this is a battle which will be fought strictly with spiritual weaponry: the shield of faith, high praise which binds the enemy, and the helmet of salvation.

The shield of faith would cover them long before they reached the brook in front of the wilderness of Jeruel, as Jehoshaphat exhorted the people, "Hear me, O Judah, and ye inhabitants of Jerusalem; Believe in the Lord your God, so shall ye be established; believe his prophets, so shall ye prosper."

The weapon of high praise would bring the Lord God right into the presence of the people, for God dwells in the midst of praises, and he inhabits the praises of his people. Attacking Judah would be an attempted assault on God himself, and God was ready ... "and when he had consulted with the people, he appointed singers unto the Lord, and that should praise the beauty of holiness, as they went out before the army, and to say, Praise the Lord; for his mercy endureth for ever." The glorious weapon of high praise, which is uplifting to the ears and spirit of man, and beautiful and most cherished by God, would have the opposite effect on the enemy. It would bring discordance, confusion, and the inability to discern who was a comrade and who was of Judah. The enemy would literally be fighting in blind enragement.

"And when they began to sing and to praise, the Lord set ambushments against the children of Ammon, Moab, and mount Seir, which were come against Judah; and they were smitten. For the children of Ammon and Moab stood up against the inhabitants of mount Seir, utterly to slay and destroy them: and when they had made an end of the inhabitants of Seir, every one helped to destroy another."

It is almost as though the deep melodies and rapturous harmonies of the singer's praises formed each spiritual molecule of the helmet of salvation until it was a formidable piece of armor before which no human or demonic force could withstand. The Hebrew for this word ambushments means to lurk, or lie in wait. Essentially, this confederacy became unable to distinguish between the spiritual and the natural, and they lay in wait for each other. In a sense of poetic justice, initially Edom appeared to be the enemy, and his forces were wiped out by his two compatriots. Imagine after the slaughter of Edom, when each Moabite appeared to Ammon to be Judah, and each Ammonite appeared to Moab as Judah. The confederacy disintegrated in one of the greatest instances of self-annihilation ever recorded.

Judah was three days in carrying back the spoil of the slaughter; an abundance of precious jewels and riches. It was almost as though God had the enemy dress up in their finest attire for the day of their death. On the fourth day, they assembled in the valley of Beracha to bless the Lord before the return to Jerusalem. And they returned with great rejoicing; with Jehoshaphat their king in the lead, and came to Jerusalem with psalteries and harps and trumpets unto the house of the Lord, for the Lord had made them rejoice over their enemies.

There are some who teach that musical instruments have no place in New Testament worship, but I would submit that the most High God is worthy of the most beautiful, soul-stirring

119

and uplifting sounds that man can offer in the sacrifice of praise. Notice they were coming to the house of the Lord with this awesome symphony ...let us never forget we are to enter his gates with thanksgiving in our hearts and come into his courts with praise. Second Chronicles Chapter 29 verse 25 shows that worship and praise with instruments in the house of the Lord is an actual directive from God "...And he set the Levites in the house of the Lord with cymbals, with psalteries, and with harps, according to the commandment of David, and of Gad the king's seer, and Nathan the prophet: for so was the commandment of the Lord by his prophets." David, Gad, and Nathan were all prophets, and David was a king; and where the word of a king is, there is power. Remember, that even at the return of the Lord and our redemption, in the day that the Lord bindeth up the breach of his people, and healeth the stroke of their wound, in every place where the grounded staff shall pass (every place where God shall appoint for punishment and correction of the enemy) it will be with tabrets (which are tambourines) and harps. So we see that God is blessed with music from instruments both in the past, in the present, and that he will even incorporate them into his future correction of the nations.

God is a Spirit; he must be worshiped in spirit and truth. He does things differently in his realm and achieves results that surpass anything contrived by man's logic. Who ever heard of sending a choir out in front of an army facing an enemy who hates you and lives, eats, and breathes your death? Jehoshaphat's experience is very relevant to us as believers in the Captivity. Generally, our forefathers would have to arm up and clash swords, throw spears, shoot arrows, and sling stones. But God provided a glimpse of his heavenly assault strategy, even before the calling out under the New Covenant. Today, we wrestle not with flesh and blood, and the weapons of our warfare are not carnal, but mighty through God to the pulling down of strongholds. Jehoshaphat got an opportunity to witness this firsthand. God has provided his personal arsenal to us, and we should be availing ourselves of it in every battle.

In conclusion, Jehoshaphat recaptured the true spirit of Judah in unity with God as in the days of David and Solomon. Toward the end of his reign, he formed an alliance with the wicked king of the northern tribes, Ahaziah. For this he received a rebuke from the Lord through the prophet Eliezer. It appears Jehoshaphat was a man of peace who deeply desired the reconciliation of the nation. Also, it can be a lonely journey to walk righteously, and it is understandable a ruler would desire a colleague on his level with whom he could fellowship. Nevertheless, light has no fellowship with darkness, and such a confederacy could not be maintained or blessed of God. Jehoshaphat is chronicled as a man who walked in the way of Asa his father, and departed not from it, doing that which was right in the sight of the Lord. Jehoshaphat's rating falls under good.

In the northern kingdom, Ahab's son Ahaziah took the throne, but his reign only lasted two years, because he maintained the wicked ways of his parents. When he suffered a debilitating injury due to a fall, he did not consult the Lord God for healing, but instead sent messengers to inquire of Baalzebub the god of Ekron whether he would recover from his disease or not. But the messengers were intercepted by Elijah the prophet, who told them to go back and tell Ahaziah he was never going to recover. Ahaziah wanted to hear this straight from Elijah himself and attempted to bring him to him by force; that is a whole other story which you can read about in the first Chapter of II Kings. Suffice it to say he died. Ahaziah's rating falls under bad.

In Judah, Jehoshaphat's son Jehoram took the throne. A common saying in the West is, 'the apple doesn't fall far from the tree,' but where Jehoram was concerned, nothing could have been further from the truth. He was a murderer, and once his father was dead and he was secure to the throne, he killed all his brothers, who were better men than he was. He also built high places, and the people of Judah followed this in committing idolatry. On top of all that, he married Ahab's daughter...this only helped him to stay steeped in wickedness.

With rebellion and disobedience comes chastisement from the Lord. The first adversary to be awakened against him was the usual hater Edom, and in rapid succession after that, Libnah, the Philistines, and the Arabians. Generally, the prophet Elijah ministered to the northern kingdom, but Jehoram's conduct earned him a letter from the prophet predicting the great plague which would befall him and his house. This manifested when God smote him with a severe disease that caused his intestines to gradually fall out. This malady opened him up to other opportunistic infections and he essentially died a human wreck. Jehoram's rating falls under bad.

Whether it was the yoking of Israel to Judah via the bringing of Ahab's daughter to the southern kingdom or mere circumstance remains to be determined, but for some reason the political intrigue and assassinations common to the northern kingdom began to increasingly manifest in the southern kingdom. Once the influence from the northern kingdom flowed to the south, Judah received evil counsel. In some cases, the bloodshed would be by divine decree as an execution of judgment, but other times it was a result of vindictiveness and an attempt to hold on to the throne. Fellowship between the northern and southern kings cost some of them their lives.

God had appointed Jehu the son of Nimshi to destroy the house of Ahab. Ahaziah king of Judah had gone to visit Joram, king of Israel, and got caught up in the slaughter. When Ahaziah's mother, Queen Athaliah—got word of her son's death, she had all the royal seed of Judah murdered. She thought she got them all, but the king's daughter rescued Joash, one of Ahaziah's sons; and he was secretly raised in the temple for six years, under the tutelage of Jehoida the priest. In his seventh year, the youth was revealed to the people and anointed king in Judah. Queen Athaliah—a Baal worshiper, was killed, the land purged of the Baalim, and Judah saw revival and rededication under the reign of Joash and the guiding counsel of Jehoida.

Once Jehoida died though, Joash turned out of the way in trying to please the princes of Judah. This brought wrath from God on Judah and Jerusalem. The Holy Ghost came upon Zechariah—the son of the deceased priest—and rebuked and admonished the people for the return to idolatry. A conspiracy was formed against Zechariah, and at the king's commandment he was stoned to death. Thus Joash the king remembered not the kindness which Jehoida his adoptive father had done to him, but slew his son.

Ultimately Syria, the perennial enemy, came against Judah and spoiled it. Joash was left with debilitating illness, and his servants (ironically an Ammonite and a Moabite) killed him on his own bed.

His son Amaziah reigned in his stead, and after avenging his father's murder, began a campaign on the Edomites. He was successful in his venture, so it is difficult to understand why he brought the gods of the Edomites back to Judah and bowed down before them and burned incense to them. God sent a prophet to him to ask him, why he was seeking after gods who could not deliver their own people? This rebuke earned the prophet a threat on his life, but not before he prophesied that God was determined to destroy Amaziah. Amaziah's own pride led him to march against the king of Israel, and his apostasy opened the door for a conspiracy against him that resulted in his death.

In the northern kingdom, Jehoahaz took the throne after Jehu, but he wrought evil in the sight of the Lord. Because the people hesitate to reform unless the leader does, Israel found itself under Syrian oppression again. At this point, Jehoahaz sought the Lord, and the Lord gave them a savior to deliver them from the Syrians.

After Jehoahaz' death, his son Joash ruled. This was the Israelite king that Amaziah pridefully challenged without provocation. He also walked in the evil ways of the Jeroboam who originally set Israel up to sin with the golden calves. His reign lasted sixteen years.

In Judah, Uzziah was made king. He was a young man when he began to reign, and his rule lasted fifty-two years. He is described as having done that which was right in the sight of the Lord. The writer of Chronicles makes an interesting observation about Uzziah:

"...he sought God in the days of Zechariah, who had understanding in the visions of God: and as long as he sought the Lord, God made him to prosper... And his name spread far abroad; for he was marvellously helped, till he was strong." This is still true today ...if you seek God and align yourself with people who are spiritually minded and spiritually strong, you will prosper, and if God helps you, you will be strong beyond means that you could ever bring to pass by yourself. Uzziah was a well-rounded person, meaning he had diverse interests and skills. He loved animal husbandry, he was a gifted civil engineer, and he also developed cutting edge battle gear for his military forces.

But when he was strong, his heart was lifted up to his destruction: for he transgressed against the Lord his God, and went into the temple of the Lord to burn incense upon the altar of incense. Azariah the priest took eighty priests with him that were not afraid to confront the king and they withstood him and reminded him it was only for the consecrated priests—the sons of Aaron—to burn incense...and they told him to go out of the sanctuary. Uzziah became enraged, but even as he was furious with them God struck him with leprosy and they forcefully removed him from the temple...he himself did not resist at this point. And he was a leper until his death.

His son Jotham reigned in his stead; he did that which was right in the sight of the Lord. The citizens of Judah were behaving corruptly, but Jotham still served the Lord. The scripture says, "... Jotham became mighty, because he prepared his ways before the Lord his God." This was really commendable considering that Jotham was a young man when he began to rule, and he was determined to walk righteously even if nobody else was going to walk with him. God gave him a great victory over the Ammonites, and they were forced to pay tribute to him.

In the northern kingdom, the second king named Jeroboam came to the throne, and held it for forty-one years. He did not depart from the idolatry Israel was steeped in. However, he did recover territory Israel had lost due to the oppression of the Syrians. After his death, his son Zechariah reigned. But his reign was very short-lived; just six months. He walked in evil idolatrous ways, and Shallum the son of Jabesh attacked him right in front of the people and assassinated him, then took the throne for himself. Zechariah was the fourth generation son of Jehu—who executed God's wrath against the house of Ahab. Even though Jehu cared little for the actual service of the Lord, God had promised him his sons would sit on the throne to the fourth generation, and God was faithful to his word.

At this point, we are pretty much looking at a race to the bottom where the northern kingdom is concerned. Shallum's conspiracy and violence against Zechariah only earned him one month on the throne, for Menahem of Tirzah came up to Samaria and assassinated him, and reigned in his stead. Menahem was likewise an idolater; and for this reason God allowed Pul (also known as Tiglath-pileser) the king of Assyria to come against the land. Menahem came up with the idea of paying Pul off with a bribe of a thousand talents of silver in exchange for him calling off his campaign. He exacted fifty shekels of silver from each mighty man of wealth to fulfill the bribe. Just so you can get an idea of how many people had to pay up, three thousand shekels equals one talent, and Pul's bribe was a thousand talents.

Menahem's son Pekahiah—continuing the practice of idolatry—took the throne upon his father's death, but he was only in power for two years before Pekah, a relative of one of his military captains conspired against him and killed him. Pekah—perpetuating the idolatry, held the throne for twenty years. It was in his days that Tiglath-pileser began to overrun the northern kingdom and take the people captive into Assyria. In perfect alignment with the law of sowing and reaping, Hoshea the son of Elah conspired against Pekah, and killed him. Hoshea assumed the throne, but his reign was only good for nine years. By that time, Assyria had a firm and unrelenting grip on Samaria. Hoshea committed evil, but not to the extent that the kings before him had done. The rulership changed in Assyria, and Hoshea had to contend with Shalmaneser, and he became subject to him and had to pay forced tribute. When Hoshea got tired of paying the annual levy, he sent messengers to So—king of Egypt, in hopes of getting help to throw off the yoke of Assyria. But Shalmaneser found out about the conspiracy, threw Hoshea in prison, and declared a war on Samaria that lasted three years. At the end of this battle, the Assyrian king exiled all the inhabitants of the northern kingdom and placed them in the cities of Halah and Habor. The tribes deported expressly by name are Reuben, Gad, and the half tribe of Manasseh. This exile removed them approximately seven hundred miles north and east of their home.

In the southern kingdom of Judah, Ahaz ascended the throne. Unfortunately, he chose to walk in the ways of the northern kingdom. He caused his son to pass through the fire, burnt incense in the high places, and sacrificed on the hills and under every green tree. He took treasures from the house of the Lord, and used them to try to bribe the king of Assyria, but it didn't do him any good. When the king of Syria and king Pekah of Israel began a military campaign against him, instead of repenting and invoking the covenant of Abraham, Isaac, and Jacob, he said to Tiglath-pileser, "I am thy son and thy servant; come up and deliver me out of the hand of the king of Syria, and out of the hand of the king of Israel, which rise up against me. And in the time of his distress did he trespass yet more against the Lord: this is that king Ahaz.

For he sacrificed unto the gods of Damascus, which smote him: and he said, Because the gods of the kings of Syria help them, therefore will I sacrifice to them, that they may help me. But they were the ruin of him, and of all Israel.

And Ahaz gathered together the vessels of the house of God, and cut in pieces the vessels of the house of God, and shut up the doors of the house of the Lord, and he made him altars in every corner of Jerusalem.

And in every several city of Judah he made high places to burn incense unto other gods, and provoked to anger the Lord God of his fathers."

Further, while going to meet the king of Assyria, he saw a pagan altar, and liked the way it looked so much, he had the pattern of it sent to the priest in Jerusalem so one like it could be made for him. And the priest went along with it. Neither does it look like anyone tried to stop Ahaz when he began marring and modifying the fixtures in the house of the Lord. He even shut up the doors to the house of the Lord! Here was a king who did not have the best interest of his people in mind, for the scripture says, "...the Lord brought Judah low because of Ahaz king of Israel; for he made Judah naked, and transgressed sore against the Lord. But God was not done showing mercy to Judah; on the contrary, he had a vessel waiting in the wings that would bring renewed dedication and revival among the people.

King Hezekiah set his heart to turn Judah and Israel back to the Lord God of their fathers. Immediately upon taking the throne, he opened the doors of the Lord's house and repaired them. He commanded the priests to sanctify themselves and cleanse the house of the Lord. The priests and the Levites undertook this challenge to completion, and also re-supplied the temple with the furnishings Ahaz had removed. With this done, the house of the Lord was properly prepared so that the priests could sacrifice and make atonement for the people. He also reinstated the musical worship. Once the people had been consecrated, they could bring their offerings to the Lord. It was a beautiful time of spiritual renewal, "And Hezekiah rejoiced, and all the people, that God had prepared the people: for the thing was done suddenly."

Have you ever been excited about a spiritual breakthrough, and been eager to share it with others so that they too might be encouraged to press on to victory? This was surely how Hezekiah felt as he dispatched invitations throughout all Judah and Israel to join him in observance of the Passover. In his communication, Hezekiah invoked the covenant God made with Abraham, Isaac, and Jacob as the incentive to honor the deliverance from Egypt. It is sad to say that upon receiving the invitation, the majority of the people laughed the messengers to scorn and mocked them. Nevertheless, God always has a remnant, and some people from the tribes of Asher and Manasseh humbled themselves and made the journey to Jerusalem. After keeping the Passover, the priests the Levites arose and blessed the people: and their voice was heard, and their prayer came up to God's holy dwelling place, even unto heaven. Spiritual renewal is followed by holy boldness, and after the completion of the Passover, the people went out to the cities of Judah and destroyed the images and groves, and demolished the high places and altars.

It is always better to be found in the place of righteousness when Satanic attack occurs, than to be given up by God for persecution because of rebellion. Right standing with God was Hezekiah's position when Sennacherib king of Assyria began his psychological warfare campaign against Judah. The object was to weaken the people's trust in the Living God and turn them against their godly king. Hezekiah had exhorted the people to "Be strong and courageous, be not afraid nor dismayed for the king of Assyria, nor for all the multitude that is with him: for there be more with us than with him: With him is an arm of flesh; but with us is the Lord our God to help us, and to fight our battles. And the people rested themselves upon the words of Hezekiah king of Judah."

This resistance of faith in the spiritual realm incited Sennacherib and his envoys to blaspheme the Lord God of Israel. They made certain to speak these things in the Judæans' language, so that the people would lose faith and surrender the city. But a powerful force was unleashed when the godly king and the prophet of the Lord Isaiah prayed together and cried to heaven. Their petition brought an angel which destroyed all Sennacherib's leaders, captains, and mighty men of valor. So he returned with shame of face to his own land. And when he went into the house of his idol god to worship, his own sons murdered him.

Sometime after this, King Hezekiah became ill, and God showed him that he would die. Many are familiar with the story of how Hezekiah prayed for the Lord to spare his life, and the sign God showed him by moving the shadow ten degrees backward. This means God actually moved the sun retrograde in its route across the sky.

True to human nature, Hezekiah became lifted up in pride and showed the magnificence of his wealth to the ambassadors of the princes of Babylon, who sent unto him to inquire of the wonder that was done in the land. This thing was from God, to test him, that he might know all that was in his heart. But he repented of his pride, and is chronicled as a king that "did that which was right in the sight of the Lord, according to all that David his father had done," and that "wrought that which was good and right and truth before the Lord his God. And in every work that he began in the service of the house of God, and in the law, and in the commandments, to seek his God, he did it with all his heart, and prospered."

Seeing Hezekiah's dedication to the Lord his God makes one wonder what was going on with his son Manasseh. Granted he was young when he began to reign at twelve years old, but there were other kings as young or younger when placed on the throne who walked righteously. Manasseh chose to depart from the way of righteousness, and descended to a level of wickedness heretofore unknown in Judah. In fact, the scripture says Manasseh seduced them to do more evil than did the nations whom the Lord destroyed before the children of Israel. Whereas the sin of pride caused some kings to stumble and sin, it seems as though Manasseh intentionally pushed the envelope as far as he could. It was almost like he had an oppositional-defiant spirit designed to undo all the good his father Hezekiah had done. In the fifty-five years he reigned, he succeeded in reversing much of the spiritual progress his father wrought.

What makes evil appear so attractive that people are willing to risk the wrath of God? It can only be a seducing spirit influencing a divided heart and prideful mind. Manasseh built again the high places his father Hezekiah had destroyed. He erected altars for Baal, and made a grove, like Ahab did. He worshiped all the host of heaven, and actually built altars for them in the two courts of the Lord! He caused his children to pass through the fire in the valley of the son of Hinnom: also he observed times, and used enchantments, and used witchcraft, and dealt with a familiar spirit, and with wizards: he wrought much evil in the sight of the Lord, to provoke him to anger. And he set a carved image, the idol which he had made, in the house of God. On top of all this, he shed innocent blood very much, till he had filled Jerusalem from one end to another.

Leaders must lead by example, and where much is given, much is required. Manasseh made Judah and the inhabitants of Jerusalem to err, and to do worse than the heathen, whom the Lord had destroyed before the children of Israel. And the Lord spake to Manasseh, and to his people: but they would not hearken. For these egregious violations, the Lord brought upon them the captains of the host of the king of Assyria, which took Manasseh among the thorns, and bound him with fetters, and carried him to Babylon. Where were Manasseh's idols now? Could the starry host of heaven save him? Did Baal help him? No, what happened was, that "Manasseh found himself in affliction, he besought the Lord his God, and humbled himself greatly before the God of his fathers, And prayed unto him: and he was intreated of him, and heard his supplication, and brought him again to Jerusalem into his kingdom. Then Manasseh knew that the Lord he was God."

After this, Manasseh brought forth the fruit of repentance in taking away the strange gods, and the idol out of the house of the Lord, and all the altars that he had built in the mount of the house of the Lord, and in Jerusalem, and cast them out of the city. And he repaired the altar of the Lord, and sacrificed thereon peace offerings and thank offerings, and commanded Judah to serve the Lord God of Israel.

It is always heartrending when one has to learn experientially by pain and disgrace rather than by faith and trust in the Lord. This is what it took to bring Manasseh to his senses. Yet, Manasseh's story is an important lesson to us about God's mercy, and how he deals with Judah as sons, chastening and correcting. Manasseh did more evil than all the kings of Judah before him, as though he were in competition with Ahab of Israel. Yet, when Manasseh repented and begged God's forgiveness, God heard him and restored him to his kingdom. The Lord Jesus Christ said, "joy shall be in heaven over one sinner that repenteth, more than over ninety and nine just persons, which need no repentance." Also God told Moses, "I will have mercy on whom I will have mercy, and I will have compassion on whom I will have compassion." God's ways are higher than our ways, and his thoughts higher than our thoughts. There is no sinner too difficult for God to reach, and no heart so hard that his Spirit cannot deal with it and convict it. We can only be in awe of God's mercies and capacity to forgive and restore.

The actions of Manasseh's son Amon, who was next on the throne, resulted in a short-lived reign and conspiratorial death. As if learning nothing from his father's humiliation at the hands of the king of Assyria, he sacrificed to the carved images his father had made, and served them. He did not repent and humble himself as his father did, but trespassed more and more. And his servants conspired against him, and slew him in his own house. But the people of the land slew all them that had conspired against king Amon; and the people of the land made Josiah his son king in his stead.

Josiah was only eight years old when he began to reign, but he quickly began seeking after the God of David his father, and declined neither to the right hand, or to the left. Seeking God leads to clarity of direction, and by the twelfth year of his reign he began to purge Judah and Jerusalem from the high places, and the groves, and the carved images, and the molten images. "And they brake down the altars of Baalim in his presence; and the images, that were on high above them, he cut down; and the groves, and the carved images, and the molten images, he brake in pieces, and made dust of them, and strowed it upon the graves of them that had sacrificed unto them. And he burnt the bones of the priests upon their altars, and cleansed Judah and Jerusalem."

In the eighteenth year of his reign after he had purged the land, Josiah commissioned the men of God to repair the house of the Lord. While they were working in the house of the Lord, Hilkiah the priest found a book of the Law of the Lord given by Moses. Hilkiah gave the book to Shaphan the scribe, and the scribe read the book to the king. "And it came to pass, when the king had heard the words of the Law, that he rent his clothes. Go, inquire of the Lord for me, and for them that are left in Israel and in Judah, concerning the words of the book that is found: for great is the wrath of the Lord that is poured out upon us, because our fathers have not kept the word of the Lord, to do after all that is written in this book. And Hilkiah, and they that the king had appointed, went to Huldah the prophetess, to speak with her about the things written in the book.

And she answered them, Thus saith the Lord God of Israel, Tell ye the man that sent you to me, Thus saith the Lord, Behold, I will bring evil upon this place, and upon the inhabitants thereof, even all the curses that are written in the book which they have read before the king of Judah: Because they have forsaken me, and have burned incense unto other gods, that they might provoke me to anger with all the works of their hands; therefore my wrath shall be poured out upon this place, and shall not be quenched. And as for the king of Judah, who sent you to inquire of the Lord, so shall ye say unto him, Thus saith the Lord God of Israel concerning the words which thou hast heard; Because thine heart was tender, and thou didst humble thy self before God, when thou heardest his words against this place, and against the inhabitants thereof, and humbledst thy self before me, and didst rend thy clothes, and weep before me; I have even heard thee also, saith the Lord. Behold, I will gather thee to thy fathers, and thou shalt be gathered to thy grave in peace, neither shall thine eyes see all the evil that I will bring upon this place, and upon the inhabitants of the same. So they brought the king word again.

Then the king sent and gathered together all the elders of Judah and Jerusalem. And the king went up into the house of the Lord, and all the men of Judah, and the inhabitants of Jerusalem, and the priests, and the Levites, and all the people, great and small: and he read in their ears all the words of the book of the covenant that was found in the house of the Lord. And the king stood in his place, and made a covenant before the Lord, to walk after the Lord, and to keep his commandments, and his testimonies, and his statutes, with all his heart, and with all his soul, to perform the words of the covenant which are written in this book. And he caused all that were present in Jerusalem and Benjamin to stand to it. And the inhabitants of Jerusalem did according to the covenant of God, the God of their fathers. And Josiah took away all the abominations out of all the countries that pertained to the children of Israel, and made all that were present in Israel to serve, even to serve the Lord their God. And all his days they departed not from following the Lord, the God of their fathers."

During the eighteenth year of Josiah's reign, he kept the Passover. The scripture says that there was no Passover like to that kept in Israel from the days of Samuel the prophet; neither did all the kings of Israel keep such a Passover as Josiah kept, and the priests, and the Levites, and all Judah and Israel that were present, and the inhabitants of Jerusalem.

It seems as though there is a pattern whereby the spirit of pride always attempts to undermine those kings which walked righteously before the Lord. After all this, when Josiah had prepared the temple, Necho king of Egypt came up to fight against Carchemish by Euphrates: and Josiah went out against him.

"But he sent ambassadors to him, saying, What have I to do with thee, thou king of Judah? I come not against thee this day, but against the house wherewith I have war: for God commanded me to make haste: forbear thee from meddling with God, who is with me, that he destroy thee not."

Nevertheless, Josiah would not turn his face from him, but disguised himself, that he might fight with him, and hearkened not unto the words of Necho from the mouth of God, and came to fight in the valley of Megiddo. Josiah was wounded by the archers, and was brought back to Jerusalem, where he died. He cut his own life short by prideful disobedience, for the scripture clearly says Necho's words were from the mouth of God. Can God speak to the ruler of a nation not expressly called to be his people? God certainly can and God does, even in this time. This is one reason we are exhorted to pray for our rulers; not so their wicked devices can come to fruition, but so we can live quiet and peaceable lives. Josiah could not have known whether the conflict in Carchemish was for the benefit of Judah, to subdue a force that might have prematurely attacked his nation. The name Carchemish means fortress of Chemosh; the supreme deity of the Moabites. Therefore, Josiah should have listened, and let Pharaoh Necho carry out this mission without interference.

After his death, Josiah's son Jehoahaz became king. But he was put down by the king of Egypt, who caused his brother Eliakim to become king over Judah and Jerusalem, and turned his name to Jehoiakim. And Necho took Jehoahaz his brother, and carried him to Egypt. Jehoiakim did evil in the sight of the Lord, and held the throne for eleven years, until Nebuchadnezzar king of Babylon bound him in fetters, and carried him to Babylon. It was this same Jehoiakim that cast the scroll of Jeremiah's words from the Lord into the fire, angry about the prophecy of exile to Babylon.

Next, Jehoiakim's son Jehoiachin sat upon the throne in Judah; also doing evil in the sight of the Lord, and his brief reign lasted all of three months and ten days, before he too, wound up in Babylon. Nebuchadnezzar made his brother Zedekiah king over Judah and Jerusalem. Zedekiah was the last king to reign in the Judæan dynasty, ruling during the ministry of the prophet Jeremiah. He did that which was evil in the sight of the Lord his God, and humbled not himself before Jeremiah the prophet speaking from the mouth of the Lord. And he also rebelled against king Nebuchadnezzar, who had made him swear by God: but he stiffened his neck, and hardened his heart from turning unto the Lord God of Israel. For this, king Nebuchadnezzar killed Zedekiah's sons before his eyes, then put out Zedekiah's eyes. He spent the remainder of his life blind in a Chaldean prison.

Israel was the possession of a God who had done what no other deity had ever or could ever do: delivered his people en masse from forced labor and a tyrannical oppressor, miraculously escorted them through a sea bed on dry ground, drowned the oppressor and his forces attempting to recapture them, supernaturally sustained them throughout a decades long trek in a hostile environment, and subdued their enemies. After all this, Israel's attitude was, "Everything would be perfect if we only had a king like all the other nations." Somewhere in the midst of the growing pains of the young nation, they forgot they were called to be peculiar treasure, a kingdom of priests, and a holy nation unto God. If Israel was destined to be a light to the nations, it was a reversal of progress to begin handling their affairs in the same manner as the other nations.

God wanted the nations all around to see what it was like for a people whose God was the Lord in every aspect of life. He wanted the nations to see how blessed all ethnicities would be if they trusted Him alone, and learned his ways and precepts. Remember, Satan stood to oppose God and turn man's heart away from the true and living God: a mission made all the easier by the deception in Eden, which transformed man's heart from innocence to deceitfulness and desperate wickedness. The battle has always been for the hearts and souls of men upon the earth; hence the prayerful petition for God's kingdom to come on earth. There were way fewer people upon the earth when Israel came out of Egypt than there are now. Can you imagine if our forefathers had followed wholeheartedly after God and been that true salt and light before the nations? Once two or three nations joined Israel in serving the Lord and others saw how blessed they were, the futility of trusting in vain idols made by men's hands would have been obvious.

So did transitioning from an absolute theocracy to a monarchy that was obligated to recognize God as the overarching and final authority help or hinder our forefathers in reaching the spiritual goal their Maker set for them? From what we have seen, Israel tends to have a real follow-the-leader mentality. When the king was godly and sought the Lord, the people were inclined to do the same, and the idolaters in the midst had great reason to fear. When the king and the prophet and the priests came together with one accord, evil was purged, revival was kindled in the hearts of the people, and the nation became a formidable force in the earth. But when the king cast the Abrahamic covenant behind him, embraced idolatry, and began to persecute and kill the prophets, the nation was dragged down with him. Further, when a king did wickedly, but repented at the last—such as Manasseh—the king himself might be spared immediate judgment, but the judgment would inevitably fall upon the posterity. Kings held great responsibility for the well-being of the people they ruled, and many failed miserably in this aspect.

Let's look at the final analysis in kingship experience, first with the northern kingdom Israel, as found in II Kings Chapter 17, verses 7-18.

"For so it was, that the children of Israel had sinned against the Lord their God, which had brought them up out of the land of Egypt, from under the hand of Pharaoh king of Egypt, and had feared other gods,

And walked in the statutes of the heathen, whom the Lord cast out from before the children of Israel, and of the kings of Israel, which they had made.

And the children of Israel did secretly those things that were not right against the Lord their God, and they built them high places in all their cities, from the tower of the watchmen to the fenced city.

And they set them up images and groves in every high hill, and under every green tree:

And there they burnt incense in all the high places, as did the heathen whom the Lord carried away before them; and wrought wicked things to provoke the Lord to anger:

For they served idols, whereof the Lord had said unto them, Ye shall not do this thing.

Yet the Lord testified against Israel, and against Judah, by all the prophets, and by all the seers, saying, Turn ye from your evil ways, and keep my commandments and my statutes, according to all the law which I commanded your fathers, and which I sent to you by my servants the prophets.

Notwithstanding they would not hear, but hardened their necks, like to the neck of their fathers, that did not believe in the Lord their God.

And they rejected his statutes, and his covenant that he made with their fathers, and his testimonies which he testified against them; and they followed vanity, and became vain, and went after the heathen that were round about them, concerning whom the Lord had charged them, that they should not do like them.

And they left all the commandments of the Lord their God, and made them molten images, even two calves, and made a grove, and worshipped all the host of heaven, and served Baal.

And they caused their sons and their daughters to pass through the fire, and used divination and enchantments, and sold themselves to do evil in the sight of the Lord, to provoke him to anger.

Therefore the Lord was very angry with Israel, and removed them out of his sight: there was none left but the tribe of Judah only."

And Judah?

"Also Judah kept not the commandments of the Lord their God, but walked in the statutes of Israel which they made." II Kings Chapter 17, verse 19.

After God's miraculous intervention to honor his covenant with Abraham, Isaac, and Jacob, and transform the nation into a unique and precious resource that would shine as a light unto the Gentiles, Israel's response was to:

*Reverence other gods

*Walk in the statutes of the heathen

*Demand a king

*Begin secret societies: worshiping on elevated heights which on the surface appeared to be for the worship of the Lord but were really for other gods

*Set up images and groves in the fertile places for fertility worship

*Burn incense in the high places

*Make wicked things

*Serve idols (the visual representation of the demonic entity)

*Refuse to listen to the prophets

*Harden their neck just as if they were an unbeliever

*Reject God's statutes and testimonies

*Reject the Abrahamic Covenant

*Actively pursue the idolatries of the neighboring heathen nations

*Forsake all the commandments of God

*Make molten images—representative of a fertility deity

*Make a grove

*Worship all the host of heaven

*Worship Baal

*Practice fiery human sacrifice

*Use divination and enchantments

*Literally sell their souls

When parsed in this manner, it becomes very clear why our forefathers were forcibly removed from the land, brought low, and carried into bondage. **As a people, we need to revisit the concept of God's honor**. He called our forefathers, covenanted with them, took the first step in preserving them and their seed, and performed many great miracles to demonstrate his power and faithfulness as he brought them into the land promised to their fathers.

The way they repaid him can be compared to Israel wading in human waste, then using God's pristine, white robe set with precious stones to wipe off their feet. They didn't value him or his care and faithfulness to them. They just didn't care. When their enemies attacked, they had no problem crying out to God for deliverance. But as soon as the coast was clear, they wanted him out of sight and out of mind. Perhaps the greatest insult was that by the time the Lord Jesus Christ arrived to reconcile the lost sheep of Israel, the people who just couldn't do without a flesh and blood king found themselves under the jurisdiction of an Edomite monarch, who himself was bound to answer to another pagan Gentile power.

We have spent a great deal of time on this subject, and now I will tell you why. It is because as a people, many of us still desire a king to go before us like all the other nations. This concept was displeasing to God in the days of Samuel the prophet, and it is equally displeasing to God today. With the 2008 United States presidential election, many were under the impression that a king had finally manifested to go forth on their behalf. By now, most if not all realize that was not the case. The Black man in the West is under a Captivity prophesied thousands of years ago—a bondage that only the Lord God can terminate. Kings do not rule during a Captivity. And providing the king is indeed of the heritage of Judah, the king would of necessity be in the Captivity, too. However, this is not likely, as a comparison of the previous captivities (Egypt and Babylon) demonstrate no Hebrew king ever exercised rule over his subjects while in bondage.

Further, Hosea Chapter 3 verses 4-5 tell us "the children of Israel shall abide many days without a king, and without a prince, and without a sacrifice, and without an image, and without an ephod, and without teraphim: Afterward shall the children of Israel return, and seek the Lord their God, and David their king; and shall fear the Lord and his goodness in the latter days."

As New Covenant believers, we should honor the nation's ruler within the context of I Peter Chapter 2 verse 17. But when it comes to an actual Deliverer, expect only one sovereign to appear on the scene to lead Captivity captive: the Risen Lamb and Conquering Lion who identified with us as a people and came first to us as his own. Hours before the crucifixion of the Lord Jesus Christ, the chief priests among our forebears foolishly insisted, "We have no king but Cæsar." Today, as joint-heirs with Christ, and members of a royal priesthood, we should be exhorting each other, "We have no king, but the Lord Jesus Christ: the Lion of the Tribe of Judah!"

Judgment for Disobedience

"For the Lord shall smite Israel, as a reed is shaken in the water, and he shall root up Israel out of this good land, which he gave to their fathers, and shall scatter them beyond the river, because they have made their groves, provoking the Lord to anger. And he shall give Israel up because of the sins of Jeroboam, who did sin, and who made Israel to sin..." I Kings Chapter 14 verse 15.

Our forefathers had been warned repeatedly since the time they came up out of Egypt that God would not tolerate wickedness and idolatry in the land. The Northern kingdom was finally carried away by the Assyrians and relocated in the cities of the Medes and the territories of Halah and Habor near the river Gozan. The Assyrian king took them and forcibly repopulated them in a direction north and east of the land of Israel.

Among these that were carried away, they took counsel among themselves, that they would leave the multitude of the heathen, and go forth into a further country, where never mankind dwelt, that they might there keep their statutes, which they never kept in their own land. And the account goes on to reveal how "they entered into Euphrates by the narrow places of the river...for the most High then shewed signs for them, and held still the flood, till they were passed over. For through that country there was a great way to go, namely, of a year and a half: and the same region is called Arsareth." If you never heard this before, it is found in II Esdras Chapter 13, in the Apocrypha; the collection of books that someone had a vested interest in removing from the Bible. It would not have been out of the question for those who escaped the Assyrian Captivity to flee crossing water and vast land masses. The Mayans of the Yucatan peninsula possess a legend that they migrated from the Far East. One version of this maintains they walked on dry ground while God held the sea still for them as attested to in the Apocryphal account.

The reason this bears such serious import is that the indigenous peoples found by the earliest European explorers to the Western lands (including North, Meso (or Central) and South America and surrounding islands) were dark and/or brown skinned—some with distinct Negroid features—and these predated the Trans-Atlantic slave trade. There were people already present in the west such as those called the California Blacks and the Washitaw Nation which inhabited the region of the Louisiana territories. Stone carvings from an even earlier time period confirm the Meso-American Olmecs were a negroid race. Even many 'native American' peoples originally had much more melanin in their skin, though today many are nearly indistinguishable from Europeans. Further, people assumed by the explorers to be "Indian" on both the North and South American continents were witnessed conducting rituals with striking similarities to the Old Covenant commandments and feasts, such as circumcision, a special booth celebration, and observance of new moons. Even the speech contained some fragmentary similarities to ancient Hebrew language.

Although the counsel of Israel was that they would go forth into a further country, where never mankind dwelt, that they might there keep their statutes, which they never kept in their own land, we must remember that by the time of exile the northern kingdom was seriously compromised by a centuries long association with idolatry. Being without the true God, a prophet, or a teaching priest, they were left with only what was committed to memory. For this reason, in addition to the remnant of Mosaic covenant observance they retained, the spirituality of the indigenous tribes of the Western world also incorporated what would be considered certain pagan beliefs and practices. Thus we see here as in Africa, the sacred totems, the wood and stone images; the belief in spirit force inhabiting animals and nature, or the use of hallucinogens during ceremonial observances. At the extreme some of these relocated Shemites reverted to ritualistic human sacrifice—the very same thing that got them expelled from the land promised to them by covenant.

The contrast of nature worship or the blending of it with monotheism prompted the missionaries accompanying the explorers to attempt to convert the natives to Christianity. Unfortunately, the light they brought with them was also darkness, due to the great divide between Catholic doctrine and the simplicity of the gospel delivered to the first century Hebrew church. And even if the doctrine had been pure, it would have been compromised by ministers of God associating themselves with the covetous explorers, who cared nothing for the people and only lusted after the rich resources of the Western lands; driven by their desire for wealth and the name they would make for themselves.

Thus we see that the northern kingdom really was scattered to the four winds. We also see that no matter where on the earth these dispersed people ended up, the Europeans also eventually arrived to subjugate them and appropriate themselves of the people's resources. Not only would the people's sovereignty and resources be removed, but their distinctive ethnicity was gradually diminished. The loss of sovereignty and resources is tied to the curses of Deuteronomy Chapter 28.

The lightening of the skin of the indigenous Western peoples can be directly attributed to the fulfillment of Noah's prophecy regarding God enlarging Japheth, with the end result that he would dwell in Shem's tents. The Hebrew word used for dwell in this instance 'shakan'—implies the idea of lodging, continuing, or permanently staying, and stems from a similar Hebrew word 'shakab" which means to lie down, for rest, including sexual connection. This same definition of dwell is directly connected to yet another Hebrew word—sikluwth; which means silliness, folly, or foolishness. The unusual correlation between dwelling, procreating, and folly seems confusing until we recall the Hebrew translation of the word for God enlarging Japheth— 'pathah'—which we defined earlier as meaning to open, be roomy in a mental or moral sense- to be or make simple or in a sinister way delude, to allure, deceive, enlarge, entice, flatter, persuade, silly (one).

What this means in terms of what we now see in the present is evidence that wherever the descendants of Shem 'set up tents', inevitably the albino descendants of Japheth would arrive to reside, and establish permanent residence. They would further entrench themselves by physically mixing with the Shemitic and Hamitic peoples. Where the folly and foolishness comes in is the need to lie and remove critical scriptural and historical resources in an attempt to blot out the identity of God's covenant people, that they might rewrite history and substitute their own version. **There are no 'Lost Tribes'; only a scattered people**.

The Lost Tribes myth is a contrivance of Esau's people which permits him to "discover" that his Anglo forebears were actually the descendants of Jacob. Between the Anglo people assuming the role of the northern tribes, and the Euro-Judaics assuming the role of the tribe of Judah, the conspiracy to erase and replace is implemented. This is the Edomite spirit of envy that goads the spiritually profane person to displace and discredit so that he might have the blessing of both worlds—spiritual and natural. Generations have been taught his account which casts him in the favorable role of undisputed conqueror and legitimate heir wherever he dwells. But in these last days, the words of the Lord Jesus Christ are fulfilled that "there is nothing covered, that shall not be revealed; and hid, that shall not be known. If God said he would scatter Israel to the four winds, then that is exactly where they went, and that is exactly where they still are. God tells us in Proverbs Chapter 11 verse 21 that "Though hand join in hand, the wicked shall not be unpunished: but the seed of the righteous shall be delivered." It does not matter how much the oppressor attempts to blend in, distort history, twist scripture, or claim he was the one that got scattered. Nothing has escaped God's eyes during man's occupancy of the earth, the rise and fall of kingdoms, or counsel taken in secret. God may allow the wicked and unregenerate to run out on a long line, but when he snaps it back, they will be broken, and that without remedy.

In the interim, God's plans to turn the Captivity of his people are right on track. Regarding the dispersal of the northern kingdom and exiles of the southern kingdom, God says, "In those days the house of Judah shall walk with the house of Israel, and they shall come together out of the land of the north to the land that I have given for an inheritance unto your fathers..." Jeremiah Chapter 3 verse 18.

Egypt or Babylon?

The prophet Jeremiah is referred to as 'the weeping prophet' because he literally cried for the destruction he saw coming on Jerusalem. He ministered to the people of Judah prior to and during the exile into Babylon. Jeremiah was the son of a priest, and a very young man when God called him—so young, in fact that he said he could not speak on God's behalf, for he was only a child. However, when God determines to use an individual, it does not matter what that person thinks of himself. Moses felt he was an ineffective communicator; Gideon said he was poor and of little rank in his family. In God's eyes our physical, intellectual, and economic handicaps mean nothing. What matters is faith and obedience.

God got straight to the point with Jeremiah:

*I knew you before you were conceived

*I sanctified you while you were still in the womb

*I ordained you a prophet to the nations

*Don't say you are a child; you're going to all to whom I will send you

*You're going to speak whatever I command you

*Don't be afraid of their faces, because I am with you to deliver you

God stretched out his hand and touched Jeremiah's mouth, continuing:

*I have put my words in your mouth

*This day I have set thee over the nations and over the kingdoms, to root out, and to pull down, and to destroy, and to throw down, to build, and to plant.

*Gird up your loins, get up, and speak to them all that I command you

*Don't be afraid of their faces, or I will confound you (break down with violence, fear, or confusion) before them

*This day I have made you a defenced city, an iron pillar, and brasen walls against the whole land, against the kings of Judah, against the princes thereof, and against the people of the land

*They shall fight against you, but they shall not prevail against you, for I am with you, to deliver you

We really should take a moment to analyze this. What we are witnessing is the real time commissioning of a true prophet of God. Many people are running to and fro today calling themselves prophets and enjoying others addressing them as such. But who among them can stand such a rigorous vetting as this? Based on Jeremiah's prophetic calling, the foundation is not whether you know God, *but God knowing, setting apart, and ordaining you*. The next level is abolishment of fear of man. Most people calling themselves prophets today are glad to give a word as long as that word does not provoke the anger of man. But truth be known, if these prophets would really speak God's heart to the people they would be run out of the lukewarm, Laodicean churches. They could forget about ministries and love offerings and being greeted in the marketplace. This is the kind of prophetic word God was going to give Jeremiah: a word

135

that would incite such rage in a backslidden people that they would fight against him! Can we find a prophet like that today?

The next stage in this calling involved assurance of divine protection, and a warning against failure to execute. This is another reason the prophetic office cannot be taken lightly. Unless one has a clear directive from the Lord, it is foolhardy to proceed just because the mantle of prophet appears prestigious. The words of the Holy Ghost filled Stephen, who was martyred for his testimony before Jerusalem's Old Covenant Hebrews, should be firmly memorized by any purporting to be a spokesperson for God today:

"Which of the prophets have not your fathers persecuted? and they have slain them which shewed before of the coming of the Just One..." Acts Chapter 7 verse 52. What this means is uttering the prophetic word is courting death. A true godly prophet will face that fact and trust God with his or her life. This is what Jeremiah was being commanded to do. God affirms his care and protection for Jeremiah twice—saying: I am with thee to deliver thee. I am sure Jeremiah listened carefully when God told him he would prophesy against the kings of Judah, implying his ministry would span the rule of more than one monarch.

This then was the opening scene when Jeremiah was called to speak to our forefathers. God already knew they were going to resist his words and persecute him. The people were steeped in idolatry and did not want to hear about their sins, no less consider repentance. They had forgotten God. On top of that, Jeremiah was tasked with telling them they were on their way to Captivity in Babylon. Complicating his message would be false prophets that would speak to the contrary and tell the people differently. The entire realm, from the king, to the priests, right on down to the common people, would reject his message. The spiritual climate was so dangerous that another contemporary prophet—Urijah—was murdered. And when Jeremiah wrote down an entire compendium of Judah's sins to be read before the elders and the king in the hope of stirring them to conviction and repentance, the ruler at the time— Jehoiakim—tossed the writing in the flames of the fireplace. Such was the disdain for the word of God. Also, he sought to take Jeremiah and his scribe Baruch into custody, but God himself hid them.

The time arrived when all of Jeremiah's words concerning the Babylonian Captivity came to pass. Nebuchadnezzar set a blockade around Jerusalem. It took about two years for the siege to exhaust the resources before the city collapsed due to famine. Zedekiah, who was king at that time, tried to escape and get away, but he was caught near Jericho and taken to Babylon in humiliation where judgment was decreed on him. Now here is God's blessing and protection on Jeremiah for his obedience: the captain of Nebuchadnezzar's guard separated Jeremiah out from the captives and gave him leave to go wherever he wanted. These were his actual words:

"The Lord thy God hath pronounced this evil upon this place. Now the Lord hath brought it, and done according as he hath said: because ye have sinned against the Lord, and have not obeyed his voice, therefore this thing is come upon you.

And now, behold, I loose thee this day from the chains which were upon thine hand. If it seem good unto thee to come with me into Babylon, come; and I will look well unto thee: but if it seem ill unto thee to come with me into Babylon, forbear: behold, all the land is before thee: whither it seemeth good and convenient for thee to go, thither go."

How sad for the people to have to hear from the mouth of a pagan the very thing their own prophet had attempted to tell them for years. Nevertheless, Jeremiah found great favor in the sight of the captain of the guard, for it was no secret he had tried to appeal to the people and ended up imprisoned because of it.

Some of the poorest of the people were permitted to remain, but they were to maintain the land; serving under the auspices of the governor King Nebuchadnezzar appointed to take control. When the new administrator assumed his duties, many Hebrews who had taken refuge among the neighboring nations of Moab, Ammon, and Edom left to return to Jerusalem, as did the military contingents which were out in the field. But almost as soon as the administrator took office, he was assassinated and the new self-appointed leader of the people began formulating plans to carry the remnant of the people to the Ammonites. When the soldiers among the people learned what this despot had done, they pursued after him and rescued the people, although the usurper himself got away. The soldiers and the people went to Bethlehem, which was close to Egypt, because they were afraid of Nebuchadnezzar, for the renegade had not only killed the leader he had appointed to administrate Jerusalem, but he had also killed Chaldean soldiers during the conspiracy. Jeremiah was with the people, having chosen the option to remain with them over going to Babylon. The people asked him for counsel from the mouth of the Lord as to what direction to take. They assured Jeremiah that whatever the Lord answered they would do, whether it was good or bad.

It was ten days before the word of the Lord returned to Jeremiah: the people were to remain in the land, and there, God promised to build and plant them, and to show mercy to them. They were not to fear the king of Babylon, because God himself would be with them to save them and deliver them from his hand.

But if they refused, and determined themselves to go to Egypt, they could expect famine, death by the sword, and pestilence, and not one of them would remain or escape from the evil God would bring upon them. If you have been following thus far along in the book, I'm sure I don't have to tell you which option they chose. <u>They decided to go to Egypt</u>. The proud men in their midst actually accused Jeremiah of lying on God. And they marshalled the entire congregation—even Jeremiah and his scribe Baruch on the trek to Egypt.

Their stubborn and rebellious ways earned them nothing but more punishment from God. They called themselves getting away from King Nebuchadnezzar, but little did they know God was going to stir him up to plan a campaign against Egypt. They themselves would be caught in the heat of the conflict, and just as Jeremiah had prophesied, none would escape. At this point in history, Nebuchadnezzar was God's servant to execute judgment on his people for rebellion, on nations, and on their false gods. When he entered Egypt, Nebuchadnezzar would smite the land, and deliver such as were for death to death; and such as were for captivity to captivity; and such as were for the sword to the sword.

Judah was not to go to Egypt; in fact, Egypt was to be a place never looked back to or desired. And how was it they were so terrified of the king of Babylon that it seemed logical to flee to Egypt, but not terrified of their awesome God and Judge who holds the power of all life and death in his hand? Could there have been an underlying motive for desiring Egypt? We actually find it in the 44th Chapter of the Book of Jeremiah. When the people arrived and began settling in at Migdol, Tahpanhes, Noph, and Pathros, they began burning incense to other gods in the land of Egypt.

This is difficult to fathom. They did not look at all the things that had happened up to that point and reflect upon how they arrived in that position. They did not consider the fulfilled prophecies of the man of God who was in their midst. They asked him for counsel at the mouth of God, but they had already made up in their minds what they were going to do. Neither did they seek God in repentance, with broken and contrite spirits. When Jeremiah confronted them with their folly and reckless choice, this is how the men of Judah actually answered him:

"As for the word that thou hast spoken unto us in the name of the Lord, we will not hearken unto thee.

But we will certainly do whatsoever thing goeth forth out of our own mouth, to burn incense unto the queen of heaven, and to pour out drink offerings unto her, as we have done, we, and our fathers, our kings, and our princes, in the cities of Judah, and in the streets of Jerusalem: for then had we plenty of victuals, and were well, and saw no evil.

But since we left off to burn incense to the queen of heaven, and to pour out drink offerings unto her, we have wanted all things, and have been consumed by the sword and by the famine.

And the women added:

And when we burned incense to the queen of heaven, and poured out drink offerings unto her, did we make her cakes to worship her, and pour out drink offerings unto her, without our men?" Jeremiah Chapter 45 verses 16-19

Jeremiah's response was that God's face was now against them for evil and not for good, and that only a small remnant would escape the sword and make it out of the land of Egypt back into the land of Judah. When God declares a Captivity for his people, they are to go where he says they must go, stay as long as he decrees they must stay, and use the downtime productively in repentance, re-dedication, and faithfulness in order to correct the spiritual condition that triggered the bondage in the first place. Some people, like Daniel and his three friends—grasped this concept, and fought the good fight of faith in spite of the humiliation of Captivity. Then there are always others—like the group that called Jeremiah a liar and told him they were going to follow through with their own plan of action—whose rebellion and unbelief lead them to devastation and utter destruction. The drive to survive independent of the One who is our only true source of Life is nothing more than a self-imposed death sentence.

Cyrus My Servant...Why Persia Was Called for Restoration

"The king's heart is in the hand of the Lord, as the rivers of water: he turneth it whithersoever he will." Proverbs Chapter 21 verse 1

"Who raised up the righteous man from the east, called him to his foot, gave the nations before him, and made him rule over kings?" Isaiah Chapter 41 verse 2

Our forefather's second Captivity was in Babylon under King Nebuchadnezzar. This is the king who originally removed Judah from their land. It was under this king that Daniel and his three friends Mishael, Hananiah, and Azariah (known by their Babylonian names of Shadrach, Meshach, and Abednego) served. Daniel's service in the Babylonian court spanned the reign of several rulers and continued into the reign of king Cyrus.

In Isaiah the 44th and 45th chapters, God speaks to Cyrus king of Persia and tells him although he (Cyrus) has not known him, God knows who he is, and has called him, named him, and girded him. This means God would surround him. God called this king, and proceeded to tell him awesome things he would do for God, among them:

*He would function as one of God's shepherds: this means he would assume a lead position in executing God's will for his people

*He would perform all God's pleasure

*He would command the reconstruction of Jerusalem and the temple

*He would oversee the freeing of God's captives

Where God guides, he provides. Here is what God promised to do for Cyrus:

*He would hold his right hand—He would personally guide him

*He would subdue the heart of kings so that they would voluntarily open their gates to him and leave them open

*God himself would go before him and make the crooked places straight

*God would demolish every obstacle that stood in Cyrus' way—breaking in pieces the gates of brass and cutting in two the bars of iron

*God would give Cyrus the treasures of darkness and hidden riches of secret places

*He would direct all his ways

God says he has raised up Cyrus in righteousness and called him for three reasons:

*that thou mayest know that I, the Lord, which call thee by thy name, am the God of Israel.

*That they may know from the rising of the sun, and from the west, that there is none beside me. I am the Lord, and there is none else.

*And most importantly, for Jacob my servant's sake, and Israel mine elect.

As God guided Cyrus in repatriating our forefathers and clearing the way for the rebuilding of the temple in Jerusalem, this king came to know assuredly just who had established him and exalted him as the conqueror of the then known world. In II Chronicles Chapter 36 verses 22-23, we read that 'the Lord stirred up the spirit of Cyrus king of Persia,' and he made both a verbal and written proclamation throughout the kingdom declaring, "All the kingdoms of the earth hath the Lord God of heaven given me; and he hath charged me to build him an house in Jerusalem, which is in Judah." Further, he exhorts the Hebrews to rise to this challenge: "Who is there among you of all his people? The Lord his God be with him, and let him go up."

These are not words that would be heard from a pagan king, except the Lord our God were leading him and guiding him. Many historians assert that Cyrus was an adherent of Zoroastrianism. Nevertheless, he was a vessel used to preserve God's elect and heritage. This was critical, because Judah's enemies continued to rage, resenting the captives return to Jerusalem, and referring to it as "a rebellious city, and hurtful to kings and provinces," in an effort to thwart the rebuilding efforts. Fortunately, king Cyrus' documented order was stored in a facility that could be compared to our National Archives and Records. A review of his proclamation by the next king, Darius—earned a sharp rebuke for the persecutors:

"Now therefore, Tatnai, governor beyond the river, Shethar-boznai, and your companions the Apharsachites, which are beyond the river, be ye far from thence: Let the work of this house of God alone; let the governor of the Jews and the elders of the Jews build this house of God in his place.

Moreover I make a decree what ye shall do to the elders of these Jews for the building of this house of God: that of the king's goods, even of the tribute beyond the river, forthwith expences be given unto these men, that they be not hindered.

And that which they have need of, both young bullocks, and rams, and lambs, for the burnt offerings of the God of heaven, wheat, salt, wine, and oil, according to the appointment of the priests which are at Jerusalem, let it be given them day by day without fail:

That they may offer sacrifices of sweet savours unto the God of heaven, and pray for the life of the king, and of his sons.

Also I have made a decree, that whosoever shall alter this word, let timber be pulled down from his house, and being set up, let him be hanged thereon; and let his house be made a dunghill for this.

And the God that hath caused his name to dwell there destroy all kings and people, that shall put to their hand to alter and to destroy this house of God which is at Jerusalem. I Darius have made a decree; let it be done with speed.

Then Tatnai, governor on this side the river, Shethar-boznai, and their companions, according to that which Darius the king had sent, so they did speedily.

And the elders of the Jews builded, and they prospered through the prophesying of Haggai the prophet and Zechariah the son of Iddo. And they builded, and finished it, according to the commandment of the God of Israel, and according to the commandment of Cyrus, and Darius, and Artaxerxes king of Persia." Ezra Chapter 6 verses 6-14

Ecclesiastes Chapter 8 verse 4 says, "Where the word of a king is, there is power: and who may say unto him, What doest thou?" The word of three different kings was behind the order to rebuild Jerusalem and the temple, *endorsed and enforced by the great and mighty King of Kings*, the Lord of Heaven and Earth. The enemies of the Hebrews sought to sabotage them, but in the end, they were effectively issued a restraining order, and forced to bless them in a way they never intended to. They were commanded to provide anything the priests needed on a daily basis for the temple sacrifices, and refrain from altering any of the king's decree on pain of death. King Darius wanted the temple rites in full function because he wanted intercession made for his life and the life of his sons! This king had enough faith in the God of Israel to believe it was vital for the Hebrew priests to pray to their God on behalf of him and his lineage.

This brief study of Cyrus is critical to our heritage not only for his role in the return from the Babylonian Captivity, but because he too, was from the line of Shem. Persia was the nation founded by Shem's son Elam. Hamitic peoples (the Egyptians and Babylonians) historically enslaved the Hebrews, and in the latter days enslavement and persecution would rise from white Japhethic people. When God got ready to move his people back into their land, he called one from the line of Shem. Thus, Noah's words come to mind again: "**Blessed be the Lord God of Shem**."

Israel's Future Unfolds before the Prophets

An interesting dynamic repeatedly surfaces in the messages of the prophets to our forebears. Although God's anger, disappointment, heartbreak, and intent to discipline are clearly expressed, inevitably the prophets also communicate God's commitment to forgive, heal, and restore his people to a glorious future that exceeds even 'the former days.' For us in these times, this perfect balance of chastening and humiliation with encouragement and fellowship with the Father and Son in heavenly places is designed to allow Christ to be formed in us that we might be transformed into the new man, which after God is created in righteousness and true holiness. When the chastening and humiliation in this present time seem unbearable, we need to remember that it is working in us the peaceable fruit of righteousness. This is best understood in the context of how often we felt our parents were unfair and too strict when we were children, but once we had children of our own, it all made perfect sense. Where our ancestors were concerned, in true parental fashion God tells them that <u>in the latter days they will consider it perfectly</u>.

The Hebrew word used here for consider means to separate mentally or distinguish, and the word perfectly means understanding as with knowledge and wisdom. What this means is in the latter days, we would come to understand our historical ancestry and relationship with God. We would then be able to look at scripture and discern the cause of our present state. We would understand that the Lord Jesus Christ was a near kinsman—a blood relative—sent first to us to turn our forebears away from their sins and reconcile them back to God. We would be able to discern the linear progression of God's dealing with man, and hone in on his trajectory despite the lies, heresies, and distortion disseminated by Esau's people, and their hatred and envy.

To illustrate the contrast of what has been and currently is against that which is to come for us, we turn to a scripture in Psalms, and two others found in Isaiah.

"O Lord our God, other lords beside thee have had dominion over us..." Isaiah Chapter 26 verse 13.

<u>This is where we find ourselves today</u>.

"But thou hast cast off, and put us to shame; and goest not forth with our armies. Thou makest us to turn back from the enemy: and they which hate us spoil for themselves. Thou hast given us like sheep appointed for meat; and hast scattered us among the heathen.

Thou sellest thy people for nought, and dost not increase thy wealth by their price. Thou makest us a reproach to our neighbours, a scorn and a derision to them that are round about us. Thou makest us a byword among the heathen, a shaking of the head among the people..." Psalms Chapter 43 verses 9-14. This speaks to our perspective toward the state of our Captivity. We know the depressing history, and see the current fallout all around us. We just have not understood why. God's hand is in this; there is no sense in being angry at the oppressor or lamenting about the unfairness of it all.

"Who gave Jacob for a spoil, and Israel to the robbers? did not the Lord, he against whom we have sinned? for they would not walk in his ways, neither were they obedient unto his law. Therefore he hath poured upon him the fury of his anger, and the strength of battle: and it hath set him on fire round about, yet he knew not; and it burned him, yet he laid it not to heart..." Isaiah Chapter 42 verses 24-25. Here God assumes full responsibility for placing us in our current position. This verse also illustrates the mind state of most of the descendants of the Trans-Atlantic slave trade: total oblivion to the fact their condition is a direct consequence of God's wrath against their forefather's rebellion.

Now, let's contrast this with the exceeding great and precious promises given us by the Lord through the prophet Jeremiah in the 30th, 31st, and 32nd chapters of his book:

"The word that came to Jeremiah from the Lord, saying, Thus speaketh the Lord God of Israel, saying, Write thee all the words that I have spoken unto thee in a book.

For, lo, the days come, saith the Lord, that I will bring again the Captivity of my people Israel and Judah, saith the Lord: and I will cause them to return to the land that I gave to their fathers, and they shall possess it.

And these are the words that the Lord spake concerning Israel and concerning Judah. For thus saith the Lord; We have heard a voice of trembling, of fear, and not of peace.

Ask ye now, and see whether a man doth travail with child? wherefore do I see every man with his hands on his loins, as a woman in travail, and all faces are turned into paleness?

Alas! for that day is great, so that none is like it: it is even the time of Jacob's trouble; but he shall be saved out of it. For it shall come to pass in that day, saith the Lord of hosts, that I will break his yoke from off thy neck, and will burst thy bonds, and strangers shall no more serve themselves of him:

But they shall serve the Lord their God, and David their king, whom I will raise up unto them.

Therefore fear thou not, O my servant Jacob, saith the Lord; neither be dismayed, O Israel: for, lo, I will save thee from afar, and thy seed from the land of their Captivity; and Jacob shall return, and shall be in rest, and be quiet, and none shall make him afraid.

For I am with thee, saith the Lord, to save thee: though I make a full end of all nations whither I have scattered thee, yet will I not make a full end of thee: but I will correct thee in measure, and will not leave thee altogether unpunished.

For thus saith the Lord, Thy bruise is incurable, and thy wound is grievous. There is none to plead thy cause, that thou mayest be bound up: thou hast no healing medicines.

All thy lovers have forgotten thee; they seek thee not; for I have wounded thee with the wound of an enemy, with the chastisement of a cruel one, for the multitude of thine iniquity; because thy sins were increased.

Why criest thou for thine affliction? thy sorrow is incurable for the multitude of thine iniquity: because thy sins were increased, I have done these things unto thee. Therefore all they that devour thee shall be devoured; and all thine adversaries, every one of them, shall go into captivity; and they that spoil thee shall be a spoil, and all that prey upon thee will I give for a prey.

For I will restore health unto thee, and I will heal thee of thy wounds, saith the Lord; because they called thee an Outcast, saying, This is Zion, whom no man seeketh after.

Thus saith the Lord; Behold, I will bring again the captivity of Jacob's tents, and have mercy on his dwellingplaces; and the city shall be builded upon her own heap, and the palace shall remain after the manner thereof.

And out of them shall proceed thanksgiving and the voice of them that make merry: and I will multiply them, and they shall not be few; I will also glorify them, and they shall not be small.

Their children also shall be as aforetime, and their congregation shall be established before me, and I will punish all that oppress them.

And their nobles shall be of themselves, and their governor shall proceed from the midst of them; and I will cause him to draw near, and he shall approach unto me: for who is this that engaged his heart to approach unto me? saith the Lord. And ye shall be my people, and I will be your God.

Behold, the whirlwind of the Lord goeth forth with fury, a continuing whirlwind: it shall fall with pain upon the head of the wicked.

The fierce anger of the Lord shall not return, until he have done it, and until he have performed the intents of his heart: in the latter days ye shall consider it.

CHAPTER 31

At the same time, saith the Lord, will I be the God of all the families of Israel, and they shall be my people.

Thus saith the Lord, The people which were left of the sword found grace in the wilderness; even Israel, when I went to cause him to rest.

The Lord hath appeared of old unto me, saying, Yea, I have loved thee with an everlasting love: therefore with lovingkindness have I drawn thee.

Again I will build thee, and thou shalt be built, O virgin of Israel: thou shalt again be adorned with thy tabrets, and shalt go forth in the dances of them that make merry.

Thou shalt yet plant vines upon the mountains of Samaria: the planters shall plant, and shall eat them as common things.

For there shall be a day, that the watchmen upon the mount Ephraim shall cry, Arise ye, and let us go up to Zion unto the Lord our God.

For thus saith the Lord; Sing with gladness for Jacob, and shout among the chief of the nations: publish ye, praise ye, and say, O Lord, save thy people, the remnant of Israel. Behold, I will bring them from the north country, and gather them from the coasts of the earth, and with them the blind and the lame, the woman with child and her that travaileth with child together: a great company shall return thither.

They shall come with weeping, and with supplications will I lead them: I will cause them to walk by the rivers of waters in a straight way, wherein they shall not stumble: for I am a father to Israel, and Ephraim is my firstborn.

Hear the word of the Lord, O ye nations, and declare it in the isles afar off, and say, He that scattered Israel will gather him, and keep him, as a shepherd doth his flock. For the Lord hath redeemed Jacob, and ransomed him from the hand of him that was stronger than he.

Therefore they shall come and sing in the height of Zion, and shall flow together to the goodness of the Lord, for wheat, and for wine, and for oil, and for the young of the flock and of the herd: and their soul shall be as a watered garden; and they shall not sorrow any more at all.

Then shall the virgin rejoice in the dance, both young men and old together: for I will turn their mourning into joy, and will comfort them, and make them rejoice from their sorrow.

And I will satiate the soul of the priests with fatness, and my people shall be satisfied with my goodness, saith the Lord.

Thus saith the Lord; A voice was heard in Ramah, lamentation, and bitter weeping; Rahel weeping for her children refused to be comforted for her children, because they were not.

Thus saith the Lord; Refrain thy voice from weeping, and thine eyes from tears: for thy work shall be rewarded, saith the Lord; and they shall come again from the land of the enemy.

And there is hope in thine end, saith the Lord, that thy children shall come again to their own border.

I have surely heard Ephraim bemoaning himself thus; Thou hast chastised me, and I was chastised, as a bullock unaccustomed to the yoke: turn thou me, and I shall be turned; for thou art the Lord my God.

Surely after that I was turned, I repented; and after that I was instructed, I smote upon my thigh: I was ashamed, yea, even confounded, because I did bear the reproach of my youth. Is Ephraim my dear son? is he a pleasant child? for since I spake against him, I do earnestly remember him still: therefore my bowels are troubled for him; I will surely have mercy upon him, saith the Lord.

Set thee up way marks, make thee high heaps: set thine heart toward the highway, even the way which thou wentest: turn again, O virgin of Israel, turn again to these thy cities.

How long wilt thou go about, O thou backsliding daughter? for the Lord hath created a new thing in the earth, A woman shall compass a man.

Thus saith the Lord of hosts, the God of Israel; As yet they shall use this speech in the land of Judah and in the cities thereof, when I shall bring again their captivity; The Lord bless thee, O habitation of justice, and mountain of holiness.

And there shall dwell in Judah itself, and in all the cities thereof together, husbandmen, and they that go forth with flocks. For I have satiated the weary soul, and I have replenished every sorrowful soul. Upon this I awaked, and beheld; and my sleep was sweet unto me.

Behold, the days come, saith the Lord, that I will sow the house of Israel and the house of Judah with the seed of man, and with the seed of beast.

And it shall come to pass, that like as I have watched over them, to pluck up, and to break down, and to throw down, and to destroy, and to afflict; so will I watch over them, to build, and to plant, saith the Lord.

In those days they shall say no more, The fathers have eaten a sour grape, and the children's teeth are set on edge.

But every one shall die for his own iniquity: every man that eateth the sour grape, his teeth shall be set on edge.

Behold, the days come, saith the Lord, that I will make a new covenant with the house of Israel, and with the house of Judah:

Not according to the covenant that I made with their fathers in the day that I took them by the hand to bring them out of the land of Egypt; which my covenant they brake, although I was an husband unto them, saith the Lord:

But this shall be the covenant that I will make with the house of Israel; After those days, saith the Lord, I will put my law in their inward parts, and write it in their hearts; and will be their God, and they shall be my people.

And they shall teach no more every man his neighbour, and every man his brother, saying, Know the Lord: for they shall all know me, from the least of them unto the greatest of them, saith the Lord: for I will forgive their iniquity, and I will remember their sin no more.

Thus saith the Lord, which giveth the sun for a light by day, and the ordinances of the moon and of the stars for a light by night, which divideth the sea when the waves thereof roar; The Lord of hosts is his name:

If those ordinances depart from before me, saith the Lord, then the seed of Israel also shall cease from being a nation before me for ever.

Thus saith the Lord; If heaven above can be measured, and the foundations of the earth searched out beneath, I will also cast off all the seed of Israel for all that they have done, saith the Lord.

Chapter 32

And now therefore thus saith the Lord, the God of Israel, concerning this city, whereof ye say, It shall be delivered into the hand of the king of Babylon by the sword, and by the famine, and by the pestilence;

Behold, I will gather them out of all countries, whither I have driven them in mine anger, and in my fury, and in great wrath; and I will bring them again unto this place, and I will cause them to dwell safely:

And they shall be my people, and I will be their God:

And I will give them one heart, and one way, that they may fear me for ever, for the good of them, and of their children after them:

And I will make an everlasting covenant with them, that I will not turn away from them, to do them good; but I will put my fear in their hearts, that they shall not depart from me.

Yea, I will rejoice over them to do them good, and I will plant them in this land assuredly with my whole heart and with my whole soul.

For thus saith the Lord; Like as I have brought all this great evil upon this people, so will I bring upon them all the good that I have promised them."

None of these prophecies have been fulfilled in their entirety. While the argument can be made that God was talking to Jeremiah about the Captivity's return from Babylon, the preponderance of the prophetic message speaks to a time yet in the future corresponding to eternal rest and glory. This did not happen after the release by the Persian kings; rather, the situation gradually degenerated to the extent that by the time the Lord Jesus Christ began his earthly ministry, Palestine was a client state of a pagan Gentile power, and the spiritual atmosphere was such that zealots were battling to preserve the last vestiges of uncorrupted worship, while the 'moderate' Pharisees and Sadducees who could be trusted to not insurrect were busy cozying up to the Edomite proxy kings who ruled over them and reported to the Romans.

So as a people we are still anticipating these exciting times to come. **And they will**. Even as the prophets foretold of the coming of the Lord Jesus Christ centuries before his advent and it came to pass that all things spoken of him would be fulfilled, even so all things must be fulfilled prophesied of Judah and Israel. We are living in exciting times, because the days are drawing nigh that these words will flesh out and become reality. Many will be stunned to see that the future restoration has little in common with the Western 'churchianity' we have become accustomed to. But if we seek God for the infilling of the Holy Ghost, put on the mind of Christ, and read the Bible in its entirety for ourselves—not just the pet prosperity scriptures—this linear plan of God will become as clear as day and you will refocus your perspective and realign your goals. You will, as your heavenly Father promised—understand it perfectly.

Let's look more in depth through the verses of this prophecy. The Lord says the days are coming when he will bring again the Captivity of his people Israel and Judah, and he will cause them to return to the land he gave to their fathers. This means we have a homeland we will be returning to. It's not the African west coast or the African interior; which are just places our ancestors fled to get out of the reach of Roman jurisdiction, and the sites their descendants were uprooted from for the Trans-Atlantic slave trade. The land referred to here is the complete geographical region God promised to our forefathers Abraham, Isaac, and Jacob. This is a much greater area than the land of Israel you hear about in the news today. II Maccabees Chapter 5 verse 19 states that God did not choose us for the sake of this land; rather, he chose the land for our sakes. This is a work God will do: he himself—by the hand of his holy angels will gather us from the four winds and bring us into the land. This is hard for some people to wrap their heads around. Well, if you believe God brought your forefathers out of Egypt with signs and supernatural wonders and a mighty outstretched hand, expect to see miraculous intervention of greater magnitude this time around.

Just prior to this deliverance comes a divine encounter which causes the inhabitants of the earth to be immobilized with fear and dread. It is also a time of trouble for us as a people, for the rage of the enemy has reached a crescendo and other prophecies tell us he is given power to make war with the saints and overcome them. The prophet Daniel also concurs this is a time of trouble, such as never was since there was a nation even to that same time; but at that time Michael—the great prince which stands for us—will stand up, and at that time, the people shall be delivered, every one that shall be found written in the book. God tells Jeremiah, in that day he will break the oppressor's yoke from off our neck, burst the bonds, and strangers will no more serve themselves of us. These events are one and the same.

The day will have arrived when we no more serve others, but are completely liberated to serve the Lord our God, and David our king, whom God will raise up over restored Israel. You probably never heard anyone in the churches say God was going to resurrect David to rule over the people. Nevertheless, this is what this verse clearly states. Some would argue this is speaking of the Lord Jesus Christ—the Root and the Offspring of David; but when the Lord Jesus Christ spoke of himself this way in his Revelation to the Apostle John, he was already resurrected. The Hebrew word for raise in this instance is defined as to rise up and to rise again. As members of the body of Christ, we are already predestinated to reign with him as kings and priests, if we have built upon the Foundation gold, silver, and precious stones. So the monarchy of David seems more in line for the people who will be gathered out and follow after the Lord with the spirit of supplication; a subject we will discuss shortly.

God says he will save us from afar. Unlike unreliable people we all know who say they are going to show up but never do, God will be right on time. It doesn't matter if your car won't start, the bus isn't running, the flights are canceled, or martial law says nobody can come out of their house. It is God himself who will save you, and your children from the land of Captivity and you are going back where you can rest, be in quiet, and none shall make you afraid. Remember, Hebrews Chapter 4 verse 9 says, There remaineth therefore a rest to the people of God.

God says he is with our people, to save them. Although he is going to make a full end of the nations where we have been scattered, he is not going to make a full end of us. But he will correct us in measure, and not leave us altogether unpunished.

Because God recognizes that our wound is grievous and our bruise and our sorrow are incurable. People shake their head at the Black man and woman in the West. The general consensus is that we are ne'er do wells—a hopeless lot. Well, this is what happens when a segment of humanity is wounded by the Holy One of Israel himself, and chastised with a cruel chastisement. All the money, social programs, and race relations efforts in the world cannot reverse the blow dealt us by our God. Only He can redeem us from this Captivity.

There is none to plead our cause; we have no healing medicines. You will find many who are willing to start foundations and non-profits for all types of causes and all types of people— even animals, but you will not see any racing to establish movements or associations that will lift the Black race in the West as a whole. Organizations established for the benefit of Blacks in the Americas provide limited assistance. But for the most part they are donor dependent, or have been forced to redefine their advocacy to include increasing numbers of clients with no historical link to the original mission: uplift of the descendants of the Trans-Atlantic slave trade. These factors influence the distribution of resources and reduce the scope of effectiveness in Black communities.

God asks us, why are you are crying about your affliction? Bottom line, he says, I have done these things unto you.

Let me stop right here and ask you, Black church member. Can you still love God with all your heart, soul, and strength knowing God has permitted this because of the sins of your forefathers? Are you willing to confess to him that he is righteous in all his ways?

Recall that God remembering his covenant and bringing us back into the land is conditional on us confessing our iniquity and the iniquity of our fathers and their trespasses, admitting we have walked contrary to God as a people, and that he has walked contrary to us and brought us into Captivity. Further, we are told to humble ourselves, and accept the punishment of our iniquity. Or will you recoil in anger and say it's not fair, he had no right to punish us for what they did...or, will you still feel that way once you understand what is in store for your oppressor?

God says everyone who is devouring us (socially/economically/psychologically) will be devoured; and all our adversaries, every one of them, will go into Captivity; and those who spoiled us shall be a spoil, and all that preyed upon us will he give for a prey. Here you can call to mind the systemic destruction of our people in this Captivity and the institutions and social constructs that drive it...at our restoration, the tables will turn and the oppressor will be in our place, while we are moved to a manner of life which far exceeds the best our adversaries could muster even after stealing the riches of this world for many years.

God is no respecter of persons. Tribulation and anguish come upon every soul that sins —to the Hebrew first, then to the Gentile. Instead of smoldering in resentment, we should be rejoicing that we have received double for our sins and have nothing to look forward to now except reconciliation and a restored kingdom; not somewhere in the vast realms of heaven— although those regions will be accessible—but right here on earth. That's why we pray for God's kingdom to come and his will to be done on earth. It is about us recovering our first dominion as sons here on the earth!

Jehovah Raapha will restore our health and heal the people of their wounds, because they called us an Outcast, saying, This is Zion, whom no man seeketh after. We have indeed been outcasts; the subject of demeaning caricatures, insulting cinemas, cruelly calculated economic sabotage, dismal treatment in the courts and criminal justice system, victims of psychological and biological warfare programs, and other non-consensual experimentation. We have been the laughingstock that no man seeks after—unless he can profit from us by sports or entertainment. But this will change at the appearing of our Lord and Savior Jesus Christ: the Lion of the Tribe of Judah.

When we return to a city that shall be rebuilt because we are not going to the works of the hands of the Gentiles that have occupied the land, but an entirely new city built from the ground up—you will constantly hear thanksgiving and merry making. And this in the midst of multitudes of people whom God has glorified. Can you imagine stepping out of your door into an atmosphere of love and greeting and praise and blessing—not just after church service, but twenty-four seven three hundred sixty, whenever and wherever you meet your brethren? A place where the children are like they were in the days of the glory of Israel: sons like plants grown up in their youth; and daughters like polished corner stones of a palace. This speaks of children that radiate strength, vitality, beauty, and purpose.

Today we struggle constantly with youth who are compromised by a wicked culture seeking to defy and overthrow all godliness we instill in our children. And many among our people have grown weary of the constant warfare and given up their children to go with the flow. God knows the constant sabotage Esau's system has perpetuated on the sons of Jacob in Captivity. He understands what it is like to do your best and then watch as family members push the self-destruct button, for he went through the same thing with Israel. In Hosea Chapter 13 verse 9 he says, "O Israel, thou hast destroyed thy self; but in me is thine help." God has not forgotten your children and grandchildren. Keep praying; he will be faithful to save them.

Two Covenants—Both Sealed by the Blood of the Lamb

The holy congregation will be established before God. Everyone will be in their proper place, and the place of their calling. From the kings and priests ruling and reigning with Christ who built on his foundation gold, silver, precious stones, and knew him in the fellowship of his sufferings, to the rest of the Captivity whose iniquity is forgiven under the new covenant whereby God's law will be written in their inward parts and their heart, the people will all be established before God as a holy congregation. This is not the same covenant as the New Covenant through Christ Jesus, for under the present covenant, we are given apostles; and some, prophets; and some, evangelists; and some, pastors and teachers; for the perfecting of the saints. We still have to receive instruction, to move from milk to meat and glory to glory. But in that day and under that covenant, they shall teach no more every man his neighbour, and every man his brother, saying, Know the Lord: for the Lord says they shall all know me, from the least of them unto the greatest of them.

Note this covenant is strictly to the house of Israel and the house of Judah—a Hebrew specific covenant which has been paid for by the shed blood of the Lamb and is formalized at his bodily return after their gathering from the corners of the earth. Gentiles, on the other hand—including descendants of the Euro-Judaic proselytes, can only avail themselves to enter the kingdom through the preaching of the cross and repentance of sins before the return of the Lord Jesus Christ. A new revelation of the vastness of God's mercies and his transforming power will be realized as this New Covenant goes into effect. All the dysfunction and self-destructive behavior associated with our people is marked for DELETE on God's program, for he has said "you shall be my people, and I will be your God." "You shall," and "I will," are spoken as directives which shall not go forth from his mouth and return to him void, but accomplish what he sent it to do. God will also turn to the people a pure language, that Judah and all the rest of the tribes may all call upon the name of the Lord, to serve him with one consent.

Any who try to oppress the people will be punished—by God. The Gentiles will quickly learn things operate differently in the Kingdom of God than they did during the heyday of the kingdoms of the world. Those who rule and administrate among the people will be of the seed of Israel and Judah. The days of trying to reason with people who cannot relate and have no desire to will cease to exist. That set up is a necessary component of the present Captivity, but do not let resentment and bitterness rise any more. Instead, rejoice for these exceeding great and precious promises which are spoken by the One who cannot lie.

These comforting words God speaks are counterbalanced by the violent rebuke of the earth and its inhabitants on the day of the Lord. His devastating fury is like a whirlwind. Think in terms of a tornado that exceeds all the known scales in intensity—except this tornado is the wrath of God. Further, he says it will continue until he has done it, and performed the intents of his heart. What could this mean in the midst of God being focused on turning our Captivity and setting us up for blessing in the earth? Simply put, it means the kingdoms of the world are firmly entrenched in their system, their way of doing things, and maintaining our Captivity, that Israel might cease from being a nation and never rise again.

Remember, Esau is of a different manner; his value system, outlook on life, and estimation of spiritual matters is diametrically opposed to God. A blessing and world dominion for the lowly and despised so-called "Negro" is not even up for consideration on his list of priorities—even if God has declared the end from the beginning and says it's already a done deal. Esau will fight to maintain the current system. Military might, nihilism and death are his forte, for it was prophesied that he would live by the sword. But remember the words of the Lord Jesus Christ: all they that take the sword shall perish with the sword. This is why God will have to rebuke and punish the nations, and, wherever Edom and Babylon the Great are found—take them all the way out.

WHAT'S IMPORTANT

Once they got into the Land of Promise, the young nation did well until the dedicated men of God and the strong shepherds passed away. But even if there wasn't a designated leader, they still had the written word, the priests, and prophets. God did not leave them without a witness, but he did want to test their hearts that they themselves might know the depths to which they would sink without him.

Israel's surrounding enemies held their breath for the moment Israel's appetite for idolatry would open the door for persecution, and they never had to wait for long. God in his compassion raised up judges when the maltreatment became too great, and as long as the judge was around, Israel would straighten up and fly right, but as soon as the judge died, they fell off the wagon again. Just how far they had strayed became obvious when the Law and commandments were pushed down the memory hole and every man began doing that which was right in his own eyes. As we saw, it was okay in the eyes of some to set up molten images right in the place designated for worship to God. We also saw the first example of men of God selling out to the highest bidder.

It was no surprise to God that the people would reject his ultimate leadership for a fallible flesh and blood entity. The path the king chose brought either blessing or destruction, with destruction becoming the predominant outcome after the death of Solomon. Strangely, in spite of all the drama and turmoil, we never see Israel come to the realization that it would be better to dispense with the entire king construct and return to letting God go before them, as in the days he delivered them and brought them through the wilderness. And as apostasy deepened over the land, the unfortunate practice developed of kings using their power to persecute and silence the prophets. Since the people had rejected God as their leader, the prophets were the lifeline to spiritual sanity and direction. When the people refused to hear them, our Father in his wisdom decided another taste of Captivity was in order. The majority of the idolatry-steeped northern tribes were deported from the land by Assyria. Refusing to stay in a strange land not of their choosing, they undertook a journey across the earth of a year and a half to reach the land 'where never mankind dwelt, that they might there keep their statutes, which they never kept in their own land.' Many centuries later, those curses God designated for them from the list in Deuteronomy Chapter 28 would overtake them, through the empirical expansion of the sons of Japheth. They watched helplessly as their livelihoods, resources, sovereignty, and dignity were stripped away. God's word never returns to him void, but accomplishes that which he sent it to do.

Judah went away into Babylon for seventy years. This period produced some of the finest heroes of the faith: Jeremiah, Daniel, Ezekiel, Ezra, and Nehemiah. These just men lived by faith, and God turned the hearts of kings and authorities in response to their brokenness, intercession, and zeal for his house and his people. We also observed how God is able to call an individual who has no prior knowledge of him and equip and strengthen him to execute righteousness in the earth—for the benefit of God's people.

Lastly, we learned that when we get out of line as a people, we should expect to be chastened. Further, God takes his own sweet time with discipline; he is not in any rush. Seventy years didn't work before, so this time around we get about six times that length. Still, with all the humiliation, deprivation, scorn, and misery gendered by the curses of Deuteronomy Chapter 28, God exhorts us that he is only correcting us in measure, rather than making a full end of us. He also unveils a glorious future of a restored kingdom—one we cannot even imagine because so much of our energy is exhausted just in trying to cope with the conditions of Captivity. We have become accustomed to the bywords and second rate status, and it is difficult to grasp that this earth will ever hold anything better. The good news is: it is your Father's good pleasure to give you the kingdom. Do not be resentful for this Captivity, but love, trust, and serve God in the beauty of holiness.

Chapter VII...Apostasy and Imbalance: A Reaction to Interference

Help, LORD; for the godly man ceaseth; for the faithful fail from among the children of men.

In the Book of Daniel Chapter 10 verse 13, we read where an angel bringing an answer in response to Daniel's prayer is hindered by the angelic prince of the kingdom of Persia. The opposition the heavenly messenger encountered cost him three weeks in earth time while he battled this entity, and the conflict raged to the intensity the great prince of our people—Michael—had to come assist him. In verse 20, the angel told Daniel that when he left he was going to fight the Persian spiritual entity again, and next in line after that the angelic prince of the kingdom of Greece would come.

We cannot begin to fathom the might of the principalities, powers, rulers of the darkness of this world, and highly placed spiritual wickedness, but the angel's account to Daniel gives a chilling perspective. We can take courage in the fact that the armor of God, the sword of his word, and praying in the Holy Ghost will enable us to stand in the face of these other-dimensional assaults. The angel's explanation also provides us with valuable insight into the alarm and call to duty that sounds in the kingdom of darkness whenever a man or woman of God begin to chasten themselves with repentance and fasting and seek the Lord for insight and understanding of his word and his plan.

We know from history—both Biblical and secular—that the Persians and later the Greeks were the entities who exerted the greatest impact on the exile and repatriation of the Hebrews. We also know that during the reign of Xerxes, Greece won a decisive victory against Persia in the battle at Salamis. The Persian star was waning, and Greece was next in line to rise. But this could not take place until Judah was back in the land and the temple rebuilt.

Zerubbabel and Sheshbazzar, who were of king David's lineage, answered Cyrus' challenge to rise up and return to Jerusalem. However, not much could get accomplished in reconstruction due to the intense hatred of the surrounding peoples, characterized by intimidation and constant disruption. God raised up Ezra; a scribe and great man of God who mobilized the people to not only return to the land, but return to God with all their heart. This was the second migration back to Judah. Work was put on hold again, while the issue of pagan intermarriage was dealt with. Ezra told the men who had married heathenish wives and gendered children that they would have to put those families away if they were to continue in the rebuilding and restoration efforts. On first hearing, this seems cruel and unreasonable, until you consider Ezra's position.

Being of priestly lineage and a scribe, Ezra had a well-rounded knowledge of the scriptures and Israel's history. He knew Moses' warning about taking spouses from the surrounding idolatrous nations, because inevitably it would cause a spiritual stumbling block. He was familiar with King Solomon's downfall toward the end of his life. Since idolatry was what got them into Captivity in the first place, it was spiritual suicide to start down that path again. This was not about any kind of racial separation either, as everyone involved was some shade of brown. This was about spiritual purity.

Judah had gone into a bondage that lasted seventy years. When people are in captivity for any prolonged period of time, they develop coping strategies. One of these strategies is an attempt to bring normalcy and purpose to life, such as a vocation, marriage and family, and obtaining the best material comforts the captivity has to offer. Some of the men of Judah had lost sight of the goal (Jerusalem) and were focused on making the best of a negative situation.

Not surprisingly, this mirrors the Black man's experience in the West today. He is in a bondage that he has not recognized is from the hand of God, nor does he anticipate any way out of it in the foreseeable future, so his goal is to make the best of life in his present circumstances. However, God does not want us to get comfortable in Captivity. The time is drawing ever closer to the return of our Lord and Savior, and his reward is with him. This does not mean refrain from marrying and raising a family, or being the best you can be in your studies or career. But always remember everything done in the natural life must be counterbalanced with a lifestyle of salt and light, wearing the armor of God, walking by faith, and dying daily to the flesh so that God is glorified in your temple.

Judah's return and reconstruction of the temple marked the Second Temple Period. Under the leadership of Ezra and exhortation and spiritual guidance of the prophets Zechariah and Haggai, the work prospered. The citizens of Judah were given local autonomy. The priestly sacrifices resumed. Ezra led the people in consecration and brought them into a renewed covenant with the Lord. Shortly thereafter, Nehemiah, the king's cupbearer, was granted permission to rebuild the walls of Jerusalem. Similar to the opposition his compatriot Ezra experienced during the rehabilitation of the temple, Nehemiah encountered hateful resistance from people representing Israel's historical enemies: Moab, Ammon, Arabia, and Philistia.

The tactic these instigators used would in our time be called psychological warfare. Mockery, insult, and ridicule were followed by a homicidal conspiracy which was supernaturally foiled, because God himself brought the conspirator's counsel to nought. The antagonism was so strong that Nehemiah and the people had to repair the wall working with one hand and gripping their sword with the other. After that, Sanballat—who held a ruling position over Samaria, attempted to lure Nehemiah away from his work on the wall, that he might kill him. When this didn't work, a lying testimony was crafted and written which stated Nehemiah had declared himself king in Judah. The threat of showing this letter to the king of Persia was an attempt to blackmail Nehemiah into cooperating with Sanballat. When that failed, false prophets were sent into the midst with words of fear and discouragement. As a last ditch effort, an intensive letter writing campaign designed to keep the returning exiles in a state of trepidation was undertaken. Nevertheless, the wall was completed in fifty-two days. During this tumultuous period, God sent the prophet Malachi to minister to the people.

With the temple rebuilt, the people re-consecrated and the city under new construction, fresh life was breathed into the Hebrew nation. At the same time, two new dynamics began to insidiously operate that would mold Judah into an entirely different construct: the beginning of the times of the Gentiles, and the addition of oral tradition to the Mosaic Law.

Mount Olympus vs Mount Zion...The Pressure to Hellenize

In the tenth chapter of Daniel, we saw the struggle God's heavenly angel was locked in against the spiritual prince of Persia. No doubt this entity did not want to relinquish Persian world domination. Indeed, history shows the forces of Persia—descended from Noah's son Shem, were gradually beaten back; with them finally capitulating to the Macedonian Alexander the Great at the battle of Issus. **Macedonia was also known as Chittim, and the Table of Nations shows 'Kittim' as a grandson of Noah through Japheth. Thus, the rise of Macedonia and Greece define the start of the times of the Gentiles**. Alexander, son of Philip the II of Macedonia, was of Greek and Macedonian extract, and a military genius, albeit from a spiritual perspective just another in a consecutive series of tools wielded by the Lord of Hosts to shape the geopolitical stage for the appearance of the Lord Jesus Christ.

Upon Alexander's untimely death at the age of thirty-three, his empire was divided among his four generals; Seleucus, Ptolemy, Lysimachus, and Cassander. Seleucus controlled the regions of Asia, eventually wresting Palestine from control of the Ptolemic rulers of Egypt. Under his sway, the influence of Hellenism—the philosophies and practices of Greek culture— kindled a battle for the hearts and minds of our ancestors. The spiritual prince of Grecia who arrived to battle the angel of God would have totally overwhelmed Judah had he not been restrained by the heavenly warrior. This is evidenced by the fact that under the reign of the Seleucid dynasties the people of Judah were compelled to resist to the point of bloodshed in order to retain the ability to serve and worship God in the Mosaic tradition.

Like a C-clamp, pressure was exerted from two directions. From one end came the apostasy of the wicked in Israel who desired to emulate the Greeks and adopted Greek names and customs, built exercise gyms, and participated in the Tyrian competitions—a sports event held in honor of the idol Hercules. From the other side came the draconian policy of Antiochus Epiphanes who decreed the people of Judah could not hold their temple sacrifices, circumcise their males, keep Sabbath, possess any of the writings of the Law and the prophets, or even identify themselves as a descendant of Judah—on pain of death. The heathen even attempted to superimpose their idolatrous images in the scrolls of the Law and prophets. This campaign was designed to make the Hebrews forget the Law, and change their ordinances. There was no prophet in that day, and many of the people lost the will to resist and gave in to the pressure to renounce their faith. These were very perilous times for our ancestors because the wicked in Israel were extremely bold to the extent they joined the heathen in persecuting those who clung to the covenant.

Howbeit, many in Israel were fully resolved that they would rather die than defile themselves and profane the holy covenant. These paid for their convictions with their lives. It was against this backdrop that Mattathias of Modin and his five sons drew their line in the sand and established a bulwark against the encroaching gates of hell. This would mark the beginning of the Hasmonaean Era.

The Resistance of the Maccabees and the Hasmonaean Era

The tipping point came the day the Seleucid king's officers arrived in Modin to enforce sacrifice to the Greek idols on the altar. Thinking to ply Mattathias with promises of wealth and royal favor, the king's emissary tried to get him to lead by example and offer the first sacrifice. Mattathias staunchly refused and in a loud voice stated his testimony to refuse the king's commandment and remain faithful to God. However, just as today, there are always people who go along to get along, and desire to curry favor with the ruling powers, thinking their allegiance to evil will save their skin. Others can't resist the lure of easy wealth. At any rate, one such person dutifully came forward to offer an idolatrous sacrifice.

At that point, Mattathias could not restrain himself and killed the apostate upon the very altar he had thought to make sacrifice on. He also killed the king's commissioner who had come to enforce the idolatrous sacrifice, and tore down the altar itself. After this, he and his sons left everything they had in the city and fled to the mountains.[13] But many people joined themselves to him; people who sought justice and were voluntarily devoted to the Law. Mattathias and his followers did everything in their power to undo the wickedness the Gentiles had wrought upon the land and the people. By him the Mosaic law was recovered out of the hand of the Gentiles and out of the hand of kings, and he did not permit the sinner to triumph. Before he died, he exhorted his sons to look to the examples of the great heroes of our faith; similar to the legacy we read in Hebrews Chapter 11. At his death, the mantle passed to his son Judas—called Maccabeus. This brother was a human illustration of the scripture, "If God be for us, who can be against us?"

The short synopsis of Judas Maccabeus is that he was a man who grieved many kings, but blessed his people and made them glad. Neither would he tolerate the foolishness of wickedness among his people, but purged them from the land whenever encountered or when their treacherous counsel was made known. Because of this he was greatly feared and renown to the utmost part of the earth.

Maccabeus' methods might appear extreme to those hearing about them today, but scripture written about him lets us know he was turning wrath away from Israel, in the same manner Phinehas the priest had dealt with Zimri and the Midianitish woman when Israel was in the wilderness. In that incident, having not even made it to the Promised Land, the people had turned away from God yet again; this time committing idolatry with the Moabites and Midianites. They became so bold with it that a man named Zimri from the tribe of Simeon brought a Midianitish woman to show off to his brethren. The wrathful justice of God fell swiftly upon Israel for that idolatry, and a plague was already breaking out among the people when this man strode into the camp with his trophy woman. That was when Phinehas the priest rose up and took them both out. In that short window, twenty-four thousand Israelites perished in the plague.

Regardless of what we think about this example of one-man judge, jury, and executioner, we need to look at God's take on it. This is what God had to say to Moses about it: "And the

---

[13] This event represented the first of dual fulfillments of the angel's words to Daniel in Daniel Chapter 11 verse 30: For the ships of Chittim shall come against him: therefore he shall be grieved, and return, and have indignation against the holy covenant: so shall he do; he shall even return, and have intelligence with them that forsake the holy covenant. And arms shall stand on his part, and they shall pollute the sanctuary of strength, and shall take away the daily sacrifice, and they shall place the abomination that maketh desolate. And such as do wickedly against the covenant shall he corrupt by flatteries: but the people that do know their God shall be strong, and do exploits. And they that understand among the people shall instruct many: yet they shall fall by the sword, and by flame, by Captivity, and by spoil, many days. This is the first fulfillment. The Lord Jesus Christ alluded to this same event, but in context of the time of the end. In the end time scenario, the temple is the body of man, the altar is the soul, and the abomination of desolation is the mark, name, and number of the Beast.

Lord spake unto Moses, saying, Phinehas, the son of Eleazar, the son of Aaron the priest, hath turned my wrath away from the children of Israel, while he was zealous for my sake among them, that I consumed not the children of Israel in my jealousy." So we can see that under the Mosaic Law, such actions were not deemed excessive when blatant wickedness was pushed in the people's faces to entice them into corruption.

The Gentile reasoning was that strength was in numbers, and based on this faulty logic, time and again they assembled massive armies composed of forces from multiple countries to overthrow Maccabeus and his men. But like his forefather Abraham who subdued the armies of five kings with only three hundred eighteen men, Judas 'The Hammer' was supernaturally empowered and undefeatable in battle. A wicked leader—Apollonius—gathered the Gentiles together, along with a great host out of Samaria; but the outcome: defeated. Seron, a prince of the army of Syria assembled a "mighty host of the ungodly" to attack Maccabeus; but the outcome: defeated.

King Antiochus became very worried about Maccabeus and went to Persia to raise more money to finance a campaign massive enough to eliminate him. In his absence, he entrusted one of his lackeys—Lysias, to manage the threat. Lysias recruited three mighty men of the king's friends to lead an army of forty thousand footmen, and seven thousand horsemen to attack Judah. In a classic case of counting chickens before they hatch, the merchants of the area brought much gold, silver, and servants to join the army in the camp in anticipation of buying the (to be) captured children of Israel for slaves; also a power of Syria and of the Philistines joined the assault; once again, the result: defeated.

The following year Lysias assembled another fighting force—this time, sixty thousand chosen footmen and five thousand horsemen. Elephants were even brought in from India; militarized and outfitted like armored vehicles, complete with the Indian who was expert in handling them. But the outcome was the same: defeated. These are just a few of the multiple battles Judas fought; each time vastly outnumbered and with inferior weapons. In the eyes of man, it looked like curtains for Maccabeus; but Syria had forgotten about the days of the prophet Elisha as told in II Kings verses 8, and 14-17 ...

"Then the king of Syria warred against Israel, and took counsel with his servants, saying, In such and such a place shall be my camp.

Therefore sent he thither horses, and chariots, and a great host: and they came by night, and compassed the city about.

And when the servant of the man of God was risen early, and gone forth, behold, an host compassed the city both with horses and chariots. And his servant said unto him, Alas, my master! how shall we do?

And he answered, Fear not: for they that be with us are more than they that be with them. And Elisha prayed, and said, Lord, I pray thee, open his eyes, that he may see.

And the Lord opened the eyes of the young man; and he saw: and, behold, the mountain was full of horses and chariots of fire round about Elisha."

Judas Maccabeus needed the supernatural favor of God, because not only was he tasked with simultaneously subduing the evil hordes assembled against him and rallying his own men to not lose heart, he also had to be wary of evil men like the wicked Alcimus trying to muscle his way in to the high priesthood; a position which would wield great power over the people. On top of that, he had to face off enemies like Nicanor who was described as bearing "deadly hate" for Israel. Then there was the ancient and ever present hatred of the children of Esau, who gladly provided aid and comfort to Israel's enemies. You can see from this description that the loathing and violence we encounter in this society has primeval roots. It never ends, it just changes nations and ethnicities. However, all Nicanor's hate could not save him. When he clashed with "The Hammer of Israel", he was just another nail, who ended up decapitated with his head hung from the tower and his proud tongue cut in pieces and left for bird food.

While we should never stop seeking the scriptures and seek God's face in prayer for strength and direction, in times of severe testing or tribulation God will sometimes exhort and encourage us with dreams and visions from his throne room. Such was the case with Maccabeus, who received a vision of the priest Onias encouraging him, and the prophet Jeremiah handing him a holy gold sword from the Lord with which he would be able to wound his adversaries. Supernaturally empowered in this manner, Maccabeus was able to achieve victory fighting under conditions that would have been suicidal for anyone else. His enemies would come out against him with battle anthems and trumpets, but he would approach them with prayer and supplication to God.

When, in the time of God's sovereign will, Judas Maccabeus died, it was in a severe battle with his archenemy Bacchides who was accompanied by none other than the wicked Alcimus who coveted the high priest position. This confirms that for a long time there have been those among our people who cloak themselves in an air of godliness and piousness but are inwardly compromised by personal vendettas and allegiance to carnal, worldly power. The duty of the high priest was to make intercession to God on behalf of the people. Judas Maccabeus was striving to bring Israel back into line with the Law and the prophets; and here was a man vying for the position of representing the people before God—intent on killing him!

It seems Judas sensed the stress of constant warfare on the nation, for before his death he wisely made a mutual treaty with the Romans; the newest power on the world block. He observed how Rome strengthened itself by prudently making alliances with nations, but in the event of threat or aggression moved with swift and deadly decisiveness. However, it appears word did not reach his new ally in time for them to assist him in his final battle. Judas Maccabeus died the way he lived: valiant like a lion and refusing to back down from the enemy.

Once Maccabeus was dead, wicked men began to flex themselves again throughout the land. Just as today, there were those of the nation of Israel who hated their own people. For this reason, Maccabeus' brother Jonathan answered the call to leadership. He also was forced to wage many battles against both the ungodly and those among his own people who seemingly existed for the purpose of sabotaging Israel. Jonathan accepted the position of high priest, bringing a measure of calm and revival to the nation. When he was assassinated by treachery, his brother Simon assumed the mantle in his stead. The rule of Simon brought a peace, blessing, and stability upon Israel that had not been seen since the Seleucids wrested Judah from the Persians and Egyptians. The Romans also renewed the treaty they had made with Maccabeus and Jonathan.

Jonathan had assumed the office of high priest by political appointment. After his death, his brother Simon took over the position, in spite of the fact they were not descended from the priestly lineage of Zadok. However, it had been mutually agreed by the people and priests, that Simon should accept this station, until there should arise a faithful prophet. They did not know—but God knew—that several generations hence, a prophet like unto Moses would appear in their midst; one who was both Faithful and the Enduring High Priest of the people.

Later successors of the Hasmonaean descent functioned not as high priests, but ruled as kings. Simon's son John Hyrcanus I effectively brought Samaria and Idumea (which is Edom) under control. Those following under him accepted titles of royalty, but this caused no little dissension because everyone knew the royal family was only from the house of David. Indeed, the Root and Offspring of Jesse would soon appear, but cloaked in human flesh as a baby whose first cries would mingle with the lowing of cattle and the bleating of sheep.

Decades of political intrigue would ensue, with internal struggles between the Sadducees; purists of the written Law, and the Pharisees—who added their oral interpretations to the Law. However, if the hearing of the word is not mixed with faith, it will not profit. And when the word of God is supplemented by personal tradition, it makes it of none effect and ultimately the tradition ends up replacing the commandment of God. There can be no doubt these extremes and excesses were a reaction to the interference of Hellenism.

The entrapment between intrusive pagan rulers who desired worship, and the vassal rulers of Judah who sought to placate the pagan's narcissistic egos caused many of the Hebrews to long for the Consolation of Israel. The Maccabean champions had revived a semblance of pride and autonomy, but that was quickly becoming eclipsed by the dawn of the powerful Roman Empire. Under Herod the Great, Palestine became a Roman protectorate, and talk of dissension or deliverance could be interpreted as seditious and lead to imprisonment or death. To add insult to injury, Herod was an Edomite. Judah was effectively controlled by a major pagan power, and micromanaged by an archenemy.

Herod manifested his true allegiance when he mounted a gold eagle—the symbol of Roman power—above the main gate of the Temple as an architectural embellishment. However, the young men who were zealous for the Law tore the Roman standard down and demolished it. How often today in churches do we observe American and often both American and Israeli flags on the platform at either side of the pulpit. No emblem of empire has any business competing for the attention of the souls of men when the gospel is preached. Jesus' kingdom is not of this world; neither should there be an attempt to mix or meld the kingdoms of this world with the kingdom from above. Yet, in the West, this is accepted as the norm.

Such was the chaotic spiritual climate when the Lord Jesus Christ, the Lion of the Tribe of Judah—began his ministry among the lost sheep of the House of Israel. The solutions he brought were not the ones the zealots wanted to hear. And the simplicity of the gospel was in stark contrast to the complex and overbearing oral interpretation of the Law on which the Pharisees prided themselves. No amount of sophistry or rhetoric could cause Jesus to snare himself with his own words. And when was the last time anyone had walked in their midst healing the sick, raising the dead, restoring the lame, and opening blind eyes? The only way to accuse him was to do so falsely ...it was impossible to even lay hands on him. His own disciples asked, "What manner of man is this?" The people marveled when he taught because he instructed as one that had authority, not as the scribes. His enemies lamented that, "The world is gone after him." Even the Gentiles i.e. Pilate's wife, knew he was a "just man," and the Roman soldier said, "Truly this was the Son of God."

The Southern Kingdom (Judah) Legalistic and Unrealistic

The Lord Jesus Christ came unto his own, but his own received him not. How could this have been, during an era when the Messiah was so longed for? Perhaps this rejection was divinely arranged so that the heart of man could be laid bare and his true nature manifested, that no flesh might glory before God. In the Book of Luke Chapter 2 verses 25-35, we read where the Holy Ghost revealed to devout Simeon that Jesus was...the glory of God's people Israel, and that he was set for the fall and rising again of many in Israel; and for a sign which would be spoken against...that the thoughts of many hearts might be revealed.

This prophetic utterance by Simeon is loaded with insight and bears exposition. In this statement, the Greek for the word 'glory' means dignity, honor, praise, and worship; 'set' means appointed; the word 'fall' means a crash or downfall; the word 'rising' speaks to resurrection or rising from the dead; 'sign' is defined as a miracle or supernatural, and 'against' means to refute or deny. Basically Simeon said the One who is our dignity, honor, praise, and worship was appointed to determine eternal death and damnation or righteous resurrection for Israel, and he would be a supernatural sign that man would attempt to refute and deny; and the divine reason behind this was so the thoughts of men's hearts might be revealed.

Christ is the only one God has appointed to be our glory, and he is the only one we can glory in. How sad that man would witness the miracles and resurrection of the Lord Jesus Christ, and still speak great words and pompous speeches to refute and deny him—especially in light of the fact that he holds the power of life and death in his hand. Ultimately, our life choices and actions will be weighed against the Word he has spoken; our thoughts and motives will be revealed, our works manifested and tried by his fire.

The inhabitants of Judah, which included the Benjamites and Levites, thought they had a handle on all things spiritual. After all, they were not worshiping a bevy of idols like their brethren in the northern kingdom had done. They possessed the Temple, which was representative of God dwelling among them—and the priests and the Levites performed the associated sacrifices and other duties according to Moses' Law. Further, although Herod the Great was a despised Edomite, he had greatly beautified the Temple, and it was a focal point of intense national pride. All the prescribed ingredients for spiritual success were seemingly there, yet the Lord Jesus Christ lamented that it would all be destroyed, because they knew not the time of their visitation.

The Greek word used here for visitation is the root for the term episcopal, and literally means to visit and inspect for the purpose of relieving. In other words, the Law was given because of transgression (remember, many in Israel were worshipping idol gods while they were in Egypt) and the Apostle Paul tells us the Law functioned as a 'schoolmaster'; an instructor, to bring them to Christ. The Law could not save Israel, but it served the purpose of defining sin and establishing the discipline and uniqueness that would set them apart from the rest of the world, and prepare their hearts for the higher level of God's righteousness dwelling in them by faith—as opposed to obeying a written code. How then, did they miss it? The testimony of the first century martyr Stephen provides keen insight.

In Acts Chapter 7 verse 51, Stephen tells the men of Israel they are stiffnecked and uncircumcised in heart and ears, and that they always resist the Holy Ghost. The word stiffnecked used here means dry, hard, or tough, harsh, severe, and obstinate, and the word resist means to oppose. There was no cutting away of the thick veil over their minds and ears so that they would be sensitive to the prompting of God's Spirit. In John Chapter 8 verse 43, Jesus said to them, "Why do ye not understand my speech? even because ye cannot hear my word." This was right before he told them, "Ye are of your father the devil, and the lusts of your father ye will do" because he knew the murderous intent of their heart. Here was Christ, the very one who gave them the Law, speaking to them about the desires of God's heart, and it was as though he was speaking a foreign language.

The Apostle Paul tells us in Hebrews Chapter 4 verse 2 that the word preached—if not mixed with faith—will not profit those who hear it. Israel had over fourteen hundred years under the Law for faith to take root and develop to the point they obeyed out of love and reverence, not just out of a fear of punishment. But this spiritual transition never took place, as they were continually compromised by their own idolatries and hardheartedness. Then, once the Gentiles began dominating them, they also had to suffer the insult of the pagan's worship. This caused the more 'pious' among them to cleave ever more zealously to the principles of the Mosaic Law in their opposition to the heathen influence. But because they were dealing strictly with the letter of the Law, and not faith, or love, or God's Spirit, they were still hardhearted and obstinate. Therefore, they dealt very cruelly and legalistically with their own people. Basically you had a segment of the population presenting that they held the key to the knowledge of God, but their hearts were mean-spirited, hypocritical, prideful, and spiritually dull. They wanted to be the gateway to God in the eyes of the people, but they themselves were blind guides. Israel was a lost flock, and the Gentiles needed a true light.

It was time for a new and living way, mercy instead of sacrifice, and the perfect fulfillment of Sinai's ordinances in all points, so that a new and better covenant could be revealed. The first man from earth could not do this, but the second man from heaven could. Christ accomplished this, and was then ready to present his body a living sacrifice for the sins of the entire world. When he was nailed to the cross, the handwriting of ordinances was also nailed to it with him. The cross represents death. Sin is the sting of death, and the Law was the strength of sin.

Therefore, it was impossible for Israel to ever be justified by the works of the Law. Jesus was manifested to destroy the works of the devil, take the heavy burden of the Law off the people through his own sinless life; exchanging it for his easy yoke under the Law of Love, and give them an everlasting spiritual Sabbath rest in him. If only they would have searched the scriptures that testified of Him, and approached him with the heart of a little child. And how heavy his heart must have been; desiring to gather them to himself, yet knowing that it could not be that a prophet perish outside of Jerusalem.

The Northern Remnant...Alienated and Out of Touch

When Jesus said he was sent to the lost sheep of the House of Israel, he was not just referring to those in Jerusalem proper and the suburbs, but also those who had escaped out of the hand of the king of Assyria during the days of the prophets and still dwelt in the northern portions of the land. By this time though, the inhabitants of the northern kingdom had intermarried with the heathen around them. This was why the people of Judah would have nothing to do with them: they considered them impure and idolaters. Judah had not forgotten about the golden calves in Dan, or the notorious king Jeroboam, who bears the pejorative title of the one who made Israel to sin.

This is how the people of Judah felt, but the Lion of the Tribe of Judah saw it differently, for man looks on the outward appearance, but God looks on the heart. That was why on the way from Judæa to Galilee, he providentially timed his journey to arrive at the mid-point—Samaria—and stopped by a well where he knew...pretty soon, a woman would be arriving to draw water. She was coming at high noon; an hour of the day when the other women of the area had already gotten their water, and she would be alone. That way she could avoid the whispers and glances directed at women who led lifestyles like hers: that of a practicing adulteress.

Often as New Covenant believers we speak of witnessing and soul winning, and indeed Proverbs Chapter 11 verse 30 advises, "...he that winneth souls is wise." How many know that the Lord Jesus Christ is the master communicator and ultimate soul winner, and Job Chapter 36 verse 22 reminds us no one can teach like God. To engage in dialogue with the Lord is to simultaneously have ones' spirit laid bare and everything brought into proper perspective. Almost as awe-inspiring is the way he sets up encounters with lost souls and meets them at a point where they can relate.

Jesus' strategy was simple, yet brilliant; he sat on the well. There, his presence was unavoidable. That in and of itself is awkward enough, in that the woman may be forced to say, "excuse me" or, avoid any conversation and fill her vessel in shamed silence. But he removes that burden by initiating the conversation and requesting a drink. The woman responds in stunned disbelief...she cannot believe a man from Judah would speak with a Samaritan; or such a woman as herself—for she knows what type of woman she is. What she doesn't know is that he also knows what type of woman she is. But he has already caught her off guard by his unorthodox approach. So she attempts to regain control of the conversation by referring to the established boundaries that exist between them.

Jesus neither acknowledges nor refutes her statement about the separation between people of the former northern kingdom and the southern kingdom. Instead, he redirects the dialogue back to the original subject: water. He then piques her curiosity by stating if she knew who had asked her for a drink, she would have asked him instead, and he would have given her living water. Now, the ice is broken, and what a dialogue begins to unfold! We must remember this is a woman who most likely in her entire life has never spoken with any one from Judah; no less engaged in casual conversation with one of their men. But something about this man has both disarmed her natural apprehension and in her spirit let her know she can speak frankly.

Her response in our modern vernacular could be interpreted as, "Seriously?? Be real." "Sir, thou hast nothing to draw with, and the well is deep: from whence then hast thou that living water? ...this well is deep; and you have nothing with which to extract water. So where is this 'living water' you have?" Now Jesus is just sitting there calmly listening to her; he has not rebuked her, or insulted her. So now she takes a little more initiative, and reminds him that she too, is of the heritage of Jacob "...Art thou greater than our father Jacob, which gave us the well, and drank thereof himself, and his children, and his cattle?"

Again, Jesus deftly sidesteps questions about his ability to deliver the living water, or how he rates against Jacob, the great patriarch of Israel. Rather, he again steers the conversation back to the original subject: water—and this time begins to elaborate on the unique qualities of this living water... "Whosoever drinketh of this water shall thirst again: But whosoever drinketh of the water that I shall give him shall never thirst; but the water that I shall give him shall be in him a well of water springing up into everlasting life."

Upon hearing this, we no longer detect skepticism in her reply. He has her convinced. She believes him. If he can produce this water, she wants it. She doesn't want to be thirsty again, and she is weary of making the trip to the well at high noon because of her stigma in the community as a whorish woman. Jesus asks her to go get her husband and come back. Now, how can she respond truthfully...without divulging the type of life she lives? So she admits, "I have no husband." The moment of truth manifests: not by her voluntary acknowledgment, but God's record where no detail is overlooked or omitted "...You have had five husbands, and the one you have right now is not yours ...you've spoken truly about this."

The realization sinks in. This is no regular man she is talking to; she is conversing with a prophet. For centuries, no prophet has ministered to the northern tribes. Now she is speaking directly to one! She seizes upon the once-in-a-life-time opportunity to get the truth about the great divide between her people and his—two groups that descended from the same father. "Our fathers worshipped in this mountain; and ye say, that in Jerusalem is the place where men ought to worship."

Indeed, she had been taught this, for during the reign of Jeroboam, the people were told Jerusalem was too great a distance to travel, and they were instructed to worship in Bethel and Dan, where the king set up two golden calves. The real reason behind Jeroboam's directive was not his concern for the distance his countrymen would have to travel, but to keep them from going to Jerusalem for any reason, lest they defect and return to the southern kingdom of Judah. By the time this woman was born, all she would have learned from Samarian history and culture was that the southern kingdom despised and disdained them, so Samaritans had their own local worship center.

Jesus' reply was a perfect combination of wisdom and truth. He didn't get caught up in the Jerusalem versus Samaria issue, although he was careful to point out that Judah knew what they worshiped, but the Samaritans didn't. God had chosen Jerusalem as his special city, and the Temple as the place he would meet his people. Man had chosen the territory of Dan as early as the time of the judges of Israel, a place that became synonymous with idolatry and apostasy. What Jesus said next was very revealing and has profound implications for our time "...the hour cometh, when ye shall neither in this mountain, nor yet at Jerusalem, worship the Father...But the hour cometh, and now is, when the true worshippers shall worship the Father in spirit and in truth: for the Father seeketh such to worship him. God is a Spirit: and they that worship him must worship him in spirit and in truth."

Essentially, what Jesus has just disclosed is a precious truth which had eluded the most esteemed teachers, priests, and scribes in Jerusalem. Because of the nature of God, God is not concerned about where people worship him, but how. The woman's reply indicates that despite the apostasy associated with the northern tribes, Messianic hope is still a significant tenet of their belief system. She is fully engaged with Jesus; trivialities about water and tribal enmities having taken a back seat to the gnawing spiritual ache inside "...I know that Messias cometh, which is called Christ: when he is come, he will tell us all things." Jesus saith unto her, "I that speak unto thee am he."

He told her what she needed to know. The rest of the story, how she left her water pot, went back to the city, and testified to the men of Samaria; how they came out to see him, and how he lodged with them for two days, is all written in the 4th Chapter of John's gospel. The Samaritans desire for Jesus to remain with them shows the hunger they had for the word of God, and the need to know that God still loved them and had not deserted them.

An interesting observation is made concerning Jesus' words to his disciples while the woman was gone into the city to get the Samaritan men. "Lift up your eyes, and look on the fields; for they are white already to harvest. And he that reapeth receiveth wages, and gathereth fruit unto life eternal: that both he that soweth and he that reapeth may rejoice together. And herein is that saying true, One soweth, and another reapeth. I sent you to reap that whereon ye bestowed no labour: other men laboured, and ye are entered into their labours." While many of the Samaritans of the woman's city believed strictly on the woman's testimony, many more believed as they listened to Jesus' teachings and declared, "...this is indeed the Christ, the Saviour of the world." Nowhere is the scripture "One soweth, and another reapeth" so clearly illustrated as what occurred in Samaria just a few years later; based on the account recorded in Acts Chapter 8 verses 5-7 "...Then Philip went down to the city of Samaria, and preached Christ unto them. And the people with one accord gave heed unto those things which Philip spake, hearing and seeing the miracles which he did.

For unclean spirits, crying with loud voice, came out of many that were possessed with them: and many taken with palsies, and that were lame, were healed.

And there was great joy in that city. But there was a certain man, called Simon, which beforetime in the same city used sorcery, and bewitched the people of Samaria, giving out that himself was some great one:

To whom they all gave heed, from the least to the greatest, saying, This man is the great power of God. And to him they had regard, because that of long time he had bewitched them with sorceries.

But when they believed Philip preaching the things concerning the kingdom of God, and the name of Jesus Christ, they were baptized, both men and women.

Then Simon himself believed also: and when he was baptized, he continued with Philip, and wondered, beholding the miracles and signs which were done. Now when the apostles which were at Jerusalem heard that Samaria had received the word of God, they sent unto them Peter and John:

Who, when they were come down, prayed for them, that they might receive the Holy Ghost: (For as yet he was fallen upon none of them: only they were baptized in the name of the Lord Jesus.) Then laid they their hands on them, and they received the Holy Ghost."

The significance here is that the northern Israelites—isolated and rejected by their southern brethren, were loved and cherished by their Kinsman Redeemer—the Star of Jacob. Many were hungry for the word of God and it seems those of the northern area were more ready to accept him as their Messiah than those from his own tribe. He taught the disciples a valuable lesson in unity and brotherhood. He demonstrated the time was at hand where those of the northern tribes need not feel condemned if they did not worship God at the Temple in Jerusalem, because God was specifically looking for worshipers who would worship him in spirit and truth. In reading this account, how often do people realize that Christ revealed this foundational precept of worshiping God in spirit and truth to a so-called outcast, rather than his own tribe who trusted that they knew everything there was to know about God! Or that he spoke to the woman about God in terms of 'the Father': indicating God still viewed her people as sons and daughters of the covenant and promises.

Jesus sowed the seed of the Word among the Samaritans, and shortly after his death and resurrection, Philip the Evangelist watered it. Then, God gave an unprecedented increase! We can also see from this account that the first century church included water immersed, Holy Ghost filled black Hebrews from the remnant of the northern tribes, in addition to the land of Judæa. This refutes the false teaching that the baptism of the Holy Ghost as demonstrated on the Day of Pentecost was only for the apostles' witness to the international assembly in Jerusalem. As Peter preached, it was—and still is—for the men and brethren of Israel, their children, those who are afar off, and as many as the Lord our God shall call.

WHAT'S IMPORTANT

The battle never lets up for the genealogical descendants of Jacob. In Israel's infancy oppression came from Egypt. After the Exodus, the nations surrounding the land God deeded to the twelve tribes were continually antagonistic. When Judah returned from the Babylonian exile, they encountered hostilities directed toward their efforts to rebuild the Temple and the city walls. As the times of the Gentiles unfolded, virulent hatred emanated from the Syrian Seleucid rulers who compelled Israel to Hellenize (adopt Greek customs) sacrifice to idols, and forsake the tenets of the Mosaic Law on pain of death. This pressure was magnified by the apostasy characterizing Israel as a whole, with many Hebrews joining the consensus of the ungodly against the righteous. Those who stood for uprightness and the covenant of the forefathers were few indeed against a mighty tide of evil. But even as many battles were fought to purge wickedness from Israel, a new era was dawning where the theater of war would transition from battlefields and guerrilla warfare to the hearts and souls of men and their choice to accept or reject the Lord Jesus Christ as the only one who could redeem and save them.

Out of this spiritual interference rose a movement to purify the national conscience and return Israel to the moorings of the Mosaic Law. One end of the spectrum taught letter strict adherence to the Law, and had hope in this life only, with no belief in resurrection. The other extreme, while believing in the resurrection of the dead, began to take the liberty of adding their tradition and analysis to the Law and representing it as the divine directives of God, thereby making the commandment of God of none effect. When the Lord Jesus Christ confronted them with their error and hypocrisy, they had too much pride to admit their wrong, and their conviction gendered resentment and hatred rather than repentance. However, whether or not they would admit their wrong, Christ's works testified that he was the Holy and Just One.

One result of the Hellenistic interference was the attempt to superimpose the symbols and images of the heathen upon the pure word of the Law and the prophets. This practice was carried forward by the Edomite king Herod the Great with the mounting of Rome's eagle standard over the Temple entrance in Jerusalem.

We saw that many descendants of the northern tribes, alienated and left to muddle on void of direction, still clung to the hope of Israel's Redeemer. After centuries of hostility, one Man walking in love broke the barrier that had been erected by the division of the kingdom after the death of Solomon. Today, the Master Witness; the Faithful and True One, has commissioned us to preach the gospel to everyone. A wise ambassador will meet people at their point of need, and reach out to them from a perspective they can relate to. The account of the woman at the well demonstrates that the vilest sinner, if won to Christ through repentance and renewal of spirit, can be transformed into a dynamic witness.

A solid parallel exists between the era we have just covered, and the times we currently live in. Since the so-called Emancipation Proclamation, success and acceptance for the Black man in the West has been based largely on how 'Hellenized' he is, or in other words, acclimated to the Greek/Roman/Anglo model. Because of this, great pressure has been exerted on the people to adapt their social mores and even worship patterns in line with those of the oppressor. Because the oppressor ultimately controls the legal, economic, and social constructs of the West, he thwarts attempts to resist acclimation by recruiting those among the Captivity who value lucre and the praise of men over absolute allegiance to God. Unfortunately, the conditions of Captivity tend to produce greater numbers on the side of those who choose to cast their lot with man, than those who place their trust solely in God, his revealed word, and his covenant promises. This means there will—at least initially—be only a remnant bearing the heat of the day and the forefront of the spiritual battle.

One reaction to such acclimation is a zealous disgust toward those who seemingly are so easily 'brainwashed' and deceived by the social engineering ploys and manipulation of the oppressor. However, we must remember that the awakening of the sons of Judah is an asynchronous process. Not everyone will come to the same realization of our identity at once. In fact, because of centuries of Captivity and the ongoing conspiracy to obscure and replace our heritage as the modern day descendants of the tribe of Judah, most people will only gain a gradual understanding—and that after moving past the initial shock and unbelief. Only then will the Biblical account make sense juxtaposed against life in the present. In communicating the connection of the Biblical scriptures to our Black brothers and sisters, we must adhere to the standard found in II Timothy Chapter 2 verses 24-25, which remind us that "...the servant of the Lord must not strive; but be gentle unto all men, apt to teach, patient, In meekness instructing those that oppose themselves." We must understand the spiritual condition of the hearts of the people of this present Captivity is basically the same as during the nascent days of the apostolic church: dry, hard, toughened, harsh, severe, and obstinate. The strong tendency to resist the Holy Ghost is still present. Some of this resistance is endemic to the inherent sinful nature of man, but with our people it is also influenced by failure to understand the Biblical root of the Captivity, the principle that God does require the past, and the reassurance that the Divine plan stipulates future justice in the form of a reciprocal Captivity for the oppressor. The natural reaction to subjugation is anger and resistance, while the infilling of the Holy Ghost requires repentance and submission: a one hundred-eighty-degree contrast.

Therefore, the witnessing of the gospel and truth of Biblical prophecy relating to our Captivity and redemption should always be prefaced with prayer and leading of the Spirit for wisdom. Dialogue should be conducted using speech seasoned with grace. Jesus himself is the prime example. During his earthly ministry, he demonstrated the ability to reach all men—from those of his own nation, to the separated brethren, to the Gentiles—with equal grace and ease. He would not break a reed that was already bruised, or quench smoking flax... Isaiah Chapter 42 verse 3.

We need to pattern our witnessing after him because we never know how close a person is to repentance and acknowledging of the truth. A person can be right on the cusp of turning from darkness to light, and it is not something readily perceived by visual observation. However, the Holy Ghost will know, so we must be sensitive to its prompting. The heart of man can be compared to a garden plot. Years of prayer and supplication by a relative who serves the Lord may cultivate the soil in preparation for receiving the seed. Someone else plants it, and over the course of time others water it. When a seed sprouts, it opens underground first in response to water and light, and is not noticeable until it emerges through the soil. Even as it gains a little height, it is still very fragile because the root is tiny and undeveloped. If someone comes along and carelessly tramples it, the plant perishes. So we should stick close to Jesus' model when communicating with others about the reality of God, the truth of His word, and the truth about our ancient heritage and covenant.

Chapter VIII...Two Kingdoms

From that time Jesus began to preach, and to say, Repent: for the kingdom of heaven is at hand.

Israel reached the zenith of glory under the reign of King Solomon. Solomon, whose name means 'Peace', was endowed with wisdom exceeded only by the Lord Jesus Christ, for God gave him a wise and an understanding heart; so that there was none like him before him, neither after him would any arise like unto him. It was a beautiful time to be alive in those days. The kingdom was quiet, because of the wisdom Solomon executed in judgment. No enemy lifted their hand against him, and in such an era of prosperity silver was as common as stones in Jerusalem.

The defining moment of the kingdom was the dedication of the Temple, the day the heavenly realm and the earthly kingdom representing it embraced; as the fire of God descended and consumed the burnt offering and sacrifices, and the massive Glory of God filled the sanctuary. Now, under the subjection of Rome and the Edomite kings who pandered to the Caesars, the people of Israel reminisced about the foregone days of glory and pondered the prophetic promise of a Deliverer who would restore them to their previous estate.

The Deliverer of Zion—Not as a King, but a Suffering Servant

Have you ever been diligently looking for something, frustrated that you can't find it; only to later discover it was right within your reach the whole time, but for some reason you never saw it? This is the case that best illustrates Israel's inability to identify and acknowledge their Savior. Sure, a few recognized right off: Simeon, Anna, the Wise Men from the East, and Jesus' cousin and herald John the Baptizer; but in each instance these were people who were actively seeking the kingdom, and the Savior's identity was revealed by God. This shows that many in those days had a strong nationalistic yearning for the restoration of the kingdom and dominion, but few were correctly seeking it through prayer and diligent examination of the scriptures. His coming was written all through the Law and the Prophets; Jesus himself said, "Search the scriptures...they are they which testify of me." Then too, our forefathers may have been as guilty as we sometimes are today of selective memory and cherry-picking scriptures. After all, Isaiah Chapter 53 verses 3-5 are not near as thrilling as Zechariah Chapter 14 verses 3-4.[14] Jesus didn't fit the profile of an intrepid leader who would stride onto the scene, crush the oppressive Roman power, and put Edom back in its place. He said he was one greater than

---

[14] Isaiah 53 verses 3-5: He is despised and rejected of men; a man of sorrows, and acquainted with grief: and we hid as it were our faces from him; he was despised, and we esteemed him not. Surely he hath borne our griefs, and carried our sorrows: yet we did esteem him stricken, smitten of God, and afflicted. But he was wounded for our transgressions, he was bruised for our iniquities: the chastisement of our peace was upon him; and with his stripes we are healed. Compare to Zechariah 14 verses 3-4: Then shall the Lord go forth, and fight against those nations, as when he fought in the day of battle. And his feet shall stand in that day upon the mount of Olives, which is before Jerusalem on the east, and the mount of Olives shall cleave in the midst thereof toward the east and toward the west, and there shall be a very great valley; and half of the mountain shall remove toward the north, and half of it toward the south.

Solomon, yet he lived as a homeless prophet, traveling on foot from city to city, village to village; dependent upon the hospitality of his closest followers. John the Baptizer said he was unworthy to untie Jesus' sandals, yet Jesus declined to receive honor from men. The Pharisees were looking for a tangible kingdom. Jesus told them the kingdom was an internal one that could not be visually observed.

Frankly, people had a problem with a Messiah that didn't fit the Deliverer archetype. So, many turned away in disillusionment. On top of that, they lacked the faith and divine revelation necessary to discern what he was saying. That was the same as being blind. If you turn away from the light—and you are already blind, you have nothing to look forward to than stumbling on in the darkness. And stumble they did. They studied and studied the Law and the Prophets, ever learning and never able to come to the knowledge of the Truth; even witnessed Jesus performing the gracious works of his Father...but still couldn't see who he was, and became offended and jealous when others acknowledged him as Messiah.

The Law of Love Contrasted with the Law of Sinai

The scriptures clearly teach that the Lord Jesus fulfilled the Law on every point without fail, and never sinned. This is what qualified him to be the perfect sinless sacrifice for both his brethren of Israel and the entire world. God's eternal justice demanded that the handwriting of ordinances given to man at Sinai be satisfied. However, no man born from the seed of Adam could ever fulfill this to the satisfaction of God's holiness. This does not mean there was fault in the Law, for Psalm Chapter 19 verse 7 states the Law is perfect. The fault rather, was in man, and his perpetual state of imperfection. The Apostle Paul explains that the decrees contained in the Law were contrary to us. The word contrary used here is defined in the Greek as an opponent, an adversary, or opposed to, and operating covertly—basically in a hidden way—and is closely linked to another word which means antagonistic. However, in spite of how that may sound, the Law was not some mean-spirited device God produced to entrap man. What the Law does do, is demonstrate just how far man has fallen from God's purity and righteousness.

Jesus' ability to fulfill God's righteous standard and remove it out of the way meant a New Covenant could be established which would exceed the written code and internalize God's righteousness in man. This would be accomplished by a never before revealed dynamic: faith working synergistically with love, enabled by the infilling of God's own Spirit in man. The Covenant sealed by the blood of Jesus would enable man to become a new creation in Christ: something the Law of Sinai could never do.

The Apostle Paul explains it this way in Galatians Chapter 5 verse 14: "For all the law is fulfilled in one word even in this; Thou shalt love thy neighbor as thyself." Romans Chapter 13 verses 8-10 assure us that "he that loveth another hath fulfilled the law. For this, Thou shalt not commit adultery, Thou shalt not kill, Thou shalt not steal, Thou shalt not bear false witness, Thou shalt not covet; and if there be any other commandment, it is briefly comprehended in this saying, namely, Thou shalt love thy neighbour as thy self. Love worketh no ill to his neighbour: therefore love is the fulfilling of the law."

The New Covenant surpasses the Law by demanding accountability in the realm of the heart from whence the issues of life proceed—long before the thoughts and intents of the heart manifest in the deeds outlawed in Sinai's code. Adultery? Don't even look on the opposite sex to lust. Murder? Stop hating. Theft? Work with your hands to provide for those in need. Lying? Let no evil communication proceed from your mouth, speak the truth in love, and remember God desires truth in the inward parts. Covetousness? Be content with such things as you have.

Notice the Covenant of Love to one's neighbor also encompasses any other commandment. This hearkens back to Jesus' statement to the Samaritan woman about God desiring to be worshiped only in spirit and truth—when the question arose of where to worship him. The encompassing of all commandments under the Covenant of Love also frees man from condemnation about when he worships, for now, not only a day—but we ourselves—must be kept holy and living sacrifices, and our Kinsman-Redeemer, the Lion of the Tribe of Judah, has called us to come unto him and he will give us Sabbath. The Greek word used for come in this instance means to come hither and follow. As in come close, and stay with him. Just as the Living Water offered to the sister at the well exceeded the natural water which one would eventually thirst for again, the Messiah who is our Sabbath rest far exceeds the six on/one off cycle, for...the Law was only a shadow of good things to come, not the very image of the things themselves...Hebrews Chapter 10 verse 1.

Jesus' teachings seemed radical and downright heretical to the Pharisees, who had practically created a scientific methodology in the interpretation and reinterpretation of the Law. By the time they got done with it—a little clarification here, some analysis and speculation there—they had made the commandment of God of none effect. However, that was what they wanted; that was the way they liked it. By developing a theology based on their own elucidation, they could remain the gatekeepers to God. The agonizing over the minutia of the Law was more about holding power over the people than love for God and the sheep of his pasture. When the Good Shepherd arrived on the scene, he cut to the chase, demystified the word, and revealed the heart of the Father toward his sons and daughters. This dealt a death blow to the Pharisaical control construct, and they declared war on Christ.

How desperate sinful, carnal man becomes when he perceives his power is slipping away from him. They sought time and time again to trap Jesus in his words, or apprehend him and take his life. But Jesus couldn't put his ministry on hold because of haters. He said, "I work and my Father works...I must work the works of him who sent me while it is day; for night cometh, and no man can work." So he kept preaching the good news of the kingdom, healing the sick, casting out demons, raising the dead, opening blind eyes, unstopping deaf ears, restoring the speech of the dumb, and feeding the masses.

He called the Pharisees out and publically humiliated them—not to make people snicker and laugh—but because what they were doing was so spiritually dangerous. Their construal of the Law and commandments was a deadly poison to anyone who ingested it. Jesus warned his disciples to beware of the leaven of the Pharisees and Sadducees. Leaven is a hidden ingredient in bread, and bread is eaten for sustenance. The idea here is that something that outwardly looks safe to consume for nourishment may be concealing something lethal. He called them hypocrites, blind guides, and whitewashed sepulchers that outwardly looked clean but inside were full of uncleanness and dead men's bones. This meant Jesus could see inside their hearts and souls and what he saw was spiritually identical to a decomposing corpse. He said they went out of the way—raveling great distances to make one convert; and only succeeded in making the convert twice the child of hell that they themselves were. By their misuse of the word, they

170

bound heavy burdens on people, whereas Jesus was offering an easy yoke. The Pharisees' worship of God had devolved to the point it was no longer about God: it was about them.

The Pharisees sat in Moses' seat—but for all this, Jesus said they were of their father the Devil. That is a very serious accusation. But it is also quite disturbing, because it means people can attempt to zealously adhere to the Mosaic Law and observe all the commandments and ordinances, and yet be a straight son of Satan and abhorred by God, spiritually dead inside, and guilty of placing heavy burdens on people who really want to serve God. This dynamic continues even to this day, with individuals and fellowships operating by either their own custom religious code or under the pretext of the Mosaic Law, keeping their followers in fear and bondage.

But the only thing that counts today is faith which works by love. If you love God and want to serve him, you need—as the Apostle Paul taught, to "be found in him, not having (your) own righteousness, which is of the Law, but that which is through the faith of Christ, the righteousness which is of God by faith..." Philippians Chapter 3 verse 9. Because "the just shall live by faith..." Hebrews Chapter 10 verse 38, and "...without faith it is impossible to please him: for he that cometh to God must believe that he is, and that he is a rewarder of them that diligently seek him..." Hebrews Chapter 11 verse 6.

I am sharing these scriptures about faith, love, and the New Covenant because some who have discovered their heritage as Hebrews feel the only way to achieve a favorable standing with God so he will turn our Captivity is to go back and do the works of the Law perfectly, where our forefathers failed. But this is a yoke which our ancestors were unable to bear, and neither can we. The good news of the kingdom is that our Elder Brother and Kinsman Redeemer stepped up and executed the righteousness of God on our behalf. Christ is the end of the Law for righteousness to every one that believeth...Romans Chapter 10 verse 4. Here are the definitions used for the Greek word end as used in the context 'end of the law': conclusion of an act or state, termination, paid—as in a levy, finally, uttermost, complete, execute, conclude, discharge a debt, accomplish, make an end, fill up, expire, finish. **Bottom line, the place you want to be is in Christ Jesus as a new creation.**

When people try to bear down on you about adhering to the Mosaic Law, stop and ask yourself if there was ever a time in the history of our ancestors when someone was able to please God without the Law. I am sure that Abel, Enoch, Job, Abraham, Isaac, Jacob, and righteous Cornelius will quickly come to mind! I submit to the reader that this is the crux of what the Lord Jesus was trying to impart in his sermons and teachings to his disciples and the people: the level of spirituality and righteousness that exceeds the Mosaic Law.

Furthermore, the righteousness which is by faith in Christ ministers life abundantly and ultimately everlasting life, while the Law can only minister death...for no person could ever keep it perfectly. That is why they had to continually sacrifice animals, with the blood as an atonement for sin. It could not wash away the sin consciousness of man, only atone for it in the sight of God. But Christ our Passover was the final sacrifice—the end of the Law for righteousness to every one that believeth!

The Apostle Paul shows that it is possible to attempt to be righteous by the standard of the Mosaic Law and still fail to be submitted to the righteousness of God. Who wants to take the risk of being told, "Depart from me, I never knew you" on that Great Day of the Lord?

"But Israel, which followed after the law of righteousness, hath not attained to the law of righteousness.

Wherefore? Because they sought it not by faith, but as it were by the works of the law. For they stumbled at that stumblingstone;

As it is written, Behold, I lay in Sion a stumblingstone and rock of offence: and whosoever believeth on him shall not be ashamed. Brethren, my heart's desire and prayer to God for Israel is, that they might be saved.

For I bear them record that they have a zeal of God, but not according to knowledge.

For they being ignorant of God's righteousness, and going about to establish their own righteousness, have not submitted themselves unto the righteousness of God.

For Christ is the end of the law for righteousness to every one that believeth." Romans Chapter 9 verses 31-33; Romans Chapter 10 verses 1-4.

It doesn't take faith to obey a written code; you just do it or face the consequences. It does take faith to please God; and he wants us to spiritually move up to the level of our patriarch Abraham:

...they which be of faith are blessed with faithful Abraham. For as many as are of the works of the law are under the curse: for it is written, Cursed is every one that continueth not in all things which are written in the book of the law to do them. But that no man is justified by the law in the sight of God, it is evident: for, The just shall live by faith. And the law is not of faith: but, The man that doeth them shall live in them. Galatians Chapter 3 verses 9-12. So, the choice is to attempt to live in the Law, or become a new creation in Christ Jesus.

Two Kingdoms...Which Will Judah Choose?

The elders and chief priests and scribes in Jerusalem held a tenuous position. Similar to many pastors and preachers today, they were greatly magnified in the people's eyes and held great sway and power over them. But in the eyes of the Gentile power that held Palestine in its grip, they were little more than toothless lions. Their powers were severely curtailed under Roman dominion, and their peculiar belief system was tolerated to the extent they did not incite the people to sedition. In fact, the pagans could logically ask the question, 'if the Hebrew's God was so all powerful, why was Palestine now a vassal of Rome?'

It is the nature of those who possess power—no matter how little they may have, to not voluntarily relinquish it. And in the mind of those who receive honor from one another and love the praise of men more than the praise of God, it is acceptable to sacrifice integrity to maintain a coveted position. So what happens when someone comes along and begins to promote a kingdom based on totally different values than that which the power seekers have always treasured...a kingdom open to the very people they despise as beneath them; a kingdom they cannot muscle their way into by virtue of wealth, politics, lineage, or influence?

Undoubtedly the answer depends upon which end of the spectrum a person occupies. If one is among the wealthy, famous, and powerful, the kingdoms of this present world present many lucrative and attractive options. However, if one is among the majority who are disdained, disenfranchised, manipulated, and crushed by the first group, the kingdoms of this world hold little appeal, and while there may be a sense of admiration for those so loftily esteemed, the realization that such prestige is reserved for an elite few triggers envy, which ultimately leads to resentment.

Those who are able to rise above the disgruntlement and anger over such economic injustice and inequity are men and women who are pursuing a higher vision than anything this world has to offer, and understand their purpose in life is to align with the High Realm, by preparing themselves for future service in it, and positioning themselves as the beacons pointing the way to it. This High Realm—the Kingdom of Heaven—was the frequent subject of Jesus' teaching and parables, and he taught using illustrations from everyday life that people could relate to. This is what Jesus said about his Father's kingdom...

*it is at hand, therefore, repent

*it belongs to the poor in spirit

*it belongs to those who are persecuted for righteousness sake

*those who teach and do his commandments will be called great in it

*you can't enter it if your righteousness doesn't exceed the righteousness of the scribes and Pharisees

*only those who do the will of the Father can enter it

*the patriarchs Abraham, Isaac, and Jacob will be there

*the least person there is greater than John the Baptist

*it has suffered violence, and the violent take it by force; men press their way into it

*there are mysteries (hidden truths) associated with it

*it is like a field sowed with good seed by the householder, but infiltrated with bad seed by an enemy

*it is like a grain of mustard seed: starting tiny but growing exponentially

*it is like leaven hid in three measures of meal

*it is like a treasure hidden in a field which makes the entire field worth purchasing *it is like a pearl so valuable it is worth selling everything you have to obtain it

*it is like a dragnet gathering good and bad fish until it is full

*the keys to it are based on discernment given by the Father into the identity of Jesus

*one cannot enter it unless they possess the heart of a little child

*it is like a king exercising clemency, who expects his subjects to follow his example

*it is virtually impossible for a rich man to enter into it

*it is like a householder needing laborers who will pay every man the agreed wage

*it is like a king preparing a marriage feast where the intended guests all either find excuses, or misuse and murder the king's ambassadors, and occasion the mass gathering of complete strangers off the street in order to fill the banquet hall

*men are shut up from it by hypocritical religious figures who aren't going there either

*it is like a man on a journey who distributed resources to his servants; expecting return on his investment when he got back

*it is like virgins waiting for the summons of the bridegroom, and only half of them have enough oil to wait out his delay

In the other gospels and the Book of Acts, the Kingdom of Heaven is called the Kingdom of God, and additional truths are revealed concerning it, such as:

*man cannot enter it unless he is born of the water and the Spirit

*we must seek it first, and trust God to take care of our earthly needs

*no one who puts their hand to the plow—and then looks back, is worthy of it

*it cannot be entered into without much tribulation

From these descriptions, it is easy to see that the composition of the Kingdom of Heaven, the character of its citizens, those found worthy to rule in it, and those welcomed to participate in the wedding festivities are diametrically opposed to the operation of the kingdoms of the world and those who are highly esteemed on earth. The manipulative skills, willingness to collude with earthly powers, sophistry, spiritual rhetoric, and pious outward appearance that characterized the scribes, chief priests and Pharisees had absolutely no relevance or place in the unseen but Everlasting Kingdom. To enter in, they would have to divest themselves of all they were, and adopt the heart of a little child. Neither would it appeal to the zealots who desired to throw off the yoke of Rome and return Judah to a theocracy, for the hour was drawing nigh when the house of Israel would no longer be judged by the Law of Moses, but by the Word which their Messiah spoke. This is found in the Gospel of John Chapter 12 verses 47-49, and is a direct fulfillment of Deuteronomy Chapter 18 verses 18-19.

Repentance and Re-Consecration Prerequisites to a Restored Kingdom

Lord, who shall abide in thy tabernacle? who shall dwell in thy holy hill?

He that walketh uprightly, and worketh righteousness, and speaketh the truth in his heart.

He that backbiteth not with his tongue, nor doeth evil to his neighbour, nor taketh up a reproach against his neighbour.

In whose eyes a vile person is contemned; but he honoureth them that fear the Lord. He that sweareth to his own hurt, and changeth not.

He that putteth not out his money to usury, nor taketh reward against the innocent. He that doeth these things shall never be moved. Psalms Chapter 15.

Central to making the way straight for the return of the Lord Jesus Christ is Judah's return to a contrite and consecrated spirit. Because the ultimate purpose of the New Covenant is not just to be saved from sin, but to rule and reign with Christ—the mindset of Judah in the close of Captivity must shift from glorying in wisdom (technology), might (personal or positional power), and riches (material wealth and prestige) to an intimate knowledge of God's heart; and his delight in the exercise of lovingkindness, judgment and righteousness in the earth...Jeremiah Chapter 9 verses 23-24. The ruling of ones' own spirit must precede the rulership of men; for God himself told David that "He that ruleth over men must be just, ruling in the fear of God." II Samuel Chapter 3 verse 23.

The benediction of Isaac's blessing in Genesis Chapter 27 verse 29, confirms the dominion was granted to our forefather Jacob "Let people serve thee, and nations bow down to thee: be lord over thy brethren, and let thy mother's sons bow down to thee: cursed be every one that curseth thee, and blessed be he that blesseth thee." The lineage of rulership proceeds further through Jacob's blessing over his sons; focusing on Judah... "Judah, thou art he whom thy brethren shall praise: thy hand shall be in the neck of thine enemies; thy father's children shall bow down before thee."

However, before honour is humility; Proverbs Chapter 15 verse 33, and these are days when servants are seen upon horses, and princes walking as servants upon the earth...Ecclesiastes Chapter 10 verse 7. Speaking of our Kinsman—the Lion of the Tribe of Judah—the Apostle John reminds us that "as he is, so are we in this world," and Jesus himself cautioned that, "The servant is not greater than his lord." Hebrews Chapter 5 verse 8 shows us that although Christ was God's Son, he learned obedience by the things which he suffered. The Greek translation for the words learned and obedience imply the Lord understood compliance and submission to authority. He was willing to do this because he came to do God's will; in the volume of the book it was written of him, and all things written of him in the scriptures had to be fulfilled.

How many of us today are able to conform to compliance and submit to godly authority as Christ our example did? The Lord may first test us on the "ground floor" level. How well do we exercise obedience in our place of employment, or other venues where we are in the position of representing Jesus before unbelievers? And within the Body of Christ, are we able to submit ourselves one to another in the reverence of God, bearing each other's burdens? Or do we have a 'big I/ little you' and one-upmanship attitude amongst each other?

The Black church in the West today is in the unique position of rulership over the household of faith, to give them meat in due season. In the renewed understanding of our heritage and purpose, God calls us blessed if we are found nourishing his flock when his Son returns. We will then be entrusted with rulership over all his goods. And the parable of the talents illustrates if we are faithful over a few things, we will be made ruler over many things; in the presence of the fullness of the joy of the Lord. The Enduring Kingdom is built on this principle: that the spirit of man mirrors the Spirit of God. This ensures that when the Kingdom of God manifests on earth, our officers are peace, our exactors righteousness, our walls Salvation, and our gates Praise, as we rule and reign with Christ as Priests of the Lord and Ministers of our God.

The Prophecy of Destruction, Diaspora, and Gentile Occupation

For a brief moment, the praise and adoration due our Messiah-King rang out in the streets of Bethphage according to the prophecy of Zechariah Chapter 9 verse 9: "Rejoice greatly, O daughter of Zion; shout, O daughter of Jerusalem: behold, thy King cometh unto thee: he is just, and having salvation; lowly, and riding upon an ass, and upon a colt the foal of an ass." It was at the mount of Olives where Jesus gave the directive to two of his disciples to unloose the ass and her colt and bring them to him. Now I might add here that Zechariah also prophesies about the second return of Christ: also at the mount of Olives, not in meekness and lowliness; but in unbridled power as the touch of his foot causes an east/west fracture on the mount; resulting in the instantaneous creation of a valley between the north and south mass of the mountain.

But on this particular day near to the Passover celebration, the people came out in droves, laying down their garments and cutting down palm branches which formed a sort of 'royal carpet' all the way to Jerusalem. The masses both went before him and behind him, shouting, "Hosanna to the Son of David: Blessed is he that cometh in the name of the Lord; Hosanna in the highest!" The adulation of the people greatly displeased the chief priests and scribes. It was shortly after this that they closed ranks with the elders of the people and Caiaphas the high priest to formulate a conspiracy to eliminate Jesus once and for all.

They ramped up their efforts to entrap him in his words and discredit him in the eyes of the people; going so far as to interrupt him as he was teaching saying, "By what authority doest thou these things? and who gave thee this authority?" The Pharisees teamed up with the Edomite government shills—the Herodians—to try to set Jesus up for sedition against Rome asking him, "Tell us therefore, What thinkest thou? Is it lawful to give tribute unto Cæsar, or not?" On their heels came the Sadducees, posing what was little more than a lecherous fantasy thinly veiled as a rhetorical question about resurrection; which was obviously out of character for them since they taught there was no resurrection, angels, or spirits. Next they trotted out someone from the legal profession to ask the very vague and potentially ensnaring question, "...which is the great commandment in the Law"?

On every point our Elder Brother and Master Counselor shut down their arguments and confounded their sensual earthly wisdom. In response, they bristled in rage and hatred which would soon escalate to murder. Further, they had no repentance or remorse for the sins of their forebears who had persecuted and killed the prophets. On top of this, Jesus foretold they would also persecute, scourge, kill, and crucify the prophets, wise men, and scribes he would send to them in the future. The blood of the righteous was upon their forefathers, their own hands, and the generation alive at that time. A monumental upheaval unequaled to anything the sons of Abraham had faced was set to go into motion: a chastisement and 'time-out' that would take generations to complete, scheduled to be served concurrent with the times of the Gentiles. In a bizarre twist of Divine justice, the very praise the religious elders of our forefathers had cringed at, "Blessed is he that cometh in the name of the Lord" would be the words their latter day descendants would have to utter to summon their Deliverer!

"O Jerusalem, Jerusalem, thou that killest the prophets, and stonest them which are sent unto thee, how often would I have gathered thy children together, even as a hen gathereth her chickens under her wings, and ye would not!

Behold, your house is left unto you desolate.

For I say unto you, **Ye shall not see me henceforth, till ye shall say, Blessed is he that cometh in the name of the Lord**...For these be the days of vengeance, that all things which are written may be fulfilled.

But woe unto them that are with child, and to them that give suck, in those days! for there shall be great distress in the land, and wrath upon this people. **And they shall fall by the edge of the sword, and shall be led away captive into all nations**: and Jerusalem shall be trodden down of the Gentiles, until the times of the Gentiles be fulfilled."

If the timeline of the future could have been unveiled to them; enabling them to see the destruction of the Temple, the razing of their beloved city, the massive genocide, their desperate flight into unfamiliar regions to escape the boundaries of Roman jurisdiction, the fulfillment of the Pentateuchal and prophetic curses of Captivity, removal of heritage, and humiliation, would it have been enough to make them stop, reconsider their actions, and reverse course?

Judah's Heart Revealed...and the Curse that Only the Cross Can Break

One of the curses listed in Deuteronomy Chapter 28 resulting from our forefather's idolatry involved continual oppression wherever Israel was scattered around the earth:

"And thou shalt grope at noonday, as the blind gropeth in darkness, and thou shalt not prosper in thy ways: and thou shalt be only oppressed and spoiled evermore, and no man shall save thee...The Lord shall send upon thee cursing, vexation, and rebuke, in all that thou settest thine hand unto for to do, until thou be destroyed, and until thou perish quickly; because of the wickedness of thy doings, whereby thou hast forsaken me...thou shalt be only oppressed and crushed always."

One way this oppression manifests in our current Captivity is the rampant inequity inherent in the criminal justice system. Disparities in sentencing laws, egotistical, overzealous prosecutors, economic barriers to obtaining private defense counsel, and the dense saturation of those who abhor Judah involved in the policing, judicial, and prison industrial complex combine to place a grievous burden on our people that we are ill-equipped to deal with.

But before we bemoan the obvious, perhaps we should travel back through time and consider the lengths our forefathers went to in order to obtain an illegal conviction on our Elder Brother and Kinsman, Jesus Christ. As we replay the events leading up to the crucifixion, we should compare the Lord's experience with that of the Black man in the judicial system of today's Captivity.

Here's what Jesus met with from his own brethren:

*His accusers used gestapo methods; arresting him by night, when he wasn't even charged with anything

*Intimidation; his adversaries brought in the equivalent of a first century swat team; shining bright lights (lanterns and torches) and a great multitude with swords and weapons—against one man

*Once he was in custody, they began a desperate search to locate a witness for the prosecution, but could find none

*Finally, false witnesses step up to testify; but none of their statements agree... additionally, the ninth commandment of the law is broken

*Jesus is then falsely accused of blasphemy—but only based on his own answer—and the testimony of one witness is insufficient to convict for the death penalty; another Mosaic law blatantly broken

*Physical and psychological abuse of the prisoner begins—mocking, scourging, spitting, physical assault, and blindfolding him and striking him—then challenging him to prophesy and identify who hit him

*The next step is collusion with the Gentiles—they take Jesus to Pilate because under Roman domination they have been stripped of their power to execute any one

*Pilate is wise enough to know a person cannot be sentenced to death simply because he acknowledges a response someone else says about him..." And Pilate asked him, saying, "Art thou the King of the Jews"? And he answered him and said, "Thou sayest it..."

*Pilate attempts to extricate himself by resorting to change of venue...since apparently Jesus is a Galilæan and Galilee is Herod's jurisdiction, he extradites him there... however, Herod is unable to extract any response from Jesus either, so he and his men mock him by

178

treating him like fake royalty and send him back to Pilate...all this succeeded in doing was strengthening the alliance between the Romans and the Edomites...so now the bond is solidified between two of Judah's oppressors...how smart was that?

*The festive atmosphere of the upcoming Passover contributes to a mob mentality among the people, as they begin chanting to Pilate for the customary annual criminal release

*The chief priests influence public opinion and further inflame the mob: scripture literally states they wanted to destroy Jesus

*They go so far as to make a veiled threat to Pilate that he would jeopardize his allegiance to Cæsar by releasing Christ...so now they are down for Rome

*Pilate releases unto them Barabbas—who for sedition and murder was cast into prison, this is who they desired; so they actually preferred a murderer over a righteous man

*Impervious to the agony and humiliation associated with this slow motion execution, or the emotions of Jesus' family who are present, the mob and the chief priests continue to mock Jesus as he is dying

From the Gentiles:

*Pilate knew the religious leader's envious motivation, and he personally found no fault in Jesus; intending to merely chastise and release him, but ended up convicting him in order to calm the unrest and save his position as procurator

*The soldiers knew Pilate found no fault, but their sadistic streak incited them to rally the entire unit, who then mocked him with a purple robe, and jammed the crown of thorns on his head, and hit him on the head with a reed and spit on him

Now, let's look at a couple of scriptures in the book of Proverbs that should have been familiar to the scribes, Pharisees, and chief priests. "Death and life are in the power of the tongue: and they that love it shall eat the fruit thereof." Proverbs Chapter 18 verse 21.

"Thou art snared with the words of thy mouth, thou art taken with the words of thy mouth." Proverbs Chapter 6 verse 2.

Based on these two proverbs about the import of words we speak, let's look at the following statements. The chief priests answered, "We have no king but Cæsar" ...John Chapter 19 verse 15. Then answered all the people, and said, "His blood be on us, and on our children" ...Matthew Chapter 27 verse 25. So:

*Framing an innocent man for spite

*Police state tactics

*Lying to get a conviction

*Twisting the accused own words to frame them for a crime worthy of the most extreme penalty

*Physical and psychological abuse dealt to the accused

*Appealing to the oppressor to effect the harshest punishment

*Influencing public opinion to legitimize resorting to the oppressor for a remedy

*Desiring to actually destroy a person

*Divesting themselves of the natural affection that checks murderous excesses under the guise of professing allegiance to the state and the good of the public

*Preferring a murderer to an innocent person

*The judicial tendency to override the conscience and pervert justice in order to please the public and retain one's position.

*The sadistic tendencies of correctional personnel toward those in custody

If any of this sounds eerily reminiscent of the Black man's relationship with the criminal justice system in the West today, perhaps it is because the apple has not fallen far from the reaping tree in terms of what our ancient forebears dealt to their Kinsman, Jesus of Nazareth. They wanted Cæsar; now we are under Esau—who personifies both the lasting hatred of Edom, and the virulent spiritual prince of Grecia. Our forefathers wanted a murderer, now our young men are mowed down by vigilantes and law enforcement acting with deadly force under a knee-jerk reaction mentality.

Our forefathers appealed to allegiance with Rome; now the media and social engineers constantly pander to the legislature to impose ever harsher laws and sentencing guidelines which will disproportionately affect the sons of Judah. Our forefathers lied and bore false witness against Christ; now, how many of the sons of Israel have spent decades incarcerated, languish on death row, or have been executed due to lying testimony, confessions extracted under duress, or suppression of exculpatory evidence? Based on the increasing number of citizens cleared by DNA forensics, the law of sowing and reaping is in full effect. This is that law:

*You always reap what you sow...

*You always reap more than what was sown...

*You always reap in a different season than when you sowed

But what sort of people are so bloodthirsty that they will accept a burden of blood guiltiness and take the liberty of passing it by oath to their future generations? The answer is only a people who are spiritually deficit, and so blinded by hatred and envy that they have lost touch with their conscience and humanity. Yet in the midst of this feeding frenzy the religious leaders in Jerusalem still felt they were holy and pious. They wouldn't even enter Pilate's judgment hall during Jesus' sham trial because they didn't want to defile themselves before Passover. They were so spiritually blind they could not see their dark, envious, and murderous hearts were already defiled beyond comprehension.

Only the righteous blood of Jesus can invalidate the blood oath imposed on us by our forebears. As a people, we need to acknowledge our forefather's great hatred and sin against the Lord Jesus Christ; repent of it, and ask the Father's forgiveness. Before you respond, "Hey—but that wasn't me," remember that God requires the past. Recall also that the great men among the godly kings and prophets who petitioned God in the time of trouble, always confessed both their sin and the sin of their forefathers. This type of prayer is pleasing and acceptable to God, because it validates his honor in the righteous judgment which has befallen us. How do I know this? Because in example after example in the scriptures when this type of prayer was prayed, God answered and moved mightily on behalf of the people. It is time to stand in the ways, and see, and ask for the old paths, where is the good way, and walk therein. This type of prayer is one of those old paths and good ways.

In concluding this section, I thought it interesting to contrast the heart of the people with the heart of their Savior—both at his death, and at his final return.

"We have no king but Cæsar."

"Father, forgive them; for they know not what they do" ...Luke Chapter 23 verse 24

"His blood be on us, and on our children."

And one shall say unto him, "What are these wounds in thine hands?"

Then he shall answer, "Those with which I was wounded in the house of my friends..." Zechariah Chapter 13 verse 6

WHAT'S IMPORTANT

As a people, we cannot conceive of a time when there was only peace and prosperity, where we could walk out the door with no fear of humiliation or retaliation due to hatred or abhorrence; when we prospered and rejoiced in the Lord because we knew we were a blessed people in a blessed land. For a brief season such a time existed, during the reign of Solomon, whose name means 'peace.' Such an era will again manifest, when one greater than Solomon— the Lion of the Tribe of Judah, returns to establish his earthly reign and return us to the land of our nativity. Eyes have not seen, nor ears heard, neither has it entered into the heart of man the wonderful things prepared for the household of faith, but God's Spirit reveals them to us, giving us hope and joyous anticipation of our Lord's return.

Nevertheless, humility is before honour, and in the case of Israel in the Captivity, chastisement and temporary removal from heritage is in effect for the purpose of turning our hearts back to the patriarchs and observing their faith, trust, and perseverance. Our Elder Brother and Kinsman Redeemer has gone before us as our example, **identifying with us as a people**. His full splendor was restrained by **captivity** in a human body, he was **temporarily**

removed from the glory he shared with the Father, and the **chastisement** of our peace was laid on him. But for the joy set before him, he endured the cross and despised the shame. Now he is set down at the right hand of the Father in heaven, until his enemies are placed under his feet.

Like many today, our forefathers could not grasp the concept of a kingdom where citizenship was predicated on the cleanness of the heart rather than the might of the hands. They could see no significance in a person possessing such great power from God, yet not using it to overthrow the oppressor. What good was it to have the kind of charisma where people from all walks of life gravitated to you, massive crowds followed you, people shoved and jostled just for the chance to touch you, your ability to communicate was personable and easy to follow; yet so authoritative that you had a captive audience whenever you sat down to teach...what good was it to have all this...yet not overthrow the Roman power? When does a king not manifest his might by conquering and accumulating as much dominion as he can? For this reason, many of the people despised Jesus.

The chief priests, scribes, Pharisees, and Sadducees hated the Light of the World because he exposed the darkness in their hearts. They were frustrated by One who was not only keeping the Law without fail, but could also expound the higher principles behind each commandment to the people. The religious leaders did not want the people to be spiritually liberated. They preferred the written code of Sinai, because their rank permitted them to interpret the commandments as they saw fit, and judge the people harshly for infractions. They sought honor one from another and loved the praise of men more than the praise of God. Yet for all their pretense in the eyes of the people as great men of God, they could not do the works of the Father—the simplest miracles. The principles of the kingdom eluded them because of their pride, and impure heart.

When their hatred finally spiraled out of control, they crafted the most nefarious conspiracy recorded in history: the murder of the Just and Holy One. They even broke their own Mosaic code of law to accomplish this—showing that Moses really meant nothing more to them than a handy historical resource they could fall back on in an attempt to justify their position and actions. In their eagerness to yoke with the state to accomplish their deadly goal, they spoke unadvisedly with their lips, and the effects of this presumptuous speech still linger among those in Captivity today. However, we see that Jesus—to his last breath—held a heart of forgiveness, and even in the world to come, will reference the crucifixion ordeal as an event that occurred 'in the house of his friends'.

We are faced with the same choices today: to humble ourselves beneath the hand of God and wait on Him to exalt us as a people...to walk in the high spiritual principles of the Kingdom, or cleave to a written code that makes it easy to judge another man's servant...to close ranks with the powers of this present world when we feel our position or credibility is threatened, or stop, listen, and consider what is being said when a righteous person exalts the kingdom of God over the kingdom of man. One kingdom is founded on the Law, sin, condemnation, and death. The other is built on faith, the righteousness of Christ, and the gift of God which is eternal life. Which kingdom will you choose?

Chapter IX...Delusion, Destruction and Dispersion

If ye transgress, I will scatter you abroad among the nations.

"And Jesus went out, and departed from the temple: and his disciples came to him for to shew him the buildings of the temple. And Jesus said unto them, See ye not all these things? verily I say unto you, There shall not be left here one stone upon another, that shall not be thrown down" ...Matthew Chapter 24 verses 1-2

"And when he was come near, he beheld the city, and wept over it, Saying, If thou hadst known, even thou, at least in this thy day, the things which belong unto thy peace! but now they are hid from thine eyes. For the days shall come upon thee, that thine enemies shall cast a trench about thee, and compass thee round, and keep thee in on every side, And shall lay thee even with the ground, and thy children within thee; and they shall not leave in thee one stone upon another; because thou knewest not the time of thy visitation" ...Luke Chapter 19 verses 41-44

The Judaizers may have congratulated themselves for routing the New Covenant believers from their midst, but ironically the intense persecution of the young Hebrew church is what saved them from the inevitable destruction of Jerusalem. After the dispersion of Christ's followers, deadly infighting began between rival groups in Judæa for control. The zealots not only wanted to lord it over their own people, but swore to never submit to Rome. The power struggle was further complicated by organized bands of robbers who terrorized the populace.

To understand the slow, agonizing death of first century Jerusalem, imagine yourself a resident trapped in a region undergoing a violent civil war—where the warring factions rob, falsely convict, and execute at will. Further, they murder anyone who tries to leave the area, suspecting them of defecting to the enemy. At the same time, organized gangs and bands of thugs roam at large, robbing and killing. No food can get into the area, and no one can get out. Everyone is succumbing to famine, but the strong rule over the weak and have the distinct advantage. Simultaneously, an enemy power has established a perimeter offensive and is bombarding the area; daily gaining a strategic advantage. This combination of anarchy, famine, and the Roman backlash against sedition ultimately caused the annihilation of the city and the Temple.

As we saw in the subsection *Evidence Points to a Black Jesus Christ*, the historian Josephus is invaluable to our history as descendants of the original Hebrews, as he himself was Hebrew and thoroughly schooled in the history, culture, and political intrigue of the nation. Jesus gave his disciples a futuristic description of Jerusalem's destruction. Josephus witnessed it with his very eyes.

The Testimony of Josephus

Any commentary on Josephus' account must be abridged, for his institutional knowledge and eye witness descriptions are detailed and voluminous. For the 'man on the street' version, I refer the reader to "The Complete Works of Josephus", with emphasis on his account of the Jewish Wars.

The spiritual condition leading to the flashpoint with Rome is aptly described in the Book of Hosea Chapter 4 verses 1-2:

"Hear the word of the Lord, ye children of Israel: for the Lord hath a controversy with the inhabitants of the land, because there is no truth, nor mercy, nor knowledge of God in the land.

By swearing, and lying, and killing, and stealing, and committing adultery, they break out, and blood toucheth blood."

The prophet Hosea's words are eerily amplified in Josephus' analysis of the rebels controlling Jerusalem in his day. Speaking of the collective factions and their cruel hand in the demise of their own people, Josephus observes:

"It is therefore impossible to go distinctly over every instance of these men's iniquity. I shall therefore speak my mind here at once briefly. That neither did any other city ever allow such miseries, nor did any age ever breed a generation more fruitful in wickedness than this was, from the beginning of the world. Finally, they brought the Hebrew nation into contempt, that they might themselves appear comparatively less impious with regard to strangers. They confessed what was true, that they were the slaves, the scum, and the spurious and abortive offspring of our nation, while they overthrew the city themselves, and forced the Romans, whether they would or no to gain a melancholy reputation, by acting gloriously against them, and did almost draw that fire upon the temple, which they seemed to think came too slowly; and indeed when they saw that temple burning from the upper city, they were neither troubled at it, nor did they shed any tears on that account, while yet these passions were discovered among the Romans themselves; which circumstances we shall speak of hereafter in the proper place, when we come to treat of such matters".[15]

What Josephus is referring to here, is that the zealots themselves set the first fires to the Temple, long before the Roman army finished the job. To them, it had become little more than a base of operations and a cache for goods and ammunition during the siege. The subterranean chambers also provided a hiding place for these wicked men, while the rest of the city suffered incomprehensible miseries. Before it was over, thousands of decomposing corpses littered the streets, and were crammed inside houses. The law of sowing and reaping manifested on an exponential scale, for at the trial of Jesus, the people had clamored for a robber and murderer to be released rather than an innocent man. Now, God required the past, and thousands of the innocent people in the city who wanted nothing to do with the zealot's delusional schemes and love for bloodshed became victims of robbery and murder.

The tyrannical nihilists controlling Jerusalem even ignored five divine omens occurring in their midst which foretold the inevitable destruction.[16] The excruciating misery that evolved in response to the Judæan sedition was not of the Roman design; this is evidenced by repeated

---

[15] The Complete Works of Josephus, The Jewish War. Book 5. Chapter 10. 5.442-445.

[16] The Complete Works of Josephus, The Jewish War. Book 6. Chapter 5. 3.288-309.

overtures to the anarchists from Titus, who had Josephus speak to the Hebrews in their own language; even recounting their history from the days of our forefather Abraham in order to bring them to their senses. According to Josephus, all of this fell on deaf ears. This devastation was what the zealots wanted. They were wicked men who hated their own people and fought only for the satisfaction of their own bloodlust and ego: brutes destined as agents to fulfill the prophecy of judgment against Jerusalem, the city that shed the blood of prophets and saints.

Literal Egypt No Longer an Option

Historically, Egypt had been counted on as the exit strategy when famine or war overwhelmed Judæa. The patriarch Abraham had sojourned there when famine paralyzed the land of Canaan. Several generations later, Jacob and his sons wound up in the land of Mizraim when famine once again reared its head; and most of you know the story of how by divine providence Joseph was sent ahead to preserve their posterity. Further down the timeline, as Nebuchadnezzar's military campaign closed in on Jerusalem, the obvious solution once again seemed to flee to Egypt; although the prophet Jeremiah cautioned the people that destruction awaited them there if they did.

This time however, escape to Egypt was not an option. This is not to say Hebrews were not already in Egypt (or many other parts of the African continent, which we will shortly discuss.) The issue rather, was those Hebrews who had the foresight to get out of Jerusalem before the zealot's tyrannical lockdown began escaped the horror of the siege. Based on Josephus' account, tens of thousands of those deported from the sacked city were sold into slavery. Those who wound up in Egypt as a result of that event were there because they were purchased to labor in the Egyptian mines.

Thus, just as the emerging Hebrew church was scattered due to persecution, taking the witness of the gospel to the furthest reaches of the Roman empire, so also the Hebrews who did not receive the witness of the apostles and were alive in Jerusalem at the end of the invasion also wound up scattered around the world, according to whatever nation they were sold to. This fulfilled Jesus' prophecy in Luke Chapter 21 verse 24, where he foretold, "they shall fall by the edge of the sword, and shall be led away captive into all nations: and Jerusalem shall be trodden down of the Gentiles, until the times of the Gentiles be fulfilled."

Where'd They Learn That? Hebrew Culture in Greater Africa

As mentioned earlier, the Hebrew people were already in Africa, and by this I am referring to the greater part of the continent that most people recognize today on the map, for as we read in the subsection *Egypt, Assyria, and Israel in the Middle—The True Africa vs the 'Middle East*, Israel has always been a part of Africa. So we are looking now at the larger body of the continent, and we can begin at the most logical and easily recognizable points: Egypt and Libya, where rather than being tiny minority enclaves—the Hebrews were deeply rooted generationally and economically.

Acts Chapter 2 verses 1-11 state that on the Day of Pentecost when the baptism of the Holy Ghost fell on one hundred twenty followers of Christ "there were dwelling at Jerusalem Jews, devout men, out of every nation under heaven...who upon hearing people who they recognized as Galileans praising God asked in amazement, "And how hear we every man in our

185

own tongue, wherein we were born? Parthians, and Medes, and Elamites, and the dwellers in Mesopotamia, and in Judæa, and Cappadocia, in Pontus, and Asia, Phrygia, and Pamphylia, in Egypt, and in the parts of Libya about Cyrene, and strangers of Rome, Jews and proselytes, Cretes and Arabians, we do hear them speak in our tongues the wonderful works of God."

They are referred to as 'devout men' because they were Hebrews who earnestly kept the holy days and were present in Jerusalem for the celebration of the Feast of Pentecost; as it was common for the Israelites to make the pilgrimage to Jerusalem on the High Holy days. Notice they said, the language where they were born, meaning these were Hebrews not born in Israel, but native to these various countries. Proselytes would have been people from other nations who were not Hebrew by descent, but had chosen to embrace their faith, as a provision was made for this under the Mosaic Law. An example is the account of the Ethiopian eunuch found in Acts Chapter 8 verses 26-39, who had come to Jerusalem to worship, and received the understanding of the gospel from Philip.

You should also know that Libya as depicted on ancient maps was considered the upper third of the African continent west back east to Egypt, not the truncated area with abnormally straight borders contrived by the British crown to simplify their empirical and resource extracting ventures. So from Biblical references alone thus far we have a Hebrew presence in Egypt (northeast on the continent), Libya (northeast/north/northwest on the continent, and Ethiopia (south). But can anyone dispute a huge landmass exists between Egypt and Ethiopia, and is it logical to believe the ancient Hebrews would shun the massive region between these two kingdoms?

That vast expanse, is identified in the Bible as the land of Cush, the eldest son of Ham. And yes, we can confirm Hebrew presence in Cushite territory by the writings of the prophet Zephaniah in Chapter 3 verse 10: "From beyond the rivers of Ethiopia my suppliants, even the daughter of my dispersed, shall bring mine offering." The Hebrew word used here for 'suppliants' is translated to incense; as increasing to a volume of smoke...hence a worshipper, and is closely related to another word meaning to burn incense in worship, intercede, or pray. You may also remember in the Book of Revelation Chapter 8 verse 4 a scenario is depicted where an...

'angel came and stood at the altar, having a golden censer; and there was given unto him much incense, that he should offer it with the prayers of all saints upon the golden altar which was before the throne.

And the smoke of the incense, which came with the prayers of the saints, ascended up before God out of the angel's hand'.

We can see from this that in the heavenly dimension prayer and worship are as a sweet savour of incense to the Lord. God says his worshipers are going to bring his offering from places beyond the rivers of Ethiopia, and specifically it will be those who have been dispersed (or scattered). We know this is referring to the end of the age, and the dispersed are descendants of the Hebrews, because the chapter ends with verses 19-20 saying, "Behold, at that time I will undo all that afflict thee: and I will save her that halteth, and gather her that was driven out; and I will get them praise and fame in every land where they have been put to shame.

At that time will I bring you again, even in the time that I gather you: for I will make you a name and a praise among all people of the earth, when I turn back your Captivity before your eyes, saith the Lord."

The descendants of the original Hebrews are the only people who fit the description of Captivity in the latter days as defined in the 28th chapter of Deuteronomy. Now all that remains to be searched out is an understanding of what rivers exist in Ethiopia, and what regions (in modern day terms) lay beyond those rivers. The country possesses eleven rivers and a lake system. Some of the main rivers are:

*The Wabi Shebele which runs southeast into Somalia, as does the Genale Dawa.
*The Omo-Ghibe which flows down to Kenya, and empties into Lake Turkana.

*The Abbay which travels south, then bends west before bearing further northwest into Sudan.

*The Tekezé also flows into Sudan.

If these points represent where the rivers terminate, and the suppliants are coming yet still from beyond those regions, we find ourselves within the jurisdiction of the ancient Cushite dominion and quickly into central, western, and southern Africa. We know that 'beyond the rivers' implies continental Africa, because the scripture does not use the term, "beyond the Great Sea, or great waters." When we factor in the historical Hebrew presence in northern Africa (such as Carthage and Tyre), consider the ancestral accounts attested to by the Lemba peoples of southeastern Africa, and the Hebraic cultural and religious practices of central and west African tribes observed by explorers and researchers, the link to the original biblical Israelites is solid and undeniable.

The fact that some tribes display a mixture of spiritualism or animism in conjunction with their Hebrewisms should not be used as criteria for dismissal of Israelite heritage. The Tabernacle (and later the Temple), priests, and prophets were the triumvirate that kept the people's spiritual focus on point. With wave after wave of migration into Africa—fleeing first from the onslaught of armies bent on conquering Palestine, and later deeper into the interior and south of the continent to escape militant Islam, the Hebrews were many days without a king, and without a prince, and without a sacrifice, and without an image, and without an ephod, and without teraphim...meaning, they had no true spiritual guidance or ongoing revelation of God's direction as he moved forward into the New Covenant. Remember, in just a few years after Joshua's death, Micah was having silver images and molten images (household gods) made, and this in a time when there were priests and prophets among the people. So whenever people do not have access to the whole counsel of God, or have access but refuse to receive the entire counsel, they can end up with an entirely abstract worship construct that bears some resemblance to the ideal, but is not the sum of the whole.

Neither should the Hebrews of Africa be measured by comparison to modern day Euro-Judaics. The Talmud, the result of centuries of carnal interpretation and reinterpretation of the Mosaic Law and Commandments appears for the most part to be a Gentile construct. I describe this as carnal interpretation because every word of God is pure, and the Law was pure for its intended purpose as a righteous tutor. The Law could only be interpreted one way—by the

187

inspiration of the Holy Ghost, and for one reason—to prepare the people to receive their Anointed Redeemer, the Christ. Jesus—who had the Spirit without measure, taught the people regarding the scriptures; **exposing the heart condition that triggered the physical act forbidden by the Law**. This is why he and he alone was qualified to expound and explicate the Law and the Commandments. Once he consummated the final sacrifice and satisfied God's justice, there was no further reason to elaborate on the handwriting of ordinances: Colossians Chapter 2 verse 14 says they were nailed to the cross with him.

By the time Jesus began his ministry, the Pharisees were already making the commandment of God of no effect by appending their carnal tradition to it. If Jesus described the efforts of his own brethren as the work of blind guides, the situation could only further deteriorate once Gentile proselytes began to add their interpretive input. One such outcome the Talmudic authors arrived at was the conclusion the Lord Jesus Christ was to be vilified and insulted with a loathing and hatred that can only be described as Satanic in its fury and mockery.

So, in observing African tribes over diverse regions of the continent, distinct expressions of the original Hebraic worship and culture have been found. These include circumcision, ritual animal sacrifice, striking blood on the door posts and lintels of their dwellings, and observance of Sabbath. Ancient Israelite commonalities manifest in each cardinal direction of the continent: from the Afro-Asiatic tribes in the north, Lembas in the south, Fulani, Yoruba, and Igbo people in the west and Nilo Saharans in the east. These practices predated the Islamic presence and persisted in spite of its often violent encroachment.

This is intriguing, as the ratio between New Covenant Holy Ghost baptized Hebrew descendants and the rest of the Hebrew descendants appears to have changed little since the Apostle Paul spoke earnestly of his brethren in Romans Chapter 10 verse 1. However, we can be greatly encouraged by the inviolate word of God that shows blindness in part is happened to Israel, but only until the fullness of the Gentiles comes in. When God knows the last Gentile that is going to repent and trust in the saving blood of his Son Jesus has entered the ark of safety, Esau's age will become a retreating echo of rage and regret, and the everlasting days of Jacob will dawn in peace and security.

The Deliverer will come out of Sion, and turn ungodliness away from Jacob. This is the covenant God has made concerning them: that he will take away their sins. They do not now understand the New Covenant; and neither should you make apologies for being a new creation in Christ Jesus. God sees them now in unbelief, but esteems them beloved on behalf of the covenant he made with our forefathers, and the gifts and callings promised to the seed of Abraham are without repentance. Those of us who are entered into Christ were able to obtain mercy through their unbelief; now God says these lost sheep of Israel will also obtain mercy through our mercy. When you consider the restoration of these millions of brethren who have been blinded in part, it is easy to understand how God could tell Abraham, "Look now toward heaven, and tell the stars, if thou be able to number them: and he said unto him, So shall thy seed be." It's not a matter of if... only a matter of how soon. May the Lord hasten his word to perform it!

WHAT'S IMPORTANT

The nationalistic hopes of a people weary of oppression were dashed when the one they thought could be Messiah accepted the death of a convicted criminal, rather than liberating Judah from Gentile rule. Jesus' presence among his brethren was a classic case of not being able to see the forest for the trees. The most learned among them failed to connect the prophecies and clues in the scriptures that this was indeed the Christ, the Son of the Living God. They had forgotten how when God manifested himself to Elijah, he was not in the wind, or the earthquake, or the fire; but in a still small voice. Jesus' method was not to cry, nor lift up, nor cause his voice to be heard in the street; meaning he was not coming as a charismatic orator to rally the crowds to revolution. The historian Josephus was one of the Hebrew brethren who had originally cast his lot with the zealots, and was likewise disillusioned with the successor to John the Baptizer who had power to work miracles, but refused to use it to break the yoke of the oppressor.

We have seen this parallel in the suffering of the Captivity, with some figures calling for retribution, and others urging restraint. The root of the problem is that the people have never realized they were under a Captivity orchestrated by a Power much higher than the oppressor. God has authored the Captivity for our discipline and to vindicate his justice; the oppressor is merely the face of it. God is watching the sand which represents the times of the Gentiles trickle through the hourglass. When the last grain drops, he himself will arise from his throne and bare his arm. No one who waits on God will ever be made ashamed. Our salvation is in returning and rest; our strength in quietness and confidence. We cannot simultaneously assume the contrite heart and spirit of supplication necessary to hasten the end of the Captivity, while railing on men for their evil, and breathing out threatenings.

We saw that Jerusalem was a city doomed to destruction for the bloodshed of the prophets, saints, and their own Kinsman-Redeemer. Yet, many of the inhabitants clung to it with nationalistic fervor, because the Temple was there. The zealots, convinced of their ability to break free from Roman control, increasingly adopted a delusional possessiveness about the city. Jerusalem became their private turf; literally a thug's paradise—with rival factions battling for control, and a beleaguered populace the prey of roving bands of robbers. Gradually, like a tightening noose, the city became a death trap to all who remained. Every successful sortie by the zealots provoked a greater show of force from the Roman military. Famine destroyed what weaponry didn't, and Jerusalem became one huge theater of death and decay.

The zealot's response to the siege of Jerusalem mirrored the sabotage of Samson, but in reverse. Samson found he had no strength against the enemy, and then he was blinded. In the case of the zealots, they were spiritually blind and thought they had sufficient strength—only to find themselves weak and powerless against the Roman war machine. Just as Samson thought he would shake himself as he always did, and wist not that God was no longer with him; so the zealots and the people felt they would gain the upper hand, because the Temple was there...but they failed to realize the presence of God had departed from it. They were on their own alone, and just as Jesus prophesied... their house was left to them desolate.

Today we see this same type of reaction in the land of our Captivity, but from the Anglo-Americans. America is the spiritual Great Babylon: the habitation of devils, hold of every foul spirit, and cage of every unclean and hateful bird. It is destined to be thrown down with violence by God—never to rise again. Yet people extol its goodness and wax on and on about how much they love their country. Some people even tear up as they gaze at the flag. They speak of America being founded on Christianity and godly principals when in truth it was founded on hypocrisy and rebellion. Is it wise and prudent to love something that is detestable to God? Punishment and great judgment are on schedule for this country; for the wicked shall be turned into hell, and all the nations that forget God. Do not make the mistake of thinking God is for this country, any more than he was for Egypt in the days of the Exodus. **Rather, in every nation he that feareth him, and worketh righteousness, is accepted with him.**

Our look at Africa showed us that many of our ancestors had the foresight to leave Judæa in advance of the Roman occupation; thus avoiding the ultimate outcome of the siege: death or the Roman slave block. We found many distinctly Hebrew practices among tribes throughout the entire continent—attesting to their heritage, and were reminded by scripture of the covenant God will honor to blot out all their sins and remember their transgression no more. Nevertheless, these brethren have been and still are the victims of Satanic torment via sponsored wars, Islamic persecution, theft of resources, apartheid conditions, slavery, and the deployment of biological warfare through vaccines and engineered plagues. God has not forgotten them; and promises in Isaiah Chapter 42 verse 16:

"And I will bring the blind by a way that they knew not; I will lead them in paths that they have not known: I will make darkness light before them, and crooked things straight. These things will I do unto them, and not forsake them."

Chapter X...Voyages of Despair...Brought to Egypt by Ships

And the Lord shall bring thee into Egypt again with ships...and there
ye shall be sold unto your enemies for bondmen and bondwomen.

The Trans-Atlantic Slave trade.

For most of our lives, this event was presented as the genesis of our history as a people. Today, based on the studies and writings of many brothers and sisters, and the gradual unveiling of our spiritual eyes, we know that is not the case; and that our true history and ancestry is represented in the pages of the Bible itself.

Islamic, Japhethic and the Sons of Belial

Since there is a wealth of information about the African Diaspora available to the public ranging from books and digital media, to historical sites, and exhibition centers such as the National Underground Railroad Freedom Center in Cincinnati, Ohio and the Lest We Forget Black Holocaust Museum of Slavery in Philadelphia, Pennsylvania, my discussion targets the key players who removed (and in some cases continue to remove) the descendants of the Hebrews from Africa.

Revelation Chapter 18 verse 13 informs us that Babylon the Great will be thrown down with violence because of her multitude of sins, and that one of the many indictments against her involves trafficking in slaves and the souls of men. We also know from I Timothy Chapter 1 verses 9-10 that the practice of menstealing—defined in the Greek as enslavers—is classified as lawless, disobedient, ungodly, sinful, unholy, profane, and ranks in the same category as homicide and sexual immorality as far as God is concerned. That being said, so far we have focused exclusively on the involvement of the descendants of Japheth with the establishment of institutionalized slavery in the Americas. But how many know as far back as eight hundred years before Hebrews arrived as slaves on the shores of the Americas, the Islamic slave trade was already thriving in Africa?

The main difference between these descendants of mixed Hamitic/Shemitic heritage and the European slave traders, was that the Europeans bought and sold to make as much money as they could as quickly as they could in a business that was fraught with its own set of peculiar risks. By contrast, in addition to the profit factor, the Muslims engaged in slave trade under cover of religious obligation. Anyone who was an infidel (a non-Muslim) was open to capture and enslavement. The Europeans would seldom if ever venture into the interior of Africa to capture slaves. Instead, they relied on relationships with various tribal entities for procurement. The Muslims, however, had already established a significant presence on the continent, and had no problem making the treks into the villages to attack and carry off slaves. Muslims are still enslaving and selling Hebrews in Africa to this day.

You will recall Deuteronomy Chapter 28 verse 37 states, 'And thou shalt become an astonishment, a proverb, and a byword, among all nations whither the Lord shall lead thee." This is borne out by a comment by Ibn Khaldoun, a 14th century Islamic historian whose writings are highly esteemed in the Muslim world:

"The only people who accept slavery are the Negroes, owing to their low degree of humanity and proximity to the animal stage."

One can see from reading speech such as this that the astonishment/proverb/byword curse has been in full operation for millennia. This is nothing more than the sinful working of man's mind by which he dehumanizes his fellow man to justify mistreatment of him. On the contrary, Black people are not in captivity status among the nations due to any subhuman status or animalistic nature. They are merely trapped in a position of subservience until their chastisement is over, and the sentence of chastisement runs concurrent with what the Bible calls the times of the Gentiles. The very fact that God has already declared the end from the beginning and stated the Gentile's time has a definite cutoff point indicates our state is temporary.

Beginning in the seventh century A.D., Muslim slave raids on Europe also regularly removed thousands of white captives from their homeland; mainly to satisfy the harems of the Turkish and Arabian sultans—a practice which contributed to the light complexions observed of the people in those regions today. We are left to wonder if this legacy of kidnapping and selling humans served to harden the European conscience toward likewise committing this same crime against others. One thing is known: when the European slave buyers arrived in the ports of Western Africa, they found already established slave markets. And to this day, in some areas of Africa such as Sudan, the risk of being kidnapped and sold into slavery by Islamists remains a present danger. Concerning the prophetic curses of Deuteronomy Chapter 28, the lesson that stands out is, 'You can run, but you cannot hide, for... among these nations shalt thou find no ease, neither shall the sole of thy foot have rest.'

As we learned in Chapter IX subsection *Where'd They Learn That? Hebrew Culture in Greater Africa*, diverse tribes across the continent of Africa retained vestiges of their ancient Hebraic culture and worship. But based on the divine principle of scattering and removal of heritage, they will never be able to unite as a nation until the return of their Kinsman Redeemer —the Lord Jesus Christ—at the end of the age, when the spirit of supplication is poured out upon them, and with one heart they acknowledge "Blessed is he that comes in the name of Lord."

Therefore, it should be understood, that although Hebrew culture could be found across the board, each nation retained distinctive tribal loyalties. This is important to understand, because often you will hear people insist, 'Blacks sold their own people into slavery'... as though somehow that absolves America of guilt concerning their part in the crimes against humanity. One tribe of Africans did not consider another tribe of Africans 'their people' any more than Polish fighting Russians and selling the captives would be called whites selling their own people. Poles would consider Poles as their own, Russians would consider Russians as their own. With this in mind, it becomes easier to understand how a tribe that retained Hebrewisms could raid another people associated with Hebrew lineage. Neither of them knew either their true heritage, or that the outcome of their actions represented the culmination of an ancient prophecy.

The kingdom of Abomey (formerly called Dahomey) was one such group who played a huge part in the procurement of slaves for the European trade. The Atlantic Ocean meets the southernmost border of their territory, and this was a main port for the boarding of captives to be shipped to the Americas. In the mid 1800's, F. E. Forbes, a commander in the service of the British Royal Navy visited Dahomey in an effort to establish dialogue with the king, for the purpose of ceasing the slave trade.

In his journals published in 1851, Forbes noted the Spartan-like military character of the nation, the Amazonian warring women, and the fact that annual slave raids took place. Forbes described Dahomey as "the dreaded oppressor of neighboring nations"[17] noting that the Yoruba people in the east were being targeted for devastation, slavery, and murder, and a populous city, home to many hundreds of Christians in the nearby Bight of Benin was "marked out as the scene of an approaching slave hunt." He also observed that human sacrifice played a significant role in their culture. Where Hebrewisms are concerned, circumcision was practiced, and when religious sacrifices were performed, "the altars are washed with the blood caught in the basins; the rest is taken round by the priests and priestesses, who as Moses commanded the leaders of Israel "strike the lintel and two side posts" of all the houses of the devotees, "with the blood that is in the basin." [18]

How strange that they would conduct this priestly ritual associated with ancient Hebrew lineage, yet possess a warped conscience which permitted them to raid villages, sell human beings into bondage, and decapitate others. These actions are reminiscent of the sons of Belial among Israel in the days of old who committed horrible atrocities in the land, and were judged worthy of death by their brethren, to put away evil out of Israel. However, in 1999 former president of Benin Mathieu Kérékou formed a conference where formal apologies were made, and ambassadors then traveled to the United States to issue statements of repentance and remorse, and seek forgiveness and reconciliation for their ancestor's part in the slave trade.

The need for more and more slaves increased in tandem with the market share for the crops they grew and harvested, and rather than rely strictly on agreements made with suppliers like the kingdom of Dahomey, Europeans began to employ the strategy of divide and conquer, whereby they would instigate feuds between tribes. The resulting conflict would enable them to replenish the supply of human cargo, keeping the slave marketing industry alive. Individual traders would also barter captives while waiting for the transport ships to arrive from Europe:

"And they have cast lots for my people; and have given a boy for an harlot, and sold a girl for wine, that they might drink..." Joel Chapter 3 verse 3.

----

[17] Forbes, Frederick E., Dahomey and the Dahomans: Being the Journals of Two Missions

to the King of Dahomey, and Residence at His Capital, in the Year 1849 and 1850.

[18] Forbes, Frederick E., Dahomey and the Dahomans: Being the Journals of Two Missions

to the King of Dahomey, and Residence at His Capital, in the Year 1849 and 1850.

Heeboe/Eboe/Igbo/Ibo and the Outpost of Ouidah/Whydah (Judah)

A 1747 map titled Accurate Map of Negroland drawn by the cartographer Eman Bower clearly shows identification of the Kingdom of Juda and Slave Coast of Whidah near Benin. Whidah or Whydah is a corruption of the French pronunciation Ouidah, and is pronounced Ahuda in Portuguese. These are all names for Judah; descendants of the original exiles from the tribe of Judah who concentrated in what was formerly the old Kingdom of Ghana, Nigeria, and Biafra. Natives from these regions identified themselves as Heeboe, Eboe, Ibo, and Igbo. These are phonetic corruptions of 'Hebrew.' There are even illustrations of these people drawn by Dutch explorers visiting the area at that time. Several decades later, the kingdom of Juda was no longer included on a map drawn by the same cartographer. Only the location 'Slave Coast' remained.

There are important memorials however, that still exist. The 'Slave Castles'—huge edifices built as holding tanks for captured Hebrews awaiting transport which were effectively dungeons—such as Elmina Castle, Cape Coast Castle, and Doree Island—are available for tourists to get a close up look at what remains as a testimony to the depths of human greed and cruelty. And in the port city of Ouidah, there is a structure aptly called 'The Door of no Return.' This was the last point many captives saw before being taken aboard the slave galleys. It stands as a stark reminder that God's word that goes forth from his mouth does not return to him void, but accomplishes what he sent it to do.

The Horrors of the Middle Passage and Psalm 68

Thy sons and thy daughters shall be given unto another people, and thine eyes shall look, and fail with longing for them all the day long: and there shall be no might in thine hand...thou shalt be only oppressed and crushed alway: So that thou shalt be mad (to rave through insanity) for the sight of thine eyes which thou shalt see. Excerpt from Deuteronomy Chapter 28 verses 32-34

Depending on the departure and destination points, the slave ships could make the journey ranging anywhere from about one-two months. During that period, the children of our people lay naked, tightly packed and shackled together in a cramped space, unable to escape the inevitable human excrement and vomit due to sea sickness. Air ventilation was reduced to the minimum, and often was insufficient in that many perished due to suffocation. Virulent outbreaks of disease were common due to the lack of sanitation. Some succumbed to starvation, while others attempted to intentionally starve themselves. Some chose suicide over slavery, some perished from despair and still others were driven to insanity. The dead were merely tossed overboard. Only our Father in heaven knows how many went to a watery grave between the eastern and western continents.

But each soul that walked through The Door of No Return, or any of the other coastal slave ports, has been carefully recorded in the heavenly archives. When the angels gather the elect from the four winds, God will raise them up...and they shall live. As it is written in Psalm Chapter 68 verse 22, 'The Lord said, I will bring again from Bashan, I will bring my people again from the depths of the sea.'

Noah had prophesied that Japheth would dwell in Shem's tents. However, this did not take place until the times of the Gentiles began. Further, the prophecy is unique because Japheth's encroachment did not stop in the land designated to our forefathers. Rather, wherever the Hebrews migrated, Japheth has also shown up to stake his claim. This is borne out by identifying the key players in the Trans-Atlantic Slave Trade:

*the Portuguese

*the Spanish

*the Dutch

*the Belgians

*the British

*the French

*the Germans

*the Italians

The Europeans maintained their involvement with Africa even as the Western slave trade was being abolished in Europe and the Americas. In a race to get the lion's share of the continent's vast resources, several of these nations began a scramble to claim as much territory as they could. If you have ever looked at a modern map of Africa and wondered how it got carved up into so many countries as opposed to archaic maps of the continent that only identify tribal nations and significant geographical features, the answer lies with the Berlin West African Conference that took place during 1884-1885. The European powers basically decided among themselves who was going to get what in Africa and formalized the agreement. The nations and tribal groups themselves did not get any say in the outcome. One can only imagine the confusion and animosity such an arrangement would bring to a populace accustomed to tribal autonomy and anciently established boundaries. At the conclusion of the conference, Europe had given itself control of all but a tiny percentage of the continent. It was with great difficulty and a significant passage of time before African nations were able to achieve their independence.

Where South Africa was concerned, European immigrants—mostly from The Netherlands and Germany, began to colonize the region around the 18th century. These immigrants were very strict Calvinists[19], and espoused a peculiar notion that they were the

---

[19] The doctrines of John Calvin, a 16th century theologian, centered around austere moral codes and the belief that certain people were predestined for salvation, and therefore could not fall from grace. Based on this line of thinking, a Christian could defraud, murder, or whatever, and still stand justified before God with no worries of condemnation because he was predestined to eternal life. The doctrine of

'chosen people'; viewing themselves as a modern version of the Old Testament Hebrews homesteading the Promised Land; despite the fact Jesus' death and resurrection abolished the Old Covenant and established the New, wherein faith works by love. Of course in their minds, if they were the new Israelites—by default, that would make the indigenous tribes idolaters and worthy of destruction. It is not difficult to see why clash after clash occurred—many violent over the years—until media coverage began to expose the wickedness of apartheid and public opinion began to weigh in.

This is a classic case of what happens to man when he professes allegiance to God, but has not received the gift of the Holy Ghost, for no man can say Jesus is the Lord, but by the Holy Ghost...I Corinthians Chapter 3 verse 3. Jude Chapter 1 verse 19 tells us that those who have not the Spirit are sensual—meaning they operate based on their senses, rather than being led by God's Spirit. Had these Afrikaaners been baptized by the Holy Ghost and led by it, they would have walked by the New Covenant guidelines that teach us to be content with such things as we have. There would have been no need to strike out and go exploring, and attempt to claim another's land as their own. And even if they did have to flee their homeland for persecution or some similar reason, two things could have been done differently: they could have sought solace on their own continent, or they could have dealt with the African tribes in a spirit of humility and love, which is the proper attitude for relating to anyone one does not know... especially, when they are a stranger entering another's house.

As unpleasant as it is to state, the truth of the matter is that the European descendants of Japheth have by their own hand brought much sorrow, bloodshed, and animosity upon themselves by barging into the lands of other people under the pretext of divine right to be settlers, colonize, and dominate. Quick to seize upon the false interpretation of the curse upon Canaan, they have failed to equally heed the curse by which Noah bound all three of his sons concerning their apportioned geographical inheritance. This fascinating account is found in the Book of Jubilees:

"And thus the sons of Noah divided unto their sons in the presence of Noah their father, and he bound them all by an oath, imprecating a curse on every one that sought to seize the portion which had not fallen to him by his lot.

And they all said, "So be it; so be it," for themselves and their sons forever throughout their generations till the day of judgment, on which the Lord God shall judge them with a sword and with fire, for all the unclean wickedness of their errors, wherewith they have filled the earth with transgression and uncleanness and fornication and sin." The Book of Jubilees Chapter 9 verses 14-15.

---

predestination flies in the face of Jesus' invitation to 'whosoever will' to come drink of the Water of Life, and the Apostle Paul's observations that some had already made shipwreck of their faith, and concerning others who had escaped the pollutions of the world through the knowledge of the Lord Jesus Christ and become entangled again, that their last end is worse than the beginning, and it would have been better for them not to have known the way of righteousness than, after they have known it, to turn from the holy commandment delivered unto them.

Invariably, the grass will always look greener on the other side of the fence, and this is exactly what happened among Noah's grandsons. But there is a right way and a wrong way to do things. Here is a case in point. At the time the geographical lands were apportioned, Japheth's son Madai did not like his land:

"And Japheth and his sons went towards the sea and dwelt in the land of their portion, and Madai saw the land of the sea and it did not please him." Now, Madai handled this disappointment in the correct manner... "and he begged a (portion) from Elam and Asshur and Arpachshad, his wife's brother, and he dwelt in the land of Media, near to his wife's brother until this day. And he called his dwelling-place, and the dwelling-place of his sons, Media, after the name of their father Madai."

Shemitic Elam's land was Persia (modern day Iran.) Centuries later, the prophet Daniel tells us the kingdom of Babylon fell to the joint forces of the Medes and Persians...Daniel Chapter 5 verse 28. Not only can we see the antiquity of the Medo-Persian relationship, but it is clear it was not affected by the curse because supplication was made for land and land was willingly granted.

Now here is an example where covetousness activated the curse. Canaan decides Shem's territory is a better deal than his own lot.

"And Ham and his sons went into the land which he was to occupy, which he acquired as his portion in the land of the south. And Canaan saw the land of Lebanon to the river of Egypt that it was very good, and he went not into the land of his inheritance to the west (that is to) the sea, and he dwelt in the land of Lebanon, eastward and westward from the border of Jordan and from the border of the sea."

His family tries to reason with him:

"And Ham, his father, and Cush and Mizraim, his brothers, said unto him: "Thou hast settled in a land which is not thine, and which did not fall to us by lot: do not do so; for if thou dost do so, thou and thy sons will fall in the land and be accursed through sedition; for by sedition ye have settled, and by sedition will thy children fall, and thou shalt be rooted out for ever. Dwell not in the dwelling of Shem; for to Shem and to his sons did it come by their lot. Cursed art thou, and cursed shalt thou be beyond all the sons of Noah, by the curse by which we bound ourselves by an oath in the presence of the holy judge, and in the presence of Noah our father."

In other words, they reminded him he was already cursed, but now if he did this thing he would be really cursed beyond all the sons of Noah. So let's see if he listened:

"But he did not hearken unto them, and dwelt in the land of Lebanon from Hamath to the entering of Egypt, he and his sons until this day ...And for this reason that land is named Canaan." This is why Genesis Chapter 12 verse 6 and Chapter 13 verse 7 speaking of Abraham's sojourning state, "the Canaanite was then in the land."

With a presumptuous spirit, Canaan assayed to occupy Shem's land. This event also gives us a grasp of how firmly the Canaanites were entrenched in the territory by the time

Israel came up out of Egypt. Their longevity and iron chariots did them no good when the day of conquest arrived. The Book of Joshua tells us that Judah went up first and drove the Canaanites out of his tribal allotment. Today, the sons of Japheth have likewise violated the millennia old oath and are occupying Shem's land, and have streamed into Africa and Asia in their quest for empire and riches—oblivious to the fact they are operating under an ancient but active curse. It would appear then, that Japheth's latter day impulse to dwell in the tents of Shem was pre-determined even as he bound himself to this oath in the presence of his father.

As New Covenant believers, we do have a mandate to go into all the world and preach the gospel (the good news of the Kingdom) healing the sick, and manifesting the power of God. But there has never been a Biblical mandate to go into all the world using missions as an icebreaker to acclimate indigenous peoples to foreign empire and colonialism. Further, the message many missionaries brought was not the pure, unadulterated gospel. They were not earnestly contending for the faith that was first delivered to the Hebrew church on the Day of Pentecost. Instead, they brought an idolatrous god made in their image and likeness, and a worship void of the power and demonstration of the Spirit. They came not in the spirit of love, but in a spirit of conceit and condescension. Such a false witness was doomed to failure.

While the system of apartheid has been formally abolished, tensions simmer, violence erupts, the indigenous people are sick and poor, and the whites and mixed multitude live in fear behind bars and gates. Now the world casts its opinion and says the region is far worse off than it was before. Well, the Hebrew people were never intended to build their house on the false European construct of democracy; which literally means mob rule. We have always been a tribal people designed to function under a theocracy with judges of our own peers to execute justice, and prophets to hold forth the vision.

It will take the return of the King of Kings to restore the years eaten by the locust, the cankerworm, the caterpillar, and the palmerworm, his great army he sent among the people. May he hasten the day.

WHAT'S IMPORTANT

The humiliation associated with the Trans-Atlantic slave trade is never a joyous topic, and so much the more because as a people we know our presence is only tolerated, rather than welcome, in a land that prides itself on freedom and justice. However, once we accept the fact that we are under a divine Captivity, and that the oppressor is merely the instrument executing it, we can turn our focus to the Restoration of the Kingdom of God, and begin the process of self-examination, repentance, and supplication.

All nations have served themselves of us in one way or another. Regarding the plight of the Hebrews, Jeremiah Chapter 50 verse 7 states, **"All that found them have devoured them: and their adversaries said, We offend not, because they have sinned against the Lord, the habitation of justice, even the Lord, the hope of their fathers."** This is equivalent to God telling us the nations know who we really are and our true heritage. The response of the children of Esau is even more callous: that we need to "just get over it." I challenge anyone to read the following verses found in the Book of Joel, Chapter 3, and then tell me if it looks like God has 'just gotten over it.' Even if we do "just get over it," the following is what the Gentiles have to look forward to, because the word has already gone forth out of the Lord's mouth concerning it.

"For, behold, in those days, and in that time, when I shall bring again the Captivity of Judah and Jerusalem,

I will also gather all nations, and will bring them down into the valley of Jehoshaphat, and will plead with them there for my people and for my heritage Israel, whom they have scattered among the nations, and parted my land.

And they have cast lots for my people; and have given a boy for an harlot, and sold a girl for wine, that they might drink.

Yea, and what have ye to do with me, O Tyre, and Zidon, and all the coasts of Palestine? will ye render me a recompence? and if ye recompense me, swiftly and speedily will I return your recompence upon your own head;

Because ye have taken my silver and my gold, and have carried into your temples my goodly pleasant things:

The children also of Judah and the children of Jerusalem have ye sold unto the Grecians, that ye might remove them far from their border.

Behold, I will raise them out of the place whither ye have sold them, and will return your recompence upon your own head:

And I will sell your sons and your daughters into the hand of the children of Judah, and they shall sell them to the Sabeans, to a people far off: for the Lord hath spoken it.

Proclaim ye this among the Gentiles; Prepare war, wake up the mighty men, let all the men of war draw near; let them come up:

Beat your plowshares into swords, and your pruninghooks into spears: let the weak say, I am strong.

Assemble yourselves, and come, all ye heathen, and gather yourselves together round about: thither cause thy mighty ones to come down, O Lord.

Let the heathen be wakened, and come up to the valley of Jehoshaphat: for there will I sit to judge all the heathen round about.

Put ye in the sickle, for the harvest is ripe: come, get you down; for the press is full, the fats overflow; for their wickedness is great.

Multitudes, multitudes in the valley of decision: for the day of the Lord is near in the valley of decision.

The sun and the moon shall be darkened, and the stars shall withdraw their shining.

The Lord also shall roar out of Zion, and utter his voice from Jerusalem; and the heavens and the earth shall shake: but the Lord will be the hope of his people, and the strength of the children of Israel.

So shall ye know that I am the Lord your God dwelling in Zion, my holy mountain: then shall Jerusalem be holy, and there shall no strangers pass through her any more.

And it shall come to pass in that day, that the mountains shall drop down new wine, and the hills shall flow with milk, and all the rivers of Judah shall flow with waters, and a fountain shall come forth of the house of the Lord, and shall water the valley of Shittim.

Egypt shall be a desolation, and Edom shall be a desolate wilderness, for the violence against the children of Judah, because they have shed innocent blood in their land.

But Judah shall dwell for ever, and Jerusalem from generation to generation.

For I will cleanse their blood that I have not cleansed: for the Lord dwelleth in Zion."

***Egypt refers to the Hamitic peoples under Islam that have and still are enslaving Judah in Africa; Edom references the European Gentiles who have profited from the Trans-Atlantic Triangle Route slavery enterprise. Tyre and Sidon refer to the present day occupants of Palestine who would resist God's judgment and vindication on behalf of his people and their restoration to their original homeland.

Chapter XI...Chastening and Discipline

You only have I known of all the families of the earth: therefore I will punish you for all your iniquities.

"He that spareth his rod hateth his son: but he that loveth him chasteneth him betimes." Proverbs Chapter 13 verse 24

"If ye endure chastening, God dealeth with you as with sons; for what son is he whom the father chasteneth not?" Hebrews Chapter 12 verse 7

When Israel Was My Son...

The relationship between the Hebrew people and God is a familial one. Whether looking back to the earliest parent/child association, or forward as mature believers in Christ to the bridegroom/spouse bond, intimacy, nurturing, guidance, and correction are inseparable from the calling of sonship.

God speaks fondly of this father-child relationship with Israel during an earlier time through the prophet Hosea in the 11th chapter of the book of the same name. The sense is that God misses this time when the innocence of childhood made his interaction with his son a delight. As I read this, I could picture visiting a family with a toddler who is cute as a button; then not seeing them again for ten or fifteen years, and the next time you run into them, the child has matured and is now acting disrespectful and giving his parents grief. The parents have done their job, and are wondering where they have failed. They are saddened and exasperated, but they do not want to give up on their child. They struggle to find the balance between firm love and harsher discipline.

In this particular scenario, God is speaking about Ephraim as representative of the Hebrews. When Israel was a child, then I loved him, and called my son out of Egypt. Just as a mother takes up her crying child to soothe it; just as a father cannot bear to see his children terrified of thunder and holds them to comfort them and let them know they are safe, so God could no longer bear the groaning of his son in Egypt, and he called him out. In fact, Isaiah Chapter 63 verse 9 tells us, 'In all their affliction he was afflicted.' But God was not the only one calling Ephraim.

As they called them, so they went from them: they sacrificed unto Baalim, and burned incense to graven images. The lure of the world was beckoning; with the fleshly pleasures and practices that were diametrically opposed to the good plan God had for his son.

I taught Ephraim also to go, taking them by their arms; but they knew not that I healed them. Here you have the picture of a baby taking his first halting steps, his arms guided by the strong hands of his father, who walks along slowly behind him. Whereas his father could cross the room in three or four strides, the tiny baby steps are observed with pleasure...the father is delighted just in that his son is learning to walk.

I drew them with cords of a man, with bands of love: and I was to them as they that take off the yoke on their jaws, and I laid meat unto them. The idea here is of the child being tied, or pledged to his parent. It is not a punitive action, but rather a gesture of love and protection, such as when a parent places a child harness on their son so he will not get separated from them in a large crowd or unfamiliar place. God was to Israel as one that took the yoke off his jaws. Here we see a picture of a plow animal that has worked all day treading corn. When the workday is over, the animal does not struggle or resist, but is eager to have the bit and the yoke removed. The animal longs for the freedom. God sensed this, and took his people out of the house of bondage. Israel didn't even have to lift their hand to find food. God brought it to them—from another dimension.

He shall not return into the land of Egypt, but the Assyrian shall be his king, because they refused to return. And the sword shall abide on his cities, and shall consume his branches, and devour them, because of their own counsels. And my people are bent to backsliding from me: though they called them to the most High, none at all would exalt him. Here, as in the case of any wise parent–God contemplates the problem with his son: in this case a persistent inclination to pull away and not keep pace with his father. And what is the best punishment to fit the transgression? Not Egypt. God's wisdom tells him submission under a pagan nation known for their cruelty in warfare will be what it takes to wake Ephraim up.

How shall I give thee up, Ephraim? How shall I deliver thee, Israel? how shall I make thee as Admah? how shall I set thee as Zeboim? mine heart is turned within me, my repentings are kindled together. What this passage in the Hebrew demonstrates is confirmation that we are created in the image and likeness of God, for we see God experiencing the same kind of deep emotional distress a parent does as they watch their child face harsh consequences at the hands of another authority. His heart is churning, he sighs deeply; he is heavy hearted and deeply affected by what he has to do.

Corrected in Measure...The Ultimate Parent... Who Can Teach Like God?

Continuing on from God's dealing with his son Ephraim, this verse captures the gist of why God is the perfect parent...I will not execute the fierceness of mine anger, I will not return to destroy Ephraim: for I am God, and not man; the Holy One in the midst of thee: and I will not enter into the city. Because God is not man, he will dispense the precise amount of discipline needed to get Ephraim back on track. God knows that pain and suffering can only go so far in influencing a person to change their ways. We ourselves know this is true because there are some people so stubborn and strong-willed that they won't submit even under torture conditions and choose death over breaking. If you are trying to deter a person from self-destructing, and it reaches the point where they just shut down and place a big **NO** sign in their mind, you have lost your battle.

God knows the perfect balance of chastening, suffering, waiting, and making himself available with open arms and a compassionate ear; to bring his sons to righteousness. God also tells his son he is the Holy One in his midst. This means that even with the destruction of the Northern Kingdom and dispersal of the people, God will not leave them...he is in their midst. In Jeremiah Chapter 31 verses 18-19, we see God's discipline resulted in the desired behavior.

A Taste of Your Own Medicine

I am sure many of you reading or listening to this book are (or have been) parents; some, like myself—from the old school, and others from more recent generations. As such, we all have our arsenal of methods designed to correct negative behavior. One time-tested strategy is 'a taste of your own medicine.'

If this method has to be used, it means you were not walking in love, in other words, loving your neighbor as yourself. In Israel's case, the commandments went out the window; and lying, theft, cheating, murder, sexual immorality, and idolatry became the standard, so that righteousness was the exception, rather than the rule. Isaiah Chapter 29 verse 21 says it was so bad, that people were marked as offenders just because somebody said something someone else didn't like, and daring to righteously reprove a wrongdoing was asking to get set up. Furthermore, getting justice in a matter was non-existent, and just one flaw or misstep in an otherwise valid case would get it thrown out—and the petitioner would get nothing.

Well, let's contrast this with life in the Captivity today and see if we have swallowed a bitter pill. We know the oppressor doesn't love us. Our presence is tolerated to the extent we can amuse him through entertainment, or keep his coffers full in the service of the prison industry. But there is no love here. We are consistently lied to—across the board—historically, and institutionally. Cheated and stolen from whether by being uninformed, misinformed, or having the economic rules arbitrarily change, so that just as we have barely recovered from one major adjustment, another looms in its place. We are encouraged and pressured to murder our children in the womb; if we get past that, there are plenty of environmental poisons and death-care masquerading as healthcare to manage our growth. If we raise our sons, Esau, who labors with witchcrafts and lives by the sword, has a drug economy, and unscrupulous agents to cull the land of young Black males.

The media and culture go into overdrive to feminize our boys and influence our girls to dress like strippers and carry themselves in a manner that is counteractive to being taken seriously in the professional world. And all around, we are surrounded by idolatrous images, and symbols of the Egyptian and Kabbalistic mystery religions. Based on this, I would draw the conclusion 'a taste of your own medicine' is one approach God is using to turn the hearts of the sons back to the fathers. He wants us to get our fill of lying, theft, cheating, murder, sexual immorality, and idolatry, so that we will cry out for his righteousness, hate every lying way, and hate sin with a perfect hatred.

Time Out

Time out is a disciplinary tactic used to stop disruptive, disobedient, or negative behavior. The object of time out is to give the child a chance to reflect on his conduct. As he watches those around him continue to enjoy fun and freedom, he must decide if the actions that got him pulled out of the group are worth continuing. And no, it doesn't matter if his Dad does own the day care. If anything, rather than being treated special, he will be made an example of; for the son is a representation of the father. Also, the father wants others at the day care to know he is a fair man, and when dealing with him, they and their children can expect equitable treatment. And if you wonder where I got that analogy, just read Jeremiah Chapter 3 verse 19!

Because we are the Lord's people, we literally had it made. Deuteronomy Chapter 32 verses 9-14 detail the care God lavished on Israel; and calls it riding on the high places of the earth. God literally spared no expense on the young nation. But verses 15-18 highlight the grave offenses our forefathers committed as their exalted status went to their heads. They forsook God. They lightly esteemed him. They provoked him to anger with strange gods. They committed abominations. They sacrificed to devils—newly created ones that even their forefathers had never heard of. They became unmindful of God, and forgot it was he that formed them. FYI, this was the sons *and* the daughters acting this way. I think you will agree—as they say—they were doing way too much: and a time out was in order.

So God says, he will hide his face from us, and see what our end is going to be. Actually he knows, but he wants *us* to come to an understanding of the result of conceit, rebellion, and idolatry. He says, he will heap mischiefs (meaning adversity, affliction, calamity, harm, and wretchedness) on us. I think we can agree this has been the lot of both our enslaved ancestors, and ourselves as their descendants. He says since we provoked him, he will provoke us to anger (meaning trouble/vex/grieve) with a foolish nation (as in a stupid, wicked, impious, and vile nation.) These are the Hebrew meanings of the words I am giving here. I don't have to name names; that is an apt description of the land of this Captivity, where the Lord our God is either a mockery or a convenience; but definitely not exalted as the Righteous Creator, King, and Judge that he is.

God goes so far as to say, I said, I would scatter them into corners, I would make the remembrance of them to cease from among men: Were it not that I feared the wrath of the enemy, lest their adversaries should behave themselves strangely, and lest they should say, Our hand is high, and the Lord hath not done all this.

Well, it certainly is the case that we have been scattered into the corners of the earth, and it is true that only a precious few historical accounts remain that link us to the once great nation renown in the world as the people the Lord God himself fought for. It is true those adversarial toward us believe they are superior because of our enslavement, and do not realize they are merely a tool being used in the hand of our Rock, who sold us and shut us up. This selling and closing us in, so that we are powerless to extricate ourselves, is the divine time out.

Work Detail

We know from the account in Exodus Chapter 1 verses 13-14 that our forefathers worked under conditions described as 'hard' and 'cruel,' for...God delivered them from working in foundries (the iron furnace), and the Egyptians made the children of Israel to serve with rigour. Being forced to learn smelting and metal working would explain how Aaron was able to fabricate the golden calf, for the Hebrews were historically shepherds. And they made their lives bitter with hard bondage, in morter, and in brick, and in all manner of service in the field: all their service, wherein they made them serve, was with rigour. The Hebrew word used for rigour is 'perek,' and means to break apart, and fracture, as with severity and cruelty. In Psalm Chapter 81 verse 6 speaking of the posterity of Joseph and by extension Israel, God says, "I removed his shoulder from the burden: his hands were delivered from the pots." The burdens were heavy loads or heavily loaded baskets the Hebrews had to carry, the pots refer to seething cauldrons, and boiling liquids. Based on this description, whatever the Egyptians had the

Hebrews doing, they took extra care to see that it was not light duty work, but as difficult as possible.

This mirrors the conditions our forefathers in the Trans-Atlantic slave trade faced. If a slave owner felt it was economically cheaper to buy a set of new slaves rather than maintain the health of the ones he had, he literally worked them to death and then replaced them. They were worked so hard their muscles would separate from the bone. The further south the plantation was, the more rigorous the labor. Hence the fear every slave had about being 'sold down river.' But conditions were even harsher on the sugar plantations in Brazil, and life was cheaper. Children as young as five were turned out to work in the field, and because sugar cane must be processed quickly, the slaves were driven relentlessly. The sugar had to be boiled in large pots; thus we see a replay of the Egyptian cauldrons.

At this point you may think, well we are not in that type of laborious bondage now. But the fact that we are not in a field working from dawn to sunset does not mean God does not see us in bondage. As long as we are working in the age of Esau under the conditions of his economic system, it is bondage. Yes, God has said man must eat bread by the sweat of his face. And yes he did say we should labor, working with our hands, and that if a man refuses to work, he should not eat. The point here is not work per say, but God's ideal plan is that man should be able to work for himself and enjoy the full fruits of his labor. He should not have to work to enrich others who care nothing for him, nor work and have a huge amount of money taken off the top under this pretext and that excuse. The laborer is worthy of his hire.

Also, it is not God's will for his people that they work diligently, and consistently have nothing to show for it, because of Esau's corrupt system manipulating the value of money, and changing laws to the convenience of the manipulators, so that year after year people must scramble to merely hold the place they were the previous year...the hope of actually getting ahead having long dissipated. This kind of system is called divers weights, and unjust balances.

Additionally, man is the one who is ordained by God to work by the sweat of his face, not the woman. Her primary duty is, as the Apostle Paul pointed out, to love her husband and children, and keep the home. Obviously, when she has these priorities under control, she is free —as the virtuous woman of Proverbs Chapter 31, to run a business on the side or invest wisely. The point is in achieving the proper work/life balance so that the husband, children, and home are prioritized, and there is no occasion for the word of God to be spoken evil of.

But how many descendants of the Trans-Atlantic slave trade have that luxury? How many brothers can afford for their wives to stay home? There are also many single mothers among our people. How many of them have to work two or even three jobs to maintain just the minimum of a decent standard of living?

Still not convinced we are in bondage? Look at the back of a one-dollar bill United States currency. The Egyptian pyramid is there to remind you of where your ancient forefathers were, and that you are back in the house of bondage today. But lest you think I read too much into things, let's see what God has to say about it:

"For the Lord will have mercy on Jacob, and will yet choose Israel, and set them in their own land: and the strangers shall be joined with them, and they shall cleave to the house of

Jacob. And the people shall take them, and bring them to their place: and the house of Israel shall possess them in the land of the Lord for servants and handmaids: and they shall take them captives, whose captives they were; and they shall rule over their oppressors.

And it shall come to pass in the day that the Lord shall give thee rest from thy sorrow, and from thy fear, and from the hard bondage wherein thou wast made to serve, That thou shalt take up this proverb against the king of Babylon, and say, How hath the oppressor ceased! the golden city ceased! The Lord hath broken the staff of the wicked, and the sceptre of the rulers.

He who smote the people in wrath with a continual stroke, he that ruled the nations in anger, is persecuted, and none hindereth. The whole earth is at rest, and is quiet: they break forth into singing." Isaiah Chapter 14 verses 1-7

Here's a different prophet talking about the same event:

"In those days the house of Judah shall walk with the house of Israel, and they shall come together out of the land of the north to the land that I have given for an inheritance unto your fathers." Jeremiah Chapter 3 verse 18 "Therefore, behold, the days come, saith the Lord, that it shall no more be said, The Lord liveth, that brought up the children of Israel out of the land of Egypt; But, The Lord liveth, that brought up the children of Israel from the land of the north, and from all the lands whither he had driven them: and I will bring them again into their land that I gave unto their fathers." Jeremiah Chapter 16 verses 14-15

These three verses tie the Lord's return to a deliverance from bondage and rest in our own land. I know it seems unreal, but it will come to pass. Maybe you are tired and weary of the day to day grind and constant setbacks, dealing with Esau's flawed and corrupt system. I have seen many decades of it, and I am tired too. But I can rejoice in the Lord because I know there is an appointed end. There remaineth yet a rest for the people of God...let us labour therefore to enter into that rest.

Loss of Privileges

The discipline of Captivity also cost us the freedom to judge our business and personal matters. The divine order was for the elders to judge 'in the gate,' and wise men and wise women were renown among the people. Today, we are at the mercy of a system that uses the symbol of a blindfolded woman to intimate justice is blind, but the truth is closer to they are blind to justice. This is not to say every judge and magistrate is crooked. What I am saying, is Esau's system is not designed to deal with a people who have been robbed and spoiled. The condition of the Black man in Captivity is best dealt with by the elders of our own people; those among them who are experienced, compassionate, and not subject to bribery and threats. Even the oppressor's legal system states we should be judged in their courts by a jury of our peers, but when was the last time you remember that happening?

I could continue, but I think I have clearly illustrated the disciplinary pressures the Lord is using in the Captivity to cause us to seek his face. Now that we know who we are, and why we are here, what is left to do except to ask him to turn our Captivity? May your Kingdom come, Lord...and your will be done on earth, as it is in heaven...Amen.

WHAT'S IMPORTANT

Any parent who truly loves their child will discipline them; for the child's own good and safety, and also that the parent might not be disgraced. I once heard something to the effect, 'there are "show and tell" children.' Some of them you can tell; others have to be shown. The Hebrew nation is clearly one with a history of having to be shown. The miracle of it all is God's steadfast faithfulness in that he continues to love us as a people...despised as we are in the eyes of the world...and he refuses to break his covenant with Abraham, Isaac, and Jacob. His mercies renew every morning, and we are not consumed.

And as difficult as it is to go through, God still tells us that he is only correcting us in measure, and that he has not dealt with us according to our iniquities. Meaning this: none of us have gotten what we really deserve. David understood this, for he said in Psalm Chapter 130 verses 2-3, "If thou, Lord, shouldest mark iniquities, O Lord, who shall stand? But there is forgiveness with thee, that thou mayest be feared."

We see what it is like to live with wickedness all around, and to be constantly vexed, grieved, and sabotaged by a culture bent on destroying us as a people. We have experienced firsthand what it means to be on the lowest rung of society ...to see strangers come into the same land and be elevated, while we are told, "Bow down, that we may go over: and we have laid our body as the ground, and as the street, to them that went over," Isaiah Chapter 51 verse 23.

We know the frustration of working—not to get ahead—but to merely maintain; and for many, just to keep going in a race to catch up. We know how that grueling pace has robbed precious time from our families and relationships, time that cannot be recovered. We know what it is to be a people beleaguered with issues and struggles for which we find no relief in the judicial system; a construct overseen by people who don't care, can't relate, and view the masses of Black people circuiting through their offices and courtrooms as job security.

We know these things. The redeeming factor is; God knows them too. And the same sentiment holds true for us today, as it did for our ancient forbears in Egypt... In all our affliction he is afflicted. He wants us to reach the point where we get serious about seeking him and his Kingdom first and foremost. For when the Kingdom comes, there is no more Captivity. It was never God's plan for his people to perpetually remain in servitude. Captivity is always temporary; it is intended as a learning experience for us, and ultimately a platform by which God judges the oppressor and receives great glory as he delivers his people. He will once again call his son out of Egypt.

Chapter XII ... Agape Love: True Gentile Christians
Bear Judah's Burden

And ye shall be hated of all men for my name's sake: but he that endureth to the end shall be saved.

The New Testament saints are commanded to bear each other's burdens, and so fulfill the law of Christ. This law is activated when we serve one another in love. We receive the capacity to love this way by the baptism and infilling of the Holy Ghost, for Romans Chapter 5 verse 5 tells us, "the love of God is shed abroad in our hearts by the Holy Ghost which is given unto us." This means that if professing Christians in the Americas had actually followed the directive of the Lord Jesus Christ, and emulated the example of the first century Hebrew church, they would have received the Holy Ghost, and been under unbearable conviction for the treatment of Judah in their midst.

How was it that worshipers could silence their conscience and shut up their bowels of compassion against their brother when the foundational commandments of Christianity are to love God with all of your heart, soul, and strength; and love your neighbor as yourself? In fact, the Apostle John tells us in I John Chapter 4 verses 20-21, "If a man say, I love God, and hateth his brother, he is a liar: for he that loveth not his brother whom he hath seen, how can he love God whom he hath not seen? And this commandment have we from him, That he who loveth God love his brother also." The Greek word used for hateth means to detest, persecute, or love less.

When worshiping in the Spirit and truth of God, such as God is seeking, an indescribable dynamic takes place. Categorizations such as age and color disappear. Yes, in the physical realm they exist, but as the Spirit of God looks on the heart, his presence arrives to dwell in the midst of the praises of his people. God is looking on the heart, and he wants us to look on the heart also, not the outward appearance. The abiding presence of the Holy Ghost is the only power that can enable people to fellowship with God and each other on the level he desires. We know God delights in this because of what John saw in the Revelation:

"After this I beheld, and, lo, a great multitude, which no man could number, of all nations, and kindreds, and people, and tongues, stood before the throne, and before the Lamb, clothed with white robes, and palms in their hands; And cried with a loud voice, saying, Salvation to our God which sitteth upon the throne, and unto the Lamb." Revelation Chapter 7 verses 9-10. Does that description sound like a segregated church to you? Or a great amalgamation of people who have one thing in common—that they love the Lord and his resurrected Son? The reality in heaven is always the perfect model for duplication on earth.

This is why I recoil when I hear people say America was founded on Christian principles. This is doublespeak and a lie to justify the nation's ungodliness and give its actions a covering of plausibility. Rather, what many Christians have done, is had a form of godliness, but denied the power thereof. There is only one Body of Christ, established on the foundation of the first century Hebrew church; repentance of sins, water immersion, and infilling of the Holy Ghost. The only godly nation is the ecclesia—the called out ones. No earthly nation can claim this foundation, for the kingdom is not of this world.

Further, the multiplicity of denominations created by denial of one or more of these three basic tenets undergirding the first century church is exceeded only by their lack of power and credibility. The only way to see the results of the original Hebrew church in this day is to retrace the steps of the apostles and duplicate their actions: the first of which was to obey instructions to wait... until they were filled with power from on high. Jesus had it without measure, John was filled with it from the womb, the disciples were baptized with it on the day of Pentecost, and they turned the world upside down. What a shame the pride of man has convinced him he does not need it now.

Today iniquity abounds, and the love of many has grown cold. We need to pray for another outpouring of the Holy Ghost such as that which fell on Azusa Street in San Francisco around 1906 under the ministry of the Black brother William J. Seymour. For a brief season, a foretaste of the great heavenly worship service seen by the Apostle John rested over San Francisco as people of all races and ethnicities came before the Lord with brokenness and repentance. There were healings and miracles, and as was said of Samaria when Philip preached—great joy in that city.

So, what does it look like when Gentiles truly bear Judah's yoke? To get a clear picture, we can cite examples with a span of twenty centuries between them. The first illustration is found in the 10th Chapter of the Book of the Acts of the Apostles:

"There was a certain man in Cæsarea called Cornelius, a centurion of the band called the Italian band,

A devout man, and one that feared God with all his house, which gave much alms to the people, and prayed to God alway.

He saw in a vision evidently about the ninth hour of the day an angel of God coming in to him, and saying unto him, Cornelius.

And when he looked on him, he was afraid, and said, What is it, Lord? And he said unto him, Thy prayers and thine alms are come up for a memorial before God. And now send men to Joppa, and call for one Simon, whose surname is Peter:

He lodgeth with one Simon a tanner, whose house is by the sea side: he shall tell thee what thou oughtest to do."

In the meantime, God was dealing with Peter, and also showed him a vision, to prepare him for the unprecedented encounter he was to have with this Gentile. Soon after this, messengers from Cornelius arrived where Peter was staying, and described their errand to him thus:

"And they said, Cornelius the centurion, a just man, and one that feareth God, and of good report among all the nation of the Jews, was warned from God by an holy angel to send for thee into his house, and to hear words of thee."

Cornelius was not selfish about this impending spiritual breakthrough. He contacted those who were near and dear to him and let them know they didn't want to miss this meeting.

"And Cornelius waited for them, and had called together his kinsmen and near friends."

When Peter arrived at Cornelius' house, Cornelius told him "...Four days ago I was fasting until this hour; and at the ninth hour I prayed in my house, and, behold, a man stood before me in bright clothing,

And said, Cornelius, thy prayer is heard, and thine alms are had in remembrance in the sight of God. Send therefore to Joppa, and call hither Simon, whose surname is Peter; he is lodged in the house of one Simon a tanner by the sea side: who, when he cometh, shall speak unto thee.

Immediately therefore I sent to thee; and thou hast well done that thou art come. Now therefore are we all here present before God, to hear all things that are commanded thee of God."

From this account, we can see that

*Cornelius was a devout man. For him, worship was a way of life.

*He brought his entire household under the reverential worship of God.

*He reached out to the poor, and did not withhold his substance.

*He was a man of prayer.

*He was just.

*He feared God.

*He didn't just talk his faith; he was known among Judah as a godly man.

*He was already involved in missions; he summoned family and friends.

*He was a man of consecration, having been found by the angel in fasting and prayer.

*His heart was open to receive all things that God commanded Peter to speak.

Peter began to preach the gospel of the Kingdom. A simple message explaining that after the ministry of John the Baptist, God anointed Jesus of Nazareth with the Holy Ghost and power, to minister to and heal those that were oppressed of the devil. And how he (Peter) was a witness of the things Jesus did both in Israel and Jerusalem, and witness to his death, burial, and resurrection. And how Jesus commissioned them to preach and testify that it is he who was ordained of God to be the Judge of the living and the dead. And that it was of Jesus which all the prophets were speaking of; and that through his name whoever believed in him would receive remission of sins.

"While Peter yet spake these words, the Holy Ghost fell on all them which heard the word.

And they of the circumcision which believed were astonished, as many as came with Peter, because that on the Gentiles also was poured out the gift of the Holy Ghost.

For they heard them speak with tongues, and magnify God. Then answered Peter, Can any man forbid water, that these should not be baptized, which have received the Holy Ghost as well as we?

And he commanded them to be baptized in the name of the Lord. Then prayed they him to tarry certain days."

What we have just seen in the example of Cornelius is a picture of the condition of the heart leading up to true Gentile conversion, and also the simplicity of the gospel. This is a far cry from the 'pray the sinner's prayer and 'ask Jesus to come into your heart' conversion methods so popular today. Neither did Peter feel the need to say anything about money, or how Cornelius could further prosper. Rather, this is an illustration of a broken and contrite heart waiting on God and desiring to be found acceptable in his sight, and a divine response granting that request.

We also see that as righteous as Cornelius was, God's certifying stamp of approval was the baptism of the Holy Ghost. And we have a clear definition of how Peter and his brethren from Joppa knew Cornelius and all that were with him had been filled with the Holy Ghost: they heard them speak with tongues and magnify God. This event was the manifestation of Peter's Pentecost sermon that the Promise from on high was also to as many as God would call; meaning the remnant He was taking out for himself from among the Gentiles to graft into the commonwealth of Israel. It clearly refutes both the teaching that the outpouring of the Holy Ghost was only for a sign to the men of Judah on that particular Pentecost, or that one is automatically filled with the Spirit as a consequence of conversion. There is a definite outward sign, so that both the believer and onlookers are witnesses that the person has been baptized with the Holy Ghost.

Closer to our time, the lives of several faithful white brothers stand out as living testimonies to this same type of first century church experience. They stood shoulder to shoulder with their Black brethren in ministry during the early part of the twentieth century. Some of these men were Southerners and knew full well the sentiment of the Reconstructionist South. But in the power of the Holy Ghost that recognizes no class or color, they actually walked out the life of the Spirit in deed and in truth.

While other congregations across the nation welcomed the outpouring of blessing, they were not willing to let it be shed abroad in their hearts. Confined to their fellowship and safely guarded from breaching the color line, they effectively quenched the Spirit. The fear of man and the desire to please men more than God hindered the witness that could have planted the seed of conviction across the nation. Yes, persecution would have resulted, but all who live godly in Christ Jesus are mandated to suffer. Like Moses, these brothers chose rather to suffer affliction with the people of God. They ministered side by side with their Black brethren in preaching the word and in sharing in ridicule and maltreatment.

It is difficult in our day to grasp just how outrageous this racial unity appeared, until one considers their behavior made them suspects of espionage and targets of vigilante abuse.

What does that tell you about this nation that people demonstrating the love of God in Christ Jesus would be perceived as subversive and enemies of the state? Nevertheless, the consecrated walk of these faithful brethren forced whites to face the inconsistency between racist segregationist attitudes and true Christian faith. And despite the persecution, these men never wavered in their firm conviction of what it means to be a sanctified, Spirit-filled Christian. Their willingness to not just get baptized in the Spirit, but actually follow its leading and obey it—gave them discernment and the holy boldness to preach the entire counsel of God.

Since the Holy Ghost leads and guides into all truth, we can only wonder how many people would have been transformed if they would have walked in the Spirit, rather than quenching it by forcing it to conform to the cultural norms of the day. Would the Spirit itself have revealed Judah's identity to Gentile Christians, preventing the deception which exists today in the form of Christian Zionism? Would it have given preachers, both Black and white— the holy boldness to tell the truth about Judah being in the midst of Captivity in the West? Instead of being caught up in prosperity theology, would the Gentile churches have blessed Judah out of their abundance, according to Romans Chapter 15 verse 27? The world would have glorified God, in seeing the infallible proof of true disciples of Christ: the holy love for one another.

The End Cannot Come... the Gospel Has Not Yet Been Preached

The Spirit of Antichrist and the Obstruction of Justice

"And this gospel of the kingdom shall be preached in all the world for a witness unto all nations; and then shall the end come..." Matthew Chapter 24 verse 14. The end is promised to come once the good news of the kingdom has been preached to all nations. Bible translators and missionary groups pride themselves on having already reached a significant portion of the world's population with the saving gospel.

But has the truth of the gospel really been preached? How can it be preached when a false image of the Lord Jesus Christ is put forth to the nations—an image that mysteriously happens to be in the likeness of the oppressor of the earth? How can it be preached when the Body and Bride of Christ is presented as a collage of denominations according to the particular fancy of their founder, rather than the singular faith that was once delivered (meaning originally transmitted) by the first century Hebrew fellowship in Jerusalem? How can it be preached when the people of his heritage whom he has temporarily set aside until the restoration of all things—are swept out of memory and replaced by a Gentile substitute which is more palatable to the Anglo-American religious taste? The life, death, resurrection, and return of the Lord Jesus Christ is an infallible truth and everlasting reality. But other than that, the Christianity preached today is little more than an amalgamation of pagan rites and rituals.[20]

In the quest to fulfill the Great Commission and take the gospel of the kingdom into all the world, how many have ever stopped to consider that the presence of the Black man in the West, through slavery and its subsequent generations serves as irrefutable proof that God is

---

[20] "Pagan Christianity?: Exploring the Roots of Our Church Practices" Frank Viola, George Barna 2008.

real, and his word as revealed in the Bible is true? Speaking truth in love in this manner may have had a much greater evangelical impact, because it would have been living proof that God is the one true God who can declare the end from the beginning, and speak forth decrees that do not return to him void, but accomplish what he sent them to do. The nations of the world looking upon our humiliated state would understand firsthand what can happen when the hand of divine discipline comes down.

But rather than present the Hebrew in Captivity in the Americas as verifiable proof of the authenticity of God's word, Esau's people have labored together to craft a substitute. This is spiritual obstruction of justice; wicked men holding the truth in unrighteousness. The Greek word used for hold means to hold down fast, possess, retain, withhold, or keep in memory. They know the truth that the Black man in the West is the true Hebrew, but they refuse to acknowledge it, or disseminate that truth that others might see the example made of us and fear God, and repent.

Often human rights activists will use the term 'crimes against humanity.' I submit that the suppression of truth regarding the identity of the people of the slave trade and their posterity is a spiritual crime against the souls of men. Who would want to deceive people about what God is doing except the spirit of antichrist? Those who promote a lie, obscure the truth, or cling to the deception because it is more agreeable to their tastes will never enter the New and holy Jerusalem, the bejeweled city of the Great King; because it is a domain of restricted access. Forbidden to enter are dogs, sorcerers, whoremongers, murderers, idolaters, and whosoever loveth and maketh a lie. The Greek word used here for maketh means to agree, appoint, or band together. **This means whoever is in agreement about keeping you in the dark about this now must face the horror of outer darkness later**.

Judah is synonymous with Jerusalem; the terms are interchangeable, as are Jacob and Israel, and Esau and Edom. This can be demonstrated by I Chronicles Chapter 6 verse 15: "And Jehozadak went into Captivity, when the Lord carried away Judah and Jerusalem by the hand of Nebuchadnezzar." Obviously Nebuchadnezzar could not dig up the entire city and take it back with him to Babylon. The account is written this way to illustrate the inseparable bond between the people and their city. Another example is found where Jesus laments, "O Jerusalem, Jerusalem, thou that killest the prophets, and stonest them which are sent unto thee." It is obvious he is speaking to the children of Judah, but he cries out to Jerusalem.

Understanding the intertwining of Judah and Jerusalem sheds new light on Jesus' words: "Jerusalem shall be trodden down of the Gentiles, until the times of the Gentiles be fulfilled." From this perspective, we can see that this is not just referring to the occupation of the old physical city in Israel, but the current oppression and treading down of our people. Zechariah Chapter 2 verse 12 reminds us that we—Judah—are the Lord's portion, and Chapter 3 verse 2 declares that God has chosen Jerusalem to rebuke Satan. If we as God's portion are synonymous with Jerusalem, and the firebrand with which he will rebuke Satan, is it any wonder why the enemy is enraged? But thanks be to God, which giveth us the victory through our Lord Jesus Christ!

The Wrath of Satan Intensifies Against Judah Worldwide

And when the dragon saw that he was cast unto the earth, he persecuted the woman which brought forth the man child...And the dragon was wroth with the woman, and went to make war with the remnant of her seed, which keep the commandments of God, and have the testimony of Jesus Christ...Revelation Chapter 12 verses 13 & 17.

Revelation Chapter 12 verse 13 clearly shows us Satan has a personal vendetta against the seed of Israel in general, and has literally declared war on the rest of her descendants that keep the commandments of God, and have the testimony of Jesus Christ. This sheds light on the turmoil and suffering tormenting Africa, and the racial hatred and disenfranchisement that characterize the West.

In the 4th Chapter and 7th verse of the Book of James, the writer exhorts the church to submit to God, resist the devil, and he will flee. We don't have to shout at him or argue, just practice a lifestyle of godly submission and holiness. We know that James had the Hebrew people in mind when he said this, because he opens his epistle in Chapter 1 verse 1 by greeting the twelve tribes which are scattered abroad.

Satan's wrath has intensified because he knows his time is short. He has to effect maximum damage in a minimum of time, so the pressure has increased from the basic contempt we experience in society to include havoc in our homes and families. Loved ones who have not submitted their lives to the Lord are often used by Satan at his whim to hinder and frustrate the saints. The delicate balance between firm boundaries and forgiveness and long suffering is repeatedly tested. Those who will not submit to the godly hierarchy in the home in order to avoid the pitfalls of Esau's biased justice system will eventually face it and deal with his flawed and God-rejecting institutions. The youth need fathers and mentors, but an incredible percentage of Black men languish in prisons unable to help their families. This guarantees the domino effect of no male guidance, a set up for the corrections system, and ultimately a vicious generational cycle of no mature males in the home.

In Africa, the people are assaulted with one genocidal scheme after another, through the proliferation of vaccines and bio-engineered pathogens. Foreigners jockey for the resources; supporting whatever leader is on the take and willing to capitulate. When the citizens complain and protest, the foreign powers provide arms and munitions to suppress their dissent. Indigenous resisters are classified as terrorists, which justifies bringing in an even heavier-handed response. This strategy of divide and conquer has been utilized repeatedly against our brothers and sisters on the African continent, leaving a trail of bloodshed, orphans, and widowhood in its wake.

A Family Affair...The Least of These My Brethren

When those who control this present world strike at the Hebrew people wherever they are scattered about the earth, they fail to realize they are striking out at God. Israel was hewn from the Rock; and Jesus testified that he came forth from the Father. While blindness in part has come on them, as many as believed on the Lord Jesus Christ gave he power to be the sons of God. When the spirit of grace and supplication is poured out on them at the time of the end and their heart turns back to the Lord, they too will be restored to the original familial relationship, and all will understand who their Elder Brother and Kinsman-Redeemer is. This is why the Apostle Paul could say, "For this cause I bow my knees unto the Father of our Lord Jesus Christ, Of whom the whole family in heaven and earth is named..." Ephesians Chapter 3 verses 14-15. The Greek word used here for family means a group of families or a whole race under a paternal line. In Amos Chapter 3 verse 2, God tells Israel, "**You only have I known of all the families of the earth: therefore I will punish you for all your iniquities**." A parent corrects his own child first, before seeking remedy against injustices perpetrated by the children of others.

We see the same theme in Isaiah's prayer in Chapter 63 verses 16-19 of his book. "Doubtless thou art our father, though Abraham be ignorant of us, and Israel acknowledge us not: thou, O Lord, art our father, our redeemer; thy name is from everlasting. O Lord, why hast thou made us to err from thy ways, and hardened our heart from thy fear? Return for thy servants' sake, the tribes of thine inheritance. The people of thy holiness have possessed it but a little while: our adversaries have trodden down thy sanctuary. We are thine: thou never barest rule over them; they were not called by thy name." Here we see clearly that the Hebrew tribes only, are those considered called by God's name.

This is why the famous petition in II Chronicles Chapter 7 verse 14 often quoted with degenerate America and the persecuting Gentiles in mind, is actually a Hebrew specific prayer. "If my people, which are called by my name, shall humble themselves, and pray, and seek my face, and turn from their wicked ways; then will I hear from heaven, and will forgive their sin, and will heal their land..." This is not a general all-purpose prayer. God is not going to heal wicked Babylon; it is destined for the fire. In fact, the scripture intones in Jeremiah Chapter 51 verse 9, "We would have healed Babylon, but she is not healed: forsake her, and let us go every one into his own country ..."

I am not discounting the Gentile brethren who are grafted into Israel, the native olive tree. But everyone who names the name of Christ must depart from iniquity. Based on Jesus' words to the Laodicean Church in Revelation Chapter 3 verses 14-19, this will be a very small remnant from the last generations. Sadly, as most of their churches solidify their allegiance to the Church of Rome rather than the faith that was first preached, they will be first among those who stoke the fires of persecution among the true saints.

This casts a whole new light on Jesus' words, "Inasmuch as ye have done it unto one of the least of these my brethren, ye have done it unto me...and, Inasmuch as ye did it not to one of the least of these, ye did it not to me." Nations will be judged on how they treated the Hebrew people. Churches and congregations will have to answer as to whether God's house was a house of prayer for all people. We ourselves, as the saints of the most High God, must walk in love toward our brethren who still have the veil over their hearts; for they are precious and beloved in the sight of God.

In meditating upon the Parable of the Ten Virgins, I gained an understanding which I think is quite relevant for our time. As the parable goes, all ten virgins took their lamps and went forth to meet the bridegroom, but only five took extra oil with them. It took the bridegroom a long time to get on the road, so they all got drowsy and fell asleep. At midnight, when the cry went out that the bridegroom was on his way, they all got up and began to trim their lamps, but the lamps of the ones who hadn't brought extra oil had gone out during the long wait. The foolish virgins wanted the wise ones to share their oil, but the wise ones pointed out there would not be enough for them both... in other words, if they tried to split what they had, everybody's lamp would end up going out. The parable closes with the foolish virgins leaving at that odd hour to buy oil, and by the time they return, they are refused access to the wedding ceremony.

I have always heard this parable interpreted as the oil representing the Holy Spirit. But I would like to present it from another perspective. The wedding celebration of the bridegroom points to the end of the age, thus the virgins point to worshipers at the end of the age. I asked myself what else oil represents in the Scriptures. The same Hebrew word is used to express oil and ointment, and in the Book of Psalms Chapter 133 I found oil signifies among other things: brethren dwelling together in unity.

The young women were all virgins, this implies they were in Christ, which is also supported by the fact they were invited to the wedding celebration. If dwelling together in unity is described as the precious oil that ran down the priest's beard and garments, and half of these virgins didn't have enough—could this allude to people who repent of their sin and get saved, but never come to understand they must really practice the commandment to love their neighbor as themselves, and love their brothers and sisters in like precious faith? The dark night that is coming when no man can work will be the time our light will have to shine the brightest. It will be the hour when the love of God in Christ for the brethren will be needed as never before, because according to Jesus, this is the litmus test by which people will recognize us as his disciples. If we don't practice it as a lifestyle now, will we really be ready for a kingdom where resurrected beings of all nations, kindreds, people, and tongues unite to worship in the beauty of holiness?

The Only Refuge and Safe Haven from the Satanic Fury

Certainly the enemy rages against us, but that does not mean we are to walk in fear. We have received exceeding great and precious promises from the Lord, and he has given us all things pertaining to life and godliness. We obtain these promises through the knowledge of God, and of Jesus our Lord. We do not receive the spirit of fear, for fear has torment. Rather, we operate in power, love, and a sound mind. These, together with daily repentance, the armor of God, the sword of his Spirit which is the word of God, and prayer, are greater than the power of darkness. We are to ask for, wait for, and actively seek the baptism of the Holy Ghost. Sanctification, discernment of error, and a dynamic witness follow the infilling of the Spirit: if we continue to walk in it.

The battles will intensify before the war is won. But God will never put more on us than we are able to bear. We are all suffering in one way or another, but none of us have had to suffer yet to the extent our brother Job did. So I encourage the saints to immerse themselves in the word of God, and continue steadfast in prayer; seeking the Lord as to what he would have you—as a son or daughter of Israel—do in these closing days.

WHAT'S IMPORTANT

Judgment begins at the house of God. It's time to tell the truth about who Israel is, and those of the tribe of Judah who have believed on Christ and received power to become the sons of God must take the lead in this. If this cannot be accomplished under the present brick and mortar construct for fear of it being misconstrued as something divisive or seditious, perhaps it is time to abandon those institutions altogether. After all, we were never intended to be known by which building we are seen entering and which church marquee graces the front lawn. Our love for our brethren, holy living, and the joy and power of the Lord are the benchmarks whereby the world must recognize us.

Because of the exceeding great and precious promises of God and the inviolable covenant with Abraham, Isaac, and Jacob, it should be with a sense of humble awe that we acknowledge our heritage. God is not revealing this to us for the purpose of boasting or bragging rights, for we are still a people in physical captivity. He is waking us up to our ancestry that we might lead the worldwide movement of repentance for ourselves, the sins of the people, and the sins of the forefathers. The descendants of the Trans-Atlantic slave trade must be the first in coming forth and acknowledging that we are here as a result of the sovereign hand of God. We need not be ashamed to admit this. We are already in a state of shame and humiliation. And we always will be as long we are in Captivity—regardless of our position or material accumulations. It's not about making ourselves look good and successful in Captivity... it's about leaving the Captivity behind altogether. There is only one way to do this: God's way—by consecration and supplication.

We must take up this mantle even as the wrath of the enemy intensifies against us. The coming days are days where we will have to stand on the literal word and promises of God, while the world is panicking around us. The lukewarm Western churches (who represent the bulk of church membership) are openly mocked for their worldliness and lack of power. They have adopted corporate business models to drive growth and income, rather than earnestly contending for the faith and trusting God to add to the church such as should be saved. They have inconveniently yoked themselves to Caesar by choosing exemption from taxation when Caesar's laws had already given them clear immunity, thus muzzling themselves from preaching the uncompromised word of God. To compensate for this failed state and lack of relevancy, they have chosen to align themselves with the powerful Roman church; rather than chastening themselves in fasting, prayer, and re-consecration.

Yet, God's timing is perfect. He never leaves himself without a witness. At precisely this critical juncture, God is raising up the sons of Zion, calling them back to remembrance of the Abrahamic Covenant and the power of the first century church. We will have to strike the balance of being as wise as serpents, yet harmless as doves. We will need to remain steadfast in prayer and keep our ears open to what the Spirit of God is saying, more than what the nightly news is saying. In short, we will need to believe the report of the Lord, that his mighty arm might be revealed on our behalf.

The ravages of generations of living in Captivity have taken their toll on our people, leaving many of them in a very low estate. They are objects of mockery and derision to the world. Yet, they are precious in the eyes of the Father and Christ. We would do well to remember these—the least of his brethren.

The word from God is if we draw nigh to him, he will draw nigh to us. God told the prophet Jeremiah that in the latter days, we would consider it (that is, the Captivity) and understand it perfectly. It's time to heed God's command to, "Call unto me, and I will answer thee, and shew thee great and mighty things, which thou knowest not."

Chapter XIII...Satanic Hate against Judah's Descendants

And when the dragon saw that he was cast unto the earth, he persecuted the woman who brought forth the man-child...And the dragon was wroth with the woman, and he went to make war with the remnant of her seed, who keep the commandments of God, and have the testimony of Jesus Christ.

How are the things of Esau searched out! how are his hidden things sought up! Obadiah Chapter 1 verse 6.

Now there was a day when the sons of God came to present themselves before the Lord, and Satan came also among them. Job Chapter 1 verse 6.

And Satan stood up against Israel, and provoked David to number Israel.

I Chronicles Chapter 21 verse 1.

Be sober, be vigilant; because your adversary the devil, as a roaring lion, walketh about, seeking whom he may devour...I Peter Chapter 5 verse 8.

Above are three classic examples of the underlying strategies of the enemy's attacks: accusation, provocateuring, and murderous aggression. These maneuvers have been used over and over again throughout the millennia against the people of God.

Why It Never Lets Up...The Origin of the Satanic War against Judah

And the Lord said unto the serpent "...I will put enmity between thee and the woman, and between thy seed and her seed; it shall bruise thy head, and thou shalt bruise his heel..." Genesis Chapter 3 verses 14-15. This ancient prophecy from the mouth of the Lord God Almighty himself set in motion the virulent animosity between Satan and the sons of God. Satan began his murderous strikes almost immediately; inciting Cain against Abel. He continued his artifices down through the Antediluvian Era, until at the time of the Flood, only eight souls were deemed righteous enough to escape judgment.

The lineage God would choose to bring forth the Seed of the Woman continued through the sons of Shem. The patriarch Abraham received a child of promise—Isaac, for God had declared that Abraham's seed was to be called in Isaac. From Isaac came the patriarch Jacob, and from among Jacob's twelve sons, the tribe of Judah. This tribe was destined to rule over the other eleven, strangle its enemies, bring forth the Conquering Lion, and rule with God. This is a heavenly calling with profound responsibilities. When our forefathers sinned, perverted justice, and killed their Kinsman-Redeemer, their exalted calling was preempted by divine chastening. Here are the gifts and callings of Judah which are without repentance:

"Judah, thou art he whom thy brethren shall praise: thy hand shall be in the neck of thine enemies; thy father's children shall bow down before thee..." Genesis Chapter 49 verse 8.

Here are verses showing the Messiah's descent from Judah, and Judah's calling to rule:

"And all the people that were in the gate, and the elders, said, We are witnesses. The Lord make the woman that is come into thine house like Rachel and like Leah, which two did build the house of Israel: and do thou worthily in Ephratah, and be famous in Bethlehem…" Ruth Chapter 4 verse 11. (Speaking of Ruth; ancestor of Christ.)

"But thou, Bethlehem Ephratah, though thou be little among the thousands of Judah, yet out of thee shall he come forth unto me that is to be ruler in Israel; whose goings forth have been from of old, from everlasting…" Micah Chapter 5 verse 2.

"And one of the elders saith unto me, Weep not: behold, the Lion of the tribe of Juda, the Root of David, hath prevailed to open the book, and to loose the seven seals thereof…" Revelation Chapter 5 verse 5.

"Ephraim compasseth me about with lies, and the house of Israel with deceit: but Judah yet ruleth with God, and is faithful with the saints…" Hosea Chapter 11 verse 12.

"But Judah shall dwell for ever, and Jerusalem from generation to generation. For I will cleanse their blood that I have not cleansed: for the Lord dwelleth in Zion…" Joel Chapter 3 verse 20-21.

"And he carried me away in the spirit to a great and high mountain, and shewed me that great city, the holy Jerusalem, descending out of heaven from God, Having the glory of God: and her light was like unto a stone most precious, even like a jasper stone, clear as crystal; And had a wall great and high, and had twelve gates, and at the gates twelve angels, and names written thereon, which are the names of the twelve tribes of the children of Israel…" Revelation Chapter 21 verses 10-12.

Through these scriptures we see Judah in both the past and future. And because we are currently serving the prophesied end time Captivity, we are proof of Judah's existence in the present. Our perpetual presence—sustained by God—is Satan's nemesis, and represents the annihilation of his kingdom through our Lord and Savior, Jesus Christ. Judah means praise, and God dwells in the midst of praise. Satan knows that once Judah awakens to their true calling as the praise of God, and begins to walk in holiness and supplication before him, his kingdom is ended forever. Since it is decreed the Ancient of Days will come and grant judgment to the saints of the most High, Satan's defeat and annihilation are a foregone conclusion. This is why his campaign to steal, kill, and destroy continues with such ferocity.

The Spiritual Dimensionality of Nations Revealed

As we noted earlier in the book, this latter day kingdom controlled by the Western powers is spiritual Babylon: the habitation of devils, hold of every foul spirit, and cage of every unclean and hateful bird. These malevolent entities are represented as occupying three different types of dwellings: the first, habitation—as a residence or permanent house; the second, hold—as a territory that is being watched and guarded; and the third, cage—a prison. It would appear then that some are right at home, having taken up a rightful residence. Others are present to watch and guard a territory and not permit the penetration of a godly witness; and still others are persecuting spirits who—like enraged inmates, will assault whoever comes within reach of their confines.

Here also manifests the spiritual prince of Grecia. This can be seen in the heavy emphasis on Greek and Roman gods, and eagle and owl symbolism that characterizes the architecture and statuary throughout the Western empires. Edom is characterized by a perpetual hatred and wrath; Philistia by an old hatred. This speaks to the contempt and loathing our people experience from other races and ethnicities. The influence of Moab is felt in the continual effort to corrupt the people by luring them into idolatry. The spirit of Sodom is evidenced by the abundance of food and luxuries, but refusal to sustain the poor and needy; in addition to a perverse delight in torture, fornication, and going after strange flesh. The Egyptian spiritual influence with its ubiquitous sun, obelisk, and pyramid imagery, serves to remind us of an ancient bondage which would have never ended unless God had intervened and rescued his son from Egypt.

Because these evil spirits have established a stronghold in the land of our Captivity, our only Rock and Refuge is in a blood covenant relationship with the Father through Christ: dwelling in the secret place of the most High and abiding under the shadow of the Almighty. These wicked and violent spirits find a ready outlet through the oppressor, who is outside of the covenant. Thus the assault continues against our people physically, psychologically, morally, and spiritually.

Bywords and Proud Speech

One method of psychological attack involves calling a person out of their name; the idea being that they will eventually come to view themselves in the same devalued manner. Isolated instances of disrespect or insult can usually be chalked up to stupidity. But when such behavior becomes the norm across a broad spectrum of society, it is more correctly interpreted as a form of psychological warfare.

Ape. Bluegum. Bootlip. Boy. Brownie. Buck. Buffie. Burrhead. Cushie. Coon. Crow. Darkie. Eight Ball. Gable. Gator Bait. Golliwog. Groid. Jigaboo/Jigga/Jigger. Jungle Bunny. Knee-Grow. Kushi. Mammy. Mau-Mau. Mulignan. Mud Person. Nigger. Negress. Nigette. Niglet. Pickaninny. Porch Monkey. Quashie. Rastus. Sambo. Schwartze. Shit Skins. Smoked Irishman. Sooty. Spearchucker. Spade. Tar-baby. Teapot. Thicklips. Wog.

Have you ever wondered why so many disparaging names were generated to refer to the people who built the Americas with their blood, sweat, and unpaid labor? The answer is found in Jeremiah Chapter 24 verse 9 "...And I will deliver them to be removed into all the kingdoms of the earth for their hurt, to be a reproach and a proverb, a taunt and a curse, in all places whither I shall drive them."

However, just because God decreed this, it cannot be taken as absolution from guilt for those who practice this speech against the children of Judah. This is because even if the oppressor does not fully understand who Judah is, he still has the teachings of Jesus, who taught that a man should love his neighbor as himself, and do unto others as you would have them do unto you. God could prophesy this decree of reproach upon his people because he knew the nations where he was going to scatter Judah would be ungodly people with only an outward profession of righteousness.

Perhaps the venue by which proud speech most effectively manifests itself is through cultural artifacts, and the realm of the visual and performing arts. The bizarre stereotypes and extreme exaggerations conceived, manufactured with zeal, and sold with pride during the Jim Crow era clearly point to what we would recognize today as a psychotic break with reality among racist whites. The stubborn refusal to meet the emancipated Hebrew on a level footing socially, intellectually, and economically drove these spiritual sons of Esau to create various images which they cherished and clung to such as:

*Illustrations of Black children as pickanninies...implying they don't need near as much invested in them as white children do

*Images depicting mature Black women as mammies...only useful as cooks, domestics, and baby sitters

*Older Black men shown as docile, grinning Sambos...past their prime, no longer a threat; but also lacking the dignity and respect that accompanies elderhood

*Young Black women recreated as wanton Jezebels...to suppress the guilt and provide justification for the raping of slave girls...they must have wanted it

*The portrayal of Black men in their prime as 'brutes' intent on defiling white women —who in the process were elevated to a demi-goddess status

*The use of Blacks to trigger nostalgic, 'feel good' emotions to sell comfort food products – such as rice and pancakes

*Lawn jockeys to communicate the wishful thinking that Black men are happy, under the most adverse conditions, to serve whites

*Young Black men shown as minstrels...for the purpose of entertaining and amusing whites

*Foolish, happy-go-lucky 'coons'...certainly not the character material for serious statesmanship or corporate responsibility

*Even international disgraces such as the degrading "Zwarte Piet" or Black Peter and his various European spinoffs; said to accompany St. Nicholas during the Christmas holidays.

As a people, we have always looked on these portrayals as humiliating and insulting, which no doubt they are. But there is a much deeper spiritual meaning behind this. In this so called 'Christian nation' a perverse sort of idolatry was being practiced among the Gentiles. Granted, it was not as violent and overt as human sacrificial murder by beating, lynching, and torching. This was a subtler approach, specifically designed to psychologically murder the Black man, and eliminate any credibility he might attain in the eyes of whites as he aggressively moved forward in the quest for equal rights.

Genesis Chapter 1 verse 27 declares, "So God created man in his own image, in the image of God created he him; male and female created he them.

According to the Bible, there was only one image wherein man was created. To say that only some men, and not others are created in the image of God is to call God a liar. Either God is right, or man is right. Accordingly, let God be true, and every man a liar. Therefore, the designing and production or printing of grotesquely distorted images of a person to demean them is blasphemous, and the cherishing of such representations is idolatry. It is nothing more than man's attempt to create something in the Satanically inspired image he wishes to see. And all of these types of images are Satanically motivated: this is obvious from the millennia old battle between the serpent, and the people under covenant with God.

Further, the exaltation of the white woman to near goddess stature was also a form of idolatry. Psalm Chapter 33 verses 13-15 state, "The Lord looketh from heaven; he beholdeth all the sons of men. From the place of his habitation he looketh upon all the inhabitants of the earth. He fashioneth their hearts alike; he considereth all their works." With that being said, there was only one group of people God ever said were gods: and that was our ancient Hebrew ancestors.

It was mentioned earlier that young Black women were portrayed as wanton Jezebels...to suppress guilt and provide justification for the raping of slave girls. That this wishful thinking type of mentality continued to persist is best expressed in the words heard in 'Brown Sugar' recorded by the English rock band the Rolling Stones, in 1971. Over four decades after its release, this song still receives airplay and is considered by many to be an oldies classic. But how many know the opening lyrics speak of a slave ship leaving the Gold Coast of Africa in route to New Orleans where the slaves will be sold to the cotton plantations? Or how the next lines reveal the slaver is raping the women because of heated Gentile passion?

Another example highlighted was the image of the foolish, happy-go-lucky 'coons'; void of character and unsuitable for serious statesmanship or corporate responsibility. The racists' need to suppress the Black man from gaining any meaningful autonomy and governance over his own affairs was fully vented in the 1915 propaganda film, 'Birth of a Nation' by D.W. Griffith. The fact that we have identified the spiritual force behind these portrayals as Satanic, and the fact that many white people today admire and laud Griffith's work and still enjoy watching the film, indicates the true spiritual state that surrounds us in our Captivity. A people who trust in their own righteousness, and lightly esteem the very clear commands of the Father and the Lord Jesus Christ will have to answer on that Great Day of the Lord...and who shall be able to stand?

Jesus said that he would judge no man, but the word that he spoke would judge man. The sentence is already spelled out for those who despise the commandments of the Lord Jesus: he will be revealed from heaven with his mighty angels, In flaming fire taking vengeance on them that know not God, and that obey not the gospel of our Lord Jesus Christ...who shall be punished with everlasting destruction from the presence of the Lord, and from the glory of his power...II Thessalonians Chapter 1 verses 8-9.

Terrorism and Vigilantism

We are constantly inundated with media coverage about inner city Black gang violence, but beyond doubt the organized gang activity of the Ku Klux Klan represents the original and much more accurate example of terror and intimidation at work. In the wake of the Civil War, a social and economic void was created in the South. Federal law could mandate change, but it was powerless to transform the hearts of men who had become comfortable with the old order of white supremacy and bristled at the prospect of Black people achieving the dignity that comes from self-sufficiency and prosperity.

Initially loosely formulated as a social club for Confederate veterans who opposed the Reconstructionist policies, the KKK evolved into the equivalent of a secret society. We have already earlier noted the Apostle Paul's observation that "the Gentiles know not God...and sacrifice unto devils." An understanding of the costumes and nomenclature of the Klan—from the white robes and tall conical hats, to the usage of titles of wizard, dragon, and Cyclops (all seeing eye) along with its numerological and philosophical association with Freemasonry—unmistakably link the driving force behind this organization to ancient Satanic paganism. Regardless of the platitudes mouthed about America being a Christian nation founded on Christian principles, the fact remains that the practicing Satanist and early luminary of the Ku Klux Klan alleged to have written ritual for them—Albert Pike, is memorialized in Washington, D.C. This represents one example where the true allegiance of this nation is identified in its architecture and statuary.

Satan comes only to steal, kill, and destroy. The murders, lynchings, fire-bombings, silent marches, and cross burnings designed to rob the populace of any sense of peace and security prove that the children of Judah were not just up against disgruntled Southerners, but an all-out Satanic assault itself. The ritual costumes the Klansmen wore hailed from pagan roots, and it was by necessity the wearers disguised themselves; as most of them were the local business owners, legal professionals, lodge members, church pastors, police, and civic leaders. Thus, it was futile for a Black person suffering injury or damages from Klan activity to appeal to the legal justice system for relief. The judge before whom he would present his case was likely someone who had been present at the scene of the crime.

The Black man during the Reconstructionist South and Jim Crow eras was effectively handicapped in defending himself against such lawlessness. His only option to protect himself, his family, and his property was to use lethal force, or at least let the marauders know he was armed, as a deterrent to a confrontation. Today, we hear much hue and cry in the West against Federal gun control laws. But how many know the push for such laws in this country was originally crafted for the purpose of preventing Black people from defending themselves against the Klan and other vigilantes? As a matter of fact, gun restrictions against our people predate the individual state 'Black Codes' and stem from the fear of insurrection of slaves, or the assistance to slaves by free Blacks. However, a nation always reaps what it sows; and today, Anglo-American citizens of the West are being systematically disarmed.

The descendants of slaves as a minority could not win a war for justice and social parity at the barrel of a gun. It became apparent that political might would be the only way to transform the socio-economic landscape and bring a semblance of equality. The prospect of Blacks using the constitutionally enshrined legislative system to upset the 'old order' sparked a fresh wave of violence and intimidation, as the Jim Crow era began the painful transition to the Civil Rights Movement.

Perhaps the name that stands out the clearest and illustrates the vigilante justice mentality common during those traumatic days is that of the innocent teenager Emmett Till.

Assaulted so violently he was grotesquely disfigured, then shot in the head and dumped in the Tallahatchie River, Till's case is a vivid example of the murderous overreaction and kangaroo court justice characterizing the South. His killers went free, and after the trial bragged about the event. It was also the tipping point that ignited the demand for justice and equal rights. More murders and more terrorism would follow until the right to vote and laws against segregation were passed. Prima facie, it would appear great strides have been made. But how much has sentiment toward the children of Judah actually changed?

If a man hates another man who is unequal socially, economically, and in terms of access to legal justice, and hates him all the more because the oppressed man wishes to become—not superior to—but only equal with him on these terms; and a third party holding more power than them both steps between them and says, "See here now: I have decreed a law that this man with less should be afforded the right to obtain the same benefits you have," can the law remove the loathing and hatred the one man has for the other?

It is impossible for legislation, or lobbying, or marching, or boycotting, or demonstrations either peaceful or violent—to change anything in a man's spirit. God has permitted man to love his neighbor as himself, with the consequence of Divine blessing for obedience, and God also permits man to hate his neighbor, with Divine consequence of dismissal from heaven's courtroom with the words, "Depart from me, ye cursed, into everlasting fire, prepared for the devil and his angels." That the oppressor's spirit has not yielded in repentance toward God—especially in the realm of vigilante justice and law enforcement—the entities most likely to have a confrontational encounter with the sons of Judah, is demonstrated by well-known events such as Trayvon Martin, of Sanford, Florida; unarmed, shot and killed by a vigilante in February 2012, and Michael Brown, of Ferguson, Missouri; unarmed, shot and killed by police in August 2014. That same month, John Crawford III was shot and killed by police in a Beavercreek, Ohio Walmart solely on the word of a 9-1-1 caller who led police to believe an imminent active shooter situation was underway. In reality, Crawford was in the pet products aisle, talking on his phone and holding an air gun he had picked up from a different section of the store. Based on the synchronization of the 9-1-1 call with the store surveillance video, Crawford remained for over six minutes in the same spot at the end of aisle, engrossed in his telephone conversation; other shoppers nonchalantly moving in and out of his vicinity, until police rushed in and shot him dead. A grand jury failed to return an indictment on the officers, triggering a Department of Justice investigation. Also, the 9-1-1 caller was not charged with inducing panic or making a false alarm.

Tragedy reared its head again in the murder of 12 year-old Tamir Rice, shot without question while holding a pellet gun near a city park in Cleveland, Ohio. Critical information relayed by the 9-1-1 caller that could have alerted police to the fact Rice was a juvenile and the gun not a real firearm was not passed on to the responding officers. This case is all the more heart-rending because the police refused to assist the mortally wounded child, and when his older sister ran up to help him, she was thrown to the ground and restrained. A grand jury refused to indict the officers. Laquan McDonald, age 17, was literally riddled with bullets as he walked away from Chicago police Officer Jason Van Dyke. And there was Corey Jones, age 31; a church musician killed by a plainclothes police officer as he waited by the side of a Florida interstate for assistance with his disabled vehicle.

The availability of media technology brought brutal excesses like the 1991 police beating of Rodney King to the mainstream. But the possibility of public scrutiny was not enough to prevent the beating death of Malice Green, the unprovoked execution of Amadou Diallo, or the sodomy assault of Abner Louima. These are the high profile cases that send shock waves through the nation. There are many other incidents that don't make the news, are committed under cover, or never come to light due to intimidation of the victim. Ultimately, events receiving news coverage become a media free-for-all for editorialists and bloggers. Internet commenters reveal the true sentiments of many American's hearts as they type under cover of anonymity. Anger and calls for action clash with pleas for restraint and both are met with scorn, ridicule, and rejoicing for the pain of our people. Underneath these disparate views and opinions lies the nagging fear that the atrocity will spark further violence. We are living in what the Bible calls the time of Jacob's trouble: a time when our mother—Jerusalem—has become a cup of trembling, and a burdensome stone to all that burden themselves with it.

So far, we have seen examples of interaction with police or citizens who somehow perceived themselves or the public to be in such great imminent danger that only murder or extreme brutality could save them. So the children of our people who are obviously not a threat to anyone don't have to fear terrorism, right?

Unfortunately, that was not the case for Carol Jenkins, a young Black woman involved in door to door sales of educational materials during the late summer of 1968. The victim of an unprovoked attack, Jenkins was brutally stabbed and left to die. It was rumored her killer felt her death was justified. The most thorough account of this civil rights era tragedy is documented in the book "The Girl in the Yellow Scarf"[21], by veteran investigative reporter Sandra Chapman.

Individual beatings, shootings, and deaths by tasering are mindboggling in themselves for their senseless brutality. But in order to really comprehend the psychopathic depths of the murderous Satanic force that bears deadly hate toward our people, we need to remember that entire towns and neighborhoods are considered fair game, too.

A recap of the misfortunes prophesied to befall our people in Deuteronomy Chapter 28 included being cursed in the city (urban areas) and the field (rural areas). The nation the Lord would bring from the ends of the earth described as a "swift eagle" would be of fierce countenance and not regard the person of the old, or show favor to the young. Most important is the imprecation that among the nations where we were scattered we would find no ease; our lives would hang in doubt before us...we would fear day and night, and have none assurance of life. We can see the outworking of this curse in events such as the Tulsa Massacre that took place in 1921.

Earlier, I mentioned the release of the propaganda film, Birth of a Nation—as a tool to demonize and discredit Black people, and incite derision and indignation toward them. The question then arises as to what was driving the need to shape public opinion of Jim Crow Era Blacks in such a negative and distorted way. The answer is that such a contrivance was

---

[21] " The Girl in the Yellow Scarf" Sandra Chapman, 2012

necessary to refute and eclipse the very real prosperity, community cohesiveness, and congenial culture that existed in the Greenwood suburb of Tulsa, Oklahoma at the turn of the twentieth century. Known as the 'Black Wall Street' and 'Little Africa', Greenwood was a thriving testament to the level of affluence and self-sufficiency Black people could achieve when provided entrepreneurial freedom and access to the same resources as their white counterparts. Whereas degradation and disenfranchisement characterized many other Black neighborhoods, Greenwood drew educated and talented people, and was looked upon as a mecca of opportunity for Blacks. Self-contained economically, it had its own school, hospital, shopping district, theater, and upscale homes. Its banks were even able to make loans to the surrounding white businesses.

Tulsa, like any other American city at the time, was home to veterans returning from World War One. Many were unable to find work after discharge. There was already a deeply entrenched Klan presence in the region. Juxtaposed to these disgruntled factions was a prosperous, self-sufficient community of people who did not and would not fit the profile and stereotype white racism had defined for it. Add to this volatile mix the widely popular Birth of a Nation film, and all that was needed was a provocation. One finally surfaced on May 31st, 1921 in the form of the never-fail strategy of a white woman accusing a Black man of sexual assault. The woman was an elevator attendant. The accused man said he had stumbled at the elevator and reached out to catch his balance; inadvertently bumping the woman in the process. Nevertheless, he was taken into custody.

The local white newspaper was a major factor in whipping the white populace into blood rage; reporting the altercation as an attempted rape. That afternoon, a lynch mob gathered at the courthouse with the intention of forcibly taking the man from the jail. The Black residents—greatly outnumbered—also gathered at the courthouse as a barrier to protect access to the man. According to eye-witness accounts, both sides were armed, but a white man attempted to wrest a gun from a Black man, and when the Black man refused to relinquish it, a shot was heard.

That marked the beginning of what can correctly be described as ethnic cleansing, a massacre, and a blood-lust feeding frenzy. Within twelve hours, Greenwood was effectively wiped from the map; abolished. National Guard units were called in, who began rounding up Blacks in Greenwood, disarming them, and taking them to internment camps. Once the people were removed from their houses, the mob would loot the home, then torch and firebomb it. Those who hid inside their homes perished in fiery infernos. Most people had little to no notice to escape the area, mothers tried to flee carrying babies and with children in tow. Nevertheless, the people were run down and executed mercilessly. The business district was looted, then torched and burned.

But there was something else that set the Tulsa massacre apart, and more clearly defines it as the 'Greenwood Extinction Operation.' Survivor's accounts indicate precise military maneuvers were underway, such as would be deployed during a siege. The morning after the man's arrest, at five a.m., a whistle blew which signaled the start of an all-out mob attack. Machine guns were observed mounted on bluffs overlooking the area, and a hail of bullets seemed to be coming from all directions. Communication lines had been cut (which at that time handled telephone and telegraph transmissions.) People trying to flee the city found the streets blocked by militia mobs, and nowhere to turn. The railroad tracks leading out of town were also blocked. At one point, a plane flew overhead; not a government plane, but most likely a privately owned bi-plane, which was not uncommon at that time. What accounts do assert, is that it dropped turpentine bombs. The National Guard troops herded people into internment camps, and afterward they were not permitted to leave unless there was a white citizen who could vouch for them. And the accused? A court later declared him innocent of any crime.

In retrospect, this event bears the hallmarks of a planned operation. In other words, the prosperity of Greenwood had provoked the ire of the white supremacy, and this tragedy likely would have eventually occurred anyway granted the necessary pretext. While mob violence can easily result in stampeding, shooting, arson, and looting, siege tactics such as severing communications, blocking exits out of a municipality, and sniper positioning of automatic weaponry require organization and prior strategizing.

Another prominent ethnic cleansing event which occurred was in Rosewood, Florida during the first week of January, 1923; this was also based on a Black on white female assault accusation (which was later revealed to be a cover for a white on white extramarital affair the woman was involved in.) These types of off the chain rage fests, along with clever contrivances like sundown laws, are part of the Captivity curse that points to us always being in doubt of our life, and not finding rest anywhere we go.

In summarizing terrorism and vigilantism against the descendants of Jacob, we must always remember the root of it is Satanic. The perpetrators are just the tool. Questions we can ask to confirm this are:

Is there a precedent for this in the lives of our ancient forebears?

Did the Tulsa Massacre present the components of a Satanic ritual sacrifice?

How could Carol Jenkin's killer savagely end her life; seemingly with no remorse?

From Daniel Chapter 11 verse 33, we can see that the sword, flame, captivity, and spoil have been used in the past against our people, and will be used again toward the time of the end. This discourse between Daniel, who was of the captives of Judah exiled to Babylon—and the messenger angel, actually begins in chapter ten, and the angel specifically states, "Now I am come to make thee understand what shall befall thy people in the latter days: for yet the vision is for many days...they shall fall by the sword, and by flame, by captivity, and by spoil, many days." We also see a parallel in the book of Obadiah in the prophecy against Edom... "For thy violence against thy brother Jacob shame shall cover thee, and thou shalt be cut off for ever...yea, thou shouldest not have looked on their affliction in the day of their calamity, nor have laid hands on their substance in the day of their calamity; Neither shouldest thou have stood in the crossway, to cut off those of his that did escape..." In the latter days, the sword is replaced by bullets, and Captivity means captured, a prisoner, and an exile. Flame means arson, firebombing, or aerial bombing, and spoil and laying hands on substance means looting. Standing in the crossway to cut off those that escape the carnage and destruction is equivalent to blocking egress out of a municipality. The Tulsa Massacre demonstrated all of these elements.

The components of a Satanic ritual sacrifice are terror, human sacrifice via bloodshed, and fiery inferno. The Tulsa Massacre also met this test.

Carol Jenkins killer had never met her, her family, or had any dealings with her. She was not a criminal or threat to anyone; she was merely a young woman in an unfamiliar area marketing educational materials and trying to meet a sales quota. So why might he have felt her death was warranted? We saw at the beginning of the chapter accusation and murderous aggression are two of the three main strategies Satan uses against the children of Judah. The woman's killer did not know why he said that, but the spirit that motivated him to kill did, for it was a spirit that predated the creation of man.

From the position of accuser, Satan could point to the blood oath of her ancestors against her Redeemer, "his blood be upon us and our children," and appoint himself as judge, jury, and executioner. From the standpoint of murderous aggressor, he saw a chance to strike a descendant of the One who crushed his head, and took the keys of hell and death out of his hand. From either perspective, Satan felt his actions were justified.

When incidents of senseless police and citizen violence are repeatedly perpetrated on our people, this is Satan in action as a provocateur. The objective is to incite the people of the Captivity to react in such a manner that Esau, who lives by the sword—will respond with a show of deadly force. When the public either smirks, shrugs it off as business as usual, or counters with "get over it," it is because Satan has convinced them; even as he convinced Carol Jenkins' killer, that they got what they deserved.

Esau's people do not have the right to arbitrarily commit violence against the sons of Jacob. When they do this, they are carrying out the directives of Satan, who is steadfast in his conviction that the descendants of the Hebrews deserve every evil thing that befalls them. And at the same time, the sons of Jacob have no right to arbitrarily commit violence against the sons of Esau, under the conviction that 'they deserve it for what they did to us.' In the case of Esau's violence against Jacob in the Captivity, it is the outworking of wrath stemming from a divine spiritual directive that predates any person alive today, and it is temporarily permitted to manifest through the vengefulness of Satan.

Although divinely permitted, Esau's wrath and persecution against Jacob will still be condemned by God in the Last Judgment, because men and their institutions must willfully reject the gospel of Jesus Christ and override their own conscience in order to carry out the directives of Satan. In the case of the sons of Jacob, it is not 'reverse racism'; for there is no such thing. It is a reaction to a previous action—a response to actions committed which provoke anger, frustration, and a desire for retribution. But only God has the right to execute justice, for the wrath of man worketh not the righteousness of God...James Chapter 1 verse 20.

God has a great stake in the human race, because of the personal sacrifice in sending his only begotten Son to redeem them, and for the honor of his own great name. For this reason, he is not willing that any should perish, but that all should come to repentance. In light of this gracious attitude toward sinful man, God is longsuffering, and prefers punishment over execution. When there are instances—such as Sodom, the Amorites, Amalek, the first century cities of Pompeii and Herculaneum, or even Babylon and Edom at the end of our age—which God considers beyond remedy, utter destruction and annihilation will be declared. However, his preferred mode of dealing with rebellious man appears to be in humbling him and bringing him into subjection under a flesh and blood taskmaster; that his pride might be broken and he might repent of his sins against God and man. When a man thus chastened sees his wrong, humbles himself, and acknowledges only God can deliver him and restore him, he is ready to be raised up again. This is why the sons of Jacob must not render evil for evil. God's declared word is that the Gentiles will go into Captivity even as Israel is restored; this is clearly written in both the Old and New Covenants. God is very effective at making his point on the consciousness of man under Captivity conditions. His desire is that the outcome will be humility and genuine love for God and ones' neighbor. When we attempt to recompense people based on our own sense of being wronged, we thwart God's judgment—which is designed to have a much greater and longer lasting impact than our puny efforts ever could.

Yes, Black on Black violence occurs, with the greatest concentration in urban areas where the oppressor has introduced the alternative economy. These incidences can be robberies, turf wars, retribution killings, gang initiations, or domestic violence. However, it is never because a Black man or woman is walking along a street or through the neighborhood and another Black person finds them suspicious, or feels he deserves death because of his blackness. That type of irrational fear—which triggers a knee-jerk reaction to use the maximum amount of force and instills a sense of dread in an armed aggressor that he is in mortal danger from an unarmed man—stems from the inalienable relationship between the Hebrew and God, the enmity between the Woman's Seed and the serpent's seed, and the reaction it creates in the unregenerate Gentile.

God told the Israelite tribes, "Ye are gods; and all of you are children of the most High. But ye shall die like men, and fall like one of the princes." A preview of this former god-man reality is presented in this description of the psychological relationship between Egypt-the house of bondage, and Judah in the future, as God rearranges the rank of the nations: "In that day shall Egypt be like unto women: and it shall be afraid and fear because of the shaking of the hand of the Lord of hosts, which he shaketh over it. And the land of Judah shall be a terror unto Egypt, every one that maketh mention thereof shall be afraid in himself, because of the counsel of the Lord of hosts, which he hath determined against it" ...Isaiah Chapter 19 verses 16-17.

Today our people are scattered; trodden down by the Gentiles, dying on the streets, and behind bars. Nevertheless, the imprint of the original stamp of Godhood remains upon us... and with it, the inevitability that we will be restored to a glory exceeding the former heights. This is what drives the oppressor to fear and kill at the slightest provocation. Neither will his hidden and unconfessed atrocities escape judgment; they will be replayed in real time with all parties present in the Celestial Courtroom. For in the vast archives of Heaven's library, there is no section that exists under the category 'Unsolved Crimes'...but all things are naked and opened unto the eyes of him with whom we have to do.

Eugenics

Man's quest to make the perfect human being and gender a perfect human race, stems from a carnal effort to attain something that can only come about through spiritual renewal. Man fell from perfection through sin and insubordination while he was in Eden. Because all human flesh descending from the original sinner bears the taint of sin, tweaking and fine-tuning can never boost man to the heights he desires. Man literally begins a journey on the road to death from the moment he draws his first breath.

Even if a flawless human body could be designed, the person himself would be corrupt, for the heart is deceitful above all things, and desperately wicked. Rather than perfection in man's constantly degenerating outer shell, God desires truth in the inward parts. God's will is that our spirit would first be perfected, and on the Last Day, we will be raised incorruptible. A perfect body will then clothe a perfect spirit. But in carnal man's warped thinking, a perfect body housing a corrupted spirit is the worthy goal. If he has to resort to merging himself with machinery, he will... in the search for perfection and glorification. The science of achieving this is called trans-humanism. But before trans-humanism, there was eugenics.

The term eugenics stems from the prefix eu—meaning good, and the suffix genos— meaning birth. Thus the word means good or noble birth. Eugenics can function two ways: either negatively, where reproduction is hindered to prevent undesirable traits, or positively, where selective breeding is employed to boost the outcome of desirable traits. We first see the negative strategy employed against our people during the pre-Exodus Captivity in Egypt. Pharaoh's genocidal command to throw the infant Hebrew males in the river ensured that the divine imprint on the children of Israel would gradually dilute. Proof of this divine imprint upon our ancestors is evidenced by Exodus Chapter 1 verse 12: "But the more they afflicted them, the more they multiplied and grew." Affliction and rigorous labor had an unexpected effect upon the Hebrew people: they experienced a population explosion. In this case, the undesirable trait was the vitality and endurance of the Hebrew male—which was perceived as a threat.

If you have been reading this book in a sequential manner, you have probably grasped the truth that our present Captivity in the West is but a modern replay of the ancient Egyptian Captivity. In retrospect, it is not surprising that the same or similar sinister schemes used in Egypt are deployed against us again. As Hebrews, we have always inherently known children are a blessing, and devastated when they were sold away from us. Therefore, it was by great craftiness of Satan that our people have been co-opted into supporting their own genocide.

The idea of racial purity—a subject of intense interest to the German dictator Adolf Hitler—gained momentum in the West in the early twentieth century; progressing quickly from a popular discussion topic to a scientifically backed mission. While the 'science' behind the movement was flawed and biased-since the supporting data for the elimination of others was provided only by white researchers, it appeared credible to many based on the works of a prominent eugenicist of the time, Francis Galton.

In the fledgling years of eugenics, stratification among our people expressed itself via deep poverty; subsistence sharecropping, limited education and menial jobs; while a minority might get the coveted opportunity to better themselves. Education was the only key to relevancy and breaking the cycle of poverty. In the shanties of the south and slums of the north, survival was the primary concern and the people's grievances were dismissed or ignored. The educated and articulate trod the delicate balance of holding a beacon of hope for the masses, while maintaining dialogue and credibility with the white power base. Thus, the elitists among our people were approached by a woman with very wicked intentions; for the purpose of conducting the public relations campaign for what she termed 'The Negro Project.'

This woman was Margaret Sanger, who—with the help of prominent figures of the period such as William E. Du Bois, and Mary McLeod Bethune—convinced Blacks that birth control was in their best interest. In a letter dated December 10, 1939 to her friend and colleague Charles J. Gamble, Sanger explains how she will co-opt Black pastors to unwittingly carry on the eugenics program, because the best way to reach the Negro is through an appeal from someone they trust from a spiritual perspective. Thus the eugenics motive was to be cloaked in spiritual care and concern. The founders of the eugenics movement against our people were smart enough to know that what a person might reject from the oppressor peddling door to door, he will accept while sitting in a pew under the sound of a voice he respects. He will not suspect the man of God of leading him astray. Attractively packaged as 'better health care', eugenics took on a respectable and benevolent appearance.

This Satanic plan of operations should never have been preached from a pulpit. Pregnancy was not the main plight of Black women. Good maternal healthcare—the basis of which is proper diet and rest—was the issue. This means the problem most affecting them was poverty, or for those who could find employment—overwork. Most Black women of the era breastfed their children, which naturally spaces births between two to three years. Further, the standard of marriage was honored and the rate of illegitimacy was much lower than it is today, as it was viewed by Blacks as scandalous. But Sanger's interest was not in addressing changes to the social and economic policies which would eliminate poverty and the need for poor women to constantly work throughout the term of their pregnancy. Her zeal was to diminish the Black sons and daughters who were now in competition with her own people for jobs and representation in their respective communities.

I am certain Du Bois and McLeod-Bethune would have recoiled in horror if they could have glimpsed into the future and seen the abortion mills that dot Black communities and the manner in which donors could contribute gifts specifically earmarked to eliminate Black babies. But where was the spirit of God in the churches that helped propagate this doctrine from hell? Was it crushed beneath that 'respectable' form of godliness that nevertheless denies the power thereof? Was any one even listening to the Spirit that leads and guides into all truth, and enables us to discern from error? Either Sanger was right, or God is right. Let's look at both of their takes on the situation:

Sanger's sentiment: the work of eugenics must not be perceived as strategy to exterminate Blacks. The use of ministers to promote our ideas will mask the true objective.

God's word: Lo, children are an heritage of the Lord: and the fruit of the womb is his reward. As arrows are in the hand of a mighty man; so are children of the youth. Happy is the man that hath his quiver full of them: they shall not be ashamed, but they shall speak with the enemies in the gate...Psalm Chapter 127 verses 3-5

Every word of God is pure: he is a shield unto them that put their trust in him... Proverbs Chapter 30 verse 5

Today, the evil fruit of Sanger's Negro Project is Planned Parenthood. To quickly locate a clinic, just go to virtually any Black neighborhood in any city. Abortion is nothing but eugenics with the deceitful, 'I care about your health and your body' packaging stripped away. Planned Parenthood makes presentations at schools, but does not counsel on abstinence. They assume it will be business as usual for our people to continue to believe the lie that they are destined to be fornicators and raise or alternately abort a bastard nation.

Question: Has eliminating our children eradicated poverty from our midst? Does it prevent terrorism and vigilante killings? How many potent and unerring arrows have been blunted, chopped and tossed to the fire? How many voices have we muted that would have spoken judgment in the gate to our enemies? The number is in the millions. Sacrificing their children to devils was one of the sins that got our forebears evicted from the land God gave them, and caused them to be scattered to the corners of the earth. It is time for us to repent for this sin on behalf of both our forefathers and our own generations, and beseech the mercies of the living God to deliver us from evil. Let us observe this timely advice from God to our forebears when they went into the Babylonian Captivity many years ago:

"Take ye wives, and beget sons and daughters; and take wives for your sons, and give your daughters to husbands, that they may bear sons and daughters; that ye may be increased there, and not diminished.

And seek the peace of the city whither I have caused you to be carried away captives, and pray unto the Lord for it: for in the peace thereof shall ye have peace..." Jeremiah Chapter 29 verses 6-7.

Economic Disenfranchisement, Sabotage, and Manipulation of the Psyche

"...he that putteth his trust in me shall possess the land, and shall inherit my holy mountain; And shall say, Cast ye up, cast ye up, prepare the way, take up the stumblingblock out of the way of my people..." Isaiah Chapter 57 verses 13-14.

America was billed as a land of opportunity for immigrants, speculators, investors, and entrepreneurs. It was new territory, under a new government; and fertile ground for innovation and invention. But there was one thing about America that was not new: and that was the sin nature that characterizes the unregenerate heart of man.

It is precisely this sinful nature in the children of Esau that has influenced them at every turn to block, sabotage, or otherwise dismantle economic prosperity for the children of Judah. Beginning with the reneged 'forty acres and a mule', inequitable sharecropping contracts, violent destruction of prosperous Black communities and business districts, exclusion from unions and trade guilds, color-based employment rejection, redlining and unscrupulous banking practices, to the present day massive ingress of undocumented aliens into the labor force, there has been an organized and systemic effort under way to ensure that the Black man in America remains on the bottom rung of the prosperity ladder. Since wealth is passed down generationally, generations of people who have nothing to show for their years of working also have nothing of tangible value to leave to their descendants, such as real estate, businesses, or investments; which are the primary vehicles by which wealth is perpetuated in the West. And because those with wealth influence monetary value and marketing trends, they can change the rules at any time, or make them up as they go along.

To state a conspiratorial effort is underway to suppress the accumulation and re-investment of wealth among our people may seem unfounded until one considers Esau cares not even for his own people and likewise sets up systems to defraud them and confiscate their wealth, such as morphing the original tax laws on commerce to include a direct tax on personal income, replacing the gold-backed standard of the dollar with fractional reserve fiat currency, and creating a private central bank that is largely controlled by offshore interests and is not a part of the United States government (the Federal Reserve.) This is a three-fold cord which is not quickly broken. It controls the ever fluctuating economic policy in the West; and whatever the aftermath, it is always crafted in such a manner as to ultimately break and impoverish the children of Jacob, and use them to line the coffers of the rich.

Such planning may take decades for the results to manifest, but the intended outcome is that the children of Judah remain slaves. A slave is not supposed to have anything. A slave is supposed to be dependent on another for his most basic needs. A slave must be controlled and dehumanized so his slavery is justifiable in the eyes of the enslaver. Slaves must breed more slaves. And the most delectable deception of all is to convince the slave he is a free man, even as the leg irons and neck yokes are being fastened upon him.

As the West began the recovery from the Great Depression, our people made slow and arduous gains in the realm of economic stability. With great sacrifice, many Black families owned farms. For those who left the south, opportunities in the North in the textile industries, steel mills, and factories created a strong blue collar labor base. Even with this progress, the specter of racism was always present, and our people were often grudgingly admitted to the workforce; the proverbial last hired/first fired. Further, even with the GI bill, Black veterans returning from the war faced hurdles in obtaining housing and higher education. In the aggregate though, the period from the 1940's to mid-1970's represented the dawn of the Black middle class, complete with stable two parent families and low illegitimacy birth rates.

Steady employment during economic upswing leads to discretionary income, which made the establishment of the Black business sector an integral part of the community. In fact, I am certain any brother or sister reading this born pre-1980s will fondly remember frequenting some Black-owned mom & pop grocer, beauty supply, repair shop, printer, hardware store, restaurant, or dry cleaner in their neighborhood. (I have not included barbers and salons because due to the very nature of the business many have been able to weather the attack against Black small business ownership.) So even with us occupying the bottom tier, a rising tide lifts all boats; and during this period, it appeared the industrial boom and consumerism economy would bring the ever elusive 'American Dream' within reach.

However, Black America could not be permitted to achieve parity with white, and it was time for the money masters—working with the private interests and social engineers—to change the rules of the game. America soon began to wage two domestic wars: both targeted at Blacks. The first was the War on Poverty; soon to be followed by the War on Drugs. These programs would have more correctly been called The War to Enslave Blacks in Poverty, and The War to Entrap Blacks with Drugs; but that would have given away their true purpose.

In 1964 during a commencement address at the historic black Howard University campus in Washington, D.C., President Lyndon B. Johnson remarked, "Freedom is not enough. You do not take a person who, for years, has been hobbled by chains and liberate him, bring him up to the starting line of a race and then say, 'you are free to compete with all the others,' and still justly believe that you have been completely fair. Thus it is not enough to just open the gates of opportunity. All our citizens must have the ability to walk through those gates."

At first hearing, this sounds noble and altruistic. But in actuality this statement is suspect because poverty had actually decreased and income increased across the board for our people at the time he uttered these words. Not only that, could he and the audience really have not been aware of Little Africa in the Greenwood suburb of Tulsa just forty-three years earlier, before the murderous massacre? The fabled Black Wall Street was a stellar example of the capabilities of a people who felt that freedom *was* enough. With a little over forty-three years between them and slavery, they did not see themselves as fresh out of chains and in need of handouts and programs. They set to work with ingenuity, entrepreneurship, and fortitude, and founded a thriving community on a self-sustaining economic base.

Yet, here was Johnson, seemingly planting the seeds of dependency in an audience who had earned Bachelors, Masters, and Doctorate degrees. While legislation designed to prevent the marginalization of qualified Blacks due to racist hiring guidelines was welcomed and needed, the long range outcome of his overall anti-poverty legislation had dire consequences among the people and ultimately worked to destabilize and demoralize them. The entire construct of the so-called War on Poverty only serves to demonstrate that moneyed interests in the West did not want to risk competition from anymore Black Wall Streets.

The anti-poverty legislation stoked the public housing project boom. Housing projects were unique in that they were complete communities within themselves. Usually constructed along public transportation routes, they could feature their own laundromat and convenience store. They were designed to have everything the residents might need right within easy access. That way, they did not have to venture out near the affluent white neighborhoods for anything. Another feature of public housing was the monotonous uniformity, such as how stalls would be constructed for a massive herding operation. There was nothing about their design to suggest creativity or aesthetics. They were nameless, faceless units intended for nameless, faceless people.

The welfare programs penalized marriage, and so disproportionately reduced benefits based on earned income that from an economic perspective, it was counterproductive to work. Many couples, needing two incomes—especially if they were ever to break the cycle of dependency—secretly lived together. This was also the era of the unannounced welfare investigator visits—in the hope of catching a man in the home. Thus began the departure from marriage which led to the predominance of single motherhood among our people. Public assistance was a vicious cycle: more children meant more income and food; at the same time, it almost guaranteed that higher education would take a back seat for many young women; and that was the very catalyst that could emancipate one from the projects/and public assistance cycle. The system was designed so that getting an increase in monthly benefits was never sufficient to actually raise one above the federal poverty threshold.

It was during Johnson's term as president 1963-1969, that another evil was introduced into the urban areas, public housing projects and the emerging subculture associated with it. This evil— which mysteriously coincided with the Vietnam War: was heroin. While certainly far from the first exposure of opiates to U.S. soil, the targeting of inner city black neighborhoods exacerbated an already negative situation. Addiction, overdose deaths, prostitution, and the crime that stems from the need to get the next fix or protect the pusher's territory began to characterize these communities. They were not safe places to live or raise children. Yet, many people were trapped in them, with no foreseeable way out.

Right on cue, another variable was thrown into the mix: Blaxploitation films. The scripture warns us as a people to envy not the oppressor and choose none of his ways. But at that time, we had not yet learned that no good can come from anything the oppressor creates. The film industry crafted a new image for youth to emulate; moving away from the demeaning supporting roles of mammies, toms, and coons, and replacing them with the starring role of Black street champion. This was a classic case of creating new gods to go before us.

While at the time it may have appeared as progress for Blacks in the entertainment industry to transition from belittling roles, the glorification of drug pushing, pimping, prostitution, and vigilante justice really only replaced one group of negative stereotypes with a different set: the over-sexualized brute, and the Jezebel. The message to a generation of youth was clear: for males, the street is where the money is to be made; for females, your physical attributes are more valuable than your intellect. In reality, the fixation on vice was in no way representative of the Black experience as a whole. Neither was any Black Robin Hood archetype ever going to arrive on the scene in the ongoing struggle between the weak and the powerful in the West. Simply put, it was the manipulation of the Black psyche, and it is probably fair to say this portrayal of Black men and women and glorification of the street set the stage for the next Satanic assault...crack cocaine.

The scourge of crack cocaine was brought to us in tandem with the massive exodus of industrial jobs overseas, and funding cuts for social support programs that provided contract jobs, job training, and family support services. The rules of the game changed yet again. Many who only needed supplemental services to stay afloat now found their meager working income placed them over the threshold to qualify for assistance. It was almost as if a perfect storm was created to destroy our young men and women.

I say it was 'brought to us', as the lid of secrecy as to how it got here was lifted long ago by the 1996 investigative journalism of San Jose Mercury News reporter Gary Webb, the trial testimony of former Los Angeles drug dealer 'Freeway' Rick Ross, and the proceedings of the Iran-Contra hearings. As the crack menace spread its tentacles across the nation, it entrenched itself in both urban and suburban areas. For those on the upper tiers of the trade, income from crack sales enabled access to the purchase of homes and automobiles; amenities which were now out of reach due to the depletion of jobs from the downsizing of the manufacturing sector. The irony was that those of our people on the upper tiers reaching for the elusive 'American Dream' carrot on a stick got there only by sacrificing their brothers and sisters on the lower tiers.

The hypocritical 'War on Drugs' spawned much self-righteous rhetoric about cleaning up communities and 'get tough' sentencing laws. It was also the impetus for an unprecedented surge in the construction of new correctional facilities across the nation; giving rise to the prison-industrial complex. The injection of such a lucrative and highly addictive substance into our neighborhoods only served to further polarize the people, as 'crack' became synonymous with 'Black'. The cultural stereotype of the violent drug dealer and crazed crackhead was indiscriminately pushed on all of us.

Generations of fathers, sons, brothers, uncles, and nephews have been caught up in the dragnet and given draconian sentences: not for being drug kingpins, but for possession of a small amount of this substance—a judicial practice which has ravaged families and communities. Suffice it to say, no Black person I have ever known either possesses the industrial or aviation capacity required to flood the United States with a product grown on plantations in South America. However, it is documented history that during the 18th century, America's mother country, Great Britain—oversaw the cultivation and production of opium poppies in India during their colonial rule. The product was then aggressively imported to China over the objections of the Qing Dynasty, triggering the famed Opium Wars.

Apparently, the apple doesn't fall far from the tree. And in the proverbial manner of history repeating itself, at the time this book is being written an influx of heroin is overtaking the West again. The resurgence of ready access to this drug on the streets also uncannily coincides with the West's presence in a region of the world that is a primary cultivator of opium poppies. All the cards are in place for a new generation to succumb to addiction, peddling, crime, and prison. The media, aware of Gary Webb's untimely death after his exposé on the source of the crack cocaine epidemic—will stick to reporting on the disturbing trends and local arrests, so we should not expect any true investigative journalism attempting to trace the source of cheap heroin into the country. Talking heads will opine that municipalities and law enforcement need more funding to combat the menace, and how tougher drug law sentencing is necessary to deter use and sales. With labor opportunities gutted and a new flood of people entering the country competing for what few jobs are left, heroin traffic will fill the void in the inner cities. As planned, those in the line of that traffic will be disproportionately Black.

Speaking through the prophet Isaiah, the Lord said that those who put their trust in him are to clear the road for his people, by removing the stumblingblocks from the midst of it. The Hebrew word used here for stumblingblocks means an enticement; something offered that will bring ruin. We are not wrestling against flesh and blood, but against spiritual wickedness controlling an end time power which God declared so wicked it would be thrown down with violence, never to rise again. Isaiah Chapter 5 verses 13-14 show us that when the people have no knowledge they go into Captivity, and that is when hell enlarges itself. But to us to whom it has been given to know the mysteries of the Kingdom and know by blood and testimony that Jesus is Lord, hell's gates cannot prevail. Do you believe God as I believe God? Prayer, preaching, and personal testimony are the spiritual weapons against the drug lie foisted upon our people.

Streets, Gangs, Gangsta Hip Hop, and Prisons

"Thy sons have fainted, they lie at the head of all the streets, as a wild bull in a net: they are full of the fury of the Lord, the rebuke of thy God…" Isaiah Chapter 51 verse 20.

A familiar sight in any urban neighborhood are the groups of young men hanging on the corners. For people of another race or not native to the locale, this often incites a sense of fear. But within the Black culture, this is neither abnormal, nor represents an organized threat, as some would suppose. I submit to the reader such a pastime is part and parcel of being Judah, and scripture appears to support it. In the book of Jeremiah Chapter 6 verse 11, the prophet, who was a very young man himself—speaks of unreservedly taking his message to the 'assembly of young men.' He knew where they hung out, and he was going to meet them on their turf and give them the word from God. In warning of the devastation that was decreed for ancient Jerusalem, he states in the 9th chapter and 21st verse that death will cut off the young men from the streets. Obviously, people of all ages and both genders use the streets, but generally the term, 'young men from the streets' predominates in the scriptures.

The congregating that is seen today however, represents a distortion of the original picture. It was the place of the elders to execute judgment and handle civil matters 'in the gate', and the young men would learn by observation. The mode of life then was much more communal and engaging than it is today, as the entire society and economic set up was different than that which we are accustomed to in Captivity. Streets are where the young men gather, but it still takes mature, disciplined men to guide and mentor them. This critical component of support and guidance has been removed by design under the massive incarceration campaign and economic disenfranchisement targeted against Black men.

Minus mature male guidance, our young men fail because they are not taking heed to the word of God, and it is not hidden in their hearts. This is a foundation best laid by the father not only in word but by lifestyle. They fail secondarily because they are not properly transitioned into manhood as they were by our ancient forebears. It is the Gentile construct under the guise of public school education to continuously memorize information of little use in successfully navigating life, rather than mastering core skills and immediately transitioning into an apprenticeship of the trade or art best suited to the individual. The Anglo-American Gentile also brought forth the artificial creation known as 'teenager' where the youth hang suspended between childhood and adulthood. This category was created to form an additional marketing segment; a revenue source for merchandisers and corporations, and at the other end of the spectrum, a resource pool for the prison-industrial complex.

Genesis Chapter 2 verse 15 tells us God took man and placed him in the garden to dress and keep it. This means he was to cultivate and protect it. These virtues of cultivation and protection should be placed in boys by their fathers, and reinforced through life experience as they mature. Ideally, as soon as youth are able to put forth their hand to start a task, see it through, and reap the rewards of their efforts, they should be afforded that opportunity. Our young men are intelligent and enterprising, but they have a scarcity of prospects as the Captivity draws to a close. The problem is compounded by the illegal drugs imported from overseas and shipped into the communities. The drug trade beckons with promises of immediate rewards—for those willing to dodge bullets and keep looking over their shoulder.

An assembly of young men congregating at the head of the streets is often perceived as a 'threat' by citizens and police alike, although a similar crowd of white youths stand a much better chance of arousing no suspicion. Stop and frisk procedures and racial profiling heighten tensions already strung high by the frustration of lack of employment, the unseasoned judgment of youth and the ever present reality that today is the day you could get tasered or shot. At the same time, the youth know that safety is in numbers. A person who is a loner can be named the perpetrator of any crime the police have been unable to solve, and he will have no witnesses who can testify otherwise.

All too often, police interaction with street congregation transitions to the ugly scene depicted in Isaiah Chapter 51 verse 20. 'Faint' and 'lying at the head of the street' depict a victim of tasering; 'as a wild bull in a net' illustrates subduing and handcuffing, and being 'full of the fury of the Lord and the rebuke of their God' speaks to the public humiliation, frustration, and inability to retaliate or vindicate ones' self.

Israel is a tribal people. Composed of twelve tribes, each clan had its own set of blessings and strong suits bestowed by God. Each tribe possessed its own territory. There was individual tribal pride, but also cohesive unity in times of national emergency or collective repentance and seeking God. In being removed from our heritage and placed in Captivity, we have lost the sense of dignity that stems from having a dedicated identity representing part of a greater whole. In this end time Captivity, a warped and distorted version of tribalism has been presented to our people in the form of gangs.

In spite of the fear-soaked media hype focusing on inner city gangs—and without providing justification for any of their nefarious deeds—it should be stressed that gangs were not brought to the West by the Hebrew. Gangs (complete with colors) existed in America's mother country, England—as far back as the late 18th century. And gangs from various European ethnicities became active on American soil after the Revolutionary War. All this was going on while the children of Judah were still officially enslaved. The enticement of the youth of Judah into gangs under the pretext of gaining respect and reputation is really nothing more than the sin of the pride of life packaged as purpose and a sense of identity. Ultimately it may involve taking a life directly or indirectly, or losing ones' own life; but regardless of whose life it is, Satan regards it as a human blood sacrifice to himself. The lure of the gang is yet another pitfall that entraps our people when we envy the oppressor and choose his ways. The influx of crack cocaine into America's urban Black neighborhoods presented a pre-packaged mini-economy for the gang presence there. The enterprise was run as efficiently as any visible corporate structure. As with any product pushed on the public under Esau's system, marketing media is an essential component to lure the customer and drive sales. So with precise timing and the full financial backing of Babylon's Satanic music industry, the next Blaxploitation upgrade was deployed, via gangsta rap and the hip hop scene.

Without getting too involved in the intricacies of the subject, rap as a genre is differentiated from gangsta hip hop, which speaks to a dedicated lifestyle. Rap is the synergistic outcome of the poetic spoken word and the rhythm intrinsic to our people. The music form itself involves a complexity of the mind and body of the artist(s) that resonates with the mind and body of the hearer. Rap could tell a story in the language of the people; or more correctly, address two sides of the story ...the lie told to the people versus the reality they actually lived. In this manner, the voice of the people and their demand for justice could still be heard without summoning the iron-fisted, jackbooted response such as befell earlier organizations, like the original Black Panthers. Precise in the beat, free-flowing with the lyrics, and serving up complex issues to the people in simple language, it was the ideal venue to highlight injustices and raise the people's conscience to matters of deep significance: something the R&B love songs and party jams could not do.

It should be no surprise then, that the genre was hijacked by the powers bent on the destruction of our people. In a rather hostile take-over, the market surreptitiously shifted to darker, more violent material that spoke to only a segment of the population that was not representative of the people as a whole, and was aggressively targeted to the youth. In recalling rap was basically an east coast/west coast development, it is not difficult to see the more malevolent lyrical content followed the highest concentrations of crack cocaine sales and

239

usage. Lyrics against injustice were replaced with what is correctly identified as the "Do what thou wilt is the whole of the law" philosophy of Satanist and occultist Aleister Crowley - common to the music industry.

The Blaxploitation brute was repackaged as the thug whose power resided in his trigger finger, and whose respect was defined—not by virtue of character—but by his cars, wardrobe, stacks of cash, and disposable harem. His drive to accumulate money, clothes, and cars was exceeded only by his willingness to execute those who crossed him, disrespected him, or got in his way. Women in the gangsta rap videos defined the new Jezebel; scantily clothed and constantly moving in the sensuous manner reminiscent of Israel's ancient golden calf celebration; thereby intimating that sexual abandon to the thug was her key to partaking in his lavish lifestyle...all made possible by the ill-gotten wealth of drug peddling.

The witchcraft of visually showing people the desired transformation of the conjurer, so that they open their minds to receive it, and ultimately imitate and act it out, was the vehicle used to remove thousands and thousands of youth and young men from their families and communities in order to populate the prison industrial complexes and line the pockets of the judicial system and private investors. To a people who never seem to achieve parity with Esau's people by playing by the right rules, a lifestyle of opulence, respect, and adulation of women can be difficult to resist; especially when you see someone you grew up with in your own neighborhood flouting wealth and prestige gained by the sale of street drugs.

A dedicated cadre of artists countered this adulteration of the genre by producing hits and entertainment media that also warned and informed. Grandmaster Flash and the Furious Five's 'The Message' and Public Enemy's 'Night of the Living Baseheads' are just two prime representations of lyrical genius turned conscious weapon. In the ensuing years, bringing a positive message became the equivalent of swimming against a relentless tide. It was as though each successive wave of performers attempted to outdo their predecessors in extremes of excess and degradation.

There are Biblically-centered artists gifted at conveying the gospel, illustrating scriptural principles such as the real life contrast between good and evil, and sharing personal testimony through spoken word and rhythm. While some might find fault with music such as this, it doesn't fit the description of 'vain repetition' when testifying of the works of the Lord or enforcing scripture and righteous principles. Through rap, it is possible to communicate the gospel on the street to people who would never darken a church door. It is just one more method of sowing the good seed of the Kingdom. Once hearts are converted, local believers can baptize and teach. As fishers of men, one of the best lures in the tackle box is a clean, sanctified vessel lyrically presenting the gospel. You have to catch a fish before you can scale him; and the ministers of Judah have liberty in Christ, as long as it is not used as a cloak of maliciousness.

But artists ministering through spoken word, like vocalists of any genre representing the gospel—must guard against tarnishing their personal testimony and above all, must not enter into the Satanic covenant with the ungodly in order to increase revenue and fame. This stumbling block can be avoided by remembering that gospel rap is just one of many ministries to encourage and edify the saints; and not a career in and of itself, or a method of becoming wealthy. We are commanded to work with our hands to earn a living; in other words, artists should have employment income rather than relying on the sales of CDs and accessories that promote the artist.

For this reason, the best candidates for ministering in music to the body of Christ are those individuals who are not seeking a vast financial reward or fame for their talents. Artists of this caliber cannot be compromised or pressured into a situation where they cave in to appeal to the mainstream, cross over to the secular, dilute the gospel, and in the extreme, become party to the Satanic covenant in the hope of maintaining wealth and popularity. Artists on this level should not expect to win awards or be headliners at sell-out venues. They must love the praise of God over that of men, and seek the honor that comes from God alone. One perspective on this is Emmett G. Price III's book, The Black Church and Hip Hop Culture: Toward Bridging the Generational Divide[22]

Perhaps the saddest thing to observe is the gansta rappers wallowing in the same worship of materialism that drives the oppressor; a lust so deeply entrenched that it grieved him for slavery to be outlawed. "It sells," they say, "and its money over everything." We can agree much selling is going on...they are selling their souls, and selling out their people for a quick thirty pieces of silver.

Those who know the unspoken codes of the secular music business know high stake collateral is attached to this kind of success. Jesus put it this way, "For what shall it profit a man, if he shall gain the whole world, and lose his own soul? Or what shall a man give in exchange for his soul?" The artists and actors who propagate this material do so to the jeopardizing of their soul. They set a stumblingblock in front of the people while justifying their own actions. In the real world, girls who imitate the gangsta thug's women will wind up with STDs, pregnant, with abortions, and not being taken seriously in other strata of society because of their dress and import.

Male youth who buy into the slick packaging will open the box to find their death or a lengthy prison sentence. The people who display the trappings of success have them only because Esau's system judged them worthy and permitted them access... and that at a very steep price. Aspiring artists would do well to remember that God said Edom is the people of his curse, and that his sword is coming down on it in judgment.

In the Testament of Judah, Chapter 4 verse 15, the great patriarch of our tribe, Judah— gives warning and exhortation to the people before his death:

"Now I have much grief, my children, because of your lewdness and witchcrafts, and idolatries which ye shall practise against the kingdom, following them that have familiar spirits, diviners, and demons of error.

Ye shall make your daughters singing girls and harlots, and ye shall mingle in the abominations of the Gentiles." He goes on to say this idolatry will bring death, the destruction

---

[22] "The Black Church and Hip Hop Culture: Toward Bridging the Generational Divide", Emmett G. Price 2012.

of the temple, and ultimately end with "the enslavement of yourselves among the Gentiles." Judah warns his posterity that this tyranny over them will persist... "Until the Lord visit you, **when with perfect heart ye repent and walk in all His commandments, and He bring you up from Captivity among the Gentiles**."

Proverbs Chapter 4 verse 23 warns us to "Keep thy heart with all diligence; for out of it are the issues of life." This means to carefully guard what enters the mind by sight or hearing; because the mind internalizes input, and "from within, out of the heart of men, proceed evil thoughts, adulteries, fornications, murders, Thefts, covetousness, wickedness, deceit, lasciviousness, an evil eye, blasphemy, pride, foolishness: All these evil things come from within, and defile the man..." Mark Chapter 7 verses 21-23. The actions on this list accurately describe to a T the subject matter of much hip hop and its associated videos. It is no coincidence when recordings boasting of deeds displeasing to God sell millions of copies, because the music is dedicated to the prince and power of the air prior to its release. Do not have men's persons in admiration because of advantage, because at the end of the day, they really don't have an advantage. For that which is highly esteemed among men is abomination in the sight of God, and their glory, and their multitude, and their pomp, and he that rejoiceth, shall descend into hell.

The elders in Judah and the mothers in Israel must put on the whole armor of God and ask him for wisdom and to open the hearts of the youth, so that they will learn, "It is better to hear the rebuke of the wise, than for a man to hear the song of fools..." Ecclesiastes Chapter 7 verse 5. We can already claim victory through our Lord Jesus Christ because there is no enchantment against Jacob, neither is there any divination against Israel...also there is no wisdom nor understanding nor counsel against the Lord....and the effectual fervent prayer of a righteous man availeth much, casting down imaginations, and every high thing that exalts itself against the knowledge of God.

"But this is a people robbed and spoiled; they are all of them snared in holes, and they are hid in prison houses: they are for a prey, and none delivereth; for a spoil, and none saith, Restore". Isaiah Chapter 42 verse 22. The fact that God saw this condition of our people and spoke through the prophet Isaiah thousands of years ago testifies to his omnipotence, omniscience, and omnipresence. Attorney and Ohio State University Law Professor Michelle Alexander[23] uncovered shocking evidence to this effect when comparing the number of Black men entangled in the criminal justice system (including corrections and community control) with those enslaved during the Antebellum period.

Speaking of the enemies of God, Psalm Chapter 83 verse 4 declares, "They have said, Come, and let us cut them off from being a nation; that the name of Israel may be no more in remembrance." When people are trapped in holes (cells), and hidden in prison houses, their remembrance is cut off. No one thinks about them, except for their family. In the case of those who have no family, social interaction with the outside world ceases to exist. They are a prey; subject to the evilness of correctional staff, other inmates, or whatever new judicial or institutional guidelines come down the pike. Whatever remedies that may exist for injury are

---

[23] "The New Jim Crow: Mass Incarceration in the Age of Colorblindness" Michelle Alexander 2012

also a double-edged sword; as most resources involved in remediation also work for the state and have first loyalty to it. If a prisoner was unfairly charged or sentenced, he must resort to pro se filings to get another hearing or ruling, and these are routinely dismissed.

They are spoiled—and there is no restoration to compensate. It has been documented that prisoners have been the subjects of non-consensual experimentation. The food and prison medical service professions serving the prisons are billion dollar industries. On the flip side of this are the impoverished families of the inmate. Because regular contact with family and social interaction are crucial to maintaining marriages, relationships, and rapport with children, a one income budget will quickly feel the impact of telephone charges and the expense involved with visiting the institution—which is usually located far away from the prisoner's home.

Life after discharge is fraught with its own set of problems. Esau's people demand that the debt is paid to society via imprisonment. Not satisfied with the completion of the sentence, he insists the prisoner obtain employment within a certain time frame as a condition of parole, regardless of the fact many felons are not highly skilled and most unskilled manufacturing jobs have already been sent overseas. At the same time, he generates employment policies that use a computer matrix to deny employment based on criminal history. He knows one of the greatest deterrents to recidivism is steady employment; so he does everything in his power to deny employment to ex-inmates. Then he goes into hysterics about supporting people on public assistance.

When you consider this scenario is happening for the possession of a small amount of marijuana, while legalization opens lucrative opportunities for monied white entrepreneurs, it is not difficult to see both the hypocrisy and the conspiracy. Reflecting on the great disparities in sentencing laws; and the way communities are set up for sabotage, jobs gutted, benefits cut, and drugs and guns then delivered courtesy of the domestic cartel of evil, it's not difficult to detect the simmering hatred masquerading as concern for public safety.

The relationship of the children of Judah in Captivity to the Western prison industrial complex is that of merely exchanging one set of shackles for another. The West was built upon the free labor of Black men and women, and it emancipated them in writing only as a last resort to rein in the Confederacy and stabilize the Union, and because it was becoming obvious how hypocritical the country looked in the eyes of the rest of the world with all the grandiloquence about freedom and liberty and rights. In his reply to a letter from New York Tribune editor Horace Greeley, Lincoln was quoted as saying, "If I could save the Union without freeing any slave I would do it, and if I could save it by freeing all the slaves I would do it; and if I could save it by freeing some and leaving others alone I would also do that. What I do about slavery, and the colored race, I do because I believe it helps to save the Union; and what I forbear, I forbear because I do not believe it would help to save the Union." The Emancipation was more a matter of political expediency than altruistic ideals or conviction about the moral turpitude of slavery. Double minded and unstable, elements of North America then behaved like violent sociopaths on temper tantrums; killing, burning, and destroying because they could no longer have the free labor they coveted. The attitude was, if they couldn't have it, no one was going to enjoy it.

Moving into the twentieth century, print, televised, and photographic media increasingly captured evidence of the forays into blood lust and unhinged rage. America saw the need to modify her approach. She smiled calmly and assumed the persona of a passive aggressive. She couldn't be perpetually uncivil when her international claim to fame was civil liberty. The problem lay in the fact that America was no longer a developing nation. Her economic base was now firmly established, and the type of manual labor slaves had provided was obsolete. There was really no more need for them, but the prospect of extracting still more profit from them was too tantalizing to resist.

She attempted to depict them as lazy, but they had asked General Sherman to secure acreage for them so they could work the land and remain separate but self-sufficient. She tried to portray them as animals and less than human, but it was obvious many of them conducted their lives and affairs with just as much or more morality than whites. She had tried convincing herself and the world that they were unreachable and unteachable, but as soon as they had the opportunity to learn to read, many became even more educated and articulate than whites. On such an undeviating trajectory of industriousness, virtue, and education, it was obvious Black people would eventually reach parity with whites. And that was unacceptable.

You may recall that during the journey to the Promised Land, Moab and Midian conspired to have Balaam curse Israel, because they saw the people were an unstoppable force. It was an unheard of thing for slaves to escape from Egypt; now they were on their way to inherit the land God had promised the patriarchs. It probably should have occurred to them that if the gods of Egypt were powerless against Israel, there wasn't anything Balaam could do. But they resorted to witchcraft anyway. Another thing unusual about this event is that there was no need for Moab and Midian's reactionary stance. Moab was the son of Abraham's nephew, Lot. Midian was the son of Abraham's second wife Keturah. Israel was not trying to take over either of their lands. Israel was going to a dedicated geographical region inhabited by the Canaanites.

Three times Balaam tried to curse Israel, and three times he failed. When he saw he could not curse that which God had already blessed, he resorted to Plan B: moral corruption. He instructed the women of Moab to entice the Israelite men with the familiar ritualistic fertility rite celebrations. They succeeded in getting them to bow down to their idols and eat food sacrificed to these demon gods. A plague kindled by the wrath of God broke out upon Israel, and struck down twenty-four thousand men before Phineas the priest executed vengeance. The strategies of Satan never change. The names, faces, and places change, but the method of operation is basically the same. He desires to corrupt us, and lead us into idolatry. This is accomplished by appealing to the lusts of the eyes, the lusts of the flesh, and the pride of life. Once caught in the trap, he accuses us before God and demands God to execute his righteous judgment against sin.

When people are suffering arduous circumstances, such as discontent and the long journey in the wilderness, or—as in our case in the end time Captivity—constant humiliation and disenfranchisement, it is tempting to look at the idolatrous world and imagine we too could have it all if we would only join them. Here in the Captivity, if the children of Jacob will not voluntarily put forth their hand to wickedness, the children of Esau literally hand them drugs and guns, and with the promise of the riches of this world, entice them to create entertainment material which will perpetuate the destruction of their own people. At the same time, Esau crafts sentencing laws and institutes law enforcement policies which target Black neighborhoods and guarantee a full catch in the dragnet to keep his drug and prison industry enterprise operating. Not content with that, he manufactures and markets destructive products with a distinct focus toward our people, such as malt liquor, and cleverly designed tobacco products.

God sees that the children of the Captivity are being forced to make the same quota of bricks without straw, even as they remain subjects of an unrelenting campaign to blot out the remembrance of them as the heirs of the Abrahamic Covenant. Just as in ancient Egypt, in all our affliction, he is afflicted. God has not forgotten the many prisoners unfairly sentenced, and stored away like shelved canned goods in a dark cellar. Prison chaplains are effectively muzzled from addressing this, but the many scriptures in the Bible alluding to the opening of the prisons are proof that God is only waiting for That Day, and That Time. Then in That Hour, these sayings will come to pass: the Lord heareth the poor, and despiseth not his prisoners...he hath broken the gates of brass, and cut the bars of iron in sunder...the Lord looseth the prisoners. It won't matter if it is a supermax prison, underground facility, or in the uttermost reaches of the universe. God has promised to save the tents of Judah first; by default, this means wherever the descendants of that tribe are found. Anyone who has a problem with this early release policy should take heed to Isaiah Chapter 49 verses 24-26:

"Shall the prey be taken from the mighty, or the lawful captive delivered?

But thus saith the Lord, Even the captives of the mighty shall be taken away, and the prey of the terrible shall be delivered: for I will contend with him that contendeth with thee, and I will save thy children.

And I will feed them that oppress thee with their own flesh; and they shall be drunken with their own blood, as with sweet wine: and all flesh shall know that I the Lord am thy Saviour and thy Redeemer, the mighty One of Jacob."

Until that day, let us remember them that are in bonds, as bound with them; and them which suffer adversity, as being ourselves also in the body.

Societal and Relational Dysfunction

From the time our forebears were captured and held in the holding tanks—the coastal 'slave castles' prior to the Voyage of No Return, the attack on the Black family was underway. Children were separated from parents; husbands and wives pulled apart and shackled in separate groups. Husbands had to endure watching their wives fondled and raped, and were helpless to protect them. It was also standard policy to shackle captives from different tribes together, to create a language barrier that would inhibit escape attempts.

Once on the slave block, families were further isolated. Sometimes a buyer would be compassionate enough to buy a mother and her child (or children) but if the buyer only needed one slave, or didn't have the money or capacity to sustain more, that family would never see each other again. If a slave married and bore children on the plantation, both the spouse and children were considered chattel property and the slave owner could sell any of them at any time. A common reason for selling slaves was to pay off debt. If a slave owner died in debt, his entire estate was auctioned off, including the slaves on it.

On the plantation, normalcy of relationships was fractured further by the class system of field negro versus house negro. Field referred to those who did the harsh sun up to sun down manual labor in the fields. Life was generally not as rigorous for those based in the house, but whippings and abuse occurred equally in both situations. Yet another subset of this was the negro overseer; appointed by the master to keep the others in check. Caught between a rock and a hard place, his option was to carry out the wishes of his master and risk the hatred of his people, or return to the same backbreaking labor they did. By virtue of his location, a house negro might, at great risk, learn to read. Or he might be entrusted with duties that gave him leave to conduct business for the master in town. It is easy to see the resentment that resulted in the wake of such freedom for some but not others.

In Chapter VI, subsection *Judgment for Disobedience*, we learned that one of the Hebrew definitions of 'dwell' in respect to Japheth dwelling in Shem's tents was 'shakan'—implying lodging, continuing, or permanently staying, and stemming from a similar Hebrew word 'shakab" which means to lie down, for rest, including sexual connection. This prophecy manifested during the Captivity via the use of enslaved women as concubines or disposable sexual objects. One well-known example revolves around the descendants of Thomas Jefferson and Sally Hemmings; an account long denied by those hoping to avoid a scandal, but finally proven in 1998 through DNA analysis. The reduction of melanin, straightening of hair, and assumption of narrower noses and thinner lips drove a deep wedge among Blacks. This was because the more European traits a Black person assumed, the more easily white people could identify with him. The effect was that this could lead to preferential treatment, although any one with so much as a drop of Black blood could be swiftly reminded of their chattel status and beaten, whipped, and humiliated. A house divided cannot stand; therefore, the color caste system was an effective tool in the divide and conquer strategy used against us.

After Emancipation, the Jim Crow era perpetuated the psychological abuse of Blacks by calling men and women out of their name. A man could command respect as a father and husband in his dwelling, but as soon as he stepped outside of it, he was reduced to "Boy", and "Nigger." Women often had an easier time finding work, as they were considered less of a threat. For men, gainful employment was much more difficult to obtain. In most whites, the emancipated Black man encountered the old hatred, and the ever present fear that lurks below the surface when one knows a great moral wrong has been committed. This continual humiliation of the Black man so that the Black woman is preferred before him economically and socially continues to be a destabilizing factor in the home and in relationships.

In tandem with the civil rights movement, yet another variable thrown into the mix was feminism. Although many would beg to differ, this author is of the opinion that the rise of the women's rights movement did nothing positive for the Black woman in America. However, I write from a spiritual, rather than a sociological perspective. Feminism became a force in the West just as Esau's system was preparing to pull the rug out from underneath our people under the guise of the War on Poverty and toxic cultural influences such as Blaxploitation.

We were designed to be a nuclear family, supportive of each other and honoring God by maintaining the proper balance of reverence and submission one toward another, with our children in subjection and obedience. The attitude that women could treat men the same way unregenerate men treat women had the effect of a deadly poison. Many Black women who wanted their 'freedom' soon found how difficult it was to go it alone, especially where raising sons was concerned. Many daughters missed out on the cherishing and stable presence of a father that would have acted as a safeguard against them taking up with the first young man they met. Single parent families perpetuated more single parent families. Men were viewed as inadequate as women made demands based more on qualities they perceived in actors and recording artists than 'real' every day guys. Chasing unrealistic dreams in this manner, many women priced themselves right out of the market.

Following the cue of those who have sold out to Satan for coveted acting roles and performing artists' positions, some sisters took it to the extreme and succeeded in generating a brand new stereotype for Black women: the loud, ghetto, confrontational female; much to the perverse glee and derision of the oppressor. In stark contrast, we are commanded to have a meek and quiet spirit, even as the great matriarch of our people, Sarah. Meek does not mean weak; it means tremendous strength under control. It is comparable to placing a bit in the mouth of a one-half ton horse. The level of the horse's power is formidable but it is guided and controlled so that no harm is done. This was also the character of Moses; a leader, prophet, husband, and father, and identified by God as 'one he knew by name.' Yet he is described as the meekest man who ever lived. How far we stray from God's ideal when we envy the oppressor and choose his ways.

Esau's distortion of the Black woman's image as bitter, argumentative, and controlling was not complete without a simultaneous agenda to feminize Black men. If a Black man won't be a thug which justifies locking him away for the alleged safety of Esau, he must be emasculated to render him non-threatening and of no significant force in his family and community. This intense need to womanize the Hebrew man is most obvious in the entertainment industry and appears to be part of the rules of engagement for those choosing the praise and adulation of man over praise from God.

Esau's system also runs interference on Black families in the realm of child-rearing. Most people of Hebrew descent instinctively follow the Biblical guidelines of corrective discipline. The oppressor's people say that is cruel and they go so far as to advise children to report their parents to authorities for using corporal punishment. Many Children's Services agencies will attempt to terminate parental rights and place the child in foster care if the parents insist on maintaining their belief system. They will demand the parents—and even caregivers who are grandparents—be 'reeducated' in the form of 'parenting classes'!

During the 1990's, the author noticed a disturbing trend in many films marketed for children. In movie after movie, there would be a scene where the child actor would scream 'I hate you' at his parents, and slam doors or some similar action. An otherwise great children's film was often undermined by these cleverly inserted demonstrations of rebellion and disrespect. Knowing what imitators children are, the addition of such scenes could hardly be a mistake.

As a people, we are warned to learn not the way of the heathen, and we instinctively know that children hitting, kicking, and screaming in anger at their parents is unacceptable behavior. Proverbs Chapter 19 verse 18 admonishes us to, 'Chasten thy son while there is hope, and let not thy soul spare for his crying." This implies there is a limited window for correcting negative behavior. To accept a child's refusal to control anger and disappointment as just a normal part of growing up, and then place the child on pharmaceutical medications when the behavior continues into his teens is unconscionable and an abdication of responsibility.

Experience has taught the Hebrew in Captivity that his sons are a perpetual target for destruction. Because of this, it is imperative young males grasp the concept of hierarchy and authority early on. It was no accident that the Apocrypha was removed from the Bible, seeing that it contained precious words of guidance for the Hebrew sons such as those found in the Wisdom of Sirach Chapter 9 verse 13 "...Keep thee far from the man that hath power to kill; so shalt thou not doubt the fear of death: and if thou come unto him, make no fault, lest he take away thy life presently: remember that thou goest in the midst of snares, and that thou walkest upon the battlements of the city."

The 'man that hath power to kill' speaks of Esau who lives by the sword; snares represents the constant risk of entrapment, presumed guilt, and profiling as a suspect i.e., walking or running while Black (meaning you must have committed a crime), shopping while Black (you must be stealing), driving while Black (you must be going to or leaving the scene of a crime or transporting drugs or stolen goods), talking on the phone while Black (you must be orchestrating a drug deal), hands in pockets while Black (you must be concealing a weapon). Battlements in the Hebrew comes from a word meaning to smite or beat down; in later language translations it alludes to the parapets and indentations on castle walls designed to shoot through; implying a militaristic confrontational attitude toward Black youth. Either definition is correct within the context of our young men today.

We live in a hypocritical society that castigates us for leaning on tried and true Biblical guidelines for child rearing, but silently nods in approval when our youth are shot and tasered. We are in the midst of a duplicitous people who try to convince us it takes a village to raise a child, when God has delegated that responsibility to the child's mother and father. When 90% of the village has a drastically different outlook on cultural and spiritual matters, and a track record of sabotage and murder, dare we trust our children to it? Until such time as God restores our judges as at the first, and our counsellors as at the beginning, and we are called the city of righteousness... the faithful city; redeemed with judgment and our converts with righteousness—it is neither prudent nor safe to entrust our children to the 'village.'

The intrusion into the Black family organism to referee in matters best decided between parents or parent and extended family is a most sinister form of divide and conquer. The oppressor does not harass because he cares about the children. He sabotages Black families because he knows once the child is out of control, he or she is another asset to support a foster parent's lifestyle, and ultimately another number on the way to the prison industrial system. In the end, your child's failure is his prosperity and job security.

A People Robbed and Spoiled...When Despair Turns Deadly

"...if ye bite and devour one another, take heed that ye be not consumed one of another..." Galatians Chapter 5 verse 15.

Whenever dialogue ensues between Blacks and whites regarding the cruelty of slavery, past actions of the Klan, and police brutality, the grievances of our people are usually countered with the issue of Black on Black violence. However, sociologists have long known that crime and violence are synonymous with poverty and disenfranchisement among any race. Stable and gainful employment goes a long way toward eliminating hostility and apathy. Stable and gainful employment is defined by jobs or self-employment paying wages high enough to actually sustain a desirable quality of life and enable people to bless those close to them and set goals to achieve those things they have been led to believe from their youth are part of being a citizen in the West. To remove stable and gainful employment from the equation while simultaneously aggressively marketing consumer goods to people with limited or no means to obtain them is a predetermined set up for a negative outcome.

When it boils down to basic human character, people of all races and ethnicities differ little when faced with the same situation. Put five people of any one race in a tiny house with one loaf of bread and two and half gallons of water, and tell them it has to last them for five days. You will soon see the struggle for hierarchy as to who feels best qualified to control the distribution of the bread and water. As hunger sets in, you will see who is likely to get aggressive or seek a pretext to use force to take over the loaf. It will become apparent who will steal, who will cheat, and who will lie.

The quiet passive person in the group may actually be trying to hatch a scheme to justify why some should forgo their ration so he can have more; for instance, if some in the group are overweight. If there is a sociopath in the group, he may cough or sneeze on the bread to taint it so that no one but he can eat it. While this is a broad illustration, the objective is to show that poverty and lack tend to bring out the worst in any people... ranging from sacrifice of character to outright violence.

Now consider that for the most part, Black people in the West are herded into the inner cities with limited stable and gainful employment opportunities and lower class amenities. Further, there is little way to obtain said amenities without going through the rigged consumer financial system established for the poor. People constantly need, but nobody has anything to give. Proverbs Chapter 19 verse 7 reminds us, "All the brethren of the poor do hate him: how much more do his friends go far from him? he pursueth them with words, yet they are wanting to him." Poor people can't ask other poor people for anything.

Drugs or alcohol may temporarily boost morale and make the reality more bearable, but the downside is that they contribute to poor judgment and dependency. Illegal enterprise appeals as a way to break the cycle of poverty, but the disadvantage to that is that one must prey upon ones' own people. And ultimately only a select few will rise to the top while the rest fall into the arrest and incarceration dragnet, and gain a criminal record which strips away what few citizen rights are left.

From time to time, I have been in conversations with white people who will tell me about how they grew up poor; the logic being that Blacks are not the only ones who had to deal with poverty and they can do better. The key to the issue is in the statement itself: "I *grew up* poor." In the majority of cases, either white privilege or a providentially timed shift in the economic sector was the catalyst that enabled them to break the cycle as they moved into adulthood. If female, marrying someone who had more to bring to the table was a way to move out of the ranks of deprivation. But for many of our people, it doesn't end with, "I grew up poor." The constantly fluctuating socio-economic landscape can lock families into a legacy of generational poverty...a revolving door of struggle which eventually degenerates from trying to get ahead, to trying to maintain, and ultimately trying to recover lost ground. It is like running to catch up with a moving car. It's not that you aren't exerting yourself to the fullest. It's that the car is designed to move twenty times faster than you.

For our people in this Captivity, honest wealth is accrued with much sacrifice and patience. Our grandparents may have saved for years to purchase a home. Perhaps we were fortunate enough to have it passed down to us. Then Esau's financial system makes the judgment call that manufacturing jobs in our area are better suited overseas. The stable and gainful employment that has enabled people to keep the homes maintained and the neighborhood clean and non-threatening is gone. Businesses close or move due to loss of paying customers.

Once the economic base is yanked, resources must be restricted to basic needs such as food and utilities. The aesthetics and extra touches associated with prosperity and home ownership take a back seat to straight financial survival. The area begins to lose its affluence and market value. Homes that housed generational families are sold to investors who then rent them out. The new occupants will generally not be former homeowners, and lack the personal attachment to the home common to property ownership. Being poor themselves, they have no incentive to keep it up.

If homeowners are still in the area and they have taken a loan out on their home, they will be forced to sell at a loss due to depreciation. They will have nothing to show for having owned a home all those years, and with no proceeds from the sale, will go forward into poverty, unless they have significant savings. As poorer and poorer people move in with no sentimental connection to the neighborhood, homeowners who stay and attempt to maintain their property will become increasingly isolated and targets for criminals, who will assume they have something of value due to the contrast in appearance compared to the rental houses.

The tipping point occurs when gentrification takes over. Massive renovation revitalizes the area, but drives up the real estate values to the extent locals can't afford property taxes or rent. Recall that the main way wealth is transferred in the West is via real estate, business ownership, or investments, and multiply this home ownership displacement scenario across municipalities nationwide since the mid 1960's. The root cause influencing Black underclass status and its associated social problems is impossible to miss.

That is just the economic side of the coin. The flip side is the human element and the psychological complexities linked to the powerlessness that is part and parcel of the latter day Captivity. To put the phenomenon of Black on Black crime in perspective, we will examine first what God said about our condition thousands of years ago, and compare it to conditions we presently see among ourselves. Remember, a thousand years is as a day in the sight of the Lord; therefore, we can safely say that God made these observations about us a few days ago.

God says we are a people that have been robbed and spoiled. The Hebrew word for robbed means to plunder, catch, and utterly take away. The Hebrew word for spoiled means for a destroyer to rob and plunder. In these particular verses of Isaiah Chapter 42 verses 22-25, God makes it clear that not only are we robbed and spoiled, but no one is petitioning that what was taken from us be restored. In other words, no one is coming forward to help us get back to our original starting point before this great theft took place.

But now God asks two questions: "Who among you will give ear to this? who will hearken and hear for the time to come?" God is saying, "Is anyone among you listening to what I'm saying about your low estate? Are you listening and hearing...because this is something you will need to understand in a time yet to come." That time is here now in this latter day Captivity, for those who have ears to hear.

But the shocking climax comes as God reveals the cause of our plunder. "Who gave Jacob for a spoil, and Israel to the robbers? did not the Lord, he against whom we have sinned? for they would not walk in his ways, neither were they obedient unto his law. Therefore he hath poured upon him the fury of his anger, and the strength of battle: and it hath set him on fire round about, yet he knew not; and it burned him, yet he laid it not to heart." Because we don't realize it is God's hand against us, it is easy to turn our frustration and anger outward toward others. People tend to strike out at those closest to them; venting at those who are actually within their reach, though they are not the root source of their injury.

Our sins have brought us to the point we are a people psychologically beaten down, and we are becoming numb to the social and cultural abuse...Isaiah Chapter 1 verses 5-6 "...Why should ye be stricken any more? ye will revolt more and more: the whole head is sick, and the whole heart faint.

From the sole of the foot even unto the head there is no soundness in it; but wounds, and bruises, and putrifying sores: they have not been closed, neither bound up, neither mollified with ointment." When a people lose sensitivity toward God, they lose sensitivity toward each other.

We are hedged in so that we cannot collectively be autonomous and self-sufficient... "For, behold, the Lord, the Lord of hosts, doth take away from Jerusalem and from Judah the stay and the staff, the whole stay of bread, and the whole stay of water." This condition of dependency on another nation's deviant economic system will remain as long as we are in a land that is not the land God covenanted to our forefathers.

Because of the Captivity in a land that is not our own, no men are able to stand who could protect the sons and daughters from abuse at the hands of Esau's people, or judges from among our peers who can judge matters peculiar to us without sitting in Esau's judicial seat. The voices of our honorable men and counselors are muted, while Esau provides megaphones and loudspeakers to childish people from our midst who will parrot and promote his sabotage and stumblingblocks "...the Lord of hosts, doth take away from Jerusalem and from Judah The mighty man, and the man of war, the judge, and the prophet, and the prudent, and the ancient, The captain of fifty, and the honourable man, and the counseller, and the cunning artificer, and the eloquent orator. And I will give children to be their princes, and babes shall rule over them."

An intense frustration stems from forced dependency upon a system designed and maintained by a hostile entity. The system is unseen and pervasive; spanning economics, culture, and institutions. The system oppresses the people; the people in turn oppress each other "...And the people shall be oppressed, every one by another, and every one by his neighbour: the child shall behave himself proudly against the ancient, and the base against the honourable."

When those among our people achieve prestige and economic success as defined by Esau's system, they are often desperately besieged by extended family and strangers alike for assistance...a burden designed to be met by a societal rather than an individual response..."When a man shall take hold of his brother of the house of his father, saying, Thou hast clothing, be thou our ruler, and let this ruin be under thy hand: In that day shall he swear, saying, I will not be an healer; for in my house is neither bread nor clothing: make me not a ruler of the people." When a brother or sister refuses to be force commissioned by family or friends, they often turn against them.

Wealth and prestige are of no avail when a nation is being pressed down by God "... For Jerusalem is ruined, and Judah is fallen: because their tongue and their doings are against the Lord, to provoke the eyes of his glory."

The women exalt pride and vanity over graciousness of spirit; causing them to be stricken in the realm of physical beauty "...Moreover the Lord saith, Because the daughters of Zion are haughty, and walk with stretched forth necks and wanton eyes, walking and mincing as they go, and making a tinkling with their feet: Therefore the Lord will smite with a scab the crown of the head of the daughters of Zion, and the Lord will discover their secret parts."

The filth of the daughters of Zion causes them to become desperate in the days just prior to the return of their Savior, and settle for concubinage over the sanctity of marriage "...And in that day seven women shall take hold of one man, saying, We will eat our own bread, and wear our own apparel: only let us be called by thy name, to take away our reproach."

A culture of partying takes precedence over celebration of God and desire to follow hard after him and stay on the cutting edge of what he is doing "...Woe unto them that rise up early in the morning, that they may follow strong drink; that continue until night, till wine inflame them! And the harp, and the viol, the tabret, and pipe, and wine, are in their feasts: but they regard not the work of the Lord, neither consider the operation of his hands."

Politicians and religious leaders are powerless to deliver from the Captivity, and many actually mislead the people down a dead-end path to destruction... "Therefore the Lord will cut off from Israel head and tail, branch and rush, in one day. The ancient and honourable, he is the head; and the prophet that teacheth lies, he is the tail. For the leaders of this people cause them to err; and they that are led of them are destroyed."

Robbed, plundered, psychologically beaten down, economically and judicially dependent, chastened and humiliated by God both physically and as a nation, void of righteous counselors, yet still crammin' and jammin' and not considering our deplorable condition is a work of the most High, nor seeking his face as to how to remedy it. Unable to self-recover from such a state, anger and resentment turns inward amongst us because we have not extended repentance and brokenness outward towards God.

is word to us in this hour is, "O Israel, thou hast destroyed thyself; but in me is thine help. I will be thy king: where is any other that may save thee in all thy cities? And thy judges of whom thou saidst, Give me a king and princes?" **To be healed of the incurable wound**

that follows us throughout our generations, we must seek God earnestly, repenting for our sins and the sins of our forefathers, and petition him to turn the Captivity and restore us:

"And ye shall seek me, and find me, when ye shall search for me with all your heart. And I will be found of you, saith the Lord: and I will turn away your Captivity, and I will gather you from all the nations, and from all the places whither I have driven you, saith the Lord; and I will bring you again into the place whence I caused you to be carried away captive" ...Jeremiah Chapter 29 verses 13-14.

The Modern Lure of Hellenism...Misdirected Loyalties

In Chapter VII, *Apostasy and Imbalance as a Reaction to Interference*, we learned that many of our forebears gave in to the pressure to Hellenize—or adopt Greek customs. It was this Hellenistic influence that the faithful in Israel strove to eradicate during the Maccabean Resistance; a period represented in the interval between the Old and New Testaments. Without a prophet and a vision from God, people of weak or dubious faith had difficulty staying true to the Lord. And people who identified with God in name only were quickly swayed to the dark side, showing their true allegiance when put to the test. Nevertheless, the faithfulness of a few went a long way in keeping the tide of evil at bay. The Book of II Maccabees Chapter 3 verses 1-3 demonstrates how a godly priest named Onias kept this charge in Jerusalem...

"Now when the holy city was inhabited with all peace, and the laws were kept very well, because of the godliness of Onias the high priest, and his hatred of wickedness,

It came to pass that even the kings themselves did honour the place, and magnify the temple with their best gifts;

Insomuch that Seleucus of Asia of his own revenues bare all the costs belonging to the service of the sacrifices."

I Maccabees Chapter 1 verses 11-15 show how Hellenism subverted this and gained a foothold:

"In those days went there out of Israel wicked men, who persuaded many, saying, Let us go and make a covenant with the heathen that are round about us: for since we departed from them we have had much sorrow.

So this device pleased them well.

Then certain of the people were so forward herein, that they went to the king, who gave them licence to do after the ordinances of the heathen:

Whereupon they built a place of exercise at Jerusalem according to the customs of the heathen:

And made themselves uncircumcised, and forsook the holy covenant, and joined themselves to the heathen, and were sold to do mischief."

II Maccabees Chapter 4 verses 7-16 provide additional background and specifics...

"But after the death of Seleucus, when Antiochus, called Epiphanes, took the kingdom, Jason the brother of Onias laboured underhand to be high priest,

Promising unto the king by intercession three hundred and threescore talents of silver, and of another revenue eighty talents:

Beside this, he promised to assign an hundred and fifty more, if he might have licence to set him up a place for exercise, and for the training up of youth in the fashions of the heathen, and to write them of Jerusalem by the name of Antiochians.

Which when the king had granted, and he had gotten into his hand the rule he forthwith brought his own nation to Greekish fashion.

And the royal privileges granted of special favour to the Jews by the means of John the father of Eupolemus, who went ambassador to Rome for amity and aid, he took away; and putting down the governments which were according to the law, he brought up new customs against the law:

For he built gladly a place of exercise under the tower itself, and brought the chief young men under his subjection, and made them wear a hat.

Now such was the height of Greek fashions, and increase of heathenish manners, through the exceeding profaneness of Jason, that ungodly wretch, and no high priest;

That the priests had no courage to serve any more at the altar, but despising the temple, and neglecting the sacrifices, hastened to be partakers of the unlawful allowance in the place of exercise, after the game of Discus called them forth;

Not setting by the honours of their fathers, but liking the glory of the Grecians best of all.

By reason whereof sore calamity came upon them: for they had them to be their enemies and avengers, whose custom they followed so earnestly, and unto whom they desired to be like in all things.

For it is not a light thing to do wickedly against the laws of God: but the time following shall declare these things."

So, with no prophet to rebuke them, and the attitude that 'we might as well enjoy the same things others enjoy', these reprobates built a huge consensus of followers, and begged permission from a pagan king to construct a fitness center in the very city that God said was consecrated to him... with the express intent of corrupting the youth of Judah.

Why was the construction of the gymnasium wicked and idolatrous before the eyes of God? Well, for one—Jerusalem was devoted to the Lord as a city holy to his presence, and the site of the Temple where God had said his presence would dwell. Introducing this Greekish influence corrupted even the priests, who began to neglect their Temple duties in order to play discus. Secondly, the youth of Judah were training to participate in the Tyrian games; an event held in honor of the idol Hercules. It is easy to see the historical link between this ancient adulation for the gods of Olympus and the modern Olympic sports competitions. Third—and most importantly, athletics is based on competition, a practice that did not exist until manifested by Satan. The devil was the first competitor—he desired to compete against God and began to envision his various triumphs...

*I will ascend into heaven...

*I will exalt my throne above the stars of God...

*I will sit also upon the mount of the congregation, in the sides of the north...

*I will ascend above the heights of the clouds...

*I will be like the most High.

Because the Gentiles sacrifice to devils, sports competition has always been a Gentile construct. In contrast, Israel has a long standing law against learning the ways of the heathen, or envying the oppressor and choosing his ways. The Maccabean account also shows that the ones the apostates so strongly desired to imitate ultimately became their enemies and avengers, and brought sore calamities upon them.

In order to play competitive sports, the opponent or opposing team must adopt a mental outlook that never existed until Satan took on his malevolent character and fell from heaven; attitudes such as intimidation and watching for weaknesses that can be exploited. Depending on the intensity of the sport (such as boxing) contenders must be ready to physically hurt the opponent. These are all tactics the devil uses against the people of God, and attitudes Black brethren can ill afford to have toward each other. It is little more than a sanitized version of gang warfare; complete with colors...a parallel universe where fans on each side perceive the opposing team as an evil to be conquered. Further, the Black sports idol plays not for his people; but for the team, its managers, and the financial backers to whom he is beholden.

The sons of Jacob are called to be a nation of kings and priests; as such, our focus must be on the perfecting of the spirit. In this hour, the winning edge is in the ability to bear the weight of the armor of God, and be expert in handling the sword of the Spirit and the shield of faith. We were never a people who organized to form teams to compete one against another. While military readiness was standard, because Israel had perennial enemies; sports competition has always been a Gentile construct.

The ancient ties to idolatry have become more manifest with the debauchery that accompanies major modern annual sporting events, and the horrific fights that are subject to take place at their conclusion. But there is a darker side to sports that seldom comes to mind; the grandiose events of old in the Roman coliseums, where the contenders were our first century Hebrew brethren and their fellow Gentile proselytes and their opponents were lions, or experienced gladiators who lived for blood lust and the coveted thumbs up signal from the emperor.

History indicates that Esau's people—who possess a different value system and estimation of spiritual matters—attempted to acclimate the sons of Jacob to pagan games during the years of chattel slavery in conjunction with celebrations that we now recognize as idolatrous. I quote here from the real life account of a former slave in "Narrative of the Life of Frederick Douglass, an American Slave."[24]

"The days between Christmas and New Year's Day are allowed as holidays; and, accordingly, we were not required to perform any labor, more than to feed and take care of the stock. This time we regarded as our own, by the grace of our masters; and we therefore used or abused it nearly as we pleased. Those of us who had families at a distance, were generally allowed to spend the whole six days in their society. This time, however, was spent in various ways. The staid, sober, thinking and industrious ones of our number would employ themselves in making corn-brooms, mats, horse-collars, and baskets; and another class of us would spend the time in hunting opossums, hares, and coons. A slave who would work during the holidays was considered by our masters as scarcely deserving them. He was regarded as one who rejected the favor of his master. It was deemed a disgrace not to get drunk at Christmas..." But by far the larger part engaged in such sports and merriments as playing ball, wrestling, running foot-races, fiddling, dancing, and drinking whisky; and this latter mode of spending the time was by far the most agreeable to the feelings of our masters.

Douglass goes on to say, "From what I know of the effect of these holidays upon the slave, I believe them to be among the most effective means in the hands of the slaveholder in keeping down the spirit of insurrection. Were the slaveholders at once to abandon this practice, I have not the slightest doubt it would lead to an immediate insurrection among the slaves. These holidays serve as conductors, or safety-valves, to carry off the rebellious spirit of enslaved humanity. But for these, the slave would be forced up to the wildest desperation; and woe betide the slaveholder, the day he ventures to remove or hinder the operation of those conductors! I warn him that, in such an event, a spirit will go forth in their midst, more to be dreaded than the most appalling earthquake.

The holidays are part and parcel of the gross fraud, wrong, and inhumanity of slavery. They are professedly a custom established by the benevolence of the slaveholders; but I undertake to say, it is the result of selfishness, and one of the grossest frauds committed upon the down-trodden slave. They do not give the slaves this time because they would not like to have their work during its continuance, but because they know it would be unsafe to deprive them of it...

From Douglass' account, it would appear there is more to the story than meets the eye in the rush to co-opt the Hebrew to join the Gentile in sports and revelry. During chattel slavery, the holidays acted as a psychological tool to manipulate the slaves; as Douglass puts it, 'a conductor—a safety valve.' They could throw the ball, but they couldn't catapult themselves off the plantation; they could wrestle each other, but they could not pin their master and declare themselves the victor over him. They could run races, but could not keep going until they escaped their bondage; they could fiddle and dance, but they were neither playing an ode to

---

[24] "Narrative of the Life of Frederick Douglass, an American Slave" Frederick Douglass 1845.

freedom nor dancing a dance of victory. They could drink to distract themselves from their true state, but when the whiskey wore off, they were still slaves.

In all honesty we must ask if sports and the Gentile's revelry do not still serve a similar purpose today: as a diversionary tool. Perhaps in the beginning, similar to our experience gaining non-subservient acting roles—it appeared different; innocuous, an opportunity seized to demonstrate we were just as good as everyone else. People like Jesse Owens, Jackie Robinson, Kenny Washington, and Earl Lloyd were a tremendous source of pride for us and made it seem as though we would finally be perceived as an asset to the nation.

Reflecting on nearly a century of Black sports figures, it is true many have devoted time to mentoring youth or established non-profits designed to give back to their communities. But what happens when they are set up before Black youth as the ultimate role model to follow to gain success in America? How many of our youth will realistically become NBA, NFL, or Major League players? And what about the lavish contracts offered to professional sports players? A strong message is sent to the young brothers that physical prowess is more valuable than mental competence and spiritual integrity.

The high dollars earned from the player's contracts…will that money find its way into the Black communities to be turned over multiple times, thereby bolstering the economic base? Will it be invested to fund Black male teachers who can relate to our young men and stand by them as mentors every step of the way from kindergarten to college graduation? Or will it more likely be invested into a clothing and accessories line viewed as so prestigious that youth will steal, fight, and kill to be seen wearing it? Black fans may say they are down for their 'team,' but they neither own an interest in the team or are financially compensated for their loyalty to it. It seems to me our focus is manipulated to align our allegiance with constructs that yield no return on personal and financial investment.

The goal of winning awards from carnal men and their corporations based on physical ability forces a person to focus on skill, technique, and physique. But in the midst of the deep spiritual warfare characteristic of the end time Captivity, each brother and sister must concentrate on developing their inner man to conform to the image of Christ. This is not to say we should neglect our health and fail to remain fit and maintain our correct weight. It doesn't mean youth should not shoot hoops, play soccer, or any number of physical activities that get their good endorphins circulating. It means that as seen from the spiritual realm, the regenerated spirit in submission to the Holy Spirit must be larger and more powerful than the person's flesh. The Apostle Paul puts it this way "… For bodily exercise profiteth little: but godliness is profitable unto all things, having promise of the life that now is, and of that which is to come." Strange as it may sound, Paul is making the claim that godliness is not just for the world to come, but will also sustain you in this present life. The reason he can make such a claim is that moderation in all things is a part of godliness.

Previously mentioned was the propensity of the sports industry to generate clothing and accessories marketing the team or star players, as a brand. This fascination with brand names actually predates the world of sports; having its roots in the fashion industry. But what is a brand? And how is value attached to it? A brand is nothing more than the dedicated trademark or identifier of a person, place, or product. If someone invests deeply in a person, place, or product that has no intrinsic worth in and of itself, they must place an artificial value on the commodity to convince you it has the capability of enhancing your self-worth and image in the eyes of others. Who has convinced the children of Judah that their image and worth is based upon values the children of Esau assign to perishable items?

True value is defined by relationships and abilities that transcend the value of currency based on a standard carnal man can manipulate and control at will. True value is shown in man's ability to succeed within the spiritual and natural realms established from eternity. The fear of the Lord is the beginning of wisdom...wisdom is the principal thing; therefore get wisdom: and with all your getting get understanding.

If we would suddenly find ourselves bereft of information technology, currency, and modern industry, people with a knowledge of shelter construction, land cultivation, animal husbandry, well digging, hunting, foraging, celestial movement, and weather forecast by observation would be far more valuable than a designer purse or pair of shoes bearing a celebrity name. And people possessing the fear of the Lord would be more greatly esteemed than any amount of gold, because they would know how to rule such a society in equity and righteous judgment. And while we are speaking of designer clothing, what on the market today compares to the shoes and garments our forebears wore which were supernaturally anointed by our Creator; able to withstand forty years of sustained use in the wilderness without wearing or degrading?

I have put forth these examples to illustrate the futility of chasing self-esteem through values defined by the oppressor and his systems. Our forefathers entered this Captivity in chains, shamefully imprinted by the searing branding irons of their purchasers. Shall we indeed exit this Captivity proudly sporting heavy chains, purchasing the oppressor's brands to self-imprint ourselves as still owned by him and bragging to our peers of how we bear his mark?

Capitalizing on Captivity...The Way of the Oppressor and Secret Societies

Repeated like a mantra through this book is the warning to envy not the oppressor, and choose none of his ways; and the admonition to learn not the ways of the heathen. Yet there have always been those in the midst of Israel who disdain that counsel and opt to be unequally yoked with the workers of iniquity. This desire to eagerly imitate the ways of the oppressor stem from a conviction that the haters of God have a distinct advantage in the affairs of this world and their personal lives. Is there any substance to such a belief? For there are two ways of looking at the wicked: the way of their earthly life while they prosper, and the end of their life when riches, power, prestige, and carnal wisdom are of no value in the hour of judgment.

Job noted the seemingly charmed life of the wicked "...

*Wherefore do the wicked live, become old, yea, are mighty in power?

*Their seed is established in their sight with them, and their offspring before their eyes.

*Their houses are safe from fear, neither is the rod of God upon them.

*Their bull gendereth, and faileth not; their cow calveth, and casteth not her calf.

*They send forth their little ones like a flock, and their children dance.

*They take the timbrel and harp, and rejoice at the sound of the organ.

*They spend their days in wealth, and in a moment go down to the grave.

*Therefore they say unto God, Depart from us; for we desire not the knowledge of thy ways.

*What is the Almighty, that we should serve him? and what profit should we have, if we pray unto him?" Job Chapter 21 verses 7-15.

The psalmist David made a similar observation "...I have seen the wicked in great power, and spreading himself like a green bay tree" Psalm 37 verse 35. In the 73rd psalm, verses 3-12 he confesses;

 "For I was envious at the foolish, when I saw the prosperity of the wicked.

*For there are no bands in their death: but their strength is firm.

*They are not in trouble as other men; neither are they plagued like other men.

*Therefore pride compasseth them about as a chain; violence covereth them as a garment.

*Their eyes stand out with fatness: they have more than heart could wish. They are corrupt, and speak wickedly concerning oppression: they speak loftily.

*They set their mouth against the heavens, and their tongue walketh through the earth.

*Therefore his people return hither: and waters of a full cup are wrung out to them.

*And they say, How doth God know? and is there knowledge in the most High?

*Behold, these are the ungodly, who prosper in the world; they increase in riches."

Satan will always offer this protected life to people, for the kingdoms of this present world are his, and he gives them to whomsoever he desires. The ideal recipient is someone who lives only for this life with no care for his eternal soul, or desire for knowledge of God. A person who relishes power, and luxuriates in all the pleasures this world can afford. A person who will not hesitate to worship Satan and signals his allegiance to others of like mind. And while the vast majority will take him up on his offer, the elect of God are called to take a different path, and shine as beacons of the true Light to expose Satan's light as the dark illumination it is.

Hebrews Chapter 11 verses 24-27 illustrate how Moses had the opportunity to bask in the position of the ruling elite and enjoy both the pleasures of sin and vast riches. But he refused the title of royalty, disregarded the wrath of the king, embraced hardship, and chose rather to suffer affliction with the people of God. Israel was still in the throes of Captivity when Moses drew his line in the sand. Life for them in Egypt would get worse before it got better. **The decision to side with the oppressor of the people of God, or take an oath into a society that will afford elite privileges stems from the desire to avoid the suffering consistent with Hebrewism and the chastening of God**.

In Chapter III, *Identity Theft...A Conspiracy of Denominational and Organizational Proportions*, we discussed the collusion among religions and institutions to obfuscate and obscure the truth of the Black man in the West as Hebrew. This self-awareness is key to bringing our consciousness to the point we forsake earthly goals for the petitioning of the turning of the Captivity. As such, all events that arise to occupy or engage the energies of the Black man in the West away from this goal must be viewed as distractions and obstacles. Social pundits, nationally known religious figures, and actors who are held in awe by the public are all used by the controlling elite to steer the Black consciousness in a direction where the focus is anywhere but on who we are, why we are here, and why nothing much has changed in the past four hundred plus years.

Political and celebrity scandals are used to manipulate the Black populace into taking sides. You may think you are listening to 'one of your own', but what is the message they are bringing? The only relevant message for this hour is that of our identity and purpose. So-called 'celebrities' cannot be relied upon to provide direction to the Hebrew in Captivity. People in these positions are either paid to represent a certain viewpoint, or owe favors which bind them to tow the party line.

Music performers especially are held up to be the face and expression of our culture, but they represent Esau's false vision for us, rather than an accurate depiction of our experience in the Captivity. Many have been compromised in a snare which forces them to bring a message antithetical to the deliverance of our people. As always, Satan has a counterfeit and corruption for God's truth. In response to Jesus' pure blood sacrifice and our repentance, God fills us with the Holy Ghost so that we can receive power to be his witnesses in the earth. In twisted contrast, Satan requires those who would attain the riches and adulation of the world to empty their self and invite a demonic spirit inside them, so that they will have power to seduce and influence minds for evil. This pact also often involves confirmation by oath and blood sacrifice.

People become caught up in the latest releases and videos, but do they really understand the songs they are singing along to? The dark world operates in duality to convey hidden messages via code words and symbols. Lyrics where the male and female subjects have attributes or invoke dedication far beyond the scope of humanity are a clue that the vocalist or group is actually praising Satan. Repeated references to the sun, a star, the light, or an angel are other giveaways. The constant hand signals covering one eye, forming a triangle, triple six A-OK sign, and the horned hand convey covert allegiance to the devil's kingdom. Proverbs Chapter 6 verses 12-13 tell us a wicked man winks with his eyes and speaks with his fingers. It goes on to say that type of person has a froward heart, continually devises mischief, and sows discord. How different from God, who tells us in Isaiah Chapter 45 verse 19 that he has not spoken in secret; as also his Son testifies in John Chapter 18 verse 20.

An interesting dynamic plays out in the music industry. Young artists will start their career with a wholesome image; thereby gaining the confidence of parents and garnering millions of fans. But at some point, the performer will commit some outrageous act or begin to appear in morally compromising apparel or situations. By this time, the fan base has already been established and followers are emotionally engaged, and the tendency is for them to let the performing artist set their trends and lifestyle.

This paradigm has its counterpart in the 'gospel' and 'Christian' music industry too, and appears to sometimes even extend to the huge mega-churches. In the Christian venue, those desiring wealth and adulation on par with the secular industry must be willing to leave the name of Jesus and reference to the Holy Ghost out of their music. They must be willing to lie to the people, steal their money, and be compromised in some type of sexual or financial scandal. They may be called upon to endorse causes antithetical to the gospel, or be placed in the same appearance venue with ungodly performers; thereby nullifying any message of conviction their song was intended to evoke.

There is nothing wrong with recording music to glorify the Lord, if the Lord has granted one with the gift of psalmistry or a beautiful voice wherewith to praise him. Even gospel rap—in reality simply scripture, artist testimony, or principles of the Kingdom as the spoken word set to music glorifies God—if the material does not mix the profane with the holy by borrowing input from the haters of God. But anyone operating in these gifts must remember that they that will be rich fall into temptation and a snare, and into many foolish and hurtful lusts, which drown men in destruction and perdition. For the love of money is the root of all evil: which while some coveted after, they have erred from the faith, and pierced themselves through with many sorrows. The focus cannot be on revenue and a name, and the witness will only be anointed as long as the artist follows after righteousness, godliness, faith, love, patience, and meekness.

Still others holding influential positions providing a platform for visibility are members of the Prince Hall Lodge: the Black version of the Gentile Freemasonry religion. It is certainly understandable in the wake of sustained persecution our people desired an organization that genders respect. Still, Freemasonry is a way that seems right to man, but the end thereof is death. Like white Freemasonry, the public mostly sees only benevolent actions on behalf of the local community. But at the uppermost degrees looms the Baphomet, and the Masonic acknowledgment that Lucifer is the light-bearer and beneficent god. Jesus said no man can serve two masters. The Apostle Paul warned us that light and darkness have no fellowship, and that we cannot simultaneously partake from the table of God and the table of devils.

In the previous subsection *The Modern Lure of Hellenism; Misdirected Loyalties*, we saw how wicked men in Israel desired the glory the Gentiles possessed..."Not setting by the honours of their fathers, but liking the glory of the Grecians best of all...but in the end it was to their own detriment...By reason whereof sore calamity came upon them: for they had them to be their enemies and avengers, whose custom they followed so earnestly, and unto whom they desired to be like in all things." Those verses go on to say, "it is not a light thing to do wickedly against the laws of God: but the time following shall declare these things." This means that the thing they desired and imitated did not immediately manifest itself as evil, but at some point those they had emulated revealed themselves to be enemies and avengers.

I have to make this point because the 33° Freemason Albert Pike—the same man who wrote the revered Masonic text Morals and Dogma, is said to have also written ritual for the

Ku Klux Klan. It is deeply troubling to think that the idolatrous 18th century move into Prince Hall Freemasonry was the spiritual trigger for the Jim Crow era brutality experience during the Klan's reign of terror. But if we take our cue from the Maccabean account, this was virtually history repeating itself. No matter how we want to view it from humanity's viewpoint, critical issues such as these must be assessed from a spiritual perspective and the word of God. Freemasonry is idolatry before the True and Living God. God is not playing about idolatry—even in the Captivity. His response to his people's involvement in this transgression has always been punishment, for the wages of sin is death. Let the reader judge the spiritual aspect of Freemasonry for himself based upon Albert Pike's own statement in Morals and Dogma:

"Lucifer, the Light-bearer! Strange and mysterious name to give to the Spirit of Darkness! Lucifer, the son of the morning! Is it he who bears the Light, and with its splendors intolerable blinds feeble, sensual or selfish Souls? Doubt it not!"[25]

If there is adoration of Satan in white Freemasonry, the identical spirit by default permeates and influences Black Freemasonry—even if the lodge members faithfully serve in their brick and mortar church. And I will grant that much of the initial involvement may have been undertaken without a full understanding of the spiritual adultery involved. But once light manifests, we must walk in the light, and turn our back on darkness.

It is now apparent Freemasonry and the Klan were deeply intertwined. Because they were Satanists, they were able to lynch, burn, pillage, murder and economically suppress our people, while nonchalantly carrying on with their daily lives, family, career, and serving in their local churches. It is an affront to our God and Creator to continue an organization patterned after a white one so instrumental in the pain and destruction of the sons and daughters of Israel. We must repent of the grievous sin of placing more confidence in the arm of flesh than that of our mighty King and Redeemer.

We must acknowledge that secret oaths and rituals conducted before an altar constructed by man is idolatry. This was one of the very sins that got our forebears forcibly removed from the land and scattered abroad the earth. It makes absolutely no sense to rekindle the madness in a strange land under Captivity! A true love for our people will cause men and women to renounce idolatry so that the Hebrew nation as a whole can be delivered. To cleave to idolatry in order to enjoy the charmed life of the wicked as described by the patriarchs Job and David is an unwise choice which will bring death and bitterness in the end. Like David we must solemnly proclaim:

"Through thy precepts I get understanding: therefore I hate every false way ...Therefore I esteem all thy precepts concerning all things to be right; and I hate every false way."

---

[25] Albert Pike, Morals and Dogma, page 321.

WHAT'S IMPORTANT

We are in a warfare that has raged since the rebellion of Lucifer and his expulsion from the heavens. By extension, his hatred and loathing of God carried over to the man and woman created in the image and likeness of God. Satan brings his assault in the form of accusation, provocateuring, and murderous aggression.

Judah and Jerusalem are inseparable contextually; both literally and spiritually and currently both are trodden down of the Gentiles. Our Kinsman-Redeemer, the Lord Jesus Christ, hails from Judah; he is both the Root and Offspring of Jesse. From eternity past, the Lion of our tribe has prevailed over Satan; although the cumulative events are still playing out in the framework of time as we perceive it until the fullness of such time is completed. Satan and his kingdom have a definite end already decreed in the everlasting Word. The same Word also decrees that Judah shall dwell for ever, and Jerusalem from generation to generation. Thus the days of Judah and Jerusalem are like those of our Redeemer: without end. The enemy is in the hapless position of fighting a war which he ultimately knows he has lost. His is a nihilist mentality and that explains the ruthlessness and cruelty that characterize his assaults.

The land of our Captivity is a habitation of devils, hold of every foul spirit, and cage of every unclean and hateful bird. The spirit behind every adversarial nation that antagonized our ancient forebears in the flesh is right at home in spiritual Babylon. Here also the high spiritual prince of Grecia struggles to maintain his hold. But God has spoken the future in past tense in saying he will bend Judah for himself, fill the bow with Ephraim, and raise up the sons of Zion against the sons of Greece. In that day, the Lord himself will be seen over us—as both commander and defender. Until that time, we put on the armor of God to stand against the myriad attacks mounted against us.

The deadly flood Satan cast out of his mouth to devour Israel and especially those who have the testimony of Jesus Christ and keep his commandments is still raging and contains all the virulent elements covered in this chapter: bywords and proud speech, terrorism and vigilantism, and the on-going practice of eugenics. Economic disenfranchisement continues, while drugs from plants that are only cultivated overseas continue to flood our neighborhoods; offering income in areas where viable employment is a distant memory. Just as legitimate job seekers compete with resumes submitted to employment recruiters, gangs compete for sales territory with hand rockets and actively recruit runners. Many of us have a family member or close associate either in prison or under some type of community control directly or indirectly stemming from this economic travesty.

Those who manage to keep their heads above these poisonous waves ultimately deal with the media mind control and the false history, false images, and false goals presented as reality. Dysfunction in the family ripples out into societal dysfunction. We live in a system that has been methodically crafted to prevent the development and expansion of economic prosperity and its associated wellbeing among the people. The result is frustration and discontent that implodes upon those who are not to blame but nevertheless first in the line of fire—those closest to the simmering anger.

Many try to move their minds past the continual assault by identifying with sports teams or celebrities. One may be constantly losing ground financially, but the boast can be made that the favored team has won the championship. Wearing something with the team's logo at least places one in the position of identifying with winning. The logic behind the manipulation of the psyche is brilliant but nevertheless a major distraction for us as a people. Fortunately, more and more are waking up to this device. To attach our self-worth to brands our oppressor waves in front of us is a discredit to our heritage and our God. The oppressor is only able to assign such exorbitant value to people, places, and things because we have not known who we truly are or realized how our value to God trumps anything this perishing world can contrive.

Some have decided to completely avoid the stigma of Captivity by choosing the path of least resistance; befriending the oppressor and assisting him in his oppression, or selling out to Satan for the money, fame, and power in this present world. Those who have chosen the way of the haters of God should not think they can walk in the counsel of the ungodly, stand in the way of sinners, and sit in the scorner's seat and still stake claim to their Hebrew descent at the redemption of Israel. Rather, they will find themselves like the chaff which the wind driveth away …the ungodly shall not stand in the judgment, nor sinners in the congregation of the righteous…the way of the ungodly shall perish.

Chapter XIV...Awakenings and Callings

Many a time have they afflicted me from my youth, may Israel now say: yet they have not prevailed against me.

Leaders, Lecturers, and Organizations

As one born during the 1950's, the author was fortunate to be exposed to a defining era of the struggle for freedom. I listened to the discussions of relatives whose grandparents were slaves, attempted to understand the comments of parents who weathered the oppression of Jim Crow, and was personally enamored with the militant aspect of the Civil Rights movement. Young though I was at the time, I could sense the tension in my parent's attitude about the divide between equal rights through strictly peaceful means, and the platform of Black pride and power; which I felt made a much more powerful statement.

In the Captivity, when leaders or organizations have risen with the capacity to mobilize our people, their efforts have been met with sabotage, slander, and infiltration; with the end result often exile, imprisonment, or assassination. Generally speaking, the key luminaries in the struggle for equality all desired access to the economic and educational resources that would grant them equal footing with white citizens. Some wanted to incorporate equality and integration with economic parity, and others eschewed it. The strategies and styles they employed and the projected outcomes they foresaw were as unique and varied as the individuals themselves. I have selected some of the better recognized warriors in the struggle in order to evaluate their efforts within the context of what we now recognize as a divine Captivity. In analyzing the role key leaders[26] played, we will see remarkable links between their persona and methods and our Biblical ancestors.

Booker T. Washington was born into slavery just seven years shy of the Emancipation Proclamation. Once he learned to read, he quickly excelled and became a student at Hampton University in Virginia. He went on to become an instructor there, and while working as a teacher, was asked to lead the newly founded Tuskegee Institute in Alabama.

Washington designed the school's curriculum to focus strongly on vocational training. He discouraged Blacks from becoming politically and socially equal with whites. Where education was concerned, he felt that students should concentrate on learning a skill or trade rather than pursue social sciences and the liberal arts. Having obtained the ability to earn income, they should then strive to show themselves dependable and stable. In this way, they would be viewed as valuable assets to their communities. According to Washington's philosophy, Black people could gain credibility in society by basically keeping their head down, doing the best they could at their particular vocation, and thereby prove themselves indispensable to American society.

---

[26] BlackPast.org™ Remembered & Reclaimed An Online Reference Guide to African American History.

Washington's views were embraced by white southerners who looked forward to Black people remaining inferior in society. White northerners supported his position because they perceived it would calm racial tensions in the south. However, his rhetoric was forcefully contested by another intellectual who had also come out of slavery: W.E.B. Du Bois. Du Bois knew that without full civil rights, any economic success gained by skilled trades would eventually be undermined.

Washington's theory was tested after African-American veterans returned from World War I. As soldiers, they had proved their worthiness in the highest manner possible: service, sacrifice, and bravery for their country. But rather than a warm welcome and hand up to get re-established, they were met with hostility and the same racist sentiment that existed before they shipped out for duty. Obviously, nothing had changed. Still, Washington's views about segregated self-sufficiency intrigued another visionary in the Black liberation movement: Marcus Garvey.

Garvey, who hailed from Jamaica, emerged as a trailblazer in the early twentieth century. A printer and publisher by trade, he understood that the pen was mightier than the sword, and in 1918 began publishing the Negro World, a newspaper devoted to the prevailing issues affecting Blacks in America. He also held speaking rallies, and his message was all the more relevant as he demonstrated the spiritual link between the biblical Hebrews and the modern Black man under oppression. Combining his talents as a speaker, writer, and organizer, he was able to build and retain a massive following. Creative, charismatic, and entrepreneurial, Garvey was an advocate of Pan-Africanism. He correctly believed that equality on American soil would never become a reality, and apparently most of our forebears in that era had also reached that consensus. At its height, his organization—the UNIA—(Universal Negro Improvement Association) claimed in excess of two million members. Although his movement was not founded upon a religious platform, he was ahead of his time in understanding that the Black race in the West was associated to the Hebrews of the Bible. Garvey 's unique ability to bring relevancy to the Christian faith by correctly linking the people with the historicity of the scriptures had a profound impact.

Garvey purchased two steamships and forged ahead with plans to repatriate Blacks in Africa, until unscrupulous business associates within the UNIA undermined the organization and left their founder charged with fraud. Garvey was imprisoned, and although his sentence was later commuted, he was exiled back to Jamaica. The UNIA was effectively neutralized, and Garvey 's movement lost momentum.

The militant nationalism of Garvey made an indelible impression upon Audley E. Moore, later to be honorably titled "Queen Mother" Moore after her visit to Ghana in 1972. A native of Louisiana, racist brutality affected her life at an early age; her great-grandmother having been raped by a slave master, and her grandfather lynched before his wife's eyes. As a young woman, Moore also found that racism was not specific to the South. It was after settling in Harlem that she began her most prolific work in organizing and lobbying for change across a broad spectrum of issues affecting poor Blacks. She became a regional director for Garvey 's UNIA.

Moore's efforts tended to be outside the traditional civil rights movement, but her focus and intensity were so great she attracted interest from multiple African leaders, who welcomed her zeal for the independence of African people everywhere. Throughout her life she served as a volunteer nurse, human rights activist, humanitarian, and spiritual leader. Her accolades are too many to be mentioned here, but one of her greatest achievements will be remembered in her mobilization of support for reparations. Moore founded the Committee for Reparations for Descendants of U. S. Slaves, garnering in excess of a million petition signatures.

During the same period, the NAACP (the National Association for the Advancement of Colored People) was organized to bring centralized leadership and national attention to the institutional injustice and deadly violence encountered by Black people. Its stated mission was to enforce the constitutional rights enshrined in the Constitution so that they applied equally to people of color.

Because of its name, many are unaware it was originally founded by white social activists following the deadly racial clash in Springfield, Illinois in 1908. Once again, the initial pretext was the white female cry of rape; an accusation which the alleged 'victim' later admitted was completely made up. Her disclosure however, was not given to the grand jury until two weeks after the riot. The aftermath of the violence included the beating and lynching of two Black citizens unrelated to her alleged incident, the burning of Black homes, and the destruction of Black businesses. Establishments of whites suspected of sympathizing with Blacks were also targeted.

The specter of the rabid viciousness that characterized the south expanding to the north spurred native Kentuckian William Walling to travel to Springfield. There, he observed the aftermath of the carnage and personally interviewed many survivors. After publishing his findings, he was contacted by Mary White Ovington, a journalist and activist based in New York. Joining these white activists were W.E.B. Du Bois, Ida Wells-Barnett, and dozens of other committed individuals across various disciplines.

Du Bois founded the group's official publication, The Crisis—which became the main voice for civil rights nationwide. The organization's model of establishing chapters across the nation fueled its growth and recognition, and attracted professionals from the legal, educational, and political science fields. This created an erudite and articulate resource pool capable of initiating the dialogue necessary to craft anti-racial legislation and maintain the pressure for its passage. The NAACP's method for bringing change embraced non-violence; a stance that gave them the higher moral ground in their face off with racial antagonism.

While criticized by some as elitist and out of touch with the man-on-the-street struggle against white violence, the NAACP nevertheless accomplished what it was best designed to do, based on the guiding principles and stated objectives that steered the organization. It crafted legislation to outlaw both lynching and the failure to prosecute anyone involved in it. The first bill passed the House but was stalled in the Senate. The second bill was not endorsed by then president Theodore Roosevelt due to his fear of losing re-election votes from the south. But over a period of three decades, the NAACP exerted sustained and unrelenting pressure on the national conscience. The end result was that without the passage of an actual law, the practice self-eliminated. Today, such a heinous crime would be dealt with for what it is: capital murder.

Beyond doubt, the NAACP's most profound accomplishments were in the realm of enforcing voting rights, advocating for equal employment opportunities and laying the legal groundwork for the landmark Brown v. Board decision, which overturned segregation in public schools. Where other movements have been relegated to the pages of history, the NAACP remains the oldest active civil rights organization in the United States, continuing its advocacy and community support.

When contemplating the involvement of white interests in the association, it must be acknowledged that it could have never achieved the victories it did without the collaboration of white social activists and fiscal support of white donors. Where other groups and voices were reactionary, responding to violence and injustice at the face to face level—the NAACP assumed a pro-active stance; working from the top down to remedy the neglect of Constitutional rights, and dismantle the protections of those who refused to apply them equally to Black citizens. The litmus test of its strength was demonstrated in the enrollment of "The Little Rock Nine": a group of Black high school students who were the first to integrate Central High School in Little Rock, Arkansas... literally risking their lives in the process.

The NAACP's staunch non-violence platform did not insulate its own members from bloodshed. Two of its representatives working in field offices in the south, Harry T. Moore, and Medgar Evers, were murdered. Moore's death by firebombing was never solved.

Malcolm X (born Malcolm Little) was the son of a preacher who was a committed follower of Marcus Garvey. According to his biography, he experienced the terror of white supremacy intimidation and violence while still a child. While serving a stint in prison, his brother would visit him and share the teachings of Islam. At this time, the Islam taking root in U.S. cities had a distinct focus on Black Nationalism and self-actualization. Upon his release, Malcolm—a gifted orator—became active in the Nation of Islam, quickly rising through the ranks.

Similar to Garvey, Malcolm X also saw the futility of expecting white America to embrace Blacks as equals or permit them to share in the prosperity and ruling voice of the nation built by their labor. At first, he advocated violent revolution to overthrow the oppressive system that marginalized and disenfranchised Black Americans, citing the success other struggling ethnicities achieved using such methods. But later, as a result of a pilgrimage to Mecca, he became convinced there was a way to both aggressively and non-violently work to improve the Black man's condition. The transformation would take place first in the United States. Once that was accomplished, Black Americans could reach out to their oppressed brothers and sisters in Africa; unifying, sharing resources and creating a worldwide solidarity of connectedness and prosperity among all Black people.

Young, dynamic, and a riveting speaker, he soon became more prominent then the religion's main leader, Elijah Muhammad. Tensions frayed even further when he became aware of moral indiscretions involving Elijah Muhammad, resulting in Malcolm X leaving the organization and founding one of his own: The Organization of African American Unity.

Malcolm X's disclosure of his mentor's moral compromise earned him enemies in the Nation of Islam. And his determination to elevate his people domestically and around the world raised the ire of the entrenched white power structure and sparked an FBI investigation. Declassified documents indicate FBI director J. Edgar Hoover's Counter Intelligence Program (or COINTELPRO) was tasked with infiltrating and discrediting Malcolm and his new Muslim Mosque. He was murdered in February of 1965.

Faith in God, conviction, and determination drove Fannie Lou Hamer to campaign for voting rights in rural Mississippi in the early 1960's. Looking at her story, one is left to wonder if women of such fortitude exist anymore. She was the youngest of a large family who earned their living by sharecropping; which is best understood as a mere subsistence lifestyle. She had to pick cotton even as a child, but still managed to learn to read and write. After marrying and being unable to bear children, she sought medical help—only to be forcibly sterilized without her consent under the pretext of removing a tumor. Eugenics was in full swing in the south, and Fannie Lou Hamer became an unsuspecting victim of it. Subsequently, she and her husband adopted and raised several poor children.

Working first with the Student Nonviolent Coordinating Committee, Mrs. Hamer went on to help found the Mississippi Freedom Democratic Party. She suffered a Klan murder attempt, and was beaten and maimed in a vicious assault while jailed for her insistence on registering to vote. Some would wonder why a person would not just give up in the face of so much adversity, but that question answers itself. It was precisely because of the severe maltreatment Blacks experienced in the Mississippi delta that she felt she had to press on. Without representatives to voice the concerns of Black Mississippians, the bias and inequities would never change. And unless the people were free to elect their representative, they would have no voice.

Fannie Lou Hamer was not a professional orator. She didn't hold degrees, or hail from a background of privilege. But she did have great faith in God. In the moments of severe trial, she would sing the praises of God to maintain her composure and that of those in the struggle around her. Her attitude was that the people would get the right to vote, or she would die trying. In 1964, as she testified on behalf of the Mississippi Freedom Democratic Party before the Democratic National Convention, President Johnson attempted to pre-empt her speech as she exposed the violence and brutality encountered by Black Mississippians in their quest to vote. But later that evening, the networks broadcast her testimony in its entirety; shocking and appalling the nation. Thank God for women like Fannie Lou Hamer, and also for men of faith like her husband, who similar to Lapidoth—the prophetess' Deborah's husband—understood the calling that was on his wife.

Perhaps the best known and revered among the advocates for our people's rights is Dr. Martin Luther King Jr., the son of a southern preacher who also took a strong stand against injustice. Because of his upbringing and the example set by his father, Dr. King was involved in various civil rights protests long before he was a household name. His national recognition came about as he headed up the Southern Leadership Conference (later to be renamed the Southern Christian Leadership Conference, or SCLC) a civil rights organization formed in response to the Montgomery Alabama Bus Boycott, and instrumental in organizing numerous other boycotts taking place across the south.

Dr. King studied the works of Mahatma Gandhi, and concluded that non-violent civil disobedience was the most prudent route to challenge the laws and attitudes undermining the basic Constitutional rights promised to all American citizens. His approach was met with fire-bombings, violent assaults, and bloodshed. However, when one rally or protest completed, another soon began. The SCLC drew ministers and supporters from all over the nation and they kept up the pressure for change.

269

It was difficult to undermine Dr. King's approach because he modeled it upon New Testament principles. As the SCLC planned strategies to dismantle the laws and policies that supported racial injustice, they were wise as serpents, but harmless as doves. The television coverage of bricks, rocks, bottles, fire hoses, and police dogs used against people who were merely sitting, marching or singing in the quest for equal rights and respect shocked and revolted the nation. No longer was the psychopathic hatred confined to back country roads and small towns with unusual names. America was forced to look in the mirror and acknowledge the gruesome, soulless entity staring back was not the epitome of freedom, liberty, and justice she claimed to be.

Together with the SCLC, Dr. King was instrumental in mobilizing the public support and national consensus critical to codifying and enforcing civil rights legislation. Due in large part to their efforts and pressure from the public, President Lyndon B. Johnson signed the Civil Rights Act into law in July of 1964. Dr. King could now turn his attention to discrimination in urban areas of the north, such as substandard housing. He concluded that integration alone could not remedy the serious inequities existing in the American economic system as a whole. He also voiced opposition to the Vietnam War. Dr. King was tolerated until he began to press forward in addressing urban poverty and the legality of the war. Declassified documents show he and the SCLC were also targets of COINTELPRO. He was murdered in April of 1968.

Working with the SCLC before Dr. King's death was a young Trinidadian who had come to New York in the early 1950's. Stokely Carmichael attended Howard University in Washington, D.C.; earning his Bachelors in Philosophy in 1964. As often as he was able, he would attend Freedom Rider events; excursions where Black and white students would ride interstate buses together to the south to make the case for desegregation. Upon reaching their destination, they would attempt to dine together at restaurants. The Freedom Riders knew full well their behavior would result in jail confinement and likely violence, but this was a price they were willing to pay again and again.

Carmichael began moving more to the forefront of the civil rights movement in the south, eventually assuming the leadership of the Student Non-Violent Coordinating Committee (or SNCC.) His approach diverged from Dr. King's in the belief Black economic self-determination was more important than integration. He based this sentiment on his observations that integration was not remedying situations such as substandard schools, or providing employment opportunities. He felt that Black progress would be manipulated and controlled as long as the economic power remained in the hands of whites, and wanted his people to have the ability to develop industry, trade, and fiscal policy independent of the white capitalist system. He also sensed that the suppression of Black enterprise was not strictly an American issue, and expanded his lectures to other nations. It was at that time that he coined the expression, 'Black Power.'

Although Carmichael stressed that Black Power referred to autonomous economic power, more moderate Blacks distanced themselves from the term for fear it would alienate whites and undermine the painstaking progress gained in the struggle for equal rights. Whites themselves read an even more extreme meaning into it; interpreting it as a rallying call for a race war.

Carmichael was named an honorary prime minister of the Black Panther Party, but resigned shortly afterward. The Black Panther Party collaborated with white revolutionary groups as part of a broad spectrum struggle against injustice, but Carmichael felt whites could not really relate to the Black experience, and that Black progress should be handled by Blacks only. He was also targeted for investigation by COINTELPRO. In 1969, he moved to West Africa.

The original Black Panther Party began in Oakland, California in 1966, and quickly developed chapters and branches throughout the United States. It is probably fair to say they were marked most intensely by COINTELPRO for infiltration and subversion, because the Panthers insisted on arming themselves—not to initiate confrontation with police—but to protect themselves and their communities from police excesses. Rather than appeal to the convenience and fickleness of the political process to address the needs of the Black community, the Panthers took a 'boots on the ground' approach to actively feed, clothe, shelter, and provide basic clinical services to the underprivileged in their neighborhoods. Many children were able to receive a nutritious breakfast before school for the first time.

The Panthers also reached out to gangs in an attempt to convince them to eschew gang warfare in favor of the higher stakes class warfare struggle. In spite of this, police violence stalked their members. Less than two years into the formation of the association, seventeen-year old unarmed Bobby Hutton was mowed down in a hail of bullets when he ran out of a house that had been tear-gassed and set on fire by police.

The shadow that eclipsed the Panther's altruistic deeds appears to be their philosophical incorporation of certain Marxist beliefs. With the West being about a quarter of a century into the Cold War, a group that was both militant and embraced tenets of the Communist Party did not garner the same type of sympathetic response as that of atrocities committed against marchers and protesters during Dr. King's crusades.

The Panthers also had harsh rhetoric for Blacks who did not want to join their movement. This made their support virtually non-existent except within the ranks of the communities they served, and COINTELPRO relentlessly assaulted the organization via varied methods of sabotage, such as provocateuring and false communications. The FBI placed an informant in the headquarters of the Chicago chapter, and in December 1969 the leader, Fred Hampton was assassinated during a Chicago police raid as he slept in his bed. Ballistics testing later determined ninety bullets were fired into the dwelling and only one fired out.

Continued harassment, intimidation, and arrests eventually splintered the Black Panther Party enough to greatly reduce its influence. Declassified FBI documents indicate that one of the stated goals of COINTELPRO was to "Prevent the rise of a "messiah" who could unify the militant Black Nationalist movement.[27] Did the death of Fred Hampton signal the close of COINTELPRO targeting? We know that at the same time North American urban areas were being flooded with drugs and guns, an identical influx was occurring in regions such as Jamaica, Trinidad, and Tobago. Bob Marley attempted to counter this with the message in his music, and

---

[27] "FBI COINTELPRO archives." FBI Records: The Vault

was looked up to by many as a spiritual leader. In response to what he perceived as the destabilization of his country and descent into a vortex of violence, he sang of self-awareness in the midst of Captivity. Marley died an untimely death at just thirty-six years of age, from an illness some have rumored was triggered by a biological agent.

Some fifteen years later, another young artist who quickly gained a huge following would also meet a violent death. Because of the media emphasis on the genre, and circumstances and people surrounding his demise, much of the public consciousness never learned of Tupac Shakur's plans to team up with other luminaries in hip hop for social and economic mobilization in America's Black urban communities. Tupac came from an activist background; his parents having been members of the original Black Panther party, so it was a logical step for him to use his platform to reach Black empowerment goals.

Admittedly, these are situations best left for the day when God shall judge the secrets of men by Jesus Christ and reveal everything man has covered. Nor does the author endeavor to endorse the lifestyles and individual philosophies of these men. The only point being made here is that whenever a Black male figure appears who is not owned and manipulated by the ruling elite of this world; that is, a person who resonates with the people and truly desires to do something to uplift them, they end up dead. And anyone who attempts to truly educate, uplift, and provide pure spiritual truth to the Hebrew in Captivity is targeted by forces with a stated agenda to neutralize them through blackmail, gang stalking, substance abuse, or sexual and financial scandals. If none of these ruses are effective, the next resort is biological attack or outright murder. It would appear Esau's system prefers leaders among our people to exist merely as a memory in the name of a street, park or school; rather than meeting them at the table in a conciliatory spirit and honestly addressing the unemployment, economic, and unfair justice burden Black people struggle under.

The controlling elite have been savvy enough to realize that successful Black nationalism was a step away from Black economic independence. The ability of Black communities to mobilize and prosper as self-sustaining entities had already been demonstrated on a micro scale in places like Tulsa, Denver and San Francisco earlier in the century. It could not be permitted to expand on a macro level. Besides, in the wake of the assassination of Dr. King and destabilization of the Black Panther party, Esau was in the process of creating new messiahs of a less threatening nature. These gods to go before the people would be designed to appeal to a culture driven by consumerism and entertainment instead of nationalism. Their unveiling was timed to coincide with the coming alternative economy. Jobs would be generated as a result; not for the community—but for the prison industrial complex.

Tears, great personal danger, and death dot the rich mosaic of faith, perseverance, wisdom, humility, courage and talent that made up the civil rights struggle. Where have we seen such a powerful force before? We have seen it in the pages of the Bible in the legacies of our forebears. The spirit of excellence that characterized Daniel, the historical shepherding abilities of the patriarchs, the ingenuity and entrepreneurialism of King Solomon and King Uzziah, the ability to gain strategic influence with the ruling elite that distinguished Esther and Ezra, the humility of Moses, the boldness of Deborah, the zeal of Jehu, the brilliant oratory of Paul, and the vehemence of the Maccabeans against the injustice perpetrated on the people...are all clearly present in our struggle for civil rights; and simply put, represent who we have always been as a people.

No one individual or group carried the day, but as a collective an undeniable impact was made on this, the land of our Captivity. When we look at the force these leaders exerted from the context of their ancient Hebraic heritage, it is not hard to understand how they weathered seemingly insurmountable obstacles, spoke truth to power, and stood firm against the very gates of hell itself.

Performing Artists

In tandem with the consensus that conditions could not continue unchallenged for Blacks in America, vocal expression arose as a strong medium to express the movement. The airways became the ideal venue to continue the drive to expose injustice, exhort and encourage, and instill a sense of pride. The music industry provided the perfect platform to counter the ever present racist propaganda and derogatory caricatures. Songs written during this period accurately captured the ethos of the struggle; reinforcing convictions and raising the consciousness of all who could hear what the artists were saying. They had a small window to work with, especially where national airplay was concerned; for activism-charged music would soon be greatly censored. Eventually, demoralization brought about by the murder of major civil rights leaders, planned economic sabotage, and the drug invasion of entire communities would silence the odes to the pride and indomitable spirit of the Black man.

Song subject matter generally fell into several categories: self-awareness and pride, hope and encouragement, criticism of injustice, and criticism of economic disenfranchisement. The list here is far from all-inclusive; but I want to highlight songs and artists which have left a powerful impact from my personal frame of reference:

Billie Holiday's 1939 rendition of 'Strange Fruit' painted a graphic reality of the South's psychopathic bloodlust without ever mentioning the term 'lynching.' Performed long before the era of music videos, the lyrical imagery was haunting. There is something about viewing violence on a screen whereby one eventually becomes desensitized. But auditory input forces the mind to form a mental image that is not easily neutralized. This song was unique in that Ms. Holiday was able—as would be said today, to 'put on blast' a taboo subject during a very volatile period.

During the time spanning the 1930's-1960's, vocalists Paul Robeson and Marian Anderson rose to prominence both domestically and internationally. Both of these talented singers dealt with the prevailing racism of the era but managed to use their platforms to support the civil rights movement.

The 60's though, marked the turning point when the civil rights movement overcame the inertia of white resistance and apathy, and gained momentum to the point it could no longer be ignored or denied. The older generation had kept the fires of struggle burning with spirituals and a cappella rallying songs. Now the gifted younger generation brought instrumental music, unique harmonies, and the ability to reach the masses via recording and airplay. It was a dynamic movement that has never again been repeated.

The assassination of Dr. King was intended to act as a psychological wrecking ball to the equal rights movement. So it was imperative the people did not lose momentum in the aftermath. Sam Cooke reminded us that 'A Change Is Gonna Come.' Curtis Mayfield and the

Impressions' song 'We're a Winner' was right on time to bolster the confidence of the people. Almost as if on cue, James Brown's epic release, 'I'm Black and I'm Proud,' stoked the fires hotter. The song was unique in that it could only truly resonate with someone who was Black. But it was much more than a pride anthem. Brown summarized the issues, the people want their fair share...they need to be able to do for themselves and reap the fruit of their own labor...they would rather die on their feet than keep living on their knees. Brown came back even harder with 'I Don't Want Nobody to Give Me Nothin'; Open Up the Door—I'll Get it Myself.' In this song, he made it clear the problem was whites blocking access to resources, employment, and education; not Blacks' refusal or inability to progress.

Speaking to the beauty and value of Black women and children was Sonny and the Checkmates' 'Black Pearl,' and Nina Simone's 'Young, Gifted, and Black'. These songs focused on the precious human qualities that made it possible to say 'I'm Black and I'm Proud' with confidence. Marvin Gaye's 'What's Goin' On' contemplated the dysfunction and needless violence that affects domestic relationships and society as a whole when communication breaks down. The Five Stairsteps brought a ray of hope and comfort that things will not always remain in the state they are for our people with 'O-o-o Child.'

The Chi-lites got straight to the point of identifying the problem in their hit, 'Power to the People.' In listening to the lyrics of the song, one realizes the same economic stranglehold present when Eugene Record and his group laid down the tracks over forty years ago still grips us today. Curtis Mayfield returned in the spirit of encouragement; exhorting us to 'Move on Up' to our destination. The title itself is deep because we can never stagnate in pits of despair and self-pity: we must remain mobile and vertical.

Some years later, and definitely with a smoother groove was McFadden and Whitehead's 'Ain't No Stoppin' Us Now.' While people across a broad listening spectrum enjoyed it, the lyrical meaning was crystal clear to Blacks. The music industry, which works in cooperation with Hollywood and intelligence agencies, had already begun to filter the types of music permitted access to the airwaves. With decades of future wars planned, they could scarce afford to have protest music influencing the youth and their voting parents.

Poets and visual artists also played a role in bringing a conscious voice to the people. Langston Hughes' classic 'Mother to Son' is just as significant today as when he penned it. Nikki Giovanni—admiringly known as 'The Truth Teller', was active in the Student Non-Violent Coordinating Committee during the civil rights movement, and continues to inspire today. Works such as hers and those of June Jordan represent the movement of Cultural Nationalism that forced the issues of racism and civil rights into the mainstream via the arts as opposed to revolutionary measures. The paintings of Romare Bearden and Faith Ringgold spoke graphically of historical black culture and struggle. These visual works are priceless; because vocal articulation of racial injustice often does little more than escalate to denial or defensive justification. But it is difficult to argue with a painting; for the artist speaks telepathically through the canvas, engaging the viewer's conscience and demanding a response.

The Quest for Civil Rights Considered in Spiritual Retrospection

Many honorable men and women among our people took up the banner for equal rights and economic autonomy; and the better known ones are the people we tend to see as the face of the movement. But countless others labored beside them in the trenches, in great financial sacrifice and in prayer vigils. Many are unnamed and unknown to us but catalogued in God's heavenly archives. Men and women hazarded their lives and subjected themselves to unspeakable persecution because they found the Constitution and Bill of Rights to be nothing more than documents of hypocrisy where Black Americans were concerned.

Efforts to achieve economic parity and self-sustainability were constantly subverted. Attempts at nationalization were sabotaged and stopped. Pleas to the government to intervene against terrorism were ignored or brushed aside. Political representation that would have taken the people's grievances to the legislative branch of government was impossible to obtain in the South. The government's own investigative agency did not want the people to have a charismatic, effective leader. Peaceful, non-violent civil disobedience was met with brutality and ultimately, murder. Leaders who called for revolution were targeted, harassed, and murdered. Organization as a nation within a nation for the preservation and protection of Black people as first priority was sabotaged by infiltration, and eventually also disabled by murder.

Can all of this be a coincidence, or is there an obvious pattern? We can better understand once we view the situation strictly from a spiritual perspective: we are still in Captivity. This is a reality in the spiritual realm and a known fact to all angelic principalities and powers, both righteous and evil. As such, we cannot demand anything of the oppressor; if we do, we are seen as captives demanding rights. Any captive demanding anything is usually met with humiliation and violence. Therefore, theoretically, we can ask, but we cannot demand.

However, scripture does not support God expecting us to appeal to the oppressor. Lobbying for laws, initiatives, increased funding for this and that, etc. has ultimately only angered those who are adversarial toward us and resent our presence. The author is convinced God is waiting for us to reach the point where we acknowledge there is none but He who can deliver us. His plan of restoration is not for things to get better and better until the days of racial hatred and discrimination are a distant memory. If anything, he is probably permitting the pressure to become intolerable so we will turn and seek his face with our entire heart in repentance and supplication for deliverance.

If you punish your child for repeatedly disobeying and tell him he must stand in the corner for an hour and think about his actions, would you cave to his demands to bring a chair so his punishment can be made more tolerable? What if he insisted you paint the wall a different color because the surface he is up close to is boring and depressing? What if he begged you to let his best friend come over so he could have someone to talk to as the hour elapsed? My guess is that as one of the children of Judah—far from capitulating, you would firmly deny his requests! Well, remember, we are hewn from a Rock that employs this same method of wise discipline.

We will only fall for the deception that racial hatred against Blacks will gradually dissipate through legal and social change if we refuse to acknowledge our Captivity is a divine punishment. Deuteronomy Chapter 28 verse 68 clearly describes coming into Egypt again by ships as coming to a land of our enemies. It matters not if the enemy relents a little now and then, or if some of the enemy's people sympathize with the captive's cause. It is still enemy territory! This means that Dr. King's dream—though noble, was exactly that—a dream... which will never become reality in this Captivity. The only certainty is the manifestation of the

Kingdom of God upon earth, and the restoration of the Hebrew. We cannot permit the quest for equality in Captivity to eclipse the very real need for the termination of the Captivity itself. We were emancipated...only to be turned over as prey to a domestic terror organization. We received the coveted right to vote...only to find that laws and policies are driven by moneyed interests; not the voice of the people. We fought valiantly for integration...only to see it ultimately used to bring in domestic and worldwide competition that undercut us out of our own demographic. We applauded hate crime laws, only to realize they have no application in the venue where they are needed by us the most... police brutality and vigilante justice.

Putting our experience in the correct context: that of a Captivity waiting to be turned—rather than that of a longsuffering, struggling people making incremental progress—goes a long way in helping us prepare our hearts and minds in submission and consecration before the Lord. While we may realize some breakthroughs during Captivity, ultimately they will either eventually be sabotaged, or eclipsed by still greater crises. The quest for civil rights was a natural outgrowth of oppression in a land that claimed to champion liberty and justice for all. It served its purpose. It is now incumbent upon us to petition heaven with repentance to turn our Captivity and restore us as a people.

Reparations or Restoration?

The quest for reparations extends as far back as 1865 with General William T. Sherman's Field Order No. 15, which set aside a four-hundred-thousand-acre tract of land extending from South Carolina down to Florida for freed slaves to establish land holdings of up to forty acres. In a meeting with Sherman, representatives on behalf of the newly emancipated slaves expressed the desire to have their own separate region where they could establish themselves apart from whites and live autonomously. In response to Sherman's directive, Congress created the Freedman's Bureau to provide legal title to the homesteads. What could have been the foundation for a Black stake in the wealth of this nation was abruptly aborted by President Andrew Johnson, who ordered the land returned to the original white owners.

Blacks who remained in the South were forced into subsistence sharecropping. Others migrated north where labor markets existed, but there were relegated to lower tier jobs and substandard housing in the urban areas. Labor unions were hostile to Blacks and held a tight grip on many industries. Some migrating west were able with much sacrifice to establish sustainable communities, but when construction of the rail lines began across the country, inevitably the developers would plan the route to intersect white municipalities, while bypassing the Black towns. Since commerce followed the trains, the tiny communities became isolated. Eventually, people stopped coming, and the residents themselves left for better prospects in the cities.

The two World Wars rallied the economy and reluctantly forced commerce and industry to include Blacks. These periods would provide some lift to the economic status of Blacks, but only in highly industrialized areas or for individual small business. Even then, prosperity was fragile at best; circumstances such as economic fluctuation, drought, adverse political influence or oppression by violent racist factions could destroy hard-won gains and leave Black families in an unrecoverable state.

Considering the history of unpaid labor, broken promises, unscrupulous sharecropping contracts, and the generational effect poverty has had upon our people, many feel reparations are justly deserved. But a judicious distribution of funds among some forty million people requires answers to many profound questions. How is the cost of such restitution quantified? We cannot answer that question without computing the cost of building a nation. How much does it cost to build a country from the third world entity America was in the 17th century to the sprawling empire it is today? And to be all-inclusive, South America and the West Indies were also built in the same manner, and Europe's commercial enterprise likewise enhanced by the commodities shipped from the West.

What about personal injury and victim compensation? Damages such as these are legally recognized today as justifiable to those who have suffered great crimes to their person and families. How would this country recompense for the personal humiliation of men and women having their naked bodies poked, prodded, and fondled? What financial restitution is sufficient for the pain and suffering associated with rape, or castration? What about the little boys and girls who were sexually abused? What is the correct price to pay for the mother's trauma of her baby ripped from her breast or children snatched from her arms, never to be seen again? How do you pay for the pain of using men and women as breeders for your personal profit? What is the price for a chopped off hand, or foot, because a slave took their chance at freedom and failed?

What is the reasonable value for being mauled by dogs? Or for slaves who served all their life and when old and feeble were turned out into the wilderness to die alone? In this day, we would treat such an action as elder abuse. So how is the value of that person's agony financially computed in modern terms? What about death at sea? If a ship set sail today and one out of every three passengers died on it and their corpses were tossed overboard, would the cruise line or shipping magnate be found not liable? And millions are on the sea floor, for God very pointedly says in Psalms Chapter 68 verse 22, "I will bring my people again from the depths of the sea." Truth be known, it is impossible for this nation or the world to ever compensate in dollars and cents for her sins against the Hebrew people—they reach unto heaven and God has the vast data archive of each injury committed either individually or collectively.

Suggested dollar amounts are bandied about in the billions, but should we really trust a ruling construct that prints money out of thin air and can devalue it in a split second with a key stroke? If the Congress and Senate approved a reparations bill today, no sooner than the funds deposited into accounts, a contrived national emergency could occur. Asset forfeiture executive orders are already on the books; and national emergencies always trump any other government services or actions. Even a conveniently timed database hack... anything like this— could instantly derail any benefit obtained. My point is: what Caesar gives, Caesar can take away.

At the risk of sounding cynical, I merely point to the track record of this nation. There has been a pattern of carrots dangling on sticks; starting from General Sherman's land offer which was subverted by a sitting President, to the sabotage of Garvey's UNIA, to the destruction of prosperous communities like Greenwood in Tulsa, to the assassination of political leaders who endeavored to uplift the Black populace. The historical trajectory of this nation simply does not lend itself to credibility in the matter of restorative justice.

Sure, reparations would be the righteous thing to do. But it takes repentance to bring forth the fruit of righteousness. When a nation is destabilizing entire Black communities via international drug trade, and locking up the men wholesale in prisons for profit, this are not a work of remorse. When a blind eye is turned to vigilante justice and police brutality is the standard operating procedure on young Black men, this does not indicate contrition for slavery. America cannot rally itself to get behind reparations because simply put, America is not sorry. As long as the American mantra is, "That was the past—get over it," you will know the critical element of repentance is missing from the equation.

But the failure of the West to repent for the travesty of slavery, and its tendency to renege on promises or protections which would aid Black prosperity are not the primary reasons to examine the feasibility of reparations. We need to step back from the worldly view of our suffering and disenfranchisement, and look at the situation strictly from a spiritual perspective. As mentioned earlier, this is Captivity, as viewed from the realm of the heavenlies. This places us in pretty much the same situation as our ancient forebears in Egypt. What kind of God would we be serving if he had laid it on Pharaoh's heart to give all the Hebrews a bonus, but still allowed them to remain in bondage, surrounded by idolatry and a people who hated them?

If you recall, he hardened Pharaoh's heart, not softened it. The account does not say, "The Egyptians said among themselves, it repenteth us that we have made the Hebrews to serve so harshly; let us bless them after all they have been through." It says, "the Egyptians made the children of Israel to serve with rigour: And they made their lives bitter with hard bondage, in morter, and in brick, and in all manner of service in the field: all their service, wherein they made them serve, was with rigour." It does not say, "They were smitten in their hearts, and repented for assisting in the genocide of the Hebrews in the slaughter of the male infants." Rather the scripture states, "every shepherd is an abomination unto the Egyptians." The Hebrew word used here for abomination 'toebah' means they found the Hebrews disgusting, and loathed and detested them.

This description of their sentiment toward the children of Israel bears an eerie resemblance to the general antipathy and resentment toward the Black man in the latter day Captivity. Also of interest is the fact that the righteous—from the time of Abel—have traditionally been shepherds. Even our Kinsman Redeemer referred to himself as the Good Shepherd, and was made like unto his brethren in all things. It is the wicked who have customarily been obsessed with the building of cities, operation of commerce, and control of the bodies and minds of men. Bottom line, God neither wanted nor expected the Egyptians to give the Hebrews anything, until it was time for his people to spoil them just before their departure. God was about deliverance, not tolerance. He did not want them to become comfortable in their bondage, when they were going to have to be physically and psychologically prepared to make a long trek through the wilderness.

God knows that the restoration of Israel will trump anything man can offer as reparation. That is why God states he is not only going to handle the restoration, but the restitution as well. He does not want his people compensated with the false banknotes of Babylon while surrounded by its devils, foul spirits, and unclean and hateful birds. Restitution will take place when the Black man is in his own land, under his own vine and fig tree. Neither will the people of God receive some paltry one-time disbursement. According to scripture the reimbursements are double, sevenfold, and a hundredfold... and these are just the ones we have been told about.

They are double "...strangers shall stand and feed your flocks, and the sons of the alien shall be your plowmen and your vinedressers.

But ye shall be named the Priests of the Lord: men shall call you the Ministers of our God: ye shall eat the riches of the Gentiles, and in their glory shall ye boast yourselves.

For your shame ye shall have double; and for confusion they shall rejoice in their portion: therefore in their land they shall possess the double: everlasting joy shall be unto them." Isaiah Chapter 60 verses 5-7

They are sevenfold "...But if he (the thief) be found, he shall restore sevenfold; he shall give all the substance of his house." Proverbs Chapter 6 verse 31

They are a hundredfold "...And every one that hath forsaken houses, or brethren, or sisters, or father, or mother, or wife, or children, or lands, for my name's sake, shall receive an hundredfold, and shall inherit everlasting life." Matthew Chapter 19 verse 29

Our mandate is to concentrate on repentance and re-consecration, and God will take care of the matter of restitution. It's difficult to conceive with our finite minds, but Zechariah Chapter 8 verses 12-15 express it best:

"For the seed shall be prosperous; the vine shall give her fruit, and the ground shall give her increase, and the heavens shall give their dew; and I will cause the remnant of this people to possess all these things.

And it shall come to pass, that as ye were a curse among the heathen, O house of Judah, and house of Israel; so will I save you, and ye shall be a blessing: fear not, but let your hands be strong.

For thus saith the Lord of hosts; As I thought to punish you, when your fathers provoked me to wrath, saith the Lord of hosts, and I repented not:

So again have I thought in these days to do well unto Jerusalem and to the house of Judah: fear ye not."

Houses and land and material prosperity cannot heal the ache of the heart of parents bereaved of their children. As our forebears entered into the judgment of the Captivity, their children were ripped away from them and they watched helplessly as they separated, never to be seen again. In other scenarios, our women bore children, but not for the pleasure of nurturing them and watching them grow up. In even crueler actions, men have been castrated, and women sterilized.

God has not forgotten this pain, and he has a great blessing in store for the people. He is going to restore children to those who lost them. Even the recipients won't be able to understand how God has done it, and it won't be as though the children are strangers, either. The prophet Isaiah foretells it like this:

"Sing, O heavens; and be joyful, O earth; and break forth into singing, O mountains: for the Lord hath comforted his people, and will have mercy upon his afflicted. But Zion said, The Lord hath forsaken me, and my Lord hath forgotten me.

Can a woman forget her sucking child, that she should not have compassion on the son of her womb? yea, they may forget, yet will I not forget thee.

Behold, I have graven thee upon the palms of my hands; thy walls are continually before me.

Thy children shall make haste; thy destroyers and they that made thee waste shall go forth of thee. Lift up thine eyes round about, and behold: all these gather themselves together, and come to thee.

As I live, saith the LORD, thou shalt surely clothe thee with them all, as with an ornament, and bind them on thee, as a bride doeth.

For thy waste and thy desolate places and the land of thy destruction, shall even now be too narrow by reason of the inhabitants, and they that swallowed thee up shall be far away. The children which thou shalt have, after thou hast lost the other, shall say again in thine ears, The place is too strait for me: give place to me that I may dwell.

Then shalt thou say in thine heart, Who hath begotten me these, seeing I have lost my children, and am desolate, a captive, and removing to and fro? and who hath brought up these? Behold, I was left alone; these, where had they been?

Thus saith the Lord God, Behold, I will lift up mine hand to the Gentiles, and set up my standard to the people: and they shall bring thy sons in their arms, and thy daughters shall be carried upon their shoulders..." Isaiah Chapter 49 verses 13-22

Remember Judah and Jerusalem are inseparable. God is telling the people, You think I have forgotten about you. I can't ever forget you. And I haven't forgotten about the children you lost, either. Praise God, his ways are higher than our ways, and his thoughts higher than our thoughts. He will bind every broken heart, dry every weeping eye, and satiate the souls of his people, for sorrow and mourning shall flee away.

Hosea Chapter 11 verse 12... Understanding How God Views Us Today

We have reached an important juncture in the prophetic message to Judah. Having obtained a comprehensive understanding of our identity and situational awareness, it is time to review the special relationship we have with God, and understand our purpose and position in these closing days.

Hosea Chapter 11 verse 12 tells us that Judah yet ruleth with God, and is faithful with the saints. The Hebrew word for ruleth used here is 'ruwd,' and means, 'to tramp about, ramble, have the dominion, lord, or rule. In this context, ramble is best defined as, 'taking a course with many turns or windings, as a stream or path'. This means wherever God is moving, whatever the twists and turns, Judah is tramping right along beside him. And as Judah moves with God in holiness and consecration, he is to claim the dominion for the kingdom of God, whether for the purpose of being a faithful witness, or interceding on behalf of his individual family. The word awman in the Hebrew to describe faithful—as in faithful with the saints, means to build up or support; to foster as a parent or nurse; to be firm or faithful, to trust or believe, to be permanent or quiet.

God has placed the Black man in America in a unique position to take the lead in building up and supporting the body of Christ. The dominion is given to our tribe, and the Conqueror came forth from our tribe. In preparing for our Lord's return and the restoration of Israel, we should be preaching, teaching, and exhorting with all diligence. Our people are hungry not only for a pure word, but to understand their purpose. We have all been slumbering through the centuries; aware that things were persistently negative but not understanding why. Now the word goes forth, "Awake thou that sleepest, and arise from the dead, and Christ shall give thee light." Those of us who shine as lights in the world in the midst of a crooked and perverse nation must share the truth of our heritage, and how Christ identifies with us in all things.

The True Awakening...the Sons of Zion vs the Sons of Greece

"And the Lord said, Shall I hide from Abraham that thing which I do;

Seeing that Abraham shall surely become a great and mighty nation, and all the nations of the earth shall be blessed in him?" Genesis Chapter 18 verses 17-18

"Surely the Lord GOD will do nothing, but he revealeth his secret unto his servants the prophets." Amos Chapter 2 verse 7

All around the world, wherever the house of Israel and the house of Judah are found, there is a sense we are on the precipice of monumental change. For those in covenant with the Lord Jesus Christ, the peace that passes all understanding is keeping their hearts and minds through the wars, rumors of wars, famines, and pestilences. For the increasing number of Black men and women in Christ who are also aware of their Hebrew heritage, sustaining strength is drawn from quietness and confidence, and the ability to be still, and know that God is God, and that he will be exalted in the earth. There is great distress of nations and men's hearts are failing them for fear. Many members of the white Western churches are becoming increasingly paranoid and arming themselves. Others are hurrying under the umbrella of the Roman Church, confident that there is security in numbers and unity.

But we are constantly reminded in the scriptures that we have no continuing city here. The same scriptures state that the earth abideth forever. This can only mean that the earth will continue to exist exactly as God has hung it upon nothing in space, but the current ruling structure and organization of the world's nations will undergo total annihilation.

Esau also senses the approach of the Day of the Lord, and his anticipation is tinged with dread. He constructs ever more powerful telescopes, in the hope of intercepting the armies of heaven that are prophesied to accompany the Lord Jesus Christ at his return. He releases doomsday movies which depict the earth obliterated or rendered uninhabitable by nuclear or natural disaster. He produces documentaries promoting interstellar space travel, which he says will be necessary to perpetuate humanity when earth is reduced to a dark, smoking cinder. He is attempting to merge his body with machines, believing trans-humanism will give him a distinct advantage over the frailties of unaltered human physiology. And the ultimate goal of his work with computer/brain interfaces is to achieve the ability to store his consciousness in the cloud; thereby continuing to exist as a sentient being even if his body is destroyed: effectively cheating death and living forever.

This is the fear and terror of the sons of Greece, who have historically trusted in their idols, and placed their confidence in sorcery, technology, military might, materialistic riches, and hedonistic pursuits. None of these things can deliver them in the day of wrath, and the beginning of sorrows is already upon them. Everything they believe in and are laboring to achieve is a lie.

When the heavens are opened revealing the Faithful and True King of Kings and Lord of Lords with his heavenly regiments, this refers to the manifestation of a vast inter-dimensional realm; and a military that dwarfs the combined armies of earth's ages. Telescopes and space weaponry will be useless in withstanding such an assault. Space telemetry will be rendered ineffective due to the shaking of the powers of heaven, the darkening of the sun and moon, displacement of all stars, and the earth reeling to and fro. Yet God has told us not to fear...Psalm Chapter 46 verses 2-3 tell us the earth will be removed, and the mountains dislodged from their foundations from severe oceanic disturbances, but we are to be still, know that he is God, and not fear, for he is our refuge.

Rather than an earth reduced to a cinder by an asteroid or the passing of the famed Planet X, we are exhorted that the meek and the seed of those that fear the Lord shall inherit the earth, and be mighty upon it. Furthermore, in Isaiah Chapter 4 verse 2, we are told, "In that day shall the branch of the Lord be beautiful and glorious, and the fruit of the earth shall be excellent and comely for them that are escaped of Israel."

Just as Noah stayed pure, God is expecting us to remain physically complete and undefiled in our generations. Man is working desperately to merge himself with technology, and enable sentient intelligence in robots which are visually indistinguishable from humans. Trans-humanism is not just the integration of bionic enhancements to the body, but also includes DNA nano-technology where electronic circuits can fuse with the building blocks of life to create self-assembling, self-replicating machinery inside the body. All this is being done in the quest for superiority and to cheat death.

In the dream Daniel interpreted for king Nebuchadnezzar, we recognize this feverish struggle to find the Philosopher's Stone. The king had dreamed of a great image with a gold head, silver torso and arms, brass belly and thighs, iron legs, and feet and toes that were a mixture of iron and clay. The feet and toes represent the last kingdom on earth before the bodily return of the Lord Jesus Christ. Daniel told the king, "Thou sawest till that a stone was cut out without hands, which smote the image upon his feet that were of iron and clay, and brake them to pieces.

Then was the iron, the clay, the brass, the silver, and the gold, broken to pieces together, and became like the chaff of the summer threshing-floors; and the wind carried them away, that no place was found for them: and the stone that smote the image became a great mountain, and filled the whole earth."

He goes on to say, "And as the toes of the feet were part of iron, and part of clay, so the kingdom shall be partly strong, and partly broken.

And whereas thou sawest iron mixed with miry clay, they shall mingle themselves with the seed of men: but they shall not cleave one to another, even as iron is not mixed with clay.

And in the days of these kings shall the God of heaven set up a kingdom, which shall never be destroyed: and the kingdom shall not be left to other people, but it shall break in pieces and consume all these kingdoms, and it shall stand for ever."

Thus the feet and toes mixed with iron (machine) and clay (human flesh) represent the last kingdom on earth before the bodily return of the Lord Jesus Christ. Lest there be any question as to who will remain and rule this kingdom after the legacy of all former kingdoms is obliterated, we need only to refer to Daniel Chapter 7 verse 27:

"And the kingdom and dominion, and the greatness of the kingdom under the whole heaven, shall be given to the people of the saints of the most High, whose kingdom is an everlasting kingdom, and all dominions shall serve and obey him."

This image represented every world government that has ever had dominion over Judah and Israel from Babylon until now. The fact that it was destroyed and reduced to fragments carried away by the wind means world governments are wicked and inferior to the kingdom of God. Psalm Chapter 1 verse 4 proves this, for it says the ungodly are like the chaff which the wind driveth away—mirroring Daniel's words.

Do not be dismayed by the ecological and societal upheaval around you, and do not be either intimidated or enticed by Esau's technological exploits. Remember that in God the Father and Christ are hidden all the treasures of wisdom and knowledge. And if God has chosen you in him, and blessed you with all spiritual blessings in heavenly places in Christ, there is absolutely no reason to walk in fear for the things coming in judgment upon the earth. These things are the predicted precursor to the outpouring of the wrath of God on a wicked and sin-loving world. We are called to perfect our love in him, and let him alone be our fear and dread.

As we awake to our purpose and calling, we have a solemn charge to keep. Our duty is to build up, support, and shepherd the saints. Those who are faithful over a few things will be designated ruler over many in the enduring kingdom on earth. Those who fed and nurtured the household of faith in due season will be granted rulership over the Lord's goods in this kingdom. Those who build upon the precious foundation of Jesus Christ with spiritual works equivalent to gold, silver, and precious stones will receive a commensurate reward. Let's take a moment to look at the spiritual composition of works which are described as priceless building materials.

Gold in the scripture relates to faith. The apostle Peter tells us that suffering and the trial of our faith is more precious than gold tried in the fire. The Lord Jesus advises the lukewarm Laodicean church to buy of him gold tried in the fire as the only way to be rich, and James Chapter 2 verse 5 tells us God has chosen the poor in this world who are rich in faith and heirs of the kingdom. Why are the poor so rich in faith? Because it takes great faith to maintain under Babylon's treacherous economic system without stealing, cheating, or committing crime.

Silver equates to the purity of God's word, the diligent application of it to the soul, testing of faith, and the skillful use of scripture to encourage and admonish the saints. Psalm Chapter 12 verses 6-7 state,

"The words of the Lord are pure words: as silver tried in a furnace of earth, purified seven times.

Thou shalt keep them, O Lord, thou shalt preserve them from this generation for ever."

Psalm Chapter 66 verses 10-11 show it also alludes to testing of integrity under affliction "... For thou, O God, hast proved us: thou hast tried us, as silver is tried. Thou broughtest us into the net; thou laidst affliction upon our loins."

The prophet Zechariah also speaks of an event where the Lord will "...bring the third part through the fire, and will refine them as silver is refined, and will try them as gold is tried: they shall call on my name, and I will hear them: I will say, It is my people: and they shall say, The Lord is my God." Zechariah Chapter 12 verse 9.

Lastly, "A word fitly spoken is like apples of gold in pictures of silver..." Proverbs Chapter 25 verse 11. We need to be mindful in our communications with one another, that the law of kindness should be in our tongue, and that we should speak healing and strength. Those of you who are familiar with colloidal silver know it is a healing and purifying agent. The same should be true with the words we speak, and the way we handle God's pure word.

Precious stones are a type of the love and fellowship between the saints as they commune among themselves in the knowledge of God's works and word. This is brought out in Malachi Chapter 3 verses 16-17...

"Then they that feared the Lord spake often one to another: and the Lord hearkened, and heard it, and a book of remembrance was written before him for them that feared the Lord, and that thought upon his name.

And they shall be mine, saith the Lord of hosts, in that day when I make up my jewels; and I will spare them, as a man spareth his own son that serveth him."

And also in Proverbs Chapter 20 verse 15 "...There is gold, and a multitude of rubies: but the lips of knowledge are a precious jewel."

It is difficult to envision now, but in the enduring Kingdom, all the stereotypes that demeaned us in the Captivity, and even our own cultural practices we established to create a sense of identity will become a distant memory, and eventually wiped away, for God shall remove all shame and humiliation from his people. Even our language will be transformed to a level of clarity and purity hitherto unknown. This is because the negative identifiers associated with us are either a result of or a response to life in Captivity. But any man in Christ is a new creation, old things are passed away, and all things become new. So although the physical Captivity is yet to be turned, the spirit of man can still be regenerated and take on the image of Christ. Not only does new life in Christ begin a mode of conduct governed by the nine fruits of the Spirit: love, joy, peace, longsuffering, gentleness, goodness, faith, meekness, and temperance; it inspires us as Hebrews to inquire more diligently into the peculiar role and relationship bestowed on us by the Father.

Our first and highest calling is to be baptized with the Holy Ghost, as our first century brethren did on the day of Pentecost after Jesus' ascension. Our Elder Brother and Kinsman Redeemer was not mouthing mere words of sentiment when he reminded his disciples he would "send the promise of my Father upon you: but tarry ye in the city of Jerusalem, until ye be endued with power from on high." Per these instructions, they couldn't even leave Jerusalem without it "...And, being assembled together with them, commanded them that they should not depart from Jerusalem, but wait for the promise of the Father, which, saith he, ye have heard of me.

For John truly baptized with water; but ye shall be baptized with the Holy Ghost not many days hence."

Jesus had told his disciples he would petition the Father for the Spirit "... I will pray the Father, and he shall give you another Comforter, that he may abide with you for ever;

Even the Spirit of truth; whom the world cannot receive, because it seeth him not, neither knoweth him: but ye know him; for he dwelleth with you, and shall be in you.

But the Comforter, which is the Holy Ghost, whom the Father will send in my name, he shall teach you all things, and bring all things to your remembrance, whatsoever I have said unto you." John Chapter 16 verses 16 and 26.

Peter acknowledges in his Pentecost sermon that God answered Christ's prayer for the Spirit to be sent to dwell inside his followers...

"Therefore being by the right hand of God exalted, **and having received of the Father the promise of the Holy Ghost, he hath shed forth this, which ye now see and hear**..." and he goes on to say, "the promise is unto you, and to your children, and to all that are afar off, even as many as the Lord our God shall call." The Hebrew word used here for 'promise' means an assent or pledge, especially a divine assurance of good. Jesus was pledging a divine assurance of good when he said the Holy Ghost would be sent to bring all things he taught to our remembrance, and give us power to be his witnesses. He also alluded to the infilling of the

Spirit as recorded in Mark Chapter 16 verse 17 ... "And these signs shall follow them that believe; In my name shall they cast out devils; they shall speak with new tongues..."

This begs the question as to why many who profess faith in Christ ignore this promise, tiptoe around it, or even outright say it is of the devil. When I hear people say they are afraid, or how will they know if it is from God, I wonder if they have ever read Luke Chapter 9 verses 11-13 "...And I say unto you, Ask, and it shall be given you; seek, and ye shall find; knock, and it shall be opened unto you.

For every one that asketh receiveth; and he that seeketh findeth; and to him that knocketh it shall be opened.

If a son shall ask bread of any of you that is a father, will he give him a stone? or if he ask a fish, will he for a fish give him a serpent?

Or if he shall ask an egg, will he offer him a scorpion?

If ye then, being evil, know how to give good gifts unto your children: how much more shall your heavenly Father give the Holy Spirit to them that ask him?"

Bread, fish, eggs, and the Holy Ghost. The first three build up and nourish the body. The other builds up and nourishes the inner man, brings glory to God and points people to His kingdom. Stones, snakes, scorpions, and a manifestation from the devil. The first three injure the physical body, and the other harms the inner man, is counterfeit, and attempts to deceive, and tear down what God has built up. Dear brothers and sisters, do you not think our Father and Creator knows the difference between them? Where is our faith that we think he would harm us?

The promise is to the house of Israel first. The only prerequisite to receiving it is repentance for our sins and genuinely committing to follow the Lord Jesus Christ and keeping his commandments. We need this mighty power to be effective witnesses of true salt and light in the closing days of the Captivity. Some people will say, "Well, I have been a witness without the infilling and I still brought people to Christ." My response to that is, very well. But do you consider your return on spiritual investment might have been thirty, sixty, or a hundredfold if you would have submitted to the instructions of the Lord Jesus?

The first century church knew the infilling of the Holy Ghost was imperative to battle the lying signs and wonders of the day. During that era, a brilliant Greek engineer and physicist named Heron of Alexander was kept busy creating engineering marvels for the pagan temples. His understanding of pneumatics and the laws of physics enabled him to design deity themed figures and props that made temple worship an awe-inspiring experience. The trick was that these lifelike images were controlled by hidden human operatives. To the worshipers however, their movement appeared to be the supernatural power of the gods.

The apostles and first century Christians did not need a temple with a 'man behind the curtain' operating controls. The 'dunamis' was residing within them wherever they went. Dunamis is the Greek word for power associated with the Holy Ghost, and actually means miraculous power force. It is the root word from which we get the modern term 'dynamite.'

Thessalonians Chapter 2 warns us the Son of Perdition will manifest just prior to the end of the age, and his coming will be after the working of Satan with all power and signs and lying wonders. II Timothy Chapter 3 verse 8 indicates Pharaoh's top sorcerers Jannes and Jambres withstood Moses in this same manner when he began to demonstrate the power of God. Revelation Chapter 13 verses 11-16 show us that the false prophet who exercises all the power of the Satanic Son of Perdition will do great wonders, so that he makes fire fall from heaven in the sight of men, and will deceive many people by these miracles. This false prophet will be able to animate an image of his Satanic master—possibly a humanoid robot—and transfer sentient powers to it.

The fear generated by this image's power to converse and kill whoever will not worship it will be what drives the world to receive the Beast's mark in their right hand or forehead. Jesus cautioned us in Matthew Chapter 24 verse 24 that if it were possible, these deceptions would fool the very elect. That's how powerful the end of days' sorcery will be. But the Holy Ghost is the Spirit of truth, and leads and guides only into truth. The advantage the elect of God will have is the ability to clearly discern between the real and the counterfeit through the leading of the Holy Ghost.

This is a spiritual warfare, and it is dangerous to attempt to minister or maintain conquered spiritual ground in an environment that is the legal domicile of devils, hold of every foul spirit, and cage of every unclean and hateful bird without the infilling of the Holy Ghost. Hell is an ever enlarging domain, and if permitted, would encroach upon and invade the spiritual dominion of the body of Christ. It has already effectively overrun institutional Christianity, and according to Matthew Chapter 16 verses 17-18, the only barrier that prevents it from prevailing against the spiritual church is the revelation that the Lord Jesus Christ is the Son of the living God. Only God can reveal this to a man or woman as something acknowledged from the heart, not just spoken from the lips. I Corinthians Chapter 12 verse 3 explains that this revelation comes from the Holy Ghost "...Wherefore I give you to understand, that no man speaking by the Spirit of God calleth Jesus accursed: and that no man can say that Jesus is the Lord, but by the Holy Ghost.

The Holy Ghost is the power that will keep our minds and guard our steps from slipping even when the warfare is most intense. We are kidding ourselves if we imagine we can be an effective witness without it, for the enemy is pulling out all stops and the battle is increasing in ferocity as he sees his reign of terror drawing to a close. Warring against principalities, powers, rulers of the darkness of this world, and spiritual wickedness in high places without the infilling of the Spirit makes no more sense than being charged by a lion and having a high-powered rifle at your disposal, but choosing to fight the beast with your bare hands instead.

If you are involved in a fellowship that teaches that the baptism of the Holy Ghost was only for the first century church, or that the initial evidence of receiving it by speaking in an unknown tongue is of the devil, I ask you to read the Gospel of John chapters 14 through 16, chapter 4 verse 24, the Gospel of Matthew chapter 3 verse 11, and the Acts of the Apostles. Then ask yourself 'qui bono'...who profits? Who stands to gain the most by discouraging you from receiving the baptism of God's spirit: the kingdom of God, or the kingdom of darkness? Who benefits the most from a church that has an outward form of godliness, but denies the power thereof? My prayer is that those of Israel who profess faith in Christ will ask God to fill them with his Spirit, for Romans Chapter 8 verses 9-11 warn us it is the seal of the authentic

Christian, the same Spirit that raised Christ from the dead, and the same spirit that will resurrect us because it dwells in us.

We also have a true calling as herald of praise unto our God. In fact, Judah means thanks and praise. Music—and I might add loud, with beat and rhythm—is an identifying characteristic of the people of Judah and Israel and intrinsic to us as a whole. It is a gift given us from God not only for his exaltation, but as supernatural weaponry to assault and overpower the realm of spiritual darkness. Today, when most people think of Black music in the West, rhythm and blues, secular rap, jazz, reggae and soca are the venues which quickly come to mind. Of course, we excel at these music forms; but I submit to you that they are all the outcome of Captivity, and a distortion of the divine gift bestowed on us. When the Captivity is turned, and God has satiated every soul, these types of music will have no more place, nor will they be missed. But there will still be much music and singing and dancing; new songs and dances yet to be expressed, because we have never known the experience of true freedom. Let's listen to Jeremiah, the young prophet, describe this time to come:

"The Lord hath appeared of old unto me, saying, Yea, I have loved thee with an everlasting love: therefore with lovingkindness have I drawn thee.

Again I will build thee, and thou shalt be built, O virgin of Israel: thou shalt again be adorned with thy tabrets, and shalt go forth in the dances of them that make merry.

For thus saith the Lord; Sing with gladness for Jacob, and shout among the chief of the nations: publish ye, praise ye, and say, O Lord, save thy people, the remnant of Israel.

For the Lord hath redeemed Jacob, and ransomed him from the hand of him that was stronger than he.

Therefore they shall come and sing in the height of Zion, and shall flow together to the goodness of the Lord, for wheat, and for wine, and for oil, and for the young of the flock and of the herd: and their soul shall be as a watered garden; and they shall not sorrow any more at all.

Then shall the virgin rejoice in the dance, both young men and old together: for I will turn their mourning into joy, and will comfort them, and make them rejoice from their sorrow.

And I will satiate the soul of the priests with fatness, and my people shall be satisfied with my goodness, saith the Lord." (Excerpts from Jeremiah Chapter 31.)

Tambourines, dancing, and God himself commanding the people to sing and shout! Young and old dancing together, feasting, rejoicing and literally no more sorrow...this calls for a whole new musical venue.

In Psalm Chapter 68 verses 24-25, David has a prophetic vision of God's victory procession "...They have seen thy goings, O God; even the goings of my God, my King, in the sanctuary. The singers went before, the players on instruments followed after; among them were the damsels playing with timbrels.

So there we see a picture of the processional order in the sanctuary to come; singers in the front, musicians behind them, and young girls playing tambourines in the mix. That is the music of rejoicing. But Judah will also arm up with music for warfare. I know it is difficult to fathom instruments that wield the same type of power as military armaments and a song so formidable that armies are rendered powerless, but that is exactly what the scriptures teach. Isaiah Chapter 30 verses 29-32 speak to this effect in the day the Lord binds up the breach of his people, and heals the stroke of their wound "...Ye shall have a song, as in the night when a holy solemnity is kept; and gladness of heart, as when one goeth with a pipe to come into the mountain of the Lord, to the mighty One of Israel.

And the Lord shall cause his glorious voice to be heard, and shall shew the lighting down of his arm, with the indignation of his anger, and with the flame of a devouring fire, with scattering, and tempest, and hailstones.

For through the voice of the LORD shall the Assyrian be beaten down, which smote with a rod.

And in every place where the grounded staff shall pass, which the LORD shall lay upon him, it shall be with tabrets and harps: and in battles of shaking will he fight with it."

Psalm Chapter 149 verses 6-9 also bear out this truth "...Let the high praises of God be in their mouth, and a two-edged sword in their hand; To execute vengeance upon the heathen, and punishments upon the people; To bind their kings with chains, and their nobles with fetters of iron; To execute upon them the judgment written: this honour have all his saints. Praise ye the Lord." I had to smile as I wrote this, because it occurred to me that in movies there is always some type of action music playing to set the mood or escalate the intensity of a fight, chase, or battle; but everyone knows in real life that's not what happens. But in the dreadful reality of the Day of the Lord, Esau's people and all the nations that join themselves to him to fight against God will have to deal with the mind-numbing effect of inter-dimensional high praise; and the sheer purity and beauty of it will torment their wicked minds; leaving them immobilized like standing sheaves before the reaper.

If you sing, worship God in the beauty of holiness, sing from the depths of your spirit, and let him anoint you with favor from heaven. Do not try to imitate the ungodly who may have mastered powerful vocal techniques, but are appealing to the sensual aspect of the hearer. Ministering unto the Lord and the body of Christ is not about sending chills down people's spines. It is about bringing such a godly impression that hearts are nudged to repentance, the weary are strengthened to keep fighting the good fight of faith, and the fallow ground of the conscience is broken to receive the good seed of the word of God.

If you write, write the psalms God has given you, and the mighty works he has done in your life, whether you are bringing a hymn, high praise, reflective worship, or gospel rap. Do not draw from the samples and inspiration of the ungodly. They are not necessary to minister effectively for the Lord; the scriptures and the Holy Ghost should be the dynamics energizing your music and lyrical content. And it grieves God's heart when we mix the profane with the holy.

The same for musical instruments; do not let carnal men tell you musical instruments are of the devil. The model for earth is heaven; harps, trumpets, and glorious harmony abound there; and those are just the instruments we know about. Pipes and tambourines are part of the conquest and worship during the installation of the kingdom of God on earth. Play as unto the Lord, and play skillfully. Make a joyful noise unto him with the most splendid melodiousness you can, for God dwells in the midst of praises, and inhabits the praise of his people.

We are also a type of the intercessor for our people. Of course, the Lord Jesus Christ, who is our faithful High Priest, is alive forever to intercede before God's throne. But there are two Old Testament examples I would like to present. The first involves Judah's intercession on behalf of Benjamin when Joseph threatened to take Benjamin as a life-time slave. Judah offered himself in Benjamin's place. We know that at that point Joseph broke down emotionally and disclosed his identity to his brethren, and the entire family was eventually reunited in Egypt. My point is that of all the brethren present, Judah came forward to make that type of sacrifice. He was a type of the Lamb of God who would one day lay down his life for his brethren. Jesus said there is no greater love than that.

The second illustration shows how Judah's presence was the only buffer between preservation and destruction. This incident took place during the reign of king Jehoram of the Northern kingdom. His father Ahab had conquered Moab during his reign, but after Ahab died, Moab rebelled and stopped paying a heavy tribute in livestock. Jehoram wanted to put down the revolt, but he was afraid to take on Moab single-handedly. So he solicited the righteous king Jehoshaphat—ruler of the southern kingdom Judah, to join him in the attack. Their approach on Moab meant they would have to take the wilderness route through Edom. Edom was not at war with Judah at that time; most likely due to Jehoshaphat's right standing with God, and the king of Edom joined them on the exploit.

After seven days in the field, they reached an area where there was no water for the host or the cattle that were following them. Faced with the specter of death before they even joined battle, the king of Israel said, "Alas! That the Lord hath called these three kings together, to deliver them into the hand of Moab!

But Jehoshaphat said, Is there not here a prophet of the Lord, that we may inquire of the Lord by him? And one of the king of Israel's servants answered and said, Here is Elisha the son of Shaphat, which poured water on the hands of Elijah.

And Jehoshaphat said, The word of the Lord is with him. So the king of Israel and Jehoshaphat and the king of Edom went down to him.

And Elisha said unto the king of Israel, What have I to do with thee? get thee to the prophets of thy father, and to the prophets of thy mother. And the king of Israel said unto him, Nay: for the Lord hath called these three kings together, to deliver them into the hand of Moab. And Elisha said, As the Lord of hosts liveth, before whom I stand, surely, were it not that I regard the presence of Jehoshaphat the king of Judah, I would not look toward thee, nor see thee.

But now bring me a minstrel. And it came to pass, when the minstrel played, that the hand of the Lord came upon him. And he said, Thus saith the Lord, Make this valley full of ditches.

For thus saith the Lord, Ye shall not see wind, neither shall ye see rain; yet that valley shall be filled with water, that ye may drink, both ye, and your cattle, and your beasts.

And this is but a light thing in the sight of the Lord: he will deliver the Moabites also into your hand...And it came to pass in the morning, when the meat offering was offered, that, behold, there came water by the way of Edom, and the country was filled with water." I Kings Chapter 3 verses 10-18 and 20

We can see from this account that the righteous presence of Judah meant the difference between life and death for the northern kingdom, and Judah's neighbor Edom. But there are several other interesting points to touch on, also. One is that a righteous man needs to preserve the things of righteousness for the righteous. In other words, Jesus warned us not to cast our pearls before swine, and the apostle Paul admonished us to do good unto all men, but especially to the household of faith.

Elisha didn't even want to speak to the king of Israel, or the king of Edom. Everyone was being gracious and approaching with a supplicatory spirit, but Elisha knew both the king of Israel and the king of Edom were idolaters at heart. I can also say with certainty that the presence of Judah in this Captivity has been the factor postponing the disastrous fate of this wicked nation. The day Judah and the tribes are sealed, it is a wrap for the West. Neither will attempts to hold us hostage stave off the inevitable, for God will say, "For I am the Lord thy God, the Holy One of Israel, thy Saviour: I gave Egypt for thy ransom, Ethiopia and Seba for thee.

Since thou wast precious in my sight, thou hast been honourable, and I have loved thee: therefore will I give men for thee, and people for thy life.

Fear not: for I am with thee: I will bring thy seed from the east, and gather thee from the west;

I will say to the north, Give up; and to the south, Keep not back: bring my sons from far, and my daughters from the ends of the earth...Isaiah Chapter 43 verses 3-6

In those days the house of Judah shall walk with the house of Israel, and they shall come together out of the land of the north to the land that I have given for an inheritance unto your fathers...Jeremiah Chapter 3 verse 18

Also...in that day there shall be a root of Jesse, which shall stand for an ensign of the people; to it shall the Gentiles seek: and his rest shall be glorious.

And it shall come to pass in that day, that the Lord shall set his hand again the second time to recover the remnant of his people, which shall be left, from Assyria, and from Egypt, and from Pathros, and from Cush, and from Elam, and from Shinar, and from Hamath, and from the islands of the sea.

And he shall set up an ensign for the nations, and shall assemble the outcasts of Israel, and gather together the dispersed of Judah from the four corners of the earth..."

Isaiah Chapter 11 verses 10-12

We also see the role of music in conjunction with the prophetic gift. This was certainly nothing new, as David was a psalmist and prophet. But I want to point out that these two ministries often operate hand in hand, complimenting each other.

Interestingly, note how when God brought the water, he orchestrated it so it came up from Edom. Despite Edom's idolatry and historical antipathy toward Judah and Israel, God provided a witness of his goodness in their own territory. Most likely, Edom was able to fill their vessels with the surplus as they returned home from the battle. Jesus reminds us in Matthew Chapter 5 verse 45 that the Father "maketh his sun to rise on the evil and on the good, and sendeth rain on the just and on the unjust."

Bottom line, you can see we hold a significant role as intercessor. Now is the time to exercise this capacity to its fullest; praying without ceasing for our families and loved ones, and the lost. Pray not only for those you know, but for those whom God intersects in your life, albeit momentarily. It may be that your prayer is the only prayer being lifted on their behalf. It may be your prayer that shifts events in the unseen realm, so that individual repents and gives God the glory in their life.

Lastly, Judah is commissioned to have dominion in the earth. Jacob's prophecy over Judah states it is our tribe that our brethren of the other tribes will praise; our hand that will ultimately strangle the enemies, and that from out of our stock would come forth the Redeemer (For Judah prevailed above his brethren, and of him came the chief ruler), and unto him will the gathering of the people be. Some centuries later as Moses blessed the tribes, he would invoke the Lord to hear the voice of Judah, and bring him unto his people...to let his hands be sufficient for him, and be a help to him from his enemies. Why would Moses ask God to bring Judah to his people? Because not every one of the tribe was brought across the Atlantic Ocean; and the other descendants still abide on the African continent or are scattered among other nations.

Judah was called first by God to go up against the Canaanites, and the victory was assured in advance. In Psalm Chapter 60 verse 7 God tells us Judah is his law-giver. Psalm Chapter 76 verse 1 tells us God is known in Judah, and his name is great in Israel. Psalm Chapter 14 verse 2 tells us when Israel went out of Egypt, the house of Jacob from a people of strange language; Judah was God's sanctuary, and Israel his dominion. And it says this exodus and God's abiding presence upon the tribe actually had a physical impact on the terrain. Joel Chapter 3 verse 20 says Judah shall dwell for ever, and Jerusalem from generation to generation. Judah is also the first named in the registry of the twelve thousand sealed out of each tribe in the end of days.

In the Testament of Judah, we draw unique insight into his divine right of rulership...In Chapter 3 verse 34-35 of his death-bed exhortation, he states "And Isaac, the father of my father, blessed me to be king in Israel, and Jacob further blessed me in like manner.

And I know that from me shall the kingdom be established."

In Chapter 4 verses 1-3 he states, "And now, my children, I command you, love Levi, that ye may abide, and exalt not yourselves against him, lest ye be utterly destroyed.

For to me the Lord gave the kingdom, and to him the priesthood, and He set the kingdom beneath the priesthood. To me He gave the things upon the earth; to him the things in the heavens."

In verses 12-14 he declares, "And there shall be continual wars in Israel; **and among men of another race shall my kingdom be brought to an end, until the salvation of Israel shall come.**

Until the appearing of the God of righteousness, that Jacob, and all the Gentiles may rest in peace. And He shall guard the might of my kingdom for ever; for the Lord sware to me with an oath that

He would not destroy the kingdom from my seed for ever."

Ours then, is a distinct role of leadership among the tribes of Israel, **even in Captivity**. Not in the sense of fleshly domination such as that which characterizes the oppressor; but as Spirit-filled vessels of praise and prayer while we wait for the kingdom to manifest on earth.

Let Brotherly Love Continue… Judah's Bond with Levi and Benjamin

Many who have studied the Hebrew heritage of the Black man will tell you the geographical location of the tribes of Israel can be pinpointed today based on identifying characteristics and blessings spoken over them in the Old Testament. Following this line of reasoning, we find the Black man in America issuing from the tribe of Judah, Blacks in the West Indies from the tribe of Benjamin, and those in Haiti from the tribe of Levi. If we search the scriptures, we find a fascinating bond of antiquity evidencing descendants from each of these tribes resided in the prime slave harvesting areas of West Africa. For Judah, Benjamin, and Levi represented the populace of Jerusalem after the kingdom split, and many fled west into Africa before its fall between 67 and 70 A.D.

In the previous section, we saw that even before the enslavement in Egypt, Judah and Levi had a unique understanding of their prophesied roles as kings and priests. We also noted Judah's intercession on behalf of his younger brother Benjamin. And when the tribes received their allotted inheritance, Benjamin's lot fell next to Judah, so there was a close association between the two tribes from early on. We also note that when Moses blessed the tribes before his death, the blessings of Judah, Levi, and Benjamin are consecutive in succession.

When Satan incited David to number Israel, his captain, Joab, refused to include the tribes of Levi and Benjamin. And who can forget David's great friendship with Jonathan, son of Saul? Jonathan, who was of the tribe of Benjamin—did everything in his power to shield David from his father's delusional wrath… even to the point of alienating himself from his father. David grieved greatly when Jonathan died in battle against the Philistines.

After Solomon's death and the kingdom split, his son Rehoboam had a distinct military advantage because of the presence of Benjamin alongside Judah: "And in every several city he put shields and spears, and made them exceeding strong, having Judah and Benjamin on his side..." II Chronicles Chapter 11 verse 12. There was also a massive exodus of Levites out of the northern kingdom "...And the priests and the Levites that were in all Israel resorted to him out of all their coasts.

For the Levites left their suburbs and their possession, and came to Judah and Jerusalem: for Jeroboam and his sons had cast them off from executing the priest's office unto the Lord:

And he ordained him priests for the high places, and for the devils, and for the calves which he had made..." II Chronicles Chapter 11 verses 13-15

Esther, who was wedded to the Persian king Ahasuerus, was of the tribe of Benjamin. And when king Cyrus of Persia gave the decree to rebuild the temple at Jerusalem, "Then rose up the chief of the fathers of Judah and Benjamin, and the priests, and the Levites, with all them whose spirit God had raised, to go up to build the house of the Lord which is in Jerusalem..." Ezra Chapter 1 verse 5. The apostle Paul was of the stock of Benjamin, and a zealous witness for the Lion of the Tribe of Judah.

In the following prophecy where all three tribes are mentioned, Jeremiah presents a beautiful picture of God's faithfulness and his intent to restore us to the land promised to the fathers:

"And I will cause the captivity of Judah and the captivity of Israel to return, and will build them, as at the first.

And I will cleanse them from all their iniquity, whereby they have sinned against me; and I will pardon all their iniquities, whereby they have sinned, and whereby they have transgressed against me.

And it shall be to me a name of joy, a praise and an honour before all the nations of the earth, which shall hear all the good that I do unto them: and they shall fear and tremble for all the goodness and for all the prosperity that I procure unto it.

In the cities of the mountains, in the cities of the vale, and in the cities of the south, and in the land of Benjamin, and in the places about Jerusalem, and in the cities of Judah, shall the flocks pass again under the hands of him that telleth them, saith the Lord.

Behold, the days come, saith the Lord, that I will perform that good thing which I have promised unto the house of Israel and to the house of Judah.

In those days, and at that time, will I cause the Branch of righteousness to grow up unto David; and he shall execute judgment and righteousness in the land.

In those days shall Judah be saved, and Jerusalem shall dwell safely: and this is the name wherewith she shall be called, The Lord our righteousness.

For thus saith the Lord; David shall never want a man to sit upon the throne of the house of Israel; Neither shall the priests the Levites want a man before me to offer burnt offerings, and to kindle meat offerings, and to do sacrifice continually. And the word of the LORD came unto Jeremiah, saying,

Thus saith the LORD; If ye can break my covenant of the day, and my covenant of the night, and that there should not be day and night in their season;

Then may also my covenant be broken with David my servant, that he should not have a son to reign upon his throne; and with the Levites the priests, my ministers.

As the host of heaven cannot be numbered, neither the sand of the sea measured: so will I multiply the seed of David my servant, and the Levites that minister unto me. Moreover the word of the LORD came to Jeremiah, saying,

Considerest thou not what this people have spoken, saying, The two families which the Lord hath chosen, he hath even cast them off? thus they have despised my people, that they should be no more a nation before them.

Thus saith the Lord; If my covenant be not with day and night, and if I have not appointed the ordinances of heaven and earth;

Then will I cast away the seed of Jacob, and David my servant, so that I will not take any of his seed to be rulers over the seed of Abraham, Isaac, and Jacob: for I will cause their Captivity to return, and have mercy on them..." Jeremiah Chapter 33 verses 7-9 and verses 13-26.

Fast forwarding to the Captivity, Marcus Garvey—who rallied our people and instilled a sense of pride in the midst of Jim Crow oppression—came to us from Jamaica, and the fiery Stokely Carmichael of the more recent civil rights movement was a native of Trinidad.

God has called forth those things which have not yet come to pass as though they already are, because he has decreed them from the beginning, and his word is forever settled in heaven. The theme of the restoration of kings and priests resonates throughout Jeremiah's prophecy; as the two families which the Lord hath chosen refers to Levi and Judah. Benjamin is specifically referred to in reference to his designated territory. This is of profound importance, because although we are presently scattered, God is already speaking of our future repatriation, both geographically and in the rendering of service.

I encourage you to begin praying for our brothers and sisters in the Caribbean, in Haiti, and in Jamaica. Pray for repentance, re-consecration, and revival. Pray for the ability to stand firm under testing and persecution, for the effectual fervent prayer of a righteous man avails much. According to this passage of scripture, the very fact that the sun rises and sets each day is a witness that our Captivity will be turned and we will be restored to the land of our forefathers. Hosea Chapter 11 verses 10-11 put it this way: "They shall walk after the Lord: he shall roar like a lion: when he shall roar, **then the children shall tremble <u>from the west</u>**. They shall tremble as a bird out of Egypt, and as a dove out of the land of Assyria: and I will place them in their houses, saith the Lord."

Tested and Proven Prayers that Judah Must Pray

If you have walked with God for any length of time, you know that prayer is a good thing, and prayer works. Did you also know we are to pray for the turning of our Captivity and the restoration of our nation? This is what the Lord Jesus Christ was speaking of when he taught his disciples to pray "thy kingdom come, thy will be done on earth as it is in heaven." God has chosen Mount Zion as his earthly regal throne, and Jerusalem as the city peculiar to him; it logically follows he desires to dwell among his people, and that is just one guarantee among many that we will be returning to the land of our forefathers. This is borne out in Micah Chapter 4 verse 8: "And thou, O tower of the flock, the strong hold of the daughter of Zion, unto thee shall it come, even the first dominion; the kingdom shall come to the daughter of Jerusalem."

God knows that once we consider and understand the reason for our present estate, we will have the impetus to petition him for deliverance. For too many years, our people have been taught they have nothing more to look forward to than an ethereal existence in heaven after death. Nothing could be further from the truth. This is not to say the saved righteous won't have unfettered access to the heavenlies. It just means that's not the sum total of what salvation and righteousness is about. We were created to exist on the earth: just without the limits of a body compromised by the effects of weakness, aging, and death in an environment subject to decay and imbalance. God's original intention was that we experience non-stop abundant life.

However, all things must be done in divine order. We have no right to ask God for the manifestation of the kingdom without acknowledging our sin as the reason for its postponement. The early Hebrew disciples thought that perhaps Jesus' resurrection signaled the reestablishment of Israel's dominion over the earth...thus they inquired, "Lord, wilt thou at this time restore again the kingdom to Israel?" Acts Chapter 1 verse 6. Of course, we know from the events that unfolded that the divine plan was for the disciples to be supernaturally empowered and the gospel preached to all nations, before the end could come. The disciples did not know the times and the seasons; that is, they were not aware Israel would go into Captivity in the West in an unknown and unnamed nation, that all the Law and Prophets might be fulfilled. From this end of the time-line then, we must first raise the prayer of repentance.

This is a difficult subject for the descendants of Israel, as most people have no point of reference to understand why they must repent; especially those to whom this book is directed— people who are already pursuing a lifestyle of righteousness and holiness. What I can tell you, is that such a prayer is in line with acknowledging God's just judgment, and prayers of this nature have always turned God's heart in favor toward his people. If you know that your life is righteous, like prophets such as Daniel, Ezra, and Jeremiah, then your prayer of repentance is for the sins of your forebears, and others in Israel. You may ask, why must I intercede for what they did? Simple answer: because many were judged in the flesh and cut off, and their descendants are not even aware a breach exists that needs to be repaired. Following are examples of acknowledgment of sin as relates to deliverance from Captivity.

Solomon's prayer at the dedication of the temple...I Kings Chapter 8 verses 46-51

"If they sin against thee, (for there is no man that sinneth not,) and thou be angry with them, and deliver them to the enemy, so that they carry them away captives unto the land of the enemy, far or near;

Yet if they shall bethink themselves in the land whither they were carried captives, and repent, and make supplication unto thee in the land of them that carried them captives, saying, We have sinned, and have done perversely, we have committed wickedness;

And so return unto thee with all their heart, and with all their soul, in the land of their enemies, which led them away captive, and pray unto thee toward their land, which thou gavest unto their fathers, the city which thou hast chosen, and the house which I have built for thy name:

Then hear thou their prayer and their supplication in heaven thy dwelling place, and maintain their cause,

And forgive thy people that have sinned against thee, and all their transgressions wherein they have transgressed against thee, and give them compassion before them who carried them captive, that they may have compassion on them:

For they be thy people, and thine inheritance, which thou broughtest forth out of Egypt, from the midst of the furnace of iron..."

Nehemiah's prayer before he arrived to rebuild Jerusalem... Nehemiah Chapter 2 verses 4-11

"And it came to pass, when I heard these words, that I sat down and wept, and mourned certain days, and fasted, and prayed before the God of heaven,

And said, I beseech thee, O Lord God of heaven, the great and terrible God, that keepeth covenant and mercy for them that love him and observe his commandments:

Let thine ear now be attentive, and thine eyes open, that thou mayest hear the prayer of thy servant, which I pray before thee now, day and night, for the children of Israel thy servants, and confess the sins of the children of Israel, which we have sinned against thee: both I and my father's house have sinned.

We have dealt very corruptly against thee, and have not kept the commandments, nor the statutes, nor the judgments, which thou commandedst thy servant Moses.

Remember, I beseech thee, the word that thou commandedst thy servant Moses, saying, If ye transgress, I will scatter you abroad among the nations:

But if ye turn unto me, and keep my commandments, and do them; though there were of you cast out unto the uttermost part of the heaven, yet will I gather them from thence, and will bring them unto the place that I have chosen to set my name there.

Now these are thy servants and thy people, whom thou hast redeemed by thy great power, and by thy strong hand.

O Lord, I beseech thee, let now thine ear be attentive to the prayer of thy servant, and to the prayer of thy servants, who desire to fear thy name: and prosper, I pray thee, thy servant this day, and grant him mercy in the sight of this man. For I was the king's cupbearer."

Excerpts from the confession of Israel and testimony of the Levites...Nehemiah Chapter 9 verses 2-3, 16-21, 30-37

"And the seed of Israel separated themselves from all strangers, and stood and confessed their sins, and the iniquities of their fathers.

And they stood up in their place, and read in the book of the law of the Lord their God one fourth part of the day; and another fourth part they confessed, and worshipped the Lord their God.

But they and our fathers dealt proudly, and hardened their necks, and hearkened not to thy commandments,

And refused to obey, neither were mindful of thy wonders that thou didst among them; but hardened their necks, and in their rebellion appointed a captain to return to their bondage: but thou art a God ready to pardon, gracious and merciful, slow to anger, and of great kindness, and forsookest them not.

Yea, when they had made them a molten calf, and said, This is thy God that brought thee up out of Egypt, and had wrought great provocations;

Yet thou in thy manifold mercies forsookest them not in the wilderness: the pillar of the cloud departed not from them by day, to lead them in the way; neither the pillar of fire by night, to shew them light, and the way wherein they should go.

Thou gavest also thy good spirit to instruct them, and withheldest not thy manna from their mouth, and gavest them water for their thirst.

Yea, forty years didst thou sustain them in the wilderness, so that they lacked nothing; their clothes waxed not old, and their feet swelled not.

Yet many years didst thou forbear them, and testifiedst against them by thy spirit in thy prophets: yet would they not give ear: therefore gavest thou them into the hand of the people of the lands.

Nevertheless for thy great mercies' sake thou didst not utterly consume them, nor forsake them; for thou art a gracious and merciful God.

Now therefore, our God, the great, the mighty, and the terrible God, who keepest covenant and mercy, let not all the trouble seem little before thee, that hath come upon us, on our kings, on our princes, and on our priests, and on our prophets, and on our fathers, and on all thy people, since the time of the kings of Assyria unto this day.

Howbeit thou art just in all that is brought upon us; for thou hast done right, but we have done wickedly:

Neither have our kings, our princes, our priests, nor our fathers, kept thy law, nor hearkened unto thy commandments and thy testimonies, wherewith thou didst testify against them.

For they have not served thee in their kingdom, and in thy great goodness that thou gavest them, and in the large and fat land which thou gavest before them, neither turned they from their wicked works.

Behold we are servants this day, and for the land that thou gavest unto our fathers to eat the fruit thereof and the good thereof, behold, we are servants in it:

And it yieldeth much increase unto the kings whom thou hast set over us because of our sins: also they have dominion over our bodies, and over our cattle, at their pleasure, and we are in great distress."

The Lamentation of Jeremiah Chapter 5...

"Remember, O Lord, what is come upon us: consider, and behold our reproach. Our inheritance is turned to strangers, our houses to aliens.

We are orphans and fatherless, our mothers are as widows.

We have drunken our water for money; our wood is sold unto us. Our necks are under persecution: we labour, and have no rest.

We have given the hand to the Egyptians, and to the Assyrians, to be satisfied with bread. Our fathers have sinned, and are not; **and we have borne their iniquities**.

Servants have ruled over us: there is none that doth deliver us out of their hand. We gat our bread with the peril of our lives because of the sword of the wilderness. Our skin was black like an oven because of the terrible famine.

They ravished the women in Zion, and the maids in the cities of Judah. Princes are hanged up by their hand: the faces of elders were not honoured. They took the young men to grind, and the children fell under the wood.

The elders have ceased from the gate, the young men from their musick. The joy of our heart is ceased; our dance is turned into mourning.

The crown is fallen from our head: woe unto us, that we have sinned! For this our heart is faint; for these things our eyes are dim.

Because of the mountain of Zion, which is desolate, the foxes walk upon it. Thou, O Lord, remainest for ever; thy throne from generation to generation. Wherefore dost thou forget us for ever, and forsake us so long time?

Turn thou us unto thee, O Lord, and we shall be turned; renew our days as of old."

The prayer of Daniel...Daniel Chapter 9 verses 3-19

"And I set my face unto the Lord God, to seek by prayer and supplications, with fasting, and sackcloth, and ashes:

And I prayed unto the Lord my God, and made my confession, and said, O Lord, the great and dreadful God, keeping the covenant and mercy to them that love him, and to them that keep his commandments;

We have sinned, and have committed iniquity, and have done wickedly, and have rebelled, even by departing from thy precepts and from thy judgments:

Neither have we hearkened unto thy servants the prophets, which spake in thy name to our kings, our princes, and our fathers, and to all the people of the land.

O Lord, righteousness belongeth unto thee, but unto us confusion of faces, as at this day; to the men of Judah, and to the inhabitants of Jerusalem, and unto all Israel, that are near, and that are far off, through all the countries whither thou hast driven them, because of their trespass that they have trespassed against thee.

O Lord, to us belongeth confusion of face, to our kings, to our princes, and to our fathers, because we have sinned against thee.

To the Lord our God belong mercies and forgivenesses, though we have rebelled against him;

Neither have we obeyed the voice of the Lord our God, to walk in his laws, which he set before us by his servants the prophets.

Yea, all Israel have transgressed thy law, even by departing, that they might not obey thy voice; therefore the curse is poured upon us, and the oath that is written in the law of Moses the servant of God, because we have sinned against him.

And he hath confirmed his words, which he spake against us, and against our judges that judged us, by bringing upon us a great evil: for under the whole heaven hath not been done as hath been done upon Jerusalem.

As it is written in the law of Moses, all this evil is come upon us: yet made we not our prayer before the Lord our God, that we might turn from our iniquities, and understand thy truth.

Therefore hath the Lord watched upon the evil, and brought it upon us: for the Lord our God is righteous in all his works which he doeth: for we obeyed not his voice.

And now, O Lord our God, that hast brought thy people forth out of the land of Egypt with a mighty hand, and hast gotten thee renown, as at this day; we have sinned, we have done wickedly. O Lord, according to all thy righteousness, I beseech thee, let thine anger and thy fury be turned away from thy city Jerusalem, thy holy mountain: because for our sins, and for the iniquities of our fathers, Jerusalem and thy people are become a reproach to all that are about us.

Now therefore, O our God, hear the prayer of thy servant, and his supplications, and cause thy face to shine upon thy sanctuary that is desolate, for the Lord's sake.

O my God, incline thine ear, and hear; open thine eyes, and behold our desolations, and the city which is called by thy name: for we do not present our supplications before thee for our righteousnesses, but for thy great mercies.

O Lord, hear; O Lord, forgive; O Lord, hearken and do; defer not, for thine own sake, O my God: for thy city and thy people are called by thy name. And whiles I was speaking, and praying, and confessing my sin and the sin of my people Israel, and presenting my supplication before the Lord my God for the holy mountain of my God;

Yea, whiles I was speaking in prayer, even the man Gabriel, whom I had seen in the vision at the beginning, being caused to fly swiftly, touched me about the time of the evening oblation.

And he informed me, and talked with me, and said, O Daniel, I am now come forth to give thee skill and understanding..."

The testimony of the prophet Joel...Joel Chapter 2 verses 10-19

"The earth shall quake before them; the heavens shall tremble: the sun and the moon shall be dark, and the stars shall withdraw their shining:

And the Lord shall utter his voice before his army: for his camp is very great: for he is strong that executeth his word: for the day of the Lord is great and very terrible; and who can abide it?

Therefore also now, saith the Lord, turn ye even to me with all your heart, and with fasting, and with weeping, and with mourning:

And rend your heart, and not your garments, and turn unto the Lord your God: for he is gracious and merciful, slow to anger, and of great kindness, and repenteth him of the evil.

Who knoweth if he will return and repent, and leave a blessing behind him; even a meat offering and a drink offering unto the Lord your God?

Blow the trumpet in Zion, sanctify a fast, call a solemn assembly:

Gather the people, sanctify the congregation, assemble the elders, gather the children, and those that suck the breasts: let the bridegroom go forth of his chamber, and the bride out of her closet.

Let the priests, the ministers of the Lord, weep between the porch and the altar, and let them say, Spare thy people, O Lord, and give not thine heritage to reproach, that the heathen should rule over them: wherefore should they say among the people, Where is their God?

Then will the Lord be jealous for his land, and pity his people.

Yea, the Lord will answer and say unto his people, Behold, I will send you corn, and wine, and oil, and ye shall be satisfied therewith: and I will no more make you a reproach among the heathen..."

The testimony of Micah...Micah Chapter 7 verses 7-9 and 18-20

"Therefore I will look unto the Lord; I will wait for the God of my salvation: my God will hear me.

Rejoice not against me, O mine enemy: when I fall, I shall arise; when I sit in darkness, the Lord shall be a light unto me.

I will bear the indignation of the Lord, because I have sinned against him, until he plead my cause, and execute judgment for me: he will bring me forth to the light, and I shall behold his righteousness. Who is a God like unto thee, that pardoneth iniquity, and passeth by the transgression of the remnant of his heritage? he retaineth not his anger for ever, because he delighteth in mercy.

He will turn again, he will have compassion upon us; he will subdue our iniquities; and thou wilt cast all their sins into the depths of the sea.

Thou wilt perform the truth to Jacob, and the mercy to Abraham, which thou hast sworn unto our fathers from the days of old."

When prayers of this nature have been offered, acknowledging our sin, the sin of our forebears, the righteousness of God's judgment, and asking forgiveness, we can then with clear conscience boldly petition for the restoration of the kingdom with the plea 'Thy kingdom come, thy will be done on earth, even as it is in heaven.' God has promised to restore the kingdom to Israel, and that Judah will reign, but it needs to be recorded in the heavenlies that Israel sought out and petitioned for it. Through the prophet Ezekiel the Lord states, "I will yet for this be inquired of by the house of Israel, to do it for them; I will increase them with men like a flock.

As the holy flock, as the flock of Jerusalem in her solemn feasts; so shall the waste cities be filled with flocks of men: and they shall know that I am the Lord. Ezekiel Chapter 36 verses 37-38.

This blessing of increase in response to inquiry is directly linked to a season of self-examination and repentance as shown in verse 31 "...Then shall ye remember your own evil ways, and your doings that were not good, and shall lothe yourselves in your own sight for your iniquities and for your abominations."

Acknowledgment of sin, repentance, and humble petition, and standing on the precious promise of the fulfillment of the Abrahamic Covenant is the first step in turning the Captivity.

Power to Be His Witnesses—the Veritas Gospel—Then, the End

Veritas is the Latin word for truth and truthfulness. And it is the Black Hebrew in the West who will bring the true gospel in the closing days of this era. As noted previously in the book, the truth of the scriptures has been hidden and the world has not been able to see that the chastisement of the Black man in the West is proof of the reality of God and the truth of his word. Had wicked men not suppressed the truth in unrighteousness, many souls might have repented in seeing prophecy unfold before their eyes.

Because the divine punishment of Israel and Judah validates the rest of the scripture, God would have been greatly exalted in the earth. Instead, a false interpretation of the Biblical account has been put forth based on the supposition that God can deal intimately with a people, call them by his name, cast out nations and set consequential blessings and curses before them and yet they can defile his holy name, re-occupy a land he banished them from, and still prosper in the earth. This is a false reality; but a lie has power, until the truth is revealed.

In Matthew Chapter 24 verse 14, Jesus tells his disciples that this gospel of the kingdom shall be preached in all the world for a witness unto all nations; and then shall the end come. The true revelation of who Israel is, our disobedience, the opening of the door of salvation to the Gentiles by virtue of our forefather's fall, and the simultaneous blessing of Christ's return for his church and Israel's restoration at the end of the age must be clearly presented.

Matthew Chapter 24 also appears to indicate offense, betrayal, affliction, and hatred will be triggered by the release of the truth of our heritage. Entire religious constructs and secular history institutions have a huge stake in continuing the misrepresentation. It will be perceived as attacking longstanding, cherished traditions and even as an attempt to undermine the faith of many. Nevertheless, Jesus taught that knowing the truth sets people free. He also said excluded from the Kingdom and relegated to outer darkness is whosoever loveth and maketh a lie.

Faith that is Rooted, Grounded, and Unshakeable

Understanding of Hebrew identity is unfamiliar territory to most Black people in the West; and especially to those who are under the Blood and Love covenant of Jesus Christ. As you move into this new reality of your heritage and the veracity of the scripture, there are a few pitfalls to avoid.

While we are grateful for those who searched out the truth of the Black man's heritage, the relationship toward God resulting from this knowledge—for the most part—excluded and denied the risen Lord Jesus Christ. Perhaps this was because of the false European image, but that lie should have been exposed just by reading the scripture in Revelation identifying Jesus as the Lion of the Tribe of Judah; since it was acknowledged the Black man in America is of Judah.

This line of reasoning that rejected Christ; who is the end of the law for righteousness to everyone that believeth—defaulted them into observance of the Mosaic Law—a covenant that was annulled even as the Levitical priesthood transitioned to the royal priesthood of Melchizedek. Not only is the Mosaic covenant fulfilled and set aside, it is inferior to the Blood and Love Covenant established through the sacrificial death of the Lord Jesus Christ. God speaks clearly concerning Christ's role in this in Hebrews Chapter 8 verses 6-13 "... But now hath he obtained a more excellent ministry, by how much also he is the mediator of a better covenant, which was established upon better promises.

For if that first covenant had been faultless, then should no place have been sought for the second.

For finding fault with them, he saith, Behold, the days come, saith the Lord, when I will make a new covenant with the house of Israel and with the house of Judah:

Not according to the covenant that I made with their fathers in the day when I took them by the hand to lead them out of the land of Egypt; because they continued not in my covenant, and I regarded them not, saith the Lord.

For this is the covenant that I will make with the house of Israel after those days, saith the Lord; I will put my laws into their mind, and write them in their hearts: and I will be to them a God, and they shall be to me a people:

And they shall not teach every man his neighbour, and every man his brother, saying, Know the Lord: for all shall know me, from the least to the greatest.

For I will be merciful to their unrighteousness, and their sins and their iniquities will I remember no more.

In that he saith, A new covenant, he hath made the first old. Now that which decayeth and waxeth old is ready to vanish away."

Galatians Chapter 2 verse 16 advises us of the futility of cleaving to the law for justification in the eyes of God ... "Knowing that a man is not justified by the works of the law, but by the faith of Jesus Christ, even we have believed in Jesus Christ, that we might be justified by the faith of Christ, and not by the works of the law: for by the works of the law shall no flesh be justified."

Galatians Chapter 3 verses 9-13 and 23-27 expound further "...So then they which be of faith are blessed with faithful Abraham.

For as many as are of the works of the law are under the curse: for it is written, Cursed is every one that continueth not in all things which are written in the book of the law to do them.

But that no man is justified by the law in the sight of God, it is evident: for, The just shall live by faith.

And the law is not of faith: but, The man that doeth them shall live in them.

Christ hath redeemed us from the curse of the law, being made a curse for us: for it is written Cursed is every one that hangeth on a tree:

But before faith came, we were kept under the law, shut up unto the faith which should afterwards be revealed. Wherefore the law was our schoolmaster to bring us unto Christ, that we might be justified by faith.

But after that faith is come, we are no longer under a schoolmaster. For ye are all the children of God by faith in Christ Jesus.

For as many of you as have been baptized into Christ have put on Christ..."

And Colossians Chapter 2 verses 14-17 show us the resurrection of Christ blotted "out the handwriting of ordinances that was against us, which was contrary to us, and took it out of the way, nailing it to his cross;

And having spoiled principalities and powers, he made a shew of them openly, triumphing over them in it.

Let no man therefore judge you in meat, or in drink, or in respect of an holy day, or of the new moon, or of the sabbath days:

Which are a shadow of things to come; but the body is of Christ."

Jesus said, "I am the way, the truth, and the life: no man cometh unto the Father, but by me..." John Chapter 14 verse 6. Worship which denies the Son of God by default denies the Father, and is similar to that of the Euro-Judaics who strive to observe the Mosaic rituals, but blaspheme the Lord Jesus. What would Moses say to these things? In Acts Chapter 3 verse 22, Peter—after healing the lame man at the temple gate Beautiful, reminded our forebears, "For Moses truly said unto the fathers, A prophet shall the Lord your God raise up unto you of your brethren, like unto me; him shall ye hear in all things whatsoever he shall say unto you.

And it shall come to pass, that every soul, which will not hear that prophet, shall be destroyed from among the people."

In Mark Chapter 9 verse 4 on the Mount of Transfiguration we see where "there appeared unto them Elias (Elijah) with Moses: and they were talking with Jesus." Clearly Moses was blessed to see the manifestation and glorification of the Prophet he foretold would be raised up from among the seed of Israel. If acknowledgement of Jesus as Lord was something false or idolatrous, obviously that was the time for Moses to speak up and make it known. Instead, he had cautioned Israel that their descendants were to hear that prophet in all things whatsoever he (would tell them.) Elijah spent his ministry combating idolatry in Israel. If acknowledgement of Jesus as Lord was something false or idolatrous, Elijah had a perfect opportunity to communicate it. Rather, we see him fellowshipping with the transfigured Christ, as would be expected of intimate friends.

Another profound point to consider is that obedience to the combined Prophet-Kinsman Redeemer-Faithful High Priest trumps discipleship to all who came before him; whether Moses or John the Baptist. We know this by John's statement to his disciples and the men of Judah who came to him with a dispute about purification. John settled the issue by saying, "He must increase, but I must decrease." He also added, "He that believeth on the Son hath everlasting life: and he that believeth not the Son shall not see life; but the wrath of God abideth on him." Romans Chapter 11 verse 26 makes it very clear the only one who can turn ungodliness away from the sons of Jacob is the Deliverer out of Sion: the Lord Jesus Christ.

Additionally, Jesus told his disciples, "Ye are they which have continued with me in my temptations. And I appoint unto you a kingdom, as my Father hath appointed unto me; That ye may eat and drink at my table in my kingdom, and sit on thrones judging the twelve tribes of Israel." Luke Chapter 22 verses 28-30. This conversation is also recorded in Matthew Chapter 19 verse 28: "And Jesus said unto them, Verily I say unto you, That ye which have followed me, in the regeneration when the Son of man shall sit in the throne of his glory, ye also shall sit upon twelve thrones, judging the twelve tribes of Israel." This is clearly a foretelling of Hebrews judging their own people, but judges who are capable of righteous administration because their spirits have been perfected through repentance and submission to Christ.

A stubborn refusal to acknowledge the New Covenant leaves a person in the precarious position of trusting in a covenant which is no longer there, while shunning the only one which God will now accept. It gives a false sense of righteousness in observing commandments and ordinances in an era when the only justification in God's eyes is faith that worketh by love. In fact, Romans Chapter 13 verses 8-10 put the matter to rest declaring, "Owe no man anything, but to love one another: for he that loveth another hath fulfilled the law.

For this, Thou shalt not commit adultery, Thou shalt not kill, Thou shalt not steal, Thou shalt not bear false witness, Thou shalt not covet; and if there be any other commandment, it is briefly comprehended in this saying, namely, Thou shalt love thy neighbour as thyself.

Love worketh no ill to his neighbour: therefore love is the fulfilling of the law."

This statement by the Apostle Paul alluding to both the commandments and law by default includes the Sabbath, a contention used by some to condemn those under the New Covenant. Some will argue that Paul was speaking to Gentiles, not Hebrews; because the letter is addressed to the Romans, but even a cursory reading of his epistle shows elaboration on tenets of Hebrew history, ritual, and observance that would have had little relevance to neophyte pagan converts. Chapters 2 verse 24 and 7 verse 1 make it very clear he is also addressing a Hebrew audience in Rome.

This is not to say the early Hebrews did not continue to worship on the seventh day by virtue of custom. And it certainly isn't an endorsement of the Roman church's idolatrous imposition of Sunday as the 'new sabbath' in a subtle attempt to pay homage to the sun god. What this does mean, is that the same principle Jesus explained to the woman at the well about the 'right' place to worship also applies to the 'right' day and time to worship: God must be worshipped in Spirit and in truth. Spirit and truth transcend all time and location, and holiness unto the Lord is a standard to be perpetually observed during every waking moment in ones' life.

The Sabbath is holy to God, and in exalting Jesus the Christ as Lord of it, the true and ultimate purpose is revealed: that our Kinsman Redeemer is the fulfillment of it, for he said, "Come unto me, all ye that labour and are heavy laden, and I will give you rest (sabbath)" and that he himself was Lord of it. This is a spiritual rest to the soul, in that we have ceased from our works, as in justification by works of the law.

Regarding the cyclical Sabbath—because it is holy, God will reinstate it purged from man's calendar tampering and pagan nomenclature. God has programmed the sun to keep the division of days, but cataclysmic disturbances are prophesied to take place in conjunction with the coming of the Son of Man, and the powers of heaven will be shaken. When the kingdom of God is established on earth and Israel restored to its inheritance in the land, time will be divinely reset and the new moons and Sabbaths established forever. Therefore,

Let no man therefore judge you in meat, or in drink, or in respect of an holy day, or of the new moon, or of the sabbath days: Which are a shadow of things to come. There still remains a rest to the people of God; our focus is to enter into that rest. In the interest of clarity, non-judgment regarding holy days should not be taken to mean pagan holidays are acceptable. They are not. This non-judgment refers to the holy days under the Mosaic law.

Do not be afraid to call upon that matchless and mighty name of Jesus: the name at which every knee shall bow, of things in heaven, and things in earth, and things under the earth; and every tongue confess—that Jesus Christ is Lord, to the glory of God the Father. The Lord Jesus Christ—that is his name and royal title; refrain not to call upon him in prayer, petition, praise, worship, or in times of peril. You have been calling on his name, and you have witnessed healing and supernatural intervention. He has made good on his declaration that all power in heaven and earth is his, and answered you faithfully in the time of trial and persecution; why let anyone shake your faith with sophistry and groundless rhetoric?

If you were not raised to speak Hebrew as a native language, there is no need to alter your communications with God for fear he will not regard your voice. God is not into semantics, as people are. He knows our thoughts before we even articulate them. He knows who we are putting our trust in. He also discerns this about all people throughout the world of whatever nation, tribe, or tongue they are. This is because God hears the heart long before the human voice articulates the words. If someone seeks to undermine your faith on the straw man argument about the name of Jesus, remember the Apostle Paul cautioned, "Who art thou that judgest another man's servant? to his own master he standeth or falleth. Yea, he shall be holden up: for God is able to make him stand." Romans Chapter 14 verse 4.

The argument will be put forth that all this time you have been calling on the Olympic god Zeus. The Greek word for Jesus used in verse 21 of the first chapter of Matthew, "And she shall bring forth a son, and thou shalt call his name JESUS: for he shall save his people from their sins" is Iēsŏus... pronounced ee-ay—sooce...the Greek pronunciation of the Hebrew pronunciation Yeh-ho-shoo-ah, meaning, Jehovah saves...and Jesus is simply the English pronunciation of the Greek. It should not be a huge surprise that a word rooted in Aramaic would be pronounced differently than the same word in Greek. In fact, if all languages and dialects in the region were similar during the time of Jesus' presence on earth, there would have been no need for Pilate to place an inscription in three different languages: Greek, Latin, and Hebrew, over the cross. All people would have been able to look at just one language and figure out what it said.

In contrast, the Greek word used for Zeus is pronounced alternately dzyooce, Dis, or deece, and answers to the supreme deity of the Greeks. When the Apostle Paul preached in the market place at Athens, if he had been referencing dzyooce, Dis, or deece, the Greeks would not have considered the gospel foolishness or some new doctrine. Instead, they would have instantly recognized him as referring to their own deity. Paul was fluent in Greek, and the Athenians clearly understood he was saying Ee-ay-sooce, not dzyooce or deece. (Reference texts I Corinthians Chapter 1 verse 23 and Acts Chapter 17 verses 18-20.)

So there is no need to speak your native tongue but alter it to Hebrew whenever you are referring to God, and there is no basis to allow word games to shipwreck your faith. The Lord has already declared his intention to turn to the people a pure language, that they may all call upon his name, to serve him with one consent when he establishes his kingdom on earth. There is no reason to change your name either. Those who overcome will be inscribed with the name of God, and the name of New Jerusalem, and our Kinsman Redeemer's new name. They will also receive a white stone with a new name written which no one knows but the recipient himself. I encourage you then, to cleave to these exceeding great and precious promises from our Lord, and be not soon shaken in your faith.

And don't be misled by people who say you are calling on an Egyptian god when you close your prayers with 'amen.' It is an actual Hebrew word meaning to trust or believe; to render faithful, and was used by Moses himself in the rehearsal of the law before Israel. Amen was the acknowledgment that all that God had spoken to them was true—including the prohibition about idolatry. It is used the same way in the Greek to express faithfulness and acknowledge that something is to be so. In Revelation Chapter 3 verse 14, the Lord Jesus Christ describes his faithfulness to the angel of the church of Laodicea by saying, "And unto the angel of the church of the Laodiceans write; These things saith the Amen, the faithful and true witness, the beginning of the creation of God..."

Trying to associate an Egyptian god who got beat down in the pre-Exodus plagues with benediction of faithful prayers to God makes about as much sense as confusing God with the Japanese fire-breathing movie monster Godzilla just because the first three letters are the same. It is just another attempt at semantics, from someone with a need to undermine people's faith. If God could be dethroned by simple machinations of men's minds like these, he would not be God. Continue to call upon the mighty name of Jesus and close your prayers with the benediction, 'Amen.'

This segues with the warning to avoid returning to Egypt in principle. While a comprehensive grasp of African studies is important, some teachers bring to bear an extreme emphasis on Afro-centricity, focusing on meta-physical power residing in melanin, and the advanced degree of scientific and philosophical knowledge that characterizes the Khemetic Mysteries. The mystery schools were the product of the Hamitic peoples who were not called into covenant with God, and sought their wisdom from sources apart from the Creator of heaven and earth.

While this melding of spiritual and gnostic disciplines is extremely ancient and has been studied and practiced for centuries, the important thing for the Black Hebrew in the West to keep in mind is that both the gods and the esoteric knowledge of Egypt were shown to be impotent and useless against I AM THAT I AM who delivered our forebears from Egypt with a mighty hand, outstretched arm, and fearful signs and wonders. Therefore, we should not seek to return to the inferior works of Ham, but recall our more excellent heritage from the godly line of Shem. Remember, in the Kingdom age, the Egyptian (along with the Assyrian) is under servitude to Judah. Why would you want to join the ranks of those to be subjugated?

Lastly, we must understand that spiritual redemption in Captivity is also a call to separate ourselves from Gentile idolatry. This may prove a stumbling block for many, but it is a step we must be willing to take. It is not about imposing legalistic restrictions on people, or being a killjoy when these festivities abound. The crux of the matter is what these celebrations truly represent, and I am not talking about rampant materialism either. I am referring to the fact that holidays celebrated in the West are actually high holy days on the calendars of occult practitioners. Witches and Satanists are fully aware of the foundational meanings behind these days; to the shame of the ignorance of those who serve the Lord Jesus Christ. The Roman Catholic Church fully knew this and attempted to 'christianize' the pagan ritual days so that the populace could continue their celebrations under the cover of religious purity. However, when it comes to idolatry, God has clearly warned us not to mix the profane with the holy.

This means the trendy little saying about 'putting Christ back in Christmas' is nothing more than a deceptive slogan to perpetuate a lie. Sure, we are all thankful the prophesied Redeemer was born of a virgin, and manifested to save his people from their sins. But that has nothing to do with the winter solstice, the Babylonian mystery religion's Tammuz, and the allusion to fertility rites associated with the wreaths and holly berries, etc. A 'mas' or mass is actually a celebration of death. The pagans know the traditional greeting really means 'merry wishes for Christ's death' in favor of the birthday of Mithras and the rebirth of Tammuz.

The bizarre amalgamation of Mithraism, Norse mythology of Jule (Yule) and Babylonian cult worship which has gradually and culturally morphed into the Christmas celebration and icons we have grown up with in the West are rooted in ancient Satanism and a spirit that exalts itself against the knowledge of God. In the same way, the fact that Jesus conquered death and is the Resurrection and Life has nothing to do with the sunrise service bringing honor to the sun, and eggs and rabbits associated with fecundity and the worship of Ishtar, the queen of heaven—at spring solstice.

The Gentiles sacrifice unto devils; <u>and this spiritual principle has never changed</u>. The familiar rituals, props, and observances are all tied to practices that got our forebears kicked out of the land and scattered across the earth. Study the Book of Ezekiel to learn about our foremothers weeping for Tammuz; study the Book of Jeremiah to find out about them baking cakes to honor the queen of heaven. I too, was raised under the standard Western tradition of these festivities. My insight into this did not come from brainwashing in a cult, or some tyrannical spiritual authority guilt-tripping me and twisting my arm to refrain. Psalm Chapter 119 verse 30 says, "The entrance of thy words giveth light; it giveth understanding unto the simple." John Chapter 16 verse 9 assures us that "the Spirit of truth... will guide you into all truth." It was through the study of these observances' true roots, and the conviction of God's Spirit that I have adopted this resolution.

Literally every festive celebration on the Western calendar is pagan in origin. From the lecherous roots of Valentine's Day, the obvious celebration of death, decay and fear associated with the witches' Satanic high holy day observance of Samhain (Halloween), to the original observance of Thanksgiving instituted to celebrate the slaughter of the Pequot Indians in Massachusetts in 1637. Since we have in excess of three-hundred days out of the calendar year to hold fellowship feasts or show special affection for a loved one, we need to take care to keep ourselves unspotted from the world. The average man or woman on the street may not know; but the practicing occultist does, as do the principalities and powers in the heavenlies. I realize under the Captivity, Esau's system is basically set up so that the only time many families are able to reunite is during the pagan holidays. But when you gather together, do not forget who you are and your true purpose, and divest yourself of the verbal expressions and festive decorations associated with these observances: for their root is to glorify sin, self, and Satan.

WHAT'S IMPORTANT

So far in the journey to make sense of our experience in the West, we have established our true identity, and that of the nations around us. We have distinguished ourselves as Shemitic Hebrews in contrast to Hamitic peoples, who are also a dark race. We have come to understand why we are here in the West, and the key events and participants that led to the usurpation of our identity. We have examined the conspiracy to blot out the memory of the Hebrew and how it permeates literature, the arts, and both secular and religious institutions. We have reviewed God's standard of dealing with us by covenant, and seen how we have historically struggled against idolatry.

We have acknowledged the epic failures of our forebears; such as a fickle heart ready to return to Egyptian idolatry, demanding a king, rejecting our true King, desiring to be like the Gentiles, and choosing to cleave to the handwriting of ordinances that ministered death, rather than the new covenant Law of love and justification by faith alone. We have seen that although we fled to the wilderness again, the word that cannot go forth and return back void to God found our forefathers, and brought them by ships again into Egypt; the house of bondage—with a yoke of iron around their necks. We understood this to be a divine punishment, that God might be honored and glorified in the sight of the nations and heavenly principalities and powers; after that he had exalted and honored our forefathers, only to be repaid by them turning to vain idols.

We have considered how a true demonstration of Gentile Christian faith should have manifested even as we were suffering persecution in the West. We looked at the intense wrath of the enemy against us, and the myriad ways it manifests to destroy us individually and collectively. We watched as honorable men and women among our people rose to the cause to put an end to the rampant violence and injustice. Most importantly, we realize and now know that although we are not confined to plantations, we are still very much in Captivity: a state of existence that only God can remediate.

An in depth look at the great loss suffered as a result of the Captivity made it obvious only God can recompense us, and the scriptures verify that he will. We learned that despite our present low estate, as far as God is concerned in the heavenlies, we still rule with him. We are being awakened individually and collectively, and we are called to purify our hearts and hands, receive the promise of the Father, and lead our brethren in praise and intercessory prayer. We

310

examined the unique bond between the Levitical priesthood and the Judæan kingship, and ponder with awe the supernatural fusion of the two roles in the order of Melchizedek, the Eternal Priest-King. The unique relationship between our tribe and the tribes of Benjamin and Levi was duly noted, along with the exhortation that we continue to support each other in prayer and in the word.

Lastly, we now have clarity regarding what to pray, and why to pray it. Up to this point, we have not had a clear course of how to act because so much of our energy was expended on reacting to the negative conditions of Captivity. But going forward, we can clearly see our path as we wait for the fulfilling of the Abrahamic Covenant. We know that in order to effectively preach the gospel, we must be willing to tell the truth about our people, and we have clear warnings of key spiritual stumbling-blocks which must be avoided. Now, it's time to let God arise, and let his enemies be scattered!

Chapter XV...Exodus Take II

And ye shall know that I am in the midst of Israel, and that I am
the Lord your God, and none else: and my people shall never be ashamed.

"Behold, the days come, saith the Lord, that I will raise unto David a righteous Branch, and a King shall reign and prosper, and shall execute judgment and justice in the earth.

In his days Judah shall be saved, and Israel shall dwell safely: and this is his name whereby he shall be called, THE LORD OUR RIGHTEOUSNESS.

Therefore, behold, the days come, saith the Lord, that they shall no more say, The Lord liveth, which brought up the children of Israel out of the land of Egypt;

But, The Lord liveth, which brought up and which led the seed of the house of Israel out of the north country, and from all countries whither I had driven them; and they shall dwell in their own land...." Jeremiah Chapter 23 verses 5-8

Why No Flesh and Blood Man Can Reverse the Situation

Beaten down and oppressed as the Black man has been in the West, he has historically striven—whether violently or non-violently—to change his situation and subordinate status. The stereotype of a docile, grinning Black man content to be a slave was a false image by which whites would assuage their conscience as they struggled to convince themselves Blacks were satisfied with their lot. However, similar to prisoners of war, behavior disguised as contentment was merely a self-preservation strategy.

In actuality, over one-hundred sixty rebellions and uprisings occurred among slaves between the 1500's and mid-1800's although the incidents associated with Toussaint L'Ouverture, Gabriel Prosser, Denmark Vesey, and Nat Turner are the ones people are most familiar with. Rebellions were often joined by Native Americans, and sometimes even sympathetic whites were organizers. In a bizarre twist, many of these plots were exposed by other slaves; whether out of insecurity of the future if the revolt succeeded, fear of reprisal if it failed, or desire of meritorious manumission: a construct by which a slave could gain his freedom by saving the lives and well-being of whites. Yet, all of these were fated to come to naught, and the descendants of the original slaves remain captive in a land that is not theirs.

In Isaiah Chapter 51 verses 17-18, God tells Jerusalem she has "drunk at the hand of the Lord the cup of his fury; thou hast drunken the dregs of the cup of trembling, and wrung them out", and "There is none to guide her among all the sons whom she hath brought forth; neither is there any that taketh her by the hand of all the sons that she hath brought up." This means that when God executes divine punishment, the best, the most brilliant, the bravest and the boldest are powerless to do anything against it. As a young nation called, nurtured, and hosted by God, we were the Samson of the world; a formidable people who could not be overcome, unless compromised by sin or idolatry. Now the Lord has hedged us in; and he has sold us...and this accounts for our human inability to throw off the yoke of oppression.

But there is a divine logic behind it, too. When FBI director J. Edgar Hoover sought to 'prevent the rise of a "Messiah" who could inspire and coalesce the militant Black Nationalist movement' he didn't realize he was actually forcing that title to be reserved for the return of our Kinsman-Redeemer. Because Jesus was made like unto his brethren in all things, at his appearance it will be obvious even in his glorified body that he is Black. The risen Messiah the oppressor so dreads will be invincible. The advanced weaponry systems he trusts in will be more harmless than foam toys. The Lord alone will be exalted in that day.

That will be the day of the Lord, and God wants to reserve the glory for our deliverance for himself.

His decree placed us in Captivity, and his formidable power alone will bring us out. No man among our people can command the myriad legions of angels to sever the wicked from among the righteous. No man among our people can flex the powers of the heavens; dimming the sun and the moon and dislodging the stars from their positions. No man among our people can convulse the earth causing the cities of the nations to fall simultaneously. No man among our people can part the ocean so that the house of Judah and the house Israel can walk together out of the land of the north to the land God has given us for an inheritance. And no man among our people can collectively bring the unregenerate Gentiles to submission. I truly believe this is why God permitted each civil rights leader to make an individual, but limited impact. It is not enough for our people to merely be lifted up and Captivity made more bearable. God's plan is that our spirits would be perfected, and we then be lifted out and repatriated in our covenant land.

Out of Egypt I Have Called My Son Redux

Thus saith the Lord of hosts; The children of Israel and the children of Judah were oppressed together: and all that took them captives held them fast; they refused to let them go. Their Redeemer is strong; the Lord of hosts is his name: he shall thoroughly plead their cause, that he may give rest to the land, and disquiet the inhabitants of Babylon...Jeremiah Chapter 50 verses 33-34.

When God says it is time to leave, it will be time to leave. Two will be in the field; one will be taken, and the other left. Two will be grinding at the mill; one will be taken, and the other left. Two will be in one bed, one will be taken and the other left. We are told to watch and be in a state of readiness.

The prophecy of coming out of Egypt is three-fold. The exodus under Moses was the first fulfillment. The return of Jesus after fleeing with his parents from Herod was the second. The termination of the latter day Captivity will be the third. But the event itself will be like the first, for Micah Chapter 7 verse 15 says...

"According to the days of thy coming out of the land of Egypt will I shew unto him marvellous things."

Esau's manipulation of mainstream history labors hard to validate the migration of the Euro-Judaics and their descendants to the newly created secular state of Israel, as a fulfillment of ancient Biblical prophecy. Many white Western churches also bought into this deception, and solicited their congregations for funds to assist the immigration. But this is a false interpretation of Biblical prophecy, and a counterfeit for the true exodus of the authentic descendants of Abraham. Not only has Esau lied about the identity of the progeny of Israel, he has remained silent as to where they are. This suppression of knowledge of the scattered exiles is yet another example of the spiritual obstruction of justice. For if the Gentiles had been made fully aware of the existence of these people, many would have observed and confessed the truth of the living God and his unerring word.

The restoration of Israel that Jesus' disciples inquired about before his ascension will not unfold like the opening of a new store rolling out an advertising campaign to attract customers and build membership. It will be an event marked by obvious supernatural anomalies as the tribal descendants of Jacob are simultaneously guided and divinely shepherded out of the countries and coasts wherever they reside. They will be protected in the wilderness during the outpouring of the wine of the wrath of God and the gathering of nations to judgment.

Where are all these latter day descendants coming from? God says, from the north, the south, the east, and the west. There they have resided, that the nations that grudgingly hosted them might be judged either as sheep or goats for the manner in which they treated these the least of Christ's brethren. We will now look at some of the lesser known posterities of Israel, such as:

The Sheedis—also known as 'Makrani'—who are descendants of African Blacks captured by Arab traders and brought to Pakistan as slaves in the 19th century.[28]

The Siddi of India—a distinct group of individuals of significant minority among the country's billions of people. They also arrived as slaves brought from Africa by Islamists and the Portuguese. They are called "Habshi" or "negro" by other Indians.[29]

The prefix 'Zanj' refers to the African people in Iran who began arriving in the 13th century. These people were brought from the Southeastern African regions by Portuguese and Islamists.

Media coverage of the Iraq war generally featured images of light brown-skinned Iraqis. But how many are aware the southern Iraq city of Basra is home to over a million Black people —also described as 'Negroes'? Because they comprise only ten percent of the population, they have no legislative voice. They are still referred to as "slave" by the balance of the populace and ravaged by poverty. Spokespersons for the Black community in Iraq describe their struggle as essentially the same as that of the American civil rights movement during the 1960's.

---

[28] "Makranis, the Negroes of Pakistan and India" Chagatai Khan, May 2009.
[29] "The Plight Of The Siddis" Sanjay Austa, africanglobe.net. 2014 May.

Writing for The Independent, journalist Andy Kershaw detailed the horrific birth defects seen at the Basrah Teaching Hospital in southern Iraq.[30] He quotes Dr. Jawad Al-Ali, the director of oncology, as saying there is an "epidemic" of cancers, and that "the number of cancer cases is doubling every year. So is the severity of the cancers, and there has been a big increase in cancer among the young." This is due to the use of depleted uranium munitions—a form of nuclear warfare—which continues to kill due to aerosolization and continued radiation release long after the initial detonation.

These groups answer to God's promise in the 11th chapter of Isaiah to bring his people from Elam (Iran), Shinar (Iraq) and Assyria, in addition to Egypt, Pathros, Cush, Hamath, and the islands of the sea.

Crisscrossing the earth, we find communities of African descendants in literally every country on the South American continent. Many already know Brazil is home to a significant Black populace, but Argentina, Bolivia, Chile, Colombia, Ecuador, Guyana, Paraguay, Peru, Suriname, Uruguay, and Venezuela also have communities of African descendants. A few were established by slaves who managed to escape and remain free long before their host country outlawed slavery. However, a common thread uniting each of them is that their ethnic group remains an economically disenfranchised minority, and the subject of both subtle and overt racism.

As pointed out earlier in the book, the worldwide African presence is not strictly a result of the slave trade. But as the right to freedom and autonomy became increasingly governed by either skin color or religious affiliation, the empirical European and Islamic advances meant the enslavement or subjugation of indigenous free men and women wherever they were found. In country after country on the earth, whether as near as Mexico, or as far as Australia—the dispersed Hebrew is found...a stark reminder of God's word forever settled in heaven: " And the Lord shall scatter thee among all people, from the one end of the earth even unto the other...and among these nations shalt thou find no ease, neither shall the sole of thy foot have rest...and thou shalt become an astonishment, a proverb, and a byword, among all nations whither the Lord shall lead thee."

The Time of Jacob's Trouble...but He Shall Be Saved out of It

We are not to fear the violent upheavals which will take place around us. We have looked into the word—and like a mirror reflection—discerned it is speaking to us and about us as Hebrews. If we believe we are the latter day descendants of the original Hebrews, we have no choice but to believe God will again perform great and supernatural miracles as he brings his people once more from Egypt, the house of bondage.

---

[30] "US Depleted Uranium Yields Chamber of Horrors in Southern Iraq" Andy Kershaw Independent Digital 2001.

In strengthening our faith regarding divine protection, we can look at God's good promises in both the Old and New Covenants. Psalm 46 speaks expressly to the Day of the Lord, but we are exhorted not to fear, in spite of the natural cataclysms and state of worldwide panic. God will be our refuge and strength, a very present help in trouble. He will be in our midst, he will help us, and that right early. Twice the psalmist says, "The Lord of hosts is with us; the God of Jacob is our refuge. Selah.

Isaiah Chapter 26 verses 19-21 give us a tiny glimpse of the sequence of events at the resurrection; notice the prophet declares he is getting up with his brethren!

"Thy dead men shall live, together with my dead body shall they arise. Awake and sing, ye that dwell in dust: for thy dew is as the dew of herbs, and the earth shall cast out the dead.

Come, my people, enter thou into thy chambers, and shut thy doors about thee: hide thyself as it were for a little moment, until the indignation be overpast.

For, behold, the Lord cometh out of his place to punish the inhabitants of the earth for their iniquity: the earth also shall disclose her blood, and shall no more cover her slain."

We see there is a hiding place the Lord will prepare; and this hiding place appears to be supernatural, and inter-dimensional. Psalm 91 indicates that "only with thine eyes shalt thou behold and see the reward of the wicked." This means you will actually observe the horrific judgment meted out to sinners, but it will not touch you. The hiding place is identified as the shadow of the Almighty. The imagery of wings and feathers denotes protection, and is the same as that alluded to by Jesus in his lament over Jerusalem in Matthew Chapter 23 verse 37.

Secular governments have issued many new laws and policies related to terrorism, but Psalm 91 tells us not to fear terror. Arrows that fly by day would relate to bullets in our day and time. God's protection is described as a fortress, and defense against traps, destruction, pestilence, and plague is assured. This is a psalm with exceeding great and precious promises, but they are conditional. The recipient must dwell in the secret place of the most High. The Hebrew word used in this psalm for dwelleth is yashab: meaning to sit down, settle down, and continue to remain, as in a state of marriage.

The protected one must also have set his love upon God. This means his heart and trust are upon God alone; implying a covenant relationship with the Almighty. These requirements bring us back to the necessity of being under the new covenant sealed by the blood of the Lord Jesus Christ: the only active covenant for propitiation of sin. Faith is involved here too, for God says, "He shall call upon me, and I will answer him." A person who doesn't relationally know God will not have the faith to call on him in times of dire peril, nor will he wait for God to answer.

More times than I can count, when God or an angel sent from him speaks to the sons and daughters of Israel, the exhortation is to "fear not." God is constantly telling us to not be afraid. Because 'fear not' and 'don't be afraid' mean the same thing, I will place 'don't be afraid' in the place of 'fear not' as though God were speaking to us in modern English vernacular, in Isaiah Chapter 41 verses 10, 13, and 14:

Don't be afraid; for I am with thee: be not dismayed; for I am thy God: I will strengthen thee; yea, I will help thee; yea, I will uphold thee with the right hand of my righteousness.

For I the Lord thy God will hold thy right hand, saying unto thee, don't be afraid; I will help thee.

Don't be afraid, thou worm Jacob, and ye men of Israel; I will help thee, saith the Lord and thy redeemer, the Holy One of Israel.

The Lord Jesus told us in Luke Chapter 21 verse 26 that men's hearts would actually fail them for fear when they see the things that are coming on the earth. When you see people losing their minds, immobilized with fear, or wilding out, remember that these are the ungodly who hated God, denied his existence, or thought their own wits or righteousness would see them through the Day of the Lord. Quite to the contrary, the scripture warns us, "if the righteous scarcely be saved, where shall the ungodly and the sinner appear?"

Yes, it will get worse for us before it gets better. The old saying goes that the darkest hour is just before the dawn. We are called to endure to the end, but our God will come, and he will save us. When we reach that point, the termination of the Captivity is literally just over the horizon. The prophet Jeremiah describes it like this:

"Alas! for that day is great, so that none is like it: it is even the time of Jacob's trouble; but he shall be saved out of it.

For it shall come to pass in that day, saith the Lord of hosts, that I will break his yoke from off thy neck, and will burst thy bonds, and strangers shall no more serve themselves of him:

But they shall serve the Lord their God, and David their king, whom I will raise up unto them.

Therefore fear thou not, O my servant Jacob, saith the Lord; neither be dismayed, O Israel: for, lo, I will save thee from afar, and thy seed from the land of their captivity; and Jacob shall return, and shall be in rest, and be quiet, and none shall make him afraid.

For I am with thee, saith the Lord, to save thee: though I make a full end of all nations whither I have scattered thee, yet will I not make a full end of thee: but I will correct thee in measure, and will not leave thee altogether unpunished..." Jeremiah Chapter 30 verses 7-11

Here, God plainly tells us the reason for our scattering and Captivity was to correct us in measure. The word measure used in this scripture passage alludes to a verdict, such as a judicial sentence under divine law for a penalty or crime. God is just. His correction has been in the proper degree to both chasten us as a people and satisfy his justice. Many of our people have been judged in the flesh, but God is the Judge of all the earth, and he will resurrect them per his righteous and merciful discretion. The outlook doesn't look very promising for the nations where we have been held captive, though. However, the heavenly scenario in Revelation Chapter 7 verse 9 shows us that people were yet found in every nation that feared God, lived righteously, and were willing to suffer for their faith.

Into the Wilderness Again...The Apostle John Sees the "Trailer"

"Thus saith the Lord God of Israel, Let my people go, that they may hold a feast unto me in the wilderness..." Exodus Chapter 5 verse 1

As mentioned earlier, the termination of the latter day Captivity will be the third fulfillment of the prophecy, "Out of Egypt I have called my son," based on Deuteronomy Chapter 28 verse 68, which foretells Israel being brought into Egypt again with ships and sold as bondmen and bondwomen—something unique to the Black man in the West during the Trans-Atlantic slave trade, since it is not necessary to travel by ship to get to physical Egypt from physical Israel. The first stop out of Egypt was the wilderness. The apostle John saw a preview of this in the form of a woman (representing Israel) who gave birth to a Man-child who was to rule all nations (the Lord Jesus Christ.) The Man-child was caught up to God and his throne (which speaks to Jesus' resurrection and ascension) and the woman fled into the wilderness into a place prepared by God, that they should feed her there a thousand two hundred and threescore days. John recaps this same observation a few verses later by saying, "And to the woman were given two wings of a great eagle, that she might fly into the wilderness, into her place, where she is nourished for a time, and times, and half a time, from the face of the serpent." This account is found in the 12th chapter of the Book of Revelation.

The Lord Jesus Christ identifies with us in all things, and following his baptism, he too was led by the Spirit into the wilderness. There, he fasted one day for each year his brethren were in the wilderness, and overcame each temptation that the Israelites failed after coming out of Egypt: the lust of the eyes, such as the sin of Achan, and Israel's seduction by the Moabite women; the lust of the flesh—as when they were whining for the fleshpots of Egypt; and the pride of life—as in the insurrection of Korah, Dathan, and Abiram.

So the scripture indicates that Israel will go into the wilderness again. This second trek into the wilderness is first alluded to in Psalm Chapter 107 verses 1-7.

"O give thanks unto the Lord, for he is good: for his mercy endureth for ever.

Let the redeemed of the Lord say so, whom he hath redeemed from the hand of the enemy; And gathered them out of the lands, from the east, and from the west, from the north, and from the south. They wandered in the wilderness in a solitary way; they found no city to dwell in. Hungry and thirsty, their soul fainted in them. Then they cried unto the Lord in their trouble, and he delivered them out of their distresses. And he led them forth by the right way, that they might go to a city of habitation."

We know this is speaking of the end of the age, because that is the only recurring theme where God gathers his people from the four cardinal directions of the earth. God has redeemed (or delivered) the descendants of the Hebrews from the enemy, but once again they are found in the wilderness. Jeremiah Chapter 31 verses 1-2 also reference this temporary wilderness habitation:

"At the same time, saith the Lord, will I be the God of all the families of Israel, and they shall be my people. Thus saith the Lord, The people which were left of the sword found grace in the wilderness; even Israel, when I went to cause him to rest."

Ezekiel Chapter 20 verses 33-38 and 41-42 speak of an end time encounter in the wilderness:

"As I live, saith the Lord God, surely with a mighty hand, and with a stretched out arm, and with fury poured out, will I rule over you: And I will bring you out from the people, and will gather you out of the countries wherein ye are scattered, with a mighty hand, and with a stretched out arm, and with fury poured out. And I will bring you into the wilderness of the people, and there will I plead with you face to face. Like as I pleaded with your fathers in the wilderness of the land of Egypt, so will I plead with you, saith the Lord God. And I will cause you to pass under the rod, and I will bring you into the bond of the covenant: And I will purge out from among you the rebels, and them that transgress against me:

I will bring them forth out of the country where they sojourn, and they shall not enter into the land of Israel: and ye shall know that I am the Lord. I will accept you with your sweet savour, when I bring you out from the people, and gather you out of the countries wherein ye have been scattered; and I will be sanctified in you before the heathen." And ye shall know that I am the Lord, when I shall bring you into the land of Israel, into the country for the which I lifted up mine hand to give it to your fathers.

This account from Ezekiel makes an interesting statement, in that the rebels and those that transgress against God will also be brought out of the land where they sojourned in Captivity, but they will not be permitted to continue to the land of covenant. This dovetails perfectly with scripture found in Psalm Chapter 67 verses 7-6 ...

"O God, when thou wentest forth before thy people, when thou didst march through the wilderness; Selah" and "he bringeth out those which are bound with chains: but the rebellious dwell in a dry land."

According to these passages, the idea is that God is going to be faithful to his promise to gather the scattered descendants of the Hebrews out of the lands of their Captivity. But he is not going to tolerate the kind of repeated foolishness that went on with the first exodus. If any of the sons and daughters don't want to submit, they will simply be rerouted to an inhospitable terrain. There will be no excuse for lack of self-control, being plain evil, or attributing the deliverance to idol gods or aliens because the very fact that people have been supernaturally removed from their surroundings will make it obvious the hand of God Almighty is at work. However, there are always some people whose ego or hardheadedness will be the undoing of them, and they will be dismissed to the dry, barren land.

Yet another reference to Israel in the wilderness before entering the covenant land is found in Hosea Chapter 2 verses 13-23, and Chapter 3 verses 4-5: "And I will visit upon her the days of Baalim, wherein she burned incense to them, and she decked herself with her earrings and her jewels, and she went after her lovers, and forgat me, saith the Lord. Therefore, behold, I will allure her, and bring her into the wilderness, and speak comfortably unto her.

And I will give her her vineyards from thence, and the valley of Achor for a door of hope: and she shall sing there, as in the days of her youth, and as in the day when she came up out of the land of Egypt.

And it shall be at that day, saith the Lord, that thou shalt call me Ishi; and shalt call me no more Baali. For I will take away the names of Baalim out of her mouth, and they shall no more be remembered by their name. And in that day will I make a covenant for them with the beasts of the field, and with the fowls of heaven, and with the creeping things of the ground: and I will break the bow and the sword and the battle out of the earth, and will make them to lie down safely.

And I will betroth thee unto me for ever; yea, I will betroth thee unto me in righteousness, and in judgment, and in lovingkindness, and in mercies. I will even betroth thee unto me in faithfulness: and thou shalt know the Lord. And it shall come to pass in that day, I will hear, saith the Lord, I will hear the heavens, and they shall hear the earth; And the earth shall hear the corn, and the wine, and the oil; and they shall hear Jezreel

And I will sow her unto me in the earth; and I will have mercy upon her that had not obtained mercy; and I will say to them which were not my people, Thou art my people; and they shall say, Thou art my God".

"For the children of Israel shall abide many days without a king, and without a prince, and without a sacrifice, and without an image, and without an ephod, and without teraphim: Afterward shall the children of Israel return, and seek the Lord their God, and David their king; and shall fear the Lord and his goodness in the latter days."

So we clearly see that a wilderness event takes place for the many descendants of the dispersed Hebrew before they come into the land promised to Abraham, Isaac, and Jacob. The people will be safe in this wild environment, because God is going to make a covenant with animals, birds, and insects so that they are not harmed. He will also cause the earth to yield increase so that the people are nourished.

Ezekiel's perspective focuses on judgment, litigation, and separation. God is going to show the people their sins and the sins of their forefathers. They will need to know why they were in the condition they were delivered from, before they enter the land of their inheritance. At that time, God will also bring them into the bond of covenant. Obviously as the history of transgression and idolatry is revealed, the desired response is repentance. The bond of the covenant is through the shed blood of Jesus, for there remains no other sacrifice for sins. The difference here is that Israel's gathering is comparative to a massive outdoor tribunal rather than the private, individual conversions we are accustomed to in the West.

Hosea's take on the wilderness encounter is more in the context of a spousal reconciliation. Here, God takes the people back to the days when their forebears disdained his goodness and forgot about him. We can sense the hurt and rejection he felt; yet, he says he will speak comfortably with Israel. This means he will commune with Israel in a tender, heart to heart manner. His words and demeanor towards those he has rescued cause Israel to burst forth in song, as in the days when they came up from Egypt. Also, Hosea says Israel will no more call God 'Baali" meaning master, but 'Ishi', which means husband. This speaks to a new level of relationship; comparable to the love relationship between Christ and the ecclesia, and the bond is likewise sealed by Jesus' blood.

Speaking of the ecclesia—the called out Body of Christ—where do they fit in during Israel's judgment in the wilderness? Israel is in the wilderness a thousand two hundred and threescore days. In another verse, John calls it time, times, and half a time. One thousand two hundred and threescore days is equal to forty-two months, or three and a half years. To find clues to the purpose of this time frame, we look for identical time frames in the scripture that are also tied to the time of the end and deliverance of God's people. The first link is found in Daniel Chapter 7 verse 25 when an angel interprets one of Daniel's visions, and describes the actions of the last world ruler just prior to the establishment of the kingdom of God on earth...

"And he shall speak great words against the most High, and shall wear out the saints of the most High, and think to change times and laws: and they shall be given into his hand until a time and times and the dividing of time." Here we see the unique measure of time described as time, times, and a dividing of time. An associated action is that the ruling power will wear out the saints of the most High.

Returning to the book of Revelation, in Chapter 13 verses 48 we find everyone on the earth worshiping the dragon (who is Satan) and his human representative (the beast.)

"And they worshipped the dragon which gave power unto the beast: and they worshipped the beast, saying, Who is like unto the beast? who is able to make war with him?

And there was given unto him a mouth speaking great things and blasphemies; and power was given unto him to continue forty and two months.

And he opened his mouth in blasphemy against God, to blaspheme his name, and his tabernacle, and them that dwell in heaven.

And it was given unto him to make war with the saints, and to overcome them: and power was given him over all kindreds, and tongues, and nations.

And all that dwell upon the earth shall worship him, whose names are not written in the book of life of the Lamb slain from the foundation of the world."

Here we have a correlation with Daniel's account. The Beast—which is the same as the Son of Perdition mentioned in II Thessalonians Chapter 2 verse 3, is permitted to reign for forty-two months, and make war against the saints and overcome them. There will be no place on the earth where any one can escape his domain.

Returning to chapter 12 of the book of Revelation, verses 15-16 show us one last attempt Satan makes to destroy the scattered of Israel with a flood, but his attack is subverted by the earth, which swallows it. It is at this juncture where we look at verse 17 and find ourselves staring back:

"And the dragon was wroth with the woman, and went to make war with the remnant of her seed, which keep the commandments of God, and have the testimony of Jesus Christ."

This is crystal clear; the remnant of Israel's seed are descendants of Hebrews. This would also include Gentiles grafted into the commonwealth of Israel through Christ. The final qualifiers are what will significantly filter out a lot of people: keeping the commandments of God and having the testimony of Jesus Christ. Many of the Gentile churches have already given their hand to Rome. Many Black churches will cease to be active once persecution of this magnitude ramps up. Verse 17 actually says Satan declares war on the descendants of Israel who keep the commandments of God and have the testimony of Jesus Christ. There is nowhere to go to escape, because he has power over all kindreds, tongues, and nations. Fellowship may be relegated to one on one meetings, but people will be encouraged to betray one another. Verse 11 shows the only way to overcome him is by the blood of the Lamb, the word of your testimony, and being willing to die for your faith if necessary.

Notice also the duality of the qualifications of the true saint. They can't keep the commandments of God and deny Jesus Christ. And they can't confess Christ but live carnally. The strait gate and narrow way are never more emphasized than during this era. Right here is where many people will find out if they truly love God, or if they have merely deluded themselves and others for years. Either we believe we are dead, and our life is hidden with Christ that we might appear with him when he appears in glory, or we don't believe it at all. But one thing I can testify is that the arm of the Lord is revealed to those who believe his report.

When it reaches this level of persecution to the point of death, look up—for your redemption draws nigh. You will know when this time is at hand, because the Son of Perdition will be revealed, and not long after that, a false religious leader will be instrumental in getting people to accept the beast's mark for economic transactions. Demonstration of allegiance will also be expected by taking his name, number, and worshiping him.

So, we are here as witnesses for at least three and a half years; salt and light in a world that is getting progressively darker and hostile to the name of Jesus and godliness. Greater Israel (scattered Hebrews) will be gathered and sheltered in the wilderness during that period for judgment, reconciliation, and entering in covenant in anticipation of repatriation, but the ecclesia—both Hebrew and Gentile—are called to endure unto the end. We will face persecution because of the wrath of Satan. But we are not appointed to the wrath of God. In fact, the vials of God's wrath will not even be poured out—until twelve thousand are sealed from each of Israel's tribes. Just because people have forgotten their heritage doesn't mean God doesn't know their historical line. And I don't have to tell you who is first in the line-up of those sealed...it is the tribe of Judah! As the tribe that is faithful with the saints, we will have to take the lead in earnestly contending for the faith. We will need to pray unceasingly for each other and for Benjamin and Levi who have historically walked beside us.

The Greek word for sealed—aphragizo—translates "to stamp with a private mark for security or preservation; by implication to keep secret, to attest." John Chapter 6 verse 27 tells us God the Father personally sealed Jesus in this manner, except when he baptized him with the Spirit, he gave it to him without measure (John Chapter 3 verse 34.) Here also is a simile of abiding in the secret place of the most High. Every time we see this usage of sealed in relation to the saints, it is referring to the Holy Ghost! The following scriptures bear this out:

"Now he which stablisheth us with you in Christ, and hath anointed us, is God; Who hath also sealed us, and given the earnest of the Spirit in our hearts."
II Corinthians Chapter 1 verses 21-22

"That we should be to the praise of his glory, who first trusted in Christ. In whom ye also trusted, after that ye heard the word of truth, the gospel of your salvation: in whom also after that ye believed, ye were sealed with that holy Spirit of promise,

"Which is the earnest of our inheritance until the redemption of the purchased possession, unto the praise of his glory." Ephesians Chapter 1 verses 12-14

"And grieve not the holy Spirit of God, whereby ye are sealed unto the day of redemption." Ephesians Chapter 4 verse 30

We have our marching orders; God wants to see twelve thousand of his Hebrew sons from each tribe baptized with and filled with the Holy Ghost for power to be his witnesses in all the world before the close of the age...just like on Pentecost, in line with his original intent for Israel to be a light to the nations. Essentially, before the curtain of grace and mercy closes on this world, God is extending another opportunity to Israel to fulfill their original commission. O the depth of the riches both of the wisdom and knowledge of God! How unsearchable are his judgments, and his ways past finding out!

At this juncture, I call to remembrance the distinction between those under the covenant of the blood of Christ (represented by his Body—the Church) and those who are gathered out of winds to reoccupy the land. We saw that those destined to rule and reign with Christ because they have suffered on behalf of his name are a tiny minority compared to the masses in the worldwide exodus that have endured humiliation and hardship strictly by virtue of Hebrew descent. We drew the comparison that Jesus was sent to all the lost sheep of the house of Israel, but he only singled out a select group for fellowship, and instruction of the hidden truths of the kingdom of God. He then entrusted this tiny cadre of followers with the care and propagation of the gospel of the kingdom—first to the house of Israel, and then to the rest of the world. We saw that the reason for such a minuscule election was that only few are chosen, and only few find the strait gate and narrow path that lead to eternal life.

We can see there is a distinct separation between the two groups, for we of the Blood and Love covenant worship God alone through Jesus Christ—having been made joint-heirs with him and given an inheritance kept, and undefiled in the heavens. In stark contrast, when God brings the mass of Hebrew descendants into the wilderness for judgment before repatriating the land, we see him having to deal with them regarding their former idolatries where they bowed down to Baalim and forgot God. Clearly this does not apply to the body of Christ, who renounced idolatry as a work of the flesh when taking on the name and yoke of Jesus. However, many if not most of Hebrew descent alive today are still practicing various forms of idolatry in the lands of their dispersion.

In God's great providence and wisdom, he has designed his plan for the end of the ages so that his Portion is purged and purified, and the suffering of his saints perfected and completed—simultaneously. Ultimately, the saints of the most High will reign jointly with the Lord Jesus Christ as bride and bridegroom, and the people will be restored to their land and their days and the days of their children multiplied in the land the Lord swore to their fathers to give them, as the days of heaven upon the earth. And for these repatriated, God says, "For, behold, I am for you, and I will turn unto you, and ye shall be tilled and sown:

And I will multiply men upon you, all the house of Israel, even all of it: and the cities shall be inhabited, and the wastes shall be builded:

And I will multiply upon you man and beast; and they shall increase and bring fruit: and I will settle you after your old estates, and will do better unto you than at your beginnings: and ye shall know that I am the Lord." Ezekiel Chapter 36 verses 9-11

Chapter XVI...The Prophecy of Enoch Fulfilled

They that hate thee shall be clothed with shame; and the dwelling place of the wicked shall come to nought.

And Enoch also, the seventh from Adam, prophesied of these, saying, Behold, the Lord cometh with ten thousands of his saints,

To execute judgment upon all, and to convince all that are ungodly among them of all their ungodly deeds which they have ungodly committed, and of all their hard speeches which ungodly sinners have spoken against him ... Jude Chapter 1 verses 14-15

Ungodly, ungodly, ungodly, ungodly. Four times the word describing the wickedness of God-rejecting sinners appears in Enoch's prophetic declaration. The prophet made this pronouncement because he saw the future unfold thousands of years ago, and declared it before he was bodily translated to the heavenly realms. This means it is a done deal: already written and must come to pass.

While the prophecy is primarily directed at the sensual, defiled false teachers and false prophets who have deceived many and led people away from the truth, Enoch says the Lord is coming to execute judgment upon all, and he is bringing his saints with him. Psalm Chapter 149 verses 6-9 show us the saints of the most High have been given the honor of executing the judgment written, and will bind the kings with chains, and their nobles with iron. They will execute vengeance on the heathen, and punishments upon the people. This is why the follower of Christ is admonished to turn the other cheek and give place to wrath and avengement in this life. To everything there is a time and season. In the judgment, the saints—possessing the spirits of just men made perfect—will execute perfect justice in the avenging work of God. Neither will this be a "battle between good and evil." The correct understanding is the execution of a verdict resulting from a High Court ruling that something was so evil as to merit complete destruction.

The Cup Removed from Zion's Hand and Given to the Nations

Thus saith thy Lord the Lord, and thy God that pleadeth the cause of his people, Behold, I have taken out of thine hand the cup of trembling, even the dregs of the cup of my fury; thou shalt no more drink it again:

But I will put it into the hand of them that afflict thee; which have said to thy soul, Bow down, that we may go over: and thou hast laid thy body as the ground, and as the street, to them that went over. Isaiah Chapter 51 verses 22-23

Enslavement, exile, poverty, ignorance. Occupants of the lowest rungs of society. A people with no say in self-direction, whose decisions are made for them by others. Requirement of honorable salutation and obeisance. How difficult for the Gentiles and the rich of the earth to envision themselves in such a position. **Yet, this is what the Biblical scriptures teach**. The prophet Isaiah lived long before my time, yet saw the future past my days—because God revealed it to him. Anger at the messengers is futile; it won't change God's word that is forever settled in heaven. The humiliation done to the children of Israel and Judah is destined to be experienced by every nation which oppressed them. They will be enslaved, for he that leadeth into captivity must go into captivity.

"I will also gather all nations, and will bring them down into the valley of Jehoshaphat, and will plead with them there for my people and for my heritage Israel, whom they have scattered among the nations, and parted my land.

And they have cast lots for my people; and have given a boy for an harlot, and sold a girl for wine, that they might drink.

The children also of Judah and the children of Jerusalem have ye sold unto the Grecians, that ye might remove them far from their border.

Behold, I will raise them out of the place whither ye have sold them, and will return your recompence upon your own head:

And I will sell your sons and your daughters into the hand of the children of Judah, and they shall sell them to the Sabeans, to a people far off: for the Lord hath spoken it." Joel Chapter 3 verses 2-3 and 6-8

Notice God said he will gather all nations, and in Joel's account, he implies someone other than the Gentiles sold the children of Judah to the Grecians (or Gentiles.) This is a specific proclamation to the Islamists who raided the villages of Judah exiled in Africa, and sold them to Gentiles. Nevertheless, all nations have participated in the revelry of spoiling Judah. Now the children of the men-stealers will be sold to Judah, but Judah won't want them, and will sell them to the Sabeans: a people described as located 'far off.'

Judah won't want to be bothered with these offspring of the men-stealers, because they will have their own set of servants already waiting. Isaiah Chapter 14 verses 1-4 illustrate how this will come to pass...

"For the Lord will have mercy on Jacob, and will yet choose Israel, and set them in their own land: and the strangers shall be joined with them, and they shall cleave to the house of Jacob.

And the people shall take them, and bring them to their place: and the house of Israel shall possess them in the land of the Lord for servants and handmaids: and they shall take them captives, whose captives they were; and they shall rule over their oppressors.

And it shall come to pass in the day that the Lord shall give thee rest from thy sorrow, and from thy fear, and from the hard bondage wherein thou wast made to serve, That thou shalt take up this proverb against the king of Babylon, and say, How hath the oppressor ceased! the golden city ceased!"

Isaiah Chapter 61 verse 5 bears this out further: "And strangers shall stand and feed your flocks, and the sons of the alien shall be your plowmen and your vinedressers."

In seeing the horrifying events coming upon the world, and the descendants of the original Hebrews supernaturally repatriated in their land, various of the Gentile nations will seek to cleave to the house Jacob; for they will perceive there is safety with them.

"Thus saith the Lord of hosts; In those days it shall come to pass, that ten men shall take hold out of all languages of the nations, even shall take hold of the skirt of him that is a Jew, saying, We will go with you: for we have heard that God is with you..." Zechariah Chapter 8 verse 23. Based on this depiction, a Hebrew just out and about is subject to be physically encountered and entreated for socialization and fellowship, from hearts hungry to know the Lord. This was what God always desired for his "Prince" that he would be a light to the Gentiles to reveal his Father, the mighty King. Now we see in the days to come, the desire of the Lord's heart is granted, as the restored Israel walks with God's laws engraved forever in their heart.

Idolatrous Inhabitants Removed; Black Israel Established in the Land

Each of the following prophecies details the same event. They speak to the destruction of Edom; a great destruction—for the violence done to the children of Judah.

The execution is likened to the treading of a winepress, and the executioner is the Lord Jesus Christ. The ruin of Edom is declared by God to be in righteousness, and undertaken on behalf of the redemption of his people. It is the day of the Lord's vengeance.

"Who is this that cometh from Edom, with dyed garments from Bozrah? this that is glorious in his apparel, travelling in the greatness of his strength? I that speak in righteousness, mighty to save.

Wherefore art thou red in thine apparel, and thy garments like him that treadeth in the winefat?

I have trodden the winepress alone; and of the people there was none with me: for I will tread them in mine anger, and trample them in my fury; and their blood shall be sprinkled upon my garments, and I will stain all my raiment. For the day of vengeance is in mine heart, and the year of my redeemed is come." Isaiah Chapter 63 verses 1-4

Isaiah Chapter 34 verses 1-8 elaborates further and shows that the devastation is the result of God's anger at the long running struggle to deny his people their rightful heritage. The imagery of the anomalies in the heavens indicates God is going to permit this misrepresentation to continue to propagate until the very end of the age. Lambs, goats, rams, unicorns, and bullocks point to God's view of the slaughter as a sacrificial restitution for the denigration of his people.

"Come near, ye nations, to hear; and hearken, ye people: let the earth hear, and all that is therein; the world, and all things that come forth of it.

For the indignation of the Lord is upon all nations, and his fury upon all their armies: he hath utterly destroyed them, he hath delivered them to the slaughter.

Their slain also shall be cast out, and their stink shall come up out of their carcases, and the mountains shall be melted with their blood.

And all the host of heaven shall be dissolved, and the heavens shall be rolled together as a scroll: and all their host shall fall down, as the leaf falleth off from the vine, and as a falling fig from the fig tree.

For my sword shall be bathed in heaven: behold, it shall come down upon Idumea, and upon the people of my curse, to judgment.

The sword of the Lord is filled with blood, it is made fat with fatness, and with the blood of lambs and goats, with the fat of the kidneys of rams: for the Lord hath a sacrifice in Bozrah, and a great slaughter in the land of Idumea.

And the unicorns shall come down with them, and the bullocks with the bulls; and their land shall be soaked with blood, and their dust made fat with fatness.

For it is the day of the Lord's vengeance, and the year of recompences for the controversy of Zion." Isaiah Chapter 34 verses 1-8

The Hebrew meaning for the word 'controversy' used in this passage means a personal or legal contest. It implies grappling, struggling, or defending a position in a debate. Although God is awakening the sons of Zion against the sons of Greece, we really don't have a dog in that fight. We don't have to face off with people and insist on proving our heritage, or that we are the rightful heirs of the land covenanted to Abraham, Isaac, and Jacob. God says vengeance is his, and that he will repay. Our strength is to be found in quietness and confidence, and the anchor of our soul is wisdom, knowledge, and the consolation that it is impossible for God to lie.

The prophet Joel associates the same heavenly cataclysms to a divine judgment and intimates that prior to this, strangers have occupied earthly Jerusalem; and Jerusalem is not considered holy in God's eyes until the strangers are removed. He exhorts the children of Judah that in the midst of the terrestrial and interstellar upheavals the Lord will be the hope of his people, and the strength of the children of Israel. Both Egypt—representing the people and lands who oppressed Judah in the latter day bondage, and Edom, representing the people and lands of those who appropriated themselves of Judah's heritage—are rendered desolate.

"The sun and the moon shall be darkened, and the stars shall withdraw their shining.

The Lord also shall roar out of Zion, and utter his voice from Jerusalem; and the heavens and the earth shall shake: but the Lord will be the hope of his people, and the strength of the children of Israel.

So shall ye know that I am the Lord your God dwelling in Zion, my holy mountain: then shall Jerusalem be holy, and there shall no strangers pass through her any more.

And it shall come to pass in that day, that the mountains shall drop down new wine, and the hills shall flow with milk, and all the rivers of Judah shall flow with waters, and a fountain shall come forth of the house of the Lord, and shall water the valley of Shittim.

Egypt shall be a desolation, and Edom shall be a desolate wilderness, for the violence against the children of Judah, because they have shed innocent blood in their land.

But Judah shall dwell for ever, and Jerusalem from generation to generation." Joel Chapter 3 verses 15-20

Lastly, we look at the end of the apostolic testimony, and see the One who told the disciples that Jerusalem would be trodden down of the Gentiles, until the times of the Gentiles were fulfilled. The sharp sword speaks to the sword bathed in heaven that Isaiah saw; the vesture dipped in blood to the staining of the garment in Bozrah; and the treading of the winepress of the fierceness and wrath of Almighty God to the vision Isaiah saw of the Lord returning in great strength from Edom.

"And I saw heaven opened, and behold a white horse; and he that sat upon him was called Faithful and True, and in righteousness he doth judge and make war.

*His eyes were as a flame of fire, and on his head were many crowns; and he had a name written, that no man knew, but he himself.

*And he was clothed with a vesture dipped in blood: and his name is called The Word of God.

*And the armies which were in heaven followed him upon white horses, clothed in fine linen, white and clean.

*And out of his mouth goeth a sharp sword, that with it he should smite the nations: and he shall rule them with a rod of iron: and he treadeth the winepress of the fierceness and wrath of Almighty God.

*And he hath on his vesture and on his thigh a name written, KING OF KINGS, AND LORD OF LORDS." Revelation Chapter 19 verses 11-16

What you are seeing here are the mighty works the Lord is going to do on our behalf as he rights every wrong and judges the nations and the pride of man in his fierce wrath. These are the same types of things he did when he delivered our forefathers from Egypt, established them in the land of covenant, and fought for the judges and righteous kings of Israel.

Because we have been in bondage for so long, and our understanding has been darkened regarding our heritage, we have seen these scriptures many times without understanding they applied to our people. The Old and New Testaments are written about us and to us, although the way has been opened through the cross for all repentant sinners to be justified by faith and continued sanctification. If we really believe God's promises, we will stand in faith and praise in these perilous times and declare, "**If God be for us, who can be against us?**"

To the Jew First, then to the Greek... the Divine Sequence of Judgment

Is God unrighteous who taketh vengeance? No, in no wise: for we have before proved both Jews and Gentiles, that they are all under sin; As it is written, There is none righteous, no, not one...excerpted from Romans Chapter 3 verses 5 and 9.

For there is no respect of persons with God. For as many as have sinned without law shall also perish without law: and as many as have sinned in the law shall be judged by the law...Romans Chapter 2 verses 11-12.

Our forefathers were given specific instructions when they came out of Egypt in the form of the law given on Sinai. Throughout Israel's history God sent all his servants the prophets, rising early and sending them, but Israel did not hearken. Further, they persecuted and killed them. Before Moses' death, he admonished them that God would raise up a prophet from among their brethren, and they were to hear that prophet. Moses warned the people that any who would not listen to the words the prophet spoke would be destroyed from among the people. Nevertheless, when Jesus manifested as a righteous prophet in the midst of his brethren, doing the miraculous works of God, he was met with hatred, jealousy, and unbelief—from a self-righteous religious elite who felt they had the handle on all things pertaining to godliness.

Our forefather's rebellion in the wilderness meant that a huge contingent never saw the land of covenant. God kept them circling around in the wilderness until all those twenty years and older who had murmured against him had perished. When their Redeemer was sent to them, they clamored to have him crucified, and a murderer granted in his stead. They also sealed their demand for his execution with a blood oath on themselves and their descendants.

This rejection of both God and his chosen Representative—his only begotten Son—occasioned the departure of God's presence from Jerusalem and activated the curses detailed by Moses and the prophets. Throughout this overall rejection of God, there was always a remnant faithful to his revealed truth. And once the saving gospel was revealed by the Hebrew disciples, there was a remnant who believed and were saved. The church at Jerusalem came under great persecution, and the saints were scattered to outlying areas and surrounding countries. This turn of events, combined with the tireless ministry of the Apostle Paul, brought the gospel to the Gentiles.

The Gentiles, however, did no better. With the reign of Constantine, the gospel would become compromised and grow cold and impotent under the strangle-hold of the Roman State Church. Over a millennia later, the work of Tyndale would translate the scriptures from Latin to the language of the common people, and the advent of the printing press would occasion their distribution to the many who sat in darkness. This delivery of the word of God came at a steep price, and ultimately cost Tyndale his life at the stake. I quote here from Foxe's Book of Martyrs to show the formidable resistance that has always characterized the satanic assault against the kingdom of God:

> "William Tyndale, the faithful minister of Christ, was born about the borders of Wales, and brought up from a child in the University of Oxford, where he, by long continuance,   increased as   well in the

knowledge of tongues, and other liberal arts, as especially in the knowledge of the Scriptures, whereunto his mind was singularly addicted; insomuch that he, lying then in Magdalen Hall, read privily to certain students and fellows of Magdalen College some parcel of divinity; instructing them in the knowledge and truth of the Scriptures. His manners and conversation being correspondent to the same, were such that all they that knew him reputed him to be a man of most virtuous disposition, and of life unspotted.

Thus he, in the University of Oxford, increasing more and more in learning, and proceeding in degrees of the schools, spying his time, removed from thence to the University of Cambridge, where he likewise made his abode a certain space. Being now further ripened in the knowledge of God's Word, leaving that university, he resorted to one Master Welch, a knight of Gloucestershire, and was there schoolmaster to his children, and in good favor with his master. As this gentleman kept a good ordinary commonly at his table, there resorted to him many times sundry abbots, deans, archdeacons, with divers other doctors, and great beneficed men; who there, together with Master Tyndale siting at the same table, did use many times to enter communication, and talk of learned men, as of Luther and of Erasmus; also of divers other controversies and questions upon the Scripture.

Then Master Tyndale, as he was learned and well practiced in God's matters, spared not to show unto them simply and plainly his judgment, and when they at any time did vary from Tyndale in opinions, he would show them in the Book, and lay plainly before them the open and manifest places of the Scriptures, to confute their errors, and confirm his sayings. And thus continued they for a certain season, reasoning and contending together divers times, until at length they waxed weary, and bare a secret grudge in their hearts against him.

As this grew on, the priests of the country, clustering together, began to grudge and storm against Tyndale, railing against him in alehouses and other places, affirming that his sayings were heresy; and accused him secretly to the chancellor, and others of the bishop's officers."

So we see thus far, that Tyndale was inspired by the work of those confronting the Church of Rome about its error, and how he would reason with them from the scripture, and how they became increasingly hostile to him. We continue from Foxe's account:

"There dwelt not far off a certain doctor, that he been chancellor to a bishop, who had been of old, familiar acquaintance with Master Tyndale, and favored him well; unto whom Master Tyndale went and opened his mind upon divers questions of the Scripture: for to him he durst be bold to disclose his heart. Unto whom the doctor said, "Do you not know that the pope is very Antichrist, whom the Scripture speaketh of? But beware what you say; for if you shall be perceived to be of that opinion, it will cost you your life."

Here we see that as early as the 16th century, the Roman Church was the enemy of whoever would know the word of God for themselves. Continuing from Foxe's account:

"Not long after, Master Tyndale happened to be in the company of a certain divine, recounted for a learned man, and, in communing and disputing with him, he drove him to that issue, that the said great doctor burst out into these blasphemous words, "We were better to be without God's laws than the pope's." Master Tyndale, hearing this, full of godly zeal, and not bearing that blasphemous saying, replied, "I defy the pope, and all his laws;" and added, "If God spared him life, ere many years he would cause a boy that driveth the plough to know more of the Scripture than he did."

Faith without works is dead; but here we see Tyndale confessing his determination to make the scriptures available to the common man. Continuing...

"Therefore, having by God's providence some aid ministered unto him by Humphrey Mummuth, and certain other good men, he took his leave of the realm, and departed into Germany, where the good man, being inflamed with a tender care and zeal of his country, refused no travail nor diligence, how, by all means possible, to reduce his brethren and countrymen of England to the same taste and understanding of God's holy Word and verity, which the Lord had endued him withal. Whereupon, considering in his mind, and conferring also with John Frith, Tyndale thought with himself no way more to conduce thereunto, than if the Scripture were turned into the vulgar speech, that the poor people might read and see the simple plain Word of God. He perceived that it was not possible to establish the lay people in any truth, except the Scriptures were so plainly laid before their eyes in their mother tongue that they might see the meaning of the text; for else, whatsoever truth should be taught them, the enemies of the truth would quench it, either with reasons of sophistry, and traditions of their own making, founded without all ground of Scripture; or else juggling with the text, expounding it in such a sense as it were impossible to gather of the text, if the right meaning thereof were seen.

Master Tyndale considered this only, or most chiefly, to be the cause of all mischief in the Church, that the Scriptures of God were hidden from the people's eyes; for so long the abominable doings and idolatries maintained by the pharisaical clergy could not be espied; and therefore all their labor was with might and main to keep it down, so that either it should not be read at all, or if it were, they would darken the right sense with the mist of their sophistry, and so entangle those who rebuked or despised their abominations; wresting the Scripture unto their own purpose, contrary unto the meaning of the text, they would so delude the unlearned lay people, that though thou felt in thy heart, and wert sure that all were false that they said, yet couldst thou not solve their subtle riddles.

For these and such other considerations this good man was stirred up of God to translate the Scripture into his mother tongue, for the profit of the simple people of his country; first setting in hand with the New Testament, which came forth in print about A.D. 1525. Cuthbert Tonstal, bishop of London, with Sir Thomas More, being sore aggrieved, despised how to destroy that false erroneous translation, as they called it."

Thus we can see the Roman Church continued running the same game as the Pharisees in Jesus' day. They insisted on interpreting the scripture for the people, but because of their own unregenerate hearts, distorted the truth of God's word; leaving the people in the dark. This was why the psalmist David said "The entrance of thy words giveth light," and "Thy word is a lamp unto my feet and a light unto my path," and Jesus said his appearance among his people meant "Light is come into the world, but men loved darkness rather than light, because their deeds were evil."

Ultimately, Tyndale was set up for entrapment which placed him in the hands of those who hated him. He was placed in prison. The account goes on...

"Master Tyndale, remaining in prison, was proffered an advocate and a procurator; the which he refused, saying that he would make answer for himself. He had so preached to them who had him in charge, and such as was there conversant with him in the Castle that they reported of him, that if he were not a good Christian man, they knew not whom they might take to be one.

At last, after much reasoning, when no reason would serve, although he deserved no death, he was condemned by virtue of the emperor's decree, made in the assembly at Augsburg. Brought forth to the place of execution, he was tied to the stake, strangled by the hangman, and afterwards consumed with fire, at the town of Vilvorde, A.D. 1536; crying at the stake with a fervent zeal, and a loud voice, "Lord! open the king of England's eyes."

Such was the power of his doctrine, and the sincerity of his life, that during the time of his imprisonment (which endured a year and a half), he converted, it is said, his keeper, the keeper's daughter, and others of his household. As touching his translation of the New Testament, because his enemies did so much carp at it, pretending it to be full of heresies, he wrote to John Frith, as followeth, "I call God to record against the day we shall appear before our Lord Jesus, that I never altered one syllable of God's Word against my conscience, nor would do this day, if all that is in earth, whether it be honor, pleasure, or riches, might be given me."

This story of Tyndale's life is important because it shows the intensity of the spiritual battle against the word of God, and the faithful witness of Gentiles who stood their ground and loved not their lives unto the death. Ultimately Tyndale's efforts brought us the scriptures we look to today for instruction in godliness, wisdom, and comfort; and this would not be the case had it been left up to the Roman Church. But now that the Gentiles had the New Testament—sealed with the blood of martyrs—with its message of repentance from sin and love as the fulfilling of the Law, were they willing to follow Christ? Or was it more advantageous to use God's word to justify their ventures and empirical pursuits?

Ultimately, we see the holy scriptures—whether Old or New Covenant, were distorted and used by the Gentiles to endorse the agenda of carnal man, and give a moral covering to robbery, slavery, and genocide. When we—the Hebrews, were given the precious oracles of God and his most precious gift of all—the only begotten of the Father—we trampled it underfoot. When the Gentiles were granted the free gift of justification by faith and citizenship into the commonwealth of Israel, in return for their lives as a living sacrifice holy and acceptable unto God, they likewise trampled it underfoot. We were brought low for our rebellion until broken and made an astonishment, a proverb, and a byword. And that is exactly what awaits Gentiles during the millennial reign of Christ.

The saints of the most High in conjunction with the house of Judah and the house of Israel will possess the kingdom, and all Gentiles who were not found in Christ at his return, that cleave to the house of Jacob will serve them. Just as our chastening was for our good and correction, theirs will be also, if they are willing to submit and humble themselves under God's hand. It will be a precious opportunity, for Daniel Chapter 12 verse 2 tells us other Gentiles will be resurrected at that time—but only to serve and ultimately be destroyed for their wickedness at the end of the millennium. This applies not only to Japhethic Gentiles, but the Hamitic and mixed multitude peoples who have historically enslaved, sold, and castrated the children of Judah and Israel in Africa.

Why the Gentiles Will Serve...God is No Respecter of Persons

And thinkest thou this, O man, that judgest them which do such things, and doest the same, that thou shalt escape the judgment of God?

Or despisest thou the riches of his goodness and forbearance and longsuffering; not knowing that the goodness of God leadeth thee to repentance?

But after thy hardness and impenitent heart treasurest up unto thy self wrath against the day of wrath and revelation of the righteous judgment of God; Who will render to every man according to his deeds:

To them who by patient continuance in well doing seek for glory and honour and immortality, eternal life:

But unto them that are contentious, and do not obey the truth, but obey unrighteousness, indignation and wrath,

Tribulation and anguish, upon every soul of man that doeth evil, of the Jew first, and also of the Gentile;

But glory, honour, and peace, to every man that worketh good, to the Jew first, and also to the Gentile:

For there is no respect of persons with God. Romans Chapter 2 verses 3-11

God would not have been righteous, and would have dishonored his own standard of holiness if he had permitted Israel to continue in idolatry, causing his name to be blasphemed among the nations, and still allowed them to reside in the land promised to the forefathers. His sense of justice demanded judgment for sin. Still, he had a sworn covenant with Abraham, Isaac, and Jacob that was infrangible. Because mercy is as big a part of God as judgment, he provided a payment for Israel's transgression by his own righteous Son, then exiled Israel from the land of covenant, while holding it in ward for them. Jeremiah Chapter 16 verse 18 and Isaiah Chapter 40 verse 2 indicate the Lord has recompensed us double for our iniquity and sin.

The postponement of Israel's repatriation was the window for the Gentiles to come into the kingdom of God. Particularly throughout the 19th and 20th centuries, men of God would come on the scene bold in the gospel and preach forcefully against sin. Revival would break out in the West, in England and in the British Isles, and many souls would be converted, but after a season the fires of conviction would cool. A smattering of churches here and there took the testimonies of Jesus and his disciples regarding the baptism of the Holy Ghost seriously, and from these fellowships sanctification, power over sin, and miracles by the power of God manifested.

However, as Western civilization increasingly prospered, seeking God decreased proportionately. Medical 'breakthroughs' challenged the need to trust God for healing. Entertainment and the ability to bring it straight into homes competed with time for Bible study, prayer, and the ability to hear God's still small voice. Progressive churches decided the baptism of the Holy Ghost was outmoded, and that they could grow and prosper quite well without it, using secular corporate growth strategies.

Without the discernment of the Spirit, churches began to wax weak, lukewarm, and powerless. It didn't appear that way initially, because outwardly, the churches were growing right along with the prosperity wave in the West. They couldn't see that they lacked faith, were blind to discernment, and unrighteous. In short, they were unaware a Laodicean transformation was taking place. But it was obvious as the decades of the sixties, seventies, eighties, and nineties successively rolled through that the church in the West was losing credibility. Amazingly, an overwhelming number of people still classified themselves as Christians, or religious.

Rather than return in repentance to scriptural moorings, the church in the West increasingly sought how to incorporate elements from other belief systems, secular philosophy, and entertainment in order to draw new members and keep their coffers full. They also found ever more creative ways to extract money from people already trapped by a burdensome economic system. They continued to incorporate pagan traditions, mixing the profane with the holy; even though many overseers—at least—knew the practices were rooted in idolatrous ritual. Preferring broken cisterns over the living water of the Holy Ghost, they voluntarily yoked themselves to the Roman Church, permitted themselves to be used as political endorsement for Caesar's empirical goals, and of their own resources and constructs, supported foreign ventures. The atrocities and toll in human suffering resulting from extraneous political and military activities morally and financially endorsed by churches has caused God's name to be blasphemed among the nations.

God would not be righteous, and would dishonor his own standard of holiness if he permitted professing Christianity to continue in lukewarmness, causing his name to be blasphemed among the nations, and still allowed them to take a seat beside men such as Tyndale, who as a true spiritual father, cared that the common poor had access to the living word, and boldly stood for the gospel—even unto death. God has no outstanding covenant on the books with the Gentiles as he has with Israel. The Gentiles received a premium offer under a broad 'whosoever will' invitation. Their simple requirement was to turn from idolatry and sexual immorality, and walk in love toward their brethren and their neighbor as they worshiped the true and living God. His sense of justice will demand that any reigning with him must be willing to bear the yoke of suffering, and purge the spirit unto holiness. Therefore, if Gentiles in the West find they must serve, it should be counted a blessing: for the opportunity for repentance and reinstatement trumps judgment to flames.

God Requires the Past...Just Judgment for the Sins of the Forefathers

The typical question from the Gentile is, "Why must I serve?? I didn't own slaves. I didn't go with the roving bands to burn and pillage and terrorize and lynch. I didn't conduct the non-consensual experiments, or craft the oppressive policies, or bring in smokable, injectable death from overseas to destabilize communities and undermine the Black man." And the simple answer is, "No, perhaps you didn't. But your forefathers did."

Herein is the bitter pill that is difficult for any of us to accept: the law of sowing and reaping. You will recall that law from earlier in the book:

*We always reap what we sow...

*We always reap more than what was sown...

*We always reap in a different season than when we sowed.

Solomon puts it another way in Ecclesiastes Chapter 3 verse 15...

"That which hath been is now; and that which is to be hath already been; and God requireth that which is past."

I didn't bake cakes to the queen of heaven, or weep for Tammuz, but my forebears did. And I have found myself in a land of Captivity that is not mine; the descendant of those who did things the Lord forbid, and sent his prophets to repeatedly warn against. If God has recompensed Israel double, how much more the nations of the world? Especially after they saw our example? The irony is that the Gentiles had the Bible, and could clearly see God's mode of operation and response to disobedience and rebellion. It was utter folly to think he would chasten his portion, and let the rest of the world slide. The righteousness of God demands that he judges impartially.

A Taste of Your Own Medicine, Work Detail, Loss of Privileges

We noted earlier the unregenerate Gentiles during the millennial reign of Christ will be the objects of enslavement, occupy the lower tiers of society, and will have to honor those they formerly enslaved and subjugated. They will now be ruled over, for when they had autonomous rule, they misused it and abused Judah, Israel, their own people, and the inhabitants of other nations. Their high titles and memorials will disappear, that God might be glorified in the branch of his planting and the work of his hands...

"The sons also of them that afflicted thee shall come bending unto thee; and all they that despised thee shall bow themselves down at the soles of thy feet; and they shall call thee, The city of the Lord, The Zion of the Holy One of Israel." Isaiah Chapter 60 verse 14

The Gentiles must serve by default, because the dominion belongs solely to the house of Judah as explained in Micah Chapter 4 verse 8: "And thou, O tower of the flock, the stronghold of the daughter of Zion, unto thee shall it come, even the first dominion; the kingdom shall come to the daughter of Jerusalem."

The sons of Jacob will have their own land: every man under his vine and under his fig tree; neither will any terrify them to force them off their property to confiscate it—the mouth of the Lord of hosts has decreed this. This means no authority will demand taxes of them to "allow" them to retain their possession. The only relation the Gentiles will have to the possessions of Israel is as laborers, for "strangers shall stand and feed your flocks, and the sons of the alien shall be your plowmen and your vinedressers." Isaiah Chapter 61 verse 5.

Even royalty of the Gentiles must bow down before the people...Isaiah Chapter 49 verses 22-23 "...Thus saith the Lord God, Behold, I will lift up mine hand to the Gentiles, and set up my standard to the people: and they shall bring thy sons in their arms, and thy daughters shall be carried upon their shoulders.

And kings shall be thy nursing fathers, and their queens thy nursing mothers: they shall bow down to thee with their face toward the earth, and lick up the dust of thy feet; and thou shalt know that I am the Lord: for they shall not be ashamed that wait for me.

Before honor is humility, and Judah and Israel have been humbled under the mighty hand of God. Now, the riches of the Gentiles will be brought into the kingdom "...But ye shall be named the Priests of the Lord: men shall call you the Ministers of our God: ye shall eat the riches of the Gentiles, and in their glory shall ye boast yourselves"...Isaiah Chapter 61 verse 6.

Ministry, intercession, worship and praise and blessing of the work of their hands is the lot of redeemed Israel "...Thy people also shall be all righteous: they shall inherit the land for ever, the branch of my planting, the work of my hands, that I may be glorified." Isaiah Chapter 60 verse 21

For your shame ye shall have double; and for confusion they shall rejoice in their portion: therefore in their land they shall possess the double: everlasting joy shall be unto them," ...Isaiah Chapter 61 verse 7.

In the verse following verse 7 God says he loves judgment; this means he is saying the subjugation of the Gentiles is only just recompense for the suffering of his people. Notice God does not revile and insult the Gentiles with names like dog, dung, bastard, etc. in the manner of those who composed the Jewish Talmud—who are Gentiles themselves. God does not need to call people out of their name, or insult their skin color and ethnic features. He merely says the Gentiles will serve as recompense for what was done to Israel, and rests it there. Because he holds all power, and no one can reverse what he has decreed, he doesn't have to resort to ad hominem attacks. Only carnal man—fearful of losing something wrongfully appropriated— will come out on the defensive, when not even under attack.

Chapter XVII...End of the Millennium and Beyond

Thou hast rebuked the heathen, thou hast destroyed the wicked, thou hast put out their name for ever and ever.

The Gentile's Last Stand...Psalm Two Goes Live

The thousand years of peace foretold by the prophets will be a time of unprecedented peace, joy, and prosperity for Israel and Judah. For the saints who spent their early earthly lives under the Blood and Love covenant of Jesus Christ, they have entered into the joy of the Lord. This is not some ethereal mist consciousness, but a very tangible existence, as expressed by Jesus in the Gospels:

"And I say unto you, That many shall come from the east and west, and shall sit down with Abraham, and Isaac, and Jacob, in the kingdom of heaven..." Matthew Chapter 8 verse 11.

"But I say unto you, I will not drink henceforth of this fruit of the vine, until that day when I drink it new with you in my Father's kingdom..." Matthew Chapter 26 verse 29.

This speaks to vibrant fellowship and activity on the part of the vast family of God, both glorified and human. And with Satan confined to the bottomless pit and his demonic host bound awaiting judgment, tranquility, beauty, and joy will characterize each day. It is an active yet restful life that only gets progressively better. In such an atmosphere, many nations will serve God voluntarily in awe and gratefulness—having realized their historical heritage was a lie and confusion:

"O Lord, my strength, and my fortress, and my refuge in the day of affliction, the Gentiles shall come unto thee from the ends of the earth, and shall say, Surely our fathers have inherited lies, vanity, and things wherein there is no profit" ...Jeremiah Chapter 16 verse 19.

"And many nations shall come, and say, Come, and let us go up to the mountain of the Lord, and to the house of the God of Jacob; and he will teach us of his ways, and we will walk in his paths: for the law shall go forth of Zion, and the word of the Lord from Jerusalem" ...Micah Chapter 4 verse 2

"And many nations shall be joined to the Lord in that day, and shall be my people: and I will dwell in the midst of thee, and thou shalt know that the Lord of hosts hath sent me unto thee" ...Zechariah Chapter 2 verse 11

"Yea, many people and strong nations shall come to seek the Lord of hosts in Jerusalem, and to pray before the Lord" ... Zechariah Chapter 8 verse 22

Additionally, all nations will be required to worship annually at the Feast of Tabernacles, and any nation that refuses to come will receive no rain:

"And it shall come to pass, that every one that is left of all the nations which came against Jerusalem shall even go up from year to year to worship the King, the Lord of hosts, and to keep the feast of tabernacles.

And it shall be, that whoso will not come up of all the families of the earth unto Jerusalem to worship the King, the Lord of hosts, even upon them shall be no rain.

And if the family of Egypt go not up, and come not, that have no rain; there shall be the plague, wherewith the Lord will smite the heathen that come not up to keep the feast of tabernacles.

This shall be the punishment of Egypt, and the punishment of all nations that come not up to keep the feast of tabernacles" ...Zechariah Chapter 14 verses 16-19

But some among the nations will bow the knee only because they are forced to. For these former oppressors of Israel, the thousand-year sentence of servitude will foster resentment, rather than repentance. This will ultimately lead to an organized rebellion, ironically timed with the release of Satan from the bottomless pit. This attempt to overthrow the kingdom of God on earth will result in their annihilation. Psalm 2 indicates the iron rod rule wielded by the Lord Jesus Christ and his Bride have incited intense bitterness in those nations who held the reins of power during the age of carnal man. They want nothing more than to throw off the restraining yoke which is enabling the rest of the world to abide in peace and harmony. A conspiracy is formed...

*"Why do the heathen rage, and the people imagine a vain thing?

*The kings of the earth set themselves, and the rulers take counsel together, against the Lord, and against his anointed, saying,

*Let us break their bands asunder, and cast away their cords from us."

But, it is a sedition doomed to failure. God predicts what will happen and warns them to ditch their plans...

*"Thou shalt break them with a rod of iron; thou shalt dash them in pieces like a potter's vessel.

*Be wise now therefore, O ye kings: be instructed, ye judges of the earth.

*Serve the Lord with fear, and rejoice with trembling.

*Kiss the Son, lest he be angry, and ye perish from the way, when his wrath is kindled but a little.

Blessed are all they that put their trust in him."

Zechariah has already hinted at the identity of one of the nations that will initially harbor dissidents: the Hamitic peoples of Egypt. But a close look at the 38th and 39th chapters of Ezekiel, and Revelation Chapter 20 verse 8 indicates the real hatred stoking the fires of the final rebellion emanates from Japheth's descendants Gog, Magog, Meshech, Tubal, Gomer, and Togarmah; joined by rebels from Persia, Ethiopia, and Libya. The apostle John provides the synopsis:

"And when the thousand years are expired, Satan shall be loosed out of his prison,

And shall go out to deceive the nations which are in the four quarters of the earth, Gog and Magog, to gather them together to battle: the number of whom is as the sand of the sea."

Revelation Chapter 20 verse 8

The prophet Ezekiel gives the blow by blow breakdown in Chapter 38... "And the word of the Lord came unto me, saying,

Son of man, set thy face against Gog, the land of Magog, the chief prince of Meshech and Tubal, and prophesy against him,

And say, Thus saith the Lord God; Behold, I am against thee, O Gog, the chief prince of Meshech and Tubal:

And I will turn thee back, and put hooks into thy jaws, and I will bring thee forth, and all thine army, horses and horsemen, all of them clothed with all sorts of armour, even a great company with bucklers and shields, all of them handling swords:

Persia, Ethiopia, and Libya with them; all of them with shield and helmet:

Gomer, and all his bands; the house of Togarmah of the north quarters, and all his bands: and many people with thee.

Be thou prepared, and prepare for thyself, thou, and all thy company that are assembled unto thee, and be thou a guard unto them.

After many days thou shalt be visited: in the latter years thou shalt come into the land that is brought back from the sword, and is gathered out of many people, against the mountains of Israel, which have been always waste: but it is brought forth out of the nations, and they shall dwell safely all of them.

Thou shalt ascend and come like a storm, thou shalt be like a cloud to cover the land, thou, and all thy bands, and many people with thee.

Thus saith the Lord God; It shall also come to pass, that at the same time shall things come into thy mind, and thou shalt think an evil thought:

And thou shalt say, I will go up to the land of unwalled villages; I will go to them that are at rest, that dwell safely, all of them dwelling without walls, and having neither bars nor gates,

To take a spoil, and to take a prey; to turn thine hand upon the desolate places that are now inhabited, and upon the people that are gathered out of the nations, which have gotten cattle and goods, that dwell in the midst of the land.

Sheba, and Dedan, and the merchants of Tarshish, with all the young lions thereof, shall say unto thee, Art thou come to take a spoil? hast thou gathered thy company to take a prey? to carry away silver and gold, to take away cattle and goods, to take a great spoil?

Therefore, son of man, prophesy and say unto Gog, Thus saith the Lord God; In that day when my people of Israel dwelleth safely, shalt thou not know it?

And thou shalt come from thy place out of the north parts, thou, and many people with thee, all of them riding upon horses, a great company, and a mighty army:

And thou shalt come up against my people of Israel, as a cloud to cover the land; it shall be in the latter days, and I will bring thee against my land, that the heathen may know me, when I shall be sanctified in thee, O Gog, before their eyes.

Thus saith the Lord God; Art thou he of whom I have spoken in old time by my servants the prophets of Israel, which prophesied in those days many years that I would bring thee against them?

And it shall come to pass at the same time when Gog shall come against the land of Israel, saith the Lord God, that my fury shall come up in my face.

For in my jealousy and in the fire of my wrath have I spoken, Surely in that day there shall be a great shaking in the land of Israel;

So that the fishes of the sea, and the fowls of the heaven, and the beasts of the field, and all creeping things that creep upon the earth, and all the men that are upon the face of the earth, shall shake at my presence, and the mountains shall be thrown down, and the steep places shall fall, and every wall shall fall to the ground.

And I will call for a sword against him throughout all my mountains, saith the Lord God: every man's sword shall be against his brother. And I will plead against him with pestilence and with blood; and I will rain upon him, and upon his bands, and upon the many people that are with him, an overflowing rain, and great hailstones, fire, and brimstone.

Thus will I magnify myself, and sanctify myself; and I will be known in the eyes of many nations, and they shall know that I am the Lord."

***Chapter 39 ***

"Therefore, thou son of man, prophesy against Gog, and say, Thus saith the Lord God; Behold, I am against thee, O Gog, the chief prince of Meshech and Tubal:

And I will turn thee back, and leave but the sixth part of thee, and will cause thee to come up from the north parts, and will bring thee upon the mountains of Israel:

And I will smite thy bow out of thy left hand, and will cause thine arrows to fall out of thy right hand.

Thou shalt fall upon the mountains of Israel, thou, and all thy bands, and the people that is with thee: I will give thee unto the ravenous birds of every sort, and to the beasts of the field to be devoured.

Thou shalt fall upon the open field: for I have spoken it, saith the Lord God.

And I will send a fire on Magog, and among them that dwell carelessly in the isles: and they shall know that I am the Lord.

So will I make my holy name known in the midst of my people Israel; and I will not let them pollute my holy name any more: and the heathen shall know that I am the Lord, the Holy One in Israel.

Behold, it is come, and it is done, saith the Lord God; this is the day whereof I have spoken.

And they that dwell in the cities of Israel shall go forth, and shall set on fire and burn the weapons, both the shields and the bucklers, the bows and the arrows, and the handstaves, and the spears, and they shall burn them with fire seven years:

So that they shall take no wood out of the field, neither cut down any out of the forests; for they shall burn the weapons with fire: and they shall spoil those that spoiled them, and rob those that robbed them, saith the Lord God.

And it shall come to pass in that day, that I will give unto Gog a place there of graves in Israel, the valley of the passengers on the east of the sea: and it shall stop the noses of the passengers: and there shall they bury Gog and all his multitude: and they shall call it The valley of Hamon-gog.

And seven months shall the house of Israel be burying of them, that they may cleanse the land.

Yea, all the people of the land shall bury them; and it shall be to them a renown the day that I shall be glorified, saith the Lord God.

And they shall sever out men of continual employment, passing through the land to bury with the passengers those that remain upon the face of the earth, to cleanse it: after the end of seven months shall they search.

And the passengers that pass through the land, when any seeth a man's bone, then shall he set up a sign by it, till the buriers have buried it in the valley of Hamon-gog. And also the name of the city shall be Hamonah. Thus shall they cleanse the land.

And, thou son of man, thus saith the Lord God; Speak unto every feathered fowl, and to every beast of the field, Assemble yourselves, and come; gather yourselves on every side to my sacrifice that I do sacrifice for you, even a great sacrifice upon the mountains of Israel, that ye may eat flesh, and drink blood.

Ye shall eat the flesh of the mighty, and drink the blood of the princes of the earth, of rams, of lambs, and of goats, of bullocks, all of them fatlings of Bashan.

And ye shall eat fat till ye be full, and drink blood till ye be drunken, of my sacrifice which I have sacrificed for you.

Thus ye shall be filled at my table with horses and chariots, with mighty men, and with all men of war, saith the Lord God.

And I will set my glory among the heathen, and all the heathen shall see my judgment that I have executed, and my hand that I have laid upon them.

So the house of Israel shall know that I am the Lord their God from that day and forward.

And the heathen shall know that the house of Israel went into captivity for their iniquity: because they trespassed against me, therefore hid I my face from them, and gave them into the hand of their enemies: so fell they all by the sword.

According to their uncleanness and according to their transgressions have I done unto them, and hid my face from them.

Therefore thus saith the Lord God; Now will I bring again the Captivity of Jacob, and have mercy upon the whole house of Israel, and will be jealous for my holy name;

After that they have borne their shame, and all their trespasses whereby they have trespassed against me, when they dwelt safely in their land, and none made them afraid.

When I have brought them again from the people, and gathered them out of their enemies' lands, and am sanctified in them in the sight of many nations;

Then shall they know that I am the Lord their God, which caused them to be led into captivity among the heathen: but I have gathered them unto their own land, and have left none of them any more there.

Neither will I hide my face any more from them: for I have poured out my spirit upon the house of Israel, saith the Lord God."

This account of the final rebellion is deeply interesting. With the Hebrew restored to his land, dwelling in safety and prosperity, who would have such an axe to grind? Who would hold a grudge that would simmer for a thousand years, until reaching a flashpoint at the slightest Satanic provocation? In chapter 38 verse 14 God makes it plain to Ezekiel that Gog knows full well the people dwelling in Israel are the Hebrews: God's portion—and that they are dwelling safely. The prophet points out that Gog and Magog are gambling on the fact that the inhabitants of Israel are dwelling in unfortified cities: essentially an easy conquest. It is not clear if Sheba, Dedan and Tarshish are observing Gog's move from a sense of envious admiration of his boldness, or shocked disbelief that he would engage in what will ultimately be a suicide mission.

Further, plans for full-spectrum dominance are not drawn up overnight. They take years of strategizing and assurance of allies and sufficient armaments. Since an attack on the kingdom of God on earth is comparable to a death wish, it would appear those attacking God's portion feel entitled to the land, and have an intense need to reestablish their former position of worldwide military supremacy. But as things stand at this point, the true descendants of the patriarchs are established in the land, and the Lord Jesus Christ has declared worldwide peace. From Gog's perspective, it will take a massive military offensive to overturn this and set the world order back as it was in the days of Japheth's glory.

To fully understand about Gog, Magog, Meshech, Tubal, Gomer, and Togarmah, identified by Ezekiel as coming out of the house of the north, and the Apostle John's seemingly conflicting observation that the nations which are in the four quarters (or winds) of the earth are Gog and Magog, we need to look at the natural, spiritual, and historical perspective. Following is a recap of the sons of Japheth:

Japheth

Sons: Gomer, Magog, Madai, Javan, Tubal, Tiras, Meschec, Ashkenaz

Grandsons: Elishah, Riphath, Tarshish, Togarmah, Kittim, Dodanim

Archaic maps drawn in the 18th and 19th centuries indicate the lands occupied by Magog, Meshech, Tubal, Gomer, and Togarmah range across a great expanse bordering and northward of the Black Sea and the Caspian Sea. Interestingly, this region was the precise domain of the ancient and powerful Khazar empire that adopted Judaism as the state religion around the 8th century. That was the site of the original, physical Gog/Magog. The kingdom ceased to exist after the 13th century, and some of the populace migrated further west into Europe and north into Russia, basically remaining in Japheth's territory; the north, and the isles. Now consider that every nation has its own overarching spiritual principality. This is a critical to understanding this prophecy because the Euro-Judaics have never been a military power with a worldwide stranglehold capable of attacking from all four winds. Historically that honor has belonged to the Anglo-American establishment. Does a link exist between ancient Gog/Magog and the Anglo-American empire? The answer is found in the heart of the City of London itself.

You will recall from Chapter II Identity Crisis sub section *Spiritual Genetics—Identified by Fruits; Rather Than After the Flesh*, "Whenever a kingdom no longer exists, or is still geographically intact—but stripped of the immense power it wielded in ancient times, God will still reference that kingdom as viable and a force to be judged, because of the malevolent spiritual principality associated with it. This means an area far removed from the ancient geographical location can literally take on the spiritual attributes of that original power, and a people generationally or racially different from the original can be influenced spiritually to emulate the original offending person/nation."

Do spiritual principalities and powers really relocate to different jurisdictions? You may be assured that the kingdom of darkness is not divided, and does whatever is necessary to maintain terrestrial coverage in the offensive against the Kingdom of God on earth. Case in point: when the Lord Jesus Christ dictated the letters to the apostle John for the angels of the seven churches during the first century, the seat of Satan was in Pergamos. Today, what was formerly Pergamos is the relatively quiet district of Bergama in western Turkey. In sharp contrast, the latter day empire known as Great Babylon (the West) is identified as the habitation of devils, hold of every foul spirit, and cage of every unclean and hateful bird. So it is apparent spiritual wickedness in high places follows the rise of kingdoms for the purpose of maintaining influence to further the objectives of the Satan. That being confirmed, we can examine a primary latter day base of operations established by these dark powers.

Eerily concurrent with the wane of the Khazarian Judaic empire was the nascent rise of the City of London in the 12th century. Similar to Rome's ancient lore of Romulus and Remus as its founders; London, England has a legend that the giants Gog and Magog are the patron founders of their city. Apparently, the citizens take this tradition quite seriously; enough so that in 1819, a juvenile reader was authored under the pseudonym Robin Goodfellow titled, The History of Gog and Magog: the Champions of London, Containing an Account of the Origin of Many Things Relative to the City.[31]

Larger than life statutes of Gog and Magog have historically adorned a massive edifice known as Guildhall, the driving force behind the city since the twelfth century and official headquarters of the City of London Corporation.[32] There have been at least three sets of these Gog/Magog 'guardians of London' statuaries since the 16th century, including the models currently installed at Guildhall. These giants are always depicted wearing full battle armor with spear, mace, sword, and arrows.

But Guildhall isn't the only place Gog and Magog are found in London. They are also part of the architecture of the St Dunstan-in-the-West church on Fleet Street. Positioned on either side of the clock, they strike the bells with their clubs on the hour and quarter hours. There is also an annual Lord Mayor's parade, where effigies of the giants are carried in the parade procession. So we can see a spiritual attachment to these entities is deeply ingrained in the Anglo conscience. From a spiritual perspective, there is no doubt these principalities have influenced political actions emanating from the region.

Now we look more in depth at the symbolism associated with one of the giants. The shield held by Magog displays a phoenix, the esoteric bird representing immolation and rebirth. Immolation refers to destruction by fire, or a sacrificial victim by fiery death. Most people have no trouble understanding the United States as a daughter of Great Britain, but how many know one of the original designs for the Great Seal of the United States featured a phoenix atop a nest of flames? The designer, William Baron, allegedly explained the immolating phoenix represented the "expiring liberty of Britain" revived by her descendants in America.

The next piece of the puzzle involves the joint effort between the British and the Khazar descendants to obtain the land God decreed to lie undisturbed until he himself gathered his covenant people at the end of the age and repatriated them. Lord Balfour, Winston Churchill,

---

[31] "The History of Gog and Magog, the Champions of London" J. Souter, London 1819.

[32] The City of London. guildhall.cityoflondon.gov.uk 2014

Theodore Herzl, and Lord Rothschild were all instrumental in the formation of the Zionist state. Political and banking might made it possible, the Anglo-American churches provided moral covering as prophecy fulfilled, and the American military has always been the sentinel and buffer to prevent dissenting powers in the region from dismantling the construct. Here we must recall the conspiracy of the enemies of God detailed in Psalm Chapter 83 verse 4 to cut off the true Israel from being a nation, that their name might never be remembered again.

The complete picture materializes with the realization that the Gentiles surviving the carnage on the Day of the Lord as the cities of the nations fall and the winepress of God's wrath is trodden will be uprooted and dispersed. Where will these exiles go? Recall how God declares he is removing the cup of his fury from Zion and placing it in the hands of those who have afflicted her, and that those who led into captivity must go into captivity. Part of the Captivity curse was to be scattered throughout the nations and to the ends of the earth, i.e. the four winds. From this perspective, it is much easier to understand how the Apostle John would describe Satan as going out "to deceive the nations which are in the four quarters of the earth, Gog and Magog, to gather them together to battle."

Since Gog and Magog were not originally in the four quarters of the earth but concentrated in the Black Sea and Caspian Sea regions, they can only refer to a people who adopted and pledged affinity to the Gog/Magog spiritual principalities. Those rulers of the darkness of this world eventually influenced them to collaborate with the actual genealogical descendants of the original Gog territory to usurp the Abrahamic covenant land in the latter days. The surprise attack on the restored Hebrew nation will be intended as payback for the divine vengeance experienced on the Day of the Lord which preceded the repatriation of the people. Remember, Psalm Chapter 2 verse 2 says the kings of the earth set themselves and the rulers take counsel against the Lord. 'Set themselves' means they will do anything so as to stay.

Verse 1 says they are literally raging, but their folly will cause God's fury to come up in his face to the extent the earth will quake and mountains will be moved out of their places. Pestilence, blood, overflowing rain, great hailstones, fire, and brimstone will be the reward of attempting to retake the land of Israel in that day. Even those of Magog who do not join the assault will die by fiery death. Thus the phoenix on the giant's shield confirms a prophetic destruction foretold in ages past. This is not the same event as the Day of the Lord, for we do not see the heavenly cataclysm of darkened sun and moon, or falling stars. ***That was the event everyone should have learned from***. The fact that Satan upon his release is able to instantly deceive these particular Gentiles indicates they never knew God and always despised his mercy. This is how the prophet Daniel could say that at the return of the Lord some would be resurrected to everlasting shame and contempt. Herein is the scripture in Amos Chapter 1 verse 11 brutally confirmed: that Esau kept his wrath forever.

God uses this horrific event as a platform to clearly inform both the heathen and each son and daughter of Jacob that they went into captivity for their iniquity, and He was the one which caused them to be led into captivity among the heathen. God's reaction to this breach of his mercy and order will be so horrendous it will leave an indelible impression on the hearts and minds of his people and the heathen alike. It is the last recorded rebellion in the scriptures, and the close of an era.

Beauty of the World to Come; Everlasting Peace and Joy

"How beautiful upon the mountains are the feet of him that bringeth good tidings, that publisheth peace; that bringeth good tidings of good, that publisheth salvation; that saith unto Zion, Thy God reigneth!" Isaiah Chapter 52 verse 7

With all insurgency eliminated, the earth is at peace and rest. When the final Court convenes, the last judgment takes place before the Great White Throne and all the dead will be judged according to their works. Those whose names are not found in the Book of Life are cast into the Lake of Fire, and ultimately Hell and the last enemy—Death—will be hurled into the Lake of Fire. All things now being subdued under the Lord Jesus Christ; in a final act of sonship and submission he subjects himself to the Father, who had delegated all power in heaven and earth to him. Now God is all and in all, and the Jubilee of Jubilees begins. Those dwelling on earth experience life on a level of tranquility, joy and prosperity heretofore unknown; for...

"Thus saith the Lord God; When I shall have gathered the house of Israel from the people among whom they are scattered, and shall be sanctified in them in the sight of the heathen, then shall they dwell in their land that I have given to my servant Jacob.

And the ransomed of the LORD shall return, and come to Zion with songs and everlasting joy upon their heads: they shall obtain joy and gladness, and sorrow and sighing shall flee away.

And they shall dwell safely therein, and shall build houses, and plant vineyards; yea, they shall dwell with confidence, when I have executed judgments upon all those that despise them round about them; and they shall know that I am the Lord their God." Ezekiel Chapter 28 verses 25-26

Never again will the children of Jacob have to fear loss, or fear having their possessions marred, or have to settle for the leftovers of the Gentiles. Rather, the gates of their city will remain open twenty-four seven all year long, that the riches and labor of the Gentiles might be brought in. It will not be a shameful whispered secret that we were the people the Lord chastised and brought low. It will be an honor to be who we are, because the world will see God's great favor and manifold mercies in restoring and exalting us. He wounded, but he has now healed. We will be made a praise in the entire earth.

"And the sons of strangers shall build up thy walls, and their kings shall minister unto thee: for in my wrath I smote thee, but in my favour have I had mercy on thee.

Therefore thy gates shall be open continually; they shall not be shut day nor night; that men may bring unto thee the forces of the Gentiles, and that their kings may be brought.

For the nation and kingdom that will not serve thee shall perish; yea, those nations shall be utterly wasted. Isaiah 60 verse 10-12

At that time will I bring you again, even in the time that I gather you: for I will make you a name and a praise among all people of the earth, when I turn back your captivity before your eyes, saith the Lord...Zephaniah Chapter 3 verse 20

348

When the Lord Jesus Christ was born of a virgin, the angels sang, "On earth peace, goodwill toward men." The stone cut out without hands that destroyed the carnal kingdoms of the earth has become a mountain that fills the entire earth. Because the earth is now filled with the knowledge of the Lord, even the animal kingdom is transformed, and their original affection for each other and humans returns.

"The wolf also shall dwell with the lamb, and the leopard shall lie down with the kid; and the calf and the young lion and the fatling together; and a little child shall lead them.

And the cow and the bear shall feed; their young ones shall lie down together: and the lion shall eat straw like the ox.

And the sucking child shall play on the hole of the asp, and the weaned child shall put his hand on the cockatrice' den.

They shall not hurt nor destroy in all my holy mountain: for the earth shall be full of the knowledge of the Lord, as the waters cover the sea..." Isaiah Chapter 11 verses 6-9

As if to emphasize how serious he is about this adjustment to nature, God shows it to Isaiah yet again:

"The wolf and the lamb shall feed together, and the lion shall eat straw like the bullock: and dust shall be the serpent's meat. They shall not hurt nor destroy in all my holy mountain, saith the Lord." Isaiah Chapter 65 verse 25

God will wipe away every tear, and the former things will be remembered no more. God himself will rejoice in his people, and joy over them with singing.

"For, behold, I create new heavens and a new earth: and the former shall not be remembered, nor come into mind.

But be ye glad and rejoice for ever in that which I create: for, behold, I create Jerusalem a rejoicing, and her people a joy.

And I will rejoice in Jerusalem, and joy in my people: and the voice of weeping shall be no more heard in her, nor the voice of crying.

Longevity of life will be the rule, rather than the exception; the people of God will be able to plan massive enterprises and creative works, and live to see their completion and thoroughly enjoy them. They will never again work to see their income sucked away by corrupt greed and theft; also sudden infant death will never again devastate the hearts of parents.

...And they shall build houses, and inhabit them; and they shall plant vineyards, and eat the fruit of them. They shall not build, and another inhabit; they shall not plant, and another eat: for as the days of a tree are the days of my people, and mine elect shall long enjoy the work of their hands.

They shall not labour in vain, nor bring forth for trouble; for they are the seed of the blessed of the Lord, and their offspring with them.

And it shall come to pass, that before they call, I will answer; and while they are yet speaking, I will hear." Isaiah Chapter 65 verses 17-24

This is Abundant Life the way God intended: as a joy to wake up in the morning, with goodness, fellowship, and repose a way of life, rather than a few fleeting hours or days a year grudgingly granted by the power-brokers of this present world before returning to the obstacle laden, unrewarding path designed and maintained by the ungodly. Micah Chapter 6 verse 8 and Amos Chapter 5 verse 24 show the kind of social order God desires:

"He hath shewed thee, O man, what is good; and what doth the Lord require of thee, but to do justly, and to love mercy, and to walk humbly with thy God? But let judgment run down as waters, and righteousness as a mighty stream." Now, the entire world operates on these principles and life on earth is joyous and something to be celebrated. Because the earth is full of the knowledge of God, the air is clean, the water is clean, food is unpolluted, the skies are unmarred, and poverty is eradicated. God says it doesn't take programs, funding, initiatives, or committees to accomplish this. All it takes is justice, mercy, humility, and righteousness. The peoples of the earth can communicate with each other and get to know each other without being previously cast as evil, backwards, or terrorists. Because no more sea will exist, people can set out to walk across the world together, sightseeing in fellowship. No one will have to cut their activities short for cruel overseers; for God has created the earth for man's enjoyment, and He will rejoice greatly in the delight of his children.

But the new heavens and earth are just the preview for the grand finale. For the New Jerusalem, sparkling like a multi-faceted gemstone, is unveiled, and descends from heaven. The true and ultimate Capital City, the mother of us all, is like a bejeweled bride in her radiance. No natural light source illuminates this city. The glory of God and light of Christ are the light, and this light illumines the path of the nations of the saved. In this City is the throne of God and his Son, and the crystal clear water of life gushes forth from it, creating a river. There also is found the tree of life with healing in its leaves; bearing twelve different types of fruit, and yielding fruit each month. And in this blessed environment, the servants of God will see him face to face, and reign for ever and ever; world without end.

Finally, the heart of God is fulfilled as his millennia old desire to dwell with man becomes a reality. All the drama and trauma that have elapsed since Adam's fall are wiped away as all things become new. Why did it take so many thousands of years and cost so much pain, death, bloodshed, and heartache?

First, because man is his own worst enemy. He is a freewill agent with the latitude to make his own choices. But since he is constrained by limitation of life, and can neither see forward to the outcome of his folly, or backward to the outcome of those who committed the same folly before him, he spends an inordinate amount of time messing up, and then either laboring to extract himself from his self-created pits, lashing out at others in blame and anger, or blindly plowing through life like a destructive, runaway train.

Secondly, because sentence against an evil work is not executed speedily, therefore the heart of the sons of men is fully set in them to do evil. Man mistakenly thinks he will get away with his deeds, without reaping what he sows, or paying what he owes.

Lastly, for millennia, many have willingly sold their souls to Satan in exchange for the fleeting riches, fame, and power offered by this perishing world; failing to realize that when they face death, none of it will be of sufficient value to redeem their soul. For this reason, sinful man labors to avoid death altogether—which is basically a fool's errand.

At times man experiences pangs of conscience for his errant ways; but in most cases, the diversions placed in his path by the Adversary of his soul, the lust of his eyes and flesh, pride, and his own desperately wicked heart override the conviction to consider his doings and repent. Man forgets that he is only dust, that Time is his enemy, and that Death stalks him from the moment he draws his first breath. The taint of Adamic sin has left man wretched and undone; regardless of how comely, intelligent, or altruistic he is. Apart from the righteousness of the Lord Jesus Christ, none of us stand a chance of reconciliation and acceptance before God. This is why the Father sent Christ: to redeem us from Adam's fall and reinstate us to a place of righteousness and fellowship with God.

God—in his great mercy—deals with man's heart and helps him often, even while man is in the midst of pride and rebellion. God waits patiently, working to bring sinful man to repentance, that he might experience true love, true freedom, and abundant life. A wise man will humble himself under God's mighty hand while the breath is still in his nostrils and the blood warm in his veins. Regardless of how we choose, all the counsel of God shall stand; everything declared will come to pass without fail. Our prayer then, is even so, come Lord Jesus...and return, O Lord, unto the many thousands of Israel!

EPILOGUE

You have just read the Message to Judah, revealing to the Black brothers and sisters in Christ the truth about their Hebrew heritage; and the rise, fall, Captivity, and future restoration of our people. My aim was to clarify our identity, our purpose, and the reason our struggle has been so long and bitter. I also endeavored to express the great favor and love God has for us as the spiritual and natural relation of the Lion of the Tribe of Judah. In this I trust I have been successful.

From now on as you read your Bible, the scriptures will come alive vibrantly as you sense you are reading about your people. From now on, as you lift your voice in praise to the Lord, you will understand you are singing to a close relative; your Near Kinsman, the Holy One of Israel and the Redeemer sent first to your people.

I am excited about the awakening of the sons of Zion, because the scripture confirms it will only take twelve thousand sealed from each tribe of Israel to unlock the judgments that break the grip of Satan and sinful man on this present world. We can hasten this sealing by keeping ourselves unspotted from the world, and petitioning God to send the outpouring of his Spirit upon our tribal brethren wherever they may be.

In disclosing who we are as a people, I have no doubt raised the ire of those who will bitterly dispute facts, and favor tradition over truth. Nevertheless, there is no way to properly interpret Biblical prophecy without exposing the counterfeit Judah and Israel and the counterfeit body of Christ. Great persecution is to be expected because of the stand I have taken, but my fear of God greatly exceeds my concerns about the retribution of man. Whatever happens to me as a result of bringing these truths, on That Day, I will stand before my Lord in the knowledge I was obedient; and as a mother in Israel and daughter of Judah...faithful with the saints.

ENDNOTES

1Regarding the original account of Josephus' description of the Lord Jesus Christ.
Die slavische Uebersetzung der Halōsis tēs Hierousalēm des Flavius Josephus, Eisler, Robert, Prague, 1930.

2 Regarding the skin color and hair texture of the Biblical Hebrews.
The ethnicity of the original Hebrews in Jerusalem is captured in a Russian iconography dated to the fourteenth century, and painted in tempura on wood panel. The painting, titled Maundy Thursday (Jesus washes the feet of the Disciples) is kept at the Pskov School of iconography in Pskov, Russia. The work is well preserved and the colors still vibrant. Clearly shown is the dark brown skin and black, curled hair of the Lord Jesus Christ and his disciples.

3 Regarding the original Europe/Africa distinction in skin color.
PINNOCK'S GUIDE TO KNOWLEDGE published August 17 1883.

4 Regarding the embedding of symbolism in architecture.
F. Tupper Saussy, Ospray Bookmakers, 1999.
RULERS OF EVIL: Useful Knowledge About Governing Bodies.

5 Regarding Constantine's Sun Day Veneration Decree.
The issue here is not whether Christians should worship God on Sunday, for New Covenant believers are free to worship God any day and at any time they choose, as long as they worship in spirit and truth. The point is that Constantine's desire was to honor the sun—a created thing—as opposed to the One who created it—and invoke the power of the state to enforce the idolatry upon the populace.

6 Regarding the skin color and hair texture of the Biblical Hebrews.
The truth of Hebrew ethnicity recognized as late as the 14th century. The ethnicity of the original Hebrews in Jerusalem is captured in a Russian iconography dated to the fourteenth century, and painted in tempura on wood panel. The painting, titled Maundy Thursday (Jesus washes the feet of the Disciples) is kept at the Pskov School of iconography in Pskov, Russia. The work is well preserved and the colors still vibrant. Clearly shown is the dark brown skin and black, curled hair of the Lord Jesus Christ and his disciples.

7 Regarding a Euro-Judaic descendant remark cryptically alluding to the true identity of the Hebrew.
Sarah Silverman, Jesus is Magic (2005).

8 Regarding the Parable of the Wheat and the Tares.

Traditionally, modern Christians have interpreted the parable of the wheat and tares as an allegory of those in church who are   just 'looking the part'—spiritual pretenders—intermingled with believers who are totally sold out for Christ. But Jesus says the field is the world—rather than a local fellowship. This implies that the difficulty in discerning the true from the false is a global phenomenon. This then reduces the question to the identity of the true spiritual body of Christ worldwide i.e., the Roman state church and nominal Christianity vs the ecclesia, and the true genealogical descendants of the Abrahamic Covenant promised end time restoration—Black descendants of slavery answering to the Old Testament prophecies of Captivity and by ships vs the Euro-Judaics under the politically constructed Zionist settlement campaign.

9 A Little History: Cyrus I Scofield and the Tribulation.
Don Nicoloff, May 2009 Idaho Observer. http://proliberty.com/observer/20090507.htm

10 Regarding the erroneous association of Black Shemitic Hebrews to the seed of Ham.
Pearl of Great Price: Abraham: Chapter 1 vs 21-25 Joseph Smith, Founder of Mormonism.

11 Regarding the true identity of enslaved Judah who was 'carried away captive into all nations.'
February 18, 2012 "Why Do So Many Jews Hate Black People?" by Alcibiades Bilzerian. thebilzerianreport.com   http://thebilzerianreport.com/why-do-so-many-jews-hate-black-people

12 Regarding the location of the true Mount Sinai.
Wyatt Archaeological Research Mt. Sinai.   www.wyattmuseum.com/mt-sinai.htm.

13 Regarding two prophesied events of Antichrist type persecution of the people of the covenant.

This event represented the first of dual fulfillments of the angel's words to Daniel in Daniel Chapter 11 verse 30: For the ships of Chittim shall come against him: therefore he shall be grieved, and return, and have indignation against the holy covenant: so shall he do; he shall even return, and have intelligence with them that forsake the holy covenant. And arms shall stand on his part, and they shall pollute the sanctuary of strength, and shall take away the daily sacrifice, and they shall place the abomination that maketh desolate. And such as do wickedly against the covenant shall he corrupt by flatteries: but the people that do know their God shall be strong, and do exploits. And they that understand among the people shall instruct many: yet they shall fall by the sword, and by flame, by Captivity, and by spoil, many days. This is the first fulfillment, because the Lord Jesus Christ alluded to this same event, but in context of the time of the end. In the end time scenario, the temple is the body of man, the altar is the soul, and the abomination of desolation is the mark, name, and number of the Beast.

14 Regarding two diametric contrasts of our Lord's appearing.

Isaiah 53 verses 3-5: He is despised and rejected of men; a man of sorrows, and acquainted with grief: and we hid as it were our faces from him; he was despised, and we esteemed him not. Surely he hath borne our griefs, and carried our sorrows: yet we did esteem him stricken, smitten of God, and afflicted. But he was wounded for our transgressions, he was bruised for our iniquities: the chastisement of our peace was upon him; and with his stripes we are healed. Compare to Zechariah 14 verses 3-4: Then shall the Lord go forth, and fight against those nations, as when he fought in the day of battle. And his feet shall stand in that day upon the mount of Olives, which is before Jerusalem on the east, and the mount of Olives shall cleave in the midst thereof toward the east and toward the west, and there shall be a very great valley; and half of the mountain shall remove toward the north, and half of it toward the south.

15 Regarding an eyewitness account of the destruction of Jerusalem.
The Complete Works of Josephus, The Jewish War. Book 5. Chapter 10. 5.442-445.

16 Regarding an eyewitness account of the destruction of Jerusalem.
The Complete Works of Josephus, The Jewish War. Book 6. Chapter 5. 3.288-309.

17 Regarding the Kingdom of Dahomey and the Slave Trade.
Forbes, Frederick E., Dahomey and the Dahomans: Being the Journals of Two Missions to the King of Dahomey, and Residence at His Capital, in the Year 1849 and 1850., Page 4.

18 Regarding Hebrewisms of the Dahomey people.
Forbes, Frederick E., Dahomey and the Dahomans: Being the Journals of Two Missions to the King of Dahomey, and Residence at His Capital, in the Year 1849 and 1850, Page 37.

19 Regarding how the doctrine of Calvinism influenced the Afrikaaners.
John Calvin was a 16th century theologian whose doctrines centered around austere moral codes and the belief that certain people were predestined for salvation, and therefore could not fall from grace. Based on this line of thinking, a Christian could defraud, murder, or whatever, and still stand justified before God with no worries of condemnation because he was predestined to eternal life. The doctrine of predestination flies in the face of Jesus' invitation to 'whosoever will' to come drink of the Water of Life, and the Apostle Paul's observations that some had already made shipwreck of their faith, and concerning others who had escaped the pollutions of the world through the knowledge of the Lord Jesus Christ and become entangled again, that their last end is worse than the beginning, and it would have been better for them not to have known the way of righteousness than, after they have known it, to turn from the holy commandment delivered unto them.

20 Regarding the contrast between the original Hebrew apostolic church and Gentile Christianity.
Pagan Christianity?: Exploring the Roots of Our Church Practices Frank Viola, George Barna. 2008 Tyndale House Publishers ISBN-13: 9781414314853.

21 Regarding the murder of Carol Jenkins.
Chapman, Sandra Prince Media Group.
May 2012 The Girl in the Yellow Scarf ISBN-978-0615607054

22 Regarding rap as a vehicle to communicate the gospel.
Price, Emmett G Scarecrow Press, 2012 The Black Church and Hip Hop Culture:
Toward Bridging the Generational Divide. ISBN-978-0-8108-8236-2

23 Regarding perspective on the Black man and criminal justice system.
Alexander, Michelle 2012 The New Press.
The New Jim Crow: Mass Incarceration in the Age of Colorblindness ISBN-13: 9781595586438

24 Regarding a former slave's perspective on the use of holidays to manage discontent.
   Narrative of the Life of Frederick Douglass, an American Slave, by Frederick Douglass 1845.

25 Regarding a perspective of Lucifer from a high-level Masonic luminary.
   Albert Pike, Morals and Dogma, page 321.

26 Comprehensive online Black history archive BlackPast.org™.
   Remembered & Reclaimed, An Online Reference Guide to African American History.

27 Regarding an excerpt from FBI COINTELPRO archives.
   FBI Records: The Vault.

28 Regarding the descendants of Israel in Pakistan, West Pakistan and India.
   Chagatai Khan, from Makranis, the Negroes of Pakistan and India, 26 May 2009,
chagataikhan.blogspot.com. References: Makranis, the Negroes of West Pakistan - John B. Edlefsen,
Khalida Shah and Mohsin Farooq Phylon (1960-), Vol. 21, No. 2 (2nd Qtr., 1960), pp. 124-130(article
consists of 7 pages) Published by: Clark Atlanta University Stable URL:
http://www.jstor.org/stable/274335
   Pakistan's Sidi keep heritage alive by By Zaffar Abbas Wednesday, 13 March, 2002, 02:52 GMT
http://news.bbc.co.uk/2/hi/south_asia/1869876.stm /
   KARACHI: Manghopirurs a living tribute to Sheedi culture July 16, 2007 Monday Jamadi-us-Sani 30,
1428 http://www.dawn.com/2007/07/16/local9.htm
   'Hoshu Sheedi Day'on March 23 Bureau Report March 21, 2007 Wednesday Rabi-ul-Awwal 1,
1428 http://www.dawn.com/2007/03/21/local34.htm] and Urdu poet Noon Meem Danish [AUTHOR: A
poet in New York By Asif Farrukhi] http://www.dawn.com/weekly/books/archive/071209/books6.htm
   'Sheedis have been hurt most by attitudes'. June 23, 2008 Monday Jamadi-us-Sani 18, 1429
http://www.dawn.com/2008/06/23/local11.htm.

29 Regarding the descendants of Israel in India.   Africa in India: The Plight of The Siddis, Sanjay Austa, 2014 May. africanearth.net.

30 Regarding bio-weapon damage to descendants of Israel in Southern Iraq US.
Depleted Uranium Yields Chamber of Horrors in Southern Iraq.
Andy Kershaw Independent Digital (UK) Ltd 2001.

31 Regarding ancient folklore ties to Great Britain and Gog and Magog.
The History of Gog and Magog, the Champions of London, J. Souter, London 1819.

32 Regarding historic and current cultural and architectural expressions of Gog and Magog as legendary British icons and patron protectors of the City of London. guildhall.cityoflondon.gov.uk 2014.

www.ingramcontent.com/pod-product-compliance
Lightning Source LLC
LaVergne TN
LVHW081332060426
835513LV00014B/1256